LAWYERS AND VAMPIRES

Lawyers and Vampires

Cultural Histories of Legal Professions

Edited by
W. WESLEY PUE
Nemetz Chair in Legal History and Professor of Law,
The University of British Columbia
and
DAVID SUGARMAN
Professor of Law, Law School, Lancaster University

OXFORD – PORTLAND OREGON
2003

Hart Publishing
Oxford and Portland, Oregon

Published in North America (US and Canada) by
Hart Publishing
c/o International Specialized Book Services
5804 NE Hassalo Street
Portland, Oregon
97213-3644
USA

Hart Publishing is a specialist legal publisher based in Oxford, England. To order further copies of this book or to request a list of other publications please write to:

Hart Publishing, Salter's Boatyard, Folly Bridge,
Abingdon Rd, Oxford OX1 4LB
Telephone: +44 (0)1865 245533 or Fax: +44 (0)1865 794882
e-mail: mail@hartpub.co.uk
WEBSITE: http//www.hartpub.co.uk

British Library Cataloguing in Publication Data
Data Available

ISBN 1–84113–312–4

Typeset by Hope Services (Abingdon) Ltd.
Printed and bound in Great Britain by
Biddles Ltd, *www.biddles.co.uk*

Preface

This book seeks to develop understandings of the historical and social functions of legal professions on a comparative basis and through interpretive lenses sensitive to the urges of 'cultural history'. The essence of a comparative 'cultural history' of legal professions is the pursuit of an understanding transcending the spatial, temporal or disciplinary boxes that conventionally constrain scholarship.

Because such work is best pursued collaboratively—perhaps it can only be pursued collaboratively—this volume presents the work of an extraordinary team of scholars, drawn from six countries on three continents. The work of each of us individually—but more especially, of the contributors as a group has been much enhanced by sustained dialogue about what it means to engage in a 'cultural history of legal professions' which has been carried on both in print and also through a series of scholarly venues including:

—meetings of the long-standing 'Working Group on Comparative Legal Professions' organised as part of the work of the International Sociological Association's Research Committee on the Sociology of Law (under the leadership of Rick Abel, Terry Halliday, Bill Felstiner, and Benoit Bastard),

—a developmental conference convened at Whistler, British Columbia under the sponsorship of the University of British Columbia's Interdisciplinary Law and Society programme,

—several meetings taking the form of panels arranged as part of the annual conferences of the [USA] Law and Society Association, the American Society for Legal History, the Australia–New Zealand Law and History Association, the Canadian Law and Society Association, and the Australia–New Zealand Studies Association of North America,

—an international workshop on 'lawyers and their socio-ethical concerns' organised by Dr JS Gandhi and hosted by Jawaharlal Nehru University's Centre for the Study of Social Systems in April 2001.

This research has been much facilitated too by concrete support provided by the University of British Columbia Library, the University of British Columbia Hampton Fund, Green College and the Interdisciplinary Law and Society Programme (University of British Columbia), the International Institute for the Sociology of Law at Onati, the Institute of Advanced Legal Studies (School of Advanced Studies, London) and the University of British Columbia's Law Endowment Fund, (which contributed to translation costs).

We are grateful too to individuals who have worked directly on the project: Joanne Chung, who provided administrative support at the University of British Columbia, Richard Hart, Mel Hamill and April Boffin of Hart Publishing,

Gisela Mutter (who provided translation from German) and Marion Macfarlane (who translated from French).

Finally, we wish to record our appreciation to the contributors to this work. They have brought great learning to our shared subject-matter. As important, they have exhibited a splendid sense of collegiality and—importantly—a sense of humour as and when needed!

W Wesley Pue
Vancouver
24 February 2003

David Sugarman
Lancaster
24 February 2003

Contents

List of Contributors

David Applebaum, Professor of History, Rowan University, Glassboro, NJ, USA

Harold Dick, Barrister and Solicitor, City of Winnipeg, Manitoba, Canada

Ann Fidler, Assistant Professor and Dean, History Department, Honors Tutorial College, Ohio University, OH, USA

Jean-Louis Halperin, University de Bourgogne, CNRS, France

Esa Konttinen, Senior Lecturer of Sociology, University of Jyräskylä, Finland

David Lemmings, Associate Professor of History, University of Newcastle, Australia

Anne McGillivray, Professor of Law, University of Manitoba, Canada

Rob McQueen, Professor of Law, Victoria University, Melbourne, Australia

Kjell Å Modéer, Lund University, Sweden

W Wesley Pue, Nemetz Chair in Legal History, Faculty of Law, University of British Columbia, Canada

John Savage, Assistant Professor, History Department, Lehigh University, PA, USA

Hannes Siegrist, Professor of Modern European History, University of Leipzig, Germany

David Sugarman, Professor of Law, Law School, Lancaster University, UK

1

Introduction: Towards a Cultural History of Lawyers

DAVID SUGARMAN AND W WESLEY PUE

I

This is the first book that directly addresses the cultural history of the legal profession. An international team of scholars canvasses wide-ranging issues concerning the culture of the legal profession and the wider cultural significance of lawyers, including consideration of the relation to cultural processes of state formation and colonisation. The essays describe and analyse significant aspects of the cultural history of the legal profession in England, Canada, Australia, France, Germany, Italy, Sweden, Switzerland, Norway and Finland. The book seeks to understand the complex ways in which lawyers were imaginatively and institutionally constructed, and their larger cultural significance. It illustrates both the diversity and the potential of a cultural approach to lawyers in history.

This book was conceived in an interdisciplinary spirit, drawing upon insights from history, law, literary, gender and visual studies. Taken together the essays offer a wide-ranging exploration of the cultural, ideological and intellectual processes through which the identity and culture of the legal profession transnationally have been developed, debated and articulated. This book aims to demonstrate some of the varied possibilities of an approach to lawyers that is both historical and culturally focussed—one which seeks to understand lawyers as both the object and the product of complex and evolving assignations of meaning, and to make an analysis of meaning an integral part of a broader effort to understand social change over time. It covers a range of subjects, including the professional formation of lawyers, lawyer's relations with each other and the state, their career structures and economic prospects, their self-image and their popular reputation. In short, this book seeks to advance a wider history of lawyers than has usually been the case through the development of comparative and cultural approaches to the history of the legal profession.

In the remainder of this Introduction we will, first, by a wave-of-the-wand treatment, indicate the cultural significance of lawyers. We will argue that while their importance has frequently been acknowledged, the history and sociology of the professions has only belatedly begun to investigate the culture of the profession and its larger cultural importance. We will then consider how and why the dominant tradition of historiography and sociology tended to neglect the comparative and cultural history of the legal profession. This will be followed by a brief overview of the development in recent years of a wider, more interdisciplinary history of lawyers. Here, we emphasise the value of work that investigates lawyers transnationally and comparatively; and the potential significance of the so-called 'cultural turn' in the human sciences for the writing of histories of the legal profession. We conclude this Introduction with an overview of the book and some brief reflections on areas, topics and approaches ripe for future exploration and development.

II

Lawyers (together with doctors and priests) have long been the butt of writers, artists and popular culture, quick to seize upon the disjunction between their lofty claims and their debased reality:

> How does an attorney sleep? First he lies on one side, then he lies on the other.
>
> How many lawyers does it take to screw in a light bulb? Three. One to Climb the ladder. One to shake it. And one to sue the ladder company.
>
> What are lawyers good for? They make used car salesmen look honest.

So caricatured, the lawyer is a self-serving pettifogger, propagating litigation and increasing the complexity and, therefore, the expense of the law.

> Darkness thus shrouded the imagery of the legal world. The Devil in person often appeared in cartoons of lawyers. They shared with him a reputation for smooth talking that cloaked sinister intentions . . . All these power-broking lawyers were dangerous because they went everywhere and knew everyone's secrets. And barristers were doubly so because they were required to plead any case, for a fee, regardless of right or wrong. Swift was one of many who denounced their ability to argue 'that *White* is *Black*, and *Black* is *White*, according as they are paid'.[1]

The 'barrage of satire'[2] that lawyers attracted often reflected the charges already levelled in parliamentary reports and debates, newspapers and magazines. Recently, the creation, transmission and re-cycling of these caricatures has been given a new lease of life through the medium of

[1] Penelope J Corfield, *Power and the Professions in Britain 1700–1850* (Routledge, London, 1995) 48–49.

[2] Corfield, *Power and the Professions in Britain 1700–1850* 42.

films, radio and TV, from court room dramas, the western, the *film noir*, to the soap opera and the documentary.

Paradoxically, perhaps, the urge to demythologise the law and demonise the legal profession has produced mixed messages—both mocking the profession for failing to conform to its own high ideals, yet nonetheless praising the rule of law and acknowledging the importance of lawyers in everyday life. Indeed, juxtaposed alongside the image of the lawyer as pettifogger is that of the larger-than-life advocate of public-interest matters—quick-witted, statesmanlike and fair-minded—much celebrated in fiction, films and TV series, notably, 'Perry Mason', 'LA Law', 'Rumpole of the Bailey' and 'Kavanah QC'.

All this attention attests to the power and influence of lawyers. As Robert Gordon put it:

> [The] facilitation of private ordering, greasing the wheels of capitalism and economic growth, is in itself an important social function. But even that function necessarily involves fitting clients' activities into a larger framework of legal regulation. Lawyers, as the field-level interpreters of the law, designers of private contractual order, and pleaders before courts and tribunals, effectively help to determine the practical content of the framework.[3]

The history of the profession illustrates how lawyers had immense opportunities open to them to use their professional roles and standing as springboards to business and political endeavours, generating great personal wealth and influence. Additionally, they were 'conceptive ideologists', that is, the creators and transmitters of specialist discourses, some of which are our most important political languages.[4] Lawyers were also institution-builders, constituting markets, states, civil society, community and colonial empires.[5] Indeed, the construction and legitimation of the liberal state and society, and the globalisation of liberal politics, probably owes much to lawyers.

In sum, loath them or love them, what lawyers do, say and write is important.

[3] Robert W Gordon, 'A Perspective from the United States' in Carol Wilton (ed) *Beyond the Law: Lawyers and Business in Canada, 1830 to 1930* (Osgoode Society, Toronto, 1990) 425–36, 429.

[4] Maureen Cain, 'The General Practice Lawyer and Client', (1979) 7 *International Journal of the Sociology of Law* 331–54.

[5] Terence Halliday, 'Lawyers as Institution-Builders: Constructing Markets, States, Civil Society and Community' in Austin Sarat, *et al* (eds), *Crossing Boundaries: Traditions and Transformations in Law and Society Research* (Northwestern University Press, Evanston, 1998).

III

The past 25 to 30 years have witnessed a sizeable aggregation of work on the histories of lawyers. This metamorphosis has been both quantitative and qualitative. The intellectual distance travelled by historians of law and legal institutions during this period has been considerable, reflecting major changes in mainstream historiography and the human sciences, as well as legal education, legal practice and society (including the reconfiguration and de-construction of law, professions and national identity). Consequently, many of the traditional concerns and assumptions of lawyers' legal history and the study of the professions have been turned on their heads.

The dominant tradition of historiography (including that pertaining to law and lawyers), at least in the period from the mid-nineteenth century to the mid-1970s, can be viewed as a species of nationalistic history, celebrating the rise of the modern nation-state. David Cannadine's description of the dominant version of British history has strong echoes with other national histories of the period—in Germany, France, the United States etc:

> To begin with, it cannot be too much stressed that they were all conceived, written and marketed as histories of *England* . . . These years may have witnessed the zenith of the British nation-state, of the United Kingdom, and the British Empire, but the nation whose history they recounted and whose identity they helped to proclaim was England. Moreover, these books were almost without exception in praise of England. They celebrated parliamentary government, the Common Law, the Church of England, ordered progress towards democracy and the avoidance of revolution. English exceptionalism was good and it was the historians task to explain it and applaud it. And they generally supposed that this history was a success story: as the authors of *1066 and All That* argued, when England ceased to be top nation, history came to a full stop.[6]

However, the dominant version of British history was merely a particular national variant of an ideology that has had universal appeal. Is there any nation that does not consider itself as unique? Around the world, historians and other human scientists helped to create and sustain the German, French, American, British, Canadian, Australian, Japanese etc exceptionalism tradition.[7] As a result, they correspondingly de-

[6] David Cannadine, 'British History as a "New Subject": Politics, Perspectives and Prospects' in Alexander Grant and Keith J Stringer (eds) *Uniting the Kingdom? The Making of British History* (Routledge, London, 1995) 12–30, 16.

[7] The most obvious Canadian reference here would be Carl Berger, *The Writing of Canadian History* (Oxford University Press, Toronto, 1976). See, generally, B Anderson, *Imagined Communities* (Verso, London, 1983); D Blackbourn and G Eley, *The Peculiarities of German History* (Oxford University Press, Oxford, 1984); Geoff Eley and

emphasised the transnational and multi-cultural elements of their legal, cultural, economic and political heritage.

This version of history writing is associated with the so-called Whig interpretation of history that consists of writing history backwards, thereby reconstituting the past as a teleology leading up to and fully manifested in the present.[8] Consequently, the complexity of life in previous times is both unified and simplified. Ironically, this linear interpretation of the past owes much to the linguistic and professional practices of the early modern common lawyers.[9]

It was further sustained by certain assumptions about the relationship between historical change and society best known as evolutionary functionalism. In the context of law and lawyers:

> . . . these notions [about historical change and the relation of law to such change] are that the natural and proper evolution of a society (or at least a 'progressive' society, to use Maine's qualification) is towards the type of liberal capitalism seen in advanced Western nations (especially the United States), and the natural and proper function of a legal system is to facilitate such an evolution.[10]

A further feature of the dominant tradition of historiography in the period *circa* 1850–1975 is its tendency to be self-consciously disciplinary; that is, informed by and constructed upon a self-referential foundation of technical expertise associated with a particular discipline or specialism. Under this optic, the human sciences were relatively self-contained and uncritical, rather than interdisciplinary, eclectic or irreverent in approach.[11]

Ronald Grigor Suny (eds), *Becoming National: A Reader* (Oxford University Press, New York, 1996); Geoffrey Cubitt (ed), *Imagining Nations* (Manchester University Press, Manchester, 1998).

[8] Herbert Butterfield, *The Whig Interpretation of History*; PBM Blaas, *Continuity and Anachronism: Parliamentary and Constitutional Development in Whig Historiography and in the Anti-Whig Reaction between 1890 and 1930* (Martinus Nijhoff, The Hague, 1978); Stefan Collini, Donald Winch, and John Burrow, *That Nobel Science of Politics: A Study in Nineteenth-Century Intellectual History* (Cambridge University Press, Cambridge, 1983); JW Burrow, *Whigs and Liberals: Continuity and Change in English Political Thought* (Clarendon Press, Oxford, 1988).

[9] See JGA Pocock, *The Ancient Constitution and the Feudal Law. Reissue with Retrospect* (Cambridge University Press, Cambridge, 1987).

[10] Robert W Gordon, 'Critical Legal Histories' (1984) 36 *Stanford Law Review* 57–126, 59. See, generally, D Sugarman, and GR Rubin, 'Towards a New History of Law and Material Society in England, 1750–1914' in GR Rubin and David Sugarman (eds), *Law, Economy and Society: Essays in the History of English Law, 1759–1914* (Professional Books, Abingdon, 1984) 1–123.

[11] With respect to the discipline of law, see Robert Stevens, *Law School*; David Sugarman, 'Legal Theory, the Common Law Mind and the Making of the Textbook Tradition' in William Twining (ed), *Legal Theory and Common Law* (Basil Blackwell, Oxford, 1986) 26–61; William Twining, *Blackstone's Tower: The English Law School* (Sweet & Maxwell, London, 1994); John Henry Schlegel, *American Legal Realism and*

Though analytically mutually distinct, these four lenses—nationalist history writing, the Whig interpretation of history, evolutionary functionalism and narrowly disciplinary—were in practice mutually supportive. Frequently they were juxtaposed together, producing the dominant vision of law and lawyers in past times. Consequently, the history of the law tended to treat the law and legal institutions as a more-or-less self-contained world or as a relatively dependent variable. The principal focus was on the evolution of legal doctrine, the formal institutional structure of the law, the ways that lawyers were organised or qualified and the biographies of eminent lawyers.[12]

Within the historiography and sociology of the profession, the dominant tradition cast its spell through the peculiarly modern concept of 'professionalisation'.[13] This talisman measured professionalism by institutional characteristics and a propensity to claim monopoly control of specialised fields of knowledge. Within this body of work the autonomy of the profession was either treated as axiomatic, or alternatively, lawyers were reduced to mere instrumentalities of classes, interests or particular types of society. What lawyers did, how they earned their bread and butter, their practices and ideas, how they dealt with clients (from the vantagepoint of both lawyers and their clients), the reputation of lawyers, and the extent to which there was access to legal advice and assistance (as well as alternatives to lawyers and litigation)—all these tended to receive short shrift.[14] In consequence, the larger role and practices of lawyers economically, politically, linguistically and culturally remained largely unaddressed or were treated as unproblematic. Analyses were largely the histories of single nations. In retrospect, they were written from a 'one nation' (or Anglocentric or Anglo-American) perspective. According to

Empirical Social Science (University of North Carolina Press, Chapel Hill, 1995); Avrom Sherr and Alan Paterson, 'Editorial: Legal Education at the Crossroads of Europe' (1995) 2 *International Journal of the Legal Profession* 5–6; Bob Hepple, 'The Renewal of the Liberal Law Degree' (1996) *Cambridge Law Journal* 470; HW Arthurs, 'The Political Economy of Canadaian Legal Education' (1998) 25 *Journal of Law and Society* 14–32; Avrom Scherr and David Sugarman, 'Introduction: Legal Education and Legal Theory', (2000) 7 *International Journal of the Legal Profession*, 7 (2000).

[12] See, further, Wilfrid Prest, 'Introduction', in W Prest (ed), *Lawyers in Early Modern Europe and America* (Croom Helm, London, 1981) 11–15.

[13] See, generally, Keith M Macdonald, *The Sociology of the Professions* (Sage, London, 1995).

[14] For an important critique of 'professionalisation', see Wilfrid R Prest, 'Why the History of the Professions is Not Written' in GR Rubin and D Sugarman (eds), *Law, Economy and Society: Essays in the History of English Law, 1750–1914* (Professional Books/Butterworths, Abingdon, 1984). See, also Michael Burrage and Rolf Torstendahl (eds), *Professions in Theory and History: Rethinking the Study of the Professions* (Sage, London, 1990); W Wesley Pue, 'In Pursuit of Better Myth: Lawyers' Histories and Histories of Lawyers' (1995) 33 *Alberta Law Review* 730–67; and Christopher W Brooks, *Lawyers, Litigation and English Society since 1450* (Hambledon Press, London, 1998).

this view, nations were separate from one another and some were naturally superior to others. Almost without exception, they were devoid of an awareness of the significance of gender, race, ethnicity and colonialism.

Since the 1970s, these attitudes, assumptions and arguments have increasingly seemed unacceptable and outmoded. Historical work on law and the legal professions, like so much else in the human sciences, has increasingly challenged the traditionalist paradigm. Scholars in a wide range of disciplines have returned to history and historical analyses in order to understand lawyers and allied professions in society. Increasingly, this work has become:

> . . . consciously interdisciplinary and informed by anthropology, sociology, literary and political studies, as well as the whole sweep of general history, not least the social history of EP Thompson and his followers, rather than constructed upon a self-referential foundation of technical legal expertise; hence law and its institutions usually appear as figures within a broad economic, political and social landscape, not as comprising a more or less self-contained theme or portrait.[15]

The new histories of the profession have significantly advanced our understanding of the profession both backward and forward in time. We now know much more about the history of the legal profession in its earliest phases in Australia, Canada, Continental Europe, England and the United States, as well as in the seventeenth, eighteenth and nineteenth centuries.[16]

[15] Wilfrid Prest, 'Notes Towards a Paper Not Given at the Plenary Session on "Cultural Histories of Legal Professions: Perspectives and Future Directions", Peyresq, France, 16–18 July 2000' (14 July 2000) 2.

[16] For example, on Australia see Bruce Kercher, *An Unruly Child. A History of Law in Australia* (Allen & Unwin, St Leonards, NSW, 1995) and the contributions of Kercher and McQueen in Robert McQueen, and W Wesley Pue (eds), *Misplaced Traditions: The Legal Profession and the British Empire. Symposium Issue, 16 (1) Law in Context*, 1999.

With respect to the considerable literature on Canada, see W Wesley Pue, 'British Maculinities, Canadian Lawyers: Canadian Legal Education, 1900–1930.' In *Misplaced Traditions: The Legal Profession and the British Empire. Symposium Issue, 16 (1)* 1999 *Law in Context*, edited by Robert McQueen and W Wesley Pue, 80–122, and the sources cited therein.

On Continental Europe, see Dietrich Rueschemeyer, *Lawyers and Their Society: A Comparative Study in the Legal Profession in Germany and the United States* (Harvard University Press, Cambridge, 1973); William J Bouwsma, 'Lawyers and Early Modern Culture' (1973) 73 *American History Review* 303–27; W Prest (ed), *Lawyers in Early Modern Europe and America* (Croom Helm, London, 1981); Ezra N Suleiman, *Private Power and Centralization in France: The Notaires and the State* (Princeton University Press, Princeton, 1987); David Bell, *Lawyers and Citizens: The Making of a Political Elite in Old Regime France* (OUP, Oxford, 19i94); Jean-Louis Halperin (ed), *Advocats Et Notaires En Europe: Les Professions Judiciaires Et Juridiques Dans L'histoire Contemporaine, Droit et Societe vol 19* (Librairie generale de droit et de jurisprudence

As we have learned more about the professions in the three centuries before the industrial revolution, so the special affiliation between professionalisation and nineteenth century capitalist society has looked increasingly problematic.

For instance, in terms of numbers of lawyers, and professional organisation and education, the English legal profession of the 1880's looks strikingly similar to that of the 1680s, although a major decline in numbers, professional organisation and education had occurred during the intervening period. This intervening period has been characterised as one of 'de-professionalisation', a significant and hitherto neglected context to the reforms of the nineteenth century.[17]

This new work on the professions in the early modern period has implicitly and explicitly challenged the efficacy of linear notions of professionalisation as a focal point for research. It is part of a wider

(LGDJ), Paris, 1996); Kenneth Ledford, *From General Estate to Special Interest: German Lawyers, 1878–1933* (Cambridge University Press, Cambridge, 1996); Terence C Halliday and Lucien Karpik (eds), *Lawyers and the Rise of Western Political Liberalism* (Clarendon Press, Oxford, 1997); Hannes Siegrist, *Advokat, Burger Und Staat: Sozialgeschichte Der Rechtsanwalte in Deutschland, Italien Und Der Schweiz (18.-20. Jh.)* 2 vols (Vittorio Klostermann, Frankfurt am Main, 1996).

On England, see David Sugarman, 'Simple Images and Complex Realities: English Lawyers and Their Relationship to Business and Politics' (1993) 11(2) *Law and History Review* 257–301; 'Who Colonized Whom?: Historical Reflections on the Intersection between Law, Lawyers and Accountants in England' in Yves Dezaley and David Sugarman (eds), *Professional Competition and Professional Power: Lawyers, Accountants and the Social Construction of Markets* (Routledge, London, 1995) 226–37; 'Bourgeois Collectivism, Professional Power and the Boundaries of the State: The Private and Public Life of the Law Society, 1825–1914' (1996) 3 *International Journal of the Legal Profession* 81–135 and the references cited therein.

On the United States, see, for example, James Willard Hurst, *The Growth of American Law* (Little, Brown and Co, Boston, 1950); Jerold S Auerbach, *Unequal Justice. Lawyers and Social Change in Modern America* (OUP, New York, 1974; RW Gordon, 'Legal Thought and Legal Practice in the Age of the American Enterprise, 1870–1920' in G Geison (ed), *Professions and Professional Ideologies in America* (Chapel Hill, 1983); Alfred S Konefsky and Andrew J King (eds), *The Papers of Daniel Webster: Legal Papers,* 3 vols (University Press of New England, Hanover, New Hampshire, 1982–4); Robert A Ferguson, *Law and Letters in American Culture* (Harvard University Press, Cambridge, 1986); Terence C Halliday, *Beyond Monopoly: Lawyers, State Crises and Professional Empowerment* (University of Chicago Press, Chicago, 1987); Michael J Powell, *From Patrician to Professional Elite: The Transformation of the New York City Bar Association* (Russell Sage, New York, 1988); Ronen Shamir, *Managing Legal Uncertainty: Elite Lawyers in the New Deal* (Duke University Press, Durham, NC, 1995).

[17] See, Christopher W Brooks, The Admissions Registers of Barnard's Inn 1620–1869, Selden Society Supp. Series-12 (Selden Society, London, 1995) and Christopher W Brooks, *Lawyers, Litigation and English Society since 1450* (Hambledon Press, London, 1998); David Sugarman, 'Bourgeois Collectivism, Professional Power and the Boundaries of the State: The Private and Public Life of the Law Society, 1825–1914' (1996) 3 *International Journal of the Legal Profession* 81–135; Lemmings, *Professors of the Law* (Oxford University Press, Oxford, New York, 2000).

movement within history and social theory that transcends two-class, patrician-plebeian models of society, and takes seriously the ideologies, institutions and practices of the middle classes—such as notions of 'gentlemanness', respectability and 'bourgeois association'. This work has fundamentally questioned some of the ways we have traditionally characterised early modern and modern society.[18]

Rather than treating the history of lawyers in a singular and unitary fashion, latter-day histories increasingly recognise the plurality of lawyers—in terms of sub-groups, culture, social composition (gentry, middling sort etc), the routes to practice (on-the-job training, apprenticeship, university education, book learning, quackery) and geographically (urban and rural)—the fragmented and de-centred character of much of the legal community and the ways in each of the histories of the several sub-groups that constituted the legal profession is characterised by its own intricate history. In part this is to problematise the category of 'lawyer'. Were 'lawyers' those people who were professionally qualified, those who were professionally qualified *and* who practised on a regular basis, or those who practised law even though they were not formally qualified as lawyers? To some extent, 'lawyer' was understood to mean different things by different people at different times. The category of 'lawyer' might embrace a wide range of sub-groupings and individuals. Yet, the demarcation line between these sub-groupings was often not clear-cut but was contested, and changed over time. There is a further problem: in the common law world at least, there are large numbers of lawyers who were not members of any professional association. Several histories of the legal profession fall into the elementary error of confusing 'lawyers' with members of law societies or bar associations. Even in the case of the English Bar—something of an ideal-type legal profession—membership of the Inns of Court was often nominal only.

Moreover, the study of lawyers from a cross-cultural perspective immediately poses the question of exactly what to compare. There are significant differences in the definition and work of lawyers in various countries. These divergences are particularly great if we compare, say, the

[18] An important by-product of some of this work has been the analysis of changing patterns of litigation over time, and its influence on the organisation and development of the legal profession, the courts and dispute resolution. See, for example, Richard L Kagan, *Lawyers and Litigants in Castille, 1500–1700* (University of North Carolina Press, Chapel Hill, 1980); Lawrence M Friedman, 'Opening the Time Capsule: A Progress Report on Studies of Courts over Time' (1990) 24(2) *Law & Society Review* 229–40; CW Brooks, 'Interpersonal Conflict and Social Tension: Civil Litigation in England, 1640–1830' in AL Beier, D Cannadine and J Rosenheim (eds) (Cambridge University Press, Cambridge, 1989) 357–99 and Brooks, *Lawyers, Litigation and English Society since 1450*. For a contemporary and comparative survey see BS Markesinis, 'Litigation Mania in England, Germany and the USA: Are We So Very Different?' (1990) *Cambridge Law Journal* 223.

common law world with other legal families or traditions, such as that of the civil law or Islamic world. It is common, for example, to translate the French 'avocat' as 'barrister' though the professional roles and concepts are not interchangeable. Similarly, even within English-derived legal systems, such as those of Manitoba, Victoria and England itself, 'barrister' can mean quite different things. It is hardly surprising, therefore, that serious and sustained cross-cultural research on lawyers has been something of a rarity.

Nonetheless, since the 1980s, the literature striving towards a comparative perspective on lawyers has grown significantly and affords some essential, albeit tentative, first steps towards a more thoroughgoing cross-cultural perspective on lawyers in society.[19] This work is beginning to produce a clearer and more precise specification of the contrasts and similarities as between the character and development of common law and civilian lawyers. Historians, legal historian and sociologists in several countries have also begun to investigate the role of lawyers in politics and state-building.[20] Studies of key lawyers' associations have sought to give greater attention to the linkages between lawyers and politics (as broadly conceived). This work has highlighted the complex and contingent ways in which elite lawyers were both a cause and effect of the limited liberal state.[21] In particular, the relationship between lawyers and liberal democracy has begun to receive significant, transnational attention.[22]

[19] Prest (ed), *Lawyers in Early Modern Europe and America*; Richard L Abel and Philip CC Lewis (eds), *Lawyers in Society. The Civil Law World* (University of California Press, Berkeley, 1988); Richard L Abel and Philip SC Lews (eds), *Lawyers in Society. Comparative Theories*. 3 vols vol 1 (University of California Press, Berkeley, 1989); Michael Burrage and Rolf Torstendahl (eds), *Professions in Theory and History: Rethinking the Study of the Professions* (Sage, London, 1990).

[20] For an early, pioneering study, see Lauro Martines, *Lawyers and Statecraft in Renaissance Florence* (Princeton University Press, Princeton, 1968).

[21] See, Terence C Halliday, *Beyond Monopoly: Lawyers, State Crises and Professional Empowerment* (University of Chicago Press, Chicago, 1987); Michael J Powell, *From Patrician to Professional Elite: The Transformation of the New York City Bar Association* (Russell Sage, New York, 1988); Christopher Brooks, 'Professions, Ideology and the Middling Sort in the Late Sixteenth and Early Seventeenth Centuries' in Jonathan Barry and Christopher Brooks (eds), *The Middling Sort of People: Culture, Society and Politics in England 1550–1800* (Macmillan, Basingstoke, Hants, 1994) 113–40; Sugarman, 'Bourgeois Collectivism, Professional Power and the Boundaries of the State: The Private and Public Life of the Law Society, 1825–1914'; Brooks, The Admissions Registers of Barnard's Inn 1620–1869; Brooks, Lawyers, Litigation and English Society since 1450. See, also, Rob McQueen's contribution to this collection.

[22] Ronen Shamir, *Managing Legal Uncertainty: Elite Lawyers in the New Deal* (Duke University Press, Durham, NC, 1995) cf Terence C Halliday, 'Politics and Civic Responsibility: Legal Elites and Cause Lawyers' (1999) 24(4) *Law and Social Inquiry* 1013–60; Terence C Halliday, and Lucien Karpik (eds), *Lawyers and the Rise of Western Political Liberalism* (Clarendon Press, Oxford, 1997) cf Stuart A Scheingold, 'Taking Weber Seriously: Lawyers, Politics and the Liberal State' (1999) 24(4) *Law and Social*

Increasingly, this literature has sought to be less parochial and Anglo-American in orientation. Thus, sensitivity to the confines of history and sociology of the professions anchored in the common law world was clearly recognised in the pioneering work of Rueschemeyer[23] and the volumes on lawyers and society edited by Abel and Lewis.[24] More recently, it is possible to talk of an increasingly thoroughgoing comparative turn which both problematises Anglo-American, taken-for-granted assumptions about the nature, scope, chronology of legal professions and professionalisation—as well as the use and non-use of the law and lawyers.

IV

In addition to its cross-national concerns, the principal focus of this book is the cultural history of lawyers (as broadly conceived). In this section we aim to explain what we mean by culture and cultural history, the kinds of questions and methods that it suggests, and some of the difficulties that it can give rise to.

Attempts to write a wider history than that of legal doctrine or of high politics have a long and distinguished pedigree. In particular, the jurist-historians of the Enlightenment created a body of work that built upon and extended the jurisprudence of legal humanists such as Bodin, and the natural law's comparative, 'laws of nations' orientation. It stressed that law was the product of time and historical development, and that it should be studied comparatively, and therefore, sociologically. The leading lights of this movement included Scotland's Kames, Smith, Robertson and Millar; England's Gibbon; the German historical school of Hugo and Savigny; and its most influential practitioner, Frances's

Inquiry 1061–82; Karpik, Lucien, *French Lawyers. A Study of Collective Action, 1274–1994* (Clarendon Press, Oxford, 1999) cf Michael Burrage, 'Escaping the Dead Hand of Rational Choice: Karpik's Historical Sociology of French Advocates' (1999) 24(4) *Law and Social Inquiry* 1083–124; Gerard Hanlon, *Lawyers, the State and the Market: Professionalism Revisisted* (Macmillan, London, 1999). See, also, Terence C Halliday, 'The Politics of Lawyers: An Emerging Agenda; (1999) 24(4) *Law and Social Inquiry* 1007–12.

[23] Dietrich Rueschemeyer, *Lawyers and Their Society: A Comparative Study of the Legal Profession in Germany and the United States* (Harvard University Press, Cambridge, 1973).

[24] Abel, Richard L, and Philip SC Lewis (eds), *Lawyers in Society. The Civil Law World* (University of California Press, Berkeley, 1988); Richard L Abel and Philip SC Lewis (eds), *Lawyers in Society. The Common Law World.* 3 vols vol 1 (University of California Press, Berkeley, 1989); Abel, Richard L, and Philip SC Lewis (eds), *Lawyers in Society. Comparative Theories.* 3 vols vol 1 (University of California Press, Berkeley, 1989).

Montesquieu. In this way the study of law became a principal way of studying society.[25]

Montesquieu's influence is difficult to overestimate. He stressed the contingency of the law, the diverse causes that fashion distinctive nation states, the need for culturally specific approaches to the study of law, and the material and cultural forces that delimit all lawmakers. It was his followers who developed these insights into histories that were sensitive to the manners and customs of particular societies and the 'spirit of the age'. It was in this context that some eighteenth century historians acquired an interest in comparative and even 'world' history.

> In 1860 the Swiss scholar Jacob Burckhardt published a study of *The Civilization of the Renaissance in Italy*, concentrating on cultural history and describing trends rather than narrating events. The sociologists of the nineteenth century . . . were extremely interested in history but rather contemptuous of professional historians. They were interested in structures, not events, and the new history owes a debt to them. . .

Thus, the cultural histories contained in this volume have '. . . a reasonably long ancestry . . .' (even if the great-great-grandparents might not recognise their descendants). What is new is not its existence so much as the fact that its practitioners are now . . . 'becoming numerous. . .'.[26]

The development and enlargement of cultural history is closely related to the formulation of new (and not so new) questions and approaches within the human sciences during the last 20 or 30 years that are sometimes referred to as the 'cultural turn.' Since at least the 1970s, the concept of 'culture' has become central to modern understandings both of political community and of personal identity. For some time now, a central issue in the human sciences has been the social construction of reality: that is, the idea that the most basic ways in which people conceive of the world, the most elementary categories that people use to organise their everyday life and understand reality—the public and private, the market, the family, the individual—are culturally and historically contingent; that is, they are manufactured by people through language, at a particular place and time. Thus, increasing attention is being paid to how a specific social reality is constructed, how people conceive of that socially constructed reality and how they interpret it to others. Whilst the cultural turn is concerned with behaviour and social structure, it lavishes most attention on the creation and diffusion of meaning, symbols and language. From this perspective, then, social life is conceived as the con-

[25] See, David Sugarman, 'Law' in John W Yolton, Roy Porter, Pat Rogers and Barbara Maria Stafford, *The Blackwell Companion to the Enlightenment* (Blackwell, Oxford, 1991) 275–77.

[26] Peter Burke, 'Overture: The New History, Its Past and Its Future' in Peter Burke (ed), *New Perspectives on Historical Writing* (Polity Press, Cambridge, 1991) 1–23, 8.

struction, interpretation and negotiation of systems of meaning. Under this optic, 'culture' widened its meaning: it refers to the history of rules and assumptions underlying everyday life.[27]

A cultural approach to law, for example, might regard law as a potent and institutional story: one of the privileged ways through which society defines and presents the world to itself. Being normative in nature, law is a way of social imagining and may come to comprise the greater lived reality of social experience. As a partially intelligible description for action, laws predispose their writers, actors and audience to certain interpretative choices and social stances.

How, then, might one characterise the cultural history of lawyers? One of its principal concerns is to describe and analyse the production, transmission and reception of the ideas and practices of lawyers in society over time: of how differing fractions within and beyond the legal community consume the practices and ideas of lawyers and their larger significance. The creation, transmission, diffusion and mediation of these discourses within and beyond the legal community is an important part of the history of the profession and of political thought.

A cultural approach to lawyers in history would also critically describe and assess the role of lawyers as potentially important actors in the complex process by which notions of national distinctiveness and personal identity were imaginatively constructed. Its concern with culture and symbols—the concerns of reputation, social standing and cultural capital—also help to explain why and when lawyers refused to undertake new fields of work or otherwise acted in ways that at first blush do not appear to accord with their material self-interest.

By deploying a cultural approach to the history of lawyers we are suggesting that legal professions:

[27] See, generally, Clifford Geertz, *The Interpretation of Cultures* (Basic Books, New York, 1973); Pierre Bourdieu, *Outline of a Theory of Practice* (Cambridge University Press, Cambridge, 1977); Stuart Hall, 'Cultural Studies: Two Paradigms' in Stuart Hall (ed), *Media, Culture and Society*, 1980; Raymond Williams, *Culture and Society* (Columbia Press, New York, 1983); Marshall Sahlins, *Culture and Practical Reason* (University of Chicago Press, Chicago, 1985); James Clifford and George E Marcus (eds), *Writing Culture: The Poetics and Politics of Ethnography* (University of California Press, Berkeley, 1986); Robert Wuthnow, *Meaning and Moral Order: Explorations in Cultural Analysis* (University of California Press, Berkeley, 1987). Roger Chartier, *Cultural History* (Polity Press, Cambridge, 1988); Lynn Hunt (ed), *The New Cultural History* (University of California Press, Berkeley, 1989); Lawrence Grossberg, Cary Nelson, and Paula Treichler, *Cultural Studies* (Routledge, New York, 1992); TL Haskell, and RF Teichgraeber III (eds), *The Culture of the Market* (Cambridge University Press, Cambridge, 1993); Joyce Appleby, Lynn Hunt, and Margaret Jacob, *Telling the Truth About History* (Norton & Company, New York, 1994); NB Dirks, G Eley, and SB Ortner, 'Introduction', in Dirks NB, G Eley and SB Ortner (eds), *Culture/Power/History* (Princeton University Press, Princeton, 1994); Bill Schwartz (ed), *The Expansion of England: Race, Ethnicity and Cultural History* (Routledge, London, 1996).

> . . . were more than the sum of . . . [their] parts, and individual . . . [lawyers] cannot be understood as simple 'economic men', who slavishly followed material gain. Like anyone else, . . . [lawyers] were self-interested and independent in varying degrees, . . . [and throughout a good deal of their history there was little guidance or restraint available with respect to the furtherance of the economic self-interest]. Nevertheless, they were all heirs to a complex of customs, working habits, role models, and ideologies . . . [that might derive] from a rich collective history which stretched back several centuries. Such a legacy certainly distinguished them from other individuals and helped to inform and constrain their behaviour; it has survived, in an adapted but still recognizable form, among contemporary . . . [lawyers] and their counterparts in former [or current] . . . colonies. So the 'culture' of . . . [lawyers] is an important subject in its own right; besides being worth investigation for its relation to . . . [popular culture, religion, political economy and other important cultures, ideas and ideologies].
>
> No culture (in this social and intellectual sense) is autonomous. . . . [Consequently, cultural histories of lawyers attempt to place lawyers and] the legal 'system' which provided their primary raison d'être, in the context of the complex (and contested) history of . . . [a particular society] and its government. This means considering their work, their clients, and the various law courts in relation to . . . [the economy and economic change, power and the culture of power, social inequality, authority and the control of definitions of reality, nation and empire building and colonialism and the intellectual trends of their day. It] also requires some attention to the important issues of their social consciousness, aspirations and allegiances . . . Put so briefly and exclusively, these issues belie their infinite scope and complexity; but while they are hardly susceptible to simple answers, they may serve as convenient yardsticks against which to measure the . . . [lawyers] working relations with clients, patrons, . . . [politicians, state servants] and other lawyers, and to assess their collective impact as the human embodiment of the law.[28]

The cultural history of lawyers also seeks to address the gendered character of the profession, for example, investigating the role of gentlemanlyness, respectability and masculinity[29] within the culture of the legal profession—the homosocial character of the legal profession—which, for example, parallels and connects to larger features of middle class Victorian culture in England and its colonies.

Additionally, it is concerned with the role of lawyers and the law in the articulation and policing of democratisation, race, ethnicity, national identity, colonialism and empire building. Once we study societies

[28] David Lemmings, *Professors of the Law. Barristers and English Legal Culture in the Eighteenth Century* (Oxford University Press, Oxford, 2000) 7–8.

[29] Cf Michael Grossberg, 'Institutionalizing Masculinity: The Law as a Masculine Profession' in Marc C Carnes and Clyde Griffen (eds), *Meanings of Manhood: Constructions of Masculinity in Victorian America* (University of Chicago Press, Chicago, 1990); Schoemaker, Robert B, *Gender in English Society, 1650–1850: The Emergence of Separate Spheres?* (Longman, London, 1998); R Collier, *Masculinity and the Law* (Routledge, London, New York, 1995).

in which divisions of class, race, and ethnicity are fundamentally constitutive, it has become clear that if we speak of culture as shared, we must now always ask 'By whom?' and 'In what ways?' and 'Under what conditions?'[30]

Elsewhere it has been observed that in Britain, France, Germany and the United States, in the period from the late eighteenth century, '. . . the law had acquired additional or indeed an entirely new legitimacy by being linked with the process of nation-building and democratization.'[31] The role of lawyers in the 'nationalisation' of the law, and legal institutions—through codes, constitutions and the resistance of the English common law to 'rationalisation'—and how this 'nationalisation' impacted on the profession, requires sustained attention. How did lawyers constitute, impose, legitimate and resist imperialism? What was the role of lawyers and religion in the 'civilising mission' in India, Africa, Ireland, Australia and Canada? And in what ways were imperial power and the imperial professions themselves (re)constituted by this process. This work is not antiquarian but topical in the light of contemporary struggles to impose particular regimes and styles of lawyering within a more globalised world.[32]

And just as lawyers are best understood as a plurality so too with the idea of culture, including legal culture. This is to acknowledge culture as multiple discourses, '. . . occasionally coming together in large systematic configuration, but more often coexisting within dynamic fields of interaction and conflict'.[33]

The essays in this book engage with some of these and other issues in order to extend, enrich and supplement more conventional histories of lawyers. Yet it should also be acknowledged that cultural history is an imprecise and contested concept. It conveys a core meaning in many historical and cultural contexts, while being sufficiently inclusive to accommodate a range of forms. It is necessarily a heterogeneous enterprise, accommodating a greater diversity of questions, concerns and

[30] Dirks, Eley, and Ortner, 'Introduction', 3.

[31] Willibald Steinmetz (ed), *Private Law and Social Inequality in the Industrial Age: Comparing Legal Cultures in Britain, France, Germany, and the United States* (OUP, Oxford, 2000) 36.

[32] DM Trubek, Y Dezalay, R Buchanan, and John R Davis, 'Global Restructuring and the Law; Studies of the Internationalization of Legal Fields and the Creation of Transnational Arenas' (1994) 44 *Case Western Reserve Law Review* 407–98; Yves Dezakay and David Sugarman (eds), *Professional Competition and Professional Power: Lawyers, Accountants and the Social Construction of Markets* (Routledge, London, 1995); Yves Dezalay and Bryant G Garth, *Dealing in Virtue: International Commercial Arbitration and the Construction of a Transnational Legal Order* (University of Chicago Press, Chicago, 1996); Avrom Sherr and David Sugarman (eds), Globalisation and Legal Education, Special Issue of the *International Journal of the Legal Profession*, 2002, in press.

[33] Dirks, Eley, and Ortner, 'Introduction', 3–4.

approaches than has conventionally been the case in historical and legal scholarship. Consequently, identifying the boundary that separates it from other forms of history writing can prove difficult. The boundary separating cultural from other types of history writing is inevitably fluid and permeable. Consequently, cultural history tends to shade into social, economic, political, intellectual, business, legal etc history—especially when it is working on accepted understandings of professional culture, and established practices, ideas and ideologies. Definitional problems also occur because 'new histories' like cultural history, 'are pushing into unfamiliar territory.'[34]

Moreover, it is important to remember the artificial, contingent and socially constructed character of conceptual categories like 'cultural', 'legal', 'social', 'economic', 'political', 'intellectual' etc. While such categories serve useful and necessary analytical purposes, they do not represent real divisions in everyday life but are invariably connected to and imbricated within each other, albeit, in a complex and contradictory fashion.

Clearly, therefore, it would be premature (and foolhardy) to attempt a single, wholly contained and universally applicable definition of the cultural history of the legal profession. Aware that the indiscriminate application of the term 'culture' threatens to deprive that word of any specific meaning, and that 'cultural history' is a contested concept, we have nonetheless sought to indicate our understanding of its meaning, parameters and utility.

V

Part I of the book addresses the formation of lawyers by way of two contrasting papers. David Lemmings' essay 'Ritual, Majesty and Mystery: Collective Life and Culture among English Barristers, Serjeants and Judges, c.1500–c.1830' describes and dissects the decline of the traditional rituals of a legal elite—their dress, their customs, their dinning requirements etc. In tracing this decline, Lemmings illuminates decisive developments in the structure and culture of the legal profession and its connections with the state and English people. In essence, Lemmings argues that the changes in the ceremonial life of the profession are illustrative of the way in which the collective life of the profession of the common law was being privatised by the middle classes. This legal elite became more inward looking and pervaded by competitive individualism—in the sense of the restriction and maximisation of returns from activities confined to an affluent minority of population.

[34] Burke, 'Overture: The New History, Its Past and Its Future', 9.

In ' "A Dry and Revolting Study": the Life and Labors of Antebellum Law Students' Ann Fidler provides a fascinating account of the life and images of antebellum law students in the United States. Fidler's essay uses textual analysis to analyse the cultural constructs that shaped the law student's experience: the rules, myths, expectations and illusions generated from within and without the legal profession. In doing so, she provides insights into one of the many ways that the law transformed the lives of individual Americans:

> William McClintick, a Chillicothe, Ohio law student wrote to a friend in 1838: 'You ask me how I like the Law, and *all about it*. To answer this, would be a task, which at present I cannot think of undertaking. *All about the Law*! Why, man, you are mad. I might as well attempt a description of the great Labyrinth of Egypt. As to my liking it, this is something more tangible. I am much better pleased that I expected to be and feel perfectly willing to continue a searcher into Legal mysteries the rest of my days. The Law, sir, is glorious. Try it yourself'.

Part II of the collection examines the relationship between lawyers and the liberal state in Continental Europe. Esa Konttinen essays a backward glance at Finland's route to legal professionalisation and the success of lawyer-officials, politically, economically and culturally. Finnish professionalisation has, throughout its history, been closely connected with a strong state and a central bureaucracy. This fact has greatly influenced the forms and content of professionalisation and the development of the legal profession. Thus, Konttinen argues that professionalisation in Finland is an example of the Continental development of the profession. He describes the cultural, educational and allied ways in which the gentry dominated the profession in the early and mid nineteenth century—in contrast to say England and the United States. Although legal culture changed during the second half of the nineteenth century, he points up the continuing significance of gentry culture within the legal profession and the ways in which the niche of lawyer-official offered a great number of the nobility a smooth transition to modern liberal-bourgeois society.

Hannes Siegrist provides a remarkable overview of Continental European developments in his 'Juridicalization, Professionalization and the Occupational Culture of the Advocate in the 19th and the early 20th centuries: A Comparison of Germany, Italy and Switzerland'. He addresses five issues. He first deals with how the legal profession was transformed during the century by comparing the situations of advocates in Germany, Italy, and Switzerland respectively. Secondly, he explicates the ratio of lawyers to the general population and its larger significance. Thirdly, he examines the relationship between supply and demand in the market for legal services, as well as the question of accessibility to law and legal advice. Fourth, he investigates the emergence of various subgroupings within the profession. Fifth, he describes some aspects of the symbolic staging of law and the legal profession: what he terms 'the myth of the law practice'; the significance of professional and honorary titles; the role of rhetoric during the ritual of a procedure; the law office as a stage for the lawyers to portray themselves; and the use of monuments and public celebrations to represent the lawyers. This wide-ranging *tour de force* explicates the quite different structural forms of legal education, organisation and practice which developed in Germany, Italy and Switzerland between the Congress of Vienna and World War I.

In 'From Rechstaat to Welfare State: Swedish Judicial Culture in Transition 1870–1970', Kjell Modéer contributes a valuable study of the transformation of judicial culture within a legal culture where judges (relative to their common law counterparts) are anonymous and where judicial biography is rare. Modéer examines a variety of sources in order to ascertain the changing meanings that judges and others attached to the life, work and cultural capital of the judge: including the ideological dimensions of judicial culture (political, philosophical and professional), the court system, the professional and ethical rules governing the judiciary the marginalisation of women as judges, the law (notably, the constitution and the code of procedure), legal education and the larger political culture. Of particular interest is his analyis of the iconography and architecture of the courtroom, and libraries and books, as a window on the mental furniture of the judiciary and their larger cultural significance.

Part III of the collection is concerned with the theme of Work and Representations. It begins with John Savage's study of the clash between the ideals of virtue and wealth in the late nineteenth-and early twentieth-century Parisian Bar. Savage characterises the culture of the Parisian Bar as a '. . . curious mixture of bourgeois values of moral probity and talent-based success, on one hand, with what can be thought of as aristocratic values of honor, prowess, even heroism. . .' In this guise it was characterised by the regulation of professional conduct that emphasised the moral and personal qualities of the advocate, masculinity, a disdain for commercialism and money-making, and the Bar's work for the public good, for example, by providing free legal counsel to the poor. This culture was attractive in part because it appeared to raise its membership above the level of the mere bourgeois. Yet, as Savage demonstrates, an economic downturn, the democratising aspirations of the Republic, the pressures generated by an increasingly overcrowded profession and the effort to admit women to the Bar when allied to larger concerns about the cultural de-generation of France—exacerbated tensions between the traditionalists and the modernisers within the profession and as between the Bar and French society. By marshalling quantitative data on changes in the size and work of the Bar, and the number of women students at university, allied to qualitative data on the ideas, ideologies and rhetoric within and beyond the Bar, Savage paints a vivid picture of the effort to reform the profession from within and without, and the backward-looking nostalgia for a past pre-democratic era that reinforced the anti-Republic, conservatism of the Bar. 'The experience of the *avocats* suggests that, in their case at least, the *fin-de-siècle* saw a cultural persistence of the Old Regime.'[35]

Jean-Louis Halperin undertakes the first detailed quantitative and qualitative study of French lawyer's fees in the nineteenth century. As with English barristers, French lawyers regarded their fees as honoraria, rather than as a salary underpinned and enforced by way of contract.[36] Halperin points out that lawyers were allowed to charge their well-off clients high fees and their less well-off clients lower fees on the principle that lawyers should be put on the same social footing as their clients. In this and other ways, they managed to develop an individual and collective strategy which made fees subject to accepted professional practices that were unwritten and advantageous for their social position. This ideology sustained the profession's claims to independence, honour and paternalism.

Anne McGillivray contributes a fascinating extended reading of Bram Stoker's *Dracula* (1897). Treating the book as a legal novel, a category in which few students of literature have thought to place it, McGillivray probes the text to reveal competing conceptions of lawyering and the legal professions amid a fear of modernity, moral de-generation and the growing disjunction between law and morality. In addition to delineating the themes of professionalism, law and modernity through the 'peculiar rationality' of Stoker's text, McGillivray demonstrates the bases of that author's legal knowledge in his lengthy stint in the legal department of the Irish civil service, and subsequent call to the Bar following his move to London.

David Applebaum contributes a fascinating study of birth and development of a major French labour union of judges, the *Syndicat de la Magistrature*, 1968–1978. Applebaum examines how middle level French judicial bureaucrats were unionised, radicalised and feminised following the political upheavals of the late 1960s. Applebaum stresses the *Syndicat's* role in creating a professional counter-culture and the refashioning of judge and citizen relations and national legal culture. He analyses its efforts to support the weaker sections of the community—employees, tenants etc—so as to do justice—and the difficulties this gave rise to. This remarkable 'story of collective challenges to the interplay of

[35] Savage's characterisation of the Paris Bar partially contradicts that of Karpik, *French Lawyers*.

[36] In this guise, lawyers were admitted to a post of honour and, therefore, the services that they provided were nominally free. Thus, the fees that they received in practice were characterised as honoraria. Cf W Wesley Pue, 'Moral Panic at the English Bar: Paternal vs Commercial Ideologies of Legal Practice in the 1860s' (1990) 15 *Law and Social Inquiry* 49–118.

state and society' derives in part from a detailed investigation of the union's own records.

The book concludes (in Part IV) with a series of essays on Lawyers and Colonialism. Rob McQueen's essay, 'Together We Fall, Divided We Stand: the Victorian Legal Profession in Crisis 1890–1940' challenges simplistic images of the homogeneity of the legal profession, and the professions assertions of 'high ethical ideals', in past times. He investigates two key moments of moral and economic panic in the life of the Australian State of Victoria's Law Society: namely the 1890s, and the period circa 1928–1936. In both these periods the profession was under significant stress. McQueen's study highlights the inevitable tension between the Law Society's role as a professional trade union, and its claims to professionalism and high ideals. Turning conventional wisdom on its head he concludes that:

> The legal profession in Victoria has always been subject to considerable division . . . the level of homogeneity claimed by both 'institutional' historians of the profession and by 'market control' theorists never appears to have existed within the profession in Victoria. Dissent and friction between sectors of the profession have been the 'norm'.

Harold Dick's essay seeks to understand the cultural chasm between Mennonites and Mennonite Lawyers in Western Canada, 1900–1939:

> To be sure, at least seven members of the legal profession in this period had been born into Mennonite homes and had grown up speaking Plattdeutsch, eating verenike, roll kuchen and zweibach and attending Mennonite churches. In addition, three of these men had attended a Mennonite High School and two had married Mennonite women. It is also true that all but one of these men practised law near Mennonite settlements for some period of time during their careers, using their connections with the Mennonites to build a clientele. Moreover, at least two of these men used their skills in an extra-legal capacity to defend the interests of the Mennonite community. . . . Nevertheless, despite these connections to the Mennonite community, none of these men can be considered Mennonites by the standards of that community at that time and, almost certainly, by their own standards as well.

Dick argues that these men were forced to abandon full participation in their ethnic, cultural and religious communities of origin, not so much because of prejudice against lawyers from immigrant communities, but because the culture inhabited by the Mennonites was fundamentally incompatible with the culture of the legal profession of the Canadian prairies. And that the incompatibilities of and conflict between these cultures in the early decades of the twentieth century made it impossible to straddle the two communities.

Finally, in his essay 'Cultural Projects and Structural Transformation in the Canadian Legal Profession', Wes Pue chronicles the attempts of some Western Canadian lawyers during the early twentieth century to effect a cultural revolution, not just of their occupation, but also its surrounding community, polity and society. Pue analyses the various impulses that underlay this effort, such as Christianity, the fear of Bolshevism as well as a concern about the law and its practitioners. The structures of professionalism themselves are found to be cultural artefacts, collapsing the 'structure'/'culture' distinction. Pue concludes that:

> Legal professionalism, like moral regulation movements, can be a manifestation of 'an anxiety of freedom that haunts modern liberal forms of rule' where there 'is no 'natural' system of order.' It is important that the developing literatures on lawyers and liberalism take into account this seemingly anti-democratic zone of professional activity, as well as the more obviously 'liberal' contributions of individual lawyers and (less often) organised legal professions alike. . . .
>
> [Most] leading lawyers would have understood the urges which led Michel Foucault to describe one project of western states as being to 'constitute the populace as a moral subject'. . . . In common cause with other prominent Canadians acting in many realms, it was very much *what Canadian lawyers were on about*. What is interesting in the work of the legal professions is the extent to which lawyers combined agendas which were explicitly moral and reforming with a profound restructuring of their profession.

VI

While the individual chapters do not provide a comprehensive basis for comparisons, they do at the very least afford a number of suggestive parallels and contrasts. The strongest initial impression of the volume is one of diversity and difference with respect to both the subject-matter of the book and the approaches adopted by the contributors. The institutional, cultural and social differences between the various nation states and their legal systems often seem very large indeed—not least as between the common law and civil law jurisdictions. Likewise the differences as between colonial and imperial centres, and provincial and urban geographical perspectives—say, Melbourne and Western Canada, contrasted with London and Paris—are often considerable. However, some common tendencies and characteristics can also be discerned, including the heterogeneity of most national legal professions, and their preoccupation with order, status (as well as economic self-interest), social exclusiveness, masculinity, legal learning and ritual. Common ground is also evident, as witnessed by the examination of professional structures in Australia, Finland, Germany, Italy and Switzerland by McQueen, Kontinnen and Siegrist respectively. Overall, the essays help us to understand the complex ways in which legal professions are culturally constructed.

Like the emerging lawyers/politics paradigm[37], cultural histories of the legal profession, such as the work in this volume, suggest that many of the most important things to know about lawyers cannot be understood within the constraints of a market control theory,[38] however valuable that may be. Rather, cultural histories of the legal profession raise more problematic and wide-ranging understandings of legal professions, their various iterations, and social roles than do approaches focussed exclusively on assessing the contributions of some lawyers to the development of liberal politics.

Although the subject-matter traversed in this book is wide-ranging, it is far from comprehensive. Several important topics require more sustained exploration, such as part-time, 'quack', 'folk-lawyers' as opposed to elite fractions within the profession ('the history of lawyers from below'), the clients' experiences of lawyers[39], the relationship between lawyers and their clients, the role and position of women, the significance of gender and the comparison between lawyers and allied occupational groups.[40] Thus, in addition to offering a broad ranging survey of current knowledge, we also hope to stimulate further work and novel lines of inquiry.

[37] See, for example, Halliday and Karpik (eds), *Lawyers and the Rise of Western Political Liberalism* (Clarendon Press, Oxford, 1997). Cf Scheingold, 'Taking Weber Seriously: Lawyers, Politics and the Liberal State'.

[38] For a critique of market control theory, see Halliday, 'The Politics of Lawyers: An Emerging Agenda.' See, also, Karpik, *French Lawyers* esp ch 8 'The Market' and W Wesley Pue, 'Trajectories of Professionalism' (1990) 19 *Manitoba Law Journal*, 384–418.

[39] See, for example, the work of Margaret Pelling.

[40] For a suggestive exemplar, see Rosemary O'Day, *The Professions in Early Modern England, 1450–1800* (Longman, Harlow, Essex, 2000).

PART I

The Formation of Lawyers

2

Ritual, Majesty and Mystery: Collective Life and Culture among English Barristers, Serjeants and Judges, c.1500–c.1830

DAVID LEMMINGS

The so-called 'upper branch' of English lawyers has traditionally been associated with a highly ritualised collective life, located in their inns, messes and courtrooms, and expressed in elaborate rituals and distinctive conventions of dress. Indeed, counsellors and judges may be unique among the lay professions for their lengthy history of participatory ceremonial. The order of serjeants at law, from which the judges were drawn until the nineteenth century, developed a complex investiture ceremony and distinctive habit by 1400, and in the fifteenth century the inns of court gave 'readings' or courses of lectures with their own extensive ceremonies.[1] But these customary institutional rituals, which were the most important ceremonies of the medieval and early modern legal profession, have not survived to the present day, although they endured for several centuries. Today the pomp and ceremony characteristic of the profession is identified primarily with state occasions, such as coronations and the opening of parliament, and the performance of public judicial duties in the provinces and at Westminster. Moreover, legal ritual is concentrated on the judges, rather than involving all the various ranks of the lawyers as participants, unlike the serjeants' creation ceremonies and inns of court readings. While modern barristers express their own sense of fellowship in the dinners and grand nights held at their inns and circuit messes, and in court they maintain a distinctive form of dress dating from the seventeenth century, their collective life is relatively private and professionally exclusive, by comparison with the great public occasions which their predecessors sponsored in the ages of Spelman and Coke.

[1] JH Baker, *The Order of Serjeants at Law* (Selden Soc, supp ser 5, 1984), 17, 88; *idem*, 'A History of English Judges' Robes', *Costume*, (1978) xii, 27; EW Ives, *The Common Lawyers of Pre-Reformation England* (Cambridge University Press, Cambridge, 1983), 41–50.

What do these contrasts mean for the changing roles of lawyers and judges in the governance of English society, and how did they occur? This essay suggests that changes in the lawyers' collective life between the sixteenth and early nineteenth centuries may illuminate decisive developments in the structure and culture of the legal profession and its connections with the state and English people. It begins with the institutional ceremonies of the late medieval and early modern inns' readers and serjeants. They seem to have represented the transmission through the generations of typically Aristotelian ideals of community solidarity and sanctioned advancement through a fixed hierarchy of ranks. But historians have drawn attention to the progressive disintegration of 'older forms of communal supervision' with post-medieval doubts about natural sociability and increasing emphasis on the competitive nature of humankind.[2] Indeed, with a massive growth in litigation after c.1560, the lawyers appear to have been transformed from a 'tight professional community' of men united by their common devotion to the corpus of English law and their membership of guild-like institutions, to a much larger collection of individuals locked in unregulated competition for advantage in an increasingly complex and national market.[3] In these circumstances it is interesting that their traditional communal rituals became progressively discordant and divisive, as the winners—a new bar elite of crown counsel and law officers—challenged symbolic representations of the old order and affirmed their superior status over the ordinary barristers and serjeants.

After considering the disintegration of these ceremonies with the decline of the inns of court and the order of serjeants, the final sections of the paper discuss the rather fragmented forms of collective life which characterised barristers and judges in the eighteenth and early nineteenth centuries. On the one hand ceremonies associated with the bar elite remained in the form of elaborate judicial ritual: indeed it is necessary to consider whether there was greater emphasis on the 'theatre of power' orchestrated by the scarlet-clad judges who were primary instruments of the increasingly powerful Georgian state.[4] On the other hand, new and

[2] For manifestations of these shifts in relation to civil litigation, see WA Champion, 'Recourse to the Law and the Meaning of the Great Litigation Decline, 1650–1750: Some Clues from the Shrewsbury Local Courts', in CW Brooks and M Lobban (eds), *Communities and Courts in Britain 1150–1900* (Hambledon, London and Rio Grande, 1997), 195–6; C Muldrew, 'The Culture of Reconciliation: Community and the Settlement of Economic Disputes in Early Modern England', *Historical Journal* (1996) xxxix, 920–21.

[3] Ives, *Common Lawyers of Pre-Reformation England*, 37; WR Prest, *The Rise of the Barristers: a Social History of the English Bar, 1560–1640* (Oxford University Press, Oxford, 1986).

[4] D Hay, 'Property, Authority, and the Criminal Law', in D Hay *et al* (eds), *Albion's Fatal Tree* (Penguin, Harmondsworth, 1975), espec 26–32. For an account of the growth of the English state in the eighteenth century (which strangely neglects law) see

increasingly utilitarian types of barristers' association emerged in the forms of independent mooting societies and exclusive bar messes which began the process of institutionalising the restrictive practices typical of the modern bar. Given the considerable decline in the volume and social reach of civil litigation after 1700, the paper concludes by assessing these associations in the light of the common charge that the modern bar approximates to a private trade union: were they merely forms of collective life which represented the middle-class 'privitisation' of the common law, in the sense of the restriction and maximisation of returns from activities confined to an affluent minority of the population?

I THE INNS OF COURT

It is appropriate to begin an historical account of legal ritual with the four inns of court, because these societies have constituted the formal institutional home of the law's upper branch since medieval times, and have survived to the present day. The origins of Gray's Inn, the Inner and Middle Temples, and Lincoln's Inn remain relatively obscure, but they may have been founded in the later thirteenth or fourteenth centuries as four among several lodging houses established for the convenience of lawyers attending the Westminster courts during the legal terms. Mere hostels which existed only to provide bed and board probably had little in the way of ceremony, but there is circumstantial evidence of legal disputation at the inns from the 1340s, and certainly by Tudor times the four societies which predominated and became known as the inns of court had evolved a complex educational system which featured case arguments and lectures delivered by senior members. Participation in these exercises became the basis for the inns' degrees of barrister and bencher or reader, and these internal ranks also became significant for advancement within the profession generally. It was therefore natural that some of the exercises, and the grades of inns' membership associated with them, became invested with dignity and symbolic importance by the performance of ceremonial acts.[5]

J Brewer, *The Sinews of Power: War, Money, and the English State 1688–1783* (Unwin Hyman, London, 1989).

[5] SE Thorne, 'The Early History of the Inns of Court with Special Reference to Gray's Inn', in *idem*, *Essays in English Legal History* (Hambledon, London, 1985), 137–54; JH Baker, *The Third University of England: The Inns of Court and the Common Law Tradition* (Selden Soc, London, 1990), espec 6–14; *idem*, 'Learning Exercises in the Medieval Inns of Court' in *idem*, *The Legal Profession and the Common Law* (Hambledon, London, 1986), 7–23; *idem*, *An Introduction to English Legal History* 3rd edn (Butterworths, London, 1990), 182–5; *idem*, 'Counsellors and Barristers' in *idem*, *The Legal Profession and the Common Law*, 109–12. Ives, *Common Lawyers of Pre-Reformation England*, 39–59; Prest, *Rise of the Barristers*, 5–6.

At their peak in the sixteenth and early seventeenth centuries, the inns of court readings were the most public and sophisticated of the societies' legal exercises, and it is therefore not surprising that they were the most ceremonious. In substance the readings were twice-yearly courses of lectures on some statute, given during the learning vacations of Lent and Autumn, and taking two or three weeks. On three days of each week (usually Monday, Wednesday and Friday) the reader, a member of the inn chosen for his learning and seniority in the society, would expound some aspect of the statute, propose doubtful questions of law raised by it, and answer relevant cases put to him by his appointed attendants and other barristers of the inn. Members of the inn participated in debate on these questions according to their seniority, and judges or serjeants who were former members of the society would also join in if they were present. The intervening days were spent in feasting and the entertainment of notable strangers to the house.[6] All these stages in the proceedings were accompanied by elaborate ceremonies, while the readers themselves were surrounded by more ritual during their year of office. These rites were described in their ideal forms by Sir William Dugdale in his *Origines Juridiciales*, first published in 1666.[7]

According to Dugdale's fullest account, which depicts reading and readers at the Middle Temple, probably in the mid-sixteenth century, the ritual associated with the readers and their duties commenced from the time of their appointment, usually six months or more before the delivery of their lectures.[8] At this time the two barristers nominated as readers for Lent and Autumn were called to the bench table, or high table of the inns' governors, at dinner time, when they bestowed a treat of wine upon the existing benchers and senior barristers 'for their first welcome'. During the time of their office, the readers were responsible for all the exercises of learning in the house, and they also presided at the inns' feasts or 'Grand Days' on All Saints' Day and Candlemas Day, when the judges and serjeants of the house who were formerly members of the house were entertained. On these feast days the readers were bound to meet the judges and serjeants, who were clad in their scarlet robes, at the lower end of the hall, and to conduct them to the table in state, carrying white staffs or rods as insignia of their office. During the meals themselves the readers were responsible for placing the various dishes before

[6] WC Richardson, *A History of the Inns of Court* (Baton Rouge, La, Claitor's, n.d. [1977]), 101–27; WR Prest, *The Inns of Court under Elizabeth and the Early Stuarts* (Longman, London, 1972), 120–24.

[7] W Dugdale, *Origines Juridiciales* 2nd edn (London, 1671), 159–60 (Inner Temple), 203–9 (Middle Temple), 247–8 (Lincoln's Inn), 276–5 [sic] (Gray's Inn).

[8] Dugdale's dating is very imprecise, although there are references to the oaths of allegiance and supremacy, and to regulations introduced *temp*. Philip and Mary and Elizabeth.

the judges, and afterwards, when the food was cleared away, they were to lead the barristers and students in the solemn 'measures' or formal dancing.[9]

The solemnity of the readers' office, and their role in the society were emphasised further by the ceremonies which were attached to the readings themselves. During the week before his reading, the reader was to forbear dining in the hall and isolate himself in his chamber, so that his first appearance should be invested with more state. Then, on the Sunday before his first lecture, he was to attend the Temple church, accompanied by those benchers in town, including two appointed as his assistants, and 12 or 14 servants in livery. That evening at dinner he took his place at the head of the bench table, and the next morning, after choosing a sub-lecturer to carry his books and papers, he began to expound his statute in the hall before the whole society, after delivering 'a grave speech, excusing his own weakness, with desire of their favourable censures'.[10] Following this first introduction, the reading progressed with lecturing and argument on the appointed days and feasting in between, with the greatest dinner being reserved for the final week, when the reader presided at 'a great and costly Feast . . . provided for the entertainment of foreign Ambassadors, Earles, Lords, and men of eminent quality'. On the day of the final lecture, after breakfast, the Reader began by making

> a grave and short speech . . . tending to the excuse of his weakness, with desire of pardon for his errors committed: which forthwith is answered by the most antient Bencher then present, who extolleth the Reader's bounty and learning, concluding with many thanks unto him.

After arguing some final cases, the reader thereupon took formal leave of the society, and prepared to travel home that evening, on which journey some of the students and other gentlemen accompanied him 'with great state and solemnity', bestowing 'a great supper' upon him at his inn that evening.[11]

The original purpose of the readings, and the office of reader, was educational. But the ceremony and ritual which surrounded the lectures and their authors reveals other, less directly practical, functions. Firstly, the readings and feasts, together with the elaborate grand days at which the readers presided, were occasions when the various ranks of the inns' past and present membership came together. Their participation in the case arguments at readings must have increased the lawyers' consciousness of common devotion to the mysteries of English law, just as, at a less elevated level, meeting and talking at dinner and elsewhere would have

[9] Dugdale, *Origines Juridiciales*, 204–5.

[10] From 1559 the reader took the oaths of supremacy and allegiance before delivering his speech.

[11] Dugdale, *Origines Juridiciales*, 206–8.

developed their corporate identity as members of one of the four legal communities. Aspects of the ceremonies described clearly acted as symbolic representations of this professional self-consciousness, which was in turn strengthened and elaborated by their performance. In this context it is significant that all the rituals of the inns, and especially those connected with the readings, took careful account of the different degrees of the participants, and ensured that they participated in strict order according to their rank and seniority. Members or senior members of the inns were constantly reminded of their place in the legal firmament by the order in which they sat down to dine, or by observing their proper turn in arguing at readings and moots. This is not so surprising in the case of the learning exercises, since the ranks of inns' membership were originally derived from them, but order of precedence was also maintained in the inns rituals which were not directly associated with legal education, such as the Grand Day feasts and revels. At the Middle Temple, for example, according to Dugdale's account, the two readers led the 'solemn measures', or dancing, on All Saints' Day in the following manner:

> . . . the Ancient of the two that hath the staff in his hand, stands at the upper end of the Bar Table; and the other with the White Rod, placeth himself at the Cupboard, in the middle of the Hall, opposite to the Judges; where the Musick being begun, he calleth twice the Master of the Revells. At the second call the Ancient, with his white staff, advanceth forward, and begins to lead the measures, followed, first by the Barristers, and then the Gentlemen under the Bar, all according to their several antiquities . . . .[12]

Orderly participation in these rites would therefore have reinforced the notion of community solidarity in the microcosm of the legal profession which each inn represented; like all effective rituals, they encouraged certainty of belief, in this case the certainty that every student, counsellor and judge was placed in a regular, unchanging order of ranks which embraced the profession and its institutional base.

Discussion of the ranks of the legal profession leads naturally to the second major function of some of the rituals which were associated with the inns' readings and readers. In the fifteenth and sixteenth centuries the delivery of readings, and election to the bench of an inn of court, were linked with promotion to the order of serjeants at law, which in turn was generally a pre-requisite for appointment to the judiciary. Not all readers became serjeants, but in practice readership carried the public status of 'apprentice at law', and the apprentices were fully fledged advocates who practised in the royal courts. The serjeants were chosen from those who had read twice in the inns of court and practised as apprentices.[13] For the

[12] Dugdale, *Origines Juridiciales*, 204.

[13] JH Baker, 'The English Legal Profession, 1450–1550', in *idem*, *The Legal Profession and the Common Law*, 78–80, 88–90.

reader himself, therefore, his appointment and the delivery of his lectures represented a change in his condition, or even assumed the proportions of a valedictory event, if he was the senior reader who was to lecture in Lent, since he would have already delivered one reading. Such a man might hope to receive a serjeant's writ in due course, which would take him from the inn of court where he had been student and barrister to one of the serjeant's inns in Fleet Street or Chancery Lane. And even a first reader was well aware that he had now attained full maturity as a member of the inn, having passed through all its ranks. Robert Callis, introducing his lectures on the Statute of Sewers at Gray's Inn in 1622, acknowledged the significance of his reading in the following way:

> My most worthy Fellows and Companions of this noble and renowned Society, the Hourglass of my puisne time [apprenticeship] is run, and I am now come to take possession of your Reader's place; . . . These twenty and six years compleat I have had continuance here, and in that time I have onely taken the measure and length of your Hall: And herein I acknowledge Grays-Inn to be the patron of my best fortunes, and yourselves the best Companions of my forepast and present life.[14]

In these circumstances it was natural that some of the ceremonies which were associated with the readers and readings functioned as rites of passage: symbolic acts which accompanied the individual's progression from one state to the next. In fact, these rituals divided into three types often identified by anthropologists; rites of separation, rites of transition, and rites of incorporation.[15] First, as has been seen, immediately before he began to read, the reader was isolated for a whole week in his chamber; this enforced separation from the fellowship of the inn no doubt emphasised his special condition, as a member who was on the threshold of metamorphosis to a new state. Secondly, during the year of his readership generally, and especially in the two or three weeks when he was lecturing, the readership's public status elevated him to a condition which was almost sacred: he was accorded precedence before all at the inn's feasts and ceremonies, accompanied by servants in livery on public occasions, and generally treated in a way that no ordinary bencher or barrister would expect. Thirdly, these rites of transition were accompanied by classical rituals of incorporation, in the form of the common meals which supplemented and concluded the reading. At the Middle Temple the process of incorporation into the new state was completed by

[14] *The reading of the Famous and Learned Robert Callis, Esq; Upon the Statute 23 H. 8 cap. 5 of Sewers: As it was delivered by him at Gray's Inn in August, 1622* 2nd edn (London, 1685), 21. Callis became a serjeant in 1627.

[15] See especially A Van Gennep, *The Rites of Passage*, trans MB Vizedom and GL Caffee (University of Chicago Press, Chicago, 1960); also V Turner, *The Ritual Process* (Penguin, Harmondsworth, 1974).

the following ritual, which took place at the first meeting of the governing parliament of benchers in the next term:

> . . . . when the Benchers . . . have dispatched their other affairs, this new Reader is sent for to come amongst them; when being come, and taking the lowest seat of the room, one of his Assistants . . . being by the Bench called to give account of the Reading, makes a great Oration unto them; declaring the great learning and charge of the Reader, together with the Statute that he read upon; . . . tending wholy to the Readers commendation. In answer whereof, the Reader makes another grave Oration, in his own excuse; magnifying the learned Arguments of his Assistants and Cupboardmen, as also the good order and behaviour of the young Gentlemen; with thanks to them all, for so patiently bearing with his infirmities. After which, the Bench gives him thanks, and so they all together sit down to Supper: at what time (and not before) the Reader is an absolute and confirmed Bencher . . .[16]

Thus it appears that the rituals and ceremonies associated with the exercises of reading at the inns of court served extra-curricular purposes, insofar as they promoted corporate solidarity within the societies and the legal profession generally, while also enabling individual lawyers to locate themselves in the established order of preferment, and affirm their progress through that order by communal acts of celebration. Dugdale's descriptions of the rituals at the Middle Temple are undoubtedly idealised, and should not be taken as evidence of their perfect and unchanging performance at all the late medieval and early modern inns. But other sources suggest that ceremonies of this kind were being performed at all the legal societies in the sixteenth century.[17] And in early Stuart times, although there are grounds to suspect that the value of reading as an educational device was being undermined by the growth of printed legal literature, contemporary accounts of readings confirm that many of the rituals were still being carried out. Indeed, the continuance of the inns' educational formalities well beyond the time when they were substantively meaningful reveals their strong attachment to the traditional rituals and ceremonies.[18]

But there was at least one important development in the ceremonies of reading at the end of the sixteenth century: individual readers were guilty of extravagance, especially in the provision of feasts for powerful outsiders, and this was encouraging a general rise in the expense of reading,

[16] Dugdale, *Origines Juridiciales*, 208.

[17] See eg the report of the royal commissioners into the state of legal education temp. Henry VIII for evidence of the insistence on order of precedence in arguing at moots and readings (Richardson, *History of the Inns of Court*, 414–17).

[18] Prest, *Inns of Court*, ch 6; *Liber Famelicus of Sir James Whitelocke*, in J Bruce (ed) (Camden soc, 1st ser lxx; 1858), 70–76. Richardson dates the decline of the educational regime at the inns from later Elizabethan period (*History of the Inns of Court*, 175–6).

which some who were called on to read simply could not afford. In 1591 the judges issued a series of orders 'for the better regulating of the readings in all the Inns of Court.' These complained of 'excessive and sumptuous charges' which were causing readers to conclude their proceedings in a shorter time than usual, and set limits to the expense, especially in the matter of feasting, 'to the intent that a mediocrity may be used frugally without excess'.[19] Like so much attempted sumptuary regulation, the orders seem to have had little effect, since further restrictions of this kind were promulgated in 1594, 1596 and 1627.[20] Sir James Whitelocke's reading of 1619 reveals the extent of the problem. His feast was attended by a galaxy of grandees, and the final cost was approximately £370, a considerable sum in the early seventeenth century. It is true that some of the cost was covered by the traditional practice according to which the readers' clients, fellow lawyers and friends made gifts of provisions and money, but he still had to pay around £240 for the privilege of acting as reader.[21]

Wealthy readers like Whitelocke were taking the opportunity of their appointment to dispense hospitality on a lavish basis among powerful courtiers, normally with the object of increasing their chances of promotion. This is important, because the increasing extravagance and expense of the readers' dinners reveals how the extra-curricular functions of the rituals identified above—the promotion of community solidarity and celebration of regular advancement through the traditional hierarchy—were being undermined by more individualistic competition and the rise of new orders among barristers. In the later sixteenth century a great increase in the volume of litigation passing through the Westminster courts caused the judges to open their bars to junior members of the inns of court; mere barristers were able to appear as well as the more senior readers or 'apprentices' who had been allowed to plead previously. In consequence there was a significant increase in the number of men called to the bar at the inns and who went on to practise the law. By the time Whitelocke delivered his reading this 'mushroom growth' among barristers anxious to take advantage of an increasingly open market was transforming them from a small community of masters and pupils, centered on the inns of court and ideally united by their institutional loyalty, to a profession whose members were divided by considerable inequalities of wealth and honour. Of course the lawyers of Westminster had always competed for honour and profit: the inns' consistent emphasis on hierarchy and loyalty were subliminal means of regulating and inhibiting

[19] Richardson, *History of the Inns of Court*, 437–9; Dugdale, *Origines Juridiciales*, 313.

[20] Richardson, *History of the Inns of Court*, 439–42, 444–45; Dugdale, *Origines Juridiciales*, 315–16, 319.

[21] Whitelocke, *Liber Famelicus*, 70–73.

human friction. But it appears that by 1600 subscription to the old ethic of community was in danger of being dissolved by a new culture of unabashed competition, and in the context of lawyering this legitimated cutting corners to secure a slice of the deluge of legal business created by England's economic growth.[22] Like many manifestations of social and economic change in the early modern period, the challenge of rising individuals and new elites was most visible in conflict over sumptuary matters.[23] As a leading barrister who earned over £600 in the year of his reading, Whitelocke was one of the winners in this lottery, and and his profligate feasting of the duke of Buckingham's allies represented a challenge to the old order which identified a new focus for loyalty: he was more interested in reading as a means to gain further advantage over his peers via court favour, than as an occasion for the legal community to confirm its traditional ties.[24]

The corrosive effects on the lawyers of this self-consciously aggressive individualism were more apparent in the reading ceremonies of the second half of the seventeenth century, and were associated with the rise of a new elite closely identified with the crown. During the civil war and interregnum the readings were not given at the inns of court, but the benchers determined to revive them with the return to 'kingly government' in 1660. As was traditional, senior barristers were called upon to read at their inns according to their seniority, irrespective of their professional success, and the readings testified to the vast differences in means between ordinary barristers and the new elite of the profession.[25] On the one hand Thomas Hardres, reader at Gray's Inn for Lent 1664, had only two servants in livery to attend him, rather than 12, while John Turner, Lent reader at the Middle Temple in the following year, was obliged to appeal for naval victuals from his wife's kinsman, Samuel Pepys, in order to supply his feast.[26] By way of contrast, three years earlier the Inner Temple reading of Sir Heneage Finch, solicitor general and future lord chancellor Nottingham, had achieved new heights of splendour and extravagance. According to Anthony Wood, Finch mounted a great feast on each of the six days which followed his reading lectures:

[22] Muldrew, 'Culture of Reconciliation', 919–21; CW Brooks, *Pettyfoggers and Vipers of the Commonwealth: the Lower Branch' of the Legal Profession in Early Modern England* (Cambridge University Press, Cambridge, 1986), chs 4–5; Prest, *Rise of the Barristers*, 5–8.

[23] See A Hunt, *Governance of the Consuming Passions: A History of Sumptuary Law* (Macmillan, Basingstoke, 1996), esp ch 7.

[24] Whitelocke, *Liber Famelicus*, 75–76; Prest, *Inns of Court*, 226–27.

[25] See D Lemmings, *Gentlemen and Barristers: the Inns of Court and the English Bar, 1680–1730* (Oxford University Press, Oxford, 1990), 78–81.

[26] JH Baker, 'Readings in Gray's Inn, their Decline and Disappearance', in *idem*, *The Legal Profession and the Common Law*, 36; *The Diary of Samuel Pepys*, in R Latham and W Matthews (eds) (Bell, London, 1970–83), vi. 28, 49.

> The first day's entertainment was of divers peers of the realm and privy counsellors, with many others of his noble friends. The second of the lord mayor, aldermen and chief citizens of London. The third . . . of the whole college of physicians, who all came in their caps and gowns. The fourth was of another long robe for all the judges and advocates (doctors of the civil law) and all the society of Doctors Commons. The fifth was of the archbishops, bishops and chief of the clergy; and the last . . . was of the King, duke of York, lord chancellor, most of the peers and great officers of court, the lords commissioners of Scotland and Ireland, &c.[27]

At this final entertainment the reader was attended by a host of servants in scarlet cloaks and white doublets; and the royal stomachs were satisfied to the accompaniment of 20 violins, which played continuously until their owners departed.[28]

Faced with this kind of ostentatious showing off, it is not surprising that some of the less distinguished barristers refused to read, presumably for fear of impoverishing themselves by attempting to compete with the likes of Finch, or incurring dishonour through revealing their parsimony.[29] In these circumstances, the institution of reading was beginning to reflect the fragmentation of the legal community, rather than affirm its solidarity. For the ordinary benchers who did read, ceremonies which represented rites of passage through the institutional ranks of the profession must have seemed hollow charades, since reading was becoming a passage to nowhere for them. The opportunities of the free market and the expansion of the profession were creating a new route to preferment, as the crown dipped into the growing pool of talented young barristers to promote those who could be moulded to serve its needs. Henceforth advancement increasingly depended on crown service in the offices of king's counsel and solicitor or attorney general, rather than progress through the ranks of the profession's ancient institutions.[30] The expense of reading was therefore fast becoming a waste of money for barristers who did not already enjoy royal office. Indeed, the delivery of a course of lectures at one of the inns was no longer a likely ticket to the degree of serjeant at law. In the 1680s Sir John Bramston, son of Charles I's chief justice, noted that his father had read twice before becoming a serjeant, and lamented the fact that a majority of the serjeants created since 1660

27 A Wood, *Athenae Oxonienses* 2nd edn (London, 1721), ii. 718–19.

28 Dugdale, *Origines Juridiciales*, 157.

29 *Master Worsley's Book on the History and Constitution of the Honourable Society of the Middle Temple*, in AR Ingpen (ed) (London, 1910), 124–5. The judges' orders for the government of the inns of court and chancery which were issued in 1664 noted that the excessive charge of readings had caused some readers to be 'much disabled thereby in their estates' (Richardson, *History of the Inns of Court*, 451; Dugdale, *Origines Juridiciales*, 323).

30 Baker, *Order of Serjeants*, 112–13; Lemmings, *Gentlemen and Barristers*, 236–45.

had not read, while many of the post-Restoration readers had 'found noe advantage'.[31] And readers no longer enjoyed privileges of precedence over other barristers in the Westminster courts, as they had previously.[32] Perhaps the only privilege remaining to them was the right to wear a tufted gown, which distinguished them from ordinary counsel appearing at the bar. But even this symbolic sumptuary privilege was challenged and lost, for Francis North donned a tufted gown when appointed king's counsel in 1668, although he was not a reader, and this type of gown became the regular dress of the crown counsel and law officers.[33]

The career of Francis North symbolises the divisions in the upper branch of the legal profession which helped to undermine the readings, and rendered their ceremonies farcical as rites which reflected the traditions of a community based on the inns of court. North's appointment as King's Counsel (hereafter KC), after only a few years at the bar, was offensive to the benchers who governed his society of the Middle Temple, because he had not followed the traditional route of preferment via seniority and reading in due course. They therefore refused to admit him to a place on the bench of their society, and were only forced to do so after North complained to the judges, who refused to hear them in court until they complied.[34] This confrontation could hardly have promoted much in the way of community solidarity in the Middle Temple and among the members of the inn generally. No doubt the ordinary benchers were offended still more in 1671, when North came to give his reading as solicitor general. Even his brother Roger North admitted that the feasting on this occasion was a 'terrible example' of extravagance, and gave the following graphic description of the way in which the dinner degenerated into disorder and conspicuous waste:

> . . . upon the grand day, as it was called, a banquet was provided to be set upon the table composed of pyramids and smaller services in form. The first pyramid was at least four foot high with stages one above another. The conveying this up to the table, through a crowd that were in full purpose to overturn it, was no small work: but, . . . it was set whole upon the table. But after it was looked on a little, all went hand over head among the rout in the hall, and far the more part

[31] *The Autobiography of Sir John Bramston, KB*, in RG Neville, Lord Braybrooke (ed) (Camden Soc, old ser, 32; 1845), 6; E Hatton, *A New View of London or, an Ample Account of that City* (London, 1708), 698.

[32] W Prynne, *Brief Animadversions on . . . the Fourth Part of the Institutes of the Lawes of England . . . by Sir Edward Cooke* (London, 1669), sig. A2; Dugdale, *Origines Juriciales*, pp 210, 212; cf Prest, *Inns of Court*, 51.

[33] JH Baker, 'History of the Gowns Worn at the English Bar', *Costume*, (1975) ix, 17.

[34] *The Lives of the Right Hon. Francis North, Baron Guilford; The Hon. Sir Dudley North; And the Hon. and Rev. Dr. John North*, in A Jessop (ed) (Everyman, London, 1890), i. 50–51. North (1637–85) was called to the bar at the Middle Temple in 1661, became KC in 1668, solicitor general 1671, attorney general 1673, lord chief justice of Common Pleas 1675, and lord keeper 1682 (*DNB*, xiv. 600–03).

was trod under foot. The entertainment the nobility had out of this, was, after they had tossed away the dishes, a view of the crowd in confusion wallowing one over another and contending for a dirty share of it.[35]

Readers who allowed the dissipation of the Restoration court to make a mockery of their customary ceremonies were destructive of the traditions which their medieval and Tudor predecessors had developed. This was an inevitable consequence of the promotion of men like North, because they had not attained professional eminence after years of continuance in the inns of court: they therefore had no respect for the inns and their rituals, and their advancement to the head of their profession represented the disintegration of the legal community which those rituals had celebrated. The readings ceased to be given at all the inns during the later 1670s, and the inns themselves progressively abandoned most of their ceremonies, along with their educational apparatus. They survived into the eighteenth century in an atrophied form, as dining clubs for a few second-rate barristers who consoled themselves with the empty privileges and luxuries which were the perquisites allocated to the members of the bench.[36]Another medieval institution of the common lawyers, the order of serjeants at law, was in a similarly decrepit state at this time, and it is appropriate to turn to the serjeants' rituals, to see how they were affected by the transformation of the legal profession.

II THE SERJEANTS AT LAW

The order of serjeants at law originated in the early fourteenth century, when the right to practise as a 'countor' or advocate in the court of Common Pleas began to be regulated by the admission of pleaders in batches at regular intervals. Those few who were admitted gained a rare privilege, in the form of a monopoly of business which passed through the principal court in England, and they became an elite body of advocates, distinguished by their wealth and great learning in the law. By the fifteenth century they had evolved into a formal fraternity, to which future members were called by royal writ, and admitted through an elaborate ceremony, which invested inclusion among the ranks of Common Pleas advocates with the dignity of an academic degree, styled serjeant at law. Receipt of a serjeant's degree became obligatory for promotion to the judicial bench, and the serjeants remained the elite of the legal profession's upper branch until the seventeenth century.[37]

35 *Lives of the Norths*, i. 98.

36 Lemmings, *Gentlemen and Barristers*, chs 2 and 4.

37 Baker, *Order of Serjeants*, chs 2–3.

The complex rituals which together comprised the serjeants' investiture ceremonies were appropriately splendid. In all there were six separate elements to the ceremonies, as they were performed from the fifteenth to the seventeenth centuries.[38] Serjeants were normally called in groups during this period, and participated in the rituals together or in immediate succession. Firstly, after they had received their serjeants' writs and made appropriate preparations, the serjeants-elect took formal leave of their inns of court, from which they were graduating to a higher fellowship, via a valedictory breakfast, which consisted principally of wine and biscuits. On these occasions the Treasurer of the inn made a formal speech to them, which traditionally expressed sadness at their departure, commended their learning and promotion as an honour to the society, and desired their friendship and protection for the future. Each serjeant-elect was then given a small sum of money, upon which the senior answered by thanking the society for all the benefits it had conferred upon him and his fellows, and promised the continuance of their friendship. Secondly, and sometimes on a day before this breakfast, the serjeants-elect went to the court of Chancery at Westminster, where their writs were returnable, declared in turn that they appered in obedience to them, and took an oath to serve the king's people as one of the serjeants at law, along with the oath of supremacy and allegiance (the latter only after 1559). The lord keeper or chancellor sometimes took the opportunity of this appearance to deliver a speech, which might take the form of a dissertation on the serjeant's degree and the trust attached to it, but this address does not seem to have been obligatory.[39] These subjects were usually reserved for the lord chief justice of England, who spoke on a subsequent occasion, when the graduands were invested with their ceremonial insignia. This third ritual represented their admission to the fraternity, and it was therefore performed by the judges, as the senior members of the serjeants' order, generally at one of the serjeants' inns or at the inn of court where the chief justice had been a member. Here the serjeants-elect attended in plain robes, and heard the chief justice's exhortation, which was often based on a biblical text and explored the serjeants' public obligations by way of the symbolism which was attached to their new robes.[40] Each new serjeant then knelt before one of the judges, who tied a white linen coif or cap under his chin and (until 1736) placed a scarlet

[38] The full ceremonies are described in *ibid*, ch 6.

[39] For speeches by the lord chancellor or keeper see *ibid*, 302–4 (1559), 314 (1594), 326–27 (1614), 333–34 (1623), 385 (1637), 395–96 (1640).

[40] *Ibid*, 280–88 (1521), 288–94 (*temp*. Henry VIII), 294–302 (1540), 324–25 (1614), 353–55 (1623), 359–60 (1625), 361–62 (1627), 366–67 (1631), 369–70 (1634), 373–74 (1637), 378–79 (1637). The lord chief justice of Common Pleas occasionally delivered a similar oration.

hood over his shoulders, thereby making him a 'brother' of the fraternity, which eventually became known as the 'order of the coif'.

The fourth stage in the proceedings was for the new serjeants to go in state to Westminster Hall, where they were to be admitted to plead in the court of Common Pleas. The serjeants walked to Westminster Hall in parti-coloured robes of murrey and blue, and were preceded by their servants, the officers of the courts, all the officers, benchers, barristers and students of each inn represented by a serjeant, and the members of their affiliate inns of chancery. The servants and officers also wore parti-coloured liveries, furnished by the serjeants, while the other lawyers wore black gowns. If all the inns of court and chancery were represented, the procession must have been a very long one, and it certainly constituted the most magnificent spectacle ever mounted by the lawyers. Upon arrival at Westminster Hall, the new serjeants attended the court of Common Pleas for the fifth step in the ceremonies. Here, after many solemn bows to the court from various parts of the hall, each serjeant made a formal demand or count in law French on behalf of a named plaintiff, which was answered by one of the old serjeants.[41] By the mid-sixteenth century the action was an artificial one, often an issue brought between peers or great officers who allowed their names to be used as patrons of the respective serjeants. After the count was over, the new serjeant took his place at the bar, according to his seniority, and his attendant or 'colt' (a barrister or bencher of his inn of court) 'gave gold', by distributing gold rings engraved with suitable mottoes to the judges and officers, as well as the peers and other grandees who attended the proceedings. This completed their formal admission as advocates in Common Pleas, and the company thereupon went on to the sixth and final stage of the creation ceremonies, the serjeants' feast.

At group calls the feast was normally held in one of the halls of the inns of court. They were sufficiently commodious to accommodate the extensive guest-list, including the lord chancellor and judges, the lord mayor and aldermen of London, and the old serjeants and crown law officers, together with various peers and great men who were connected with the new members of the order. The feasting had been spread over seven days in medieval and early Tudor times, and the king had sometimes attended. By the sixteenth century it had become a single dinner, but it remained the third public feast in England, which attracted visiting foreign dignitaries, and involved considerable culinary extravagance and other entertainment. Even in 1736, at the last general call of serjeants, the 'sumptuous dinner' in the Middle Temple hall was accompanied by 'A

[41] These formal pleadings were sometimes repeated at other stages in the proceedings. See for example Serjeant Bridgman's account of the 1623 call, when the counts were made three times (*ibid*, 335–49).

very good band of musick', and one of the galleries was fitted up 'for Ladys to sit to see the company at Dinner'.[42]

Unlike the inns of court readings, the serjeants' creations were purely ceremonial.[43] Although they served to 'make' serjeants, they had no directly practical function, in the form of legal education or real litigation. Even the crucial 'counting' in Common Pleas, which admitted the new serjeants to the court, was a ritual act, rather than the beginning of his substantive practice in that court. It therefore follows that the creation ceremonies served oblique purposes, although these ends were important enough to the profession for them to be preserved for two and a half centuries. What were these purposes? Like the inns' readings, at one level the creation ceremonies functioned as rites of passage, by which the promotion of individuals through the regular grades of the profession was acknowledged and celebrated among the legal community. The first stage of this process was the valedictory breakfast at the serjeant-elect's inn of court. The ritual speeches made on this occasion show that the participants interpreted the event as the end of an apprenticeship, during which the future serjeant had learned the law through regular study and participation in the society's exercises. Thus, according to Dugdale's account of the Treasurer's or senior bencher's speech, he

> rehearseth the manner of learning and study, giving lawd and praise to them [i.e. the serjeants elect] that have well used them, showing what worship and profit cometh and groweth by reasons of the same, in proof whereof, those new Serjeants for their cunning, discretion, and wisdom be called by the King's Highness, and his honourable Council, to the great promotion and dignity of the office of a Serjeant of the Law . . .[44]

Henceforth, as serjeants, they were masters rather than apprentices, and the leave-taking ceremony therefore marked the end of their former state, their symbolic death as members of the inns and students of the law. Indeed, by the end of the seventeenth century it was being compared explicitly with a funeral.[45]

The ceremonies of swearing in Chancery, coifing before all the judges and counting in the Common Pleas were intermediate stages in this process of graduation, by which the serjeants-elect assumed the insignia

[42] W Downing, *Observations on the Constitution Customs and Usuage of the Honourable Society of the Middle Temple*, (London, 1896), 230.

[43] In medieval and early Renaissance times, the rituals regularly included a visit to St. Paul's, where one of the old serjeants made a speech and the new ones were assigned pillars in the north aisle. Before the Reformation these may have served as places for the serjeants to meet clients but this practice had certainly ceased by the mid-16th century, along with the ceremony (Baker, *Order of Serjeants*, 101–4).

[44] Dugdale, *Origines Juridiciales*, 114; cf *ibid*, 121; Whitelocke, *Liber Famelicus*, 82.

[45] H Chauncy, *The Historical Antiquities of Hertfordshire* (London, 1700), i. 153.

and began to perform the duties associated with their new condition. Again, the speeches delivered on these occasions, usually by the lord chief justice of England or the lord chancellor or keeper, reinforced the notion of an orderly advancement through the profession's ranks, and drew attention to the ritual as symbolic of a change of state or condition within this hierarchy. In 1521, for example, the chief justice reminded the new serjeants that

> The tabard and hood which you wear is the reward of justice for your demerits and deservings, whereby you are known and distinct from the rest of your faculty. For, as we see in degrees of school, the doctor . . . by his apparell is known from other of the graduates, so you by this tabard and hood are known from the residue which be students of the law.'[46]

And in 1614 Lord Chancellor Egerton was even more explicit, setting promotion to the degree of serjeant and the rites attached to it within the context of the traditional order of legal preferment, passage through which assumed the proportions of a divinely inevitable progress:

> For lex divinitatis est, infima et media, duci ad suprema. For first you were under the Bar, from thence you rise to the Bar, from thence to the Bench, and so to this place, which is the chiefest. So that God calls you to his own law.'[47]

So in the words of these senior members of the profession, the creation ceremonies appear as rites which reflected and enforced the certainty and stability of legal institutions which had remained unchanged for generations. As JH Baker has pointed out, the judges who presided at the coifing ceremony had inherited the leadership of an ancient fellowship, and for those who took this trust seriously, the investiture in coif and hood symbolised the transmission of their responsibility to a new generation, and the maintenance of an uninterrupted line of succession.[48]

The serjeants' feast which concluded the creation ceremonies clearly represents the final stage in these rites of passage; after the rites of separation associated with leaving the inns of court and those of transition represented by coifing and pleading in Common Pleas, the new serjeants were finally incorporated into the order by enjoying a celebratory feast in common with the judges and old serjeants. Other members of the legal profession were also present, as they were at some of the preceding ceremonies, and, as long as they were conscientiously performed, these rituals may therefore be regarded as occasions which served to promote solidarity and common consciousness among the various members of the legal community, just as some of the acts associated with reading at the

[46] Baker, *Order of Serjeants*, 287–8.

[47] *Ibid*, 326; cf E Chamberlayne, *Angliae Notitia, or the Present State of Great Britain*, part ii 1st edn (London, 1671), 432–4.

[48] Baker, *Order of Serjeants*, 89.

inns of court did. As in the case of the readings, rank and precedence were carefully represented: at the serjeants' feasts the judges, old serjeants and law officers were placed before the new serjeants, and the members of the inns of court were relegated to the role of mere servants, with even the benchers sometimes condescending to wait upon the peers and other dignitaries, while junior members attended to their inferiors.[49]

Order of precedence was most important in the great procession in which the serjeants walked to Westminster Hall, to the extent that even the menial officers of the inns of court walked in order. According to a contemporary account of the procedure observed on this occasion, after the coifing ceremony

> the judges and the old serjeants go in their coaches to Westminster, whilst the others put on their party-coloured robes in order to walk publicly to Westminster Hall. Which was done in the usuall following manner; viz: first the Warden of the Fleet's officers to sweep and clear the way, then the inns of chancery of each house, the youngest going first, and so the next in seniority, then should follow the old serjeants' clerkes . . ., and then the students, barristers and benchers of Lincoln's Inn, preceded by the officers and servants of their house in their gownes and jackets, then the gentlemen of the Middle Temple in the same form and manner, and lastly the Inner Temple followed them,[50] preceded by their porter, the two turnspits, the second cook and pannierman, the head washpot and fourth butler, the third butler and the chief cook, the second and chief butler, and the steward alone, then the students, barristers and benchers, two and two, and lastly the new serjeants, one by one, beginning with the youngest, supported by two clerks and two staff men with their coat armour painted thereon, till the whole procession closed.[51]

This public procession is especially important in the context of the legal community. Although it was not an annual event, it was the only ceremony which embraced all the lawyers below the judicial bench, including members of the 'upper' and 'lower' branches of the profession. As such, it was a living representation of the hierarchy which was often referred to by the senior members of the profession, ranging from the most junior clerk or attorney who was a member of one of the inns of chancery to the serjeants 'graduating' from the inns of court. If there was any occasion on which ritual served to bind the lawyers into a real professional family, rather than a collection of individuals dedicated only to their own interest, the serjeants' procession provided the best opportunity for achieving this end. Moreover, it was a public event. So far it has appeared that the serjeants' creation ceremonies fulfilled functions similar to those served by the rituals associated with reading, in that they

[49] Dugdale, *Origines Juriciales*, 118–19, 124.

[50] Gray's Inn was not represented in this procession because no barrister of that house was made a serjeant.

[51] Baker, *Order of Serjeants*, 422 (call of 1724).

acted as rites of passage, and, ideally, helped to create a sense of community among the lawyers. But the serjeants' creations were crucially different in at least one respect from the inns of court readings; they were not merely 'internal' events, of importance to the lawyers; rather some of the pomp and ceremony was conducted in public, and it is reasonable to suppose that it was designed to impress the common people. It is easy to see why this was so. Between 1400 and 1600 admission to the degree of serjeant was a fair promise of advancement to the judicial bench; if only a serjeant was to live long enough, and death created vacancies among the judges, there was a very good chance that he would become a judge himself. And in the meantime, he was quite likely to be called upon to officiate as an assize commissioner, thereby performing the functions of a judge on circuit. In effect, during Tudor times at least, serjeants and judges were genuinely members of the same order, whose essential functions were judicial.[52] The speeches made by the judges themselves at the creation ceremonies confirm this, since the chief justice frequently reminded the new serjeants that they were becoming 'ministers' of the king's law.[53] The ritual of becoming a serjeant therefore represented not only entry to an elite body of advocates; more importantly, it assumed the proportions of the assumption of royal authority and power. Some of the ceremonies were therefore conducted in public; because the new serjeants were being presented as instruments of the crown, whose splendour and majesty was clearly designed to awe the people who watched them parade through the streets of London.

Of course the communication of this royal power, and the other 'internal' functions of the creation ceremonies as rites which reflected and reinforced the cohesive hierarchy of the legal profession, were dependent on the survival of the serjeants as the elite of the legal community. The meaning of these symbols therefore declined in the seventeenth century and after, as the order of serjeants, like the inns of court, was undermined by the transformation which spread through the profession. In the context of a more openly competitive working environment, and the increased application of royal prerogative power to nurture a cadre of dependent lawyers and judges, the serjeants gradually declined into a body of counsellors who were inferior to, and distinct from, the outstanding barristers who became senior judges.[54] Although its full impact on the mentalité, of the bar only became clear in the eighteenth century, this degenerative process was manifested in the creation ceremonies as early as 1606, when Sir Edward Coke was made a serjeant merely in order

[52] Ives, *Common Lawyers*, 66–67, 74–75.

[53] Baker, *Order of Serjeants*, 291–2, 294–5 (calls *temp*. Henry VIII).

[54] For the further application of royal patronage among barristers after 1660 see D Lemmings, 'The Independence of the Judiciary in Eighteenth-Century England', in P Birks (ed), *The Life of the Law* (Hambledon, London, 1993), 128–9.

to be formally qualified for immediate appointment as chief justice of Common Pleas. Coke's promotion from attorney general to chief justice represented the new route to preferment, mentioned previously, by which the leaders of the profession were chosen from the ranks of the crown counsel, rather than from the practising serjeants. His creation as serjeant was merely a formality, which invested a barrister who had enjoyed rapid success in the expanding market for legal talent with the trappings of the medieval elite—increasingly becoming an elite in name only after 1600. Coke was made a serjeant alone; significantly, he managed to avoid the public procession and was invested with the coif in the treasury of Common Pleas immediately before he was admitted to the court and sworn in as chief justice. As an aggressive and acquisitive individualist and an officer of state who was effectively bypassing the order of serjeants, no doubt he thought the ceremony which attached to the degree was inappropriate.[55] This view was certainly shared by others, since 'private' calls of judges-elect with the minimum of ceremony continued. Later in 1606 Humphrey Winch was made a serjeant in order to be chief baron of the Exchequer in Ireland, but he gave no rings, had no procession, and avoided the celebratory feast. And in 1625 two men who were intended for the judicial bench were created serjeants in the vacation without any ceremony at all. Tradition re-asserted itself on this occasion: the judges conferred and declared the creation void, condemning the omission of the ceremonies and the making of serjeants so 'easily and hastily' as detracting from the 'solemnity and dignity' of the degree, a practice which they said would be of dangerous consequences for the order if it was allowed to continue.[56]

The creation ceremonies survived for another century, but although the private calls of judges-elect generally included some of the rituals, the full ceremonies were confined to the 'public' calls of several serjeants. This increasing division in the performance of the ceremonies seems to have been a conscious process. The speeches of the chief justices on these occasions sometimes distinguished between the creations of ordinary, practising serjeants, and those of the future judges, to the effect that the rituals and robes, together with the traditional obligations of the coif which they represented, were regarded as being of lesser significance for those men who were intended for the bench. As Sir Thomas Richardson had put it in 1634, when investing a chief justice in Common Pleas, 'you are not to remain at the bar as a common soldier to be armed but to be a

[55] Note, however, that Coke spoke eloquently of the honour and dignity invested in the order of serjeants when he presided, as chief justice, at the general call of serjeants in 1614 (Baker, *Order of Serjeants*, 328).

[56] *Ibid*, 105–6, 358–59, 362–63.

judge'.[57] By 1700, at which time the order of serjeants was most definitely a second rank of senior advocates, compared with the new elite of king's counsel, the rituals were merely curiosities—relics of an order with a glorious past. All the efforts of Serjeant Sir Henry Chauncy, who lovingly detailed the ceremonies in his *Historical Antiquities of Hertfordshire*, could not restore their original meaning, at a time when the legal community was in decay, and the practising serjeants were no longer powerful and wealthy advocates who could expect to become judges.[58] The full ceremonies were performed for the last time in 1736; after this there was no public procession, and the other rituals which pre-supposed the existence of a community of lawyers—the valedictory breakfasts at the inns, and the serjeants' feasts—were commuted in the later eighteenth century for monetary payments to the society of serjeants.[59] In 1755 the lord chief justice of Common Pleas, who had never practised as a serjeant, proposed that the serjeants should lose their monopoly of business in his court. At the time it was argued that this innovation might have resulted in the end of the order, and it was rejected by the other judges.[60] In fact the order of serjeants itself continued to survive until the early twentieth century, when the last serjeant died, but its privileges were abolished in Victorian times.[61]

A consciousness on the part of elite barristers that they were different and superior seems to have assisted in the gradual destruction of this institution, just as full subscription to the culture of openly competitive individualism which underwrote the litigation boom of early modern England undermined the inns of court readings and their ceremonies. A final demonstration of their impact on the serjeants' rituals appears in the diary of Sir Dudley Ryder, who became a serjeant in 1754 as a step to the chief justiceship of England. Like Coke, for Ryder becoming a serjeant was a mere formality: he had risen to be attorney general by serving the government in the House of Commons, and he had no real interest in the creation ceremonies, beyond a desire to carry them through without any taint of parsimony.[62] In his diary, the surviving rituals were reduced to the level of a list of chores which have to be undertaken, preferably by his junior, Henry Bathurst, who was becoming a

57 *Ibid*, 372 (call of Sir John Finch, 1634). He went on to remind Finch of his obligation to advance the king's prerogative. See also *ibid*, 419 (call of Sir Edward Ward, 1695).

58 Chauncy, *Historical Antiquities of Hertfordshire* (1700), i. 150–58.

59 Baker, *Order of Serjeants*, 106.

60 'Observations touching the Antiquity and Dignity of the Degree of Serjeant-at-Law', in E Wynne (ed), *A Miscellany, Containing Several Law Tracts* (London, 1765), 227–31, 368–87.

61 Baker, *Order of Serjeants*, 115–29.

62 For Ryder's career see R Sedgwick, *The House of Commons 1715–54* (HMSO, London, 1970), ii. 397.

serjeant and judge at the same time, or by Counsellor Brown, his attendant barrister:

> Be thinking of the motto for [the] ring, speak to Brown and Bathurst; [consider] of the speech, of the coach of state and horses, of persons to make the robes, [how] to provide the dinner, [and] the wine of all sorts; *get Bathurst to undertake all this*.[63]

Ryder went through the motions of the serjeants' creation ceremonies without any apparent consciousness of their original meaning for the profession of which he was a member.[64] He clearly regarded the degree of serjeant at law as an insignificant dignity, for he commented acidly 'nobody will accept of the degree but to be a judge'.[65] His successor as chief justice and head of the serjeants' order, Lord Mansfield, seems to have held similar views, since he was said to have laughed when presiding at the coifing of new members.[66] The rituals of the profession, and the ancient institutions which they celebrated, could not long survive men such as these.

III JUDICIAL MAJESTY AND THE EIGHTEENTH-CENTURY STATE

By the mid-eighteenth century, almost all the ceremonies which had been associated with the ancient institutions of the barristers had ceased to exist, or were in the process of terminal decay. Legal ritual and ceremony did not disappear altogether, however, although it was much restricted in scope. Indeed, despite the decline of their traditional institutions, there was collective life of a sort among eighteenth-century barristers, and its distinctive rites and rituals provide important clues to understanding their history. Moreover, while they were not generated within the inns of court, such customary activities as there were did indicate some pride in the maintenance of a common fellowship among groups of barristers, albeit of a rather narrower and more defensive nature. Crucially, however, where participants in the celebratory occasions of the medieval and early

[63] Sandon Hall, Staffordshire, Harrowby MSS., xxvii, pt. 4a, 28–9: diary for 8 Apr 1754 (emphasis added).

[64] See also an account of Sir Lloyd Kenyon's creation as a serjeant in 1788, on becoming lord chief justice, which appeared in an early law magazine. Upon taking formal leave of the Middle Temple, Kenyon gave a very short loyal speech which paraphrased the famous speech of Sir Robert Callis (given at his reading in 1622), and after undergoing the 'ancient and ridiculous' ritual of his investiture in coif and hood, in Common Pleas, he almost forgot to distribute gold rings (*The Templar; or, Monthly Register* (1789), i. 302–5).

[65] Sandon Hall, Staffordshire, Harrowby MSS., xxvii, pt. 4a, p 28.

[66] JH Baker, 'A History of the Order of Serjeants at Law' (Unpublished PhD thesis, University of London, 1968), i. 406.

modern inns often depicted the practice of law as a satisfying public service which united all lawyers, like Ryder and Mansfield, Georgian judges and barristers seem to have come away from their own ceremonies, dinners and associations with little more than a heightened consciousness of their collective professional status and individual superiority.[67] Depending on their particular eminence, they were inclined to look down on mere barristers, ungentlemanly attorneys and simple-minded non-lawyers. This awareness of professional and social exclusivity can be seen most clearly in two principal areas: the judges' and barristers' participation in the increasingly ritualistic administration of the criminal law, and the activities of private messes and other associations of working barristers. It is appropriate to consider them separately because it is arguable that the culture of the eighteenth-century bar was partially divided: there were the 'great counsel' who were eligible to become leading judges and quasi-ministers, and the ordinary barristers, men who only associated in the interests of preserving their livelihood.

The administration of criminal justice involved the performance of much ritual, but it was hardly 'internal' to the legal profession. Rather it was a matter of public display and theatre, and it centred on the judges, as the main actors in the drama. For example, they travelled around their circuits in style. When Sir Dudley Ryder first went out on circuit as chief justice of England in 1754 his coach was preceded by a crier and a tipstaff, and he was also attended by his marshal and clerk, the porter of the circuit, two footmen and several grooms, all in livery. The chief justice's horses were covered with a cloth on which his arms were embroidered, and the whole retinue of both assize judges required up to 20 horses in all, to pull the coaches and seat the servants and officers.[68] This cavalcade must have presented a considerable spectacle by itself, as it travelled the turnpikes between assize towns. Moreover, it was enormously augmented at the border of each county, where the judges were met by the sheriff with his officers and the local gentry, all on horseback or in their own coaches. The whole procession then travelled on to the assize town, which it entered to the accompaniment of church bells and trumpets, preceded by the sheriff's men, armed with pikes or halberts.

The awesome effect was no doubt reinforced throughout the duration of the assizes, as the judges proceeded with the sheriff and his men to and from the court room to their lodgings, or to the town hall, where they were dined by the corporation. Indeed, the ritual was also carried into the courtroom. Here the court divided into two sides: one judge heard civil

[67] For Sir Nicholas Bacon's emphasis on the public service performed by those who 'gyve liefe to the lawe' see Baker, *Serjeants at Law*, 303 ('the servyce of the lawe ought of righte to be taken for an highe and grate servyce in the commonwealth').

[68] Lincoln's Inn, Harrowby TSS, doc 19(f), 1–2: Ryder's Assize diary, 5 Aug 1754; cf *The Long Vacation* (1691), 3.

causes depending in the central courts by right of the fiction of nisi prius, while the other undertook the criminal work, under the commissions of gaol delivery and oyer and terminer.[69] The proceedings were at their most theatrical in the criminal court. Here, according to sumptuary regulations issued in 1635, the judge was to wear the full dress of scarlet robe and mantle, trimmed with minniver, while by the eighteenth century the civil judge was permitted to appear in a black silk gown.[70] Thus arrayed in scarlet, the criminal judge was invested with the power of judicial death in capital cases, after the jury had passed their verdict. To add to the impact, he donned a black cap before pronouncing the awful death sentence, to the effect that the prisoner was to be taken away and hanged by the neck until dead. (After 1752, in cases of murder he might even order the body of the executed to be given thereafter to the surgeons for dissection, or hanged in chains at some prominent spot.[71]) Mercy also had its solemn rites: in the case of an assizes where no one was condemned to suffer in this way, the sheriff presented the judge with a pair of spotless white gloves, symbolising the fact that no blood lay on his hands, and the sword of justice had remained sheathed.[72]

Of course there is not much controversy as to the meaning of lavish judicial displays like these (which were also performed at London oyer and terminer and gaol delivery sessions, when the city officials entertained the judges, and on the occasions when the judges attended the House of Lords). They were simply designed to represent the power and authority vested in the judges by the crown, and in the case of the criminal proceedings, the devolved agency of life or death. As such they may appear to be relatively uninteresting in the context of the history of lawyers, because these devices had been used in the same way during Tudor and Stuart times. But there are reasons to believe that the administration of criminal law and its theatre became more significant in the overall context of governing eighteenth-century society, and this point is related to the development of the legal profession during these years.

A previous generation of historians has suggested that the eighteenth century was characterised by a decline in the popular appeal of the monarchy, and in the role of the crown as a symbol of power and author-

[69] Although civil cases were commenced in the central courts and local juries were formally summoned to Westminster, a proviso was always added 'unless before then' (*nisi prius* in Latin), the royal justices should come into the county. In practice they always did, and the case was tried at the assizes. The commission of gaol delivery was to try and deliver the prisoners from the gaol mentioned, while that of oyer and terminer was 'to enquire into, hear and determine the offences specified' (see Baker, *Introduction to English Legal History*, 20, 24).

[70] JH Baker, 'A History of English Judges' Robes', *Costume*, xii (1978), 32, 36.

[71] By the 'murder act' (25 Geo. II, c. 37).

[72] JS Cockburn, *A History of English Assizes* (Cambridge University Press, Cambridge, 1972) 297–302.

ity which might compel obedience and maintain order among the common people. These authors have also suggested that the established church, riddled with absenteeism and emasculated by the decay of its courts, had lost its power as an agency of social control. In these circumstances, Douglas Hay has argued that the law and its administration became much more important as an instrument of the state which legitimised and transmitted the power of the ruling classes—the landed oligarchy of gentry and aristocracy. And he has interpreted the ritualistic majesty of the criminal law, described previously, as one of the elements of this 'ruling-class conspiracy', which aimed to subordinate and subjugate the common people, in the absence of a police force or standing army.[73] Of course some of the background supports to this thesis have been undermined recently: JCD Clark has insisted that eighteenth-century England was a 'confessional state', in which divine-right kingship was translated into a theory of governance which was not much less powerful than that which sustained the Stuarts.[74] And Linda Colley has described the 'apotheothis' of George III as a symbol for popular loyalty in the later eighteenth century.[75] Moreover, research on the prosecution of offences has undermined Hay's characterisation of Hanoverian justice as a narrowly patrician versus plebeian system: prosecutors were often people from the middling groups of English society, and occasionally they came from the bottom of the social scale.[76] But although Hay seems to have been carried away by his perception of a sophisticated Gramscian legitimating ideology behind the law, and his account of what 'law' meant to contemporaries is regrettably one-dimensional, nevertheless evidence remains that the elite of the legal profession *was* partly assimilated by the growth of the state in the eighteenth century.[77] So it would not be surprising if Georgian judges and barristers actively subscribed to socially-coercive and exclusive 'shows'.

[73] Hay, 'Property, Authority and the Criminal Law', 17–63.

[74] JCD Clark, *English Society, 1688–1832* (Cambridge University Press, Cambridge, 1985), esp ch 3.

[75] L Colley, 'The Apotheosis of George III: Loyalty, Royalty and the British Nation 1760–1820', *Past and Present*, cii (1984), 94–129; *idem*, *Britons: Forging the Nation 1707–1837* (Yale University Press, New Haven, CT, 1992), ch 5.

[76] JH Langbein, 'Albion's Fatal Flaws', *Past and Present*, xcviii (1983), 101–102; P King, 'Decision-Makers and Decision-Making in the English Criminal Law, 1750–1800', *Historical Journal*, xxvii (1984), 27–34; JM Beattie, *Crime and the Courts in England 1660–1800* (Oxford University Press, Oxford, 1986), 192–7.

[77] For criticisms of Hay see D Sugarman, 'Theory and Practice in Law and History: a Prologue to the Study of the Relationship between Law and Economy from a Socio-historical Perspective', in *Law, State and Society*, ed B Fryer *et al* (Croom Helm, London, 1981), 81–94. And for alternative contemporary understandings and expectations of law see D Lemmings, *Professors of the Law: Barristers and English Legal Culture in the Eighteenth Century* (Oxford University Press, Oxford, 2000), esp ch 1.

Despite the arguments of whig historians about the growth of judicial 'independence' from the crown after 1689, analysis of judges' career patterns shows that the process by which advancement depended upon crown service continued and was intensified after the Glorious Revolution. Certainly the most senior Georgian judges were frequently tried and trusted men who had served many years as crown counsel and law officers, and with the increased importance of parliament they were roles which required advocacy in the House of Commons, as well as in Westminster Hall. This had important implications for the role of the judicial bench, and its relations with government. The first point to make is that the judiciary was 'politicised' in the eighteenth century, and thoroughly so at the senior levels. As a close attendant on the monarch, the chancellor had always been forced to become a politician, but the Glorious Revolution inaugurated a century or more which saw an uninterrupted line of chancellors who were active parliamentarians before they ascended the woolsack: Hardwicke, Thurlow, Loughborough and Eldon are the most obvious examples of the type.[78] Moreover, after 1689, lawyer-politicians became the norm among the chief justices of the common law courts too. Of the 28 chiefs appointed to King's Bench and Common Pleas between 1689 and 1820, 24 were former MPs, and many of them were career parliamentarians who had served as principal government or party spokesmen in the House of Commons, often in the capacity of attorney or solicitor general.[79] So although the influence of politics and the application of state power had certainly touched the judiciary before, the days of chief justices who were enthusiastic amateurs in politics and government (like the Restoration judges Sir Francis Pemberton, Sir William Scroggs, Sir Edmund Saunders and Sir George Jeffreys), were passing after 1689. And secondly, as suggested above, since they were professional politicians and crown counsel their post-Revolution successors were surely likely to have been preoccupied with affairs of state as much as they were with law and justice. After all, as MPs judges had debated the 'bloody code', and those who had been law officers had drafted and promoted it; as crown counsel they had been the indicters and prosecutors of jacobite rebels, radical authors and 'jacobin' conspirators. So Sir William Blackstone may have been thinking of his own times, as well as remembering the seventeenth century, when he wrote 'Nothing . . . is more to be avoided, in a free constitution, than

[78] E Foss, *The Judges of England* (Longmans, London, 1848–69), viii. 178–97, 374–85, 385–98, ix. 39–52.

[79] The exceptions were Sir Charles Abbott (Lord Tenterden), chief justice of King's Bench 1818–32; Thomas Reeve, chief justice of Common Pleas 1736–7; Sir John Eardley Wilmot, chief justice of Common Pleas 1766–71; and Sir James Eyre, chief justice of Common Pleas 1793–99.

uniting the provinces of a judge and minister of state.'[80] The clearest evidence of contemporary judges acting as 'ministers of state' is during the first two-thirds of the eighteenth century, among judges with the longest records of crown service.

It is notorious that the early Hanoverian state was repressive and interventionist in its use of the criminal law: after 1715 the government used the courts to prosecute perceived political and public order challenges; and several important criminal statutes were enacted, including the Riot Act (1715), the Transportation Act (1718) and the Black Act (1723).[81] But it is less well known that some early eighteenth-century judges who were excessively zealous and severe in its service were long-term intimates of the whig ministers. For example Sir Francis Page, the 'hanging judge' of Pope, Fielding, and Johnson, had been a political pamphleteer and client of the Whig junto in Queen Anne's time, and spent several years as king's serjeant and MP before becoming a baron of the Exchequer in 1718. The fact that in February 1722 he was charged with infringing the privileges of the House of Commons by attempting to corrupt the corporation of Banbury suggests he continued to be an enthusiastic politician.[82] Also Sir Robert Eyre, successively a judge of King's Bench, lord chief baron of Exchequer, and lord chief justice of Common Pleas, and in 1729–30 one of several judges suspected of 'screening' the prison gaolers who were being investigated by an anti-government committee of enquiry into the state of the prisons, was another long-term client of the whig ministers, having been an MP, solicitor general and defender of Whig pamphleteers from the judicial bench.[83] As Edward Thompson has pointed out, Page was the senior judge selected to preside over the special commission

[80] Blackstone, *Commentaries* (Clarendon Press, Oxford, 1765–69), i. 260.

[81] JM Beattie, 'Scales of Justice: Defence Counsel and the English Criminal Trial in the Eighteenth and Nineteenth Centuries', *Law and History Review*, 225; *idem*, 'The Cabinet and the Management of Death at Tyburn after the Revolution of 1688–1689, in *The Revolution of 1688–1689: Changing Perspectives*, ed LG Schwoerer (Cambridge University Press, Cambridge, 1992), esp 218–9, 232–3.

[82] He only escaped censure by four votes. Foss, *Judges of England*, viii. 143–46; San Marino, Calif., Huntington Lib., Stowe (Brydges) MSS., ST57/18, 378: [James Brydges, Duke of Chandos] to 'Mr Attorny Generall' [Sir Robert Raymond], 11 Feb 1722. For Page's reputation as a severe judge see Pope, in J Sutherland (ed), *The Dunciad*, 2nd edn (Methuen, London, 1953), 343; *idem*, in J Butt (ed), *Imitations of Horace*, 2nd edn (Methuen, London, 1953), 13; S Johnson, 'An Account of the Life of Mr Richard Savage, Son of the Earl Rivers', in P Crutwell (ed), *Selected Writings* (Penguin, Harmondsworth, 1968), 67–8; H Fielding, *The History of Tom Jones* (Penguin, Harmondsworth, 1966), 410–11.

[83] Foss, *Judges*, viii. 121–2; G Holmes, *British Politics in the Age of Anne* (Macmillan, London, 1967), 186; British Library, Additional MSS, 32,686 ff. 383–6: Duke of Newcastle to Lord Townshend, 1 Nov 1723; AA Hanham, 'Whig Opposition to Sir Robert Walpole in the House of Commons, 1727–1734' (Unpublished PhD thesis, University of Leicester, 1992), esp 245, 251–6.; *A Complete Collection of State Trials*, TB Howell (ed) (London, 1809–26), xvii. 619–26.

which tried the 'Windsor Blacks' in June 1723, and when the trial of several 'Waltham Blacks' was removed from the Hampshire assizes to King's Bench in November of the same year, the judge on the bench was Sir Robert Eyre.[84] Indeed, their selection for this service appears to be significant of political closeness to the government, because recent work has shown that there were links between the Blacks and the jacobites who were involved in the Atterbury Plot of 1722.[85]

The two most famous judges of the period were also actively complicit with ministers of state. Lord Hardwicke, lord chief justice of King's Bench between 1733 and 1737, and Lord Mansfield, who occupied the same office between 1756 and 1788, were lawyers who had been raised in continuous government service during the ascendency of Walpole and the Pelhams (1722–1756), a period when one party monopolised government, and a small group of ministers controlled legal appointments. As virtually government ministers themselves, it would not be surprising if they were more preoccupied with the interests of the state, if not the ruling elite, than they were with the strict interpretation of the law. Certainly they were not backward in deploying modern penal statutes. Thompson has shown that in 1736 Hardwicke extended the infamous Black Act against deer stealing, contrary to the words of the statute, to condemn two turnpike rioters who were not involved in poaching game. Was it a coincidence that he had been solicitor general when the act became law, and must have assisted in drafting it? Certainly he went on to preside over the administration of the criminal law, as chief justice of England and lord chancellor, for over twenty years in the mid-eighteenth century. Thompson has also revealed that in 1767 Mansfield, one of Hardwicke's successors as lord chief justice, used a dubious precedent from a case tried under the Black Act to extend the provisions of the Riot Act, in this case to condemn a man who had shouted encouragement to rioters pulling down a dwelling house in Norwich. And in the following year, at the height of the anti-government Wilkite agitation, he applied the same precedent to affirm the capital conviction of three unarmed coal-heavers under the clause of the Black Act which referred to shooting at persons in dwelling houses, on the grounds that they partipated in a violent attack where others had used firearms. The chief justice reached these decisions—which along with Hardwicke's pioneering ruling of 1736 were crucial in establishing the broad construction of the Black Act—despite his knowledge that Sir Michael Foster, another judge (and significantly never an MP or law officer), had written a learned argument which condemned the extension of the Act to include 'aiding and abet-

[84] EP Thompson, *Whigs and Hunters* (Penguin, Harmondsworth, 1977), 74, 146, 151–3, 211–12.

[85] E Cruickshanks and H Erskine-Hill, 'The Waltham Black Act and Jacobitism', *Journal of British Studies*, (1985) xxiv, 358–65.

ting' offenders, an argument which he had forced Foster to suppress. At the time he had privately admitted to Foster that his (ie Foster's) interpretation was right in respect of strict legal reasoning, but in his subsequent rulings he failed to acknowledge the 'former authorities' which the other judge had cited.[86]

Given the consanguinity between members of the judiciary and ministers preoccupied with maintaining public order and increasing the efficacy of the criminal law, perhaps we should expect an increase in judicial 'majesty' during the eighteenth century. The Hanoverian period was once regarded as an era of stability at home and expansion abroad, but historians of crime have shown how there was increasing concern about violent offences against property in this period, especially in the urban areas, and in London above all. According to JM Beattie, the increasing incidence of reported crimes in the press, particularly after the conclusion of the wars which ended in 1748, 1763 and 1782, may well have encouraged their readers to believe that 'society was in some danger of being overwhelmed with crime.'[87] The nervousness of the social elite was no doubt increased, and focussed on the problem of controlling the lower orders, by the popular disturbances which threatened the peace in the 1760s, 1780s and 1790s. At times like this it was comforting to be reminded of the intimidating pomp and ceremony which surrounded the judges. Eighteenth-century lawyers were clearly aware of the public impression made by judicial display. The future lord chancellor Charles Pratt, for example, riding the western circuit as a barrister in 1749, described an anti-turnpike riot which occurred near Bristol, involving around 700 of the country people. The rioters were only temporarily dispersed by a force of sailors marshalled by the city authorities, but Pratt believed the affair would be settled finally when the assize judge arrived in the town. As he wrote to his future wife,

> I do not in my own opinion believe these fellows will be Hardy or audacious enough to attack a Judge, for such men are more terrified with the awful appearance of a Civil Magistrate than an armed force.[88]

Indeed, there are signs that the 'awful appearance' of the judges was accentuated in the eighteenth century, and this was accompanied by some other changes in the dignity of the judiciary which appeared to invest them with more state authority. The macabre theatre of the judges' role

[86] Thompson, *Whigs and Hunters*, 210–11, 250–54; L Radzinowicz, *A History of English Criminal Law and its Administration from 1750* (Stevens and Sons, London, 1948–86) 52–8, 71–2, 77–8; G Rudé, *Wilkes and Liberty* (Oxford University Press, Oxford, 1962), 38–9, 47, 97.

[87] Beattie, *Crime and the Courts*, 213–35.

[88] Kent Archives Office, Camden MSS., U840 C1/30: Pratt to Elizabeth Jeffreys, 5 Aug, 1749.

in the criminal law assumed larger proportions simply because the statute book was being loaded with capital crimes, and the assize commissioners or Old Bailey judges therefore donned the black cap more frequently, even if they often recommended the secretary of state to reprieve condemned men and women after sentence. This was also the century when junior judges, those who were not chiefs in the common law courts, began to be addressed as 'my lord', rather than merely 'sir'.[89] And after 1714 the chief justices of King's Bench were frequently made peers of the realm, a dignity not readily accorded to their predecessors.

Thus it appears that the upper branch of the legal profession and the judiciary were drawn more closely within the orbit of the state during the Hanoverian period. Hanoverian barristers tended to be advanced via government service in the House of Commons, rather than through the customary ranks, and with the traditional rituals, of the legal inns. It is therefore not surprising that the high ceremonial of the profession was identified with the state in the eighteenth century, since its leaders were long-standing servants of the crown. The elaborate processions, scarlet robes, full-bottomed wigs and black caps of the eighteenth-century judiciary were the residue of a culture whose traditional institutional customs had been destroyed in the welter of competition for profit and prestige occasioned by the Tudor-Stuart growth of litigation, and the Stuart-Georgian intensification of government influence over the leading lawyers. But if these were the rituals of the winners, and the profession had effectively been shorn of its more inclusive ceremonial, were there alternative rituals and ceremonies among mere barristers? As we shall see even ordinary barristers may have placed more emphasis on their participation in state-judicial legal ritual, because in the eighteenth century common law seems to have become more consciously exclusive and the bar was more explicitly socially elitist. But collective life among barristers also took new forms, which were characteristic of changes in the role and status of the bar.

IV LAWYERLY MYSTERY AND BARRISTERS' TRADE UNIONISM

Lawyers were among the chief executors of the constitutional settlement made in 1689, by which 'the rule of law' helped to constitute and legitimate the state. Of course they were also beneficiaries: like the barristers who attended the quasi-royal 'levees' routinely given by the lord chancellor and lord chief justice at their houses, in a small way, they shared in the state power invested in the profession, and were pleased at being so

[89] Foss, *Judges of England*, viii. 200–201.

distinguished.[90] Indeed the barristers who accompanied the judges on circuit were conscious of sharing in the power of the state. Thus Dudley Ryder, travelling the circuit as a junior barrister in the 1720s, congratulated himself on the impression made on the ordinary country folk by the imposing parade of judges and counsel on entering the assize towns:

> . . . if we have few Diversions of our own we have a considerable Quantity of that kind of reflected pleasure which all great folks feel in the sense of having communicated happiness to others. . . . If I may compare Great things with small I may say that like the Sun in its Diurnal circuit Joy & gladness accompanys us as we pass along & we make Day wherever we appear. The young men & Maidens putt on their best faces & clothes & stare at us with their mouths wide open in humble admiration.[91]

Ryder's pride in being part of the judges' grand perambulations represented his awareness of being an insider on an occasion which was designed to awe and impress the common people.

In various ways, rather than consciousness of justice as a public good, the collective life of eighteenth-century barristers nourished a culture which was becoming self-consciously exclusive. Blackstone seems to have understood this very well, and essayed to correct the problem: his attempt to found a school of common law at Oxford is perhaps best explained as a subtle effort at legal reform, by which the law might become 'a science, which is universal in its use and extent, accommodated to each individual, yet comprehending the whole community'.[92] He was certainly aware that many contemporary critics of English law believed mystery and exclusivity were the primary characteristics of lawyerly learning, as well as judicial ritual. Indeed, in a paragraph which was excised from the published life of his brother Francis, the Restoration barrister Roger North connected the two and acknowledged the utility of law as coercive magic:

> . . . as for those that Reason popularly, saying why should Law be made a mystery, and all people not be lett into the very penetralia of it, and so the science or profession be damned all at once, I answer in a word, viz. for reverence: for that gives more force to laws, in the sense of common people, than Reason it selfe. I grant it would be rare if all people were wise: but it is found that much the greater part are otherwise, & tied up more by shows, than realities; I may with as fair a pretence ask, why such a stir with the Halberts, Trumpets, & Scarlet, at the

[90] See eg *Morning Chronicle, and London Advertiser*, 1 Feb 1779: 'Yesterday evening the Lord Chancellor had a levee at his House in Great Ormond Street, as had likewise Lord Mansfield at his house in Bloomsbury-square.'

[91] Sandon Hall, Harrowby MSS, vol. vi, ff. 69–69v: draft, Dudley Ryder to 'Dear Jo' [cousin Rev J Billio], c.1720s.

[92] Blackstone, *Commentaries*, i. 27. See D Lemmings, 'Blackstone and Law Reform by Education: Preparation for the Bar and Lawyerly Culture in Eighteenth-Century England', *Law and History Review* (1998) xvi, 211–55.

> assizes, & solemn Robes upon the Benches, and at the bars of Judicature! Might not all such vain expense, superflous cloth, & empty noise & show be better spared, & Judges sit like justices of the peace, or stewards of courts in their ordinary habits! I know it will be Answered, for dignity: or as I said before, Reverence, true; but for what reason is that dignity needful, but to amuse the common people, who are terrified, & engaged more by exterior appearances than by real authority![93]

Admittedly, such a repressive and socially divisive interpretation of 'the rule of law' might have been born of extreme circumstances (North was a high Tory who lived through the Exclusion Crisis and the Revolution of 1688), and the passage did not survive to be printed. But although the common lawyers had long taken pride in their mystery and their elite associations, there are signs that by the end of the eighteenth century barristers who reflected on their collective role and controlled their institutions regarded social exclusivity and intimidatory coercion as worthy ends in themselves. At this time the inns of court developed new conservative vigour, while the circuit barristers institutionalised their association in semi-formal messes; in the process they not only expressed an unprecedented superiority complex towards the uneducated and unpropertied, but also re-intensified their discrimination against attorneys.

As remarked earlier, by the eighteenth century the inns of court had degenerated into mere dining clubs for barristers and benchers. Their condition was not assisted by a major decline in the volume of civil litigation from the late seventeenth century, a recession in the primary source of barristers' work which must have made a career at the bar less attractive.[94] Not surprisingly, admissions declined markedly in mid-century, and although there were several isolated attempts to provide courses of lectures in place of the readings and legal exercises, none of them succeeded in becoming fully established. Law students were left to

[93] BL, Add. MSS. 32,508 (Life of Lord Guilford), f. 28 (after 1700). Dudley Ryder was also pleased about his access to the exclusive knowledge of the law. See Harrowby MSS, vol ii., f. 311: Ryder to 'Dear Cousin', c.1720s ('I don't know whether it may not be some entertainment to you to be let into a secret [ie. that law has rational foundations] that generally shocks the Lay gens (as we of the Law call them) & has been looked upon as unintelligible to any but such as have made it the business of at least a great part of their lives').

[94] CW Brooks, 'Interpersonal Conflict and Social Tension: Civil Litigation in England, 1640–1830', in AL Beier *et al* (eds), *The First Modern Society* (Cambridge University Press, Cambridge, 1989), 360–67; H Horwitz and P Polden, 'Continuity or Change in the Court of Chancery in the Seventeenth and Eighteenth Centuries?', *Journal of British Studies* (1996) xxxv, 29–32; WA Champion, 'Litigation in the Boroughs: the Shrewsbury *Curia Parva*, 1480–1730', *Journal of Legal History* (1994) xv, 205–7, 211, 216–18; *idem*, 'Recourse to the Law and the Meaning of the Great Litigation Decline, 1650–1750: Some Clues from the Shrewsbury Local Courts', in CW Brooks and M Lobban (eds), *Communities and Courts in Britain 1150–1900* (Hambledon, London, 1997), 179–98.

learn the law by private reading, attendance on the courts and participation in private mooting societies or debating clubs.[95] But while their corporate life was considerably impoverished by comparison with its former glory, the benchers of the inns retained their valuable monopoly over admission to the bar, a privilege which guaranteed the minimum of recruits necessary for survival. At the end of the century there was a marked revival in numbers of law suits, admissions and calls to the bar at the inns, and barristers practising in Westminster Hall. There are signs that late-Georgian litigation was derived from a more restrictive section of the population than the broadly-based clientele who had resorted to the courts during the litigation boom of the sixteenth and early seventeenth centuries, however.[96] So it is probably no coincidence that although there are traces of a revival in the bar's collective life around that time, and there was a limited return to institutional controls over individual practice, they assumed forms which were noticeably more socially elitist and professionally defensive than the confident fellowship of their medieval and early modern predecessors.

One important ingredient of the bar's collective self-esteem at the end of the eighteenth century was its enhanced social status. While 'patriotic' barristers like Erskine (and Camden, Dunning and Glyn before him) espoused popular causes, in so far as he was becoming more 'polite', the ideal barrister was self-consciously snobbish, rather than virtuous. By 1840 an admiring commentator was able to say

> The high social position occupied by the bar in modern times is unquestionable. With the highest honours of the state open to him, the barrister is entitled to take rank amongst the gentry-classes of the kingdom.[97]

Indeed, it was social elitism, rather than educational utility, which lay behind the principal shift in the structure of legal education: from clerical apprenticeship to university and pupillage. Thus while *The Barrister: or Strictures on the Education Proper for the Bar*, first published in 1791, paid due attention to the need for barristers to have a public education, its importance here was not principally, as for Blackstone, that liberal learning might serve as a means to rationalise the administration of law. Rather the point was to ensure they were bred in a gentlemanly environment. Where Blackstone had criticised apprenticeship with an attorney for its potential to narrow the mind into rote learning of the forms of practice, for *The Barrister*, its most serious dangers were social and moral: in an attorney's office, the student would be liable to 'loss of every

[95] Lemmings, 'Blackstone and Law Reform by Education', 211–55.

[96] Brooks, 'Interpersonal Conflict', 361–4; Lemmings, *Gentlemen and Barristers*, 10; *idem*, *Professors of the Law*, esp ch 3.

[97] [A Polson] *Law and Lawyers; or Sketches and Illustrations of Legal History and Biography* (London, 1840), i. 162.

sentiment of decency, morality and religion'.[98] By contrast, at one of the universities, after the public school (preferably Eton or Westminster), rather than developing habits of 'vulgar conviviality' with people of 'inferior stations', 'habitual intercourse with men of literature and fashion' would breed cultivated gentlemen able 'to take a respectable station among the most elevated ranks of society'.[99]

Correspondingly, while the inns of court cherished their 'honourable' status, and at the end of the eighteenth century their members celebrated the revival of their aristocratic associations, their residual importance was as 'gatekeeping', institutions. Above all, and despite the fragmentation of their educational regime and collective rituals, the benchers found a role in the maintenance and protection of the bar as a closed association of polite gentlemen. To this end they exploited the monopoly privileges which sustained their culture. Thus in 1798, when the inns were recovering their numbers, their benchers acted to capitalise on their assets and limit access to their market. After a meeting of benchers from all four inns, common regulations were introduced to enforce minimum attendance at dinner of those students who were keeping 'terms' towards their call, and every such person who had not resided for two years in one of the universities was ordered to pay a deposit of £100, returnable on call or on leaving the inn.[100] These regulations also coincided with the final phase in the long drawn out process by which practising attorneys were excluded from the inns of court: the four inns' regulations for call to the bar which were promulgated in 1762 excluded attorneys or solicitors who had not ceased to practise for two years, and after 1793 they took effective steps to prevent them from qualifying for the bar while continuing to practise their profession.[101]

There is also contemporaneous evidence of more elitist and exclusive attitudes among barristers who joined the bar messes attached to each circuit. Circuit messes did not appear overnight: in the 1690s one barrister on the Home circuit commented on the enhanced good fellowship of unequal acquaintances thrown together by their common 'Pilgrimage after mony'; a loose sense of community that acted to relieve the boredom and ameliorate the losses of briefless men by sharing their expenses of 'dyet' and accommodation among the other and more fortunate barristers who went the circuit.[102] And they had their own private dinners,

[98] *The Barrister* 2nd edn (London, 1818), 21, also p 29.

[99] *Ibid*, 15–16, 23, 26, 34.

[100] *A Calendar of the Inner Temple Records*, FA Inderwick and RA Roberts (eds) (London, 1896–1936), v. 633. The £100 deposit was in addition to admission fees and the bond taken for payment of duties.

[101] *Ibid*, v. 142–3; HH Bellot, 'The Exclusion of Attorneys from the Inns of Court', *Law Quarterly Review* (1910) xxvi, 143–5.

[102] Hertfordshire RO, Panshanger Papers, D/EP F81/51: William Cowper to Judith Cowper, 10 Aug, 1693; and *ibid*, D/EP F81/82: same to same, 4 Aug, 1696 ('Here

separate from the occasions when they joined the circuit judges to dine. Charles Pratt, the future Lord Chancellor Camden, recorded enjoying a private dinner with 50 of his fellow circuiteers at Bath in September 1753, and Nicholas Ridley, a newly-called barrister, dined with his 'brethren of the long robe' on his arrival at Durham to attend the assizes there in 1773.[103] Ultimately the bar mess developed around the masculine camaderie and high jinks which were also found among public school boys and members of gentleman's clubs, and they found their clearest expression in the collective organisation of exclusive dinners at the assize towns. (Chancery leaders—who formed a self-conscious 'bar' of their own by the later eighteenth century—may have had an equivalent in their own regular dinners, such as the one organised by Charles Yorke in July 1769.[104]) The important point to understand is that although these practitioners' gatherings partook of the usual eating, ritual toasting, and wagering common to drinking and dining clubs, the eighteenth-century circuit mess was not (unlike urban coffee houses and clubs) merely a free association of independent individuals. Although not yet fully institutionalised, the mess was assuming the right to regulate and adjudicate relations among its members and outsiders: to be precise, it was developing rules of etiquette designed to insulate barristers from 'improper' contact with clients, witnesses and especially attorneys.[105] For besides electing officers to preside at gatherings and juniors to address the details of arranging for transportation of the baggage waggon and payment of wine and food, the messes usually constituted themselves as courts for the symbolic 'trial' of members who were presented for infringing the society's conventions.

The fortuitous survival of records for the Midland circuit mess during the 1780s and 1790s enables us to analyse the substance of their proceedings. Admittedly, most were jocular; misdemeanours were commonly punished by fines of a few shillings or a bottle of wine, and offences included 'appearing in a coloured coat at the Assembly at Derby', as well as being a bigamist, in the case of a barrister 'married by the [local]

[Maidstone] is little business & little of that falls to my share, so that [I] shall pay, at this place, half costs'). The northern and home circuits both had a 'common purse' in the 1780s, when Boswell travelled them; he estimated the cost of going the full circuit, lasting 30 days, at 'about fifty pounds' (*Boswell: The English Experiment 1785–1789*, IS Lustig and FA Pottle (eds) (McGraw-Hill, New York, 1986), 85, 89, 270).

[103] Kent Archives Office, Camden MSS., U840 C1/39: Pratt to Elizabeth Pratt (his wife), 5 Sept, 1753; Northumberland County Record Office, Ridley MSS., ZR1 32/1/2: Ridley's diary for 4–5 Aug, 1773.

[104] British Library, Additional MSS, 35, 362, ff. 249–50: Charles Yorke to Lord Hardwicke, 22 July 1769.

[105] Compare R Cock, 'The Bar at Assizes: Barristers on Three Nineteenth-century Circuits', *Kingston Law Review*, (1976) vi, 36–52, who emphasises the informality and irregularity of the early bar messes.

Newspapers' to more than one woman. Even the attempted prohibitions against social contact with attorneys have a humorous tone. In March 1784 several barristers were fined for dancing with attorneys' sisters at the assize ball, and in August 1790 another group was indicted for fishing and eating mutton chops with attorneys.[106] But charges of dining, drinking or travelling with attorneys and their relatives were virtually continuous, and they must be read in the context of the contemporaneous concerns about junior barristers not keeping their proper 'distance' from mere 'practisers'. The circuit mess—a club of working barristers free to deploy their collective social power in accordance with their own interests and prejudices—was continuing and extending the inns' policy to promote total social segregation from attorneys.

Clearly, although the bar's fastidiousness about contact with attorneys can be dressed up as the development of modern 'professionalism', by way of enforcing 'principles of independence and merit' it was also a matter of power relations.[107] Barristers were promoting their dominant position in the administration of law against the danger of 'interested friendship', which might ultimately lead to the calamity of '*no Barristers but Attorneys Clerks*'.[108] While their modern apologists insist that the bar's supremacy ensures litigation and doctrinal development are controlled by the best-educated lawyers, such an argument has less force for an age when legal education was haphazard, and procedure irrational. Indeed, we may suspect that the exclusion of attorneys from habits of social intercourse with barristers helped to preserve the courts and the common law from consumer-led grass-roots reform. In the eighteenth century the main targets of individual suitors' complaints were attorneys and solicitors, because they had taken over the business of dealing with litigants in the first instance, and they presented the final bill.[109] As one member of the exposed 'lower branch' grumbled, despite 'the large Fees to Counsel', 'we bear all the reproach, and suffer for their Sins (they are out of our Clients hearing and reach)'. His preferred solution was legislative intervention 'to reform the many dilatory and chargeable Customs, Rules and Forms of the several Courts, and by that Means

[106] Bodleian Lib., Records of Midland and Oxford Circuits, 1773–1806, vol. 1, ff. 26, 58, 61: courts at Warwick, 1784 and 1790, and Leicester, 1791. I am grateful to Raymond Cocks for helping me to locate these records.

[107] D Duman, 'The English Bar in the Georgian Era', in W Prest (ed), *Lawyers in Early Modern Europe and America* (Croom Helm, London, 1981), 103–4. For an early 19th-century explanation of the rules of etiquette applied by the bar mess, see [Polson] *Law and Lawyers*, i. 136–8 ('They serve effectually to prevent any of those petty arts by which vulgar and cunning pettyfoggers might attempt to obtain practice').

[108] Ruggles, *The Barrister*, 27.

[109] See Lemmings, *Gentlemen and Barristers*, 125–6; *idem*, *Professors of the Law*, ch 2.1.

render Justice speedy'.[110] In this context unregulated contact with unsympathetic litigants and their representatives would have been uncomfortable and perhaps ultimately damaging, and it was convenient for barristers who maintained their social and ethical superiority over attorneys to associate any defects in the administration of law with 'a blameable degree of intermixture in habits of interest, among . . . the Barristers and the Practisers [ie attorneys]'.[111] Moreover, they clearly understood their collective power to order the conduct of suits to their own advantage, for the eighteenth-century bar mess was already developing those restrictive practices which subsequently led to the bar being compared with a trade union.[112]

The Midland circuit mess certainly paid sustained attention to working conventions which appeared to protect their own livelihoods. In 1785 Mr. Balguy was presented 'for taking a brief for a Plaintiff in which four witnesses were examined without a Junior', and Mr. Dayrell 'for holding a brief for a Defendant with three witnesses, . . . without a junior'. Although the first charge was withdrawn, and the second attracted a fine of one 'Bottle', it is clear that the mess was subtly reminding its members that they should insist on the retention of another counsel in full trials.[113] This pressure anticipated and exceeded in scope the controversial nineteenth-century rules about retaining two counsel when the leader was a crown counsel.[114] Moreover, another counsel was presented and fined for taking a brief at the 1784 Warwick summer assizes without a fee, and Mr. Rastall was fined 'for advising with both sides in a Cause, & before Briefs were delivered, recommending a Compromise to be effected upon fair & equal Terms by the unconditional submission of one Party.'[115] Rulings like these sit uneasily with traditional prescriptions for ethical counsel and advocacy, especially the oft-repeated injunction to promote settlement among the parties, and the enduring ideal of the good lawyer, who offers his services freely, merely accepting fees as gratuitous rewards for his services.[116] On the face of it, they seem

[110] *Proposals Humbly Offer'd to the Parliament, for Remedying the Great Charge and Delay of Suits at Law, and in Equity*, 3rd edn (London, 1724), 14–15.

[111] See *The Barrister*, vii–xi, xiv–xv.

[112] For the beginnings of that debate, see D Duman, *The English and Colonial Bars in the Nineteenth Century* (Croom Helm, London, 1983), 48.

[113] Bodleian Library, Oxford, records of the Midland and Oxford circuits, 1773–1806, vol 1, ff. 30–31: Warwick, 1785.

[114] Duman, *English and Colonial Bars in the Nineteenth Century*, 44–5; B Abel-Smith and R Stevens, *Lawyers and the Courts: A Sociological Study of the English Legal System 1750–1965* (Heinemann, London, 1967), 56, 223; R Cocks, *Foundations of the Modern Bar* (Sweet & Maxwell, London, 1983), 87–88.

[115] Bodleian Lib., Records of Midland and Oxford Circuits, vol 1, ff. 31–32: Warwick, March, 1785.

[116] In the 16th and early 17th centuries these precepts were frequently repeated by the presiding judges at the creation of serjeants (Baker, *Serjeants at Law*, 280–81, 352,

to represent simple collective self-interest on the part of established barristers.[117]

It therefore appears that while the bar's collective life was fragmented during the eighteenth century, and the traditional rituals and ceremonies based on the inns and the order of serjeants decayed, groups of working barristers nevertheless maintained and ultimately refreshed a sense of corporate consciousness. Above all, of course, they continued to identify with their traditional role as 'professors' of the common law. But the apparent contraction of litigation to a relatively small section of the population, and the evident exclusivity of the bar's attitudes and restrictive practices, suggests the common law had indeed been partly 'privatised' and even 'trade-unionised' since Tudor-Stuart times. Indeed, if one focus of the bar's corporate activities and self-consciousness centred in the protection and maximisation of their litigation mystery, their close identification with the 'majesty' of criminal proceedings may imply another perspective on the common law as principally representative of the state and the propertied, rather than the hallowed symbol of every 'Englishman's Birthright'. As the author of *The Barrister* put it, writing in the aftermath of the French Revolution, barristers and judges certainly owed a vague duty to 'the sacred source of all justice'; but more concretely, their exclusive education and associations were expected to inspire the barrister with an essentially negative political trust. As a fully paid-up member of the new and consciously conservative elite of the propertied and politely educated, he would defend the status quo against modern liberal heresies:

> the laws of this country, administered by such men, will preserve through the world, a deep-rooted respect in the opinion of *mankind*; for that constitution which is our palladium, whatever freedom of government the present spirit of liberty, that diffuses itself so far and wide throughout the globe, may obtain for the many millions of fellow-creatures, who have hitherto been the slaves of despotism.[118]

Under this optic, the constitution was opposed to liberty, law was a weapon against the threat of disorder and dis-appropriation from below, and the barristers and judges were their front-line soldiers. Indeed, in the nineteenth century it appears that the benchers of the inns of court followed similar instincts in their regulation of the profession, by intimidat-

378, 396). For more discussion of the 'good lawyer' ideology see Lemmings, *Professors of the Law*, ch 8.

[117] For further disciplinary and etiquette developments which rendered the bar 'more cohesive, more exclusory and more narrow' see WW Pue, 'Exorcising Professional Demons: Charles Rann Kennedy and the Transition to the Modern Bar', *Law and History Review* (1987) v, 135–74.

[118] *The Barrister*, preface, xii–xiv (original emphasis). The book had appeared originally as occasional essays in *The World*, during 1791.

ing and/or excluding radicals, reformers, and other political deviants: a sustained policy that 'substantially inhibited the flourishing of liberal legal practices'.[119] The barristers had always been private practitioners, and their institutions were voluntary bodies; but they had long acknowledged public responsibilities and trusts, and the common law was popularly supposed to be available to all, not least as a bulwark against the state and the over-mighty. By contrast, to paraphrase Edward Thompson, the forms of collective life characteristic of many barristers and some senior judges during the eighteenth century suggest they were 'consenting adults in their own corruption' in so far as they consented to and even acknowledged a contraction in the social reach and constitutional trust of the lawyers and the courts.[120]

[119] WW Pue, 'Lawyers and Political Liberalism in Eighteenth- and Nineteenth-Century England', in TC Halliday and L Karpik, *Lawyers and the Rise of Western Political Liberalism: Europe and America from the Eighteenth to Twentieth Centuries* (Oxford University Press, Oxford, 1997), 167–206 (quoting 197).

[120] EP Thompson, *Customs in Common* (Penguin, Harmondsworth, 1991), 32. Cf WD Rubinstein, 'The End of "Old Corruption" in Britain 1780–1860', *Past and Present* ci (1983), for 'the genuine nexus which had been built up between the Pitt-Liverpool Tories and the older, more conservative segments of the middle classes like the East India Company and the legal profession' (77).

3

'A Dry and Revolting Study: The Life and Labours of Antebellum Law Students

ANN FIDLER

The popular nineteenth-century novelist, Oliver Bounderby, faced a difficult technical dilemma in the writing of his book, *The Law Student: Or, the Struggles of a Heart* (1850). His protagonist, the handsome, virile Fred Stanton, leaves his deceptively placid hometown to study law in New York City. This period of legal study was necessary if Fred had any chance of defeating the villain (a crooked lawyer), rescuing a family fortune, and securing the love of a beautiful young woman. Yet Bounderby, in making his main character a law student, saddled himself with the onerous task of describing a pastime in which reading a 'Story' meant subjecting oneself to Story on Bailments, Story on Bills of Exchange, or Story on Equity Jurisprudence.[1] His resolution of this difficulty in the course of two succinct paragraphs was masterful. Bounderby's underlying strategy surfaced in the first sentence of his discussion of Fred's career as a law student : 'The life of a student, like the history of a happy nation, does not offer generally many very striking points which the historian can seize'.[2]

Although most legal historians have not had the inestimable pleasure of reading *The Law Student*, a large number subscribe to Bounderby's proposition. As a result, little is known about the ways and means of antebellum law students. Instead, the scholar's gaze has been steadily fixed upon the more tangible topic of the institutional evolution of the law school, the men who pounded its podiums, and the development of its curriculum. Lost in the midst of the general crusade to understand the might and majesty of the law school are the individuals who were subject to its dictates. Antebellum law students are rarely glimpsed in discussions of legal education, and are practically invisible in the historiography of

[1] These are the colloquial titles of works by Joseph Story, the famous antebellum lawyer, jurist, and law professor.

[2] Oliver Bounderby, *The Law Student: Or, The Struggles of a Heart* (Samuel French, New York, 1850), 33.

the legal profession and legal culture. Yet the days spent reading law transformed laymen into lawyers. The ordering of their identity as lawyers began in an environment filled with ink-splattered commonplace books and dog-eared copies of Blackstone. Through a range of encounters, law students developed beliefs about the nature of law, its applications and their responsibilities to community, country and each other. As a result, the habits and the habitats of antebellum law students offer fertile ground for cultivating knowledge about law, lawyers, and legal culture in the nineteenth-century.

Contrary to Bounderby's assertion, there are a number of 'striking points' which historians can 'seize' upon when constructing a history of antebellum law students. This essay seizes upon some of the cultural constructs that shaped the law student experience. My research on Northern law students suggests that would-be lawyers possessed a distinctive culture derived from a cavalcade of rules, rituals, myths, expectations and illusions generated from within and without the legal profession. This unique culture produced a trans-regional community of law students based upon images of legal study, common methodologies, and exposure to particular legal texts. Cultural comity amongst law students provided the medium in which a post-bellum national legal culture would take root. In the following pages, the lives and labours of antebellum law students will be discussed in an attempt to extend present knowledge beyond the boundaries of Bounderby.

CULTURE AND THINGS LEGAL: GENERALITIES AND PARTICULARITIES OF AN EVOLVING DISCOURSE

Before entering the law offices and law school classrooms of the past, some preliminary observations need to be made about legal culture in general and antebellum legal culture in particular. Legal culture is a concept that has received considerable attention in the historical work of the past decade, but the intersection between culture and things legal is not well understood. The chief difficulty with legal culture lies in finding an adequate meaning for the term in the midst of a historical discourse that is still evolving. Like all things cultural, it is a pot-pourri of possibilities lacking the sharp edges that contribute to a good definition. Lawrence M Friedman made an early attempt to pin down legal culture by describing it as a filter between legal agents and society at large made up of 'ideas, attitudes, beliefs, expectations, and opinions about law' engendered by legal institutions.[3] Kermit L Hall changed legal culture from a passive

[3] Lawrence M Friedman, *Law and Society: An Introduction* (Prentice-Hall, Englewood Cliffs, NJ, 1977), 7.

screening device into an active 'matrix of values, attitudes, and assumptions' responsible for shaping 'both the operation and the perception of the law'.[4] Hall along with David J Bodenhamer and James W Ely also argued that legal culture contained important sectional and regional elements.[5] What was common to most discussions of legal culture in the 1980s was the sense that the ideas and values that fuelled legal culture emanated from formal legal institutions and the legal profession.[6] In a 1991 article, Michael Grossberg suggests that this core assumption about culture and things legal is too static and exclusive. Entities existing outside of traditional legal enclosures, such as litigants, popular ideology, and informal institutions, are overshadowed by a preoccupation with legal rules and rule makers. Grossberg suggests that legal culture is more fruitfully understood as an arena of conflict occupied by a myriad of subcultures capable of influencing law, and in turn, being influenced by it.[7] This description of legal culture is useful for the study of antebellum law students, because legal pupils occupied a transitional position between the layman and the lawyer. Being neither fish nor fowl, a law student cannot be fully understood from the perspective of the legal profession or from that of the lay world. A thorough historical account of the antebellum law student must include an attempt to place him within his own unique cultural environment as well as those of the profession and communities that he was destined to serve.

The depiction of legal culture as a product of the interaction of subcultures also accommodates the complicated nature of the antebellum legal universe. The mode, men and manners of legal practice were in a state of flux before the Civil War. The lax licensing requirements of the expanding West drew well-educated men from the East as well as the ill-educated sons of humble farmers to the bar. Mingling of the posh and poor in the growing commercial cities and small agricultural settlements resulted in a bar subject to an assortment of internal struggles ranging from large matters like legal ethics to small ones like legal etiquette. Meanwhile, beyond the bar, laymen engaged the profession in a variety of tussles. An extensive set of legal reforms that altered or attempted to

[4] Kermit L Hall, *The Magic Mirror: Law in American History* (Oxford University Press, New York, 1989), 6.

[5] See, Kermit L Hall, 'The Legal Culture of the Great Plains', *Great Plains Quarterly* (1992) 12, 86–98; Kermit L Hall and James W Ely, Jr (eds), *An Uncertain Tradition: Constitutionalism and the History of the South* (University of Georgia Press, Athens, 1988); David J Bodenhamer and James W Ely, Jr (eds), *Ambivalent Legacy: A Legal History of the South* (University Press of Missouri, Jackson, 1984).

[6] For example, most of the 11 essays included in Bodenhamer and Ely's *Ambivalent Legacy* focus upon questions of jurisprudence, the legal profession, courts, specific cases and other apparatus connected with traditional legal institutions and actors.

[7] Michael Grossberg, ' "Fighting Faiths" and the Challenges of Legal History,' (1991) 25 *Journal of Social History*, 191–201, 195–196.

alter the selection of judges, the jurisdictions of courts, the right to practice law, the bounds of legal procedure and the purview of the common law were championed by laymen. Fugitive slaves, capital punishment opponents, and temperance types also scaled the legal ramparts.

The best overall description of antebellum legal culture resides in the work of R Kent Newmyer. Undaunted by the kaleidoscopic nature of the legal landscape, Newmyer constructs an elegant synthesis that finds an embryonic national legal culture flourishing in New England.[8] His thesis is of particular interest to a discussion of antebellum law students because he designates Harvard Law School as the engine of both a regional and a national legal culture. Newmyer argues that persuasive, prolific New Englanders such as Joseph Story shaped the legal and cultural agenda of the law school for the purpose of infusing their conservative ideals on a fragmented region and nation.[9] The doyens of the law school aligned it with powerful regional economic interests and cultural institutions, multiplying the influence already exerted by its graduates stocking the bench and bar. Newmyer believes that New England legal culture contained in the writings of its faculty and the notes of its students spread across the North, counteracting the 'centrifugal tendencies' of the prevailing ragtag system of legal apprenticeship.[10] In this manner, a pathway was constructed for the formation of a post-bellum national legal culture amenable to legal conservatism. Although Newmyer's discussion contains much of value, his focus on the role of the formal structures and strictures of the law produces an incomplete picture of antebellum legal culture in the North. It is a vision of a legal universe controlled by professors in which law students appear only in the form of vectors who transport the wisdom of Harvard Law School to the wilds of the Northwest. Reinserting law students and their milieu into the equation produces a more detailed understanding of the nature of antebellum legal culture.

A close reading of the diaries and letters of antebellum law students does reveal elements of experiential commonality that transcend the diversity in legal education inherent in a mix of apprenticeships and law school attendance, in settings ranging from the rural Northwest to urban New England. The basis for this commonality is not simply the imprint of the Harvard Law School curriculum, however, but stems from a more extensive and complex body of influences prevalent in antebellum legal education. The connatural experiences of law students are illustrated by a brief comparison of the legal training of Charles Sumner, scion of a

[8] R Kent Newmyer, 'Harvard Law School, New England Legal Culture, and the Antebellum Origins of American Jurisprudence,' in David Thelen (ed), *The Constitution and American Life* (Cornell University Press, Ithaca, 1988), 154–175.

[9] *Ibid*, 157.

[10] *Ibid*, 162.

Boston lawyer, and student at Harvard Law School between 1831–1833, with that of Albert G Riddle, heir to the poverty and distress of Ohio pioneers, who studied with Seabury Ford of Burton, Ohio, between 1838–1840.

During the time Sumner was at Harvard, Joseph Story—Newmyer's candidate for the catalyst of antebellum legal culture—published his first two monographs: *Commentaries on the Law of Bailments* (1832) and *Commentaries on the Constitution of the United States* (1833). Although Story's *Commentaries* oeuvre was in its infancy, Sumner, as a favourite pupil of Story's, absorbed much of his teacher's jurisprudential outlook in the form of lectures. By 1840, the year that Riddle ended his apprenticeship, four more monographs by Story were published.[11] Yet a reading list included in Riddle's unpublished memoir does not include any works by Story even though the young Buckeye was the student of a prominent Yale-educated attorney in possession of a well-stocked law library. (See, Appendix). Despite the disparities in their educational experience and curriculum, Sumner and Riddle shared many beliefs and expectations concerning law and lawyers.

Undoubtedly, Story maintained an important presence in the Northwest, especially if the work of his student Timothy Walker, founder of the Cincinnati Law School, is taken into account. Volumes penned by Story, however, were not ubiquitous in the rapidly settling western ranges. Michael H. Harris notes that Story's books did not appear frequently in private antebellum law libraries in Indiana.[12] Clearly, there were additional elements, including images of legal study, methodologies for studying law, and other books, that assisted in the creation of the cultural comity that existed between Sumner and Riddle.

MEASURING UP: IMAGES OF LEGAL STUDY

Antebellum folklore and lawyer jokes suggest that attorneys became members of the legal profession through the time-honoured tradition of selling their souls to the devil. Unfortunately, it was not that simple. Once the decision was made to embark upon a life of legal toil, a young man needed to obtain some instruction in the rudiments of legal practice. In the period before the Civil War, apprenticeship, law school, or a combination of both were the chief educational choices available to law students. Each option involved the relatively glamourless activities of

[11] *Commentaries on the Conflict of Laws* (1834); *Commentaries on Equity Jurisprudence* (1836); *Commentaries on Equity Pleading* (1838); *Commentaries on the Law of Agency* (1839).

[12] Michael H Harris, 'The Frontier Lawyer's Library; Southern Indiana, 1800–1850, as a Test Case,' (1972) 26 *The American Journal of Legal History*, 239–251, 250.

learning the law by means of reading, writing, and observing. In addition to imparting knowledge, an apprenticeship or a term at law school laid the foundations for a life lived within an occupation.

Despite its rather mundane nature, legal study was a subject of interest to antebellum Americans. Popular culture was rife with conflicting imagery associated with learning the law. The value of legal study, what it entailed, and whether it could be properly borne by the human mind and body formed subjects of general discussion. How did this imagery generated outside the legal profession affect would-be lawyers' perception of themselves and their task? What can it tell us about the substance and structure of legal culture?

In the view of the anonymous author of the 1846 satirical novel *Law and Laziness*, the study of law contributed little to the formation of citizens worthy to guide the course of a nation. 'There is no place like a law-office,' he observed, 'for making a fashionable acquaintance, and doing the least work with the greatest ease'.[13] In a letter in 1819 to the *Scioto Gazette*, a resident of Chillicothe, Ohio made clear his manifest displeasure at the contributions made by law students in his community.

> Every lawyer's 'prentice must be continually dabbling in political affairs, and weekly annoying the public with a farrago of impudence and stupidity. No town in the state is more infested with these creatures than Chillicothe; and if the corporation could pass an ordinance to ferret out from their borough such pestiferous nuisances, they would contribute more to the dignity of the place and the peace of the citizens, than they have by any of the previous laudable endeavors toward order and morality.[14]

Although judged lazy and meddlesome by some, there were other viewpoints regarding the usefulness of law students. Tocqueville observed in 1835 that the pursuit of legal knowledge was a worthy enterprise, as it provided 'security against the excesses of democracy'.[15] A Circleville, Ohio attorney felt that a number of advantages accrued to society from the popularity of legal studies. In an 1849 article on the legal profession, he presented a catalogue of benefits to society derived from the study of law.

> It sharpens and invigorates the understanding. It teaches men to reason and reflect . . . No mind capable of the comprehension of its spirit, ever found there encouragement to chicane, fraud, or immorality. It adds force to virtue by more

[13] *Law and Laziness; or, Students At Law of Leisure* (Golden Rule Office, New York, 1846), 6.

[14] Quoted in James M Miller, *The Genesis of Western Culture: The Upper Ohio Valley, 1800–1825* (The Ohio State Archaeological and Historical Society, Columbus, 1938), 61.

[15] Alexis de Tocqueville, *Democracy in America* (Alfred A Knopf, New York, 1980), I, 272.

> clearly defining the rights and duties of persons, and it strengthens wavering principles by the sanctions of its wisdom. . . . This study renders men more obedient subjects of government. . . . There are few minds that, on perusal of Blackstone, Kent, and Story, do not warm, glow and burn with the love of right, and the sentiments of rational patriotism.[16]

The discussion over the value of legal study was not confined to the sphere of curmudgeons, commentators and counsellors-at-law. The topic was also the subject of public lectures and debating society discussions across the nation. In 1837, John E Moler witnessed such a debate at Dickinson College in Carlisle, Pennsylvania. The debate was entitled 'Which is more beneficial to the world a doctor or a lawyer?'[17] No record of the outcome of the actual proceedings survives, but Moler's decision to become a physician is somewhat suggestive.

Faced with conflicting opinions about the value of studying the law, young men considering legal careers frequently turned to their elders for advice. The counsel given by laymen often contained imagery that reflected the popular understanding of what legal study entailed. In 1825, Alexander Chase replied to his brother Salmon's request for career consultation with a discussion of 'the advantages public and private of each of the learned professions.' Alexander, a geologist, cautioned Salmon that the law presented a significant amount of mental labour. Law dragged behind it a

> formidable train of ponderous quartos and folios of maxims and opinions expressed in the technical jargon and elegant obscurity of centuries long past, to say nothing of the thousands of volumes of later date.—To become a good Lawyer it is requisite that you should not only be master of all these but that you should have a competent knowledge of all the other sciences, of the arts, and a thorough acquaintance with ancient and modern History—In fine you must become an universal scholar.[18]

Alexander Chase's thoughts reflected a widespread perception of the depth and breadth of the enterprise of legal study present in both law and lay circles.

The depiction of the attorney as the consummate bookworm was the natural outcome of a profession in which books played such a prominent role. As Thomas Jefferson observed in 1769, 'a lawyer without books

[16] 'The Profession of the Law,' (Dec 1849) ns 2 *The Western Law Journal*, 97–113, 99–100.

[17] 26 Feb 1837, Journal of John Engle Moler, Ohio Historical Society, Columbus, Ohio.

[18] Alexander Ralston Chase to Salmon P Chase, 4 Nov 1825, *The Salmon P. Chase Papers: Correspondence, 1823–1857* (ed) John Niven (Kent State University Press, Kent, OH, 1994), II, 4–5.

would be a workman without tools'.[19] Attorneys toted books into court as ammunition for their legal arguments. Lawyers travelling on circuit carried a volume or two. Portraits of counsellors-at-law always contained a tasteful scattering of law books. Legal offices frequently displayed libraries ranged in plain view of the client's chair. While generally modest in scale, these personal law libraries were known even to those who had no reason to consult an attorney. Quite often, the lawyer's office contained the largest collection of books in a particular locale. All of these books signalled to laymen a concern, if not a passion, for knowledge. In many small towns, lawyers were often the most literate, although not necessarily the best educated, members of the community. William Dean Howells, who in 1855 spent a month as a student in the Jefferson, Ohio law office of Benjamin Wade, observed: 'There were lawyers, of those abounding at every county-seat, who were fond of reading, and imparted their tastes to the young men studying in their offices'.[20]

There is no record of a single antebellum lawyer actually achieving the mastery of the 'thousands of volumes of law' described by Alexander Chase. In fact, the combination of lenient licensing standards and the perfunctory nature of most bar examinations enabled men to join the profession on the strength of having read an armful of books. Yet the belief in the necessity of comprehensive and arduous learning persisted despite the actuality of the low threshold of admission.[21] The image of the attorney as a man of hard-won erudition was a useful concept and therefore carefully cultivated by the antebellum profession. In 1835, William Rawle, Jr declared that in addition to a detailed understanding of 'the whole volume of legal science,' a lawyer needed 'a deep and accurate knowledge of history, . . . some acquaintance with the useful and even the elegant arts and sciences, familiarity with polite literature, and . . . profound and frequent study of the sacred volume' to 'successfully perform the varied duties of his calling'.[22] The existence of a link between intellectual pursuits and the practice of law enabled lawyers to claim a

[19] Thomas Jefferson to Thomas Turpin, 5 Feb 1769, *The Papers of Thomas Jefferson*, (ed) Julian P Boyd (Princeton University Press, Princeton, 1950), I, 24.

[20] William Dean Howells, *Years of My Youth and Three Essays* (Indiana University Press, Bloomington, 1975), 92. The prevalence of lawyers among the ranks of the well read is discussed in Ronald J Zboray's examination of the charge records of the New York Society Library for the years 1847–49 and 1854–56. His work reveals that the largest group of male patrons were lawyers. Zboray, *A Fictive People: Antebellum Economic Development and the American Reading Public* (Oxford University Press, New York, 1993), 159–160.

[21] See Robert A Ferguson, *Law and Letters in American Culture* (Harvard University Press, Cambridge, Mass, 1984), 28–30.

[22] William Rawle, Jr, 'An Address Delivered Before the Law Academy of Philadelphia on the 6th of May, 1835,' *The American Jurist and Law Magazine* 15 (April 1836) 233–235, 233.

range of abilities that ostensibly fitted them for leadership in governmental and social spheres. Members of the bar also vainly hoped that public recognition of a high intellectual threshold of the bar would serve as a damper against the penetration of the profession by a dreaded cavalcade of threadbare schoolmasters and disgruntled farmers.

The concept of the well-read, learned lawyer was a durable one capable of co-existing with the other popular vision of attorneys as malingering blots of pestilence upon thc commonweal. Not surprisingly, the image of the erudite lawyer found its strongest reinforcement in the speeches of lawyers and law professors, but traces of it can be found in the personal correspondence and diaries of law students. Many law students felt the necessity of measuring up to the archetype of the antebellum attorney. Fiscal difficulties forced Calvin Fletcher, an Ohio law student, to divide his time between teaching and the study of law. Although he was supervised by an attorney, his reading was limited and took place in fits and starts. On the eve of his official admission to the bar, Fletcher measured himself against the omnipresent ideal.

> I found myself very incapabl[e] in my profession as a Lawyer. Much application must [be] given before I can expect to reap an agreeable and ful[l] harvest. I find myself very ignorant of the world and destitute of that fund of book knowledge that is necessary for to acquit myself with honor and eclat at the bar.[23]

Throughout his years of active practice, this strongly ingrained sense of deficiency caused Fletcher to pursue a programme of reading designed to remedy his nescience.

Individuals whose lack of resources curtailed the scope of their studies were not the only law students to experience the pressure generated by the inability to measure up to the ideal. The legal education of another Ohio law student, Rutherford B Hayes, was not undercut by the restrictive forces of money and time. Hayes had the leisure to pursue the path of the universal scholar through the study of language and literature. Despite his considerable accomplishments, however, he too felt that his progress was insufficient. Like Fletcher, Hayes looked to the future for a remedy of his shortcomings.

> My deficiencies are so many and apparent that I fear no exertion I can now make will prepare me for entrance into business as well as I could wish. But what I leave undone now may be finished, partially at least, during the intervals of leisure which for many years to come I am to expect.[24]

[23] 6 Dec 1820, *The Diary of Calvin Fletcher* (ed) Gayle Thornbrough (Indiana Historical Society, Indianapolis, 1972), I, 19.

[24] 21 Sept 1844, *Diary and Letters of Rutherford Birchard Hayes* (ed) Charles R Williams (The Ohio State Archaeological and Historical Society, Columbus, 1922), I, 159–160 (hereafter cited as *RBH Diary*).

While some law students felt obliged to scourge themselves for their perceived failings, the institutions in which they received their education, be they offices or law schools, seemed unconcerned with forging would-be lawyers in the mould of universal scholars. Generous lipservice was given to the concept, but the goal of acquiring profound and extensive knowledge through deep, broad reading was a task left solely to the discretion of the individual. Some students, prodded by ambition or fear, took up the challenge. Peter Zinn, who studied law under the direction of a Cincinnati lawyer, set up an evening reading schedule that included works of history, literature, foreign languages and natural sciences.[25] Young men who attended law schools often followed suit. Law students at schools attached to universities were sometimes aided in this pursuit by being granted permission to partake of the offerings of other departments. Rutherford B Hayes took advantage of Harvard University's policy of granting its law students the

> privilege of attending all the public lectures of the University gratis; and the opportunity of instruction in the modern languages on the payment of $10 per annum for each language studied.[26]

The conception of law student as universal scholar was frequently overshadowed by another popular representation of legal study—the stultifying dryness and dullness of reading the law. Unlike the previous notion, which was the product of lay observation and professional puffery, the popular understanding of the tedium inherent in legal reading drew heavily on the commentary of would-be lawyers. American law students of the past were instrumental in the creation of a minor branch of literature consisting chiefly of complaints about studying law. Their groans and grumbles appeared in correspondence, doggerel, reminiscences, biographies and newspapers from the eighteenth century onwards.[27] One of the primary themes of this genre was that the study of law added little relish to the circumstances of living. William Wirt, who studied law in the 1780s, ventured his opinion on the nature of the pursuit in an 1814 letter to a law student.

> The law is to many, at first, and at last too, a dry and revolting study. It is hard and laborious; it is a dark and intricate labyrinth, through which they grope in constant uncertainty and perplexity—the most painful of all states of mind.[28]

[25] See, Peter Zinn Diary, Cincinnati Historical Society, Cincinnati, Ohio, 218, 229–230, 236–237.

[26] 'The Law Institution of Harvard University,' *The American Jurist and Law Magazine* (July 1830) 4, 217–220, 218; *RBH Diary*, I, 115, 120, 147, 148.

[27] For a choice selection of 18th-century grumbles see, Jay F Alexander, 'Legal Careers in Eighteenth Century America,' (1985) 23 *Duquesne Law Review*, 631–658.

[28] William Wirt to Francis Gilmore, 13 July 1814, John P Kennedy, *Memoirs of the Life of William Wirt* (Lea & Blanchard, Philadelphia, 1849), I, 376.

Wirt's words were echoed and underscored by many others, insuring that young antebellum men possessed ample knowledge of this outlook on legal study. As a result, those committed to the path of the law fretted about what lay ahead, and those who wavered engaged in a fair amount of foot-dragging and soul-searching. Individuals who took the plunge emerged divided on the question of law's tedium. Mathew Birchard began studying medicine and then switched to law in 1824. He observed:

> I yet have this to say of the two studies. So far as I remember that of medicine was more captivating & always interesting. *Law was dry & Dull* for a long time. It required much study before I could feel an absorbing interest in it. I think it much the dullest for a beginner.[29]

Richard Henry Dana, who studied law at Harvard in 1838, offered a different assessment.

> From the very first recitation it became exceedingly interesting to me; & I have never yet found it dry or irksome. After studying law about a year & a half, I told Professor Greenleaf that I had not come across any dry places yet. 'No Sir,' said he, '& you never will. A man who begins it properly & studies it philosophically, will never find it dry'.[30]

In the popular understanding of the law student existence, reading the law not only exposed young men to dull books, but also threatened their personal health. As a result, state and national constitutions were not the only constitutions that concerned law students. In Albert G. Riddle's *Bart Ridgeley; A Story of Northern Ohio*, an autobiographical novel recounting its author's youth, law student days and early legal practice, the eponymous main character returns to the office of his law instructor, General Ford, after consuming the first volume of Blackstone in the space of a week. The General scolds Bart:

> I don't know but there is a man in the world who, without having seen a law book before, has taken up and mastered the first volume of Blackstone in a week, but I never heard of him. . . . It will not do for you to go on in this way; you should read up a library in a year, if you lived, but will die in six months, at this rate.

With tears in his eyes, Bart said: 'Do not fear [for] me, General; I am strong and healthy; besides, there are a good many things worse than death'.[31]

Albert G Riddle's belief that legal study took a significant toll on the mind and body stemmed from the death of his brother Harrison, who

[29] Mathew Birchard, Autobiographical Sketch, Western Reserve Historical Society, Cleveland, Ohio.

[30] Richard Henry Dana, Jr, *An Autobiographical Sketch, 1815–1842* (ed) Robert F Metzdorf (Shoe String Press, Hamden, CT, 1953), 78.

[31] Albert G Riddle, *Bart Ridgeley; A Story of Northern Ohio* (Nichols and Hall, Boston, 1873), 104.

died shortly after being admitted to the Ohio bar. The Riddle family was convinced that a gruelling course of legal study killed Harrison. Albert, who was at his brother's deathbed, concluded,

> Nothing but utter exhaustion appeared to be his ailing, in which his mind seemed to share—the penalty of his two years, unremitting and intense study—not the law alone, but kindred studies.[32]

When Albert later declared his intentions to become a lawyer, his mother and elder brothers declared their opposition, citing the fate of Harrison, but the young man managed to prevail. Like his alter-ego Bart, he was willing to take the risk, believing 'that his own elasticity and power of endurance would carry him forward and through, unscathed'.[33] Rutherford B Hayes also acknowledged the debilitating effects of legal study. While at Harvard Law School, he declared:

> If I ever have any students I shall earnestly advise them to take respite enough to prevent them from becoming disgusted and wearied out with study. . . . A few months of close application can be easily borne by a young man of regular habits and good constitution, but continual study seems to dry up the fountains of the heart, cramp the intellect, sour the temper, and ruin health.[34]

The concerns raised by Riddle and Hayes illustrate how cultural concepts from outside the legal profession influenced internal discussions of legal study. Most antebellum Americans were convinced that periods of concentrated study were dangerous to the well-being of young men. They were led and confirmed in this belief by a group of medical experts whose work focused on the brain as the primary engine of physical health. In 1832, Dr Amariah Brigham published his influential *Remarks on the Influence of Mental Cultivation and Mental Excitement Upon Health*. Directed at a lay audience, Brigham's work sought to warn parents against the 'injury they may do their children by too early cultivating their minds.'[35] Adults engaged in strenuous mental labours, Brigham concluded, were also subject to the potentially damaging effects of brain drain. The mind possessed the ability to produce disease, consequently 'if we do admit that the brain is the organ by which the mind acts, we must acknowledge the necessity of guarding this organ most carefully, of exercising it with extreme caution, of not endangering its delicate structure at any period of life by too much labor.' In defence of his physiological theory, Brigham quoted from Plutarch: ' "Should the body sue the

[32] Albert G Riddle, 'Fifty-Five Years of Lawyer Life, 1840–1895,' 28, Albert G. Riddle Papers, Western Reserve Historical Society.

[33] Riddle, *Bart Ridgeley*, 168.

[34] 18 May 1844, *RBH Diary*, I, 151.

[35] Amariah Brigham, *Remarks on the Influence of Mental Cultivation and Mental Excitement Upon Health* (1833; reprint, Scholars' Facsimiles & Reprints, Delmar, NY, 1973), 47.

mind before the court of judicature for damages, it would be found that the mind would prove to have been a ruinous tenant to its landlord" '.[36] Joan Burbick points out how the emphasis on 'privileging the brain' by Brigham and other medical writers dovetailed with changes in antebellum society. 'The rising class of managers and professionals knew the key to their wealth and supposed happiness lay in their ability to be mental laborers. . . . With mental labor came a sense that the mind could easily become exhausted and worn out. Manual labor exercised the body and could produce strength, but mental labor seemed to rest upon an inertia for most of the body while the brain worked surrounded by an abyss of strain, delusions, and torments. The efforts of the mind could easily turn upon the user and extract a nasty revenge'.[37] Under this scenario, legal study was considered a risk even for the healthy, but for those in poor physical condition it was unthinkable. Albert G Riddle observed that the son of his late partner 'has not yet developed the bodily vigor and hardihood' to sustain him as a law student.[38] George W Brown used his weak constitution to head off his father's efforts to arrange a legal apprenticeship. Brown reminded his father in an 1831 letter: 'It requires good health for the practice of law as for most anything else, especially strong lungs, which I have not'.[39]

[36] *Ibid*, 32, 188.

[37] Joan Burbick, *Healing the Republic: The Language of Health and the Culture of Nationalism in Nineteenth-Century America* (Cambridge University Press, Cambridge, 1994), 156.

The role of the mind in the untimely demise of students took root firmly in antebellum popular culture, but not everyone subscribed to it. The Reverend Daniel Wise acknowledged the prevalent belief that being a serious student was an unhealthy occupation, however, he doubted that strenuous mental activity had anything to do with the deaths of young men. Wise preferred to locate the source of ill-health in the abuse of a lower organ. 'When I am told of a sickly student, that he is 'studying himself to death,' . . . I study his countenance, and there, too often, read the real, melancholy truth in his dull, averted, sunken eye, discolored skin, pimpled forehead, and timid manner. These signs proclaim that the young man is, in some way, violating the laws of his physical nature. He is secretly destroying himself! . . . He is sapping the source of life with his own guilty hands, and erelong, will be a mind in ruins, or a heap of dust.' Daniel Wise, *The Young Man's Counselor; or, Sketches and Illustrations of the Duties and Dangers of Young Men. Designed to be a Guide to Success in this Life, and to Happiness in the Life Which is to Come* (Swormstedt & Poe, Cincinnati, 1856), 119–120.

[38] Albert G Riddle, *History of Geauga and Lake Counties* (Williams Brothers, Philadelphia, 1878), 99.

[39] George C Wing (ed), *Early Years on the Western Reserve With Extracts From Letters of Ephraim Brown and Family* (Arthur H Clark Co, Cleveland, 1916), 120.

The belief in the necessity of good overall health for the undertaking of legal study persisted after the Civil War. Joel Prentiss Bishop devoted the first chapter of his book for law students to a discussion of 'physical capacity.' See, Bishop, *The First Book of Law; Explaining the Nature, Sources, Books, and Practical Applications of Legal Science, and Methods of Study and Practice* (Little, Brown, & Co, Boston, 1868), 1–4.

The emphasis on the debilitating effects of concentrated study also assisted in the project of legitimating law as a manly and exclusive endeavour. A desire to forge firm links between masculinity and the legal profession emerged during the antebellum period.[40] The devotion to books and pens that allowed attorneys to lay claim to an exalted national role also prompted visions of soft-bodied men sapped by idleness. Imagery emphasising that law students must be fit, healthy and in possession of great stamina to avoid being crushed by the demands of legal study helped lawyers to augment the belief that law was an exclusively masculine domain. Before embarking on his legal studies in 1842, Rutherford B Hayes wrote in his diary: 'The life of a truly great lawyer must be one of severe and intense application; he treads no 'primrose path;' every step is one of toil and difficulty; it is not by sudden, vigorous efforts that he is to succeed, but by patient, enduring energy, which never hesitates, never falters, but pushes on to the last. . . . Now is the time to acquire the habits which will enable me to endure its hardships; and if I make a right use of my present opportunities, my after life will be as happy as it is laborious'.[41]

While there were certainly exceptions, neither death, nor dullness, nor the prospect of eternal diligence stayed most antebellum law students from attorneys' offices or law school classrooms. Heroic visions of the ends of legal study kept law students at their appointed task. Charles Sumner wrote to another law student in 1831:

> Tower, we have struck the true profession; the one in which the mind is the most sharpened and quickened, and the duties of which, properly discharged, are most vital to the interests of the country.[42]

Popular representations of legal study, however, were an important part of law student culture. Each law book was measured for tedium, every bout of ill health scrutinised, and the ideal of the true lawyer continually sighed after. In the same letter, Sumner admitted that he despaired when confronted by 'the vast weight which a lawyer must bear up under'.[43]

Images of the content, consequences and expectations of reading the law functioned as a common denominator for young men making the journey between the lay and the legal world. These depictions also

[40] See, E Anthony Rotundo, *American Manhood: Transformations in Masculinity from the Revolution to the Modern Era* (Basic Books, New York, 1993), 169–174; Michael Grossberg, 'Institutionalizing Masculinity: The Law as a Masculine Profession,' in MC Carnes and C Griffen (eds), *Meanings for Manhood: Constructions of Masculinity in Victorian America* (University of Chicago Press, Chicago, 1990), 133–151.

[41] 6 Jan 1842, *RBH Diary*, I, 82–83.

[42] Charles Sumner to Charlemagne Tower, 29 September 1831, Edward L. Pierce, *Memoirs and Letters of Charles Sumner*, 2nd edn (S Low, Marston, Searle, & Rivington, London, 1878), I, 111.

[43] *Ibid.*

coloured the lay understanding of the law student experience. As a result, the prevailing imagery of legal study provided a two-way channel through which would-be attorneys and laymen communicated about the nature and value of reading the law. One instance of the functioning of this cultural exchange can be seen in *Law and Laziness* which plays with the commonplaces concerning law students in a mock exposé that purports to reveal that instead of being colourless drones, antebellum law students in New York were actually colourless lazybones. The novel details a group of law students' efforts to avoid, postpone and mitigate the business of learning the law until shortly before the bar examination. In words that echo those of Alexander Chase, the author observed

> there are Chitty, Phillips, Kent, the Revised Statues, &c., to be familiar with; some thousand reports to be consulted; and Graham and Burrill to be got by heart, at leisure moments—all in three weeks.

The author wryly notes, 'Somewhere in history there is an infant wonder who did this in a year and died of the effort'.[44] Yet the novel's chivvying of law students has a serious purpose. The author wants to provoke discussion about the course of legal study and the effects of restricting admission to the bar. Humorous treatment of the popular imagery surrounding law students provides him with an effective means of communicating his concerns.

BY THE BOOK: THE MECHANICS OF READING THE LAW

Upon entering an office or law school, the new acolyte of the law was introduced to books from whence a good portion of his sense and sensibility about the law was to be garnered. It was the task of the law student to read the books at least once, to take notes upon them in a commonplace notebook, and on occasion to answer questions about their contents. This course of 'steady, systematic, dutiful reading,' as one antebellum attorney characterised it, laid the groundwork for a career in the law.[45] Oliver Bounderby, with his unerring instinct for compression, presented a terse description of the process.

> Three years rolled on over the head of Stanton in the office where he was endeavoring to master the noble science whose history is adorned with the names of Bacon, Coke, Blackstone, and a thousand others shining as bright as those. The history of one day in this period would pretty nearly be the history of it all. Hard

[44] *Law and Laziness*, 20.

[45] George W Houk, *A Sketch of the Dayton Bench and Bar* (United Brethren Publishing House, Dayton, 1889), 47.

> and unremitting study, and the closest attention to all the mysteries of the profession he sought to attain, seemed to be his only thoughts.[46]

The antebellum syllabus of legal reading rarely encompassed thousands of bright, shiny books, but it was variable. Reading lists reflected the publication of new material, the content of libraries and the preferences of instructors. There was, however, some overlap in titles and subject matter. A comparison between the reading done by two Ohio antebellum legal apprentices—Albert G Riddle and Peter Zinn—and the books assigned by three antebellum law schools—Indiana, Harvard and Cincinnati—yields a total of 38 titles (see, Appendix).[47] Titles read by three or more parties were Blackstone's *Commentaries* (all five), Kent's *Commentaries* (Zinn, Indiana, Harvard), and Chitty on Contracts (Cincinnati, Harvard, Indiana). Other congruities existed in the realm of subject matter. Riddle, Zinn and the students attending the law schools all read preliminary studies of the law and works concerning pleading under common law procedure. Subjects studied by four parties (Riddle, Indiana, Harvard, Cincinnati) included evidence under common law procedure and the principles related to chancery law and procedure. Other similarities included overviews examining matters like equity, common law procedural concerns and contracts. Differences between reading assignments existed in not only the treatises chosen on a particular topic, but in the absence or presence of readings on certain subjects.[48] Only one or two lists included works on criminal law, criminal procedure, legal history, statutory law, common law practice, negotiable contracts, sales, equity pleading and practice, partnership, constitutional law, corporations, international law, insurance, maritime contracts, agency, bailments, or commercial law.

The titles of books provide clues to the scope and direction of particular legal educations, but the practice of judging books by their covers cannot be condoned. Legal historians still pick up these crumbling volumes on occasion to stiffen the resolve of arguments, but each 'black letter' law book coaxed out of storage seems grey and lifeless under the fluorescent lights of the modern law library. For antebellum law students, however, these law books were more than cowhide containers of legal pronouncements. They were instruments of fortune and futility that engaged and

[46] Bounderby, *The Law Student*, 33.

[47] Sources for these reading lists are noted in the Appendix. The lists cannot be thought of as definitive as most students ventured beyond their assigned reading. The comparison of lists was undertaken to give some sense of what was considered core reading for antebellum law students.

[48] The range of titles assigned for a single topic of study can be seen in the reading lists. For example, there are three different texts devoted to the procedural aspects of equity—Fonblanque's *Equity* (Riddle), Story's *Equity Jurisprudence* (Indiana, Harvard), and Holcombe's *Introduction to Equity* (Cincinnati).

enraged young men in equal proportions. Blackstone and his minions must be understood as part of a dialogue that was taking place between self, other students, society and the profession. The mechanics of reading and the coping strategies that students developed help explain why law students underwent similar intellectual experiences despite variations in the content and the context of their studies.

On his first day as a law student, George W Van Horne knew that there would be difficult times ahead, but on that date in 1853 his enthusiasm for legal study knew no bounds.

> Comparatively a stranger to the 'Republic of Letters,' untutored in the Sciences, and upon no familiar terms with the classics, I perceive at once that my future success does not depend on what *has* been accomplished but rather, upon *present* unwearied action, just appreciation of present advantages, an unflinching purpose, an energy of will, that bows before, and yields to no opposing obstacle.[49]

While few antebellum law students could equal Van Horne's exuberance, many shared his lack of preparation for the often byzantine task of reading the law. Given what is known about antebellum culture and education, this observation may seem surprising. The ostensible task of the law student was the digestion of a battery of topics through which the structure, function and operation of the law would be slowly revealed. On the surface, literary socialisation in the period seemed well suited to such an endeavour. Education tended to encourage the capacity for rote memorisation and compartmentalisation while trimming the sails of imagination. Common practices associated with reading the Bible emphasised the turning of discrete narratives into a complex maze of strictures that gave purpose and form to faith. Meanwhile, the dictates of self-culture promoted the virtues of steady, serious reading. Young antebellum men of all walks of life were urged to devote any available leisure time to works of a serious, factual nature, and from the reading lists that survive it is evident that while novels and newspapers proved tempting, the advice was often followed. Taken together these common antebellum strategies of selecting and processing reading material suggest that a happy match existed between the project of legal study and the skills of young men. Yet most law students struggled and fumed over the task set before them.

Ronald Zboray, in his work on antebellum reading and publishing, suggests that the standard picture of literary socialisation needs adjusting. He points out that an antebellum individual's reading capacity and interpretative capability depended upon religious, familial and educational forums that were increasingly fractured. Bible reading was altered by a proliferation of sects with divergent ideas on the interpretation and

[49] Mildred Throne (ed), 'The Diary of a Law Student, 1853–1855,' *Iowa Journal of History* (1957) 55, 167–186, 169.

use of scripture. Familial lines of power in regard to the responsibilities of raising middle-class children shifted in a way that altered reading practices within the home. Zboray notes that attentive mothers sheltered their charges from the dreary technical and competitive aspects of the lives of their fathers by selecting reading material that dealt with the formation of personal character.[50] At the other end of the social scale, parental attention to reading of any variety was rare for children in large families of low incomes and little leisure. In the schoolroom, the experience of reading was anything but standard as pupils were exposed to a wide array of inept pedagogy. As a consequence, large numbers of law students were rendered ill-equipped for their studies.

Under these circumstances, the first challenge that many youths faced in reading the law was learning the mechanics of *how* to read the law. That task involved not only understanding the means of translating printed words into accessible knowledge, but figuring out how to deal with limitations imposed by abilities, resources and instruction. Those who suffered the least in regard to the prospect of legal reading were generally young men who had attended a college or university. While time spent at an institution of higher education did not translate into greater comprehension of the material, it did ease the transition into legal study by providing exposure to classical languages, history and the methodology of scientific thought. These were subjects that aided in developing a feel for the logic and rhythms of legal reading. While a student at Harvard Law School, Rutherford B Hayes advised some friends at Kenyon College:

> For the student who has the industry and the ability to master the difficulties of his college course, will not be apt to grapple unsuccessfully with the difficulties of the *study* of law.[51]

A college or university sojourn also provided some young men with the *savior faire* necessary for dealing with the amorphous task set before them. Exposure to higher education taught some students the fine art of academic coasting—knowing when it was absolutely necessary to push and when it was possible to sit back and enjoy the ride. Charles Matchett, studying at Cincinnati Law School, confided to his journal:

> It may be my misfortune to fail. As far as I am concerned in the failure I care but little: but when I reflect that I have an aged and venerable Father at home, whose

[50] 'The reading a mother encouraged did not so much ready her child to deal with a society of contracts, technical manuals, account books, or law, as provide the morality, feelings, and discipline that might make the world a better place.' Zboray, *Fictive People*, 86.

[51] Rutherford B Hayes to the President and Members of the Phi Zeta Club, 30 Jan 1844, *RBH Diary*, I, 140.

> most anxious care is for my success; I must strive with all my might to make the case otherwise.

The desire to succeed, however, did not interfere with his active social life that included frequent attendance at concerts, lyceums, plays, the occasional snowball fight and 'the Balloon assention by Moris Goddard on a live Pony in company with his wife'.[52] In college, Matchett had learned that academic work need not be an obstacle to a daily round of pleasure.

Although it offered some advantages, college exposure could not completely resolve the strain of dealing with the volumes of volumes, the swift passage of time and the fragility of powers of concentration. Most students, regardless of educational background, sought a method, philosophy, or short-cut to help them get through. Rutherford B Hayes believed that 'mental discipline' was indispensable to legal study. He noted in his diary:

> The important powers to be disciplined in studying a work like Blackstone, are the memory and attention. The other great powers of the mind, [such] as apprehension, judgement, and reasoning, are of necessity called into action.[53]

In an attempt to impose mental discipline Hayes instituted a regime of study. It forbade the reading of newspapers, and required him to rise at seven and retire at ten, spending six hours a day studying law, two hours at German, and another two reading the English divine, William Chillingsworth.[54] Peter Zinn's daily diary entries often ended with the phrase 'mad at myself.' He charted the course of each day's progress and often found himself lacking. As a consequence, Zinn constructed a complicated schedule of checks and balances that in theory promoted intense industry while setting aside time for the purpose of banishing care. His diary then recorded his progress in his 'rules for my government.' After two weeks of the cumbersome regime, he decided to abandon it, and notations such as 'tolerably mad at self and truly miserable' begin to appear again.[55]

The establishment of a regime was a practice urged upon law students for centuries. William Fulbecke published one of the earliest English guides to the proper study of the law in 1600. The subtitle of the book indicated its general purpose: '*Wherein is Shewed, What Things Ought to be Observed and Used of Them that are Addicted to the Study of the Law*'[56]. Twenty-eight years later, Edward Coke, in his commentary upon

[52] 20 Jan, 13 April 1856, Charles G Matchett Journal, Cincinnati Historical Society, 11, 22.

[53] 19 Nov 1842, *RBH Diary*, I, 109.

[54] 26 Nov 1842, *RBH Diary*, I, 110.

[55] Zinn Diary, 217, 218, 234.

[56] William Fulbecke, *A Direction or Preparative to the Study of the Lawe* (1600; reprint, Garland, New York, 1980).

Thomas Littleton's work on the common law of real property, advised students to dedicate six hours to sleep, six hours to reading, four hours to discussion, two to eating and the final waking hours to spiritual matters.[57] In antebellum America, David Hoffman in the second edition of *A Course of Legal Study* (1836) enlarged upon his predecessor's directives by pointing out the importance of method. He wrote:

> In the various pursuits of man throughout life, method is no less important than industry. If the latter brings us with certainty to the contemplated end, the former facilitates our progress, designates the paths which are the least incumbered, and leads us directly, and often without fatigue, to the object of pursuit. . . . [H]e who has been uniformly the most methodical, though he may not have seen, heard, read, and reflected more than another, has certainly acquired more, both in extent and quality.[58]

Rutherford B Hayes considered Hoffman's advice in his diary:

> Hoffman . . . gives a number of resolutions proper for a law student to make on setting out his journey into the dreary wilderness (the figure is true if not in good taste) of the law. He prescribes a course of study, which, if adopted and faithfully pursued, cannot fail to render a man an able lawyer. Now, why not adopt the resolutions, *deo juvante*, and pursue the course? . . . Method and regularity are necessary in this, as in all great undertakings, for anything worthy the name of success.[59]

In the antebellum context, the devotion to regimes among law students not only grew out of the task set before them, but was coloured by expectations imposed upon all young men by a changing society. In the past two decades, social and cultural historians have probed the portmanteaus and psyches of youths living before the Civil War.[60] Their work

[57] The epigram in Latin appears in the first American edition of Coke on Littleton. JH Thomas (ed), *A Systematic Arrangement of Lord Coke's First Institute of the Laws of England* (Robert Small, Philadelphia, 1827) I, 5. Henry Venard, an antebellum law student studying under Clement Vallandigham in Dayton, Ohio, paraphrased Coke's daily directions to a letter to a friend. '[I] would like to have you here to talk with for one of the directions given to students by sir E. Coke is to read all Morning and talk all afternoon and I can not follow that direction because I have no person to talk with . . . .' Henry Venard to William R Moore, 13 May 1850, William R. Moore Papers, Ohio Historical Society. See also, Charles Sumner, 'The Employment of Time. Lecture Before the Boston Lyceum . . ., February 18, 1846,' *The Works of Charles Sumner* (Lee and Shepard, Boston, 1874), I, 184–213, 200–201.

[58] David Hoffman, *A Course of Legal Study*, 2nd edn (Joseph Neal, Baltimore, 1836), 19.

[59] 27 Oct 1843, *RBH Diary*, I, 121.

[60] See, Rotundo, *American Manhood:*; Rodney D Olsen, *Dancing in Chains: The Youth of William Dean Howells* (New York University Press, New York, 1991); Robert Wiebe, *The Opening of American Society: From the Adoption of the Constitution to the Eve of Disunion* (Knopf, New York, 1984); Karen Halttunen, *Confidence Men and Painted Women: A Study of Middle-class Culture in America, 1830–1870* (Yale

reveals a generation of young people possessed by a self-consciousness of epic proportions generated by a society absorbing the effects of the dissolution of social boundaries. Older Americans, alarmed at the unravelling of the previous century's mechanisms of control, sought to create new means of inculcating responsibility and proper behaviour among adolescents. The youth was warned that his life would consist of an unending, solitary struggle against the corruptions engendered by the desires of his mind and body.[61] Lollygags and dillydalliers received no quarter at the frontiers of antebellum adolescence.

In such an atmosphere, every episode of neglect warranted critical evaluation as law students struggled to control all facets of their lives. Thus, the evening spent chatting in the parlour was measured against the unread volume of Kent left lying on the desk. This milieu of self-scrutiny encouraged the belief that small lapses could contaminate an individual's character leading inexorably to disgrace, disease, dissipation, and disinheritance.[62] Salmon P Chase abandoned any pretense of careful, regimented study as the bar examination approached in December of 1829. Chase admitted: 'I read superficially but my object was rather to finish a certain number of books before I applied for admission to the bar than to acquire legal knowledge.' The tactic, however, caused him considerable concern.

> I have given strength to a habit of superficial reading which was strong before. It will not now be easy to eradicate it and substitute for it a habit of close attention and patient reflection. Yet this must be done or my admission to the bar will do me little good.[63]

In an enterprise like studying the law, achievement was difficult to measure, and the daily round of work largely devoid of any means of confirming legal ability. The construction of rigid, often elaborate schedules detailing the metes and bounds of reading, eating and sleeping offered a means of regulating the self and judging progress. Regardless of the contents of the reading list, these regimes offered a refuge from anxiety. As David Hoffman assured his readers,

University Press, New Haven, 1982); Mary P Ryan, *Cradle of the Middle Class: The Family in Oneida County, New York, 1790–1865* (Cambridge University Press, New York, 1981); Carroll Smith-Rosenberg, 'Sex as Symbol in Victorian Purity: An Ethnohistorical Analysis of Jacksonian America,' in J Demos and SS Boocock (eds), *Turning Points: Historical and Sociological Essays on the Family* (The University of Chicago Press, Chicago, 1978), 212–247; Allan S Horlick, *Country Boys and Merchant Princes: The Social Control of Young Men in New York* (Bucknell University Press, Lewisburg, PA, 1975).

[61] See, Halttunen, *Confidence Men*, 25; Wiebe, *Opening of American Society*, 271.

[62] See, Lewis Perry, *Boats Against the Current: American Culture Between Revolution and Modernity, 1820–1860* (Oxford University Press, New York, 1993), 194.

[63] 1–2 & c Dec 1829, *Journal of Salmon P. Chase*, I, 30.

> Method places in our hands both a torch and clue, to guide us through the surest and easiest ways: it agreeably impresses the mind with confidence, amidst the greatest difficulties, and presents the most distinct and lively pictures of all that is worthy of notice in our path; and finally brings us to the end of our journey, improved, invigorated, and delighted.[64]

BLACKSTONE AS TOUCHSTONE: THE CULTURAL ROLE OF THE *COMMENTARIES*

Popular representations of legal study along with strategies for coping with reading the law provide a means of probing the socialisation of those engaged in the enterprise of becoming an attorney. The process through which young men learned to be lawyers was also shaped by the reading of particular works in the law student canon. The urtext of antebellum law students was William Blackstone's ubiquitous *Commentaries on the Laws of England*. Blackstone became inseparable from the practice of law because it presented a comprehensible and comprehensive summary of that incomprehensible and incompressible system that underpinned American legal activities—the common law. Before Blackstone, Americans tried to learn the common law from works of their sixteenth and seventeenth century legal forefathers. It was a daunting task that embittered and disgusted an entire generation of lawyers. Thus, the arrival of Blackstone was hailed as a kind of miracle. Elevated by a host of heartfelt hosannas, Blackstone became a fixture in the antebellum law office, but like any familiar, albeit valuable furnishing, it was cleaned, painted and re-upholstered many times as a variety of men tried to nationalise, regionalise, individualise or accessorise its contents.[65] Some even possessed the temerity to criticise Blackstone as the inculcator of unwholesome political ideas or point out its general irrelevance to a rapidly changing world of practice and procedure.[66] Regardless of renovation or reproach, however, Blackstone, in one form or another, remained the linchpin of antebellum legal education. Its influence endured beyond pupillage, providing practitioners with a span of com-

[64] Hoffman, *Course of Legal Study*, 20.

[65] See, Craig E Klafter, *Reason Over Precedents: Origins of American Legal Thought* (Greenwood Press, Westport, CT, 1993), 31–47, for a discussion of how St. George Tucker shaped his influential edition of the *Commentaries*.

[66] See, 'Study of the Law,' in Michael H Hoeflich (ed), *The Gladsome Light of Jurisprudence: Learning the Law in England and the United States in the 18th and 19th Centuries* (Greenwood Press, New York, 1988), 201–213, 206–207 (First published in *The Southern Literary Messenger* (1837) 3, 25–31); Julius S Waterman, 'Thomas Jefferson and Blackstone's Commentaries,' in DH Flaherty (ed), *Essays in the History of Early American Law* (University of North Carolina Press, Chapel Hill, 1969), 451–488, 457–472.

mon ground on which the edifice of a national legal culture would be constructed after the Civil War.

Because of its importance to the process of learning the law, the *Commentaries* played a highly visible role in the lives of law students. Blackstone served as a catalyst of professional identity, functioned as a site of social and cultural communion for law students and furnished a generation of lawyers with a rudimentary understanding of the nature and operation of law. Other books, such as James Kent's *Commentaries on American Law* (1826–1830) and Timothy Walker's *Introduction to American Law* (1837), were widely read by law students and contributed to the antebellum understanding of law. Neither Kent nor Walker's works, however, achieved Blackstone's status as a cultural cynosure. Charles Sumner wrote to a fellow law student in 1832:

> Truly, the English commentator [Blackstone] is a glorious man; he brings such a method, such a flow of language and allusion and illustration to every topic! I have heard a sensible lawyer place Kent *above* him; but, in my opinion, sooner ought the earth to be above the clear and azure-built heavens![67]

Blackstone occupied the centre of a ceaseless discussion that included panegyrics by Joseph Story, pot-shots by Thomas Jefferson and parody in the form of Gilbert Abbott Beckett's *The Comic Blackstone* (1844). Despite the significance of Blackstone, the cultural relationship between the antebellum legal community and the *Commentaries* remains largely unexplored.[68] In past historical studies of attorneys before the Civil War, Blackstone appears as a prop. It rests in a saddlebag, on the desk or in Abraham Lincoln's case, apocryphally in the bottom of a barrel of junk. Yet when Blackstone is seen through the eyes of law students, it transcends its status as object and becomes a force with which to be reckoned.

Legal study either in an office or in a law school typically began with a foray into the *Commentaries*. To get started, as one antebellum law student put it, you had to 'open Justice Blackstone & then, Crocket like, "go ahead" '.[69] In an 1831 letter welcoming a pupil to his office, Philip Doddridge advised the young man to begin reading Blackstone immediately. 'This book,' Doddridge wrote, 'should be read with more ease than

[67] Charles Sumner to Charlemagne Tower, 31 Jan 1832, *Memoirs*, I, 113. Sumner's appreciation for Kent deepened after a year of legal study. He declared in an 1833 letter to Tower: 'I have had from him [Kent] a great deal of elegant instruction. His Commentaries are not wholly appreciated by the student upon a first perusal; they are hardly elementary enough.' Sumner to Charlemagne Tower, 12 June 1833, *Memoirs*, I, 119–120.

[68] An exception is Robert A Ferguson who addresses the cultural influences of Blackstone on the lawyer-writer, and the development of early American literature. See, *Law and Letters*, 30–33, 92.

[69] William McClintick to William S Gregg, 8 July 1840, William S Gregg Papers, Ohio Historical Society.

any one in any language except the bible and by every one who would wish to excell. Not a sentence should be left unstudied'.[70] Blackstone was the McGuffey Reader of the legal set, and as such its style, substance, and imagery created a common legal framework upon which antebellum lawyers secured their ideology and convictions concerning law and its practice.

Four volumes comprised the *Commentaries*. The first tackled the rights of persons and the role of government. The second dealt with property law. The third looked at civil procedure and remedies, while the final volume took on criminal law. The scope of Blackstone is broad and its pages are laden with detail, but it presented complex information in a structured, easily digestible fashion. The readability of Blackstone gave heart to many law students who feared the dry complexities of the law. In fact, some judged Blackstone to be too accessible. *Law and Laziness* took aim at the congenial nature of the *Commentaries*.

> That grim Sphynx with his riddles, Coke upon Lyttleton, no longer frowns at the gates of the law and frightens away the children. . . . But Blackstone opens, invitingly, an airy and ornamental portal to the traveller, in search of a profession and tempts him to enter on the thorny path, and tangled labyrinths beyond. He has made law fashionable; inundated the profession with young men of bad habits and good families; and created the order of students of leisure.[71]

Blackstone's position as the polestar of the antebellum law student was not just a result of his way with words, but was also a product of the economic realities of legal practice. Law books were expensive and as a result most lawyers' libraries were small. Without much capital to invest in books, attorneys tended to purchase used editions of texts that covered a broad range of subjects in a single volume.[72] The *Commentaries* met both criteria as it was considered to be a comprehensive work readily available for secondhand purchase. A young man in search of a legal career might have difficulty in finding a preceptor, the wherewithal to pursue his studies, or a roof to sleep under, but a copy of Blackstone was always within reach.

Blackstone had an influential role in the creation of legal identity, in part, because its fame transgressed the boundaries of the legal world and spilled into popular culture. Therefore, even before a law student turned a single page, he was acquainted with the name and the fame of

[70] Philip Doddridge to Waltman Willey, 5 Aug 1831, Western Reserve Historical Society.

[71] *Law and Laziness*, 21.

[72] See, Harris, 'Frontier Lawyer's Library', 244–245. Newmyer paints a different picture of lawyer's book-buying strategies: 'By publishing individual volumes on specific subjects, rather than massive works like those of William Blackstone and James Kent, Story made it possible for lawyers to buy only what they needed at a price that they could afford.' Newmyer, 'Harvard Law School,' 163.

Blackstone. For lawyers, a copy of the *Commentaries* was the iconographic equivalent of the blacksmith's anvil. An 1859 painting by David Gilmore Blythe entitled *The Lawyer's Dream* depicts an old man snoozing away amidst the clutter of his office. A viewer knows that the figure is a lawyer because in the foreground of the picture lies a large book with the name Blackstone emblazoned across the cover.[73] The prominence of the *Commentaries* within society heightened the law student's first encounter with the work, often transforming it into a moment of personal significance. George W Van Horne wrote on the day he began his legal apprenticeship:

> language of mind is not adequate for the illustration of the emotions and aspirations, which glow in my bosom, as for the first time I am honoured with an introduction to the immortal Blackstone.[74]

Reading Blackstone was an outward sign of a commitment to the idea of becoming an attorney. As the first weeks of legal study progressed, the name of Blackstone appeared repeatedly in letters as law students sought to establish their legal identities in the eyes of individuals who had heretofore known them only in their mundane incarnations as sons, brothers, or friends. Ros Buchanan, who studied law in Ohio, gave notice of his new status in an 1836 letter to a college friend. 'Here I come—clear the track—I am no longer Ros—but ahem! Why Sir, I am *Mr. Lawyer*.' Mr. Lawyer continued chastising his friend for failing to keep an appointment, saying,

> You deserve banishment everlasting, and by golly, you shall have it. For with Blackstone in one hand and a box of cegars in the other I will send you beyond the region of Hen peck where you shall eat grass like an oxen, forever, and forevermore.[75]

The mere mention of Blackstone served as a powerful identifier, but the contents of the book were equally important to the development of a sense of self as lawyer. In particular, the specialised vocabulary and imagery found in Blackstone provided the means through which law students could ground their legal identity. It would take many months before a young man could present an argument before a tribunal, but in the course of the first week of reading Blackstone, words such as *non compos* or *laches* tripped off the tongue providing his first tangible

[73] *The Lawyer's Dream*, oil on canvas by David Gilmore Blythe (1815–1865) 61.6 × 51.4 cm. (241/4 × 20 1/4 in.), 1859, The Carnegie Museum of Art, Pittsburgh, PA. The link between Blackstone and the legal profession is symbolised by the large padlock and chain that secures the book to the lawyer's desk. The message is that Blackstone belongs unreservedly to members of the legal profession who render its contents inaccessible by their unchallenged possession.

[74] Throne, 'Diary of a Law Student,' 169.

[75] Ros Buchanan to William S Gregg, 20 Sept 1836, Gregg Papers.

connection to the profession. The technical vocabulary of the law came in for considerable criticism by laymen and some lawyers. Timothy Walker, in the 1844 edition of his *Introduction to American Law*, observed that professionals like to

> create a monopoly of their acquisitions, by employing a language not generally understood, nor easily acquired; and when a phraseology, however barbarous or inelegant, has been consecrated by time, it is very difficult to change it.[76]

In the initial stages of their professional journey, however, law students were not inclined to ponder unduly the obscurity of law's language. Like the passwords of a secret society, the specialised vocabulary found in the *Commentaries* provided law students with a sense of inclusion and the authority of technical knowledge. These young men were discovering what David Sugarman has called 'the special power of lawyers to do things with words'.[77]

Imagery found in the text gave students another means of transforming their understanding of themselves and the role of the lawyer. For instance, in Volume One, the most familiar and personal human relationships are categorised and put into a legal context. Law students studied a chapter on parents and children in which the affections and aversions of family life were metamorphosed into particulars concerning a range of enforceable duties and responsibilities. In the pages of Blackstone, issues that many law students were intimately acquainted with such as punishment, education and the extent of parental power, were quickly and cleanly brought under law's dominion. The imagery of hearth and home as vessels of the law continued in another chapter focusing on the realm of husbands and wives. Marriage, intones Blackstone, is considered in no other light than a civil contract

> allowing it to be good and valid in all cases, where the parties at the time of making it were, in the first place, *willing* to contract; secondly, *able* to contract; and, lastly, actually *did* contract, in the proper forms and solemnities required by law.[78]

[76] Timothy Walker, *Introduction to American Law, Designed as a First Book for Students*, 2nd edn (U P James, Cincinnati, 1844), 2.

[77] David Sugarman, 'Simple Images and Complex Realities: English Lawyers and Their Relationship to Business and Politics, 1750–1950,' *Law and History Review* (1993) 11, 257–301, 293.

[78] William Blackstone, *Commentaries on the Laws of England* (1765, reprint, University of Chicago Press, Chicago, 1979), I, 421.

Gilbert Abbott Beckett parodied this famous passage in his popular satirical work of 1844, *The Comic Blackstone:* 'To make a marriage three things are required;—first, that the parties *will* marry; secondly that they *can*; and thirdly, that they *do*; though to us it seems that if they *do*, it matters little whether they *will*, and if they *will*, it is of little consequence whether they *can*; for if they *do*, they *do*; and if they *will* they *must*; because where there is a *will* there is a *way*, and therefore they *can* if they *choose*; and if they

The influence of this perspective of marital relations is evident in a passage from the diary of Calvin Fletcher, an Ohio lawyer newly admitted to the bar, who reflected on his marriage proposal of the previous day. He wrote:

> I will here suggest my reasons for these ingagements that I am about to fulfil so that I shall be able here after to satisfy myself and if not myself others that may have an inspection of this Book, that I deliberately went into the marriage contract being sensible of all the disadvantages under which I labor.[79]

Contact with imagery of parents and wives as legal entities did not wring all the sentimentality out of young male minds, but it did supply them with a new understanding of the lines of power, duty and authority in the institutions of marriage and family.

The *Commentaries* also formed a site of social and cultural communion for law students. Peter Zinn, Albert G Riddle and students of the law schools at Cincinnati, Harvard, and Indiana did not all share the experience of reading Espinasse's *Nisi Prius*, but every last one of them read Blackstone. From the provisions supplied by the *Commentaries*—an emerging legal identity, a new vocabulary, and a different way of viewing the familiar—law students fashioned a shared consciousness of the process of legal study. Few students knew much about the actual life and career of Sir William, but in antebellum law offices the historical man was of no concern. Blackstone was removed from the context of his life and refashioned as the law student's particular friend. George W Van Horne wrote of Blackstone in his journal as though the old fellow had dropped in for tea.

> Attended closely the companionship of Blackstone in conversation about the Clergy of England, and before eve'g had the pleasure of relating to Mr. Ladd the facts gathered from the interview with the learned gentleman.[80]

Law students thought of Blackstone as a benign old man—wise but a bit old-fashioned. In this guise, Blackstone became part of the language of frolic and friendship shared by law students. Blackstone, having penned a few poems himself, might have enjoyed Josiah Scott's doggerel description of the labours of a legal pupil. One stanza read: 'I sometimes at the lasses look,/ Sometimes hurrah for Jackson!/ Sometimes I read a musty book/ Compiled by old Judge Blackstone'.[81]

don't, it is because they *won't*, which brings us to the conclusion, that if they *do*, it is absurd to speculate upon whether they *will* or *can* marry.' Beckett, *The Comic Blackstone* (Carey and Hart, Philadelphia, 1844), 83.

[79] 4 Feb 1821, *Diary of Calvin Fletcher*, I , 24.

[80] Throne, 'Diary of a Law Student,' 172.

[81] RC Colmery, *A Memoir of the Life and Character of Josiah Scott* (Cott & Hann, Columbus, OH, 1881), 15.

While the reading of Blackstone brought students together, it also served as a means of making distinctions among them. In the world of the antebellum law student it wasn't enough just to read Blackstone, among your peers what mattered was how fast you read it. I have labelled this phenomenon as 'Blackstone velocity quotient.' Young men unsure of their abilities and intellectual talents wanted a measurement that could be communicated to others that might act to bolster self-esteem and give a much-needed sense of progress. Many believed that the rapid consumption of Blackstone was a portent of legal aptitude and future success. Rutherford B Hayes noted his Blackstone macho quotient in an 1842 entry in his diary in which he claimed to be plowing through the *Commentaries* at a pace of 150 pages per week.[82] Albert G Riddle left Hayes in the dust. He took only a week to read each volume.[83]

Blackstone assisted in the socialisation of law students not only by encouraging the development of a legal identity and a sense of community but by instilling a basic understanding of the nature and operation of law. To glimpse the *Commentaries*' role in the latter enterprise, it is necessary to try and reconstruct the experience of reading Volumes One through Four through the eyes of a prototypical antebellum law student. The young man sits in an attorney's office on the verge of opening up Volume One. At that moment what does the youth know about the ways of the law? For the law student, like so many laymen, the notion of law possesses three functional dimensions—it is a compendium of rules written down in a statute book somewhere that regulates actions, it is a dimly realised consciousness concerning rights and it is a process which brings together community members, lawyers and judges in an adversarial setting. As the law student settles back in his chair and begins to read, he quickly discovers that law is a complex mixture composed of a dizzying spectrum of custom, authority, Latin phrases and people with tricky names like Puffendorf. With each page he turns, the youth witnesses how law surrounds the mighty and the minute. When he closes the final volume, his general, unfocused ideas about the province of law give way to inchoative understanding of the law as the rational, orderly engine of society.

In reading the *Commentaries*, the law student passes through his first stage of legal study—the Blackstone moment. He has seen that law provides pragmatic solutions to complex problems; that authority matters to the correct interpretation of the law; and that law is a science and its components are arranged in a manner consistent with its natural structure. The Blackstone moment was recorded by Rutherford B Hayes in an 1842 diary entry.

[82] 19 Nov 1842, *RBH Diary*, I, 108.

[83] Riddle, 'Fifty-Five Years of Lawyer Life,' 42.

> Blackstone's' style is so clear that his meaning is seldom obscure, and he is so perspicuous in the statement of the reasons for what he says and in his explanations, that great exertion is not requisite to comprehend him. As it is all plain reading, the attention is the only power especially exercised.[84]

The Blackstone moment conferred a sense of control and offered the possibility for mastery of complexities, but for most antebellum law students it was brutally brief. The further law students ventured from the *Commentaries*, the clearer it became that what was orderly and rational was William Blackstone's mind and that the daily law of town, state and nation was bewilderment's finest creation. Peter Zinn, a post-Blackstone law student confronted with the task of understanding the practical applications of the law of contracts, declared:

> the head of contracts contains so many nice points of law, and the decisions are so conflicting, that we often get entangled and almost wholly lost in the mist of the many apparent contradictory decisions. Express and implied frauds—symbolical, and delivery in fact—personal property in and out of possession . . . afford a field of investigation as intricate and as difficult of exploration as the swamps of Florida.[85]

Although the premise of a neatly packaged legal system was undermined, a residue of the Blackstone moment remained, providing a critical link between antebellum attorneys. The study of Blackstone gave counsellors-at-law the materials necessary to make their peace with the difficult and cantankerous conundrum known as the law. Law might exhibit signs of being as pathless as a swamp, but the lawyer whose livelihood depended on his ability to navigate among the mangroves and moss needed to feel that there were some common principles to use in steering. The belief that law at its core was orderly, rational, and necessary for individuals and society in general was critical for the practice of law and the development of the American legal profession.[86] Evidence of the presence of this understanding of the basic nature of law and its operation can be found in the large and small moments of antebellum law. It spilled over into the structure and strictures of antebellum legal treatises, into the philosophies and goals of the developing law schools, into the continued preference for Blackstone when it came time to educate the next batch of lawyers, and into the countless number of times that antebellum lawyers reached for their copies of the *Commentaries* when confronted with a difficult problem. Blackstone was always there to be made use of and when it no longer inspired the roaring flames of a novice's reverence

[84] 19 Nov 1842, *RBH Diary*, I, 108.

[85] 20 March 1841, Zinn Diary, 166.

[86] Grant Gilmore argued that the influence of Blackstone was the result of his ability to convince others of the comforting idea that law was knowable and incontrovertible. Gilmore, *The Ages of American Law* (Yale University Press, New Haven, 1977), 64–68.

at least it could coax a spark of respect for the book's utility. Josiah Quincy in his 1832 speech at the dedication of the Dane Law College at Harvard stated:

> If we were to say that all the improvements, which have been introduced into the study and the science of the law since the middle of the last century, were the consequence of the publication of the single work of Blackstone, we should assert, perhaps, more than we could prove, though possibly not more than is true.[87]

Scholars who hope to understand the creation and sustenance of the legal culture that flourished among nineteenth-century lawyers must take note of Quincy's words. As Robert A Ferguson observes:

> These encomiums to Blackstone deserve careful attention because they point to the source of the lawyer's epistemological self-confidence, his peculiar ability to convert general knowledge into design and then power into places where others found only confusion.[88]

The socialisation of the antebellum law student did not produce a profession without rancour and disagreement. Once admitted to the bar, the pressure of internal disputes, lay calls for reform, particular regional legal concerns and the realities of practice in the local courts tended to dilute the strength of the cultural comity acquired through legal study. Yet the cultural lessons of law student days retained a place in the words, thoughts and deeds of the men who populated the nineteenth century legal world. Contained within a law student culture that linked the Northern half of the country together through key legal works, disciplined study, and devotion to a common endeavour were the seeds of a national legal culture that matured after the Civil War.

Listening to the voices of antebellum law students assists in the pursuit of broad historical questions, but it also provides insight into one of the many ways that law transformed the lives of individual Americans. William McClintick, a Chillicothe, Ohio law student wrote to a friend in 1838:

> You ask me how I like the Law, and all about it. To answer this, would be a task, which at present I cannot think of undertaking. All about the Law! Why, man, you are mad. I might as well attempt a description of the great Labyrinth of Egypt. As to my liking it, this is something more tangible. I am much better pleased that I expected to be and feel perfectly willing to continue a searcher into Legal mysteries the rest of my days. The Law, sir, is glorious. Try it yourself.[89]

[87] Josiah Quincy, *An Address Delivered at the Dedication of Dane Law College in Harvard University, October 23, 1832* (EW Metcalf and Co, Cambridge, 1832), 14.

[88] Ferguson, *Law and Letters*, 31.

[89] William McClintick to William Gregg, 28 April 1838, Gregg Papers.

Appendix
The Reading of Antebellum Law Students

The title, date and place of initial publication, and subject category for each book is presented on its first appearance in a reading list. Subject categories are based on those used by Timothy Walker in his 'Catalogue of a Select Law Library,' *The Western Law Journal* 1 (July 1844): 458–465, although where necessary, additional classifications not found in the original have been furnished. Many of the books appearing in these reading lists went through several editions. A number of the English works were annotated or amended to reflect the needs of American legal practice. Thus, an antebellum law student assigned to read a work like Chitty on Contracts probably read one of the annotated American editions printed in Massachusetts and Pennsylvania between 1827–1860.

1. Albert G. Riddle. Student of Seabury Ford, Burton, Ohio, 1838–1840. List represents books read in a two-year period.
Source: Albert G Riddle, 'Fifty-Five Years of Lawyer Life, 1840–1895,' Albert G Riddle Papers, Western Reserve Historical Society.

William Blackstone, *Commentaries on the Laws of England* (England, 1765–1769). [Preliminary Studies—Elementary].

Isaac Espinasse, *A Digest of the Law of Actions and Trials at Nisi Prius* (England, 1789). [Common Law Procedure—Practice].

Charles Butler, *Horae Juridicae Subsecivae* (England, 1804). [Civil and Canon Law].

Thomas Peak, *Compendium of the Law of Evidence* (England, 1801). [Common Law Procedure—Evidence].

Joseph Chitty, Jr, *Precedents in Pleading with Notes on Practice, Pleading, and Evidence* (England, 1836–1838). [Common Law Procedure—Pleadings].

Joseph Chitty, *Criminal Law; Comprising the Practice, Pleadings, and Evidence with Precedents* (England, 1816). [Crimes and Criminal Procedure].

John Fonblanque, *Treatise of Equity* (England, 1793–1794). [Chancery Law and Procedure—Principles].

Matthew Hale, *The History of the Common Law of England* (England, 1713). [Preliminary Studies—Historical].

William Hawkins, *Pleas of the Crown* (England, 1716–1721). [Crimes and Criminal Procedure].

Matthew Bacon, *A New Abridgement of the Law* (England, 1736). [Abridgements and Digests—General].

Salmon P. Chase, *Statutes of Ohio and of the Northwestern Territory, 1788–1833* (United States, 1833–1835). [Statutory Law—Particular States].

Riddles' reading list also indicates that he studied a work by Powell. Presumably this is John J Powell (1755?–1801) who wrote a series of books on contracts, devises and mortgages. Riddle also read 'Ch J Swift's, Treaties,' a work whose full title, name of author, and date I have been unable to locate.

2. Peter Zinn. Student of William Corry, Cincinnati, Ohio, 1841–1842. List represents books read in a fifteen-month period.
Source: Peter Zinn Diary, Cincinnati Historical Society.

Blackstone's *Commentaries*.

Timothy Walker, *Introduction to American Law, Designed as a First Book for Students* (United States, 1837). [Preliminary Studies—Elementary].

James Kent, *Commentaries on American Law* (United States, 1826–1830). [Preliminary Studies—Elementary].

Francis Hilliard, *Elements of the Law* (United States, 1835). [Preliminary Studies—Elementary].

Joseph R Swan, *Statutes of the State of Ohio* (United States, 1841). [Statutory Law—Particular States].

James Gould, *A Treatise on the Principles of Pleading, in Civil Actions* (United States, 1832). [Common Law Procedure—Pleading].

3. Required Texts, Indiana University School of Law, 1843. List represents books assigned for a twelve-month course of study.
Source: 'The Law Department of Indiana University, at Bloomington,' *The Western Law Journal* 1 (November 1843): 92.

Blackstone's *Commentaries*.

Kent's *Commentaries*.

Chitty on Pleading.

Joseph Chitty, Jr, *A Practical Treatise on the Law of Contracts, not Under Seal; and Upon the Usual Defences to Actions Thereon* (England, 1826). [Personal Property and Contracts—General].

Henry J Stephen, *Principles of Pleading in Civil Actions* (England, 1824). [Common Law Procedure—Pleading].

Joseph Chitty, *Bills of Exchange, Checks on Bankers, Promissory Notes, Banker's Cash Notes, and Bank-Notes* (England, 1799). [Personal Property and Contracts—Negotiable Contracts].

Thomas Starkie, *Practical Treatise on the Law of Evidence* (England, 1824). [Common Law Procedure—Evidence].

Joseph Story, *Commentaries on the Constitution of the United States* (United States, 1833). [Constitutional Law].

Joseph Story, *Commentaries on Equity Jurisprudence* (United States, 1836). [Chancery Law and Procedure—Principles].

Joseph Story, *Commentaries on Equity Pleadings* (United States, 1838). [Chancery Law and Procedure—Practice and Pleadings].

4. Required Texts, Harvard University School of Law, 1844. List represents books assigned for a two-year course of study.
Source: 'Law School in Harvard University,' *The Western Law Journal* 1 (January 1844): 184–187.

Blackstone's *Commentaries*.
Kent's *Commentaries*.
Chitty on Contracts.
Chitty on Pleading.
Starkie on Evidence.
Stephen on Pleading.
Story on Equity Jurisprudence.
Story on Equity Pleadings.
Story's Commentaries on the Constitution.

Joseph K Angell and Samuel Ames, *Law of Private Corporations, Aggregate* (United States, 1832). [Law of Persons—Corporations].

Simon Greenleaf, *A Treatise on the Law of Evidence* (United States, 1842–53). [Common Law Procedure—Evidence].

George Long, *A Treatise on the Law Relative to Sales of Personal Property* (England, 1821). [Personal Property and Contracts—Sales].

Charles Abbott, *Law Relative to Merchant Ships and Seamen* (England, 1802). [Personal Property and Contracts—Maritime Contracts].

Samuel Marshall, *Law of Insurance* (England, 1802). [Personal Property and Contracts—Insurance].

Joseph Story, *Commentaries on the Law of Agency* (United States, 1839). [Law of Persons—Master and Servant].

Joseph Story, *Commentaries on the Law of Bailments* (United States, 1832). [Personal Property and Contracts—Bailments].

Joseph Story, *Commentaries on the Conflict of Laws, Foreign and Domestic* (United States, 1834). [International Law].

Joseph Story, *Commentaries on the Law of Bills of Exchange, Foreign and Inland* (United States, 1843). [Personal Property and Contracts—Negotiable Contracts].

Joseph Story, *Commentaries on the Law of Partnership* (United States, 1841). [Law of Persons—Partnership].

William Cruise, *A Digest of the Laws of England Respecting Real Property* (England, 1804). [Law of Real Property—General].

5. Required Texts, Cincinnati Law School, 1849. List represents books assigned for an eight-month course of study.
Source: 'Law Department of the Cincinnati College,' *The Western Law Journal*, n.s. 2 (November 1849): 96.

Blackstone's *Commentaries*.
Walker's *Introduction to American Law*.
Chitty on Contracts.
Gould on Pleading.
Greenleaf on Evidence.
James P Holcombe, *Introduction to Equity Jurisprudence* (United States, 1846). [Chancery Law and Procedure—Principles].
John W Smith, *A Compendium of Mercantile Law* (England, 1834). [Personal Property and Contracts—Commercial Law].

PART II

Lawyers and the Liberal State

4

'Finland's Route' of Professionalisation and Lawyer-Officials

ESA KONTTINEN

THE THEORY AND VARYING HISTORICAL LINES OF PROFESSIONALISATION

The theory of professions was long based one-sidedly on Anglo-American experience, Britain and the United States being known as the real 'native countries of professionalism' and 'native countries of the theory of professions'. While Anglo-American theoretical work on professions earlier yielded 'universal' models of various kinds—which were widely used, often in a rather unreflective manner, in the analysis of educated occupations in other countries as well—awareness of diverging lines of development has grown in recent years. As a result of this awareness, scholars have taken seriously the need for more adequate theoretical concepts for describing the various lines of the professionalization process (eg Freidson 1994, 5–6). It has been emphasised that careful analysis is needed to understand the forms and development of professionalisation in individual societies (e.g. McClelland 1990). On a general level, in Western societies the main contribution of this search is a clear specification of two great lines of development, the Anglo-American and the Continental one.

Following Randall Collins (1990, 15–18), these two routes can be described as follows. A typical Anglo route was the formation of monopolistic practitioner groups operating in the market for services. An occupation became a high-status profession by forming itself independently of the state. Occupational groups struggled with each other in the market for specialised services. These groups, which were effectively organised and adequately qualified, succeeded in convincing the buyers of services of their exclusive quality, and sooner or later they would exclude the competitive groups and monopolise specific services. A specialised education was the usual exclusory criterion. This monopolistic position gave these groups economic and social rewards. The privileged position of a highly specialised and educated occupational group with high status is called a profession.

The Anglo model of professionalisation thus manifests free competition of occupational groups in the market of services. It is, then, quite natural that occupational groups and their associations should be at the centre of the theory. The state had, to a large extent, a legitimating role as an official guarantor of the professional position. Occupational groups even founded educational institutes of their own.

A typical Continental route was quite different. The primary driving force behind the development of Continental professions was the growth of the state. Office in state bureaucracy was the key here. On the one hand, academic education and a university degree as a precondition for state office, and on the other hand, the connections of bureaucrats to old status groups—above all to the nobility—gave the officials high status. The nobility is here a model status group which gives its aura to bureaucrats; then the credential revolution carries this aura further and further to other occupations. In societies like France and Germany, the bureaucratic state not only legitimated and controlled professional posts, but even organised them and their educational institutions.

In the course of the nineteenth century continental societies, too, were liberated, and a new type of civil society was able to develop. There was now more room for independent occupational associations; as a result, the Continental model moved towards the Anglo route. However, bureaucracy, academic credentialing and a quasi-aristocratic lifestyle were fused to a high degree. This characterises the Continental image of a profession much more than its Anglo counterpart.

It is important to understand these descriptions as ideal types, as Collins himself does: as guiding methodological principles rather than factors predetermining the course of investigation. Collins says that in any historical case, variations of these two types of condition may lie anywhere on the continuum and involve mixtures of both types. For instance, there are remarkable differences between the professionalisation processes in Germany and France, both strong state societies. Professions may also vary considerably in a given society. Therefore, Collins prefers to talk broadly about *socially idealised occupations organised as closed associational communities*. This definition of profession includes 'bureaucratic office-holders', 'licensed market-monopolisers', and 'esoteric knowledge-holders'.

In what follows I analyse the professionalisation process in Finland within this general scheme. I focus on the nineteenth-century Finnish society, on the period when important professional structures were formed, structures which constituted an important basis for later developments. Even today we can discern the influence of structural formations dating back to the early nineteenth century. This holds eg for the social position of lawyers in the Finnish society of our days.

I begin by analysing the formation of the Finnish professional field in general, paving the way for the study of the legal profession. How were professional and occupational fields structured in this society? How were they determined by the main societal institutions, the leading classes and the state bureaucracy? Which role did the professional field in general and the legal profession in particular play in this whole? My general argument is that this macro context or 'professional macro system' is of central importance for the understanding of the overall development of any individual profession in its early history.

At first sight it is clear that professionalisation in nineteenth-century Finland is an example of the Continental line of development. A strong central bureaucracy was built immediately after Finland was separated from Sweden and annexed to Russia in 1809 as her Grand Duchy (the position of Finland up to the year 1917, when Finland gained her independence). Since then, the central bureaucracy has without question been in a key position in the construction of a number of social institutions in Finnish society.

Therefore, we must pay attention to the central bureaucracy and its policies. However, this is not enough. To have a better understanding of the dynamics of this society we need to have an overview of the positions and characteristics of the old status groups in the power structure. A careful analysis of these status groups is particularly important in the case of Finland. This is because in Finland their interests were connected, for specific historical reasons, exceptionally tightly with the professional field. This dependency, for its part, shaped in a crucial manner some of the main professional structures in this field. (See also Konttinen 1996a.)

THE BUREAUCRACY-CENTRED SOCIETY: A SOURCE FOR A HOMOGENEOUS EDUCATIONAL BASIS FOR PROFESSIONS

There are good reasons for describing the early period of the Grand Duchy of Finland as a bureaucratic society. The central bureaucracy, with the Senate as its peak and a Russian Governor General as its leader, controlled and organised the entire social life in an authoritative manner. The Russian Emperor governed through the bureaucracy, which, however, had in many spheres of social policy a fairly wide autonomy. The position of the Senate was strengthened by the fact that the Diet of Four Estates was summoned together only in 1863 (after the Porvoo Diet in 1810). The political position of the Grand Duchy was very fragile, and political and social life were strictly controlled by top bureaucrats in an attempt to avoid giving Russia any grounds for reducing Finland's autonomy.

Partly for this reason, the founding of professional associations was not possible during this period. Occupational groups themselves were weak, but also the origins were strictly controlled by the bureaucrats. True, the first Finnish nationwide professional association, *The Finnish Society of Physicians,* was founded as early as 1835. However, during its early days it was not a unique professional association: its basic activities consisted above all of practical matters like lending books for physicians. Furthermore, the founding of this association had been proposed by one of Finland's leading bureaucrats.

It was *the central bureaucracy* that organised occupations. In some cases a state organ (like the physicians' *Collegium Medicum*) was established to arrange the speciality. For a number of emerging professions, like that of educated architects, a department of the central bureaucracy itself functioned as an educational and training institution.

Market economy was underdeveloped; only a few per cent of the population worked in industry. Freedom of trade did not begin to develop until the second half of the 1800s. As regards educated occupations, the free markets for services were extremely narrow. Reflecting the centrality of bureaucracy, public office was practically the only form of professional career. Unlike in the more developed European countries, there were no noteworthy private bases for professional markets in Finnish society. Only wealthier noblemen could employ private teachers or clergymen. Sometimes, as in the case of a handful of physicians, architects and lawyers, professionals could earn additional income by selling their services to private persons. Although a private basis for professional jobs started to emerge at the end of the century, public office has provided the basic occupational identity for a great number of professions and professionals.

There was only one university in the Grand Duchy, the University of Helsinki. It had its origin in Turku Academy, founded in 1640 and transferred to Helsinki in 1828. The main task of the university was to produce educated personnel for public office—state officials, clergymen, teachers, lawyers and physicians. There did not exist any private educational institutions for the education of professionals.

Thus, if the professional field was so undeveloped, why should one understand this period as so important for the future professional developments, as I have argued? First, the fact that the field of professions with their educational institutions was organised and controlled from a single locus, the central bureaucracy, resulted in an apparent *homogeneity of professional definitions,* a feature which was to characterise the Finnish professional field for a long time. While during the same period (and also in the second half of the century) particularly in the United States, but also in Great Britain, there were plenty of different occupational groups competing with each other for privileged professional status, in Finland there emerged quite clear-cut professional definitions as early as the first half of the nineteenth century. A specialised university education was required of physicians, clergymen and teachers, as well as for practice in state office and in court.[1]

Secondly, modern, uniform *degree requirements* can be traced back to these circumstances. The importance of academic degrees to professions can largely be explained by the need of the bureaucracy for rationally qualified personnel. When the Finnish central administration was established in 1809, there were few qualified personnel for its use, and the central administration soon fell into crisis. As an attempt at a more rational administration, specialised degrees for state officials were developed, first in 1814 and more systematically in 1817 (Klinge 1989). It was ordered that a university degree was a necessary condition for practice in specialised posts in the state administration. These degrees, which included the study of both general cultural subjects and specialised *juridical* subjects, greatly contributed to the increased importance of the modern university degree for practice in professional posts: they formed a general model. The decision to make juridical subjects the main degree requirements crucially influenced the future of the legal profession. The occupation of lawyer-official in the service of the central bureaucracy was to form the most important branch of this profession far into the future.

Even more importantly, the whole occupational field, its hierarchies and composition, as well as the positions of a number of individual professions in the field underwent a relatively stable development during this period. To proceed with the analysis, we need to know that the early nineteenth-century Finnish society was an agrarian one, in which the main social institutions were close to each other, as were professions, the bureaucracy and formal education. In this undifferentiated totality, the old status groups—the leading estates—continued to have the primary position.

THE BUREAUCRACY, SOCIAL CLASSES AND PROFESSIONS

If the central bureaucracy exercised a lot of power in society, then it is not irrelevant to ask who was steering the ship. Indeed, as for early professionalisation in Finland, the class orientations of those in power were a highly significant factor: a lot of power in internal matters remained in the hands of top bureaucrats. Here we approach the legal profession as well.

[1] It is true that there were rigid hierarchies in the posts of eg teachers and clergy professions (Suolahti 1919; Hanho 1955), but these hierarchies were stable and determined by the general social hierarchy of the society. The top positions of professions were in the hands of the leading status groups, the nobility and the clergy, and there was little competition between occupational subgroups.

A key phenomenon here is that—following the earlier Swedish practice—top positions of the established bureaucracy were given by the emperor Alexander I to the members of the nobility after the Finnish War in 1809. The proportion of noblemen among of the Senators soon grew to 65–70 per cent (See Mikkeli 1954, 42, Table 1). By this seemingly odd decision concerning the recently defeated enemy (as well as by some other decisions), the emperor kept the leading status groups loyal to the mother country and determined to repel separation efforts.

For historical reasons, the Finnish nobility was a narrow and also a relatively weak stratum. Since very early times there had been an exceptionally broad stratum of independent peasants in Sweden and particularly in Finland, with the result that the land-owning base of the nobility was weak (for a comparative perspective, see Anderson 1980; Blum 1978). It was so weak indeed that state office became a more important source of income and status than land-owning. During 1721–1803, only three percent of noblemen were without public office in Finland (Wirilander 1974, 192). But in Sweden, practically only one post was reserved for Finnish noblemen: that of army officer. In 1800, 93 per cent of the Finnish noble office-holders served in the army (*ibid*, 185). It was thus unfortunate from the viewpoint of this office-holding nobility that, after the Finnish War in 1809, Finnish troops were disbanded by the Russian emperor. The Finnish nobility fell into deep crisis. On this basis we can understand how important it was for members of the First Estate to have the central bureaucracy under its control. Risto Alapuro (1988, 25) has stated that the central bureaucracy now became a stronghold for the nobility. In these high posts of the bureaucracy noblemen could defend the position of their estate.

In addition to the nobility, there was another old status group that was important from the viewpoint of early professionalisation: the Clergy, or the Second (or Learned) estate, as it was also called. Clergymen formed the broadest professional stratum in the Finnish side of the country from the seventeenth century onwards (on the grounds for that, see Konttinen 1991a, 83–89). This stratum consisted not only of clergymen, but also of school and university teachers. Before the period of the Grand Duchy, the Finnish nobility had been involved in the profession of army officer and estranged itself from university education, and the whole range of education, from school to university, had been left to the Church. Consequently, both leading groups identified with specific professions. The nobility, in particular, had avoided professions other than the military. This division of labour directed the habituses of these leading status groups in divergent directions—a factor which deepened their conflict. But after the 1809 change, under the control of Russia, this conflict could not take a violent form, but one of peaceful competition.

What is important from the viewpoint of professionalisation is that the main societal locus, or 'the form of social existence', of both status groups were *professions*. Thus, in Finland the hierarchical relationships of professions followed the hierarchical relationships of the social classes. This fact had important consequences for the development of the professional field.

The competition between the leading status groups over material and social rewards directly concerned the professions. After the nobility had won the leading posts in the bureaucracy, the professional field was divided into privileged and 'oppressed' sections. The professions of the nobility—no longer so much the profession of army officer as that of lawyer-official—were the winners, and the clerical profession was the loser. The numbers of clergymen no longer increased and those social fields, above all school education, that had been previously under the absolute control of the Church, were now placed under the control of the Senate. The position of school teachers was the worst of all. Because of the old habitus of the nobility, the development of public schools was not in the interest of the bureaucracy.

Having adopted modern principles—education and academic degrees—as a precondition for entrance to higher social positions in the bureaucracy and society, noblemen and other gentry-officials were also learning to use these modern principles as social exclusion criteria. This dual function of modern university education (which had already been stressed by Max Weber, 1985, 576–579) was effectively put into use during this period. Interestingly, earlier in the eighteenth century the university had been remarkably open to the lower classes, such as sons of peasants, artisans and burghers. But access by the common people to the university was now experienced as a threat by noblemen and bureaucrats, since the university was a route to higher positions in the bureaucracy—now so important for noblemen, too. However, it was no longer possible to formally restrict access by the common people to the university. From a broader perspective, the leading position of the nobility was no longer absolute. Thus, the principle means of guaranteeing positions in the bureaucracy for the nobility and other gentry was by way of *educational policy*, making it as difficult as possible for the common people to enter the university. This exclusion policy was clearly put forward by some leading bureaucrats, and it was systematically enforced particularly from the 1820s until the beginning of the 1850s (see Konttinen 1996b). Largely as a result of this policy, the proportion of the common people among university students fell dramatically, and they made up only a small minority of students until the last decades of the century.

This structural class tension produced a *gentry university* and a broad gap between gentry occupations and non-gentry occupations like artisans. An important structural feature resulting from this tendency was—

together with the dominance of the bureaucracy—that non-gentry occupational groups had no chance in this society to even compete for the status of a proper profession. The field of educated professions really was a separate field excluded from the competition of lower occupations. This line of development differed sharply from that of the United States and Great Britain, where there was an 'open market' for competition for professional privileges and status. The case of the German states shows that the central factor here is not only the bureaucracy itself. In the German states of that period lower occupations as well as the middle strata had fairly good chances of social ascent through the university system. Here, too, the explanation can be found in the class system. The social ascent was made possible by the so-called *Bildungsbürgertum* at the head of the bureaucracy. This educated middle class had gained its position of power particularly following the Napoleonic wars and broadened the public sector and higher education. Doors were opened for the lower middle classes as well (Titze 1983). In the Grand Duchy of Finland the doors were closed on the common people by the bureaucrats.

LAWYER-OFFICIALS: AT THE PEAK

Owing to the social exclusion policies of the bureaucracy, the field of educated professions remained narrow in the first half of the nineteenth century. This class of gentry was divided into privileged and 'proletarian' poles. Deriving from the position of the bureaucracy in society, the nobility controlling it, and from the close link between the nobility and the profession of lawyer-officials, it is to be expected that lawyer-officials were amongst the privileged.

A critic of the central administration in the early 1900s gives us a description of the early Finnish bureaucratic stratum (Nevanlinna 1907). This bureaucrat, a gentry person with a law degree, was working for the state bureaucracy. He had a large income, commensurate with his social position in the bureaucracy. With all the symbols of the gentry—a university education, abundant leisure time (four to five working hours or less per day), his work under his own control, a gentry life style and great prestige—he was at the very peak of society.

It was quite logical that legal education should become a very typical education for members of the Senate (Konttinen 1991b, 511; Tyynilä 1992, 369). During 1809–1909 a great majority of the members of the Senate and Senators were lawyers by profession. Data by Stenvall (1996, 57) show that those with a legal education had a strong, dominant position particularly in the executive committees in the Senate from the time its establishment until the end of the Grand Duchy (1917). For instance, in 1850 13 out of the 17 top officials in these committees were lawyers, and in 1900, as many as 33 out of 36. This dominant position of lawyers at the top of the bureaucracy, in turn, strengthened the status of all lawyers. Lawyer officials, as the core group of the gentry and the bureaucracy, could have much power and high status also for the reason that the challenger (above all the bourgeoisie) of the new society were still weak.

To give an example, it was originally these connections and structures, created in the early period of the Grand Duchy, which formed the basis for the fact that, after Finland gained her independence in 1917, so many of the presidents of the republic have been lawyers by education. A legal education was for a long time one of the most important qualifications for higher posts in political life. In fact, as for the presidents of the republic, this situation has changed only in the last two or three decades, during which legal education has lost its monopoly.

One special feature of the Finnish lawyer-official in the nineteenth century is worth mentioning here. His work in the bureaucracy was characterised by strong formality and formal procedures—in fact, especially in the early period, it expressed strict formality rather than effective formal rationality in the Weberian sense. This observance of formalities can be partly explained by his weak qualification in the early period: it was an attempt to make up for the lack of real qualifications. It was naturally also a result of the history of the bureaucratic stratum and its poor educational standards. In addition, juridical studies at the universities laid stress on legal paragraphs and the like. Furthermore, the emphasis on formal procedures gave a bureaucrat an advantageous opportunity to move from one post to another. Similar procedures, ie secretarial tasks, were adapted for use in the non-specialised parts of the bureaucracy (Nevanlinna 1907; Stenvall 1995, 83).

The political position of the Grand Duchy, too, favoured strict formal legalism and the legal profession. The culture of political life during the first decades of the Grand Duchy was characterised by powerful legalism. Legal issues became a central legitimation basis particularly in matters which were important in terms of the political position of the Grand Duchy. This was not only, or even basically, a result of the position of lawyers in the bureaucracy, but rather of the fragile political situation of the Grand Duchy as part of Russia. Emphasis on law was a means for top bureaucrats to secure the autonomy of the country. Attempts by Russia to reduce the internal autonomy of Finland were repelled by appealing to strict legal procedures. But this was possible only as long as this emphasis on lawfulness was successfully communicated to Finnish citizens as well. A young bureaucrat expressed this attitude in his letter in 1845:

> Is it not enough that our fragile independence is dependent on the regent's more or less humane attitude [. . .] In such a country as ours, forms are more important than elsewhere. As long as it is considered essential to respect the form, the con-

tent is respected as well—if the form is interfered with, the content will very soon be altered as well.

The Vice-Chancellor of the university stressed during a dispute that 'everywhere, in every situation, the juridical view becomes dominant' (citations from Selleck 1961, 47). As a by-product of this emphasis, the position of the legal representatives of this legalism was strengthened. In certain competitive situations with rival groups, the bureaucrats themselves learned to make use of legalism to ensure their own position as a status group (for an example of this, see Nurmio 1947; Konttinen 1991a, 136–141).

As a result of the bureaucratic structure and the interests of those exercising power in it, as late as the 1870s the clerical and the legal professions were many times broader in terms of number of members than any other educated occupation (See Konttinen 1991b, 517). In the first half of the nineteenth century, there were only a few dozen of formally educated physicians and a few architects in the country (for teachers, as well as for physicians, the situation had already changed by the 1870s). In terms off the numbers of members, the clearest change compared with the situation in the eighteenth century was that lawyer-officials had 'replaced' army officers. The change was an expression of the changed importance of these professions for the old status groups and for the bureaucracy. The clerical profession had remained the core profession of the Learned Estate, and lawyer-officials had become the most important profession of the nobility and other office-gentry.

Early nineteenth-century Finnish society was still a society of old estates in its very essence. The members of professions defined themselves as members of the estates and the gentry rather than as members of the professions or the specialism in concern. This holds particularly for the core professions of the leading status groups. For instance, lawyer-officials identified themselves above all as gentry groups of officials and nobility (those who were members of this estate). Distinct identities based on occupational characteristics could to some extent develop mainly within those professions which were outside the core of the leading estates—including, for example, secondary school teachers and physicians. Receiving little support from the leading classes, these professions were more dependent on other sources of status.

Interestingly, it was this context in which the core section of the Finnish nobility began to adopt characteristics of modern society. The adoption of university education—clearly a feature of modern society—was a relatively painless change in orientation for them, following their crisis and the weak landowning position underlying it. By comparison, in Russia the landowning basis of the nobility was much stronger, and therefore they were more traditionally oriented. Indeed, the Russian nobility opposed the idea of making university degrees a precondition for state office (see Wortman 1976, 40–42). In Finland, by contrast, noblemen and other bureaucratic strata soon learned to make use of higher education and degrees as social exclusion criteria for entrance to privileged social positions (see Konttinen 1996b). As a consequence of adopting these features of modern society, the posts in the central bureaucracy offered a great number of noblemen and other members of old status groups a convenient opportunity to adapt themselves to an emerging modern liberal-bourgeois society.

TOWARDS A LIBERAL-BOURGEOIS SOCIETY AND THE EMERGENCE OF PROFESSIONAL ASSOCIATIONS

In the second half of the nineteenth century Finnish society was still an agrarian one in its very essence. In 1890, only seven per cent of the population was located in the industrial sector. However, new elements of liberal-bourgeois society were strengthening in many areas of social life. Again, the impetus for change came from outside.

The year 1855 was the turning point. Russia was defeated by Western powers in the Crimean war, and she was forced to change both politically and socially. Alexander II started deep social reforms in Russia. This wave of liberalism immediately reached the Grand Duchy of Finland, and various spheres of social life were liberated. Liberal persons were appointed as members of the Senate, and the nationalists, called Fennocists, now had an opportunity to act freely (it may be worth mentioning that they did not demand the separation of the country from Russia). Soon economic life was liberated and school education was developed to meet the needs of broader social strata. The Diet of Four Estates was again summoned together in 1863. However, the old political decision-making structure of the Diet remained unchanged until the year 1905, when Finland got a modern type of parliament with free, secret and equal elections.

The simple model of bureaucracy-centred societal development changed into a much more complex one. Various political groups could now compete with each other for the direction of the social development of the Grand Duchy. Opportunities grew for the strengthening of a new type of civil society (a recent study: Liikanen 1995). There had been elementary forms of independent civil society since the end of the eighteenth century (Stenius 1987)—and also during the strict bureaucratic order—but now liberalism allowed associational life to have a strong breakthrough. However, free founding of voluntary associations did not become possible until the beginning of the 1890s.

It was during the second half of the nineteenth century that one of the most important structures of modern professions became reality in

Finland. Modern *professional associations* came to birth. They were no longer merely practical extensions of the bureaucracy. They were now independent, in many cases active, and in some cases remarkably influential and successful in promoting their aims.

A few elementary forms of professional organisations had already emerged during the period of the strict bureaucracy. Now, after the liberal turn, this process could strengthen. *The Finnish Society for Physicians,* originally founded in 1835, gradually became a more effective professional organisation. The association arranged nationwide meetings in which common issues were discussed. The institution of annual meetings was also the next stage in the formation of another professional association, that of secondary school teachers. *The Pedagogical Association in Finland* was founded by permission of the Senate in 1864. *The Juridical Association in Finland* had its beginning in 1862 and engineers' and architects' common *Technological Association in Finland* in 1872 (officially in 1884). A number of new professional associations were founded in the 1880s and the 1890s.

The original motive behind the founding of these associations was not successful competition in the market of services with other occupational groups in the sense emphasized in the neo-Weberian approach to the study of professions, as was the case eg in the United States. The central social structures of the Grand Duchy in the early nineteenth century prevented such a competitive situation between occupational groups from emerging in the Finnish occupational markets. This situation prevailed until about the end of the 1880s. The bureaucratic order had made the relationships between professional occupations comparatively clear-cut, and the culture of competition was still weak in this field of social activity. Associations expressed the will of their elites *to develop the specialism*—in many cases scientifically. They also provided the opportunity for members to participate in discussions about policies concerning the specialism.

The associations of that time above all contributed to the strengthening of the identity of the members of occupational groups around their specialism and the core group of the profession. For secondary school teachers, this period saw a clear separation from the Clergy and the building of identity around the science of education and educational specialism at the university (Paunu 1954; Rinne & Jauhiainen 1988, 165–177). The professorship in educational science was founded at the University of Helsinki in 1852, and there were close connections between the professor and school teachers in developing educational subjects for the teaching profession.

Associations and annual general meetings were important not only to professional identity. They also influenced the various aspects of state policy concerning the specialism. This was the central task of the teaching profession from the second half of the 1850s onwards. In the changed circumstances opportunities for professional and economic reforms opened up. It has been stressed that teachers (together with educational scientists) themselves were important agents of the reforms within the teaching profession (Hanho 1955, 136; Rinne & Jauhiainen 1988, 169). Their originally miserable economic position was improved on several occasions in the second half of the century. Education as a profession was also improved by means of teacher training and by stricter specialisation in the science of education. As a result of these developments, teachers in state secondary schools became esteemed professionals and 'full members' of the gentry (the position of teachers in private schools was weaker).

The case of architects (Salokannel 1993) and educated physicians (Vuolio 1991) also prove that professional associations could be fairly successful in their attempts to improve the social position and status of their members. As for architects, it was above all the rise of the industrial bourgeoisie at the end of the nineteenth century that offered them challenging new tasks. The years around the turn of the century were a period of real triumph for private architectural firms. Indeed, in this country with a strong state, the position of private architects became so strong that in 1910 they proposed the abolition of the Department of Public Buildings in the central bureaucracy.

During the last decades of the century, there were a number of basic tendencies in Finnish society that influenced the dynamics of professional groups. As part of the modernisation process, the functions of the state became more specific and, as an expression of this, administrative functions departed from professional ones. An undifferentiated situation shifted towards more specialised institutions. For physicians, the professional functions of *Collegium Medicum* weakened, and in the reform of 1878 professors of medicine lost their earlier position in the state administration. This administrative differentiation, for its part, not only allowed but even forced professions to develop their associations as organisations for planning and using strategies in relation to the state.

THE FINNISH JURIDICAL ASSOCIATION

In the case of lawyers as well, a new association, *The Finnish Juridical Association* (1862) and its periodical strengthened their awareness around legal issues, which were defined as being of central interest in the original rules of the association (Konttinen 1991b, 514). Here we can see well the emphasis on legalism, referred to above. This emphasis can also be seen as a tendency of the strengthening of the specialism in the profession. However, the functions of this association were clearly broader.

In its early stage it functioned as a forum in which a broader societal elite could discuss important legal issues and wider societal questions.

The importance of the bureaucratic field as a career domain for lawyers increased until the end of the nineteenth century. The court system had employed 45 per cent of all lawyers in 1879, but by 1898 the proportion had dropped to 33 per cent, while the proportion of those working in administration had grown from 36 to 42 per cent, respectively. By contrast, business life continued to be of little importance. In 1898 only six per cent of lawyers made a living in business, mostly as bank managers. (Konttinen 1991b, 515.)

The Juridical Association in its beginnings reflected the core status position of the occupation of lawyer-official. Officials in the Senate formed the core group of the association. Interestingly, lawyers employed by the court system seem to have been a much less important group in its central department in Helsinki. Membership was not limited to those with a degree in law, but the members also included eg army officers, still a high status occupation closely linked with the nobility. A few teachers were also included. More than one third of the members of the central department of the association in Helsinki were noblemen.

At that time, lawyer-officials did not need an organisation to promote their economic and social position. They could secure social and economic rewards through their positions in the central bureaucracy. In the general departments of the central administration they had no challengers for a long time. In contrast, in specialist sectors of the administration particular professions, such as architects and physicians had a more prominent position.

Although identification with the specialism grew in importance in the second half of the nineteenth century, the members of educated professions preserved their gentry identity. Both features lived side by side in the professions. University education continued to have class determinants and offered the members of educated professions cultural capital and high status. The members of the gentry professions also represented the gentry characteristics in their lifestyle. They were dressed in upper-class style, associated with other members of the gentry, and often kept several household servants. This cultural characteristics were maintained well into the twentieth century among the old professions such as physicians, lawyers or secondary school teachers.

PREPARING FOR COMPETITION

Partly as an expression of the sharpening competition in the services market and partly as a result of the shaping of the identities of the members of occupations around science-based specialism, professional associations developed in the direction of stricter occupational *monopolies* maintained by educational criteria. Associations accepted as their members only those who had the required university degree. As already mentioned, during its early days *the Finnish Juridical Association* also granted membership to individuals belonging to the non-juridical elite. The change in orientation occurred at the end of the century, and at the end of the first decade of the twentieth century there were only a handful of non-jurist members in the association. *The Association of Finnish-Minded Lawyers*, originally founded in 1898, restricted, in its original rules, membership of the association to those with a law degree. During this period, the association of architects refused membership to applicants who did not have the required education. The result of these differentiation processes was that the specialised scientific body of knowledge grew in importance as a basic identity factor of the members of professions. More clearly than before, specialist education began to be used in the competition for professional privileges among occupational groups.

The professional markets grew and became more specialised as a result of economic, scientific and societal development during the last decades of the nineteenth century. More markets for qualified technical and commercial manpower opened up, and education for such occupations as agronomists and nurses was developed by the state. As shown by our overview of architects, the private bases for professions widened as well.

These processes brought to the occupational field more and more groups that were comparable with each other. As a result, and of great importance to professional and occupational dynamics, a competitive situation developed and strengthened between them. This structural process began to intensify in the 1890s, and since then the struggle among occupational groups over the delimitation of various tasks has been a basic structural characteristic of the Finnish occupational and professional field. There have been continuous disputes about the division of labour between, for example, technicians and engineers, architects and engineers, and the position of lawyers and other educated groups within state administration. The grounding of professional associations' monopolies in education can be understood as a preparation for increasing competition. At the same time this process manifested itself in the detachment of educated occupational groups from the traditional society and their adaptation to the modern era.

As regards professional group dynamics, another factor, not following from the occupational principle, was also of importance. As a result of the strengthening of the nationalist Fennocist movement (which had originated in the 1840s), the struggle over the position of the Finnish language divided the educated upper class in two: those who defended the position of Swedish (which had been the language of the upper class and had officially been used in higher school education and in official state affairs) and the supporters of Finnish. This struggle, which was a characteristic feature of social life during the last decades of the century and at the beginning of the twentieth century as well, divided all educated occupations in two, and both sides had an association of their own. In the medical profession, an association of the supporters of the Finnish language, *Duodecim*, had a considerable influence on occupational competition. The leaders of *Duodecim* used skilful double tactics in relation to municipalities and the state (Vuolio 1991). Negotiating with each side in turn, they succeeded in having an autonomous and protected position, on which the almost mythical image of the municipal practitioner among the Finnish people was to be partly based. Underlying this success, however, was their Fennocist ideology and the resulting support among leaders in the state and rural communes.

The founding of *The Association of Finnish-Minded Lawyers* in 1898 was also an expression of this language dispute. And since the Finnish-minded were gaining victory in this struggle, together with the fact that lawyer-officials were still at the top of the hierarchy, it is understandable that the leaders of this association were securing high positions in the future Finnish society. Indeed, three leading figures (KJ Ståhlberg, PE Svinhufvud and JK Paasikivi) of the young association were later elected presidents of the Republic of Finland.

PUBLIC ADMINISTRATION AND THE LEGAL PROFESSION

I have focused my analysis of the legal profession solely on lawyer-officials, and bypassed jurists in the service of the system of courts and other spheres of social life. In the Finnish case, indeed, this profession triumphed and reached its high status precisely within this sector. It was also the central administration that grew in importance in the recruitment of those with a law degree during the nineteenth century. On the basis of their primary source of income, only five percent of lawyers were attorneys. (Konttinen 1991b, 515). Economic life was still underdeveloped and did not yet need a lot of specialised legal services.

However, a few decades earlier the system of courts had been the most important employer of jurists. The growing importance of administration was connected with the broadening and ongoing specialisation of civil administration. Heikki Ylikangas (1991, 32) has estimated that the number of higher officials in the central administration was roughly ten times greater in the last year of the Grand Duchy (1917) than in 1809.

Lawyers in higher office in the departments of the Senate had no challengers in nineteenth-century Finland. It seemed to be self-evident that lawyers were recruited for the posts in the non-specialised departments of the Senate. This practice seems to have been continuously strengthened during the nineteenth century (Stenvall 1995, 57). In these posts general administrative qualifications—knowledge and mastery of administrative procedures—were emphasised, rather than knowledge of the contents of special legal domains (ibid.). Accordingly, moving into a post in some other department was easy for these office-holders. There developed a set of complex rules for recruitment as a form of promotion. Naturally, this was a favourable state of affairs from the viewpoint of these office-holders themselves.

While these general procedural qualifications were emphasised in the ministries, there developed another division of central administration that emphasised specialised areas of knowledge: central administrative boards, like the National Board of Health, the National Board for Building, and so on. To the task of serving these organisations professional specialists of a given specialism were appointed, some of them professors at the university. Thus, the position of lawyers in these organisations remained relatively weak. For instance, in 1890, among the 63 higher officials in these boards there were only 14 lawyers (Stenvall 1995, 62).

During the first years of the twentieth century, severe criticism was directed against the position of power of lawyers in the officialdom of the ministries. In particular, the emphasis on formal procedural knowledge and the neglect of specialist areas of knowledge were criticised (see Stenvall 1995,72; Nevanlinna 1907).

It can be seen (Konttinen 1991a) that the breakdown, in 1905, of the old political decision-making structure of the society of estates and the establishment of the modern parliamentary system weakened the position of lawyers in the highest political organisations. However, in the higher posts of ministries their position remained relatively unchanged until the country became independent. After that, during the decades between the world wars, a steady decline took place. In particular, humanistic, technical, agricultural and commercial education increased in importance. However, in spite of these changes, the long line of jurist dominance in the recruitment for higher office in ministries and administrative boards of the state apparatus is manifest even today (Stenvall 1995, 212–213; Ståhlberg 1983).

'FINLAND'S ROUTE' AND THE SUCCESS OF LAWYER-OFFICIALS

Finnish professionalisation has throughout its history been closely connected with the strong state. This fact has greatly influenced the form and content of professionalisation and particularly the development of the legal profession. However, on the basis of our analysis it is clear that, to be able to understand the concrete forms and processes of professionalisation, the state cannot be studied in isolation but in the context of other social structures and processes.

One lesson from the viewpoint of professionalisation is that the role of the state has not remained the same during its long existence. In the context of larger societal structures, its varying societal character has provided different frameworks for professionalisation. The first period of the central bureaucracy, 1809–1854, was characterised by its 'absolute' position in societal policy-making. The bureaucracy had other fields of social life under its strict control. However, the central bureaucracy must not be understood as a neutral locus of power but, on the contrary, as biased towards the interests and habitus of those in power. Generally speaking, only those professions and institutions which accorded with their interests and habitus could develop during this period. However, in all this defensiveness of the old status group, one crucial modern element of modernisation had a strong push: the modern curriculum in the education of the professions. In the centralised system every true profession ultimately had the same kind of educational structure. On the other hand, under the strict control of the bureaucracy, another central feature of modern professions, nationwide professional associations, could not emerge during this period. Furthermore, we cannot yet speak about any major free market elements in the professionalisation process.

As a professionalisation period, the second half of the nineteenth century clearly differed from the first one. This was caused by the profound change in societal dynamics. The central bureaucracy lost its earlier position as the only locus of societal development. However, it was not the broadening of free markets for services that formed the new basic element in the professionalisation process, but the emergence of a new type of civil society with new nationalist ideals. Nationwide professional associations could emerge as part of this liberalisation process. In some cases they proved to be quite effective in their policies aimed at strengthening their professional status and economic and social position. In these new circumstances, the centrality of the state to professionalisation could be seen, among others, in the fact that it was the professional groups whose interests coincided with those of the new power holders (the Liberals and the Fennocists) in the state that were able to promote their position. The state still controlled and strictly organised the educational institutions of professions. From this period onwards, thanks to the contribution of the Fennocist movement, more professional and semi-professional services were brought to rural areas.

For the first time in a broader sense, free market demand for professions emerged at the end of the nineteenth century. This made it possible for successful professional projects to be launched independently of the state, as the case of private architects shows. A general structural tendency in the professionalisation process, very typical of the modern occupational field, was strengthening at the end of the century: competition over occupational boundaries with neighbouring occupational groups. On the one hand this was made possible by the free founding of voluntary associations, on the other hand by the ongoing specialisation—the continuous emergence of distinct occupational groups.

On a general level, Finnish professionalisation in the second half of the nineteenth century manifested an increasing independence from the structures of the old society of estates. The professions and occupations, as groups with their specific identities based on the scientific specialism, generally became a field of their own, relatively separate from the state and the leading social classes. The members of the professions identified themselves increasingly with the specialism in question. However, they preserved for long the cultural capital they had gained as members of the gentry. The old gentry character of educated professions remained, in a symbolic sense, visible far into the twentieth century. In this process of losing old class determinants, of preserving old status symbols, and of constructing new identities around scientific specialism and the occupational group, the members of the educated professions became members of the upper middle class.

The course of lawyer-officials from the old society to the emerging liberal-bourgeoisie may have been the easiest among all occupations. They had the support of the two central structures of society: the state and the leading social classes. This support structure was formed as early as the early nineteenth century in the construction of the central bureaucracy. And it could also be maintained in the second half of the century, since legal issues and the legal profession were also in the interest of the new power holders, the Liberals and the Fennocists. The prominent position of lawyers in the state administration was self-evident. This occupation had no real challengers in this agrarian country, where economic groups were still weak. And once the higher administrative posts had been occupied, it was easy to defend these privileged posts. Under these circumstances, the occupation of lawyer-officials offered a number of the members of the leading status group of the old society—the nobility—a smooth transition to modern liberal-bourgeois society.

REFERENCES

Alapuro, Risto *State and Revolution in Finland* (University of California Press, Berkeley, 1988).

Anderson, Perry *Lineages of the Absolutist State* (Verso, London, 1980).

Blum, Jerome *The End of the Old Order in Rural Europe* (Princeton University Press, Princeton, 1978).

Collins, Randall 'Changing Conceptions in the Sociology of Professions'. In R Torstendahl and M Burrage (eds), *The Formation of Professions* (Sage, London, 1990) 11–23.

Elovainio, Päivi 'Tieteiden eriytyminen Suomen korkeakouluissa'. *Sosiologia* (1972) 9 (6), 242–260.

Freidson, Eliot *Professionalism reborn. Theory, Prophecy and Policy* (Polity Press, Cambridge, 1994).

Hanho, JT *Suomen oppikoululaitoksen historia II* (WSOY, Porvoo, 1955).

Kiuasmaa, Kyösti *Oppikoulu 1880–1980. Oppikoulu ja sen opettajat koulujärjestyksestä peruskouluun* (Pohjoinen, Oulu, 1982).

Klinge, Matti 'Yliopisto ja virkamieskorkeakoulu', in M Klinge, R Knapas, A Leikola and J Strömberg, *Keisarillinen Aleksanterin-yliopisto 1808–1917* (Otava, Helsinki, 1989) 333–417.

Konttinen, Esa *Perinteisesti moderniin. Professioiden yhteiskunnallinen synty Suomessa* (Vastapaino, Tampere, 1991(a)).

—— 'Professionalization as Status Adaptation. The Nobility, the Bureaucracy, and the Modernization of the Legal Profession in Finland'. *Law & Social Inquiry* (1991(b) 16 (3), 201–230.

—— 'A Continental Way to Professionalization: On the Formation of the "Finnish Route" ', in Hannu Simola and Thomas S Popkewitz (eds), *Professionalization and Education,* (1996(a)), 52–76. Department of Teacher Education, University of Helsinki, Research Report 169.

—— 'Central Bureaucracy and the Restriction of Education in Early Nineteenth-Century Finland'. *Scandinavian Journal of History* 1996(b) 21 (3), 201–220.

Liikanen, Ilkka *Fennomania ja kansa. Joukkojärjestäytymisen läpimurto ja Suomalaisen puolueen synty*. Historiallisia tutkimuksia 191 (Suomen historiallinen seura, Helsinki, 1995).

McClelland, Charles E 'Escape from freedom? Reflections on German professionalization, 1870–1933', in Torstendahl & Burrage (eds), *The Formation of Professions* (Sage, London, 1990) 97–113.

Mikkeli, Anna-Liisa *Aatelin osuus Suomen suuriruhtinaskunnan virkamiehistöstä 19. vuosisadalla*. (Pro gradu thesis in the Finnish history. University of Helsinki, 1954).

Nevanlinna, Ernst *Virkamiesolomme. Millaiset ne ovat ja millaiset niiden pitäisi olla* (Suomalainen Kustannus Oy Kansa, Helsinki, 1907).

Nurmio, Yrjö *Taistelu suomen kielen asemasta 1800-luvun puolivälissä: vuoden 1850 kielisäännöksen syntyhistorian, voimassaolon ja kumoamisen selvittelyä* (WSOY, Porvoo, 1947).

Paunu, Eira 'Oppikoulunopettajiston muodostuminen itsenäiseksi virkakunnaksi.' *Suomen Kirkkohistoriallisen Seuran vuosikirja* [1954] 41–42, 83–20, June 1996–97. Helsinki.

Peltonen, Matti 'A Bourgeoisie Bureaucracy? The New Mentality of Finnish Aristocracy at the Beginning of the Period of Autonomy' in Matti Peltonen (ed), *State, Culture & Bourgeoisie. Aspects of the Peculiarity of the Finnish*, (Publications of the Research Unit for Contemporary Culture 13. University of Jyväskylä, 1989) 33–53.

Rinne, Risto and Jauhiainen, Jari *Koulutus, professionalisoituminen ja valtio. Julkisen sektorin koulutettujen reproduktioammattikuntien muotoutuminen*

Suomessa. Turun yliopiston kasvatustieteiden tiedekunta. Julkaisusarja A (1988) 128.

Salokannel, Mervi 'Arkkitehdin ammatin professionalisaatio', in E Konttinen (ed), *Ammattikunnat, yhteiskunta ja valtio. Suomalaisten professioiden kehityskuvia* 1993, 45–77. Jyväskylän yliopiston sosiologian laitoksen julkaisuja 55.

Screen, JEO *The Entry of Finnish Officers into Russian Military Service 1809–1917* (PhD Thesis, University of London, 1976).

Selleck, Roberta *The Language Issue in Finnish Political Discussion: 1809–1863* (PhD Thesis, Radcliffe College. Cambridge, Mass, 1961).

Stenius, Henrik *Frivilligt, jämligt, samfällt. Föreningväsendets utveckling i Finland fram till 1900-talets början med speciell hänsyn till massorganisationprincipens genombrott*. Skrifter utgivna av Svenska Litteratursällskapet i Finland. Ekenäs, 1987.

Stenvall, Jari *Herrasmiestaidoista asiantuntijatietoon*. The Committee for Administrative History in Finland. Helsinki: Painatuskeskus, 1995.

Ståhlberg, Krister 'De staligt anställda i Finland'. In L Lundquist and K Ståhlberg (eds), *Byråkrater i Norden*, 80–127. Publications of the research institute of the Åbo Akademi Foundation. Åbo, 1983.

Suolahti, Gunnar *Suomen papisto 1600– ja 1700-luvuilla* (WSOY, Porvoo, 1919).

Titze, Hartmut 'Enrollment Expansion and Academic Overcrowding in Germany', in KH Jarausch (ed), *The Transformation of Higher Learning 1860–1930* (The University of Chicago Press, Chicago, 1983) 57–88.

Tyynilä, Markku *Senaatti. Tutkimus hallituskonselji-senaatista 1809–1918*. Hallintohistoriallisia tutkimuksia 5. Helsinki, 1992.

Weber, Max *Wirtschaft und Gesellschaft* (JCB Mohr, Tübingen, 1985).

Wirilander, Kaarlo *Herrasväkeä. Suomen säätyläistö 1721–1870*. Historiallisia tutkimuksia 93 (Suomen historiallinen seura, Helsinki, 1974).

Wortman, Richard S *The Development of Russian Legal Consciousness* (The University of Chicago Press, Chicago, 1976).

Vuolio, Vesa *Lunastettu vapaus. Kunnanlääkärin ammatillisen autonomian muotoutuminen*. Jyväskylän yliopiston sosiologian laitoksen julkaisuja 49, 1991.

Ylikangas, Heikki Keskushallinnan virkamiesten rekrytointi Suomessa ajanjaksolla 1909–1984. Report from the Committee for Administrative History in Finland. Helsinki, 1991.

5

Juridicalisation, Professionalisation and the Occupational Culture of the Advocate in the Nineteenth and the early Twentieth centuries: A Comparison of Germany, Italy and Switzerland[1]

HANNES SIEGRIST (TRANS G MUTTER)

In the eighteenth and nineteenth centuries, the modern state occupied the chief role in juridicalisation. In the process of codification, the state enacted binding laws for its territory, settled procedures, homogenised and systematised norms and doctrines, and enforced its statutes with the help of its hierarchically structured administrative and judicial organ. Along with this went the process of professionalisation, involving the transformation of both the juristic professions and their functional roles. The knowledge and opinions of the jurists were being homogenised as a result of newly created and reformed occupational training and examinations. The state regulated admission to the profession and had control over the legal practice. The jurists gained a central role within society as a functional and value-forming elite in the process of creating, developing and applying the constitutional law and as well as of enforcing the concept of legality. Non-juristic influences were being forced back in the course of the juridicalisation and professionalisation. The demands for social control on the part of old levels of authority and of new social groups were being restricted or brought into the realm of legality.

A comparison of the international and intercultural components of juridicalisation and professionalisation reveals that the juristic functions, roles, and professional behaviours were carried out according to each system and legal culture. Similarly varied was the relationship between jurists of the state, lawyers with private practices and legal laymen.

[1] If not otherwise indicated, all references apply to Hannes Siegrist, *Advokat, Bürger und Staat. Sozialgeschichte der Rechtsanwälte in Deutschland, Italien und der Schweiz (18–20 Jahrhundert)* (Vittorio Klostermann, Frankfurt/Main, 1996).

Generally it can be said that, by means of juridicalisation and professionalisation, the bureaucratic authoritarian states curtailed the influence of lawyers on legal affairs and pushed legal laymen into a marginal role. Liberal and democratic states, on the other hand, permitted their lawyers and legal laymen more freedom, allowing them to gain some influence in the process of juridicalisation. Differences in the extent to which the constitutions of each nation were developed must be interpreted against this background.

In general, one can discern different types of juridicalisation according to what role the lawyers occupied in this process. In the bureaucratic authoritarian states and police-states of the early nineteenth century, the professors and the jurists holding official offices claimed the leading role in the process of juridicalisation and professionalisation, while the lawyers were being disciplined by the state. In liberal societies, the leading role was shared by the official jurists representing the state and by the lawyers representing the so called state-free social sphere. In democratic societies, the lawyers, together with the so-called legal laymen, set the standards. Depending on the type of professionalisation that was taking place, the advocates developed a specific interest in juridicalisation which affected the quality and quantity of supply and demand in the market of juristic services.

Juridicalisation and professionalisation affected the processes of social control, socio-cultural integration and political pilotage. In an attempt to guarantee that arising conflicts would be solved in legal forms and that the social circumstances would be stabilised, the state saw to it that functions and responsibilities as well as structures and mechanisms were being lawfully regulated. In this sense, law gained its importance as an agent that contributed to the re-formation of society. Moreover, symbols and rituals played a role, ensuring that the society, which had initially been established on a legal-rational basis, was also now able to develop into a legal community. Relatively complex societies suffered from a high degree of social, cultural and political inequality and instability. Therefore, it was necessary to have symbols with which one could identify, together with legal, occupational and social rituals, to support the process of building a community. At the same time, the process of juridicalisation and professionalisation also had in a certain sense a destabilising effect: it brought about change in the existing circumstances and awakened new desires. Juridicalisation and professionalisation contributed therefore to a changing view of how society and law were perceived and interpreted. They also led to the establishment of individual and collective strategies supporting the transformation. The form of the professionalisation and juridicalisation determined the lawyers' performance and their way of legitimising themselves. Being professionals who dealt with central social values like honour, property, freedom and order, the lawyers relied on being trusted by the people. The foundation on which this trust was based was also determined by the form of juridicalisation and professionalisation.

These points summarise the main problems which occupied the legislators, jurists and legal laymen during the political-social changes and the institutional and legal reforms of the nineteenth century.

By focusing on four selected aspects, these problems shall be further illustrated in the following chapters. The first chapter deals with how the profession of the lawyer was transformed during the nineteenth century by comparing the situations of advocates in Germany, Italy and Switzerland respectively. The second chapter, after having first looked at the ratio of lawyers to the general population in specific regions, discusses the relationship between supply and demand in the market for legal services, as well as the question of accessibility to law and legal advice. The third chapter examines the emergence of a variety of social types within the legal profession which developed as a result of the occupational tradition, the legal and political regulations and the professional and social practices of the lawyers. Chapter four outlines some aspects of the symbolic staging of law and the legal profession: the myth of the law practice; the significance of professional and honorary titles; the role of rhetoric during the ritual of a procedure; the law office as stage for the lawyers to portray themselves; and the use of monuments and public celebrations to represent the lawyers. This work is based on the belief that in regards to juridicalisation and professionalisation substantial timely divergences as well as regional and national differences existed. This holds true, despite the considerable similarities in the development of law and the administration of justice that prevailed in the states and nations on European territory. [2]

1. TYPES OF PROFESSIONALISATION

Lawyers offer legal service and service that relates to the law. They professionally mediate according to their field-oriented knowledge, their specific attitudes and the trust that is placed in them by society when dealing with conflicts concerning central social goods and values. This definition of the occupational and functional role of the lawyer is, in a sense, independent of time and valid for all the societies that are here being investigated. Nevertheless, variations developed as a result of the specific historical and social processes in the individual states and legal territories.

[2] See for example Helmut Coing (ed) *Handbuch der Quellen und Literatur der neueren europäischen Privatrechtsgeschichte*, 3 vols (each of them consisting in turn of a number of volumes) (Beck, Munich, 1976) ff.

At the turn of the nineteenth century, as part of the profound political, institutional, legal, social and economic changes that took place at this time, the legal profession, which was at this point already a richly varied occupation, was being fundamentally transformed. States, legislators, bureaucrats, lawyers and interested legal laymen were in competition with each other in an attempt to control the construction of the occupation. The legal profession was, on the one hand, an institution regulated by procedural law, and on the other, a profession. This transformation of the legal profession may be termed 'professionalisation'. Its result is reflected in the various types of the 'profession' that existed at the time. Both the movement toward and the result of the professionalisation were dependent on legal and professional models, social interests and needs, common political and economic ideas about rules and order, as well as on the distribution of power within each individual state. Of these factors, the images and narratives about the profession and about society affected just as strongly the professionalisation process as did the involved interests .

In the early nineteenth century, three models of the profession served as guidelines for the transformation and re-construction of the legal profession. These models were closely related to common social-political and legal concepts. First, some viewed the legal profession (the term is used here to include those professionals also labelled 'Advokat', 'Rechsanwalt', 'avvocato', 'procuratore' and so on) as an adjunct of the constitutionally rationalised and standardised administration of law. It was for them not more than a secondary authority, implementing the politics which guaranteed the public weal and the authority of the state. The second group oriented itself on the model of a field-oriented 'independent profession' that was examined and guided by a special ethic. It could independently offer its services on the market. Historical models for this version of the profession existed in the *ancien régime*, when society was still organised by estates of the realm. However, the model had to be adjusted to the needs and constraints of the state and civil society of Europe after the French Revolution. The third group demanded the complete de-regularisation of the profession. In this model, each citizen should be able to take on the function of representing the law and of giving legal advice and maintaining a private practice. Just as other professions were de-regularised as a result of the abolishing the *Zünften und Gilden* (guilds) and the introduction of liberality and economic freedom, in which process they had lost their class privileges, so, they argued, should the legal profession be de-regularised.

The first two models of the profession were setting the standard in large parts of Europe between 1750 and 1850, in the first wave of the transformation and re-definition of the lawyers' and jurists' occupation. The initiative for juridicalising and professionalising the legal profession came from the state and the political climate of the time. The question of professionalising the legal profession presented a secondary aspect in the general 'institutional and legal revolution.' Models of the liberal independent profession of the advocate were only hesitantly and often reluctantly accepted by the legislators. Even states which were de-regularising numerous other professions and occupations and were attributing to them the status of a 'private business' disapproved of a liberally organised market and an independent professional business for the legal profession. Exceptions to this reluctance were evident in France after the Revolution as well as in Switzerland, where the legal profession was de-regularised between 1790 and 1870.

The professional situation finally gained a stable footing in the next step of its development around the year 1840. Three fundamentally different legal-institutional types of the legal profession emerged: the professional holding an official office (*'Amtsprofession'*), the independent profession *('freier wissenschaftlicher Beruf')*, and the advocate maintaining a private law practice (*'freies Advokatengewerbe')*. The first type involved the bearing of a public office and required the degree of an officially examined profession. This category of the profession was the result of 'professionalisation orchestrated by the ruling class'. The state made the legal profession similar to that of judges and of juridically educated high officials in terms of education and examination procedures. The state also comprehensively regulated the social status and the professional role of the lawyer. The legal profession was essentially defined as advocacy at court and was declared a full profession within the system of the constitutional administration of justice. The state structured the market and the professional opportunities by appointing judicial districts, by determining the *Numerus clausus* (the ratio of lawyers to population), and by implementing regulations for fees. The state guaranteed its appointed lawyers a monopoly of function and a living standard that was in accordance with their status, but made it difficult for them to perform other juristic as well as economic, administrative, cultural and political activities. It also granted lawyers a monopoly of representation before the court *(Anwaltsmonopol)*, which guaranteed their formal superiority over legal laymen and clients. Because the state restrictively administered the market for legal services, it also controlled not only the lawyers, but also access by its subjects and citizens to legal advice and to justice. The state held lawyers back in their efforts to develop an independent professional and educated identity and an occupational autonomy by forbidding them until the 1840s to publicly discuss legislation as well denying their right to belong to and establish societies and bar associations. Lawyers had little influence on the socialisation of junior lawyers and on the development of law as a science. Their influence was limited because the practical and theoretical training of future lawyers took place at state institutions, with the result they received the education of a civil servant. Further, the lawyers could not act as professors at universities nor set examinations. Their role was instead to support the state by implementing (and not interpreting) its judicial and general public interest politics. The state clearly dominated the four-sided relationship that existed between state, law, clients and lawyers.

The second widely adopted model involved the shifting of the legal profession into an independent profession. In the course of a 'moderate professionalisation orchestrated from above', the training, examination, and conferment of degrees was being lawfully regulated and delegated to institutions of higher learning and to examination committees. In a few German states, in some Swiss cantons, and in Italian and other Western European states, lawyers actively participated in the qualification of future lawyers. They acted as university professors or were masters to an apprentice of the legal profession. Further, by being political figures in legislative assemblies, by being legal publicists and commentators, lawyers were able to play a part in contributing to the doctrine and theoretical field of law. After completion of the prescribed training and examination, graduates of law were in principle free to assume the profession of the advocate. They could expand their professional field of activity by taking part in the administration of justice as well as duties related to education, the economy, publication and the church. Advocates were forced to act independently in a relatively free market and cultivated, as a result, a more open attitude towards the acquisition of income and towards the needs of their clients. Advocates emerged for this reason as universal experts in the field of mediation and as counsellors for citizens who needed help with their various circumstances. This fact worked in a specific way to intensify the juridicalisation of the relationship between client and advocate.

The third model was that of the private law practice, which had little or no regulations or procedures in place in regards to training, occupational practices, acquisition of income and status of the lawyer. This model asserted itself in some areas which had not formerly belonged to the Roman-legal territory and in areas in which the legal profession could not fall back on a strong tradition. Private law practices were established in other regions as a result of a politic that focused on de-regularisation and de-professionalisation, in accordance with its market-liberal, liberal-democratic and equality-promoting concepts. In this political climate, it was assumed that each active citizen who was of age and entitled to act should be able to choose his occupation freely and should be able to practice his profession within the realm of the common laws. In this system, the life of the advocate was largely determined by opportunities and restraints. Their position was relatively strong because of an increasing demand for legal advice and other mediating services. The advocate, however, had to be flexible to the needs of the market and to the needs of the public sector. While balancing the demands of the law, the constitutional administration of justice and the legal interests of the individual, the lawyer had to find and define his own role. The trust which was bestowed on him was mainly based on his individual social, economic, cultural and political assets and on his knowledge rather than on the prestige of an official professional title or on the collectively agreed upon 'honour and dignity of the advocate's status'. Like their colleagues in the system of the 'independent law profession', these advocates adopted civilian strategies to build their careers and tended to accumulate status and position in the areas of law, regency, culture and economics. The basic position from which individuals would be recruited for other, more advanced work within the profession, and which also was influential on other legal occupations, was that of lawyer. The legal profession did not signify a caste. Lawyers understood themselves as legally qualified experts in the mediation of legal, economic, political, social and cultural problems.

Within the framework of a liberal bourgeois society, the establishment of a professional identity was often carried out without the existence of legal regulations to show the way; that is to say, it was accomplished within a process that I have called 'informal professionalisation' or—if this development was predominately brought about and influenced by civilian groups—'civilian professionalisation'. For example, market forces together with controlling and sanctioning social mechanisms in Switzerland made it possible for the educational level of advocates in cantons (in which the legal education was not, or was only vaguely, regulated) to be not substantially lower than in states where strict educational and professional regulations existed.

Around the 1840s and 1850s, the ideal type of the occupation and professional conduct, as described above, existed only in a few states in its pure form. In most states, two or more forms of the profession of the lawyer stood side by side. For example, the legal profession consisted of two divisions: the official office of the lawyer for the courts *('Prokurator', 'Avoué', 'Anwalt', 'Patrocinatore')* and the independent educated profession of the 'advocate'. Some states allowed the combination of the two roles within one person. The small number of appointed lawyers of the court predominately took on the formal and ritual responsibilities of a trial. Advocates, on the other hand, took on the legal valuation of the case and acted, as well, as independent legal experts in the market for juristic services. The significance of this functional and professional differentiation was a recurring controversial topic among the contemporaries. For example, when the Prussian government attempted, in the newly annexed Rhineprovince, to combine the profession of the advocate with that of the lawyer for the courts *('Anwalt')*, in an attempt to introduce the integrated Prussian model of the official office *(die Amtsprofession)*, some advocates and courts of justice opposed the move. They argued that it was difficult to combine the training that was rigidly focused on the forms of procedure with a similarly rigorous training on the subject matter of an action.[3] In the year 1819, the *Geheime Staatsrat* (privy counsellor) Daniels, who was a former advocate in Cologne, made a strong recommendation to the Prussian government to maintain the profession of the independent advocate. His reasoning was that this profession most suitably met the interests of the public as well as the requirements of running a business. He argued that the legal profession would allow a 'young man' who was equipped with the necessary theoretical and practical knowledge to test his 'virtues and talents'. It would enable him to concentrate, independent of his work as procurator, on the scientific part of jurisprudence and on court practice. This would permit the young advocate, who could not yet hope to be considered for an official office, to advertise his talents publicly and to make himself known in a favourable light. Daniels argued further that access to a larger pool of available advocates would be beneficial to civilian clients, who could thus more freely choose an agent.[4]

The two-part division of the legal profession, as discussed above, was in the tradition of Roman and Canon law as well as of Napoleonic occupational legislation that had been introduced into Western and Southern Europe. Yet, the retention of the two-part division reveals a fundamental conflict in the processes of juridicalisation and professionalisation: the state was unable to impose its strategies against the habits and demands of social and juristic elite groups. The division incorporated a compromise between the authoritarian state, committed to its politics of professionalisation and justice, and the social elite, demanding law and the dispensation of justice. This construction of the profession may also be categorised as 'moderate professionalisation orchestrated from above.' It was typical of societies in which parts of the aristocracy favouring decentralisation, civilian elites, clients and lawyers could demand a say in the construction of law and the legal profession.

The question of how the above types and combinations of the profession spread themselves across European territory about 1840 shall be discussed next.

The model of the official office *(die Amtsprofession)* was valid without restriction in the biggest German states like Prussia, Bavaria, Austria and

[3] Nordrhein-Westfälisches Hauptstaatsarchiv Düsseldorf, Abteilung 2, Rheinisches Behördenarchiv, Schloß Kalkum, OLG Cologne 11/1265, Institut der Advocat-Anwälte in der Rheinprovinz, Cologne 29.9.1832.

[4] Nordrhein-Westfälisches Hauptstaatsarchiv Düsseldorf, Abteilung 2, Rheinisches Behördenarchiv, Schloß Kalkum, OLG Cologne 11/1015, Gutachten Daniels und Boelling an Großkanzler Beyme, 1819.

some smaller German principalities as well as in the former Kingdom of Lombardy-Venetia, of the House of Habsburg. Areas in which only the model of the independent legal professions could be found (like Bremen) were rare in Germany. The number of such territories was greater in Italy (Papal State, Modena) and in Switzerland (some larger cantons). Around 1840, the profession of the lawyer solely in the form of an independent business could only be found in some very heterogeneous and decentralised Swiss cantons, or in smaller cantons. At times, however, it appeared as if the model of the independent law business would assert itself generally in Switzerland. In the 1840s and 1850s Lucerne and Geneva joined this group temporarily, as did the democratically-ruled Zurich in the 1870s. Not until 1898–99 did Zurich, after a referendum, again declare the legal profession a regulated 'scientific profession'.

Numerous and various legal professions existed simultaneously in most European states. In wide parts of Italy, in several medium-sized and smaller German states as well as in the Prussian Rhineprovince, which was a later addition to the Prussian state, the legal profession was divided in two types: the official office *('die Amtsprofession')* of the lawyer of the court and the independent profession *('freier Beruf')* of the advocate. This system no longer existed in Switzerland; here, by contrast, the coexistence of the educated independent profession and the independent business was quite common. In addition, the older combination of the official office and the private law business still existed.

In many Swiss cantons, advocacy as a private business was officially recognised and socially legitimate. In Germany and Italy, on the other hand, legislation made it impossible for advocacy as a private business to exist officially. Nevertheless, this category existed effectively in these countries also since the code of procedure allowed so-called law consultants (*Rechtskonsulenten*), commissioners of procedure (*Prozeßbeauftragten*), or individuals exercising a mandate (*Mandatierten*) to appear before the lower courts. Literate artisans who were knowledgeable in law, teachers, and low-paid civil servants who, acting as advocates, operated a private law business were to be found in all territories, although only in small numbers. Still, the lawyers occasionally fought against them energetically and called them dishonest, uneducated and money-hungry *'Winkeladvokaten'* (pettifogging lawyers). The lawyers saw in them a threat to law and order, to legality, and to the citizen who was seeking legal protection. Lawyers strengthened their own professional image in that they slandered that of the *Winkeladvokaten*.

It is noteworthy that in Europe in the first half of the nineteenth century there were many routes to professionalisation, resulting in a variety of professions and occupations. The regional distribution of the different types of the profession reveals the dominant occurrence of certain types in each of the (future) national states, of which each country produced at least two distinctly developed models. For a while it appeared as if the model of the official office (*Amtsprofession*) would assert itself still more in Germany and in Italy. This changed, however, in the 1860s where, as in all of Europe, the legal profession was changed in accordance with the liberal spirit of the time; that is, the profession underwent a transformation which may be characterised as 'liberal professionalisation'. In the 1860s and 1870s, during the general political liberalisation and construction of national laws for the legal profession, the official office, '*die Amtsprofession*', was transformed into an 'independent profession'. More and more Swiss Cantons in the late nineteenth and the early twentieth centuries adopted the practice of transforming the 'independent law business' into an 'independent scientific profession'. Another practice was to further standardise the already-existing 'independent profession'. Sometimes this simply meant that tendencies that were already informally established were legally sanctioned. The 'independent legal profession' resulting from the liberal regulation of the occupation was also introduced in the Austrian-Hungarian countries and in Russia in 1868 and 1874 respectively. Along with the scientifically educated, examined and certified advocates, who enjoyed some privileges yet did not hold a monopoly for practising law, numerous independent advocates continued to practice their business. In this sense, the circumstances were similar to those in parts of Switzerland and to those in the United States of America, where the legal profession had become independent as a result of the de-regularisation efforts of the 1830s. This independent status of the legal profession prevailed in Switzerland as well as in the United States for some time, before it was again standardised under pressure from educational institutions and of independent occupational associations in these countries.

2. MARKET POLITICS FOR LEGAL SERVICES AND ACCESSIBILITY TO LAW

In the nineteenth century, governments, advocates and clients regarded the ratio of lawyers to citizens, that is, the number of lawyers in relation to the number of citizens, as an indicator of how intense juridicalisation was as well as an indicator of the particular type of juridicalisation that was being carried out. It was also regarded as an indicator of the availability of legal advice. This ratio is a point of reference, indicating a number of things: principles for piloting, strategies for controlling, the supply and demand of legal services in the marketplace, distribution of power and traditions. Generally speaking, the ratio of lawyers to citizens was lower in states that employed the system of the *Amtsprofession* (the official office) or, in other words, the '*Konzessionssystem*' (franchise system) than in those states that allowed private law practices characterised by independent legal professionals, where supply and demand were regulated by the market.

In the franchise system *(Konzessionssystem)*, the state determined the number of lawyers in such a way that, without encouraging a quarrelsome disposition in people, the most necessary and valid needs of its citizens and subjects could be met. The courts evaluated the demand for lawyers and analysed the numbers in terms of utilising the courts and the activities of the lawyers. Following this process of accounting, the courts calculated the necessary number of lawyers needed to serve a given number of people, which was then approved by the ministry of justice. The ratio of lawyers was low around 1840 in Prussia (excepting the Rhineprovince) and Bavaria: 1:10,100 and 1:12,200 respectively. The average ratio in Prussia was approximately 1:20,000 in the Upper Scilesian judicial district *(Oberlandesgerichtsbezirken)* and 1:6,000 in the Western provinces, which were more urbanised and economically more developed. The ratio was even lower in the Habsburg Monarchy, where the decline from East to West was still more pronounced: 1:20,000. The highest ration in the Habsburg Monarchy, 1:5,000, was found in highly populated, urbanised and (relatively) economically developed Lombardy.[5] Karl Czoernig, a high-ranking Vienna official who was very familiar with the circumstances in Lombardy, called the advocates of Lombardy 'hair splitters' and 'trouble makers'. He argued that the individualistic, egotistical and materialistic society of the North-Italian kingdom were lacking in trust for their king, their government and for the organic makeup of their society, and that the civilians, for this reason, would seek the advice of advocates for any petty issue that arose.

The low number of lawyers in the Eastern- and Middle-European territories points to a professionalisation engineered by the ruling class and to a selective and restrictive juridicalisation strategy in these states. The reason for the low ratio of lawyers to citizens was determined not only by the lower demand for legal advice in areas that were less urbanised or socially, educationally and economically backwards, but also by the fact that the state artificially limited the availability of lawyers. Another reason was that the state discriminated against large portions of its citizens legally and administratively, namely the rural population and the socially lower status groups as well as the non-German population. The state was limited, however, in enforcing its strategies of juridicalisation towards the traditional elite since some Austrian and Prussian regions adhered to the system of patrimonial jurisdiction *(Patrimonialgerichtsbarkeit)*.

[5] Numbers for the Habsburg Monarchy around the year 1860: Alexander Brix, *Organisation der Advokatur* (Braumüller, Wien, 1868), S. VII; für die Lombardei um 1840: Siegrist, Advokat, see n 1 above, p 90.

The ratio of lawyers to citizens was visibly higher in Central and Western Germany, as well as in Italy, Switzerland and most Western-European countries. Around 1840, the average for all German states was approximately 1:6,000. The ratio in Württemberg (which had no *numerus clausus*) as well as in Baden and in the Duchy of Hesse (which had a *numerus clausus*) was between 1:6,000 and 1:10,000. The Prussian Rhineprovince and the Monarchy of Hannover, where the legal profession was accessible but the number of lawyers and procurators (*Prokuratoren*) was limited, were included in the group of regions that had a ratio of 1:2,000 and 1:6,000 respectively. The ratio in most Italian states and Swiss cantons was also around these proportions. The German states Hamburg and Mecklenburg, in which an independent legal profession existed, had a ratio between 1:1,000 and 1:2,000. In the Monarchy of Saxony, where the *numerus clausus* was regulated very loosely and where, at this time, many lawyers still occupied an office as judge, the ratio was also between 1:1,000 and 1:2,000. In regions where both types of the legal profession were customary, such as Naples/the Monarchy of Sicily and Tuscany and the Swiss cantons of Geneva, Lucerne, Tessin and Baselland, the ratio was 1:2,000.

After the liberalisation of the legal professions and the implementation of national legislation for lawyers (introduced in Italy in 1874, in Germany in 1878, in Austria in 1868), which had the abolition of the *numerus clausus* at its centre, the ratio of lawyers to population commonly decreased. The ratio decreased in Germany from 1:11,000 in 1880 to 1:8,000 in 1900 to 1:5,000 in 1920 to 1:3,000 in the early 1930s. In Italy, the country usually wrongly accused of being an exception, the ratio stagnated between 1880 and 1920 at the level of 1:2,000. The ratio in Switzerland was always between 1:2,000 and 1:3,000. However, regional differences remained, if only in a limited area, since the regions which formerly had fewer lawyers improved their ratio. The number of lawyers in areas with a traditionally high ratio remained steady despite a relatively low growth rate.

In Germany where, until the 1920s, the ratio of lawyers to citizens had been relatively low, while the transformation of the legal profession had been especially distinct, critical voices appeared soon after the liberalisation. It was feared that the position of lawyers and the quality of the administration of justice might suffer as a result of the changes. Some divisions of the legal profession insisted that the *numerus clauses* should be re-instated, but were unable to assert their claim even within their own professional group. In the so-called *Überfüllungsdebatte*, a debate about the flooding of the market with lawyers, supporters and opponents of the *numerus clausus* likewise revived arguments, and models of the former franchise system *(Konzessionssystem)* of the state were put forward. The supporters of the *numerus clausus* did not interpret the rising number of lawyers and the decreased ratio of lawyers to citizens as a chance for juridicalisation, even though new occupational territory was opening up. Rather, they viewed this development as a danger to their professional and civil status and as a threat to the legal culture as it was affected by the intensified business competition. In Italy, and especially in Switzerland, the *Überfüllungsdebatte*—the debate about the flooding of the market with lawyers—was less heated. This shows that the lawyers in these countries, because of their older tradition of professional independence and (sometimes) independent business activity, acted more aggressively and more freely in the market than the German lawyers did. The Swiss and Italian lawyers were prepared to adjust to the coming legal requirements.

In all countries, most lawyers, because of increasing demands for legal services by the socially insignificant and by the working classes, were reluctant to become more closely involved in the (potential) mega market until the early decades of the twentieth century. These groups were seeking legal advice about labour disputes, accident insurance, withdrawal notices, rental issues and family rights, fields of law that were not yet fully integrated into the system. Because of their particular training, many lawyers lacked familiarity with such areas. Traditionally, lawyers had focused on the more lucrative area of private law, serving property owners.

It can be argued that the professional and social advancement of the lawyer of the nineteenth century was directly linked to the establishment of modern civil law, which was primarily focused on the needs of prosperous property owners. In the late nineteenth and early twentieth centuries, even liberal jurists repeatedly acknowledged the validity of this fact. The expansion of the rights of defence lawyers also affected criminal law, which therefore increasingly became a mass business during the nineteenth century. Still, the field of criminal defence, except for a small minority of specialists, remained in economic and professional terms a less interesting professional activity.

Some lawyers were directly responsible for propagating the belief among the population that they, the population, were excluded from the law and that the lawyers only reluctantly represented them. This belief arose because lawyers were, in some areas of the law, less active and demonstrated a disinterested attitude towards the problems and legal needs of the lower classes and labourers. The assumption that the advocates preferred representing the wealthy and the middle class rather than the socially insignificant and lower class was widespread and resulted in an emotional and ideological rejection of legal profession. This rejection found its expression in the socialist demand for the abolition of the legal profession or for the transfer of its ownership to the state, and for the establishment of a commonly understandable law.

Unions, churches, women's associations, and private and communal charities all insisted that the lower classes be included in the process of juridicalisation. Since the 1890s, these organisations had been establishing legal aid offices for labourers and domestic servants, where they could receive legal advice—for example, answers to questions about labour contracts or liabilities—from knowledgeable legal laymen, or sometimes from employed lawyers. The influence on the process of the juridicalisation of a small minority of lawyers committed to a social-philantrophist, union-friendly and socialist conception should also not be underestimated. They helped to advance the process with their engagement in fields of legal advice, publication and politics.

3. SPECIALISTS AND UNIVERSALISTS

The process of juridicalisation and professionalisation in the nineteenth and early twentieth centuries was in many ways determined by the interests and needs of the middle class, from which lawyers, judges and senior civil servants were being recruited. Studies about the social antecedents and the marriage circles of lawyers in the different countries reveal that lawyers frequently came from overlapping social circles: the educated middle class; the trade, business and industry bourgeoisie; the high ranks of the civil service; and the independent professionals. Because of their proximity to the middle class, lawyers enriched the legal culture with their specific attitudes and expectations.

The social and professional advancement of lawyers in the nineteenth and early twentieth centuries was closely connected to the rise of the middle class, alongside the expansion of the constitutional state and the systematic juridicalisation of more and more social institutions. The professional-social role of lawyers was determined by the characteristics and dynamics of the expansion of the constitutional state as well as by the growth of middle-class society within each individual state. For example, in Prussia, before the appearance of the German liberal legislation for the legal profession of 1878, the judicial commissaries *(Justizkommisare)* were restricted to their role before the court and during a procedure.[6] Rudolf Gneist, a publishing pioneer for an independent legal profession, who was familiar with the situation in other countries, argued in 1867 that the Prussian judicial commissaries were insufficiently active in terms of the administration of property and mediating credit, and that they acted comparatively rarely as counsel of choice for families

[6] Some judicial commissaries performed also functions of the notariate, which was in Prussia compatible with the legal profession, unlike in most other European territories. This function of the notariate was predominatly awarded to deserving lawyers.

and companies. He argued that '*Winkeladvocaten*' (pettifogging lawyers) were drafting large numbers of petitions, designing contracts, and arranging commission dealings because of the inability of the commissaries to cover the needs of the public. He suggested that many trials might be avoided if lawyers were present when contracts were being drafted. Gneist argued that insufficient engagement on the part of judicial commissaries in this type of service was leading to lawyers' dependency on the state and to a break-down of trust in their relationship with their clients.[7]

My collective-biographical research about the life and the profession of lawyers in terms of their sideline economic activity[8] in German, Swiss and Italian cities has shown that German lawyers often acted less as supervisory or administrative board members, as corporation trustees, as administrators of property, or as other appointed executives than did their Italian and Swiss colleagues. This difference remained in Germany through the late nineteenth and early twentieth centuries, when a conspicuous minority of lawyers started to take professional advantage of the rising economic trend and of the expansion of businesses. Still, the figure of the lawyer dealing with business continued in Switzerland and in Italy to be more common and more widely legitimised than in large parts of Germany. This was due to the occupational tradition and to the more flexible professional ethic of Swiss and Italian lawyers as compared to the traditional role of the lawyer of the court in Germany, which tended to remain static since he saw himself as the 'acting organ of the administration of law'.

Lawyers in Switzerland and Italy more often took on additional functions in the administration of law,[9] for example as judges in a secondary office or as trustees in public organisations. The office of judge, because judges were elected, was still accessible to lawyers in Switzerland at a later point, while in Germany the posts of judges, even in the lower courts, had been transferred into life-long positions for established civil servants. The political changes and the specific rules for recruiting judges to the lower courts (*Prätur)* led, in Italy, to improved communication between judges and advocates.

Swiss and Italian advocates were generally more engaged in the functional fields of 'theory', 'culture', 'publication' and 'politics' than were

[7] Rudolf Gneist, *Freie Advokatur. Die erste Forderung aller Justizreform in Preußen* 2nd edn (Springer, Berlin, 1911 (1st edn Berlin, 1867), 64–74.

[8] If one considers the function of representation and support at court as well as general legal advice as fundamental functions of the legal profession, then all other activities are secondary. However, sometimes the secondary functions within the whole field of activity were more important than the fundamental function.

[9] This does not include the notary's office, since only northern Germany allowed the combination of legal practice with that of the notary.

German lawyers. The political-legal and professional circumstances were affected by the political activity of lawyers. Swiss advocates profited relatively early on from the expansion of political rights which were a result of liberalisation and democratisation, which some of them had been fighting for. Disciples of protest, reform and revolutionary movements, with a civil-liberal, democratic and nationalistic agenda, could also be found in Germany; however, lawyers here were generally less able to establish themselves successfully in politics. Up until the early twentieth century, the role of the political advocate in Germany was less common and less accepted than in Switzerland, Italy and numerous other Western European and now also Eastern European counties.

This comparison of general tendencies in the various nations obscures at times the significant regional differences that existed within national borders. In German states, in which the legal profession was already, by the early nineteenth century, completely or partially an independent profession and where the political circumstances were more liberal than in other states, patterns similar to those in Italy and Switzerland can be found. The tendency to combine public office and functions existed in all three countries. The professional and social practices of lawyers were therefore dependent on the regulations of the profession and on the constitution as well as on the social and political distributions of power: in states in which the system of official office dominated and in which constitutional society was less developed, the advocates tended to be highly specialised. The life and ambition of this type of professional and field-oriented advocate were primarily determined by his profession and by his service to the administration of justice of the state. In states in which the legal profession was an independent profession or even a private business and in which the political order was more liberal, the ideal of the 'universal jurist' *('Universaljurist')* and the 'complete citizen' *('der komplette Bürger')* arose. When in the early 1840s the southern German liberal Friedrich List admired the situation in 'constitutional states' like France, England and the United States of America, he was referring precisely to this notion of the advocate. In these countries the advocates were not viewed 'as instruments of the state' but rather 'counsel of families and as individuals'. In places where the individual and rights of the individual were highly valued, advocates equipped with erudition, diligence, and talent could reap not only the professional and private but also the public trust of citizens. Thus satisfied, so argued List, the citizen would then elect advocates into legislative assemblies, governments and the courts.[10]

The combination of different roles—such as advocate-professor, advocate-publisher, businessman-lawyer, pensioner-advocate and

[10] Friedrich List, 'Advocat', in Carl von Rotteck u. Carl Welcker (eds), *Staatslexikon oder Enzyklopädie der Staatswissenschaften*, vol 1, 2nd edn (Hammerich, Altona, 1846), 362–377.

advocate-politician—was more common in states in which occupations were relatively freely regulated. In such states, lawyers were allowed to practise a variety of activities and mediating functions. The dominant existing blueprint of the profession, together with economic, social and political reasons, made this sometimes a requirement rather than a choice. The accumulation of a number of these secondary roles within one person led to the appearance of a new social type: the 'universal jurist' or the 'complete citizen'. The (more or less) 'complete citizen' gained a special significance in relatively open societies: that is, in societies in which the elite was regionally and professionally segmented, in which bureaucracy was less pronounced, and which had a liberal or democratic constitution and political culture. This type of jurist is found relatively early in Switzerland and, since the late nineteenth century, also increasingly in liberal Italy and in certain German regions. The 'complete citizen' also established himself over time in areas of the Habsburg Monarchy, in the new states of the region of the former Ottoman Empire and finally in Tsarist Russia.[11] The advocates in these states took on numerous leadership positions in the nationalistic and liberal movements and, in time, represented a significant part of the elite of the state. They helped to shape the juridicalisation, the constitutional state and the political culture. They created a 'culture of the advocate' which spread to the whole of society. In other words, advocates—insofar as they played a central role—created in professional, juristic, social and political terms a functional and symbolic connection between values, attitudes, practices and mechanisms.

The rise of the culture of the advocate was fostered by the fact that lawyers played a significant political and field-oriented role in the important phases of expanding the legal and constitutional states as well as in the juridicalisation of social interactions. The modern legal culture expanded in all areas of life as a result of lawyers' practice of combining legal, political and economic functions and roles. Critics, however,

[11] Jörg Baberowski, *Autokratie und Justiz. Zum Verhältnis von Rechtsstaatlichkeit und Rückständigkeit im ausgehenden Zarenreich* (Klostermann, Frankfurt/Main, 1995); Charles E McClelland, Stephan Merl and Hannes Siegrist (eds), Professionen im modernen Osteuropa (Duncker and Humblot, Berlin, 1995); Franz Kübl, *Geschichte der österreichischen Advokatur* (Oesterr, Rechtanwaltskammertag, Wien, 1981); Wolfgang Höpken, 'Zwischen Bürokratie and Bürgertum: "Bürgerliche Berufe" in Südosteuropa', in Wolfgang Höpken and Holm Sundhaussen (eds), *Eliten in Südosteuropa* (Suedosteuropa Gesellschaft, Munich, 1998) 69–103; Maria M Kovacs, *Liberal Professions and Illiberal Politics. Hungary from the Habsburgs to the Holocaust* (Woodrow Wilson Centre Press, Washington, 1994); Chara Argyriadis, 'Da notaio ad avvocato. Metamorfosi del giurista e trasformazioni sociali nella Grecia del XIX secolo', in Aldo Mazzacane und Cristina Vano (Hg.), *Università e professioni giuridiche in Europa nell'età liberale* (Jovens, Naples, 1994) 371–388; Witold Wolodkiewicz, 'La professione di avvocato nei territori polacchi tra Otto e Novecento', in Mazzacane und Vano (eds), 335–347.

warned that this mixing of the different spheres would contaminate the law with non-legal conceptions and interests. Rival groups and democratic-egalitarian movements repeatedly accused advocates of seeking hegemony by attempting to act as mediators and to take over élite-functions, and of blurring distinctions and combining interests and thus constructing an 'advocate supremacy'. In states that had an 'advocate culture', lawyers were made entirely responsible for deficiencies in law and politics. In this sense, lawyers experienced a similar fate to that of the judicially educated civil servants who, living in states with a 'bureaucratic culture', were treated with hostility. These civil servants were seen as representative of 'bureaucratisation' and of the mediation monopoly that was bestowed by the state and were, for this reason, disliked. In societies where advocates handled the interests of society in a less bureaucratic and formalised way, providing personalised and informal client-focused mediation, lawyers became, in a wider sense, mediation experts. That this was not unique to small states nor specific to backward societies could be shown by comparing them with the USA and France.

4. MYTHS, SYMBOLS, AND RITUALS

The habit of identifying the law with the lawyer was, at certain times, also brought about by the 'myths about the lawyer'. These myths consisted basically of established historical images and narratives about the advocate, concerning his role when dealing with questions of law and freedom as well as guilt and redemption. Because of the ongoing transformation affecting law and the profession as well as new social needs, interests and experiences, these myths were repeatedly being questioned. Lawyers were consequently forced to bring their myths in line with the prevailing circumstances of their time. At first, lawyers liked to remind the public of the biblical and antique myths, from Moses to Cicero, in relation to lawyers and legislators. Then they referred to the role of the advocate as the supporter of the legal Occidental-Christian civilizations of the High Middle Ages and of early modern times. Finally, they emphasised the role of the advocate as pioneer of modern progress and the constitutional state, as creator and protector of civil society, as helper of citizens, as independent guarantor of freedom and as unconditional servant of law and the general public interest.

The advocate's effort to construct their myths was repeatedly disrupted by criticism of other societal elites and professional groups. Members of the aristocracy and clergy were afraid of losing their power and influence as a result of the modern juridicalisation. They accused lawyers of destroying the ancient law and the law of God and called them usurpers and revolutionaries, as well as *Rabulisten* (manipulators of law) and formalists. They further accused advocates of ignoring the traditional and Christian idea of justice, while they were performing their questionable practices. On the other hand, the supporters of 'professionalisation orchestrated from above' opposed the idea of an independent legal profession. They were seeking to fuse the myth of the servant of the law with the myth of the strong state that was committed to the general public interest. Depending on the time and on the individual country, specifically inflected myths about the advocate developed against this background. These myths determined the image that the lawyer had of himself and that others had of him which in turn affected his professional ethics and regulated his social status.

The rules and customary prescriptions outlining honourable, task-oriented and morally correct conduct during a trial and in interactions with colleagues, clients, judges and representatives of the state sought a professional performance that adhered to the office and the status of the advocate. These rules were determined by old professional practices, by norms for the law of procedure, and by the disciplinary verdicts of the ordinary courts, or by the rulings of disciplinary committees which started to appear in Italy and Germany around the middle of the nineteenth century.

The rules and regulations were hesitantly developed further by the jurisdiction of the disciplinary committees and in public discussions, but in principle they remained outside the realm of rational negotiations. The lawyers' attempt to fit their professional-social performance to new requirements and needs was, at times, made very difficult. As a result, sub-groups of the legal profession adhered only in appearance to the rules regarding their occupation. This trend gave rise to a double-sided moral which was partially accepted. Despite their contradictory nature, the rules of professional conduct together with the myths were effective in symbolically integrating the occupationally, socially, culturally and economically heterogeneous group of professionals at specific events. Further, the identification of the citizen with the law and the lawyer was frequently encouraged by these rules of conduct and by the myths.

During the transition to modern law, that is, during the emergence of the constitutional state and a society that was based on a rational contract, procedural law lost some of its magical character. The requirements of the new law of procedure supported rationalisation, yet allowed rituals and a certain sacral tendency to remain part of the court proceedings. By observing the procedural and professional rituals, judges and lawyers supported the idea that all participants involved in a conflict and in a procedure could identify with the law and experience themselves as part of a politically and culturally legitimate legal community.

Lawyers, independent of the construction of their profession and their social status, remained experts in private and social crises and borderline situations that could harm the individual or threaten common stability and order. Finding themselves in the difficult role of mediator, lawyers knew that the rationalised legal procedure and the systematised knowledge of law alone were not sufficient to guarantee social integrity and that an emotional identification with symbols could not be omitted. Mediating between socio-cultural groups and different interested parties and mentalities, lawyers had to consider that diverse social groups would respond to different symbols and that one group might experience a specific symbol unlike another group. This explains why lawyers paid particular attention to rituals and symbols in an attempt to soften the dividing effects of conflicts and tensions among diverse parties. The citizen's trust in lawyers and the degree of his acceptance of the juridicalisation were influenced by the way lawyers transposed the formal-rational law into practice when it involved conflicts between the state and society or between any two rival parties.

In states or in legal territories where proceedings were conducted in written form (especially in the early and mid-nineteenth century, but also later), lawyers had fewer chances to present themselves to their clients and to an audience. Written proceedings separated the participants of a trial from each other, both temporally and spatially, since the relevant parties were not present to witness the drawing up of the documents. This written mode of procedure did not truly uphold a legal community, as was demanded by civil law reformers and liberal-minded lawyers who advocated that a procedure should be public and actively involve the relevant parties. Public and oral proceedings, which were, depending on each individual state, sooner or later introduced, met the demands of the reform-minded citizens and lawyers much more closely. Judicial procedure gained a new rational and symbolic significance with the introduction of public and oral proceedings: the liturgy of the proceedings encouraged the construction of a legal community and legitimised the practice of law. This situation—even though it was not always stated in this manner—was one of the major topics among the jurists of the nineteenth century, when they discussed the reform of procedural law.

During the liturgy of a procedure, all participants embodied a symbolic role and represented a higher or transcendental idea. Juridicalisation was fostered by enabling the audience to identify with the symbols of law and with the performers of the rituals, as well as with the lawyer and his complex role as servant of the law and as representative of the individual. The lawyer's activity was assessed not only on the basis of his knowledge and the end result of the trial, but also on the basis of his conduct: how well he played his role and how well he could articulate reason and emotion.

After the introduction of oral and public procedure, the rhetoric of the advocate gained new significance during the nineteenth century. In other words, the staging of gestures and symbols, in combination with the use of legal jargon which was supposed to support the legal findings and encourage the formation of a temporary legal community between the representatives of the relevant parties and the public, was becoming paramount. Being a communicative device, the lawyer's oratory was built on his understanding of emotions, which could be used to awaken feelings in the addressed parties that could then be stirred in a certain direction.

Artful speech was more valued in France and in parts of Italy than it was in most German states. For example, Prussia's Frederic II rejected the use of oratory during a procedure with the following words: 'I don't want theatrical coups in justice!' Such dislike for oratory dissipated when Napoleon introduced oral proceedings into the courts of his conquered German territories. Some advocates and legal laymen began to appreciate the new form of procedure. For example, in 1814 the senate of Hamburg decided to adhere to the practice of oral proceedings at its commercial court. It ignored the complaints of a few advocates:

> We Germans do not like to plead. It is against our language and nature. Also, Germans are serious and more introverted, and it is equally a fault as it is a virtue of the German people that the gift of rhetoric is seldom among them. It would be better, therefore, if Hamburg would conduct its defence in the quiet of a study, allowing a more mature thinking process, and if it would trade its war of speech for a thorough knowledge in the form of clear writing. As everyone knows, this opinion reflects the general German sentiment on the topic.[12]

However, this reference to the character of the German people, in an attempt to explain their lack of desire to talk, did not convince the majority of Hamburg's advocates and merchants, nor did it justify the abolition of the use of oratory in the courts. The German Rhineland, where French law remained intact after Napoleon had left, preserved the use of oratory in the courts. Liberal lawyers from other parts of Germany flocked to the Rhineland in the 1840s to acquaint themselves with the promising proceedings at the *Schwurgericht* (the crown court) Oratory having been rejected in large parts of Germany for a long time, was after the 1830s successfully revived by the liberal reform movement and the jury court was increasingly introduced into civil and criminal law.

However, judging by the way in which rhetoric was viewed around 1900 in Germany, even by lawyers who at times were loath to give it up, the art of speech was regarded as a questionable tool and as a device that interfered with an educated approach during a procedure. In his memoirs, published in 1910, Fritz Friedmann, a Berlin lawyer, describes the work habits of a number of well-known Berlin criminal defence lawyers.

[12] Cited in W Treue und G Commichau, 'Zur Geschichte einer Hamburgischen Anwaltssozietät 1822–1972', (1972) 17 *Tradition. Zeitschrift für Firmengeschichte und Unternehmerbiographie* 49–82, at 51.

These lawyers had taken on large quantities of petty cases, and consequently their defence during those trials, because of the sheer volume, had been sloppy. One of those defence lawyers, Friedmann writes, had handled small cases such as these by the dozen, neglecting, as a result, to make legal arguments. Instead, he attempted to make his case by focusing on the person, that is, he tried to convince with tears and sniffles.[13] Acting like a preacher or a popular speaker, this lawyer lost the confidence of the judges. Still, the popularity of such lawyers was not always lost. The defence lawyer, Joseph Grommes (1826–1889) of Cologne, had been immensely popular among the common folk of the city on the Rhine. To be told that one was so bad that not even Grommes would be able to acquit one[14] (a frequent saying among the market women of Cologne) was considered to be a most terrible insult. The Bavarian advocate and writer Ludwig Thoma describes the habits of rural advocates at around the same time. Rhetoric was a popular artifice among these rural lawyers because it was expected by their clients and because it impressed the audience. According to Thoma, rhetoric helped to overcome the gap between the 'educated' and the 'folk' and, at the same time, offered a bit of entertainment in a monotonous rural life. Thoma also tells of a few advocates in Traunstein (where he had been a post-graduate judicial service trainee) who tried to out-do each other by using coarse language so that their Bavarian jokes gained a reputation.[15]

In Southern Italy, defence lawyers talented in rhetoric were not only admired by the public but also by members of the circle of advocates. One of these famous criminal defence lawyers was Nicola Amore (1830–1894) of Naples. His style of pleading at the bar was compared by some to a wild creek, forcefully pulling with it everything on its route over cliffs and abysses down into the valley. Others compared his style to the eruption of Vesuvius, carrying all obstacles along with its lava stream. Again, others associated him with the famous French speaker Mirabeau. Amore was regarded as an artist in his choice of defence strategy. His admirers praised his well-structured oral pleadings, enriched with technical, scientific and literary knowledge, in which he tended to build surprising twists that enabled him to dramatise his case. It was said that Amore had embodied hope for many, but horror for his opponents, whom he attacked valiantly, not unlike the manner in which General Garibaldi of the *Freischaren* had attacked his rivals.[16]

[13] Fritz Friedmann, *Was ich erlebte! Memoiren, Vol 1* (Pulvermacher, Berlin, 1910) 119f.

[14] *Ibid* Friedmann, 158f.

[15] Ludwig Thoma, *Erinnerungen* (Piper, Munich, 1980) 105.

[16] Saverio Cilibrizzi, *Nicola Amore. Principe del foro italiano e grande sindaco di Napoli* (Naples) 70–82.

The reputation of these southern-Italian advocates, who were called 'orators' ('*oratori*'), was based on the older tradition of the occupation, on a deep scepticism towards the state and the possibility of human rights, and on an ideal of justice that was philosophically founded or deeply rooted in the public culture. During the south-north migration, this pattern spread to the northern regions of Italy, where it had been originally just as uncommon and unwelcome as it had been in Prussia.

In Switzerland also, where advocates—because of the strong presence of legal laymen in the courts—occupied a distinct role in making a science out of law and in spreading the systematic legal concept, rhetoric was in some cantons an accepted device. The judges in these regions did not interfere much with rhetorical overplay in their court rooms. To maintain their reputation as educated jurists, advocates agreed among themselves to refrain at times from excessive use of rhetorical devices.

Professional and honorary titles identified lawyers as being trustworthy, which was a necessary requirement, enabling them to perform their work. Furthermore, their titles influenced the manner in which lawyers were perceived by their clients and the public. In the early nineteenth century, some states adopted the practice of granting lawyers distinguished social and professional honorary titles, with the result that the old academic titles like '*Doktor*' (used for the holder of a PhD) or '*Lizentiat*' (Licentiate) faded in comparison. In Prussia (with the exception of the Rhineprovince), the examined and appointed lawyers carried the titel of '*Justizkommisar*' (judicial commissary); in Bavaria the title '*Königlicher Advokat*' (advocate of the King) was used; and in most other states, titles like '*Hofgerichtsadvokat*' (advocate of the regency court), '*Advokat*' (advocate), '*Anwalt*' (lawyer) or '*Prokurator*' (attorney) were given. Deserving advocates in Prussia received the title '*Justizrat*' (judicial counsellor) or in a few cases even the title '*Geheimer Justizrat*', which were titles that had originally been reserved for civil servants. Other states bestowed deserving advocates with the title '*Rat*' (counsellor).

Since the middle of the nineteenth century, the professional title of '*Rechtsanwalt*' (lawyer) became more common in German states, and in 1879, with the introduction of a new statute regulating the legal profession, it became standard throughout Germany. From this time on, some German states abstained from granting older and industrious lawyers additional titles. Württemberg and the Hanseatic towns quite consciously never introduced the title *Justizrat*, being afraid that this classification could lead to the belief that titles were indications of good and bad lawyers.[17] Prussia, on the other hand, continued to grant older lawyers the title of *Justizrat*. Bavaria, following Prussia's example, introduced the title of *Justizrat* in 1886. The result of this was that lawyers in

[17] W Kiefe, 'Der bayerische "Justizrat" ' (1921) *Juristische Wochenschrift* 35–38.

these states, who did not receive a title and who were by-passed by younger colleagues, were suspected of having something wrong with them. In 1894, a diligent 64-year-old lawyer in Cologne complained to the president of the Higher Regional Court that he still had not been nominated to become *Justizrat* because he had been sentenced in 1886 to a disciplinary punishment by the disciplinary commissioners of the bar association. He claimed that, because of this, his emotional state was 'horrible' and that he was now a 'marked man'. Joy and peace had subsequently become strangers to him and to his family.[18] In some German states until the end of the Empire, the granting of the title of *Justizrat* was used as an instrument both to discipline and motivate lawyers. This title for lawyers also helped to strengthen the trust of the audience in the legal profession and in the administration of law. Professional titles like *Justizrat* that were only bestowed on certain members of the profession, however, were forbidden in the Weimarer Republic. Bavaria, on the other hand, adhered to the practice of granting titles until the Supreme Court of the German Reich decided against it in 1929.

Italy and Switzerland did not grant titles to promote members of the legal profession as was done in Germany with the title of *Justizrat*. Advocates refused to let the state interfere with their professional reputation and social status. To be an advocate already imparted social glamour on the person in both countries. Even ministers, high civil servants, and professors carried the title of advocate, a practice that would not have been imaginable in Germany. The title '*Avvocato*' was supplemented by Italian advocates with titles for political offices, like '*Onorevole*' (Member of Parliament), and with honorary titles granted by the state, like '*Cavaliere*' (knight), indicating the bearer of an honorary decoration of the fifth class granted by the state. Some Italian advocates also carried, in addition to their professional title, the honorary title of '*Commendatore*', identifying them as bearers of a decoration of the third class. Lawyers in Germany also belonged to the group that supported the state and were, therefore, honoured with decorations. A few of them received the Prussian honorary decoration *Roter Adler-Orden*, indicting a fourth-class decoration. This honour was similar to that of the Italian '*Cavaliere*', but there was no title used in addressing its bearer. Italian advocates had a strong presence in parliament, government and administration. For this reason they, unlike their German counterparts, had some influence in the granting of titles. No such constitutionally organised institution existed in democratic-liberal Switzerland.

The most important place for lawyers to have contact with their clients, where they could demonstrate themselves as professionals and as

[18] Nordrhein-Westfälisches Hauptstaatsarchiv Düsseldorf, Abteilung 2, Rheinisches Behördenarchiv, Schloß Kalkum, OLG Cologne 11/990, Bl. 105/64ff.

representatives of the law, was their office. It became customary for lawyers to receive their clients in their law office, sooner or later, all over Europe. This was not only for practical reasons. In addition, it was based on the continuously renewed professional rule that legal experts, independent legal professionals, or professionals holding an official office should not be required to pursue their clients, and that they should not offer their services publicly as if legal advice was a commodity like any other. Legal advicc, it was felt, should be given at a suitable, appropriate and neutral place instead.

The law office as distinguished 'abode of the law' was emphasised by its furnishings. The occupational performance of lawyers was culturally and professionally consecrated by the bookcases containing old and new collections of law books, documents of legal commentaries and reference books, together with the classics of legal literature as well as classical and national fiction. The first visitor to knock at the door of the young rural advocate Ludwig Thoma in Dachau in 1890 was a bookseller, one who specialised in supplying the libraries of notaries and lawyers. He convinced the novice of the legal profession that books were essential to an advocate so that he could make a good impression upon clients. He advised Thoma to buy the most important volumes and commentaries about law as well as a collection of old verdicts. The young advocate should in addition, according to the bookseller, acquire beautifully bound official journals and gazettes of ordinances. Despite being outdated, he argued, these would look good in the office and would cost Thoma little, if he paid by instalments.[19]

In his 1897 publication Handbook for the Lawyer, the Italian advocate Domenico Giurati recommended a library for the advocate that was even more comprehensive. According to Giurati, lawyers should not only be in possession of the *Corpus Juris*, but should also have statute books and collections of verdicts as well as encyclopaedias, such as the French encyclopaedia by Dalloz, the *Enciclopedia giuridica*, published in Milan and the *Digesto Italiano*. In addition, Giurati recommended literature about rhetoric and about the construction of pleadings at the bar as well as some of the classics of the history of law and legal philosophy, such as those by Savigny, Hugo and Sclopis. He finally suggested some classics of jurisprudence: Cicero, Montesquieu, Rossi, Beccaria, Brissot, Nicolini, Bentham, Bordeaux, Brougham, Hello, Casanova, Cormenin and a number of more recent specialised volumes by Italian authors.[20] It was a given

[19] Ludwig Thoma, *Vom Advokaten zum Literaten. Unbekannte Briefe*, ed and commentary by Richard Lemp (Piper, Munich, 1979) 58–72.

[20] For information about the authors see Michael Stolleis (ed), *Juristen. Ein biographisches Lexikon. Von der Antike bis zum 20. Jahrhundert* (CH Beck, Munich, 1995).

for Giurati that the works by Homer, Virgil, Horace, Dante, Machiavelli, Boccaccio and Alfieri should be found in the bookcases of any advocate, as well as the classics of world literature from Shakespeare to Victor Hugo, Cervantes and Goethe, and finally the works of the modern Italian authors, such as Foscolo, Monti, Leopardi and Manzoni.[21]

The furnishings of the law office differed somewhat according to the income, status, milieu, clientele, taste, needs, region and nation of its occupant. However, the set-up of the office had to a certain extent to be civil and functional. An illustration of this can be seen in the following description, taken from the schedule of estate assets of an averagely wealthy Bavarian advocate at the Regional Court:

> 1 sofa; 1 table with 9 different chairs; 1 desk on which are placed statute books and encyclopaedias as well as 1 small pendulum-clock; 1 oven on which a statue of a Black woman is placed; 1 book cabinet; 1 carved figurine on a stand; 1 more sculpture representing two boys; 1 pendulum clock; 1 easel; 1 book cabinet. As requested, this book cabinet has been sealed because it contains many volumes of books about law. Approximately 21 pictures and photographs are on the wall as well as 1 stuffed eagle.[22]

A law office equipped in this fashion helped to create a professional as well as private atmosphere that fostered trust.

Attempting to ensure the solidarity of the legal profession and to exhibit advocates publicly as leading exponents of law, culture and society, advocates consciously staged congresses, funeral services and events at which monuments for their fellow legal professionals were erected and unveiled. By comparing these events on the international stage, it can be seen that, in terms of the cultural set-up of social celebrations and social clubs, significant similarities existed in European countries. At the same time, there were also differences resulting from the specific characteristics of each society and from the type of legal profession that prevailed. Rome, the new capital of the centralised national state, functioned as the monumental stage for the irregularly held congresses of Italian advocates. In two federations, Switzerland and Germany, the national congresses were held more frequently in the regional capital cities and were less pompous. Italian advocates viewed their assemblies as actual congresses of jurists and, in broad terms, as professional and field-oriented conventions. The German '*Anwaltstage*' (lawyer's congress), on the other hand, had the character of a convention held by a professional group, even though common jurisprudential problems were at the heart of the meeting. In Switzerland and in Italy, funeral services of high-ranking liberal advocate-politicians were attended by the highest dignitaries of the

[21] Domenico Giurati, *Come si fa l'avvocato* (Livorno, 1897) 191–215.

[22] Staatsarchiv Landshut, 166N, 14, 159, Nr. 183/33, Nachlaßprotokoll Dr. Georg Schreiner, 1.8.1933.

state along with people of civil prominence, while high society in some German states avoided such events.

A specifically Italian speciality was the creation of monuments honouring advocates and signifying the identification of lawyers with the profession, law and nation. In 1882, the Chamber of Lawyers in Naples held an exhibition of marble sculptures featuring exemplary advocates and jurists. The opening of the exhibition was attended by the Minister of Justice, Zanardelli, and other distinguished dignitaries representing politics and the economy. After the exhibition, the sculptures were permanently placed in the court house Castelcapuano, transforming it into a *'Capitol'* or *'Pantheon'* of the great legal consultants and defence lawyers of Naples.[23] In 1897, the executive board of the Chamber of Advocates in Florence collected money for the purpose of purchasing a monument in remembrance of their late president of the board, the national-liberal politician Augusto Barazzuoli (1830–1896). In 1898, the board also organized a fund-raising event, collecting for the purchase of a memorial stone for the former president of their board and politician Adriano Mari.[24] In a letter sent all over Italy in 1909, the board of the Chamber of Advocates in Naples requested donations for a monument to honour the advocate and minister Emanuele Gianturco. The letter stated that Gianturco, an 'athlete with superior eloquence' who had fought a 'forensic battle' and entered an 'honourable struggle for justice', had always remained a true advocate.[25]

The events involving the unveiling of monuments in the presence of members of the political, cultural and legal elite always turned into celebrations of the civil jurists and advocates, who exploited this effect to bolster their own identity and, at the same time, to demonstrate to society the value of law, education, morals and a noble mind. By means of the placing of these politicians and *'principi del foro'* (advocate kings) next to the deceased great jurists and politicians of the past, the myth of the advocate was stabilised and the belief in justice strengthened.

V. CONCLUSION

In summary, it may be said that in the nineteenth century the problems surrounding the connection between juridicalisation and professionalisation were frequently discussed, amid controversy, among jurists and the public. My illustrations have shown that some insights into the 'social history of law' can be gained by examining this problematic topic. The

[23] S Cilibrizzi, 134f.

[24] Archivio del ordine degli avvocati, Firenze, Filza 29, 1897, No 27; Filza 30, 1898, No 32.

[25] Archivio del ordine degli avvocati, Firenze, Filza 39, 1909.

professional and social opportunities for lawyers were strongly dependent upon the legal and political system of each particular society. A variety of types of professionalisation processes existed in Europe, resulting in a number of professional and social types of the legal profession. Correspondingly, specific forms of juridicalisation and of occupational-cultural practices of the legal profession went along with this development. Over time, the situation in the European states became more similar. The legal profession had frequently been the object of the codifying and professionalising politics of the state. However, lawyers also developed during these processes their own functional and symbolic strategies, thus determining what kinds of professionalisation and juridicalisation of social interaction took place and how intense they were.

6

From 'Rechtsstaat' to 'Welfare-State': Swedish Judicial Culture in Transition 1870–1970

KJELL Å MODÉER

1. INTRODUCTION

On 1 January 1995 Sweden became a member of the European Union. The referendum on this membership divided Sweden in two parts, those for and those against. Those in favour of membership gained 52 per cent, those against 47.5 per cent. Those in favour were generally urban, male southeners. Those against were rural, female and came from the northern part of Sweden. The referendum, however, also divided Sweden from a cultural point of view. Sweden has, in postwar years given a political impression of being a very homogeneous country. Sweden, as the archetype of the welfare state, did not need any international comparison. The political culture was a very strong state-orientated and domestic one. The 'folk-home'-ideology meant a rural, social and small-scale model transplanted into the modern urban Sweden.

The political discourse surrounding Swedish membership brought new, supra-national aspects to the Swedish parliamentary system. The homogenous front collapsed and suddenly showed a new divided front. The conservative and the liberal parties represented a new radical platform. They were in favour of the EU and wanted Sweden to participate in constructing the future of Europe. The dominant Swedish political party, the Social democrats, was divided. There was an outspoken section of the party that wanted to uphold the traditional national welfare state ideology. The board of the Social democrats, however, was in favour and many voters trusted their leaders.

Membership of the EU has had an impact not only on the political life of Sweden but also—and very much so—on the life of the legal arena. As of 1 January 1995, the Swedish national legal culture has become a part of a supra-national legal—and judicial—culture. The supra-national European courts in Luxembourg and Strasbourg have a daily impact on the Swedish Bar and judiciary. At the beginning of the 1990s the decade was named 'the decade of the jurists'. Such rhetoric has not only been a challenge to the more international orientated younger section of jurists, it has also been a challenge for the Swedish judge, who up until now, has lived in a very close, and national orientated judicial culture. Questions like: 'What is Swedish judicial culture?' were previously not on the agenda. Now, however, all new statutes from the EU and the European Convention of Human Rights have to be taken into consideration in the Swedish courts.

Sweden is, with the help of its representatives, bringing its judicial culture into the institutions of the EU. There is a need to identify the role of the Swedish judge, and his/her cultural roots, briefly to identify the judicial culture and to place it on the European map.[1]

2. SWEDEN AND LEGAL CULTURE

Legal cultures are always in transition. A homogeneous legal culture also has continuity, a national heritage, built into its systems.

The two German professors of comparative law, Konrad Zweigert and Hein Kötz, have defined the European legal systems in terms of legal families, the roman, the German, the Anglo-American, the socialist one (now obsolete) and the Scandinavian. They found Scandinavian legal culture specific, on the one hand because in these countries they did not find modern codes as in Germany and France, but on the other hand they are civil law countries with a legal system based on statutes. Roman law had also played a role in the legal history of the countries but not as dominating as that in the Roman law countries.[2] This concept of *families of law* (Rechtsfamilien) has recently been questioned in the legal discourse.[3]

But more specifically, how can you identify legal culture in a country and what is the difference between legal culture and judicial culture. *Legal culture* is the more general term. It tries to identify and describe how the law influences a specific society and vice versa at a particular time. *Judicial culture* however, focuses on the actors in a more specific arena: the professional actors in the courtroom—judges, prosecutors, attorneys and lawyers.

[1] Cf Kjell Å Modéer, *Den svenska domarkulturen—europeiska och nationella förebilder*, (Lund 1994), also in SOU 1994:99. This work was published as a part of a legislative draft given in 1994 by a Swedish governmental committee.

[2] K Zweigert & H Kötz (transl Tony Weir), *An Introduction to Comparative Law*, 3rd edn (Oxford University Press, Oxford, 1998, 276 ff.

[3] Hein Kötz, Abschied von der Rechtskreislehre?, Zeitschrift für europäische Privatrecht 1998, 493 ff. Cf the discussion on comparative law, eg Mark Van Hoecke and Mark Warrington, 'Legal Cultures, Legal Paradigms and Legal Doctrine: Towards a New Model for Comparative Law' (1998) 47 *International and Comparative Law Quarterly*, 495 ff; Ugo Mattei, 'Three Patterns of Law: Taxonomy and Change in the World's Legal Systems' (1997) 45 *The American Journal of Comparative Law*, 5 ff.

This more specific culture also needs more specific analytical instruments. Are the parameters you need to be able to identify and evaluate a judicial culture others than when you are identifying a legal culture? Judicial culture is to be sought within the judiciary itself; it is the internal culture of the actors in the courthouse. In the Anglo-American world there is a huge literature of judicial biographers from Alphons Mason to Laura Kalman and Gerald Gunter. This art of literature provides the opportunity of looking at the single judge and his/her legal and political philosophy and helps to establish a pattern. This art of literature, however, is a rare phenomenon in continental Europe, where there is no system of case law and where the single actor as a civil servant by tradition has been a part of a secret corporate body. So it is necessary to find other parameters in order to identify a judicial culture such as that of Sweden. This article is an attempt to identify and describe the parameters and transition of this specific culture. Political scientists have already formulated a model for the modern history of Swedish political culture.[4] This chronology in three parts will be used as a periodisation of the judicial culture:

1. The idealistic civil-servant state 1870–1932
2. The corporativistic state 1932–1976
3. The party-bound (divided) state 1976–to the present.

3. DIACHRONIC PERSPECTIVE 1870–1970

This article will look at the period from the peak of the individualistic liberal Rechtsstaat around 1870 to a similar peak of the strong social welfare state in the 1970s.

The '*Rechtsstaat*' was a product of Germany in the mid-nineteenth century. It represented a state seeking to reduce the extent to which it interfered in lives of its citizens. It represents the legalistic guarantees of the society and the statutes as a rule of law. The role of lawyers in this society was to protect the legal rights of the small and poor citizen against the state. The perspective was individualistic, the goals and aims idealistic.

The *Welfare state* on the other hand brought about a new look at the case of 'The citizen vs The State'. The perspectives were changed around. The social state promoted collectivist and corporativist programmes. The role of jurists became instead to support the state as 'social engineers' when it constructed a new order in which the individualistic perspective became more and more diffuse and jurists became more and

[4] Jörgen Hermansson, *Politik som intressekamp. Parlamentariskt beslutsfattande och organiserade intressen i Sverige*, (Stockholm 1993).

more pragmatic. From a political scientist's perspective it was a transition from a weak to a strong state, from individualism to corporativism, from idealism to pragmatism. From a legal perspective emphasise shifted from civil, private law to public law.

Those two state models also represent two forms of strong homogeneous cultures. The first one is an international archetype found all over continental Europe in the last century; the other is extremely national. Sweden even became a model for the left wing democrats in the US in the 1930s, the New Dealers.[5]

4. HISTORICAL FUNDAMENTS FOR SWEDISH JUDICIAL CULTURE

In trying to identify the roots of modern Swedish judicial culture one can identify two international and one national phenomena, namely (1) legal education and (2) the constitution as the contract between the citizen and the Nation, the state, and finally (3) the hierarchical court system.

4.1. Legal education

The emergence of professional jurists was important in the absolutistic era and in the National-State, in which national history, language and culture were emphasised. In the mid-eighteenth century legal education offered by the Faculties of Law was, for the first time, regulated by the state. From that time a specific law degree was offered by the Universities, a law degree with which young jurists might prove their authority.[6] From 1749 the law degree became the entrance ticket to practice in the courts. Legal education in Sweden was to a great extent an education for civil servants, a school for judges, where within a couple of years students became knowledgeable in law (lagfaren).

At that time judges were the only professional legal group in the courtroom. The Swedish code of 1734 stipulated that the representatives of the parties in the courts should be wise and sensible but there was no claim to be knowledgeable in legal matters. There still is no such requirement. This is a product of rural times when the legislator considered it unreasonable that parties in the district courts should have to have educated and trained lawyers from the capital. This has had an immense effect on the Swedish Bar, which up to 1900 principally was illiterate in legal

[5] Gunnar Myrdal was a catalyst in this perspective.—Cf Kjell Å Modéer, *The Runner-up: A New Deal-Lawyer as Catalyst*. [Unpublished manuscript, 1995, Stanford & UC Berkeley.]

[6] Lars Björne, *Patrioter och institutionalister. Den nordiska rättsvetenskapens historia, Del 1, Tiden före 1815*, Rättshistoriskt bibliotek, vol 52, Lund 1995.

matters. The erection of the professional Swedish Bar was a result of the *Rechtsstaat* culture of the late nineteenth Century.

Legal education and legal science in Sweden in the late nineteenth century developed under strong influence from Germany.[7] The course of study became increasingly more theoretical and scientific, and took four years instead of two. Both from a qualitative as well as a quantitative perspective the education improved and became more scientific. Theoretical questions were raised; political issues and aims were formalised into statutes or legal definitions and rules.

From the seventeenth century legal training for young jurists was provided in the courts of appeal. It was an apprentice-system in which the older judges served as mentors for the young clerks. This mentoring-system (from the German 'Auskultantensystem') was transplanted from Germany into the Swedish Courts of Appeal.[8]

In summary, Swedish judicial culture in the nineteenth century was formed by legal education and training, by law professors at the Faculties of Law and by senior judges in the Courts of Appeal.

4.2. The Constitution

The political theories developed during the Enlightenment discussed and identified the role of the judge from a constitutional perspective. The theory of separation of power, as introduced by Montesquieu in his work *The Spirit of the Laws* 1748, had a great impact on several constitutions from the American in 1787 to the Norwegian in 1814 and the Danish in 1849. It is important to emphasise that for Montesquieu the autonomy of the courts did not imply strong political power for the judge. The judge stood under the laws, as a passive implementer of the very detailed codes of the time. First with John Marshall and the case of *Marbury v Madison* in 1803 the American Supreme Court introduced judicial review as a powerful political instrument. Following the introduction of more abstract legal rules, with the doctrine of precedents the role of the continental European judges developed from passive implementers to dynamic creators of legal rules and principles. The 'separation of power' principle evolved from a relatively weak position to a strong one in political life.

Rousseau took a different position with his principle of the sovereignty of the people. He preferred parliament as a democratic forum for the political system. In his view the professional judges of the absolutistic era had shown their shortcomings by being servants of the king and his power. The British jury system was his model for judicial reform.

[7] Jan-Olof Sundell, *Tysk påverkan på svensk civilrättsdoktrin 1870–1914*, (Diss, Uppsala, 1987), Rättshistoriskt bibliotek, vol 40, Lund 1987.

[8] David Gaunt, *Utbildning till statens tjänst. En kollektivbiografi av stormaktstidens hovrättsauskultanter*, Studia Historica Upsaliensia 63 (Diss, Uppsala, 1975).

Montesquieu and Rousseau are, however, two representatives of the two modern constitutional theories which are of great importance for judicial culture. Montesquieu represents autonomy, political power and elitism. Rousseau represents the concept of parliament, democracy and lay-judges.

In Sweden the Constitution of 1809 brought an end to the absolutistic regime from 1772. The separation of power principle was implemented with autonomous courts and judges who could not be removed. There were, however, still historical elements in the judicial culture. The king still chaired sessions in the High Court of Justice. Swedish people could still appeal to the King in Court, as they had done since the Middle Ages. This was, of course, an anomaly for the French successor to the Swedish throne, Jean Baptiste Bernadotte, who refused to chair sessions in the High Court, and after him no king ever did. This constitutional rule was abolished in 1909.

The Constitution of 1809 became the second oldest constitution of the world. Throughout the 160 years or more that it was in use the judges, through constitutional practice, gained a stronger position. A governmental investigation in 1941 stated, inter alia, that judicial review was a principle accepted in Swedish constitutional practice.

The 1809 Constitution was succeeded in 1974 by a new one, dominated by the 'sovereignty of the people' principle. In its preamble it stated, 'All public power emanates from the people'. As will be shown below, the new Constitution has had a significant impact on the development of modern Swedish judicial culture.

4.3. The Court-system

Since the Middle Ages Sweden has had a hierarchical court system with district courts at its base and the King's court at the top. In the early seventeenth century the court system developed the structure it has had until recent times (with the reform of court organisation in 1970).

The lower district courts in towns (rådhusrätt) and in the countryside (häradsrätt) were not professionalised until the end of the seventeenth century. At that time enough jurists were educated in the universities and trained to make it possible for the King to implement a reform that set up a legally-trained judge in each district court. The judge should not only have knowledge of the law, he should also have his residence in his territory (jurisdiction). Farmers were required to build courthouses and hand over farms to the judges.

In the rural district courts most of the judges were laymen. They formed the *nämnd*. Twelve farmers of the district took part in the court sessions, chaired by the professional judge (häradshövding). The main rule was that the unanimous opinion of the 12 laymen was the opinion of the court, even if the professional judge was of another opinion. If just one of the laymen, however, voted with the professional judge their vote won.

In the district court we can identify one essential aspect of Swedish judicial culture. The professional judge appointed by the king was responsible for implementing the legal system, the written law. The laymen represented the local authorities, the customs and common sense. It was a marriage between elitism and state control on the one hand and democracy and proximity to the local environment on the other. This culture was oral and open to the public and in earlier times the sessions were held in the open air. It was a culture dominated by social control. The members of the local society took part as audience in the sessions which were held regularly three times a year.

By contrast the Courts of Appeal (hovrätter) and other High Courts of Justice were professional courts. Not only from a judicial point of view were they superior to the lower courts, but also appeals were made to them, they administered all the courts within their jurisdiction (including the training of young judges) and controlled the lower courts so that they adhered to the king's codes and statutes. This was, as in other continental European countries, a closed and secrete environment, a strong hierarchic culture, filled with internal conflicts and disciplinary bullying towards clerks and other subordinated judges. In the Court of Appeal there were separate groups of judges, including members belonging to the King's council, members of the nobility and the learned members (educated in law). The Court of Appeal was a King's court with parallels all over Europe, and the formalism and the social classes of the time imprinted themselves on its culture.

Passing through those two judicial cultures was essential for the careers of the members of the judiciary in Sweden from the seventeenth century onwards.

5. THE COURTHOUSE: JUDICIAL ICONOGRAPHY AND ARCHITECTURE

The courtroom and its frame, the courthouse, reflect the judicial culture in its contemporary society. In engravings from the seventeenth and eighteenth centuries, the European courtroom is drawn depicting the status and dignity of the judges, sitting in their red robes and wigs, every detail reflecting the society of its time both realistically and in symbols. You cannot interpret those engravings without knowing the iconography, either from roman and Greek mythology, as the figures of Justitia and Prudentia, or in more concrete form, as the dog in the front of the engraving symbolises the principle of public access to the courtroom.

The courtroom of the nineteenth century was one of the public arenas for the Rechtsstaat. Another public arena was the Parliament. The idea of representative democracy was concretised in impressive parliament buildings all over the western hemisphere, constructed in neo-classical or Palladian style. In Budapest, Vienna and Berlin, the parliament buildings symbolised the power of the democratic legislator, in Berlin even devoted to the German people; the motto *'Dem Deutschen Volke'* was carved out in the stone of the front gable of the building.

The courthouses were theatres for criminal justice. In Paris on the Ile de la Cité the Palais de Justice, with roots back in the late fifteenth century, was renovated during the time of Napoleon III to suit the modern criminal justice, with jury and attorneys for the defence.[9] The bench was raised on a podium, the prosecutors, attorneys, defendant, witnesses and the public—all had to use their separate entrances in the formal procedure. The setting was traditional. The big hall for the meetings between the actors and the audience. The staircase leading to the court immensely high and wide, symbolising the high court as a legal cathedral of its time. The huge courthouses, built in the same neoclassical style, were also to be found in Brussels,[10] London,[11] Berlin and Leipzig.[12] They were all constructed between 1850–1870.

The courthouses are an important iconographic and architectural parameter of the European judicial culture of the nineteenth century. In Sweden there are hundreds of them. Most of more than 400 district courthouses in Sweden were constructed in the period between 1870–1930. Together with the first generation of trained professional architects (from the Institutes of Technology) the chief judges of the local district identified the symbols for the sacred activities in courthouses. The buildings were created as Temples of Justice.

The courthouse was built as a parallel to the parish church.[13] The architects also consciously combined the European view of the courthouse as a holy temple to Justitia, with national romantic elements, typical for the period around 1900. Architects created the buildings as icons for the professional work produced in them. They also helped judges to identify themselves as icons for the liberal *Rechtsstaat*. This

[9] Katherine Fisher Taylor, *In the Theater of Criminal Justice: The Palais de Justice in Second Empire Paris* (Princeton University Press, Princeton NJ, 1994).

[10] Pierre Loze, *Le Palais de Justice de Bruxelles, Monument XIXe* (Atelier Vokaer, Bruxelles, 1983).

[11] David B Brownlee, *The Law Courts. The Architecture of George Edmund Street* (MIT Press, Cambridge,Mass, 1984).

[12] K Klemmer, R Wassermann and TMWessel, *Deutsche Gerichtsgebäude: Von der Dorflinde über den Justizpalast zum Haus des Rechts* (Beck, München, 1993).

[13] Kjell Å Modéer, Det heliga rummet. Domstolsbyggnadernas roll i det civila samhället, *Lakimies* (Helsinki) 7–8/2000, 1060 ff.

idealistic view of the role of the judge was also supported by the constitutional doctrine in Sweden at that time. It supported a metaphysical view of the institutions of the state. To the professional judges were delivered powers from the king and the parliament, which made them special civil servants. Like priests who received their vocation from God to enter their profession, judges had to have a similar vocation when sworn in to serve in court.

The courthouses from that period also were built as mansions for the chief judge. In the cellar was the archive for judicial records and cells for those who had been arrested. On the ground floor all the judicial activities took place, with the courtroom dominating at the centre. The secretariat and rooms for attorneys and prosecutors were also located there. On the first floor was the private home of the chief judge and his family, with rooms for maids and servants, a setting totally reflecting the status of the chief judge and his social responsibilities. On the second floor were rooms for the clerks, who lived as members of the family up to the 1930s without salary but with free food and lodging. There were also rooms for the 12 laymen who often had to stay over night when the proceedings endured late in the evenings. To sum up, the courthouse was a living house filled with judicial, legal and social activities, a mirror of judicial culture.

A quite new method of constructing courthouses was introduced in the 1930s. In art and architecture the older emblematic national style was replaced by functionalism. In Sweden this style was introduced in 1930, at a great exhibition in Stockholm where this more strict style was demonstrated for the first time. It was, however, not only an architectural style that was introduced, it was also a new cultural style. The cultivated citizen became a part of the Swedish bourgeoisie of the twentieth century.[14] Owner occupied houses (egnahem) and apartment houses built by tenant-owned societies were to be found in newly erected suburbs in the cities. The heavy, bourgeois urban lifestyle, draped in red velvet, thick carpets and indoor palms, was replaced with a more functional and 'bare' style of architecture with big windows befitting a lifestyle much more affiliated to nature and with furniture in bright natural wood materials. This new functional style was also to be seen in the models of public buildings. The courthouses built from 1935 onwards were often constructed in red or yellow brick and were influenced by this new style on the one hand emphasising the surrounding nature (not social constructs) and on the other hand the more legal and bureaucratic *functions* of the courthouses more than the social. The magnificent flats for the chief-judges were abolished in the drawings of the new houses, although

[14] Jonas Frykman & Orvar Lövgren, *Den kultiverade människan* (Liber, Lund, 1979) 221 ff.

not in all. The court administrators, the secretariat, its employees and typewriters were the winners, when this new period started.

6. LEGAL PROCEDURE

An essential part of the judicial culture of Sweden is to be found in the Code of Procedure. The Code sets the standard for the possibilities—and obstacles—for the judge on the bench. In 1870 the judge totally dominated the court sessions. He was the leading actor. He mastered the sessions in every case by following the manual in the Code of Procedure as a ritual; analogous to the sacred ritual that clergyman went through in mass in church every Sunday.

There were also sacred elements in the Code of Procedure. The Court messenger had to ring a bell up on the roof of the Court, to summon the citizens to the open and public court sessions. The local clergyman had to start the session by preaching a sermon. And in front of the judge was placed the bible. All oaths were to be given with the 'hand on the book'. The Christian judge mastered all these elements. The judge, as a Swedish civil servant, had to be a member of the Swedish state church.

The essential part of the Code of Procedure emanated originally from canon law. The inquisition was used as the main principle of criminal procedure until the advent of the new Code of Procedure in 1948.

The new Code of 1948 introduced not only the adversorial system in the courtroom. It also introduced oral procedure in the Courts of Appeal and in the High Court of Justice. January 1948 literally meant a revolution for the judiciary in those courts.

Still more important was that lawyers (and the Bar Association) and prosecutors became important figures in the courtroom together with the judge. For the Swedish judiciary this was a radical reform, and especially for the older generation of judges it was difficult to accept the professional actors on the floor playing an independent role in the procedure. It was, however, also a question of professionalism. Still around 1950 prosecutors were not trained in law and the Bar only accounted for around 800 trained members. Around 1970, when the older generation of judges had left the bench and a young, skillful, generation of prosecutors and attorneys had entered the scene, a new modern judicial culture began to be implemented.

To the modernities of the Swedish legal procedure from around 1970 belongs the role of the layman. There was, from a political (eg social democratic) point of view, a suspicion towards the conservative-regarded judiciary. One way to break up this elitist culture was to 'democratise' the courts and to give more individual responsibility to laymen. The collective vote-system was abolished, the number of laymen was reduced to five and each layman got a single vote. Some years later, from 1974, laymen were also introduced in the courts of appeal. To these courts this was a revolution as significant as that of 1948. Chief Judges in those courts also publicly told the lay judges they were not welcome in Court. This part of the reform is still controversial, which shows that there has been a problem in adjusting to the modern judicial culture in the traditionally more professional courts.

The result of this reform has been that the national organisation of laymen regularly makes claims for legal vocational training. Parliament, however, has consistently declined to permit the growth of a quasi-professional group of magistrates. Many of the lay judges, however, feel uncomfortable with this system. In a couple of cases, made public by the media, lay judges have not managed to handle their new position, which has resulted in cries from the media of lack of confidence in the court system.

Formality is a part of the rule of law. It constitutes predictability, and it is good for the public who need to have confidence in the judiciary. Formality is a good thing both for a clever judge to interpret extensively and for an immature young judge to use rigidly. Together with the Constitution, the Code of Procedure is an important legal framework for the culture of the judiciary.

The Code of Procedure also includes important ethical rules for judges. In the judge's oath, all the requisites of the judge are listed, such as what is permitted and what is prohibited. The standards for the good judge are also to be found in another historical Swedish legal document, The Rules of the Judge (*Domarreglerna*) from the 1540s and since the codes were printed in the early seventeenth century, also a part of the Swedish Code. These rules, to a great extent, are taken from the Bible, from Thomistic ethical thoughts and from the medieval European codes. 'A good judge is better than a good law, because he can always manage a convenient decision', is one of the often-quoted rules. Even if those rules are still reproduced in the Swedish Code they have been looked upon as obsolete until recent times. The European Convention of Human Rights and its Article 6 on parties' rights to a fair trial, however, has again made these historical rulings interesting.

7. LIBRARIES AND BOOKS: JUDGES AND LAWYERS INSTRUMENT

Printed legal materials in different forms such as textbooks, commentaries and precedents are another means of identifying judicial culture. Which books were read by jurists at the time of the *Rechtsstaat* and how did it change over time?

First some comments on the book collections. In the 1870s there were very few public collections of law books in Sweden. Neither in the law faculties nor in the courthouses were any substantial book collections to be found. The book catalogues that were kept show how these collections consisted to a great extent of statutes and ordinances.[15]

Judges and lawyers kept books of their own. Private book collections from the *Rechtsstaat* generations can be identified through book auction catalogues. Even if they do not indicate whether jurists have read the books, they indicate their interests within their cognitive structures.

The book collection of the permanent Law Commission has been kept and shows the immense influence of France and Germany in the late nineteenth century Swedish legal culture.[16]

Legal science was an important part of the literature. Academic dissertations appeared frequently among the books of the jurists. Cases from the High Court of Justice began to be published in the 1870s, indicating the need for this material in the courts. Also the first Scandinavian law journal appeared towards the end of the nineteenth century.

The book collections went from being private to being public. As the printed legal material increased, a judge was no longer able to maintain his own professional library. In the postwar era the courts started to build up their own libraries. This was also a change of culture, from an individualist one, where the single judge worked at home with his own study and library, to a more collectivistic environment where he went to work in the morning, worked in his chambers and used the court's library.

Rudolph von Jhering is an example of the influence of German legal scientists upon Swedish jurists during the first decades of the twentieth century. His work *'Kampf ums Recht'* was mostly read by the idealistic jurists. In 1941, during WW II—when neutral Sweden was under great political pressure—a new translation made by a Swedish judge was published. In a district court of Stockholm it is still to be found in the library, however in an unfolded copy. . .[17]

8. MALE JUDICIAL CULTURE

Swedish judicial culture was traditionally male, and during the century described, it remained principally male, even if increasingly more women entered professional positions.

Until about 1900 women were excluded from the legal profession. The first women who pursued a legal education graduated from the universities around 1905. The first generation of women lawyers went to the bar, as all

[15] eg in Göta Court of Appeal in the 1880's the collection of books was listed on two sheets of paper. Kjell Å Modéer, *Historiska rättskällor. En introduktion i rättshistoria*, 2 edn (Nergelius & Santérus, Stockholm, 1997) 164.

[16] Today in the Law Library, Lund University.

[17] Södra Roslags tingsrätt, Stockholm.

public positions of civil servants were reserved for male jurists. After changes to the Constitution, those position were opened to women in 1923.

But even if, in theory, there was the possibility of women becoming judges, it wasn't until after WW II that female judges first entered the scene.

The first female member of the High Court of Justice was appointed in 1968 (Ingrid Gärde Widemar) and the first female district court judge (Anna-Lisa Vinberg, Gothenburg) in 1963.

Still in the 1970s men dominated recruitment to the judiciary.

During the last 25 years there have been great changes in the numbers of women entering the profession, which has been more marked in the public rather than the private sector. Female members of the Swedish Bar Association still account for not more than about 10 per cent whilst within the judiciary and among the state prosecutors there is a majority of female professionals.

To a great extent the women who entered the Swedish legal profession during this period up to 1970 had to adjust their professional careers to the dominant male culture.

9. IDEALISM AND IDEOLOGY

One essential parameter of judicial culture is legal ideology.[18] From an ideological and philosophical point of view there was a radical change in the 1910s as the professor of philosophy Axel Hägerström in Uppsala attacked the idealistic philosophy, which for decades had dominated the universities. Two Uppsala law students, Vilhelm Lundstedt [1882–1955] and Karl Olivecrona [1897–1980], listened to Hägerström's lectures, and under his influence one decade later they became the most important creators of the school of Scandinavian legal realism. The realists abolished all forms of metaphysics in law. There were no rights (of property, for example) in a traditional sense; Law was regarded as technical facts operated by jurists. One consequence was that the Uppsala School was critical to international public law and its inability to construct valid sanctions to be implemented within the legal system in the nation state.

Two members of the School, both professors of civil law in Uppsala, Vilhelm Lundstedt and Östen Undén [1886–1974], also played an important role in political life from the 1930s onward.[19] They were both social democrats, and the Uppsala School fitted very well into the political

[18] Cf Roger Cotterrell, 'The Concept of Legal Culture', & Lawrence M Friedman, 'The Concept of Legal Culture: A Reply', both in David Nelken (ed), *Comparative Legal Cultures* (Dartmouth, Aldershot, 1996) 13ff and 33 ff.

[19] Lundstedt was MP 1929–48 and Undén was Secretary of State 1924–26, 1945–92.

platform of modern Swedish social democracy at the time the party came into office in 1932. The Social Democratic Party remained in power for more or less 44 years.

Law students educated at Uppsala and Lund from the 1930s onwards learned about this anti-metaphysical, anti-authoritarian and pragmatic legal philosophy. They learned that law was a technique and that the role of jurists was to be technicians, to help society in constructing a new society as 'social engineers'. Social engineering had nothing to do with power, they argued. Jurists were simply executing the will of the legislator. For more than half a century this was the fundamental philosophical platform of Swedish political and judicial culture.

By taking the ideologies as a parameter for measuring judicial culture the result is, that there is an important delay in the incorporation of ideology into judicial culture. This has to do with the closed career system in civil law countries, especially in Sweden. If you graduated with a law degree in the 1930s you reached the peak of your career in the judiciary some 25 years later. From that time (around the 1930s) young clerks were placed on a career path that continuously and successively, with merits such as ability and skill, took them to the higher ranks of the career. For some years they dwelled in the political culture. Every judge with ambitions of reaching senior positions had to work as secretary to governmental committees working with drafts for future legislation. Many of the contemporary judges in top positions spent several years as 'social engineers' in this political world, during the time that Olof Palme served as Prime Minister between 1969–1976. This period is of importance in understanding the transition of judicial culture in modern Sweden.

10. POLITICAL CULTURE AND JUDICIAL CULTURE: THE SOCIAL DEMOCRATIC GOVERNMENT OF OLOF PALME 1969–1976

During this period the modern national judicial culture was formed. It was not a revolution; it was the result of a continuous ideological transition since the 1930s. By this time law students who had graduated in the early 1950s had reached positions in the Department of Justice. This department grew dramatically in the 1960s as a result of the immense legislative work in different fields such as family law, labour law, consumer law, social security law, rent control legislation and legal aid—all fields in which Sweden pioneered legislation in which the state safeguarded the weaker party to a contract.

The Constitution of 1809 provided that the High Court of Justice should consider every legislative change before bills were ratified by Parliament. This form of 'judicial preview' was compulsory. Its purpose was to ensure that the new legislation was in accordance with the Constitution.

In the 1960s there were recurring conflicts between the Law Council and the Government. It was a cultural conflict, between the conservative-regarded judiciary and the progressive politicians. In 1971 Parliament adopted a law, stating that 'judicial preview' in the future did not have to be compulsory. The government could decide if the proposed legislation should be considered by the Law Council or not.

A quite new organisation of district courts in 1970 centralised responsibility for the administration of the courthouses from the local communities to a central authority in Stockholm. From that time on, all renovations were made in the same functionalist style. New courthouses were built like government agency buildings—anonymous, sterile and bureaucratic and senior judges were obliged to move out of the old courthouses. The old prestigeous podiums for the bench were dismantled. The judiciary was increasingly regarded more as bureaucrats than as civil servants.

Another way of getting rid of a conservative judiciary was to take away power from them in terms of jurisdiction. New courts were erected for special purposes. From 1929 the Labour Court became a model for other courts such as consumer courts and tenants courts, in all of which the parties were represented by representatives of the unions or other corporative organisations. Corporative and lay members were further means of reducing the importance of the professional judiciary.

The older members of the judiciary felt uncomfortable with the new political order. Many of the younger members, however, saw the possibility of rapid advancement and adjusted themselves to the contemporary political culture.

It was not only the judiciary that was the focus of reform. The Bar was also a target for reform. One way to compete with the private Bar was to open up law firms, driven by state money. From 1973 about 150 lawyers were employed by the state to work in public law firms. The intention on the government's part was to successively raise the number of state lawyers, but the depression became an obstacle and this reform was never successful. Today state owned law firms have been abolished and its employees have turned to private practice.

The new Constitution adopted in 1974 did not result in any debate at all within the judiciary,[20] in spite of radical changes to the position of the judicial branch. Thereafter the judiciary retaind its autonomy, but it was regulated by the 'Administration and Justice' section of the Constitution. More important was that the separation of power doctrine was replaced by the sovereignty of the people doctrine. To a great extent the judiciary became executors of the legislators. Judicial review was regulated as an instrument to be used only if legislation was evidently contrary to the constitution. The

[20] Gustav Petrén, Domstolarna enligt 1974 års regeringsform (*Svensk*, *juristtidning*, 1975) 1 ff.

judiciary has never found this to be the case. The rulings in the Constitution not only removed power from the judges, it also made them passive. A Swedish judge has to follow the preparatory papers of the legislation given by the government and Parliament when the statute is adopted. In these papers the *Zeitgeist*, the ideology, the political purpose and the pragmatic interpretation is to be found.

In summary, the political culture of the 1970s has played an important part in the development of the Swedish judiciary. Swedish judicial culture was homogenous and national. It also had an anti-idealistic character. This judicial culture was a corporativist one.

11. CONCLUSIONS

In this article I have tried to describe the judicial culture by highlighting some significant aspects of the culture.

— **The ideological dimensions.** These encompass not only strict political ideologies, but more philosophical ideologies and professional ones. The political ideologies of course, to some extent influence the judicial culture, for instance by nominating or appointing the judiciary, or as shown in the Swedish example, by letting the judiciary take part in legislative work.

— **Professional and ethical rules** for the judiciary are given an official position in judicial culture. They can be on the idealistic side, as shown in the historical Rules of the Judge. They can also be more pragmatic as in the rulings of the Disciplinary Committee of the Judiciary.

— **The legal dimensions.** The Constitution and the Code of Procedure constitute a legal basis for the judicial culture. Autonomy, authority, status and formalism are all qualities of the judicial culture identified in the Constitution and in the legislation as previously mentioned.

— **The local environment of the judge.** The importance of the courthouse, its decorative façades and architectural symbols, has been emphasised. European as well as local (national) cultural elements can be identified in the courthouses as an important part of the judicial culture.

— **Legal education and training.** Continuity within a judicial culture is also dependent on the career system itself. From the moment law students begin their legal education they contribute to the legal system and the judicial culture. Swedish legal education has, for a long time, been orientated towards the public sector and the judicial career.

— **The judicial career.** The Swedish career-system is contrary to the recruitment system of judges in the Anglo-American legal system.

Traditionally the career path takes Swedish judges into three different environments: the district court, the Court of Appeal and the Department of Justice, each with its own character and culture. The district court with its closeness to the local social environment including the laymen in court, the Court of Appeal with its more formalistic and collegiate work and the Department of Justice with its more politically orientated tasks. From his/her time as a clerk to work in the Department as an expert the judge is continually confronted by other judges who more or less consciously influence him or her. The career system in that sense is fostering what Max Weber called a 'honoratiores' system, a strict elitist culture.[21]

At last a reflection related to the future. In the light of the more democratic aims the Welfare State in Sweden has introduced into judicial culture it would not be surprising if, in the near future, as Swedish judges are entering the European courts and their legal systems, these were a collision with other European judicial cultures, in which the separation of power principle, political power and elitist attitudes—actually the *Rechtsstaat* model—remain as dominating aspects parts of the judicial culture. Perhaps the judicial culture of the Welfare state was just a historical parenthesis. . .

[21] Max Weber, *Economy and Society: An Outline of Interpretive Sociology* (ed) Guenther Toth and Claus Wittich (University of California Press, Berkeley, 1978) 784 ff.

PART III

Work and Representations

7

The Problems of Wealth and Virtue: The Paris Bar and the Generation of the Fin-de-Siècle

JOHN SAVAGE

In November of 1899, just a few weeks into the new school term, shouts filled an amphitheatre crowded with law students as they subjected a classmate to an aggressive verbal attack. On the entrance of the professor, the crowd quietened down but the student in question, the son of a government minister, took the opportunity to shout '*Vive la République!*' which led to an even louder chorus of rebuke and a chaotic situation the professor was powerless to stop. Several more days of disturbances followed.[1] The student's father, Georges Trouillot, had recently been given a ministerial appointment in the new Radical Republican government brought into office in the wake of the Dreyfus Affair. In fact, the timing of the outburst points to the political overtones of the students' display. The incident was but one in a series of confrontations between republican and anti-republican factions at the Law Faculty and throughout the Latin Quarter, including a habit on the part of law students of starting fights with the mostly pro-Dreyfusard students at the Faculty of Letters. In at least one case, a law professor joined in the attack on a republican student. It became a commonplace of the *fin-de-siècle* for the press and public to see the Law Faculty as a bastion of conservatism and political reaction.[2]

This incident points to how the image of the '*République des Avocats*' is ultimately misleading. The association between lawyers and the early, triumphant Third Republic does not square with the nature of the independent legal profession in the late nineteenth century.[3] By the end of the century, nationalism and anti-Semitism had made inroads among stu-

[1] Archives de la Préfecture de Police [APP] Ba 23. Report of 30 Nov 1899. The incident is also discussed in *Le Temps*, 2 Dec, 1899, 3, which describes it as a '*manifestation nationaliste*'.

[2] *L'Aurore*, 22 Dec 1899.

[3] Philip Nord, *The Republican Moment: Struggles for Democracy in Nineteenth-century France* (Harvard University Press, Cambridge, MA, 1995), ch six.

dents at the Law Faculty as they had among a number of groups in French society. There was, however, another dimension to these tensions within the Law faculty, one that can be brought to light with some additional context. First of all, Trouillot, the minister in question, was not simply a standing member of a republican government. He was probably best known to the students as the author of a bill in Parliament that would have opened up the profession of *avocat* to all holders of the degree of *licence*, eliminating the requirement of being approved by the Order of Advocates itself.[4] Indeed, it is likely because of this that Trouillot had recently been struck off the register of the Paris Order by its governing council, an event that was followed closely in the press. Finally, his disbarment was overturned in court on the basis that the professional hearings had not observed due process, causing an uproar among leading advocates, who saw the sovereignty of their professional body compromised.[5]

It might be argued that, for these law students, the Republic stood for something more than just an abstract political ideology. For one thing, the Republic meant the promise of social mobility, the 'end of the notables' in Daniel Halévy's phrase, and the birth of a merit-based society.[6] These goals were to be achieved largely through the democratisation of education, a central focus of early republican policy. And while some of the students in that amphitheatre were beneficiaries of this greater openness, it represented a cultural problem to them. In general, compared to their Anglo-American counterparts in this period, the French middle classes had a more ambiguous relationship with the idea of social mobility. The rapid growth of industrial wealth during the mid-nineteenth century did not eliminate the longing for aristocratic status that traditionally characterised the bourgeoisie. The resulting malaise made examples of meritocracy in France more explicitly aristocratic. This ambiguous sensibility, caught between ideals of wealth and virtue, clashed directly with the republican rhetoric of social mobility that was powerfully captured in Léon Gambetta's idea of the '*nouvelles couches*': the rising new strata that would lead a society based on talent rather than privilege. The practical problem faced by these young students, the challenge of being successful in an increasingly overcrowded profession, was in a certain way analogous to a deeper problem raised by the Republic, that is, the problem of the democratisation of elites. As this broader student population demanded entry into the legal profession, leaders of the Paris Bar were forced to reevaluate the boundaries of professional identity in fundamental ways.

4 *Le Temps*, 29 March, 1893, 2.

5 *Gazette du Palais*, 1898, vol. 2, 609.

6 Daniel Halévy, *La Fin des Notables* (Grasset, Paris, 1930).

LAWYERS AND BOURGEOIS: ENTERING THE BAR

For a young man entering the Law Faculty in the late-nineteenth century, the Bar represented an honourable profession, an occupation that enjoyed a social status tied to the moral standards set by its leaders. Like the bourgeoisie itself, there were barriers to entering the Bar that were in part financial, but also linked to habits and mores, to a moral code that excluded some aspirants and created a sense of value and identity for those who belonged. Indeed, the advocate's moral probity was deemed crucial to justifying his unusual status as the only legal professional who was not a state employee. As defenders of property, and civil society in general, before the state, parallels between the specific traits of advocates and a broadly defined bourgeois culture are not difficult to find. The Order of Advocates was quintessentially meritocratic, but also had a time-honoured tradition of providing free legal assistance to the poor, a practice that could serve as a model of nineteenth century paternalism. In addition to these features, one might add a professional culture deeply ingrained with what Robert Nye has called 'male codes of honor'.[7] In fact, issues of masculinity provide a key to understanding the curious mixture of bourgeois values of moral probity and talent-based success, on the one hand, and what can be thought of as aristocratic values of honor, prowess, even heroism—all of which were associated with the great orators of the nineteenth century French Bar on the other. Indeed, I would argue that the tensions of *fin-de-siècle* bourgeois culture are nowhere better illustrated than in the case of the legal profession, where the important role of such codes of honour made membership far more than an economic proposition.

For the sake of comparison, a world of difference separates the French context from the situation of American lawyers. For example, in an article that appeared in a magazine called *The Law Student's Helper* entitled 'My first year as a Lawyer—What money I made and how I made it', the author describes the difficulties of starting out in the profession in the 1880s. He tells of the 'shabby' room he was forced to use to meet with clients, the various strategies used in letters to solicit business, and how much of his income came from collecting debts. The article ends with a fully itemised list of fees and expenses for that year.[8] Detailing such financial aspects of practice would be greeted with horror, and immediate sanctions, in France. Of course much of the difference between this American account and that of an *avocat* has to do with the division

[7] Robert Nye, *Masculinity and Male Codes of Honor in Modern France* (Oxford University Press, New York, 1993).

[8] *The Law Student's Helper*, Jan–Feb 1893, 9–11.

of labour among French legal professionals, the fact that others, *avoués, notaires,* or *agréés* handled matters of money.[9] But another major contrast is that the advocate was under the scrutiny of the disciplinary council of his Order in ways that went well beyond American Bar associations.

Professional ethics were intimately bound together with standards of bourgeois morality. The advocate was of course subject to more rigorous standards of speech and behaviour than were required by the law. But the efforts of the disciplinary council to ensure the independence of the Order also focused on his personal and moral qualities. The notion of *dignité* was by no means purely abstract. In practice, this requirement meant, for example, that a young aspirant to the profession would be visited by a member of the Council of Discipline who would verify that his place of residence was worthy of a practicing advocate. This examination followed a number of set criteria, from the importance of having a servant answer the door, to the clear separation of work and living areas and the size and content of the library. According to a typical description of the period, the young lawyer needed

> 'a parlor or a waiting room that is, if not luxurious, at least comfortable, an office with a desk and library, with a sufficient number of chairs to seat several clients, as well as the officers of the court who may accompany them'.[10]

The lawyer was also required to reside within the city limits of the seat of the district in which he practiced. In Paris, this meant that lawyers pleading cases in suburbs that were part of the Department of the Seine had to live in the city, not the poorer outlying *faubourgs.* The importance of having an acceptable *cabinet* was the most concrete requirement for a potential member of the Order, one that only young men of some means could hope to fulfill. The advocate was formally required to own his own furniture and thus restricted from dwelling in any kind of boarding house.[11] Indeed, he was not allowed to conduct professional matters anywhere else:

[9] *Avoué* is generally translated as solicitor and *notaire* as notary. These were both considered *offices* that were purchased from the state, putting these professions out of reach of young men of modest backgrounds. The term *agréés* refers to those lawyers admitted to plead before commercial courts, a lucrative practice forbidden to members of the Order of Advocates. See Jean-Louis Halpérin, *Les professions judiciaires et juridiques dans l'histoire contemporaine* (Institut d'Etudes Judiciaires, Université de Lyon III, Lyon, 1992), 73.

[10] René Lafon, *Pour Devenir Avocat* (Schleicher frères, Paris, 1899), 160.

[11] Saint Georges, *Les Chemins de la Vie: le Barreau* (A. Mame et fils, Tours, 1900), 95; Ernest Cresson, *Usages et règles de la profession d'avocat, jurisprudence, ordonnances, décrets et lois* vol. 1, (L. Larose et Forcel, Paris, 1888), 63.

> 'the advocate who accepts an appointment from a client in a café is wanting in professional conduct, and the fact of having visited the client to receive money constitutes inappropriate behavior (une inconvenance)'.[12]

These requirements, formally stated by the Council of Discipline, were ostensibly meant to insure the advocate's dignity and independence. The association of moral qualities with the nature of the interior space of the home further attests to the link between professional guidelines and bourgeois status.[13]

For those young aspirants who could not present the Council with evidence of a proper office, there was little chance of earning enough money to finance one-self through the cases they might plead. In effect, professional rules made earning a living difficult. Barred from any kind of advertising or solicitation; untested, and largely untrained in the real demands of the courtroom, the young *stagiaire* (intern) faced significant obstacles in establishing a practice. In particular, young lawyers who pleaded the cases of legal assistance were strictly forbidden from receiving payment of any kind. Even once they had in fact found a willing client with a legitimate case, professional rules stated that fees could never be requested in writing. Honoraria were to be offered spontaneously as a 'present' in exchange for the advocate's aid, not as remuneration for a service rendered.[14] As a result, faced with a client who would not pay his bill, an advocate had no recourse before the courts, since suing for fees could and did lead to disciplinary hearings before the Council. It was well known that clients familiar with this system were prepared to take advantage of young interns.[15] What is striking is that in these cases, the Council did not seek to protect the lawyer, but enforced the rules that stopped him from demanding payment. The advocate was barred even from discussing any aspect of the subject of honoraria with officers of the court or prosecutors. Such an infraction was punishable by the most severe sanction, disbarment.[16]

During the period of the *stage,* the advocate was not allowed to engage in any activities that were deemed incompatible with his profession, including serving as a clerk for a solicitor, or even giving Latin or French lessons to private students.[17] This meant that, in addition to the years of

[12] Decision of Council of Discipline cited by Gaston Leroux, *La Fronde*, 15 Nov 1900.

[13] Nord, *The Republican Moment*, ch 9.

[14] Decision of 30 April, 1867: '*L'honoraire offert par le client doit toujours constituer, de la part de celui-ci, une rémunération essentiellement volontaire et spontanée*'. Mollot, *Règles de la profession d'avocat* (Durand, Paris, 1866), vol. 1, 79.

[15] Lafon, *Pour Devenir Avocat*, 92.

[16] Mollot, *Règles de la profession*, vol. 1, 77.

[17] 'La Presse Judiciaire Parisienne', *Le Palais de justice de Paris, son monde et ses moeurs* (Librairies-imprimeries réunies, Paris, 1892), 123; 128.

study at the Law Faculty, no real income could be earned for at least another three years.[18] These practices demonstrate the implicit social selection at work in the standards of the profession. Interns were allowed to request their official admission to the Order's register after three years attending the *stage*. If they did not do so at that time, they were *required* to request admission after five years as a *stagiaire*. At this point, the treasurer of the Order would inform the young man that he had to choose between registering on the Order's official roll, and thus being subject to the *patente*, a tax levied on professionals and businessmen, or leaving the practice of law altogether.

The residency requirement guaranteed that the Council of Discipline could keep an eye on the members of their Order, including their financial situation, and make sure that their private lives were sufficiently 'dignified'. This surveillance could be quite rigorous. The Council's reach extended well into the home of the advocate, and touched on areas having nothing to do with professional life. According to a decision reached by the Council of Discipline in 1880, 'Particularly unfortunate scenes, both within the home of the advocate and in public, with respect to a quarrel started in a public house (*brasserie*), warrant severe punishments'.[19] As is made clear by a decision of 1887, social contacts could also be subject to the approval of the Council:

> 'To trouble the public peace by inappropriate acts, to frequent cafés with little decency and in such a manner as to attract humiliating sarcasm, to degrade oneself with certain company, is to face the most severe penalties'.[20]

These constraints extended to a rule against being seen at trade-union meetings.

The power of the *Conseil de l'Ordre* can be understood partly in terms of the importance of the young advocate having good relations with senior members of the profession, as they were a crucial source of finding work and gaining recognition. The opportunity to work with a well-known senior advocate was highly prized, and could guarantee professional success. But it was not easy to find ways to get the attention of these figures, outside of an impressive display of oratory before the *Conference du stage*. How was a young advocate without connections

[18] Paul Jacquemart, ed., *Professions et Métiers, Guide pour le Choix d'une Carrière à l'Usage des Familles et de la Jeunesse*, vol. 1 'Les professions libérales', (A. Colin, Paris, 1891), 158.

[19] Decision of 13 July, 1880, quoted in Gaston Leroux, *Sur Mon Chemin* (E. Flammarion, Paris, 1900), 183.

[20] Decision of 2 Feb 1887, quoted in Leroux, *Sur mon Chemin*, 183. In the same decision, the Council declared its right to examine and appreciate, 'documents officially produced against an advocate in a case of marital separation (*séparation de corps*)'. Several other disciplinary actions related to morality are cited by Cresson, *Usages et Règles*, 88.

supposed to get his first cases? According to Mollot's professional manual, the clients were to find the advocate in his office; 'what triumph would there be without obstacles?' he wrote.[21] In practice, the nature of legal procedure made a relationship with an *avoué*, or solicitor, imperative. The challenge for a young intern was somehow to get the attention of a solicitor who could then give him work. This could happen if he turned his banal case of legal assistance into a brilliant legal argument, though opportunities of this kind were in short supply. One solicitor also recommended that the young advocate arrange to be seen in the main hall of the *Palais de justice*, 'with a briefcase that looks a bit heavy, filled with anything, a melon if necessary'.[22] The relationship with the solicitor was to remain informal: setting up any type of formal agreement was strictly forbidden.[23]

Starting in the 1860s, the rigidity of professional rules began to be challenged as increasing numbers of young men sought to enter the Bar. Law faculties around France absorbed more and more students produced in this period of growing access to higher education. According to a study undertaken by the Ministry of Education in 1865, advanced study in law was the goal of the single largest group of students at the secondary level.[24] The figure of the briefless barrister was certainly not new, he had been a favourite subject for writers and publicists under the July Monarchy in particular. But the phenomenon differed from that described by Balzac in that a much smaller proportion of the young advocates had independent means. They sought more often to earn their living as quickly as possible, and were less likely to seek the title simply as a mark of social rank, as was common among provincial notables in earlier years, or with the goal of a political career in mind.[25] In addition to this, the figure of the 'gentleman lawyer' was dealt a severe blow in mid-century with the imposition of the *patente* tax on all practising advocates.

By the mid-1860s, several periodicals were founded in order to serve the interests of the new generation of advocates. The editors of these journals sought specifically to facilitate the entry of young men into the profession, given the great number of obstacles they were likely to encounter. One goal was to publish the oratory of remarkable young lawyers in

[21] Mollot, *Règles de la profession*, vol. 1, 74.

[22] *Le Palais de Justice de Paris*, 147.

[23] Mollot, *Règles de la profession*, vol. 1, 76–77.

[24] 15% of students in lycée hoped to study law (the largest single group); Patrick Harrigan, *Mobility, Elites and Education in French Society of the Second Empire* (Wilfrid Laurier University Press, Waterloo, Ontario, 1980), 32.

[25] Lenore O'Boyle, 'The problem of an excess of educated men in Europe: 1800–1850', (1970) 2(4) *Journal of Modern History*.

order to publicise their talents and attract clients.[26] These journals did not hesitate to point to the artificial nature of the rules of the Paris Bar as a major hindrance to young lawyers attempting to practise their trade. One editorialist published a mock 'letter to the *bâtonnier*', the president of the Order, satirising the naïve expectations of those first entering the Bar and lamenting the difficulties of the first years of professional life:

> Ambitious! Alas, yes, that has always been the worst of my faults. At 15, I dreamed of being Demosthenes; at 18, Berryer; at 20, with all due respect, to becoming *bâtonnier*; at 22, to being the great lawyer of my region; from there it kept getting lower; at 23, I dreamed only of earning an honest living, at 24, pleading once, any kind of case, so that my friends wouldn't make fun of me too much. . . .[27]

The parodic sketch of the young provincial getting his first taste of the real professional world in Paris was mirrored in true accounts in later years. Steered away from putting a plaque on his door, so that no one was aware of his title or his existence, the young intern faced a visit by a member of the Council of Discipline,

> 'A man who came to see me explained very clearly that with my two straw chairs and light wooden table, I was compromising the dignity of the Order, and he indicated to me the minimum number of armchairs and quality of wood that were necessary before one could begin to uphold the law and combat injustice'.[28]

What began as a schoolboyish joke on the part of a handful of young lawyers foreshadowed issues that came to a head during the Third Republic, when professional rules of conduct were formally challenged due to their elitism. Critics attacked the Order not only in the name of the clients they served, but also in the name of the republican ideal of social mobility, for those whose professional ambitions were frustrated.

THE BAR AND THE REPUBLIC

By 1879, the Third Republic had fought off the most immediate threats to its existence and had proven itself to be, at least for the moment, the regime that divided Frenchmen the least. In this year, republicans finally reached a majority in the Chamber of Deputies and began to push legislation through under the guidance of Jules Ferry. Having survived the first years of the new regime, these legislators went about the task of rethink-

[26] See, for example *Le Barreau, Journal du Palais* 1, 16 Nov 1865. The journal's goals were applauded by the president of the Bar in its second issue: 1 Dec 1865, 125.

[27] Modestin 'Lettre d'un stagiaire à M. le Bâtonnier sur la profession d'avocat', *La Conférence*, 23, 5 April 1865, 738.

[28] Modestin, 'Lettre d'un stagiaire', 739.

ing French society and political life from a republican perspective. While historians have paid much attention to Ferry's colonial and educational legislation, less has been written about the vast reforms undertaken in the justice system in this period. After the failed attempts to purge the magistracy in the early 1870s, the legal system remained a bastion of conservatism. It took years, for example, for the courtroom itself to display evidence of the republican state. Only after the republican majority was achieved in the Chamber of Deputies was a 'humble plaster bust' of the republic introduced. One journalist described the reaction at the *Palais de Justice*,

> 'There were restrained smiles, hushed whispers and tragic gestures. This effigy was a profanation whose arrival had, under the most unreal pretexts, been put off for the previous eight years'.[29]

The greatest battle was over the removal of magistrates who were named before the advent of the republican regime and whose positions were protected by *inamovibilité*, life-long appointment to the bench. True to their traditional distrust for judicial power, republicans felt that previous attempts to purify the legal system had been too moderate, and a number of leaders qualified the magistracy as a 'third power' that threatened to offset republican gains in the legislative branch. What followed has been described by Jean-Pierre Royer as a 'judicial revolution' between 1879–1883.[30] One initiative focused on replacing standing judges by introducing elections. This idea had the support of many radicals as well as a good number of moderate republicans, who saw in it a way to bring a direct popular voice in legal affairs. The decree of June 1882 establishing that judges at all levels would be elected by universal suffrage is evidence of the generalised suspicion of the magistracy on the part of republican lawmakers. The measure was adopted as being the only policy consistent with the Republic, and gave satisfaction to the Radical programme. Very soon, however, the weaknesses of the sweeping law came to the surface. Critics objected that a huge number of offices would be affected immediately, and these would then become open to men of insufficient qualifications. Within just a few months, the measure was reversed by the Chamber. The idea of elected judges had been popular in part because it offered a means to rid the nation of the magistrates appointed by Napoleon III. By the following year, a new measure was passed that addressed that issue directly. The law of 30 August 1883 set in motion an aggressive purging of the magistracy, in which the simple

[29] Achille Dalsème, *A Travers le Palais* (E. Dentu, Paris, 1881), 73.

[30] The President of the Republic himself, Jules Grévy, compared the magistracy to a barrel of vinegar, that 'stubbornly remains vinegar, no matter how much good wine I pour in..'. Cited by Jean-Pierre Royer, *Histoire de la Justice en France* (Presses Universitaires de France, Paris, 1995), 580.

denunciation of a judge for having anti-republican opinions was sufficient to have him removed from the bench.[31] In opposition to angry objections from judges, who declared their independence to be under attack, republican leaders responded that the principle of life-long appointment was incompatible with the Republic itself, which demanded direct accountability from its representatives. The result of the law was that approximately one thousand judges were fired within just a few weeks.[32] Not a few of these, it can be pointed out, turned to the Bar as a second career.

Attention to the problem of conservative standing magistrates in the early 1880s naturally led to scrutiny of other aspects of the legal system that seemed inconsistent with republican principles. At first, the Order of Advocates was spared the scrutiny of the republican state, as the lawyers were more often seen as a countervailing influence to the reactionary bench.[33] In addition to this, a favourable decision of the Council of State over the issue of the legal identity of the Order of Advocates appeared in 1881. According to this decision, the Bar was not an *établissement public*, since it had the right to be a party to legal cases with no need for prior authorisation from the State. However, it was not to be considered an organisation with a purely civil status either, since it could not accept or hold funds in its own name.[34] This legal ambiguity meant that it was unclear whether the Order was under the jurisdiction of civil or administrative law, an uncertainty that leaders of the legal profession cited as evidence of its special mission, and a status that was somehow outside the categories of positive law. This logic was the key argument for the absolute sovereignty of the Council of Discipline over its decisions for decades to come.[35]

Nevertheless, republican attacks on the independence of the judiciary made some lawyers nervous, and justifiably so. It was in Paris that the first serious challenge to the legitimacy of the Order of Advocates appeared since the Commune. In November 1883, a proposal to abolish the 'monopoly' of the advocates was submitted to the *Conseil Général de Paris* by a young council member and advocate, Joseph Henri Michelin.

[31] Royer, *Histoire de la Justice*, 599.

[32] Jean-Pierre Machelon, 'L'Epuration Républicaine: La loi du 30 Août 1883', in *Les Epurations de la Magistrature de la Révolution à la Liberation* (Loysel, Paris, 1994), 87–103.

[33] Dalsème, *A travers le palais*, 120.

[34] C. B. [Charles Beudant], 'Questions Administratives, jurisprudence de Conseil d'Etat', (1881) 49 *Revue Pratique de Droit Français*, 404–5.

[35] Charles Dejongh, 'De la Personnalité Morale de l'Ordre des Avocats en France et en Belgique', (1902) 29 *Journal de Droit International Privé*, 784. On the issue of the Order's sovereignty, see my dissertation, 'Advocates of the Republic: The Paris Bar and Legal Culture in early Third Republic France, 1870–1914', (New York University, 1999), ch 2.

He proposed to 'suppress' the Order of Advocates in the name of free access to justice and in order to do away with the procedural inefficiency of the present legal system. Michelin attacked this 'worst of all monopolies', the advocate's right to plead in court, that required a lawyer not only to have a law degree, but to be approved by the *Conseil de l'Ordre*.

Discussion of the proposal in the municipal council was heated, to say the least. To a chorus of protests from several of the lawyers present, Michelin was defended by an associate who argued that 'even the most worthy plaintiffs rarely find an advocate to defend them, if beforehand a certain sum of money has not been deposited'.[36] Other colleagues were incensed at this display of disrespect toward the Bar. One council member responded that the claims were absurd, that the Order provided defense at no cost and that lawyers did not even accept money for their services. In response to this a man named Weber spoke up, first citing cases of prospective members of the Bar being refused for their political beliefs, and finally revealing that he himself had suffered from the tyranny of the Order's governing council, having been rejected from the register due to his involvement in business dealings. Weber accused the Council of Discipline of being more concerned with his 'liberal' politics than anything else. After three sessions of discussion, Michelin's statement was finally approved by the comfortable margin of 42 to 15.[37]

The following year, Michelin was elected as a deputy to the National Assembly representing the department of the Seine. He was a Radical Socialist and sat with the group known as the *extrême gauche intransigeante*. Like many of his colleagues, he soon became enamoured with the populist nationalism General Boulanger. While Michelin was registered with the Bar, he did not practice law but rather devoted his attention to his political career and editing the radical journal *L'Action*. His proposal to do away with the Paris Bar in the Municipal Council was submitted to the Ministry of Justice, which then gave it to the parliamentary committee that considered questions of civil procedure. Meanwhile, he brought his motion to the National Assembly, where it became the first of a series of attempts over the next twenty years to curtail or do away with the Bar's monopoly on legal services.

Michelin based his bill on two major ideas. First, that the lawyers' 'privilege' contributed significantly to the high cost of justice, as well as the overly complicated nature of the legal system. A private individual seeking to go to court over some injustice had to hire an *avoué*, as well as an *avocat*, since the former had no right to plead cases orally before the courts, thus doubling the cost of justice. 'This state of things cannot last

[36] Archives de Paris [AP] D 2 N[1].48C 55. 'Voeu tendant à la suppression du monopole des avocats', report of 6 Oct 1884.

[37] AP D2N[1].48 C 55 Conseil Général de Paris, report of 10 Oct 1884.

any longer', he declared, 'Justice must, in effect, be organized in the interest of those who use the system and not those who profit from it'.[38] Secondly, Michelin brought out the political nature of the profession, pointing to the case of former members of the Commune who had been refused admission to the Bar, but also what he claimed was the conservative Catholic bias of the *Conseil*, which made one's spiritual beliefs subject to their approval: 'There is here an incontestable abuse and a very real violation of the principle of freedom of conscience'.[39] Michelin suggested that the Bar be replaced by an open system of legal defence, where all plaintiffs could speak for themselves before a judge or have someone of their choosing do it for them. Advocates themselves could continue to exist, but they would not be regulated by a professional body and they would no longer have a monopoly on the practice of speaking in court.

The Bill was examined by a parliamentary commission which was to decide its merits as a subject of debate in the Chamber of Deputies. This was a decisive stage of the legislative process. Given the large amount of legislation submitted by deputies, the commissions performed the important function of triage to determine which proposals were worthy of their colleagues' attention.[40] Within the commission, serious criticisms of the proposal were again voiced by lawyers. The conservative deputy Keller argued that

> 'the corporation of advocates as it is organized offers guarantees of knowledge and honor. In leaving these guarantees behind, precious for the public and especially for weaker parties (petits justiciables), we would be favoring the agents d'affaires ('businessmen' acting as officious counsel) to the detriment of the public good'.[41]

Despite the clear support of a number of members of the Bar for Keller, the commission voted to prolong the life of the Bill and to present it on the floor of Parliament.

The report that was drafted by the commission showed no evidence of its internal disagreements, and was remarkably aggressive toward the Bar, calling it an 'arbitrary and abusive organization', and referring to its suppression during the Revolution in the name of 'freedom of labor' as 'a great act of patriotism and logic'.[42] Colfavru, speaking before the Chamber of Deputies in favour of Michelin's Bill, was passionate about the underlying justice of doing away with the legal profession. The Order

[38] *Journal Officiel*, Annexe 498, 1 March, 1886, 1176.

[39] *Journal Officiel*, Annexe 498, 1 March, 1886, 1176.

[40] R. K. Gooch, *The French Parliamentary Committee System* (Archon Books, Hamden, Connecticut, 1969), 156–7.

[41] Archives Nationales [AN] C*II 853, Quatrième Commision d'Initiative Parlementaire, 19 March, 1886.

[42] *Journal Officiel* Annexe 670, 15 April, 1886, 1371.

of Advocates, he claimed, was an 'anachronism' that recalled the privileges of the Old Regime,

> . . . with the difference that [since the Revolution] political passions have had a much bigger role in the *conseils*, which have stopped at no violence, and persecuted the proudest of independent spirits to the point of ostracism. How many men of character and talent have been rejected in this way or excluded from a career that gave them assurances, as solemn as they were insincere, that it was open to all men of learning, with no limitations on the person or his opinions![43]

He argued that the only possible objections came from

> 'certain advocates who have but a tepid affection for democratic institutions, and who, with dubious personal motives, pretend to protect the interests of their fellow citizens while reserving the exclusive right to defend them'.

As for the *agents d'affaire*, Colfavru did not seek to whitewash their character, instead laying the blame for their existence directly on the Bar itself:

> 'it is the intolerance of the Council of Discipline that leads to the recruitment of this phalanx, of whom the great number of advocates forego neither the assistance nor the cooperation'.[44]

The commission's approval of Michelin's proposal encouraged similar initiatives to be launched, as they had a much better chance of being heard since they could be grouped together with the first bill. Vergoin, a moderate republican, proposed a 'transformation' of the profession. His bill focused on how internal resentments within the profession had taken on a public dimension. He noted what he called '*les bizarreries*' of the Order's rules, and again emphasised the sinister potential of the *Conseils de l'Ordre*, 'worrisome jurisdictions that are these secret tribunals . . .'. which he saw as a danger to the public, but also 'for the advocates themselves, alternatively subject to anonymous evaluations and inquisitorial affronts from colleagues and equals'. Vergoin made plain that these sentiments were especially directed at the Paris Bar, 'where the severity of the council's rules reaches its greatest intensity'. His proposal sheds light on how lawyers were perceived as being out of step with the times and ultimately even incapable of performing their basic function because of their strange professional culture. The advocate was seen as a member of a

> 'closed caste . . . condemned by its special rules to an isolation from practical life, the consequence of which sometimes goes so far as to corrupt the sense of Justice itself and the very notion of Truth'.[45]

[43] *Journal Officiel* Annexe 670, 15 April, 1886, 1371.
[44] *Journal Officiel* Annexe 670, 15 April, 1886, 1371.
[45] *Journal Officiel* Annexe 1260, 18 Nov 1886, 519–520.

Responses to the various Bills introduced in Parliament showed there was widespread sympathy for the proposed measures. Even the mainstream *Le Temps*, a newspaper commonly read by lawyers and businessmen, suggested that the spirit of the recent parliamentary initiatives was not misdirected and that it was in fact time to open the doors of the Order to a wider public.[46] However, the next issue of the paper contained a rather barbed response from Edmond Allou, a former *bâtonnier* who was among the most senior members of the Paris Bar. He started out by expressing shock at the ideas in the parliamentary proposals, and asked sarcastically whether soon everyone would want to be allowed to practice medicine. As for the idea of abolishing the Bar altogether, he wrote:

> 'If we could succeed in realizing this strange progress today, I would wish as a vengeance on our reformers a great trial with the defense led, naturally, by officious counsel, and elected magistrates to judge it'.[47]

There was certainly no attempt by an ageing doyen of the profession like Allou to justify his opposition to the democratic principle. He made no bones about admitting that the corpus of lawyers did enjoy a monopoly over pleading in court, he simply justified this as being for the public's own good. Indeed, this sort of paternalist rhetoric is how many older members of the profession met outside criticism. The comments of members of the Bar reflect pride in their elitism, and an underlying distaste for the democratisation of legal institutions. In his speech to the young interns of the Bar in November 1886, the *bâtonnier* Martini denounced the Order's critics in these terms:

> 'they sacrifice the public interest to that invidious and lowly spirit of false democracy that seeks to curb everything, men and institutions, to its level of vulgar mediocrity. They take umbrage at our Order: they want to do away with it, and their dream is to debase our profession by opening it up to those unworthy of practicing it'.[48]

But over time, leaders of the profession began to make a greater effort to respond to their critics. Though the fundamental ideas changed little, defenders of the Order sought to explain exactly how the Bar worked for the public good. In a speech responding to the parliamentary attacks, Charles Rivière emphasised that the Order of Advocates 'is a public institution, invested with a high social mission'. He drew a distinction between the Bar and other liberal professions over this idea of *service public*. Because its function was so closely tied to the state, the Bar's com-

[46] *Le Temps*, 23 March, 1886, 1.

[47] *Le Temps*, 1 April, 1886, 1.

[48] Martini, *De la suppression de l'Ordre des Avocats*, 1886, 27. The speech also appears in *Bulletin de la société amicale des secrétaires and anciens secrétaires de la conférence du stage* [*BSCA*], (1886) 26–62.

mitment to the public good was all the more manifest than that of physicians, scientists, engineers or philosophers. Yet Rivière emphasized that this link to the State had to be carefully circumscribed. The State should have no role in naming or monitoring members of the profession. Here, once again, the honour of the profession was at stake. Such increased state control of the profession would represent, '. . . the end of our glorious traditions, the ruin of the moral grandeur of our Order, the lowering of our profession to the level of a vulgar trade'.[49]

Leaders of the Paris Bar insisted on the important contributions the profession made to civil society. The best example of this, and the practice increasingly publicised by members of the Order, was the tradition of providing free legal counsel to the poor. Senior lawyers invoked *assistance judiciaire* as evidence of the selflessness and social conscience of the profession. Starting in the early 1880s, for example, the *bâtonnier* would invariably conclude his annual speech to the interns with a ritual enumeration of the cases of assistance, specifically presented as a justification for the profession. But the issue of legal assistance was not so clear-cut, since it could serve both as evidence of the Order's mission of public service, and also the exploitation of young lawyers of modest backgrounds. In the last years of the century, it was the subject of the difficulty of entering the legal profession, as well as other *professions libérales*, that began to capture the interest of publicists. In fact, interest in careerism led to a proliferation of new publications that served as guides to the best possible occupations according to a young man's talents, sensibilities and goals. Career guides also stressed the difficulty of preparatory studies for the work, its social standing and later possibilities for advancement. Through the decades that preceded the First World War, career guides emphasised the risks inherent in seeking a position as an advocate.

Authors noted that studies were long and expensive, and did not guarantee the ability to practise. '*Les débuts*', as one book remarked, often meant fifteen years or more.[50] According to another author, by the time the young advocate took his oath, he had cost his family 20,000 francs, and wouldn't earn any significant income for a good ten years after that.[51] All emphasised the need for some independent means in order to become an advocate. Indeed, Cresson's manual itself recommended an income of no less than 6,000 *livres* in order to survive in the profession. Although they stressed the great social prestige of the *homme de loi*, the guides invariably warned that such rewards awaited only a tiny number of aspirants, and the typical advocate could end up far less well off than less ambitious professionals. Without a fortune, the advocate

[49] Charles Rivière, *De la Suppression de l'Ordre des Avocats: Réponse à la Proposition Michelin* (Imprimerie de Mougin-Rusand, Lyon, 1886), 13, 15.

[50] Lafon, *Pour devenir avocat*, 78.

[51] Jacquemart, *Professions et Métiers*, 153, 156.

'would always have more trouble balancing his budget than the typical ministerial assistant, however modest one may imagine the surroundings (*appartements*) of the latter'.[52]

The guides never failed to mention the role of the Council of Discipline among the obstacles faced by young lawyers. While such books tended to make light of the rhetoric of professional manuals and the speeches of the *stage*, they nevertheless underlined how these rules presented very real constraints for the young advocate trying to earn a living. In one early and extreme example, a presentation of the profession to young readers published in 1881, the author went as far as to recount the story of an impoverished young advocate who had a promising career ahead of him after obtaining his degree from the faculty, but had been unable to get any cases and lived in poverty. In desperation he threw himself at a client, but was reprimanded by the Council for this act of solicitation, and ended up starving to death in his lonely attic-room.[53] In a serial published in the 1890s, another author devoted his efforts to exposing 'the ravages that a narrow and false conception of the profession of advocate can cause to a pure and honest soul'. Accused of calumny by members of the Bar, no less a figure than Raymond Poincaré came to the author's defence.[54] Such stories could not have encouraged young aspirants to the Bar. The prospect of earning the title of advocate and yet not being able to support even a moderate existence was daunting, and the Bar's traditional restrictions were presented as central to the task.

The theme of the overcrowding of professional life became fully articulated at the turn of the century with the publication of a tract by Henry Bérenger, former head of the student association of the University of Paris. Bérenger lashed out at the general system of higher education that he saw as 'a veritable factory for producing proletarians.'[55] He denounced the promise of meritocratic social mobility under the Republic as nothing but a sham, and contended that thousands of young people were destined to a life of severe disillusionment after believing they could accede to a higher station by preparing to enter the liberal professions: 'what good is this democratic dupery of liberal professions accessible to the People?'[56] Bérenger argued that rather than giving young people an honest trade they could be proud of and that would earn them a decent living, the Republican regime was simply generating bitterness by feeding off of the inflated expectations of students, without even

[52] Lafon, *Pour devenir avocat*, 75.

[53] Dalsème, *A travers le palais*, 78.

[54] The author in question was Masson-Forestier. *Le Temps,* 9 Nov 1896, 3.

[55] Henry Bérenger, *Les Prolétaires Intellectuels en France* (Editions de la Revue, Paris, 1901), 39.

[56] Bérenger, *Les proletaires intellectuels*, 41.

giving them any practical expertise in return. Indeed, for Bérenger this lack of 'real' or applied knowledge characterised the course of study for all of the liberal professions, the implication being that the obligatory diplomas were artificial requirements aimed at draining the savings of middle class students.

Bérenger claimed that the worst of the liberal professions by far was the Bar, where the greatest number of students imagined themselves to be headed. He maintained that no more than one in twelve advocates earned even enough to live on, and even these would make virtually nothing in their first ten years of practice.[57] The experience of years of poverty and idleness presented a veritable social danger for this new class, which Bérenger clearly meant to stand as a dark reflection of the much vaunted *nouvelles couches*, where acrimony overtook precisely those young men whose personal honour and devotion to their career had to be completely above suspicion.[58] Like Maurice Barrès, whose novel *Les Déracinés* undoubtedly inspired him, Bérenger's tract attempted to capitalise on the frustrations of a middle-class that had been promised so much by the Republic.

THE DEMOGRAPHIC EXPANSION

But how accurate was the notion of an 'intellectual proletariat', in particular as it applied to the legal profession? Were the numbers of young lawyers in Paris really multiplying at a rate greater than that of the population as a whole, the expansion of the economy, or than what had been seen in the earlier periods? The statistics thrown around by publicists like Bérenger were dubious at best, though they were often taken up by the mainstream press and even lawyers themselves. Most importantly, however, such figures rarely attempted to show the evolution in context over any significant period of time. Table 1 shows the progression of advocates registered at the Paris Bar as well as the figure for the total number of advocates in France. The three columns on the right refer to the corresponding numbers of *stagiaires*, the young graduates of the law faculty considering a career in the Bar.

These figures show the steady expansion of the Paris Bar starting in the 1880s and an overall increase of more than 150 per cent before the First World War. More striking than this absolute increase, however, is the dramatic shift in the weight of the Parisians as a proportion of the total population of lawyers in France. From less than one in six in the early years of the Republic, nearly one in every three French advocates were registered

[57] Bérenger, *Les proletaires intellectuels*, 9.

[58] Bérenger, *Les proletaires intellectuels*, 20.

Table 1: Advocates and Stagiaires, *1872–1913*

	Advocates			*Stagiaires*		
	Paris	France	% in Paris	Paris	France	% in Paris
1872	613	3,969	15.4	831	2,156	38.5
1875	701	4,025	17.4	772	2,277	33.9
1880	739	4,121	17.9	791	2,147	36.8
1885	832	4,279	19.4	1,043	2,567	40.6
1890	947	4,430	21.4	1,000	2,454	40.7
1895	1,035	4,426	23.4	967	2,393	40.4
1900	1,142	4,492	25.4	939	2,197	42.7
1905	1,247	4,638	26.9	919	2,202	41.7
1910	1,352	4,660	29.0	1,002	2,545	39.4
1913	1,583	5,023	31.5	905	2,288	39.6

Sources: *Compte Général de l'Administration de la Justice*, *Tableau de l'Ordre des Avocats* and *Annuaire des Professions Judiciaires et Juridiques*.

at the Paris Bar by World War I.[59] Indeed, the overall growth of the population of lawyers nationally is roughly equal to that of the Paris Bar alone. Outside of Paris, the profession was in stagnation,[60]and in many regions the early Third Republic was a period of desertion of the Bar.[61]

[59] It should be noted that no figure in the period preceding World War I approaches the number of advocates *per capita* achieved in France under the July Monarchy. Jean-Louis Halperin has found that relative to the general population, there was one advocate for every 6,969 inhabitants in France in 1830, and one for every 8,519 inhabitants in 1900 (Halpérin, *Les professions judiciaires et juridiques*). However, it is crucial to emphasise the important differences in the social composition of the Bar at these times. By the end of the 19th century, the figure of the 'gentleman lawyer' who rarely practiced was in decline. The amount of litigation had also increased markedly by the end of the century.

[60] The number of advocates registered *outside* of Paris was as follows:

1872: 3,356	1895: 3,391
1875: 3,326	1900: 3,350
1880: 3,382	1905: 3,391
1885: 3,447	1910: 3,308
1890: 3,483	1913: 3,440

Source: Table 1.

[61] Pascal Plas has found this to be the case in Limoges and the Limousin, for example. 'Le Barreau, carrefour des elites locales: l'exemple limousin' in Sylvie Gillaume, (ed) *Les Elites Fin-de-Siècle* (Editions de la M.S.H.A., Bordeaux, 1992), 76 n 52.

At the same time, the number of Parisian *stagiaires*, after a weaker period in the 1870s and early 1880s, remained approximately stable as a proportion of the national total at about 40 per cent. This large figure shows that those *stagiaires* who ended up in other careers were more often found in the capital, as one might expect, given this population's common parallel interests in politics, government work, journalism or big business. Until 1891 there were more interns than advocates registered in Paris, whilst this was never close to being the case elsewhere in France. Over time, however, the interns' openness to other careers declined significantly, with a greater and greater proportion entering the Bar, and the *stage* gradually losing its position as a starting point for a variety of elite careers. It is not possible to say with great precision what this proportion was. However, it is clear that only a fraction of the *stagiaires*, no more than one in ten, as Bérenger and others suggested, ended up practising at the Bar in the long run.[62]

The dramatic increase of Parisian lawyers as a proportion of the profession nationally is a key to understanding the importance of the Paris *Conseil de l'Ordre* within the profession, and the conflicting interests that led to tensions with provincial orders in later years. But did this redistribution simply reflect a booming demand for legal services in the capital? The above figures do not tell us anything specific about the relative availability of work for the advocates. The following table provides statistics for the number of civil cases registered on the *rôle*, that is, the calendar of court cases in both Paris and France, as well as the number of cases argued before the *Tribunal Correctionnel*, the court that considered minor crimes (*délits*), and the serious criminal cases before the *Cour d'Assises*. This last category included the most spectacular and notorious criminal cases. Yet although it received the most attention from the press and epitomised the public's notion of the lawyers' work, the Assizes provided only a fraction of the number of cases available to advocates *(See Table 2)*.

This table is not an exact statement of the number of cases pleaded by advocates in a given year. Many of the cases listed on the *rôle*, for example, were rescheduled or abandoned. Nevertheless, the figures provide a solid *index* of the litigiousness of French society and the demand for the

[62] Given that the *stage* lasted at least 3 years and no more than 5 years, then the potential number of entrants in a given year should be about one fourth of the total number of interns in that year. This leads to a figure of about 200–250 *each year,* yet there is nothing close to this level, but rather something closer to 25 per year at the very most, that is, about one-tenth of the total number of potential new members on the register. Comparing this figure to the large proportion of students who declared their intentions to pursue entry into the Bar suggests the significant degree of 'self-elimination' among aspirants to the profession.

Table 2.: Civil and Criminal Cases, 1870–1910

	Paris			France		
	Rôle	Trib. Cor.	Assises	*Rôle*	Trib. Cor.	Assises
1870	21,923	18,692*	302	138,999	142,520*	2,796
1875	23,347	19,919	586	163,180	167,214	3,736
1880	21,978	22,043	341	176,145	170,260	3,258
1885	31,987	n.a.	n.a.	200,169	n.a.	n.a.
1890	30,025	25,271	301	189,879	191,766	2,982
1895	26,198	24,830	306	182,686	196,295	2,526
1900	28,289	19,278	266	183,860	167,179	2,283
1905	34,921	19,208	236	188,859	173,804	2,236
1910	39,174	26,584	251	182,531	181,046	2,160

* figures for 1869.
Source: *Compte Général de l'Administration de la Justice Civile et Commerciale*.

services of advocates from one period to another.[63] The table demonstrates that periods of stagnation in the demand for legal services, likely tied to economic downturn, characterised the evolution of the case-load both in Paris and in France as a whole. This lack of growth appeared first in the 1870s, during the period of Depression that affected the whole of Europe. After rising in the early 1880s, the number of civil cases declined from a peak in 1887 and reached a low point in 1896. Thereafter, there is again a healthy increase through the remaining pre-war years. Using this information to create an index of the demand for legal services, it is possible to get a sense of the availability of work for members of the legal profession by contrasting this series with that of the total number of advocates. The resulting data is arranged in Table 3.

This table shows a relatively small difference in the number of cases per advocate at the outset of the Third Republic when comparing Paris and the rest of France. From the early 1870s until nearly the end of the century, however, there is healthy growth in this proportion nationally, while

[63] On the notion of litigiousness in French society, cf. Bernard Schnapper 'Pour une géographie des mentalités judiciaires: la litigiosité en France au XIXe siècle' in *Voies Nouvelles en Histoires du Droit: la justice, la famille, la répression pénale (XVIème-XXème siècles)*, (Presses Universitaires de France, Paris, 1991), 395–419.

Table 3: Work Index, 1870–1913

	Total Cases *(Paris)*	Work *Index*	Total Cases *(France)*	Work *Index*
1870	40,917	63.6*	284,315	72.0*
1875	43,852	62.6	334,130	83.0
1880	44,362	60.0	349,663	84.9
1890	55,597	58.7	384,627	86.8
1895	52,334	49.6	381,507	86.1
1900	47,803	41.9	353,322	78.7
1905	54,365	43.6	364,899	78.7
1910	66,009	48.8	365,737	78.5
1913	62,313	39.4	379,900	75.6

*advocate figures are from 1871.
Source: Tables 2.1 and 2.2.

Paris sees a drop of more than one third in the available cases per lawyer by 1900. In the 1890s, there were just over half as many cases per advocate in Paris as in France, and in 1905 there were more than 80% more cases per lawyer. Thus, more than the absolute numbers of advocates, this relation demonstrates the important disparity between the situation of the Paris Bar, despite its heavy proportion of the national profession, and that of provincial advocates. The table also shows that the main change over time occurred in the category of civil cases, which include commercial cases heard by civil courts. At the same time, an increasing proportion of the cases in this list, indeed those most likely to be available to the youngest members of the profession, were not a source of income for the advocates at all. Nor in general were they a source of future paying clients. The legal assistance caseload was overwhelmingly given to advocates with little experience or clientèle of their own. This was especially true in Paris, where all but a few cases were handed out to advocates in their first few years of practice. The defenders were named by the *bâtonnier* from the list of advocates registered in the *stage*. As the following table shows, the number of cases of legal assistance increased fourfold in the period 1875–1905.[64]

[64] A similar increase occurred nationally, with the proportion of cases in Paris staying steady at about one-fifth of that total throughout the period 1870–1914.

Table 4: Legal Assistance in Paris, 1872–1913

1872	5,107	1895	14,447
1875	5,112	1900	17,400
1880	6,646	1905	20,565
1885	10,632	1910	20,675
1890	13,025	1913	23,547

Source: Compte Général de l'Administration de la Justice Civile et Commerciale.

When the *bâtonnier* Martini declared to his young audience that their role in legal assistance 'never has seemed a burden to you', he may well have heard some shuffling in the ranks.[65] Ten years later, the *bâtonnier* Pouillet spoke of how these cases could lead to greater things, given enough time: '. . . within their humble milieu, you will gain real popularity, and your clientele will form, little by little, out of the recognition of your clients from legal assistance'.[66] He admitted, however, that this waiting would be an economic burden for some, 'it is not here that one risks suddenly coming into a fortune'.[67] By this time, even the leaders of the Order admitted that this essentially free service was taken advantage of by plaintiffs who were not always among the truly poor. It was not only that the number of cases of legal assistance was growing, but that they made an increasingly significant proportion of the total number of court cases. Whereas, in the 1860s, cases of legal assistance had made up only a small minority of the cases in the register of the civil court of the Seine, this proportion grew dramatically in later years. By 1875, nearly one-fifth of all cases before the civil court were the result of initial requests for legal assistance. This figure rose to nearly 40 per cent in 1890, and well over half of all cases in 1900, more than double the proportion for France as a whole.[68] This evolution illustrates the tremendous role of unpaid services provided by young aspirants to the profession, particularly in the Paris Bar.

[65] *BSCA* 8, 1886, 40.

[66] *BSCA* 18, 1896, 114.

[67] *BSCA* 18, 1896, 116.

[68] These statistics were compiled using the technique employed by Bernard Schnapper for the whole of France, which showed the proportion reaching about one-quarter at the same time. For Paris, statistics had to be adjusted to exclude affairs from the *Tribunal de Paix* and *Tribunal de Commerce*. The specific results are as follows: 1875: 19.7%, 1880: 27.2%, 1890: 39.0%, 1900: 55.4%. 'Rapport au Président de la Republique sur l'Administration de la Justice Civile et Commerciale en France et en Algerie pendant les Années 1881 à 1900', *Compte générale de l'Administration de la Justice . . .*, v–xlvi.

THE PUSH FOR REFORM

By the turn of the century, demands for the reform of professional standards from within the Order itself joined the parliamentary initiatives. Critics distributed pamphlets at the *Palais de Justice* or wrote articles in the press that often focused on the economic difficulties of young members of the profession. A pamphlet published by Antonin Oudart deplored the huge amount of unpaid work given to young lawyers. Like several of the parliamentary critics, he invoked the language of freedom of labour to argue his case.[69] Oudart noted also that the system was a windfall for the lowly *agent d'affaires*, who were able to steer their clients to the free services of an advocate, and then demand a fee they could keep for themselves. It was indeed a common strategy for young advocates to resort to collaboration with an *agent d'affaires* in order to find clients. This tactic was just one of the ways that professional rules were bent and even broken on a regular basis. According to a reformer named Jacques Bonzon, reflecting on his years as a young advocate in the 1890s, for referrals, the best bet was friendship with a judge, a prison guard or owner of a large bar (ie a public house).[70]

The reality was that advocates did demand payment for their services. The important principle was to avoid any public statement, or any record of the transaction that could be used as evidence in court; the demands had to be made within the sanctuary of the advocate's office.[71] The most common way around the rules appears to have been a letter to the client, declaring '*il manque une pièce à votre dossier.*' If the confused client asked which document was missing, some advocates would go further, writing '*il manque la pièce de vin* [*vingt* = twenty] . . .'.[72] Often lawyers would not plead until the payment had been made. It also happened that two opposing advocates agreed to stall a case interminably if one of their clients had not made payment. Other tactics could be used to solicit cases. Reports were common, for example, of lawyers who would attempt to bribe courtroom guards to steer clients their way when they had the chance.[73] But such actions always carried the danger of being found out. They were not ignored by the Council of Discipline, which was active in punishing far less substantive infractions. The large number

[69] Antonin Oudart, *Situation du Barreau de France*. 1902, 3.

[70] Jacques Bonzon, 'La Lutte Sociale dans le Prétoire', in *Les Echos Parisiens* 1 July, 1911, 3.

[71] See, for example, *Le Palais de Justice de Paris*, 131.

[72] Leroux, *Sur mon Chemin*, 191. Jean de Bonnefon, 'La Suppression de l'Ordre des Avocats', in (1901) 25 *La France Judiciaire*, 183.

[73] *Le Temps*, 8 March, 1894, 1; Lafon also suggests this tactic to young lawyers, *Pour Devenir Avocat*, 93.

of cases touching on the advocate's official place of residence in the last decades of the century is evidence of the Council's growing concern about maintaining control over the expanding population of lawyers.

The Council was empowered to deliver one of a series of different sanctions against advocates who were guilty of infractions. These included formal reprimand, suspension for up to one year, and disbarment. The most common form of sanction was *avertissement*, or warning. This could be presented in writing or informally, as a *non-lieu avec avertissement paternel*. As Cresson writes, 'when the mistake is excusable, it is not punished in the legal sense of the word; a remark suffices, and this remark is feared'.[74] It seems he was right about this. Gaston Leroux, a young advocate who became a court journalist and later a successful novelist, wrote of the profound humiliation caused by the Council's reprimands, which became known to the world of the *Palais de Justice*. Leroux described the case of a young *stagiaire* who had gone to plead a case in the provinces, but had failed to pay homage to the local *bâtonnier*. On his return to Paris, he found himself 'dragged' into the office of his own *bâtonnier* and given a serious tongue-lashing.[75]

Leroux had had similar experiences as a young lawyer. He once gave in and finally paid a plumbing bill for work that had never been done, since the *bâtonnier* had called on him every week about it: 'One can no longer owe a tailor for three shirts without them sticking their noses into it!'[76] For Leroux, the worst aspect of this intense scrutiny was precisely that it compromised the lawyer's sense of self-respect. Advocates would run to the Council to relate rumours about a colleague, or demand they sanction a competitor. He denounced their desire 'to intervene in the most private affairs of the advocates they have "under their blade", which leads them to welcome story-tellers and back-room gossips, who lead them to order inquests concerning events that have no bearing on the profession of advocate, never distinguishing the man from the professional, which allows them, in a word, all tyranny . . .'.[77]

The actions of the disciplinary council appear to have increased with the growing population of lawyers at the end of the century, as leaders of the profession recognised the difficult financial situation faced by many younger lawyers. The fact that more cases went to appeal illustrates that advocates were not only willing to defy the rules, but to challenge the council's right to carry out disciplinary action based on those rules.[78] Professional speeches of this period took up the theme of patience as the

[74] Cresson, *Usages et Règles*, vol. 2, 147.
[75] Leroux, *Sur mon Chemin*, 182.
[76] Leroux, *Sur mon Chemin*, 182.
[77] Leroux, *Sur mon Chemin*, 180–81.
[78] For example, *Gazette du Palais*, 1896, vol. 1, 118–120; 1898, vol.1, 653.

greatest of virtues for the young advocate. For leaders like Nicolet, *bâtonnier* in 1878, the problem had been one of unrealistic and immature ambitions that would soon give way to common sense.[79] By the turn of the century, the rhetoric was both more realistic and more pointed. While assuring the interns before him that 'the Council of Discipline is a family court whose justice is above all paternal', the *bâtonnier* of 1895 recognized that what pushed young advocates to break the rules of the Order was sometimes pure economic necessity.[80] A few years later, the *bâtonnier* Danet was direct and frank with the *stagiaires* in a way that his predecessors would not have dared. His speech was a clear warning to continue to observe the rules as described in the advocates' professional manuals:

> The prolonged wait for clients, slow to show confidence in you, will lead you to disillusion, at times even an inner rebellion . . . prefer waiting to compromise. Know to resist all solicitations coming from unscrupulous intermediaries, who are never disinterested and seek to exploit your inexperience: they can only wound your dignity and compromise your honor![81]

Danet was referring once again to the *agents d'affaires*, and his speech shows an awareness that young advocates were tempted by the methods of these outlaw professionals. Attention to the *agents* during the *stage* only intensified in this period. Charles Rivière attempted to explain the phenomenon to his audience, saying that while a few were honest business people, others came to the practice out of frustration with their vulgar lot in life:

> 'they did not know how to keep themselves within the honest and mediocre living that the future promised them, they abandoned their regular function and threw themselves into what is called, in a phrase that is as vague as it is descriptive, *les affaires* [business]'.[82]

Among the 'types' who turned to this occupation, he included '. . . the advocate barred from the register of his order, his heart filled with a bitter desire for vengeance, giving his hateful advice, pushing his clients to the extremities of the Law . . .'.[83]

What sorts of practices were employed by the *agents d'affaires*? In an article entitled '*Les Affaires*', one *jurisconsulte*, as he referred to himself, explained some of the strategies he used to get clients. Businessmen like himself had the advantage over advocates, he wrote, in that they could go

79 *BSCA* 1, 1879, 37.

80 *BSCA* 17, 1895, 49.

81 *BSCA* 24, 1902, 108. The contrast with the message of Cresson when he served as bâtonnier, which denied any sort of problems of this nature, could not be more stark; *BSCA* 12, 1890, 31–63.

82 Rivière, *De la suppression*, 7.

83 Rivière, *De la suppression*, 7.

out and find cases. Doing so effectively was simply a matter of creativity. He recalled that in the mid-1880s, at the time of the legalization of divorce, one agency made a fortune by researching all of the marital separations (*separations de corps*) of the previous 15 or 20 years, and sending out letters to them. For a time, the agency processed as many as 25 divorces per day. He recommended that anyone starting out should go to their local shopkeepers and offer to take care of any debtors they were having trouble with, in exchange for a percentage of the money recovered. On the other hand, one could find the names of people being sued through payoffs to bailiffs or clerks, and contact them with an offer of services.[84] Finally, he proudly recounted his most recent tactic:

> A short time ago, one of my clients was deceased, Boulevard Voltaire. One hour after the declaration of death at the *mairie*, the widow received the following note: Madame, I have learned of the death of *Monsieur* your husband. His will could be the cause of difficulties. It would be in your interest, Madame, to come and see me immediately.[85]

Faced with a client with little money but a strong case, an *agent d'affaires* could engage the process of *assistance judiciaire*, finding an advocate who would do the early work on the case, and then take over and charge a contingency fee if it was successful.[86]

Despite such abuses, the governing council insisted on the importance of refusing any form of payment from the assisted party, even when they won a judgment from the court. The *bâtonnier* Pouillet explained the rules governing cases of legal assistance:

> The advocate, in this case, can not only not request payment; but he cannot receive any, in any form, even if his client, saved by him, acquires a fortune; even if years pass between the court decision and the day payment is offered; even if, in the meantime, (the advocate) has himself become poor.[87]

Rather than becoming more flexible with respect to such rules of conduct, the Council repeatedly chose to reaffirm them in the last decades of the century.[88] This inflexibility was the principal target of parliamentary reformers like Maurice Vergoin and advocates like Paul Moysen, who wrote the most influential pamphlet criticizing the Council of Discipline. Moysen's *Réformes Pratiques* was the object of much debate among lawyers at the turn of the century. Declaring the traditions of the Order antiquated and contrary to the interests of young advocates in particular,

[84] Jules Gourbeyre, 'Les Affaires', in *L'Avocat, Journal Hebdomodaire de Droit pour Tous*, 17, 4 March 1897, 2.

[85] Gourbeyre, 'Les Affaires', 2.

[86] Gourbeyre, 'Les Affaires', 2.

[87] *BSCA* 8, 1896, 111.

[88] AN AD XIXj 57, Decision of 7 Nov 1899.

Moysen called for a professional body that would be 'more active, more dynamic, less sterile in its results'.[89]

In a manner similar to Vergoin and his supporters, Moysen saw the liberalisation of the profession as a means of saving it from itself. Already Vergoin had argued that greater flexibility and realism were the only antidotes to the threat from unregulated competitors: 'the democratic organization of the Bar being the only remedy for the invasion of the *agents d'affaires*, the only barrier that can legitimately and victoriously oppose their ever-increasing activity'. His vision of overhauling the profession was based upon the idea that the advocate was a *mandataire*, that is, worked under a contract to provide services to a client in exchange for a fee. Publicly recognizing this status would mean that advocates could plead before all courts, including the commercial and administrative jurisdictions that were closed to them so long as they were forbidden from accepting the *mandat*. This softening of the least practical of the Bar's rules would be a boon to the profession, opening up new fields of legal practice that were heretofore closed off. He pointed to the *Tribunal de Commerce* as an example of the governing council's ineffectiveness in protecting the interests of the profession. Because of professional rules governing 'independence', advocates were virtually excluded from this jurisdiction. Complaints over its inaccessibility were not new, but there was an increasing sense that the governing council was at fault for doing nothing.[90]

Moysen also asserted the need to open up the Bar to business practices that he saw as an unavoidable feature of the modern world, and dared to suggest that lawyers be allowed not only to sue for honoraria, but that they be able to charge fees on a contingency basis.[91] Like other authors who called for change, Moysen emphasised the difficulties for young advocates. It was imperative to open up other jurisdictions to advocates by relaxing the rules governing the legal mandate. The general decline in the amount of available work for young lawyers coupled with the dramatic increase in the number of cases brought before the *Tribunaux de Commerce* raised the anger of reform-minded lawyers. As several authors pointed out, advocates were allowed to plead before these courts throughout much of the South of France. In cities like Marseilles this activity gave young lawyers an income of 25 francs per case, which often represented their only imcome.[92]

[89] Paul Moysen, *Le Barreau de Paris, Réformes Pratiques* (Wattier frères, Paris, 1898), 12.

[90] Léon Oudin, *Un abus judiciaire: le monopole illégale des agréés près les tribunaux de commerce, étude juridique*, (Paris, 1879).

[91] Moysen, *Réformes Pratiques*, 25.

[92] Lafon, *Pour devenir avocat*, 169n.

A formal proposal was drafted by a group of reformist advocates seeking a moderate position that would not compromise the dignity of the Order, but nevertheless open up access to the commercial courts. In response, the Council of Discipline of the Paris Order stood firm:

> 'All mandates are contrary to the fundamental tradition of the Order . . . this proposal written to the Council, however cautious it may seem, could expose advocates to responsibilities they have always avoided, thanks to the even greater caution of their tradition'.[93]

Thus, reformers within the profession around the turn of the century often echoed the points made by parliamentary critics of earlier years. Such critics were not always in favour of abolishing the Bar altogether. Vergoin, for one, recognised that the changes he proposed for the Bar were more than cosmetic. They would mean abandoning a fiction that was at the heart of the advocate's identity. But he tried to explain that this should not be seen as bringing dishonour upon the legal profession, that greater freedom meant dignity as well. Vergoin looked forward to the time 'when the advocate, free from that point to address all forms of litigation without reservation, would become in the full and honourable sense of the word, a businessman . . .'.[94]

L'OFFICE VIRILE

Throughout its history, the legal profession was spoken of as a masculine profession, the art of oratory described as a distinctly 'male talent', in the words of the *bâtonnier* Nicolet.[95] Leaders of the Order spoke of it as a *confraternité*. The language of brotherhood was linked to professional ethics in that advocates needed to be able to trust each other, in particular to know that they had not withheld any case-evidence during a trial. Within the language of honour and dignity, masculinity worked as a mainly unspoken, but fundamental first principle. The bond among *confrères* was reinforced throughout the period of socialisation in the *stage*. Yet it was more than simply professional, it was tied to a rhetoric of honour that harked back to medieval roots. Lawyers did not hesitate to refer to the Order as a 'knighthood' (*une chevalerie*). In addition to this, in the nineteenth century it was clear that the professional ideal of *indépendance* was restricted to men, in that only they could be true legal subjects, *pères de familles*. As we have seen, any man who was not master of his own legal affairs, or even his financial situation, could not hope to be admitted to the Order of Advocates.

93 AN AD XIXj 57, Decision of June 13, 1899.

94 *Journal Officiel* Annexe 1260, 18 Nov, 1886, 520.

95 'L'Impatience d'Arriver', *BSCA* 1, 1879, 48.

But the masculine virtues of the advocate were most apparent in his singular talent and exclusive function, public speech. In his book on the legal profession, Henri Joly traces the ideal advocate back to ancient Greece, emphasising above all the 'robust chest and virile aspect' of Gorgias.[96] The masculinity of the advocate had to do with the physicality of public speaking, having a booming voice to fill a courtroom and hold the attention of a rapt audience for hours on end. Great oratory also relied on the supposedly male characteristics of reason, logic and clarity, as opposed to subtlety, intrigue or prevarication: its directness, its very publicity made it masculine. As one commentator put it, advocates are men because their speech shows a measure of restraint, 'men's character being less quick, more reflective than women's'.[97] Another author admitted that women could sometimes speak well, but to a fault. They were ultimately 'too sensitive' and especially too easily filled with 'naïve good faith'.[98] Yet leaders of the Bar frequently spoke of the virility of the great orators of the nineteenth century as a kind of fiery passion. In fact, since the 1860s more and more commentators had decried the loss of these qualities, and the decline of eloquence was often described in gender terms.

Older members of the profession seemed to agree that this decline was linked to the appearance of a new generation at the Bar. The young generation seemed more interested in getting through their studies as quickly as possible and earning a living. In his study of the Paris Bar, Maurice Joly noted that the young generation had a long way to go to catch up with its predecessors. The hallowed advocates of past decades such as Berryer (father and son), Dupin, Odilon Barrot or Marie had become famous as lawyers by the age of 30 or 35 and then launched successful careers in politics, which had been their main goal. As their professional objectives became more mundane, Joly argued, the advocates' blood seemed to have cooled over the decades. 'What seems to be lacking the most in the advocates of this generation', he wrote, 'is that fire of the soul . . . that passion and enthusiasm'. Their eloquence had lost its 'virile audacity'. Joly qualified the young generation as '*l'école des affaires*', who only seemed interested in the law as a form of business, a money-making proposition and no longer a true vocation. As a result, they were more dedicated to a greater technical mastery of the law, but their style of speaking had become dry, uninteresting and hence less 'virile'.[99] By the 1870s, a chorus of voices joined Joly in deploring the death of eloquence

[96] Henri Joly, *Le Barreau de Paris* (Paris, 1863), 7.

[97] Raymond Arnstein, *l'Avocat* (Paris, 1883), 13.

[98] Lafon, *Pour devenir avocat*, 183.

[99] Maurice Joly, *Le Barreau de Paris, Etudes politiques et littéraires* (Paris, 1863), 224–225; 237.

at the Bar.[100] In this sense, the democratisation and rationalisation of the profession were perceived as a threat, not only to its moral dignity, but to the masculinity of the Order.

In the mid-1880s, a small handful of women began to challenge this all-male bastion, starting with studies at the law faculty. Increased access to education had also been accorded to women, of course, with the establishment of a programme of *études primaires supérieures* for women being a central plank of the platform of republican educational reform. Yet while many women completed the *bac-ès lettres*, the most common prerequisite to higher study in law, the law faculty had strikingly low numbers of women students through the *fin-de-siècle* period (*See Table 5*). The first woman registered at the Paris Law Faculty in 1884. Like a good proportion of those who followed, she was a foreigner, a Rumanian named Sarmisa Bilcesco, who was ultimately awarded her doctorate in 1890.[101] The first French woman to complete an advanced degree in law was Jeanne Chauvin, a woman of 30 who already had degrees in letters, science and philosophy before entering the law faculty. On the day of her doctoral defense in 1892 a large crowd gathered well in advance of the scheduled time, filling the hall and stairway outside of the examination room. Professor Charles Beudant's attempts to disperse the crowd were unsuccessful, and he was forced to suspend the session until another day.[102]

While some of these spectators simply came to see the oddity of a woman-lawyer, many were fellow students angry about the precedent that was being established. According to *L'Illustration*, crowds of young men filled the amphitheater, 'loudly protesting' the event.[103] In the context of the demographic expansion of the period, many students saw Chauvin as the beacon of a further overcrowding of the law faculty, and the Bar itself. Chauvin's thesis was certainly topical. It was later published as '*Etude Historique sur les Professions Accessibles aux Femmes* . . .'. During her defense, she endured some pointed questions from her committee. According to one press account, Beudant wondered whether,

[100] For example, Jules Jeanneney, 'Sur l'Eloquence Judiciaire dans les Temps Modernes', *BSCA* 13, 1891, especially 133–4 on the dryness, and unpoetic nature of present eloquence. According to the *bâtonnier* Barboux, in 'Des Conditions de l'Eloquence Judiciaire', *BSCA* 4, 1882, 41: great eloquence is no longer really desirable in the courtroom, '*une discussion toute pedestre, donnant les raisons commes elles viennent; une langue sobre, nette, familière, à égale distance de la vulgarité et de l'éloquence, est l'instrument naturel d'une société démocratique, éprise d'utilité et de sciences exactes, et convaincue que, dans un discours comme ailleurs, on peut intervertir l'ordre des facteurs sans changer le produit*'.

[101] AN AJ[16] 1690. Bilcesko did not seek admission to the Paris *stage*, but was admitted to the Bar of Bucharest in 1891.

[102] *Le Temps*, 3 July, 1892.

[103] *L'Illustration* 2577, 16 July, 1892, 47.

Table 5: Women Students in France, 1875–1898

	1875–1888	1888–1898
Law		
certificat/bac	2	—
licence	1	4
doctorat	—	2
Letters		
bac	87	98
licence	2	7
Sciences		
bac (all forms)	130	84
licence	—	54
doctorat	—	2
Medicine		
officiat	4	28
doctorat	35	131
Pharmacy		
2ème classe	1	11
1ère classe	—	2

Source: Statistiques de l'Enseignement Supérieur.

in addition to the two known genders, she wished to introduce '*le genre neutre*.' Professor Larnaude remarked that what France really needed was a higher birthrate. Chauvin replied that she felt sure the women around him could provide him with more than enough babies.[104] Yet she was successful ('*le candidat admise*'), and all members of the committee awarded her with the highest mark, the *boule blanche*.[105]

Chauvin got her doctorate in order to teach law in an *Ecole Supérieur des Jeunes Filles*. But after a few years of being unable to find steady work she decided to practice law, and requested entry to the Bar in September 1897. This request presented series of complications. First of all, the fact

[104] This retrospective account appeared in *L'Eclair*, 17 Nov 1900.

[105] While it is tempting to see in Jeanne Chauvin an early heroine of the liberal feminist movement, this is tempered by the fact that her dissertation was devoted to showing that the subjection of women in the professions was the result of Jewish influences introduced in the Middle Ages, see p 11 of the thesis. The subtitle was '. . . *influence du sémitisme sur l'évolution de la position économique de la femme dans la société*'.

that she had fulfilled the formal requirements for admission was made possible by the educational policies of the republican state. As Chauvin herself argued, in awarding the various degrees she had earned, 'the state, by a kind of tacit contract, has engaged itself to open the careers to which they give access completely and without reservation'.[106] For its part, the Order was far from enthusiastic about the prospect of a woman in its ranks. In a speech to the *stagiaires* in November of that year, Ducreux chose the topic of 'Women's Rights in French Society', which turned out to be a conservative diatribe laced with references to the author Ferdinand Brunétière. The speaker touched only in passing on the issue of women in the legal profession, but left no doubt as to his feelings when he claimed that, whether in politics or at the Bar, 'the morality of a people risks being lost when the public life of women begins'.[107] Chauvin's request to practise law in 1897 marked a moment of confrontation between the State and the Order over the issue of the sovereignty of its decisions.

In late November, Chauvin presented herself at the official oath-taking ceremony for new advocates. Ployer, the president of the Bar, submitted a list of names to the court that did not include hers. Assisted by a solicitor who requested that she be allowed to speak, Chauvin was given the floor by the presiding magistrate. At this moment, another lawyer designated by the Order jumped in to explain why she should not, arguing that since 'the conditions for being registered on the *tableau* of advocates of the Court of Paris (are) conditions of morality and dignity', it was not possible for her to be admitted.[108] For the Order, the issue was that Chauvin had not been admitted to the *stage*, the training period that focused on the 'moral qualities' of the profession, and therefore she could not be allowed to take the professional oath. On this point, the Order's argument won out, despite the contrary predictions of an experienced court journalist like Albert Bataille, himself excluded from practice by the Council some years earlier.[109] The case of Jeanne Chauvin is thus a key to understanding a number of issues faced by the Bar at the turn of the century. In addition to the anxiety over the demographic expansion in the profession and the sovereignty of the Order with respect to the state, the admission of women raised the question of the rationalisation of antiquated rules and ideals related to the 'moral qualities' of the advocate.

In response to the Court's decision, the former premier Léon Bourgeois himself, assisted by a future premier who was a member of the

[106] *L'Illustration* 2854, 6 Nov 1897, 364.

[107] Ducreux, 'Les Droits des Femmes dans la Société Française' *BSCA* vol. 20, 1898, given 20 Nov, 1897, 180.

[108] *Gazette des Tribunaux*, 25 Nov 1897.

[109] Bibliothèque Marguerite Durand (MD), Dossier Jeanne Chauvin.

Paris Bar, Raymond Poincaré, initiated a parliamentary proposal demanding the admission of women to the Bar. They explicitly questioned the ability of the courts to initiate change when long-standing practices were at stake, and suggested that legislative means were the only ones that might yield results.[110] Bourgeois's argument was paradoxical. He used the Order's own view of itself as a private body to claim its obligation to allow women to practice law.

> 'If the profession of advocate could be seen as constituting an extension of the state, there would be serious reasons to exclude women. But this is not the case; the advocate is not a *fonctionnaire* [civil servant], and the law has no business knowing the gender of people who practice a profession (that is) in any degree separate from (the state)'.[111]

Bourgeois was responding to one of the main arguments used against the admission of women to the Bar. In certain exceptional situations, advocates could be called upon to fill the role of *substitut*, in order to complete the required number of magistrates presiding over certain kinds of cases. Such events were rare, and largely restricted to small jurisdictions where few judges were available. Since legally, women could not yet act as judges, this role would be closed to them. Bourgeois's emphasis on the private nature of the profession showed that he felt the Order should be treated the same as any other group in civil society.

Opponents of the measure treated the whole idea with derision. 'Deputies are named to vote on serious laws, not on bedroom farces [*des canevas d'opérette*]', declared Massubuau, member of the anti-Semitic faction. Yet arguments against the admission of women were not particularly sober. One deputy tried to use the sixteenth century prohibition against wearing a beard or moustache at the bar as evidence that women couldn't be advocates.[112] The most common objections had to do with the appearance of feminine traits in the public sphere:

> 'excellent minds could doubt the smooth functioning of Justice if, in the land of old French gallantry, the advocate at the bar could make up for the lack of an argument not only with the seduction of words, but her own person'.[113]

Apparently, judges would be incapable of objective decisions in the physical presence of a woman. For its part, the press took up Chauvin's cause from the beginning, and columnists and caricaturists had a field day speculating on the sexual tensions that would result in the courtroom if women were to become lawyers. According to one journalist,

[110] *Annales de la Chambre, Documents Parlementaires* SE 1898, annexe 469, 400–402.
[111] AN C 7412, Commission de la Réforme Judiciaire, régistre 1, 1 April, 1898.
[112] Fernand Corcos, *Les Avocates*, 18–19.
[113] AN C 7412, Commission de la Réforme Judiciaire, régistre 1, 1 April, 1898.

Chauvin's name appeared in print 6,935 times in 1898 alone.[114] Some press accounts expressed ambivalence about the real impact of the legislation, pointing out that women-advocates would be just as unlikely to earn a living as men.[115]

Following on Bourgeois's initial proposal, another Parisian lawyer, René Viviani, took over the initiative in the next legislature and brought it to term. He was assisted by leading figures of the left such as Millerand and Poincaré, as well as lesser known deputies who had been involved in previous legislation that challenged the Order's monopoly, Maurice-Faure and Trouillot. The law of 1 December 1900 finally opened the profession to women. Rather than give Jeanne Chauvin the satisfaction of being the first woman at the Bar, however, the Paris Council proceeded to admit Olga Petit, a Russian woman married to a lawyer, since she had not been associated with the legislative initiative. The number of women who actually practised law before World War I remained very small.[116] But their admission marked a very public defeat for the Bar's claim to sovereignty and independence, and, for many older lawyers, more evidence of the decline of the gendered ideal of professional honour. To them, the admission of women to the Bar was merely a symbol of a longer decay of the dignity of the Order, linked to the process of democratisation.

HONOUR AND VIOLENCE

In response to the first wave of parliamentary attacks on the outdated rules imposed by the Council of Discipline, the outraged *bâtonnier* Martini vowed that he would never allow his colleagues to become 'vile solicitors'.[117] In the mid-1880s, the language of 'careers open to talent' and 'traditional privilege' had clearly identifiable political overtones. The issue of the opening of the profession brought a response from the leaders of the Bar that was sharply anti-republican in tenor. It showed that they saw professional values as being deeply at odds with the democratic ideals of the regime. Faced with attacks in parliament, Martini's language was defiant:

> 'No matter what they say, this is not a question of abolishing a monopoly, our institution cannot be condemned in the name of National Sovereignty, Universal

[114] MD, Dossier Jeanne Chauvin.

[115] *La Liberté*, 4 Aug 1899. According to *L'Evenement* of 2 July, 1899, 'The bitterness of the profession of advocate will not give sustenance to many young women, but it will gnaw at the meager income of many young men'.

[116] In 1910 there were sixteen *avocates parisiennes*, but most had not pleaded more than a handful of cases. *Les Echos Parisiens*, 1 Nov 1910, 5.

[117] Martini, *De la suppression*, 46.

> Suffrage and the Republic, or the grand principles of freedom of labor and freedom of conscience'.[118]

Leaders of the Bar decried not only these public attacks, but what they saw as a decline of standards of honour within the profession. They warned that the greater involvement in business practices would compromise the very identity of the profession, and steadily lower its status. One advocate linked this process to the Order's experience after the French Revolution,

> What will happen when the mob replaces the elite, and when advocates plead as businessmen, with the shop doors open, in the name of laws that protect freedom of commerce! (With) the pursuit of cases falling into piracy and the client-trade, those newcomers who first appeared long ago, following the first ruin of the Order, will reappear, but made worse by the modern fury of the struggle for survival.[119]

The author remarked that a new form of eloquence would accompany this professional degradation, one increasingly concerned with efficiency and practicality. Indeed, the obsession with the decline of eloquence in this period best illustrates the anxiety over the loss of a sacred professional identity:

> 'One will speak as a dignified court bailiff, and those *agents d'affaires* who give themselves license to criticize, will no longer denounce an oration for being too literary. The word *talent* will have but one meaning . . . *talent* will be a currency *(une monnaie)* . . .'.[120]

The proposals made by reformers from within the Bar at the turn of the century, echoing parliamentary critics, show how the rhetoric of honor and virtue that the lawyers' professional identity was built on left even many advocates unconvinced. But the reformist movement met with similar responses. In answer to the wave of tracts and proposals of 1898, the *bâtonnier* Ployer again evoked the evils of commercialism to his audience of young interns:

> Do you wish to be bankruptcy clearing houses, business liquidators, or rent-collectors? And do you think that the day after a trial, when the judge has paid you off and applied a tax, you could still, taking up your robes, have before him that freedom of judgment, that independence of language and that kind of equality of authority?[121]

But how did the younger generation of advocates take such injunctions to observe the traditional rules? Certainly, at the level of the *stage*, there

[118] Martini, *De la suppression*, 26.

[119] Julien Munier-Jolain, *Les Epoques de l'Eloquence Judiciaire en France* (Perrin, Paris, 1888), 193.

[120] Munier-Jolain, *Les Epoques de l'Eloquence*, 194.

[121] *BSCA*, 20, 1898.

was a degree of cynicism, and getting the interns to attend regularly was a perennial problem. But it is striking how little impact the reformers had on the decisions of the Council. Paul Moysen reported that the response to his pamphlet was overwhelmingly positive among lawyers. Virtually all the letters he received were from members of the Bar who were in favor of some professional reform.[122] But Moysen's own candidacy for the *Conseil de l'Ordre* was not successful in the year his piece drew so much attention.[123] Why was it that demands for reform did not translate into overturning the standing members of the governing council?

An analysis of the Council over the entire period 1870–1914 shows that the average age of its members increased steadily. That is, when new members were appointed, they tended to be very senior advocates. Earlier in the 19th century, by contrast, it had been common for some members to have practised for as little as 10 or 15 years. While at least six members of the council had been registered at the Bar for less than 25 years in the 1870s, this figure fell to just two or three starting in 1880.[124] Elections to the Council took place each summer, and the 'campaign season' started in the spring. The elections constituted perhaps the most concrete example of sociability among lawyers in the Order. It was a time when, even if for reasons of material interest, all embraced the rhetoric of *confraternité*. Reformers tended to mock the annual ritual, which by all accounts included a good deal of wining and dining: 'It is in the springtime that every advocate, if he doesn't have enough cases to plead, at least has enough to eat. Since, in the first days of July, the ballots are cast'.[125] For once, generational dependence was reversed, as more senior advocates needed to count on younger ones for their vote. But each time there was vacancy on the Council, the young proved easy to seduce. According to *Les Echos Parisiens*, 'the little act of "vote for me" begins in the same classic and gastronomic way'.[126] For the candidates, election had a serious side: being appointed to the Council was worth an extra 50,000 francs of annual income, by one account.[127]

The Paris Bar was unusual in France in that elections were not open to all members of the Order. Only advocates who had been registered for at least ten years were allowed to cast ballots. This fact certainly accounts

[122] *Le Temps*, 23 June, 1898, 3.

[123] *Le Temps*, 3 July, 1898, 4.

[124] These figures are derived from the lists of the Council members recorded in the annual volumes of the *Almanach National*, 1871–1919.

[125] Jacques Bonzon, 'La lutte sociale dans le prétoire' *Les Echos Parisiens* 1 July, 1911, 2.

[126] *Les Echos Parisiens*, 25 Jan 1905, 4. In a later issue, the paper presented a moral issue in mock-seriousness: should an advocate refuse invitations to dinner made by a candidate to the Council if he is not intending to vote for them? *Les Echos Parisiens*, 5 July, 1907, 5.

[127] Bonzon, 'La Lutte Sociale dans le Prétoire', 2.

for some of the success of conservative candidates for the Council. But by the turn of the century, the students that had completed their training in the early 1880s were becoming mature advocates in positions of prominence. The steady growth in numbers also suggests that the age pyramid in the Order favoured this generation over their elders. Yet it seems that by the time they had been on the register for 10 years, these lawyers, who as youths had been accused of only being concerned with money, had become defenders of the traditions of the Order. For all of the artifice of the *Conference du stage*, the younger generation of lawyers identified with their older colleagues, and embraced much of their rhetoric of honour and dignity.

By 1901, the socialist deputy Jules Coutant, denounced the Order in Parliament as being governed by 'an almost total heredity and, most often, the near impossibility for young men of working class families' to be admitted. The reason for this exclusion was not the difficulty of the training, he argued, but the obscure and anachronistic rules of the Order.[128] Did the sense of identification with members of the Council extend to younger cohorts of the turn of the century? The student demonstrations of the period provide some insight into what the profession stood for among its potential members. For one thing, student violence and unrest were, in their own way, an expression of the 'masculinity' of the professions in this period.[129] Frustration over the lack of career outlets led to many of the outbursts that occurred in the Latin Quarter in the 1890s and 1900s. Professors who were judged too harsh in their grading were the object of a number of such demonstrations.[130]

In January 1903, a group of mainly first year law students marched in protest to their professor of Roman law, Jobbé-Duval. In addition to seeing Roman law as an impractical waste of time, the students claimed he was being too hard on them, giving out the dreaded *boule noire* far too frequently in their exams.[131] Further, they reproached his tendency to discuss issues in class that would not be included in the final examination. Unlike the explicitly political rallies of the period, resentment toward this professor sparked demonstrations and rioting that lasted for

[128] Jules Coutant, *Journal Officiel, Documents Parlementaires de la Chambre . . .* Annexe 2253, Session Ordinaire of 12 March, 1901, 202.

[129] Cf in the American case: Stephen H. Norwood, 'The Student as Strikebreaker: College Youth and the Crisis of Masculinity in the early 20th century' (1994) 28(2) *Journal of Social History*, 330–49.

[130] For example, demonstrations against Professors Cuq and Bartin. Archives de la Prefecture de Police [APP] B[a] 23, reports of 27–29 Dec 1905 and APP B[a] 1523, 20 Nov 1906. See also AN[16] 1796, meeting of 20 Jan 1898 where professor Lainé is bothered by hecklers; AN AJ[16] 1798, meetings of 14–18 Nov 1912 when arson is committed in an amphitheater due to overcrowding.

[131] APP B[a] 23. report of 15 Jan 1903. *La Libre Parole*, 17 Jan 1903.

two full weeks, despite a significant response from the police. It can also be noted that although the demonstration did not seem to be planned by any student or outside organisation, it did follow a week of similar demonstrations at the Faculty of Medicine. Most striking perhaps, as professor Jobbé-Duval himself remarked, was that these were students in their first year who had not yet faced him or any other professor in an examination.[132] Like the medical students they were imitating, these law students were reacting to the general atmosphere of overcrowding in the Latin Quarter they felt had a direct impact on their own futures. It was not the specific experience of failing an examination that led students into the street, but the sense that the professors were more demanding than they had been in the past.

In 1905, third-year students threatened to riot if the hour of their civil law course was not changed, as many of them worked afternoons as clerks for notaries or solicitors in order to get some knowledge of legal procedure.[133] The incident demonstrates how anxiety over the transition to professional life was often behind the students' actions. But students did not direct their anger against the rules and restrictions of the Bar. More often, students blamed republican policies of openness that led to overcrowding in higher education. In the context of an increasingly difficult job market, that which had been considered the domain of upper class privilege, the *licence de droit* and the social status that went along with it, seemed increasingly cheapened.

These references to student violence return us to our point of departure, the conflict over the Dreyfus Affair. It is striking in the upheaval over Captain Dreyfus how little was heard from the Bar, given its strong stance as a collective institution in opposition to the imperial regime of Napoleon III. By the turn of the century, the *intellectuel universel* seems to have replaced the heroic *avocat* of earlier times in such public controversies.[134] As it has often been pointed out, the Dreyfus Affair was about more than anti-Semitism; it was, in a certain way, a referendum on the Republic. *L'Affaire* especially brought out all of the hidden anxiety of the middle classes over the rapid change in social life of the *fin-de-siècle* decades. This anxiety was often expressed over issues of masculinity and personal honour. As Robert Nye has pointed out, the Republic itself was thought of in gendered terms, as its birth out of the defeat at Sedan created a kind of imperative of virility.[135] But by the 1890s, the image of the Republic was that of a prostitute, *la gueuze*: masculinity had lost out to money. It seems that the same revulsion at the monetary aspects of the

[132] *Le Petit Bleu*, 22 Jan 1903.

[133] APP B^a 23. report of 7 Nov 1905.

[134] See Christophe Charle, 'Le Declin de la République des Avocats', in Pierre Birnbaum, (ed.), *La France de l'Affaire Dreyfus* (Gallimard, Paris, 1994), 56–86.

[135] Nye, *Masculinity and Male Codes of Honor.*

profession are what led advocates to oppose the admission of women to the Bar. Proponents of that measure consistently cited the United States as a model for the acceptance of women lawyers, without understanding that the American lawyer-businessmen represented the worst fate for the French *avocats*. As we have seen, the monetarisation of the profession was not only seen as a threat to the advocate's honor, but also as the loss of his literary artistry, both of which were deeply tied to a sense of manhood.

In France, the notion of an 'educated intelligence' as a foundation of middle-class identity was arguably more important than it was in either Britain or the United States.[136] Education and professional expertise served not only to secure distance from lower class occupations, but also to emulate and appropriate aristocratic codes of honor and virtue. In the Latin Quarter, anti-republican violence expressed students' fears over tightening standards and increased competition. For many students, the law faculty did not just represent the opportunity of a good bourgeois occupation. A career at the Bar meant being above money, outside of the throng of *mere* bourgeois. The sense of a proletarianisation of the liberal professions meant a cheapening of their value to young hopefuls.

Within the Bar, the reformers of the turn of the century sought to put the profession 'in step' with the modern world. Invoking the language of openness and freedom of opportunity, they attempted to challenge the sheer inertia of the Bar's traditional rhetoric. Yet just as they had rejected the project of meritocratic opening of higher education as law students, the generation of the *fin-de-siècle* refused arguments cast in terms of economic liberalism for professional reform. The rhetoric of freedom of labour did not sway the majority of the advocates, despite the remarkable obstacles posed to professional practice by the reaffirmation of traditional rules. In this way the continued 'privilege' of the Bar went hand in hand with the social 'privilege' of the law student.

Rather than promoting a republicanisation of the legal profession, the demographic shift of the late nineteenth century galvanised a backward looking rhetoric among lawyers, a nostalgia for a past, pre-democratic era. Young lawyers embraced traditionalism even as the wave of new lawyers continued to surge, and until World War I career guides issued warnings away from entering the profession.[137] It was for these reasons that the most radical of the reformers, Jacques Bonzon, showed little

[136] Burton Bledstein, *The Culture of Professionalism: The Middle Class and the Development of Higher Education in America* (Norton, New York, 1976). Harold Perkin, *The Rise of Professional Society* (Routledge, New York, 1989).

[137] Jean Lievin, *Les Meilleurs Professions pour faire Fortune après la Guerre* (les Éditions pratiques et documentaires, Paris, 1916), 10; 24. Louis Debray, *Rapport présenté au nom de la Commission d'Etudes sur les mesures propres à éviter l'encombrement de la Faculté de Droit de Paris* (Paris, 1910).

interest in trying to effect change through the mechanism of the Bar itself. Bonzon wrote that such changes had to come from outside intervention, namely through legislative action.[138] Hence the ambiguous modernity of the 19th century Bar, defender of the citizen-individual before the state, the advocate also claimed a professional organisation that dates from the eighteenth century. The experience of the *avocats* suggests that, in their case at least, the *fin-de-siècle* saw a cultural persistence of the 'Old Regime'.

[138] Jacques Bonzon, *La Réforme du Barreau* (Edition des *Echos parisiens*, Paris, 1905).

8

Text and Subtext: French Lawyers' Fees in the Nineteenth Century

JEAN-LOUIS HALPÉRIN(TRANS M MACFARLANE)

Nineteenth-century French lawyers have left us little evidence as to the amount of their fees.[1] Their predecessors under the Ancien Régime had already resisted attempts by the royal authority to impose a fee scale on them or at least to make them provide their clients with receipts.[2] After Napoleon reinstated the *ordres d'avocats*,[3] the French Bar succeeded in developing a 'disinterestedness ethic' according to which fees were of minimal importance to any lawyer worth his salt.[4] On the basis of legal texts which did not impose a fee scale on lawyers, contrary to what happened in the case of *avoués* and *notaires'* and an interpretation rooted in tradition, the *Conseil de l'Ordre de Paris* established a whole 'fee theory'

[1] Literature on fees up until 1914 deals almost exclusively with the issue of the admissibility of the lawyer's legal action for payment of his fees. This is true in particular of the doctoral thesis in law by the lawyer H Labouret *Des honoraires des avocats* (Dufréney, Lille, 1906).

[2] P-J-J-G Guyot, *Répertoire universel et raisonné de jurisprudence* (Paris, 1784) t. I, '*Avocat*', 796; D Dalloz, *Répertoire méthodique et alphabétique de législation, de doctrine et de jurisprudence* (Paris, 1846) t. V, '*Avocat*', 459–463, recalls the main attempts made by the royal authority to legislate on lawyers' fees, from the 1274 decree (setting a maximum of 30 *livres*) to the 1579 Blois decree obliging lawyers to provide a written receipt for their fees. Rejecting this provision, Parisian lawyers went on strike in 1602; this episode led to the publication of the *Dialogue des avocats,* by A Loisel. Cf DA Bell, *Lawyers and Citizens* (Oxford University Press, Oxford, 1994) 45; J-L Gazzaniga, 'Jalons pour une histoire de la profession d'avocat des origines à la Révolution française', in *Les Petites Affiches*, 70 (12 June 1989) 28–29.

[3] MP Fitzsimmons, *The Parisian Order of Barristers and the French Revolution* (Harvard University Press, Harvard, 1987). Abolished in September 1790, the *ordres d'avocats* were re-established by the decree issued on 14 December 1810. This text stipulated, among other authoritative provisions, that lawyers would mention their fees at the foot of their accounts and would give a receipt for their fees for oral arguments (s 44). This provision never gained acceptance among lawyers and was abandoned in the decree issued on 20 November 1822, which governed discipline in the profession throughout the nineteenth century. The disciplinary council of each Bar was expected to uphold the 'principles of moderation, disinterestedness and integrity on which the honour of the *ordre des avocats* was based'.

[4] Cf in particular L Karpik, *Les avocats. Entre l'État, le public et le marché. XIIIe–XXe siècle* (Gallimard, Paris, 1995), Bibliothèque des sciences humaines, 158–160.

which became the norm in almost all Bars and gained partial acceptance among judges. There were no restrictions on fees, which lawyers were free to set at their own discretion for each client and each case. Thus, the Bar was a 'liberal profession' with greater independence from the state than officers of the court (*avoués* and *notaires*), who were government-appointed and subject to a fee scale. The contract between a lawyer and his client was neither a contract for the hire of services nor a power of attorney; this commitment was presented as an 'innominate agreement,' a 'service' or an 'office' which created a legitimate obligation to provide fair compensation.[5] Not only did this compensation termed a 'fee' and not a 'salary' have to be modest, but it was also supposed to be freely offered by the client. As the finishing touch to this intellectual construct aimed at reinforcing the lawyer's independence from his client, lawyers were prohibited from bringing an action to prosecute clients who refused to pay their fees. Following a letter from the president of the *Ordre de Paris* in 1819, the *Conseil de l'Ordre* threatened to disbar any lawyer who took legal action in order to obtain his fees, and the legality of this disciplinary decision was gradually acknowledged by courts during the nineteenth century.

Contrary to what many nineteenth-century French lawyers thought, this concept of fees was not peculiar to the French Bar. While German and Italian lawyers had been subject to a fee scale, English barristers were not, and they also defended the prohibition of legal action in this area.[6] However, it is possible to acquire a relatively good knowledge of barristers' incomes.[7] Investigation seems more difficult in the case of French lawyers, and we have first to attempt to gather all available numerical evidence about nineteenth-century lawyers' fees. Based on these few quantitative data, it is possible to speculate further as to whether or not there was an economy or a market associated with the legal profession during the 1810–1914 period.

Rather surprisingly, the best evidence we have available about the amount of nineteenth-century French lawyers' fees is of a judicial nature. Despite the threats of disbarment hanging over lawyers who took legal action in order to obtain their fees, several cases did arise which led

[5] M Mollot, *Règles de la profession d'avocat*, 2nd edn (Durand et Pedone-Lauriel, Paris, 1866) t. I, 6–15 and 115–122. In 1842, the date of the first edition of his work, this lawyer started to collect the rules and accepted practices of the lawyer's profession, basing himself on the decisions of the *Conseil de l'Ordre* of the Paris Bar.

[6] J-L Halperin (ed), *Avocats et notaires en Europe. Les professions judiciaires et juridiques dans l'histoire contemporaine* (LGDJ, Paris, 1996) '*Droit et société*', 242–243.

[7] D Duman, *The English and Colonial Bars in the Nineteenth Century* (Croom Helm, London, 1983) 144–146, quoting in particular the figures of a parliamentary committee in 1850.

lawyers to discuss their fees in the presence of judges, which is precisely what the *conseils de l'ordre* wanted to avoid in order to prevent the judiciary from exercising any control over financial relations between lawyers and their clients. Although only some of these legal decisions have been published, they provide a varied selection of situations and invaluable information on fees. Further delving into court records may provide valuable additional information in the future.

The most common situation, likely to spark proceedings relating to a lawyer's fees, resulted from the duality of the professions of lawyer and *avoué*.[8] In civil cases, parties were obliged to appoint an *avoué* as their representative before the court of first instance as well as the Court of Appeal. The *avoué,* who was responsible for all pleadings, was his client's legal agent and was paid according to a fee scale which was set by regulation in 1807. In this situation, the litigant had first to approach the *avoué,* and it was not unusual for the latter to choose for himself the lawyer responsible for arguing the case. The *avoué* sometimes paid the lawyer his fees and then included them in the bill of expenses he presented to the client. As nobody challenged the *avoué*'s right to take legal action against a recalcitrant debtor, a legal challenge concerning an *avoué*'s claims against his party could lead to discussion about the lawyer's fees.

Throughout the nineteenth century, judgments and decisions maintained that, as the legal agent, the *avoué* was perfectly at liberty to choose the lawyer, advance fees for his client, and then request recovery of the amount paid.[9] The only issue that might cause difficulties was that of evidence in the absence of a written contract.[10] This 'hypocritical' system

[8] This duality, which is comparable in certain respects to that between barristers and solicitors, was based on texts from the Consulate and the Empire, which had revived a tradition from the Ancien Régime. Taking advantage of the law passed on 28 April 1816, which enabled them to make money out of the right to introduce their successor to the Ministry of Justice, *avoués* bought their positions, and *avoué* posts were subject to a *numerus clausus*. J-L Halperin, 'Les avoués au XIXe siècle, des rentiers de la Justice?' *Histoire de la Justice*, 4 (1991) 99–120.

[9] J-B Sirey, *Recueil des lois et arrêts* [hereinafter *S*], 1829, 2, 286 (Limoges, 10 August 1829); 1830, 2, 159 (Bourges, 26 April 1830); 1832, 2, 581 (Toulouse, 11 May 1831); 1833, 2, 128 and 484 (Montpellier, 12 March 1832, and Toulouse, 20 March 1833); 1839, 2, 230 (Paris, 22 November 1838); 1841, 2, 271 (Caen, 30 December 1840); 1846, 2, 191 (Colmar, 22 January 1846); 1887, 2, 97 (Aix, 26 May 1886).

[10] *S* 1853, 1, 370 (Applic. 2 May 1853: in the absence of an express agreement between the lawyer and the *avoué,* there is mention of a quasi-contract in a dispute between a lawyer and the heirs to an *avoué*); *S*. 1869, 2, 304 (*Tribunal de Nîmes,* 2 December 1868); *Dalloz Périodique* [hereinafter *DP*] 1879, 2, 95 (Poitiers, 21 January 1879, referring to business management). On the subject of this development in case law, cf *Répertoire encyclopédique du droit français,* by Fernand Labori (1889) t. II, '*Avocat*', 82. M Mollot, *op. cit.*, t. II, p 261 refers to a decision by the *Conseil de l'Ordre de Paris* in 1860, imposing a penalty for the lawyer's suit against the *avoué* as an indirect way of violating a professional duty.

was likely to satisfy all professionals. In material terms, the *avoué* was sure of recovering his funds, and the lawyer relied on the *avoué*'s guarantee. Symbolically, the *avoué* obtained legal confirmation of his role as *dominus litis,* which made many lawyers dependent on his choices, while lawyers preserved the distinction between their 'noble' profession and the duties of *avoués*, who were paid set fees.

There are other, less common, hypotheses which could lead the courts to consider a lawyer's fee claim: in the case of a counterclaim for compensation by a lawyer who was being sued by his client, who was simultaneously his creditor,[11] when a deceased lawyer's heirs sought to rebuild estate assets,[12] or, very exceptionally, when the heirs to an estate challenged a mortgage taken out as security for payment of a lawyer's fees.[13] Finally, lawyers sometimes took the initiative and went to court themselves in order to recover outstanding fees. This action, to which all creditors could have recourse under common law, was in no way contrary to legislation, even though it ran counter to the professional practices proclaimed and defended by the Paris Bar. From the first half of the nineteenth century onwards, lawyers from Marseille, Grenoble and Nantes brought actions for recovery of fees, with the judges' approval and apparently without fear of disciplinary action being taken by their *ordre.*[14] A few lawyers then relied on these favourable precedents to make legal claims for their fees, running the risk, particularly in Paris, of legal action being taken before the *Conseil de l'ordre.* Although this kind of action was infrequent, it bears witness to the resistance among judges and a number of lawyers to the tradition defended, more or less fervently, by the Paris Bar authorities.[15]

[11] *S* 1845, 2, 655 (Dijon, 24 Jan 1842), *DP* 1846, 1, 161.

[12] *DP* 1892, 2, 287 (Lyons, 5 Nov 1891).

[13] *DP* 1890, 2, 281 (Agen, 4 March 1889). This case was exceptional in more ways than one: a servant, designated residuary legatee by his master, had been accused of murdering him; the servant was acquitted, but the bequest having been revoked on grounds of ingratitude, the legitimate heirs of the deceased then discovered that the property of the estate was mortgaged up to the hilt in the lawyer's favour, which led to a lawsuit.

[14] *S* 1834, 2, 377 (Aix, 12 March 1834, referring to a Marseilles lawyer); *S* 1839, 2, 152 (Grenoble, 2 May 1838: in this case, the client accused the lawyer of betraying him by not travelling to Grenoble). As early as 1870, a *tribunal de paix* in Paris considered the tolerance of 'many provincial Bars' with regard to actions for the recovery of fees to be common knowledge (*DP* 1870, 3, 78).

[15] *S* 1853, 1, 114 (Applic. 4 Jan 1853: the Paris Court of Appeal had allowed the legal action brought by the lawyer on whom the penalty of a warning had been imposed by the *Conseil de l'Ordre*; the *Cour de cassation* rejected the appeal on the grounds of excess of functions against the disciplinary decision); *DP* 1853, 2, 149 (Orleans, 28 Jan 1853: the trainee lawyer, who had taken his clients to court, had been subject to disciplinary action); *S* 1861, 2, 529 (Bordeaux, 10 April 1861: a lawyer from Angoulême had taken action against several of his clients before the justice of the peace and had been disciplined by the *Conseil de l'Ordre;* the court of appeal quashed the legal action).

Most of these court decisions provide us with figures indicating the amount of lawyers' fees. In a few cases, fees are under 100 francs.[16] Fees of 100 francs and especially 200 francs are very often quoted.[17] Above that level, higher amounts had to be justified by a special situation which was verified by judges: the lawyer's claim against his client could be the balance of an account relating to several cases, or fees over 1,000 francs could be explained by the nature of the case, especially when it was a criminal trial in the *cour d'assises*.[18] In most cases, fees were not considered to be excessive by judges, who took into account 'the difficulties of the case and the significance of the interests involved'. Sometimes, judges referred consideration of fees to the lawyers' disciplinary council or proceeded themselves with the taxation of costs.[19] Although judges were sometimes nostalgic for the 'stern and honourable' practices of lawyers in days gone by,[20] they all acknowledged the licitness of actions for recovery of fees and felt that lawyers were entitled to fair compensation for services rendered to clients, since the Bar's former principles of generosity were no longer in tune with legislation and common practice.[21]

[16] *S* 1829, 2, 30 (Rouen, 17 May 1828: 80 francs paid to two lawyers who were consulted and advised against pursuing legal action); *S* 1830, 2, 159 (Bourges, 26 April 1830: 80 francs for defence fees); *DP* 1853, 2, 149 (Orleans, 28 Jan 1853: the trainee lawyer claimed 48 francs and 85 centimes for several trips and for having consulted documents at a *notaire*'s office; court costs had increased the claim to 220 francs).

[17] *S* 1829, 2, 85 (200 francs in fees) and 286 (100 francs for arguing a case); *S* 1833, 2, 128 (200 francs in fees); *S* 1841, 2, 271 (200 francs in fees); *S* 1858, 2, 187 (200 francs in fees for arguing a case on appeal); *DP* 1870, 2, 778 (200 francs in fees for arguing a case); *DP* 1879, 2, 95 (100 francs in fees).

[18] *S* 1833, 2, 484 (Toulouse, 20 March 1833: 2,400 francs in fees for numerous written statements in a separation of property case); *S* 1839, 2, 152 (Grenoble, 2 May 1838: 1,200 francs in fees for travel and a defence before the Grenoble *cour d'assises*; the case led to a judgment of dismissal by the *Cour de cassation* in 1839, *S* 1839, 1, 474); *S* 1853, 1, 114 (Req. 4 Jan 1853: 171,000 francs in fees claimed by a lawyer from a railway company for arguing 174 cases and making 291 settlements); *DP* 1876, 1, 161 (4,290 francs for several cases on behalf of a wine merchant); *DP* 1890, 2, 281 (Agen, 4 March 1889: 2 000 francs in fees judged to be 'very adequate payment in the *cour d'assises*'); *DP* 1892, 2, 287 (Lyons, 5 Nov 1891: 3,000 francs in fees, a figure given for several cases in the accounts of the deceased lawyer); *S* 1903, 2, 5 (Caen, 1 March 1902: 940 francs in fees for various cases).

[19] *S* 1834, 2, 377 (Aix, 12 March 1834: referral to the *conseil de l'ordre*); *DP* 1868, 4, 248 (Crim. 11 Feb 1867: the magistrates of the *cour d'assises* had sovereign power to reduce the lawyer's fees); *DP* 1890, 2, 281 (rejection of an extra payment of 3,000 francs on the acquittal of the accused, who were servants of modest means); *DP* 1892, 2, 287 (a reduction from 3,000 to 2,000 francs due to the scant resources and the age of the client).

[20] *S* 1830, 2, 159 (Bourges, 26 April 1830).

[21] *S* 1861, 2, 529 (Bordeaux, 10 April 1861: the magistrates defend the action for recovery of fees, which they consider preferable to 'secret practices'). As noted in the *Répertoire Labori* (*op. cit.*, 1889, t. II, '*Avocat*', at 82), such a precedent created a curious situation: the same lawyer could be allowed to take legal action to recover his fees and be subjected to disciplinary action for so doing. Although the *Cour de cassation* had,

Judges were clearly not shocked at the amounts involved in these trials, which suggests that such amounts were in keeping with lawyers' everyday practice.

Comparable figures appear in the other, more scattered, documents which provide evidence of the amounts of French lawyers' fees in the nineteenth century. First of all, there are disciplinary decisions by the *conseils de l'ordre* of the various Bars. Thus, in Lyon, the records of the deliberations of the *Conseil de l'Ordre* show fees ranging from 50 to 1,000 francs from 1871 to 1896;[22] in each case, it is not the amount of these fees that is challenged, but rather the unscrupulous way in which they were claimed by the lawyer. The same holds true in Dijon, for more modest amounts.[23] Disciplinary decisions by the Paris Bar, reported by Mollot to back up the disinterestedness theory, also refer to fees ranging from 45 to 1,000 francs.[24] Unfortunately, we only have a very small number of private documents dealing with lawyers' incomes. Not all lawyers kept accounts: taxes did not apply to professional income, but were levied via the *patente* on the rent of office premises; many of them destroyed their own archives, and very few have left written evidence about their fees. The case of César Colmet Daâge, who had a notebook of fees which was studied by his great grandson, Félix Colmet Daâge, is quite exceptional. We thus know that this great Parisian lawyer, who, at his death in 1866, was the senior member of the *ordre,* generally charged 300, 500, 800 or 1,000 francs for arguing cases and that his fees for a case came to 3,000 francs only three times in nine years.[25] We also know from the personal papers of Waldeck-Rousseau, who was a prominent business lawyer before becoming president of the Council in 1899, that he made on average 80 to 100 francs on each of the 300 cases he pleaded annually from 1875 onwards, and that his fees could reach 10,000 francs per year for a major business company.[26] A letter in 1899 from Labori, one of Alfred Dreyfus' lawyers, indicates 5,000 francs in fees for Zola's

in 1853, legitimised this independence of legal action and disciplinary proceedings, the Bordeaux court had been more logical by nullifying disciplinary proceedings against the lawyer involved, in 1861.

[22] Record of deliberations of the *Conseil de l'Ordre de Lyon* (preserved at the Bar of Lyons), 9 July 1872 (discussion on fees ranging from 50 to 500 francs for the defence of a soldier before a court martial), 12 Nov 1878 (1,000 francs as a retainer in a criminal case), 13 May 1879 (550 francs in fees for concluding a trial with a settlement).

[23] Record of the deliberations of the *Conseil de l'Ordre de Dijon,* 29 April 1832 (50 or 80 francs in fees in a lesser criminal case), 16 Aug 1835 (113, 50 francs in fees for two arguments and documents in separation of property proceedings).

[24] A Mollot, *op. cit.*, t. II, 254–268.

[25] F Colmet Daage, *Malaise au Palais* (Paris, Messein, 1953) 34–35. The same author states that, in the mid-nineteenth century, a Parisian lawyer, even a trainee, was not allowed to argue a case for less than 100 francs.

[26] P Sorlin, *Waldeck-Rousseau* (Arts Thesis, Colin, Paris, 1966) 152–153.

defence and 20,000 francs in fees received from Mathieu Dreyfus.[27] Dupin reportedly received 50,000 francs in fees from the Duke of Orleans for advising him in a settlement with the Théâtre Français, and Billaut reportedly received 12,000 francs for arguing in a parricide case in Limoges, in 1850.[28]

Other evidence, which is far more imprecise and should be treated warily, deals with the annual incomes of fairly well-known lawyers. From 1852 to 1858, for instance, Jules Favre reportedly earned from 150,000 to 300,000 francs a year.[29] Another prominent Parisian lawyer during the Second Empire allegedly started out with an annual income of between 16,000 and 20,000 francs, which later reached an average of 50,000 and then 100,000 francs.[30] At the beginning of the Third Republic, Barboux reportedly had an annual income of a mere 12,000 to 15,000 francs in fees before becoming president of the *Ordre de Paris* in 1880–1881.[31] In 1909, Viscount D'Avenel, in his *Histoire économique de la propriété, des salaires,* was of the opinion that there were no more than about ten lawyers in his day who 'regularly earned 100 000 francs a year', about 15 who earned between 50,000 and 100,000 francs, about 30 who earned between 30,000 and 50,000 francs, and about 60 who earned between 10,000 and 30,000 francs, while the rest earned no more than 10,000 francs a year.[32] The same author estimated fees to be between 50 and 2,000 francs, the average commonly charged being between 300 and 400 francs. These figures tally with those mentioned in other sources and confirm the validity of the sample provided by court decisions. Noting this wide range of fees and incomes, D'Avenel wrote: '. . . here as elsewhere, prices obey economic laws, which are totally independent of people or things'. Consideration of the nature of the economic laws which would have determined their amounts is essential to the study of French lawyers' fees in the nineteenth century.

[27] Y Ozanam, 'L'avocat de Zola et de Dreyfus: Fernand Labori (1860–1917)' [forthcoming in *Histoire de la Justice*, 1998].

[28] A Damien, *Les avocats du temps passé* (H Lefèbvre, Versailles, 1973) 377. The author cites the case of a Versailles lawyer who claimed 30 francs for defending a gardener brought before a criminal court in 1869.

[29] P-A Perrod, *Jules Favre, avocat de la liberté* (La Manufacture, Lyons, 1988) 167.

[30] A Damien, '*Avocats*' in J Tulard (ed), *Dictionnaire du Second Empire* (Fayard, Paris, 1995) 90. This is probably Bétolaud.

[31] R Allou and C Chenu, *Les grands avocats du siècle* (A Pedone, Paris, 1894) 345.

[32] G D'Avenel, *Histoire économique de la propriété, des salaires, des denrées et de tous les prix en général depuis l'an 1200 jusqu'à l'an 1800* (Paris, 1909) t. V, 251–256. Good examples of provincial lawyers' incomes, averaging from 6,000 to 7,000 francs a year, are provided in the thesis by P Plas, *Avocats et barreaux dans le ressort de la Cour d'appel de Limoges de la Révolution française à la seconde guerre mondiale* (doctorate in history, Paris IV, 1997) 1190.

'The lawyer's knowledge, eloquence and integrity are not goods; when called upon by misfortune and poverty, they are given freely; they are not sold': these were the noble sentiments taught to young lawyers by Cresson's manual in 1896.[33] Through its disinterestedness and its fee theory, the nineteenth-century French Bar wanted to give the impression of being free of all economic calculation. Yet, despite this 'money taboo' and the discretion maintained by the world of the law courts regarding fee amounts, economic considerations were not foreign to the legal profession: it is significant that the *Répertoire Dalloz* reproduced in 1846, under '*Avocat*', a passage by Adam Smith on fees.[34] It would also have been possible to quote the *Cours d'économie politique,* by Pellegrino Rossi,[35] speculating as to whether the laws of free competition could be applied to what would have to be called a legal services 'market'. Today, analyses are still at odds on this point and on the appropriateness of the term 'market'. The neo-Weberian concept of a combined effort by lawyers to exploit their clients has not really convinced French authors, who prefer to refer to an 'economy of restraint'[36] or even the 'false issue of income'.[37] However, the figures we have given do show that fees were not arbitrarily set; although they vary considerably in amount from lawyer to lawyer, client to client and case to case, they nonetheless fall within a certain range, which suggests that, in this area, there were indeed practices which, while unspoken, were known and often observed. Therefore, the question of the role of fees still remains, even after market logic has been discounted.

Classical economists, like Smith or Rossi, knew for a fact that intellectual production did not obey the same rules as 'purely mechanical' production. Lawyers, like doctors and artists, were not subject to ordinary rules of competition when dealing with their clients. Countless factors prevented a legal services market from developing in nineteenth-century France. Although French lawyers had a monopoly—that of arguing cases before the Court of Appeal and, barring exceptions, before courts of first instance and *cours d'assises*, they were in no position to engage in competition over the amount of their fees. First of all, many lawyers did not 'chase after' cases and did not wish to fight with their colleagues over the apportioning of cases. Although the number of dilettante lawyers dwindled during the nineteenth century—along with the number of Bar

[33] EG Cresson, *Abrégé des usages et règles de la profession d'avocat* (L Larose, Paris, 1896) 133.

[34] D Dalloz, *op. cit.*, t. V, 260, 511.

[35] P Rossi, *Cours d'économie politique* (Joubert, Paris, 1840) t. I, 294–295.

[36] L Karpik, *op. cit.*, at 15 (quoting the works of Larson) and 152–171 (the liberal Bar allegedly was not subject to market logic due to the economy of restraint).

[37] P Plas, *op. cit.*, 1178: whatever their income, by virtue of their origins or their means, lawyers belonged to the middle-class world.

members, which decreased from 1848 onwards, stabilising around 4,000 and 4,500 from 1860 to 1900[38]—there always remained a significant body of lawyers who were men of private means or property owners, who argued cases occasionally and tended to disrupt the homogeneity of service supply. In the case of lawyers in name only, it would be preferable to speak of a lack of interest in the practice of arguing in court rather than of virtuous disinterestedness. The very fact that many professionals did not need their fees to survive distorted the way the law of supply and demand operated between lawyers and clients.

Competition between active or 'militant' lawyers could not take the form of a fee war. Since lawyers were categorically forbidden from engaging in any form of publicity, they had to wait for clients to come to them. Touting moderate fees would have been particularly inappropriate. For young lawyers, building up a client base was a lengthy process which relied on a complex network of relationships involving *avoués* and, in certain cases, business agents who referred litigants to this or that Bar member. This practice was considered contrary to Bar practices and could lead to sanctions determined by the *Conseil de l'Ordre*. Disciplinary litigation proves the existence of various methods to drum up business: reference is made to visiting cards being left in prisons, rumours being spread or newspaper articles being begged for in order to enhance the image of a counsel for the defence by boasting about the rate of acquittals obtained, or even secret pacts between lawyers, *avoués* and business agents.[39] All these practices, which were considered incompatible with the dignity of the Bar, were aimed at increasing client numbers, but they never consisted in offering lower fees than those charged by colleagues.

Finally, there was a considerable number of cases in which the lawyer had to provide his services free of charge: official appointments in criminal cases and arguments in favour of the poorest individuals, who could be assisted on a charitable basis during the first half of the nineteenth century, until a law passed on 22 January 1851, gave them the benefit of legal aid. In addition, there were cases in which the lawyer made do with very modest fees out of sympathy for badly-off clients, whether they were insolvent criminals or, in the late nineteenth century, trades associations without resources.[40] Certainly, this burden of free or almost free defence

[38] J-L Halperin, 'Les sources statistiques de l'histoire des avocats en France aux XVIIIe et XIXe siècles' in *Revue de la Société Internationale d'Histoire de la Profession d'Avocat* (1991) (3) 55–74.

[39] Cf J-L Halperin, *Avocats et notaires en Europe, op. cit.*, 226 and 235–36. The case judged by the Agen Court in 1889 (*above* n 13) gives the example of a lawyer who bragged, 'in a boastful display of poor taste, of having obtained seventy-two acquittals before the Gers *cours d'assises* in the space of nine years'.

[40] N Olszak, 'Les avocats et l'acculturation juridique du mouvement ouvrier', *Revue Internationale d'Histoire de la Profession d'Avocat* (1993), 5, 189–212.

was mainly shouldered by the youngest lawyers—Bars made sure they handed these kinds of cases on to trainees—and this may have been an additional factor which increased the amounts of open fees received for other cases. Again, however, not every lawyer was able to play on his fees in the way a service provider would have done in a competitive market. As for clients, they were unable to choose their lawyers on the basis of their fees; as their hands were also tied by these networks which put litigants in contact with representatives of the law, clients were rarely in a position to discuss fee amounts with a lawyer who was always at liberty to refuse to handle their cases. For the poorest individuals subject to trial—before the 1851 law, or just above the eligibility threshold for legal aid after that date—access to justice was very expensive due to legal costs, ie the legal taxes levied by the state and fixed-rate emoluments paid to *huissiers* and *avoués*.[41] On the other hand, the litigant who won his trial was released from payment of these expenses, which were charged to the other party. The same did not hold for fees, which were still owed by the party who hired the lawyer. It is hardly conceivable that litigants would ask for lower fees before their trials ended . . . and, once a case was decided, whatever the outcome, the client acting in bad faith could hope to gain more from his dishonesty in failing to pay his lawyer than from applying to the appropriate authorities for a reduction. The general view was that the litigant who found the fees too high should approach the council of the *Ordre* to which the lawyer belonged: he had very little hope of obtaining a hearing and could not obtain reimbursement of fees which he had paid voluntarily. At the very most, he could hope that the lawyer, challenged before the *Conseil de l'Ordre,* would take the initiative by refunding the fees in part. There was no recourse against these types of decisions by the Bar authorities, as litigation provides no examples of an application for fee reduction, which would have been the sole basis for legal action. Again, fees did not result from a power relationship between lawyers and clients which would have obeyed the laws of supply and demand. The overall stability of fees during the nineteenth century—with perhaps an upward trend after 1830—contrasts with the ebb and flow of judicial litigation which determined the number of cases likely to be dealt with by representatives of the law.

This economic inertia relating to fees does not mean that fee-setting was unimportant or exempt from rules established by common professional practices. It must first be remembered that, during the nineteenth century, an increasing number of lawyers needed their fees to make a living. Having been subject to the *patente*—a tax proportional to the office

[41] H Crespin, *Les frais de justice au XIXe siècle*, Travaux et recherches Panthéon-Assas Paris II (Paris, LGDJ, 1995). For *avoués,* average emoluments were between 75 and 120 francs for ordinary civil cases: J-L Halperin, 'Les avoués au XIXe siècle, des rentiers de la Justice?', *op. cit.*, 113.

rental, levied regardless of whether or not the profession was actually being practised—since a law passed on 18 May 1850, lawyers could not always make do with their private fortunes or parental assistance. In addition, there was always a small number of lawyers of more modest origins, who had no capital at their disposal when they started their careers. Although the democratisation of recruitment to the Bar is very relative,[42] the trend toward professionalisation is undeniable: in the second half of the nineteenth century, many lawyers worked extremely hard to earn a living, and, despite their efforts, it was not unusual for them to leave a meagre inheritance when they died.[43] Despite warnings from the *conseils de l'ordre,* more and more lawyers demanded an advance from their clients. In these circumstances, it is not surprising that fees came to well over the 15 francs per argument stipulated in section 80 of the 1807 Schedule of Costs and Expenses, which lawyers preferred to leave to the *avoués*. After 1850, the trend was to look for good institutional clients—towns, railway or insurance companies, industrial or business companies—who gave lawyers some hope of decent fees on a regular basis.

Fees, which were relatively high in amount compared to the wages of nineteenth-century workers or employees, were 'fair compensation for services rendered'. All work deserves a reward, as judges maintained to justify actions for recovery of fees. There is no longer any doubt that, in the nineteenth century, the intellectual work carried out by the liberal professions had a value, as did the salaried work of the manual trades. In 1854, the liberal jurist Renouard proposed replacing the sections of the *Code civil* dealing with the hire of services with new provisions on 'the provision of services contract'. For this eminent judge, who had been a lawyer early in his career, the liberal professions which provide services through their intellectual work must fit into the framework of this provision of services contract. Although 'words may display tact and language may show modesty' 'which may justify the use of the noble term *honoraires* for lawyers' fees' Renouard challenges the distinctions drawn between the 'aristocracy' of the working world and workers.[44] In Italy, there developed during the same period a whole body of thought on fees, which were both the lawyer's remuneration and 'a tribute to his honour'.[45]

[42] J-L Halperin, *Avocats et notaires en Europe, op. cit.*, 206–08: study of the professions of the fathers of lawyers from Lyons registered between 1872 and 1914 indicates that this democratisation had hardly begun on the eve of World War I.

[43] P Sorlin, *op. cit.*, 95. Figures we have noted in the declarations of succession of a few lawyers from Lyons who died between 1841 and 1890 indicate inheritances ranging from 3,000 to 1,000.000 francs.

[44] A-C Renouard, 'Mémoire sur le contrat de prestation de travail' in *Séances et travaux de l'Académie des sciences morales et politiques* (1854) t. XXVII, 189–193.

[45] P Beneduce, *Il corpo eloquente. Identificazione del giurista nell'Italia liberale* (Il Mulino, Bologna, 1996) 322–330. The principles used for calculating fees in the nineteenth century are already set out in the treatise *De salario*, by Zacchia, published in 1658.

The terms used in decisions of the court or disciplinary decisions clarify the 'customary' method of calculating fees, which had first to be in proportion to the importance of the case. The fee-scale thus provides us with a grid for interpreting the hierarchy established by the Bar between the various types of litigation. To start off with, 'minor' cases—argued before the justice of the peace for civil cases or the *tribunal correctionnel* for misdemeanours—were of little interest to lawyers. In these areas, a lawyer's assistance was not obligatory, the amounts at stake were small (less than 200 francs in most cases), and litigants were often poorly off. There was not much to be expected of an offender who was brought before the *tribunal correctionnel,* apart from a few cases involving honour or the press. Under these circumstances, lawyers did not rush to the Bar to plead these minor cases which brought in a few dozen francs. The lawyer's real work—'the bread-and-butter work of law firms', as Pascal Plas puts it—consisted of oral arguments delivered before a civil court of first instance or court of appeal. The lawyer had a monopoly in this and had to carry out a thorough study of legislation, precedents and doctrine. At the Court of Appeal level, it was still quite common in the nineteenth century for detailed statements of case to be written and sometimes printed. As soon as it was more than a case of routine and purely factual proceedings, fees amounted to hundreds of francs. In fact, most clients could afford access to this rich man's justice, often involving property, marriage contracts or inheritances. These well-off litigants also had to pay their *avoué,* and lawyers probably made it a point of honour to charge fees that at least equalled the emoluments received by the *avoué*. Competition between professions vying for the 'legal field', as Pierre Bourdieu puts it,[46] was also a factor in fee calculation. In the second half of the nineteenth century, this group of lucrative cases included an increasing number of commercial cases. Although lawyers had long had reservations about arguing cases in commercial courts or practical difficulties in doing so, they realised what profits they could make by having among their clients a railway company—we came across an example with figures from as early as the 1840–50 period—or large industrial companies. For a minority of 'business lawyers', this commercial litigation combined the advantages of regular income based on the repetition of advice or minor trials with the opportunity for exceptionally high fees, as demonstrated by the Waldeck-Rousseau example.

Finally, oral arguments in criminal cases, delivered before the *cours d'assises,* could, in certain circumstances, command fees amounting to several thousand francs. Certainly, defence was free or almost free of charge for a large number of accused who had the benefit of a lawyer

[46] P Bourdieu, 'La force du droit. Éléments pour une sociologie du champ juridique' in *Actes de la recherche en science sociale*, 64, (Sept 1986), 4.

appointed by the court or who belonged to the neediest classes. However, the *assises* also offered 'prestigious' trials of a political nature for violation of the press laws or crimes against moral standards, in which well-off clients found themselves involved—as the accused or as victims, in the latter case also assisted by a lawyer as civil parties. And, as their honour, and sometimes their lives, were at stake, no price was too high! In the criminal justice system, these major cases paid for the others, and this system of 'social' equalisation was perfect for a lawyer who was building his reputation based on all case files by obtaining acquittals. In addition to the stars of the Bar with their prestigious clients, there was in the provinces a small group of lawyers who argued in the *cour d'assises* several dozen times during their careers and who might occasionally charge fees of 2,000 or 3,000 francs.[47]

Fee calculation according to the importance of the case had to follow certain rules which left room for considerable flexibility. Lawyers were, of course, forbidden from matching fees to the value of the dispute, according to whether or not the outcome of the trial was favourable. The prohibition of such a *de quota litis* pact seems to have been universally respected, except in certain areas such as assessment procedures for expropriation compensation. More subtly, flat fees were also forbidden: lawyers could not set their fees as soon as they read the case file, based on where it stood in the scale of values which we have tried to reconstruct. Fees could not be determined in advance, as the lawyer's 'good offices' were only known at the end of the trial. There again, the desire to measure the work actually done by the lawyer was coupled with a roundabout way of taking the result into account, without saying as much!

It is significant that texts say nothing about the lawyer's fame as a factor in fee calculation. On the contrary, the *Répertoire Dalloz* considers unfair the rules for fee assessment proposed by Adam Smith in his explanations of the 'lottery of the law'. According to Adam Smith, only one lawyer to every 20 managed to have a successful career, and his fees had to pay for the lengthy and expensive education of his 20 less fortunate colleagues. This economic calculation seemed repugnant to French jurists, doubtless because it related to exceptional cases. The fees of the most famous lawyers were not subject to any rules: they were not necessarily excessive, as fame attracted a large number of cases. In any case, they did not lead to public challenges and mostly remained secret. For the profession as a whole, the important thing was not these extreme cases; competition occurred more between the various legal professions than between lawyers themselves.

Finally, it is repeated, in paternalistic tones, that fees had to be proportionate to the client's wealth. A good lawyer should not be

[47] P Plas, *op. cit.*, 1029–1036.

'uncompromising' toward 'unfortunate' litigants who were 'reduced to working for a living'. This is as much as to say that he could charge his well-off clients high fees. This form of compensation was all the more necessary because it put the lawyer on the same social footing as the distinguished individuals whom he accepted to defend. For a rich middle-class person, safeguarding his property, his honour, and even his life, could well account for a substantial portion of his annual income. For the lawyer, his work could not be valued below this gentleman's standard of living. Adam Smith wrote, very accurately, that the compensation of lawyers should be 'able to give them the rank in society which is demanded by such considerable confidence'.[48] Common practices with regard to fees were also standards aimed at 'appointing' or 'establishing' the place of lawyers in a money-based class society. In 1872, the senior member of the Bar in Lyons deplored a tendency to 'put fees before professional dignity'.[49] We believe, on the contrary, that nineteenth-century lawyers made fees a component part of their professional dignity. By remaining 'assessors' of the amount of their compensation, while projecting the image of a disinterested profession,[50] they managed to develop an individual and collective strategy which made fees subject to accepted professional practices that were unwritten and advantageous to their social position.

[48] A Smith, *An Inquiry into the Nature and Causes of the Wealth of Nations*, RH Campbell and AS Skinner (eds) (Oxford, 1976) vol I, 122.

[49] Record of the deliberations of the Bar in Lyons, 7 Aug 1872, and 29 July 1884 ('the exaggerated development of the financial aspect of the profession of lawyer represents a danger for the future of the Bar').

[50] For a comparison with England, cf D Sugarman, 'Simple Images and Complex Realities: English Lawyers and Their Relationship to Business and Politics, 1750–1950', *Law and History Review* (Fall 1993) 11(2), 257–301.

9

'He Would Have Made a Wonderful Solicitor': Law, Modernity and Professionalism in Bram Stoker's Dracula

ANNE McGILLIVRAY*

> *Let me begin with facts—bare, meagre facts, verified by books and figures, and of which there can be no doubt. . . . Last evening, when the Count came into my room he began by asking me questions on legal matters and on the doing of certain kinds of business. I had spent the day wearily over books, and, simply to keep my mind occupied, went over some of the matters I had been examined in at Lincoln's Inn. There was a certain method in the Count's inquiries. . . .*
>
> *First, he asked if a man in England might have two solicitors, or more. I told him he might have a dozen if he wished, but that it would not be wise to have more than one solicitor engaged in one transaction, as only one could act at a time . . . we solicitors had a system of agency one for the other, so that local work could be done locally on instruction from any solicitor. . . . 'But,' said he, 'I could be at liberty to direct myself. Is it not so?'*
>
> *'Of course,' I replied; 'and such is often done by men of business, who do not like the whole of their affairs to be known by any one person.'*
>
> *'Good!' he said, and then went on to ask about the means of making consignments and the forms to be gone through, and of all sorts of difficulties which might arise, but by foresight could be guarded against. I explained all these things to him to the best of my ability, and he certainly left me under the impression that he would have made a wonderful solicitor, for there was nothing that he did not think of or foresee (p 34).*
>
> *Jonathan Harker's Diary*[1]

* *Professor of Law, University of Manitoba.* *I am grateful to W Wesley Pue and David Sugarman for their support and suggestions; to the Librarians of the Inns of Court and the Registrars of the Law Societies of the United Kingdom and Northern Ireland for their helpful replies to my queries; and to Winnipeg playwright Kristjan Peterson, whose coffee shop suggestions toward a dramatic plotting of* Dracula *at the onset of this project led me to see Harker as Dracula's chief legal and moral opposite,* contra *academia as well as Hollywood.*

[1] Bram Stoker, *Dracula* (Archibald Constable, London, 1897). Page references are to Leonard Wolf (ed), *The Annotated Dracula* (Ballasting, New York, 1975).

A LEGAL NOVEL

A 'legal novel' for John Henry Wigmore is one in which 'the principles or the profession of the law form a main part of the author's themes'.[2] His 'List of 100 Legal Novels' (1908) was to enable the lawyer 'to familiarize himself with those features of his profession which have been taken up into general thought and literature.' *Dracula* (1897) reflects competing images of lawyering and the legal professions amid *fin-de-siècle* fear of modernity, moral degeneration and the growing disjunction between law and morality. The novel is not on Wigmore's list.[3] Its gothic obsession with blood and seduction, pollution and degeneration, perversion and predation, death and disease exclude it as belonging 'to a class whose influence is bad'.[4] If being a literary classic is a touchstone of canonical inclusion, *Dracula* was named the 100th title in the Oxford University Press World Classic Series, with the editorial comment that the other 99 authors would turn over in their graves if they knew of its elevation. If longevity and popularity count, the novel celebrated its 100th anniversary on 26 May 1997, never having been out of print. This Article is a reading of *Dracula* as a legal novel.

The novel drew mixed reviews. The *Daily Mail* was enthusiastic.

> In seeking a parallel to this weird, powerful and horrible story . . . our minds revert to such tales as . . . *Frankenstein* . . . But *Dracula* is even more appalling in its gloomy fascination than any of these![5]

Stoker's mother concurred.

> My dear, Dracula is splendid, a thousand miles beyond anything you have written before . . . No book since Mrs. Shelley's *Frankenstein* or indeed any other at all has come near yours in originality, or terror—Poe is nowhere.

The comparison is apt. The noble but monstrous vampire and the noble monster created by a monstrous scientist trace a common literary descent in the gothic tradition. They owe their immediate genesis to anxieties about science and morality in the first century to see itself as modern.

[2] John Henry Wigmore, 'A List of 100 Legal Novels' (1908) 2 *Illinois Law Review* 574, 576. For a brief introduction to the field, see Anne McGillivray, '*Recherche Sublime*: An Introduction to Law and Literature' in Evelyn J Hinz, Trevor Anderson and Anne McGillivray (eds), *Adversaria: Literature and the Law* (1994) 27 *Mosaic: A Journal for the Interdisciplinary Study of Literature* 1.

[3] Nor has *Dracula* appeared on law and literature lists since produced until Elizabeth Villiers Gemmette (ed), *Law in Literature: An Annotated Bibliography of Law-Related Works* (Whitston, Troy, NY, 1998).

[4] Wigmore, n 2 at 26–7.

[5] Daniel Farson, *The Man Who Wrote Dracula: A Biography of Bram Stoker* (Michael Joseph, London, 1975) at 162 *et seq*.

Mary Wollstonecraft, aged 16 and eloping with the poet Shelley, stayed in Geneva with Byron and his doctor-lover John Polidori in 1814. Inspired by Byron's rainy afternoon dare to write a ghost story in the German mode, Wollstonecraft began *Frankenstein* (1818).[6] The novel inaugurated science fiction. Polidori's offering, *The Vampyre* (1819),[7] introduced the vampire noble into the gothic tradition. His Lord Ruthven was precursor to Sheridan Le Fanu's *Camilla* (1872) featuring the vamping of young girls by the Countess Mircalla who in turn prepared the way for Count Dracula.[8] *Frankenstein* and *Dracula* interrogate science, morality and professionalism at the opening and closing of the nineteenth century. The scientist Frankenstein combines the arcane science of alchemy with the modern science of galvanism to create a monster, thus usurping the generative power of god and mother. The scientist Van Helsing combines the arcane science of vampirology with an astonishing array of modern

[6] Wollstonecraft records her visit to Castle Frankenstein, family seat of Count Frankenstein. Inhabited by bats and owls, its last human resident was the alchemist Konrad Dippel (1673–1734). Born at the castle, Dippel studied theology, medicine and alchemy, returned when the family had died out and styled himself Dippel Frankensteina. Dippel exhumed graves and vivisected animals in an attempt to engender life in the dead. His sole discovery is prussic acid, made by boiling up bones, hair and dried blood; see Radu Florescu discussed in John Harlow, 'Body snatcher gave jolt to tale of Frankenstein', *The Sunday Times*, 22 Sept 1996. That Dippel is the source of her Dr Frankenstein does not detract from her exploration of the moral dilemma and the suffering of the monster and his creator.

[7] Published in the *New Monthly Magazine* and rumoured to have been written by Byron (he submitted a story fragment in support), *The Vampyre* was a popular sensation. A play based on the work was staged throughout Europe on a double bill with *Frankenstein.* Polidori translated Walpole's *The Castle of Otranto,* the first Gothic novel, into Italian. James B Twitchell, *Dreadful Pleasures: An Anatomy of Modern Horror* (Oxford University Press, Oxford, 1985) ch 3.

[8] 'The grave of the Countess Mircalla was opened . . . The features, though a hundred and fifty years had passed since her funeral, were tinted with the warmth of life. . . . The two medical men . . . attested to the marvellous fact, that there was a faint but appreciable respiration, and a corresponding action of the heart. The limbs were perfectly flexible, the flesh elastic; and the leaden coffin floated with blood. . . . Here, then, were all the admitted signs and proofs of vampirism. The body, therefore, in accordance with the ancient practice, was raised, and a sharp stake driven through the heart of the vampire, who uttered a piercing shriek . . .' Farson, n 5 at 137. Dracula's literary antecedents include Goethe's *The Bride of Corinth*, Burger's *Lenore,* Robert Southey's ballad *Thalaba the Destroyer* and Thomas Preskett Prest's serial penny dreadful written in 1847 *Varney the Vampyre or, The feast of blood* (London, 1847; reprinted Penny Numbers, 1853; full text, Electronic Text Center, University of Virginia Library. http://etext.lib.virginia.edu/toc/modeng/public/AeVarl.html. 'The figure turns half round, and the light falls upon the face. It is perfectly white—perfectly bloodless. The eyes look like polished tin; the lips are drawn back . . . Is she going mad? . . . . He drags her head to the bed's edge . . . With a plunge he seizes her neck in his fang-like teeth—a gush of blood, and a hideous sucking noise follows. *The girl has swooned, and the vampire is at his hideous repast!*' This was followed by, among others, Guy du Maupassant and Arthur Conan Doyle's story of a spinster vampire published with Stoker's *The Watter's Mou.*

sciences to slay a monster, obeying the legal and moral dictates of god and father. Frankenstein's monster is a new-born innocent corrupted by his creator's rejection. Dracula is ancient, lustful and corrupting. Despite their moral opposition, the monsters have much in common. They are avid to learn, intellectually brilliant, starved for company, hunted as killers and hated as unnaturally-animate flesh deriving from the crypt. Both must cope with the complex social systems and mores of contemporary English society. Frankenstein's monster employs a quasi-legal rhetoric. Dracula retains solicitors and studies the law.

The *Spectator* objected to the novel's modern setting. This

> clever but cadaverous romance . . . would have been all the more effective if he had chosen an earlier period. The up-to-dateness of the book—the phonograph diaries, typewriters and so on—hardly fits in with the medieval methods which ultimately secure the victory for Count Dracula's foes.[9]

The 'up-to-dateness' includes shorthand, phonography, typewriting, telegraphy and the excellent late-Victorian postal and railway services. Dracula's solicitor Jonathan Harker brings photographs of the London estate purchased for Dracula.[10] 'I could not enter [the house] as I had not the key . . . but I have taken with my kodak views of it from various points.' Dracula approves of the estate's medieval origins, gothic chapel, crypt and Poe-etic tarn, 'a deep, dark-looking pond or small lake' (p 30). 'I myself am of an old family, and to live in a new house would kill me.' Although photography had been used from the mid-1800s in the study of degeneracy,[11] and psychiatrist John Seward, head of an asylum next door to the estate, would have known of this, there are no 'kodak views' of Dracula. Proof that vampires cannot be photographed would wait until Hollywood met Dracula. The novel juxtaposes the tropes of modernity against 'that which mere modernity cannot kill' (p 38). When the vampire abandons his gothic Transylvania for the modern streets of London, the threat is not only to its peoples but to modernity itself.

Dracula is foreign, ur-catholic, carnal. His foes celebrate a morality that is English, protestant, chauvinist and chaste. Dracula's alchemical

[9] *The Atheneum* described it as 'highly sensational . . . wanting in the constructive art as well as in the higher literary sense. It reads at times like a mere series of grotesquely incredible events; but there are better moments that show more power, even though these are never productive of the tremor such subjects evoke under the hand of a master.' *Punch* called it 'ingenious.' Reviewers accept the novel's sexual connotations because the vampire is merely obeying the dictates of his nature, suggests C Bentley, 'The Monster in the Bedroom: Sexual Symbolism in Bram Stoker's *Dracula*' (1972) *Literature and Psychology* 22; reprinted, ML Carter (ed), *Dracula: The Vampire and the Critics* (Ann Arbour, Michigan, UMI Research Press, 1988), 32.

[10] Dracula's estate bears the ominous name Carfax, from'quatre-face' or crossroad, where the bodies of witches and suicides were staked and buried.

[11] Daniel Pick, *Faces of Degeneration: A European Disorder, c. 1848–1918* (Cambridge University Press, Cambridge, 1993).

knowledge and demonic powers learned at the Scholomance, the devil's school, include shape shifting into beasts, insects, light and fog; hypnotism, telepathy and control of the elements; and control of such lower life forms as rats, wolves and bats. Against these powers, the vampire-fighters array the modern knowledges of law, medicine, psychiatry, hypnotism, criminology, metaphysics, physiognomy, weaponry and campaign planning, yet the scientific method is deconstructed even as it is employed. Van Helsing lectures his former student John Seward:

> You are a clever man, friend John; you reason well, and your wit is bold, but you are too prejudiced. You do not let your eyes see nor your ears hear, and that which is outside your daily life is not of account to you. . . . Ah, it is the fault of our science, that it wants to explain all; and if it explain not, then it says there is nothing to explain (p 172)

The Enlightenment celebration of science, interrogated and disrupted in *Frankenstein*, culminated in the mid-Victorian cult of science.[12] By the close of the nineteenth century, this yielded to an insecurity about science and morality, a deepening moral and social pluralism and the historic sense of dislocation named 'modernity'.[13] The meaning of modernity in the nineteenth century ranged from imperialism to sexism to the sense of a new era. Josie Harris describes the condition as[14]

> a widely diffused sense of living in a peculiarly 'modern' age . . . '[W]e moderns' was widely used as a self-explanatory expression . . . by economists, lawyers, scientists [and] by the 1870s the term was being widely used to describe 'the way we live now': the age of evolution, plutocracy, gaslight, and feminism. . . . This sense of the unique dominance of the present time was immensely reinforced over the next thirty years. . . . This sense of living in a new epoch . . . could be seen in the emergence during the 1890s of the 'new woman'. . . . [M]odernity meant the continuous advance of human and institutional rationality . . . [and for the Irish] a lurking grief at the memory of a lost domain.

Evolution, with its contingents of progress and degeneracy, is central to modernity. Framed as social Darwinism, evolution meant to late Victorians the gaining of social spaces through 'the continual advance of human and institutional rationality.' Irrationality means the losing of social spaces. It is thus a constant threat to human progress. Irrationality

[12] RA Cosgrove, 'The Reception of Analytical Jurisprudence: The Victorian debate on the Separation of Law and Morality, 1860–1900' cited in GR Rubin and David Sugarman, *Law, Economy and Society, 1750–1914: Essays in the History of English Law* (Professional Books, Abingdon, 1984), 78.

[13] Jose Harris, *Private Lives, Public Spirit: A Social History of Britain 1870–1914* (Oxford University Press, Oxford, 1993). Harris stresses the pluralism of the period and quotes HG Wells. 'The grey expanse of life today is grey, not in its essence, but because of the minute, confused mingling and mutual cancelling of many-coloured lives' (p 13).

[14] Harris, n 13, 32–36.

was embodied by the close of the century in the alien, the Jew, the central European immigrant, the criminal, the degenerate, women and children.

Evolutionary thought shaped nineteenth-century beliefs. Erasmus Darwin's *The Temple of Nature* (post 1803) celebrates evolution in heroic couplets at the dawn of the new century. Evolution is the divine engineering of Reproduction, multiplying species and culminating in the survival of Happiness:

> Shout round the globe, how Reproduction strives
> With vanquish'd Death—and Happiness survives;
> How life increasing peoples every clime
> And young renascent Nature conquers Time.

The paradigm-shaking work of his grandson Charles, *On the Origin of Species* (1859), is a darker view of evolution, a determinism guided not by a divine mind intent on renewal and perfection but by the accruing accidents of natural selection. It is genetically driven, environmentally determined, selfish and blind. No divine hand is apparent. Signs of divinity in property and class, filial piety and the great chain of being itself had been challenged in liberal discourse during Erasmus' century and, in law, by a new barristry fighting old corruption.[15] A Darwinian positivism owing more to the eighteenth-century spirit of Erasmus than the nineteenth-century spirit of Charles informed the new science of law after 1860. Law's entity, Peter Fitzpatrick writes,[16]

> is sustained despite the process of change by presenting transition as a step from one ordered state containing the entity to another—from the primitive to the modern, and so on. The transition is always one from the simple to the complex, from the unified to the diverse . . . differentiation is always accompanied by a continued social integration, an encompassing order which law itself sustains. The entity in evolving responds to and overcomes the inadequacies of its prior form.

Law's project is sustained by differentiation, from its origins in simple custom to the diversity and complexity of the common law, 'from the primitive to the modern'. Law's processes are the natural processes of evolution driven by law's version of the divine, or disembodied hand rather than the blind trial and error painstakingly set out in *On the Origin of Species*. Stoker has been accused of 'making law out of lore'[17]

[15] On the rise of legal advocacy in the development and defence of liberalism, see W Wesley Pue, 'Lawyers and Political Liberalism in Eighteenth- and Nineteenth-Century England' in Terence C Halliday and Lucien Karpik (eds), *Lawyers and the Rise of Western Political Liberalism: Europe and North America in the Eighteenth to Twentieth Centuries* (Clarendon, Oxford, 1997).

[16] On the impact of the history of evolutionary theory on HLA Hart's *The Concept of Law* (1961), see Peter Fitzpatrick (ed), *Dangerous Supplements: Resistance and Renewal in Jurisprudence* (Duke University Press, Durham, North Carolina, 1991).

[17] Wolf, n 1.

in rationalising the rules of vampirology. The phrase aptly describes the work of classical jurists in the last half of the nineteenth century. In this project, the vast lore of the common law was to be arranged according to genus and species, its doctrines, principles and rules taxonomised by origin, type and order. Law was to be a science, 'clear, rational, internally coherent and systematised'.[18] In aim and method, the project was imbued with evolutionary positivism and the supremacy of Anglo-Saxon culture. The transformation was less orderly than hoped. Law remains plagued by random mutation ('weird cases')[19] and the living fossils of lost doctrines resurrected. Its revision as a modern science did not eliminate its monsters, nor was the disappearance of evil from jurisprudence entirely satisfactory to the late-Victorian mind. *Dracula* embraces these contradictions.

Of the host of folkloric and fictional vampires extant by the close of the nineteenth century, only Dracula survived the transition from the gothic to the (post) modern. Modernity is *Dracula's* strength. It represents more than new tools to fight old vampires or new strategies of a smart vampire needing *lebensraum*. It functions as a touchstone of change, a crystal reflecting and refracting images of science, morality and law in complex linked facets. The *fin-de-siècle* Darwinian pessimism played out in fears of alterity, moral degeneration and racial decay also underlay professional debates about the modernisation of the legal professions. These fears are embodied in Count Dracula.

'I COULD NOT REPRESS A SHUDDER': IMAGES OF DEGENERATION

I now had an opportunity of observing him, and found him of a very marked physiognomy. His face was a strong—a very strong—aquiline, with high bridge of the thin nose and peculiarly arched nostrils; with lofty domed forehead. . . . His eyebrows were very massive, almost meeting across the nose. . . . The mouth, so far as I could see it under the heavy moustache, was fixed and rather cruel-looking, with peculiarly sharp teeth . . . his ears were pale, and at the tops extremely pointed . . .. The general effect was one of extraordinary pallor. . . . Hitherto I had noticed the backs of his hands as they lay on his knees in the fire-light, and they had seemed rather white and fine; but seeing them now close to me, I could not but notice that they were rather coarse. . . . Strange to say, there were hairs in the centre of the palm. The nails were long and fine, and cut to a sharp point. As the Count leaned over me and his hands touched me, I could not

[18] David Sugarman, '"A Hatred of Disorder": Legal Science, Liberalism and Imperialism' in Fitzpatrick, n 16 at 39.

[19] Cf Susan Sage Heinzelman, 'Hard Cases, Easy Cases and Weird Cases: Canon Formation in Law and Literature' (1988) 21 *Mosaic: A Journal for the Interdisciplinary Study of Literature* 59.

repress a shudder. It may have been that his breath was rank, but a horrible feeling of nausea came over me, which, do what I would, I could not conceal. The Count, evidently noticing, drew back; and with a grim sort of smile, which showed more than he had yet done his protuberant teeth, sat himself down again on his own side of the fireplace (pp 21–2).

Jonathan Harker's Diary

The ancient Greek practice of physiognomy, reading the face, head and body to know the mind, was elevated to a science in the late eighteenth century. Nineteenth-century studies of character and deviance relied on physiognamy and informed the nascent discipline of criminology.[20] Jonathan Harker, newly-admitted solicitor, studies his first client, Count Dracula, in his Transylvanian castle. Expecting nobility, Harker is disturbed by hints of degeneracy. Pallor and hairy palms reflect exhausting and perverse sexual practices. Pointed ears and teeth are traits of degeneration, of genetic reversal, atavistic throwbacks to primitive human forms.[21] Coarse hands signal common blood or manual labour unsuited to a noble station in life. Harker literally gags on Dracula's degeneracy, the rank breath of the blood-eater, the stench of the crypt. Mina Murray Harker later encounters this stench in her moments with the Count. Lucy Westenra, Mina's friend and Dracula's first English conquest, experiences physiognomy as an act of love. In a letter to Mina, she describes her suitor Dr Seward as 'an excellent *parti*, being handsome, well off, and of good birth. Just fancy! He is only nine-and-twenty, and he has an immense lunatic asylum under his own care.'

> I can fancy what a wonderful power he must have over his patients. He has a curious habit of looking one straight in the face, as if trying to read one's thoughts. He tries this on very much with me, but I flatter myself he has got a tough nut to crack. I know that from my glass. Do you ever try to read your own face? *I do*, and I can tell you it is not a bad study, and gives you more trouble than you can well fancy if you have never tried it. He says that I afford him a curious psychological study, and I humbly think I do (pp 58–9).

The novel returns to the analysis of Dracula, now drawing upon behaviourist theories of degeneracy. The continental polymath and leader of the vampire-fighters Dr Van Helsing expounds on 'the philosophy of crime', explaining to Mina that Dracula is 'predestinate to crime' whose 'child-brain' compels him 'to do the same thing every time' (p 299). He invites her comments. She immediately spots its theoretical underpinnings:

[20] Stoker's library included Lavater's five-volume *Essays on Physiognamy* (1789). Barbara Belford, *Bram Stoker: A Biography of the Author of Dracula* (Alfred A Knopf, New York, 1996).

[21] 'He who rejects with scorn the belief that his own canines, and their occasional great development in other men, are due to our early progenitors having been provided with these formidable weapons, will probably reveal by sneering the line of his descent.

> The Count is a criminal and of criminal type. Nordau and Lombroso would so classify him, and *qua* criminal he is of imperfectly formed mind. Thus, in a difficulty he has to seek resource in habit. His past is a clue . . . as a criminal, he is selfish; and as his intellect is small and his action is based on selfishness, he confines himself to one purpose. That purpose is remorseless (p 300).

Dracula is written to Lombroso's physiognomy of the atavism,[22] while Nordeau's *Degeneration* (1892) ties degeneracy to genius.[23] Lombroso predicts behavioural atavism under stress. Mina calls upon this in referencing the history of the Count's historical *persona*, Vlad Tepes Dracula the Impaler, to predict Dracula's next course of action. 'As he fled back over the Danube, leaving his forces to be cut to pieces, so now he is intent on being safe, careless of all.' Degeneration theory predicts Dracula's flight to Transylvania.

Dracula's task in the 'corridor between the centuries' for Daniel Pick was to 'represent, externalise and kill off a distinct constellation of contemporary fears' of corruption and degeneration.[24] *Dracula* 'sensationalised the horrors of degeneration and charted reassuringly the

For though he no longer intends, nor has the power, to use these teeth as weapons, he will unconsciously retract his "snarling muscles" . . . so as to expose them ready for action, like a dog preparing to fight.' Charles Darwin, *The Descent of Man and Selection in Relation to Sex* 1 (J Murray, London, 1872), p 127, quoted in Pick, n 11 at 171. Dracula's teeth are 'protuberant.' The lengthening of Mina's and Lucy's canines in their vampiric transformations is marked. 'She seemed like a nightmare of Lucy as she lay there; the pointed teeth, the bloodstained voluptuous mouth—which it made one shudder to see—the whole carnal and unspiritual appearance, seeming like a devilish mocker of Lucy's sweet purity' (*Dracula*, p 174).

[22] Gena Lombroso Ferrero's *Criminal Man According to the Classification of Cesare Lombroso* (GP Putnam, New York and London, 1911) summarises her father's work. The nose of the atavism is 'often aquiline like the beak of a bird of prey.' 'Aquiline,' writes Harker of Dracula's nose,'beaky,' writes Mina, who sees him once in the streets. 'I was looking at a very beautiful girl, in a big cartwheel hat, sitting in a victoria outside Giuliano's. . . . [A] tall, thin man, with a beaky nose and black moustache and pointed beard . . . was also observing the pretty girl. . . . His face was not a good face; it was hard, and cruel, and sensual, and his big white teeth, that looked all the whiter because his lips were so red, were pointed like an animal's.' Jonathan says, 'I believe it is the Count, but he has grown young' (p 157). 'The eyebrows are bushy and tend to meet across the nose', Lombroso writes, and the Count's 'eyebrows were very massive, almost meeting across the nose'. The ear of the criminal is 'a relic of the pointed ear' with a 'a protuberance on the upper part of the posterior margin,' and so are Dracula's. Lombroso's criminal is sensual, lazy, vain, impulsive and able to endure pain. Wolf, n 1, annotation, 300.

[23] Nordeau devotes a chapter to Oscar Wilde linking homosexuality, artistic ability and moral degeneracy. Wilde was Stoker's Dublin, meeting at his mother Lady Wilde's nationalist cultural salons. At the height of the 1895 run of his play 'The Importance of Being Ernest', Wilde was sentenced to two years' hard labour for buying sex from young boys, recently criminalised in legislation aimed at the 'white slave trade' in girls.

[24] Pick, n 11, 174.

process of their confinement and containment'. Although Krafft-Ebing and Freud were known in Stoker's day, the novel 'seems insistently and tantalisingly pre-Freudian, still caught up in the terms of Victorian degenerationism'.[25] Fears of degeneration and racial pollution haunted imperialist societies. Social evolution and evolutionary anthropology supported imperialist discourses on the indigenous peoples of the Americas and Australia. If not regressed from an original edenic state prior to European contact, they were, at the least, frozen in time and unable to progress and would die out in the face of a superior civilisation.[26] Degeneration theory turned to the scrutiny of the Other within the home population.[27] Women, children and immigrants were vectors of moral or medical plague threatening the health of late nineteenth-century England.

A 'fearful enigma',[28] the vampire is the ultimate Other, the stranger in our midst, a predator and plague vector driven by brute appetite. His metaphor is the parasite polluting the blood that is metonym of life, class and racial purity. Social parasitism is a disease of advanced cultures. 'I long to go through the crowded streets of your mighty London, to be in the midst of whirl and rush of humanity, to share its life, its change, its death,' the Count tells Harker (p 23). His threat reflects contemporary panics about syphilis, prostitution, addiction, feeble-mindedness and insanity. In his sole speech to the vampire-fighters, Dracula articulates the threat posed by this genius among parasites:

> You think to baffle me, you—with your pale faces all in a row, like sheep in a butcher's shop. You shall be sorry yet, each one of you. . . . My revenge is just begun! I have spread it over centuries, and time is on my side. Your girls that you

[25] 'Stoker's text was paralysed at a threshold of uncertainty, at the turning point between a psychiatric positivism (which the novel derided), and the glimpsed possibility of a new exploration of the unconscious. The rejection of conventional science in the novel was conceived to involve not so much a leap into the future as a return to earlier knowledge.' Pick, n 11, 171.

[26] Such theories recast in scientific discourse the older presumptions of cultural supremacy and desuetude and were used to justify destruction of First Nations cultures in North America. See Anne McGillivray, 'Therapies of Freedom: The Colonization of Aboriginal Childhood' in McGillivray (ed), *Governing Childhood* (Dartmouth, Aldershot, 1997). Darwinism was turned to the defence of rapacious Victorian business practices and the new behavioural sciences. Children of the socially unfit, for example, might be saved but would remain peripheral members of the dominant culture. Criminality was reconstructed according to Darwinian ideas replacing good and evil with environmental and genetic theories of diminished responsibility; see Martin J Wiener, *Reconstructing the Criminal: Culture, Law and Policy in England, 1830–1914* (Cambridge University Press, New York, 1990). 'The moral problems of the nineteenth century were becoming the administrative ones of the twentieth century' (p 201).

[27] Pick, n 11, 39.

[28] Pick, n 11, 171.

> all love are mine already; and through them you and others shall yet be mine—my creatures, to do my bidding and to be my jackals when I want to feed (p 271).

But his parasitism does not always kill and Mina proves that he does not always get his girl. His bite grants, at least to some, eternal life, enhanced strength and sexualised beauty[29] and this suggests that the relationship between vampire and victim more closely resembles the evolutionary strategy of *symbiosis*, a mutually interdependent partnership between different species in which each contributes to the other's success. The destabilising inference of the vampire as symbion is that we need the vampire as much as he needs us. His bite is irresistible or desired.

Evolutionary theory in *Dracula* is a nineteenth-century jumble of social Darwinism, speciation and a pre-Darwinian Lamarckism. Seward's patient, the lunatic Renfield, undertakes a Lamarckian experiment.[30] Anticipating the coming of 'the Master' and crying 'the blood is the life', he first eats flies, then feeds flies to a sparrow and eats the sparrow, working his way up the food chain from simple to complex organisms to obtain prolonged life through 'the blood'. He is killed by his 'master', Dracula, and does not become a vampire. Similar confusion about evolution, alterity and degeneration, modernity and professionalism, suffused nineteenth-century debates about the future of the legal profession.

[29] *Contra Dracula* critics, I find few contradictions in Stoker's vampirology. Vampires can kill outright, with or without taking blood (eg Dracula's murder of the madman Renfield). We are not told whether the baby consumed by the *lamia* or the murdered seamen of Dracula's ship *The Demeter* become vampires. Although the Transylvanian forest crawls with vampires, none has the Count's gifts. Part-vampires like Mina may be explained as a matter of increasing doses, as Lucy becomes fully vampire after repeated bites, but the London infants she bites live untouched save for marks as of dogs or rats at the throat, and the memory of a 'bloofer [beautiful] lady' (p 161). One exception may be the 'emaciated child' found under a furze bush in Hampstead Heath (p 162) whose fate, vampiric or otherwise, is not recorded. Of the hundreds of vampire movies, *Lost Boys* is most attuned to Stoker's curable vampires.

[30] Jean Lamarcke's *Philosophie zoologique* (Paris, 1809) and *Histoire des animaux sans vertebres* (1815–22) predate Darwin's *Origin of Species* (1859) but it was Lamarcke who first upset the eighteenth-century vision of evolution as emanating from God. He argued that acquired characteristics were heritable (the giraffe, for example, got its long neck by generations of short-necked creatures reaching for higher branches of trees). Darwin disproved the thesis and it would seem that it was rejected by Stoker, as seen in the depiction of Renfield's experiments. Lamarckism was adopted by the Soviet Union and Darwin was proscribed. For experimental national socialism, it is more useful to believe in environmental determinism (you can get used to anything by the second generation) than in genetic predisposition to preferred niches, social or natural.

'YOU FORGET THAT I AM A LAWYER': PETTIFOGGERS AND LEGAL GENTLEMEN

> *Under the circumstances, Van Helsing and I took it upon ourselves to examine papers, etc. He insisted upon looking over Lucy's papers himself. I asked him why, for I feared that he, being a foreigner, might not be quite aware of English legal requirements, and so might in ignorance make some unnecessary trouble. He answered me:- 'I know, I know. You forget that I am a lawyer as well as a doctor. But this is not altogether for the law. You knew that, when you avoided the coroner. I have more than him to avoid' (p 149).*
>
> *Dr Seward's Diary*

'I suppose that we women are such cowards that we think a man will save us from fears, and we marry him,' Lucy writes to Mina. 'It seems that a man always does find a girl alone' (p 61). But it is Dracula who finds this girl alone and she is not saved. Lucy articulates her desires. 'Why can't they let a girl marry three men, or as many as want her, and save all this trouble? But this is heresy, and I must not say it' (p 62). Her heretical and polygynous desire is fulfilled, through a marriage of blood transfused from her suitors Lord Arthur Godalming, Dr Seward and the Texan adventurer *Quincey* Morris (and, as a last resort, Van Helsing). Van Helsing likens the transfusions to the consummation of marriage. He advises one donor, 'A brave man's blood is the best thing on this earth when a woman is in trouble' (p 139). He alone suspects that Lucy's fatal anaemia is caused by the bloodsucking of a vampire. Lucy's last record is her diary descriptions of her mother's death by heart failure and Dracula's final fatal return. 'The air seems full of specks, floating and circling in the draught from the window, and the lights burn blue and dim' (p 135).

Professionalism is central in the fight against Dracula, modernity arrayed against irrationality and old powers. But professionalism also provides the cover for wrongdoing. Seward uses his medical privileges to avoid a coroner's inquest. Van Helsing adds to his impossible list of credentials—'MD, DPh, DLit, etc, etc'—a handy law degree, never again mentioned, to justify his theft of Lucy's diary. When he proposes a search of Dracula's Piccadilly house for 'deeds of purchase, keys and other things . . . book of cheques' (p 259) that will provide clues to his other London lairs, Jonathan Harker cries enthusiastically, 'We shall break in if need be' (p 260). Godalming demurs.

> *Quincey* and I will find a locksmith. You had better not come with us in case there should be any difficulty; for under the circumstances it wouldn't seem so bad for us to break into an empty house. But you are a solicitor and the Incorporated Law Society might tell you that you should have known better (p 265).

Godalming instead relies on his status as a gentleman and peer to carry off the break-in. A smaller code, that of the Law Society, is observed. A greater one, the sanctity of private property, is broken.

The crimes committed or abetted by lawyers Van Helsing and Harker include theft, destruction of evidence (burning Dracula's title deeds), burglary, interfering with a dead body (the staking of the *lamia* and the beheading of Dracula) and falsification of documents. Seward records Lucy's staking by her fiancé Godalming. It reads as rape:

> The thing in the coffin writhed; and a hideous, bloodcurdling screech came from the opened red lips. The body shook and quivered and twisted in wild contortions; the sharp white teeth champed together till the lips were cut, and the mouth was smeared with a crimson foam. But Arthur never faltered. He looked like a figure of Thor as his untrembling arm rose and fell, driving deeper and deeper the mercy-bearing stake . . . his face was set, and high duty seemed to shine through it . . . the writhing and quivering of the body became less and the teeth ceased to champ, and the face to quiver. Finally it lay still. The terrible task was over. The Professor and I sawed the top off the stake, leaving the point of it in the body. Then we cut off the head and filled the mouth with garlic. We soldered up the leaden coffin, screwed on the coffin-lid and came away (p 194–5).

Lucy's erotic and lascivious beauty and night stalking (the 'bloofer lady' who preys on small children) lead Godalming to demand,'Has there been any mistake? . . . . Has she been buried alive?' (p. 185). Van Helsing prevaricates. 'I did not say she was alive . . .. I go no further than to say she may be Un-Dead'. If vampires are Un-Dead, is this murder? It is not murder if the victim is dead, nor if the victim is not human, but what is an 'Un-dead'? Destroying its body releases the vampire to God's justice rather than perpetual damnation, according with the belief, extant until Stoker's day, that execution so releases the criminal. When staked, Lucy loses her vampiric eroticism and becomes her familiar worn but beatific self. Yet Van Helsing, the enthusiastic author of her staking, experiences the staking of Dracula's other *lamia* in his Transylvanian crypt as murder. 'She lay in her vampire sleep, so full of life and voluptuous beauty that I shudder as though I have come to do murder' (p 324).

'Has she been buried alive?' Godalming's question has a long medico-legal history. Vampires and witches are closely linked. Witches as described in the 1486 *Malleus Maleficarum,*[31] the legal handbook for the inquisition of witches, share much with vampires. Female witches prey on men and the male organ, draining potency, and gain demonic powers through sexual congress with the devil. The devil sends *incubi* and *succubi* to seduce sleepers, polluting psyche and semen, perhaps getting women with monstrous offspring. Witches, like vampires, glory in blood,

[31] Heinrich Kramer and James Sprenger, *Malleus Maleficarum*, 1468 (tr. Montague Summers, Dover, New York, 1971).

are most powerful at night and can fly, shapeshift and command fog and lower animals. Witches are killed by burning at the stake, vampires by staking or burning. That vampires were people prematurely buried and escaping their graves in amnesiac states is noted by Dom Calumet in 1746.[32]

> We are told that dead men . . . return from their tombs, are heard to speak, walk about . . . injure both men and animals whose blood they drain. . . . Nor can the men deliver themselves unless they dig the corpses up . . . and drive a sharp stake through these bodies, cut off the heads, tear out the hearts; or else they burn the bodies to ashes. It seems impossible not to subscribe to the prevailing belief that these apparitions do actually come forth from their graves. . . . It suffices to explain how vampires have been dragged from the grave and made to speak, shout, scream and bleed: they were still alive.

The Sorbonne has condemned such attacks, he writes, and it is 'astonishing that the magistrates and secular bodies have not employed their authority and legal force to put an end to it'.[33] Vampire lore echoes in plague tales told to the invalid child Stoker by his mother Charlotte.[34] A cholera epidemic in Sligo during her girlhood killed two-thirds of the townspeople. The starving drank the blood of cattle. Stricken travellers were pushed into pits and buried alive. A villager searched for his wife's body in a barn filled with hundreds of corpses and carried her home. She lived to a ripe old age. By Stoker's day, history was fading into myth, with the development of more subtle technologies for determining death. Fear of live burials and living dead survived.[35]

[32] Farson, n 5, 109–114.

[33] Science continues to stalk irrationality and there are numerous medical theories of vampirism. Decomposing corpses exhumed may be ruddy in colour, gasses produced push blood from the lungs to the mouth and staking releases intestinal gasses with a sound like a human cry. Rabies plagues in Eastern Europe were seven times more likely to affect men than women and animal victims were most often dogs, bats and wolves, named as the familiars of Dracula. Rabies induces aggressiveness including biting, which transmits the virus, teeth-baring, froth of a bloody fluid at the mouth, hyper-sexuality (male patients had intercourse up to 30 times a day), insomnia and nightwalking, and hypersensitivity to such stimuli as garlic and mirrors. An eighteenth-century rabies test was to hold a mirror before the patient; if he could stand the sight of his own image, he was not rabid; see J Gomez-Alonso, *Neurology* September 1998. Biochemist David Dolphin suggests that 'vampires' suffer from the rare hereditary disease of porphyria (a form of which may have affected George III). This induces photosensitivity, lesions causing recession of lip and gum giving a fanged appearance, and destruction of nose and fingers giving an animal appearance. The condition is treated by injecting hemes, the pigment of red blood; garlic contains alkaloids that destroy a heme protein; see Paul Sieveking, 'The truth behind a vampire's blood lust,' *The Sunday Telegraph,* 18 Oct 1998.

[34] Belford, n 20, 22.

[35] Edgar Allan Poe's 'The Premature Burial' (1840) draws on these fears. *R v Kitching* (1976), 32 CCC (2d) 159 (Manitoba Court of Appeal) places the problem in a current medico-legal context. Two Winnipeg 'bouncers' were convicted of manslaughter in the

The lawyer Van Helsing's polymathic knowledge, decisive action and noble purpose is contrasted with the pettifogging family solicitor, the genial and foolish Mr Marquand of Wholeman, Sons, Marquand & Lidderdale. Marquand is called in on the morning of the deaths of Lucy and her mother, after Van Helsing's theft of Lucy's diary. Her mother had bequeathed the Westenra estate to Lucy's fiancé Godalming and Marquand explains that, in drafting the will, he tried to preserve Lucy's financial independence by making her sole beneficiary. He was resisted by his client:

> Frankly we did our best to prevent such a testamentary disposition, and point out certain contingencies that might leave her daughter either penniless or not so free as she should be to act regarding a matrimonial alliance. Indeed, we pressed the matter so far that we almost came into collision, for she asked us if we were or were not prepared to carry out her wishes. Of course, we had then no alternative but to accept. We were right in principle, and ninety-nine times out of a hundred we should have proved, by the logic of events, the accuracy of our judgment.

'Events' as understood by Marquand have proved him wrong:

> Frankly, however, I must admit that in this case any other form of disposition would have rendered impossible the carrying out of her wishes. For by her predeceasing her daughter the latter would have come into possession of the property, and, even had she only survived her mother by five minutes, her property would, in case there were no will—and a will was a practical impossibility in such a case—have been treated at her decease as under intestacy. In which case Lord Godalming, though so dear a friend, would have had no claim in the world; and the inheritors, being remote, would not be likely to abandon their just rights, for sentimental reasons regarding a perfect stranger. I assure you, my dear sirs, I am rejoiced at the result, perfectly rejoiced (p 152–3).

Seward acidly remarks, 'He was a good fellow, but his rejoicing at the one little part—in which he was officially interested—of so great a tragedy, was an object-lesson in the limitations of sympathetic understanding' (p 153). Van Helsing's theft of the diary and its entry showing that her mother in fact predeceased her (and the maids know it, having laid out the body) has preserved the estate for Lord Godalming. Stoker restates a classic wills problem found in basic law school texts, and works in a vampiric twist.

Marquand is not the only pettifogger in the novel. Dracula's ship *The Demeter*, storm-driven with her dead captain lashed to the wheel and all hands lost, enters Whitby Harbour. The only survivor is a large dog,

brutal eviction of a club patron, causing irreversible and total brain damage. The victim was maintained on life support so that his kidneys could be harvested. The accused argued on appeal that the doctors killed the victim by removing his kidneys. The Court ruled that brain death is the point at which death occurs. The case resurrects another Poe tale, 'The Tell-tale Heart.'

Dracula in changed shape, which swims to shore and disappears.[36] The *Dailygraph* reports a law student's analysis of salvage rights:

> The fact that a coastguard was the first on board may save some complications, later on, in the Admiralty Court; for coastguards cannot claim the salvage which is the right of the first civilian entering on a derelict. Already the legal tongues are wagging, and one young law student is loudly asserting that the rights of the owner are already completely sacrificed, his property being held in contravention of the statutes of mortmain, since the tiller, as emblemship, if not proof, of delegated possession, is held in a *dead hand* (p 83).

The analys is a piece of legal casuistry. *Mortmain*, law's 'dead hand', applies only to corporately-held lands and tenements. As corporations, like vampires, are eternal and never die a natural death, this may be a coded Stoker joke. The salvage in any event is worthless, except to Dracula, as it consists entirely of boxes of earth from his castle crypt. The *Dailygraph* updates its report on the 'derelict ship':

> It turned out that the schooner is a Russian from Varna, and is called the *Demeter*. She is most entirely in ballast of silver sand, with only a small amount of cargo—a number of great wooden boxes filled with mould. This cargo was consigned to a Whitby solicitor, Mr SF Billington, of 7, The Crescent, who this morning went aboard and formally took possession of the goods consigned to him. The Russian consul, too, acting for the charter-party, took formal possession of the ship, and paid all harbour dues, etc. Nothing is talked about here today except the strange coincidence; the officials of the Board of Trade have been most exacting in seeing that every compliance has been made with existing regulations. As the matter is to be a 'nine days' wonder,' they are evidently determined that there shall be no cause of after complaint (p 83).

Seward 'saw the invoice, and took note of it: "Fifty cases of common earth, to be used for experimental purposes" ' (p 202). The carter's invoice for removal, issued by Dracula's solicitor Billington who boarded *The Demeter* and took formal possession of his client's 'goods', is later recorded (p 97–8):

> Herewith please receive invoice of goods sent by Great Northern Railway. Same are to be delivered at Carfax, near Purfleet, immediately on receipt at goods station King's Cross. The house is presently empty, but enclosed please find keys, all of which are labelled. You will please deposit the boxes, fifty in number, which for the consignment, in the partially ruined building forming part of the house and marked 'A' on the rough diagram enclosed. Your agent will easily recognise the locality, as it is the ancient chapel of the mansion.

[36] 'A good deal of interest was abroad concerning the dog which landed after the ship struck, and more than a few of the members of the S.P.C.A., which is very strong in Whitby, have tried to befriend the animal. To the general disappointment, however, it was not to be found. . . . There are some who look with dread . . . lest later on it should in itself become a danger, for it is evidently a fierce brute' (p 83).

Having taken Harker's advice to retain other solicitors, Dracula reclaims his cargo and stashes it throughout London—Carfax, Piccadilly, Mile End, Bermondsey (p 266).

The solicitor is not, professionally speaking, a match for the vampire. He is a pettifogger who delights in narrow legal arcana and in proliferating confusion about the law and who sees law as bounded in forms and documents. He is typified by the genial Marquand, the casuistical law student and the uninquisitive solicitor Billington, whose name denotes his financial bottom line. His profession limits him to strict performance in a limited arena and he cannot (or may not) compass the bounds of good and evil. High birth and social station presumptively confer compassion, public-spiritedness and honour, qualities that Seward finds sadly lacking in Mr Marquand and clearly lacking in professional dogsbodies like Billington. The privileges enjoyed by the noble Godalming are shared by barristers in a professional construct linking 'blood' with both ethical behaviour and the performance of the larger interests of justice. The expectation justifies both means and ends. As Kafka observes in *The Problem of Our Laws*, what the nobles do is right because the nobles do it.[37]

The legal gentleman is of high birth, educated at the right schools and initiated into law by the exclusive Inns of Court. He eschews formalised legal education and regards professional discipline as superfluous and insulting. By professional designation, he is the 'the larger-than-life advocate of public-interest matters—quick-witted, statesmanlike and fair-minded'.[38] The lawyer-scientist Van Helsing and the statesman-noble Vlad Tepes Dracula represent this ideal. Van Helsing, writes his former pupil Seward, is arbitrary but open-minded,

> a philosopher and a metaphysician, and one of the most advanced scientists of his day [with] an iron nerve, a temper of the ice-brook, an indomitable resolution, self-command, and toleration . . . and the kindliest and truest heart that beats (p 109).

These qualities

> form the equipment for the noble work he is doing for mankind, work both in theory and in practice, for his views are as wide as his all-embracing sympathy. I tell you these facts that you may know why I have such confidence in him.

Even so, Van Helsing frequently must justify his actions to his followers. He compares himself with Dracula and dares his danger. 'We, however,

[37] For an exegesis, see Frederick C DeCoste, 'Kafka, Legal Theorizing and Redemption' in *Adversaria*, n 2.

[38] David Sugarman, 'Simple Images and Complex Realities: English Lawyers and Their Relationship to Business and Politics, 1750–1950' (1993) 11 *Law and History Review* 257 at 300.

are not all selfish, and we believe that God is with us. . . . We shall follow [Dracula]; and we shall not flinch; even if we peril ourselves that we become like him' (p 301). As a lawyer, he is a pragmatist and moral relativist, dealing with law's relationship to morality by variously deferring one to the other.[39] Harker praises Dracula for his legal knowledge (p 34) and Van Helsing praises his advocacy for his people. 'He was in life a most wonderful man.' Dracula, like Van Helsing, is a polymath:[40]

> Soldier, statesman, and alchemist—which latter was the highest development of the science-knowledge of his time. He had a mighty brain, a learning beyond compare, and a heart that knew no fear and no remorse. He dared even to attend the Scholomance, and there was no branch of knowledge of his time that he did not essay (p 267).

But if Dracula is a lawyer, he is a bloodsucker. His nobility cloaks his corruption. He 'who can flourish in the midst of diseases that kill off whole peoples' (p 282) is a plague vector. 'Early political commentators on the growth of the modern legal profession constantly talked of swarms of lawyers infecting the commonwealth like the plague,' Peter Goodrich writes.[41] Robert Burton, analysing the mental health of the English nation in *The Anatomie of Melancholy* (1628), terms the legal professions

> a general mischief in our times, an unsensible plague, and never so many of them . . . and for the most part a supercilious, bad, covetous, litigious generation of men . . . gowned vultures, *que ex iniuriam vivunt et sanguine civium*, thieves and seminaries of discord . . . irreligious Harpies.

[39] On lawyering and pragmatism, see Thomas Grey, *The Wallace Stevens Case: Law and the Practice of Poetry* (Harvard University Press, Cambridge, 1991), reviewed in Anne McGillivray, 'Different Voices, Different Choices: Playing at Law and Literature' (1992) 7 *Canadian Journal of Law and Society* 253.

[40] Stoker met Arminius Vambery, Hungarian adventurer and holder of the Chair of Oriental Languages at the University of Pesth, 30 April 1990. Vambery is mentioned as Van Helsing's friend (p 267). The meeting may have inspired Stoker's designation of Dracula as the Wallachian Vlad Tepes Vth the Impaler Dracula, 'of the devil' (1431–1476). The Impaler was many wicked things but not a vampire. He made mothers eat their babies, split open a mistress to confirm her pregnancy and rounded up beggars for a feast, then burnt the hall around them. When Turkish envoys refused to remove their fezzes in his presence, he ordered their hats nailed to their heads. He staked enemies in his courtyard, choosing transverse or horizontal spits, held high or low, and dined amidst their cries and corpses. When a *boyar* objected to the noise and smell, he had him staked above the clamour. Vlad Tepes is revered as a Romanian national hero, freeing the region from the Turks and preserving Christianity. His fame as a vampire was a state embarrassment but Dracula has now become a staple of the new Romanian tourist trade.

[41] Quoted in Peter Goodrich, *Oedipus Lex: Psychoanalysis, History, Law* (University of California Press, Berkeley, 1995) at 5.

A plague of lawyers, gowned vultures drawing life from the injury and the blood of the people—these enduring images of the legal profession are evoked in the person of Dracula.[42]

Praising Dracula's abilities, Van Helsing mirrors his own strengths—the embrace of multiple knowledge at boundaries and cutting edges, stalwart resolve, new science and old alchemies. Dracula's genius is Nordau's degeneracy. He is Un-Dead, with a child's brain, morally undeveloped yet capable of rapid learning and a devious cleverness. In Van Helsing's broken English:

> [he] study new tongues. He learn new social life; new environment of old ways, the politic, the law, the finance, the science, the habit of a new land and a new people . . . He have done this alone; all alone! from a ruin tomb in a forgotten land. What more may he not do when the greater world of thought is open to him (p 282).

What does Van Helsing expect from Dracula's exposure to the greater world of thought— enhanced predation or voluntary redemption? We do not know. The world of thought does not open further to Dracula, thanks to Van Helsing. Dracula's morality, like Van Helsing's, is pragmatic but it resides in an appetite that Dracula feels no need to justify. Van Helsing's lament initiates the stock trope of all good scientists, up against an evil intellect. 'Oh! if such a one was to come from God, and not the Devil, what a force for good might he not be in this old world of ours' (p 282).

Images of lawyering in *Dracula* are not simple binary oppositions. They reflect complex post-1850 professional debates about the relationship between law and lawyering, law and morality. 'The period *circa* 1860 to 1900,' write Sugarman and Rubin, 'is of special interest in the study of the legal professions'.[43]

> It is in this period that the assumption of a moral basis to the legal system is challenged by Austin in England and Holmes in America. Indeed in a whole series of ways the relationship between the individual and the state was being re-examined . . . provok[ing] a significant debate concerning the separation (or otherwise) of law and morality.

Is the separation of law and morality a sign of progress or degeneration? *Dracula* interrogates this gap, an abyss where monsters lurk.[44] But the novel is more subtly concerned with another kind of lawyer and a more

[42] A tired joke remaking the law school rounds at the time of writing is: Q. Where do vampires learn to suck blood? A. At law school.

[43] Rubin and Sugarman, n 12, 78–9.

[44] Demonised female offenders like Karla Homolka draw coded metaphors of vampirism and witchery from the gap between evil and psychiatric explanation in law; see Anne McGillivray, ' "A moral vacuity in her which is difficult, if not impossible, to explain": Law, Psychiatry and the Remaking of Karla Homolka' (1998) *Intl J Legal Profession* 255–88.

modern image of lawyering than the pettifogging solicitor and the barrister-advocate, whether noble or corrupt. This was a modern image originating from within the legal profession itself and meant to fuse, at least in moral aim, the two branches of the legal profession. This is the neutral technician of law. Its embodiment is the solicitor Jonathan Harker.

'THE FACE IN THE MIRROR': THE NEUTRAL TECHNICIAN OF LAW

> *What sort of place had I come to, and among what kind of people? What sort of grim adventure was it on which I had embarked? Was this a customary incident in the life of a solicitor's clerk sent out to explain the purchase of a London estate to a foreigner? Solicitor's clerk! Mina would not like that. Solicitor—for just before leaving for London I got word that my examination was successful; and I am now a full-blown solicitor! I began to rub my eyes and pinch myself to see if I were awake. It all seemed like a horrible nightmare to me . . .* (p 19).
>
> *Jonathan Harker's Diary*

Dracula is pitted in critical and popular works against Van Helsing and the three adventurers,[45] informed and inspired by 'the angel' Mina, with her ineffectual solicitor husband in tow. Jonathan Harker's absence from much of the plot (although he appears more often than Dracula) lends some support to this interpretation. But Dracula does not see it this way. His model and the enemy he singles out for special revenge is the young solicitor. Harker is the first to meet the Count and the first to be seduced and horrified by vampirism. 'Harker Jonathan', the Count calls him, drawing our attention to his role as 'Harker' while apologising for the misplaced patronym. His Englishness and his technical legal knowledge are desired by Dracula, as is his blood, briefly, and his wife. It is Harker who delivers the first blow to the vampire in his Transylvanian crypt, scarring his forehead, the second blow in London, slashing his coat, sending coins and documents cascading from his pockets and provoking Dracula's 'sheep' speech (p 271), and the final fatal blow in Transylvania that cuts his throat. The young solicitor takes on the old bloodsucker and defeats the professional paradigm.

Harker is the neutral technician of law, combining 'the characteristically 'legal' skills of counsellor, drafter, and advocate'.[46] This image of

[45] *Quincey*, Seward and Godalming are old friends who, having shared in exotic adventures, are now suitors for the hand in marriage of Lucy Westenra.

[46] 'Lawyers sometimes see themselves as neutral technicians . . .' Rubin and Sugarman, n 12, 78–9.

lawyering offered a reconciliation of conflicts within and between the legal professions of the day:[47]

> between different messes and other forms of regional divisions; the tensions between the traditional habits of the profession and the demands for organised legal education, examinations and more centralised control; and the tensions between an attachment to mere practical and technical skill and the demand for a more scientific jurisprudence.

The paradigm embraces a scientific jurisprudence, up-to-date law office technologies (Mina prepares herself to be legal secretary to Jonathan by mastering shorthand, touch-typewriting and the dictaphone), and education, clerkship and Law Society examination (as the novel opens, Harker has been informed that he has passed). The neutral technician is constrained to ethics by loyalty to his firm and principal, and by the discipline of the 'Incorporated Law Society' from whose censure Harker is spared, in the break and entering of Dracula's house. In this paradigm of lawyering, the law is a neutral mirror of the lawyer's expectations of and for the client, and of the client's expectations of law. The face in law's mirror is at once that of lawyer and client.

Harker, of the Exeter firm of Peter Hawkins, Solicitor, travels to the Carpathians on instruction from his principal to complete a real estate transaction for Count Dracula of Transylvania, Hawkins having suffered an attack of gout. Dracula has chosen the firm for reasons of privacy. He wants to buy a London property but does not wish his affairs known in London. Wealthy, foreign and noble, he is an outstanding and unusual client for a one-man provincial law firm to have landed. Harker bears a letter of introduction from Hawkins. One passage 'gave me a thrill of pleasure' (p 21).

> He is a young man, full of energy and talent in his own way, and of a very faithful disposition. He is discreet and silent, and has grown into manhood in my service. He will be ready to attend on you when you will during his stay, and shall take your instructions in all matters.

And so Harker does. Buoyed by his new-won professionalism, he forgets the peasants' warnings, the terror of his night journey and the enigma of Dracula, in the wonders of Dracula's library:

> In the library I found, to my great delight, a vast number of English books, whole shelves full of them, and bound volumes of magazine and newspapers. A table in the centre was littered with English magazine and newspapers, though none of them were of very recent date. The books were of the most varied kind—history, geography, politics, political economy, botany, geology, law—all relating to England and English life and customs and manners. There were even such books

[47] Rubin and Sugarman, n 12, 94, citing R Cocks, *Foundations of the Modern Bar* (Sweet & Maxwell, London, 1983). See also Richard L Abel, *The Legal Profession in England and Wales* (Blackwell, 1988), 38 *et seq.*

> of reference as the London Directory, the 'Red' and 'Blue' books, Whitaker's Almanack, the Army and Navy Lists, and—it somehow gladdened my heart to see it—the Law List (p 23).

This is a lawyer's library. By his books, Dracula has come to know the object of his desire, 'your great England, and to know her is to love her.' (p 23). The portent of the Count's longing for 'its life, its change, its death' is missed by Harker but his services to the Count are spelled out. In addition to his legal duties, he is to tutor the Count in English and Englishness.

> You come to me not alone as agent of my friend Peter Hawkins, of Exeter, to tell my all about my new estate in London. You shall, I trust, rest here with me a while, so that by our talking I may learn the English intonation; and I would that you tell me when I make error, even of the smallest, in my speaking (p 24).

He spends the following nights interrogating Harker on every subject 'regarding my dear new country of England' (p 27). His object is to pass as English and be loved by them.

> Here I am noble; I am *boyar*; the common people know me and I am master. But a stranger in a strange land, he is no one; men know him not—and to know not is to care not for (p 23).

The good lawyer and guest, Harker 'felt under obligation to meet my host's wishes in every way.' As the lawyer must transform the client into law's terms, so the client transforms the lawyer. Harker, shaving, hears Dracula entering the room but cannot see him in his shaving mirror.

> [I]t amazed me that I had not seen him, since the reflection of the glass covered the whole room behind me . . . But there was no reflection of him in the mirror! . . . there was no sign of a man in it, *except myself* (p 27, emphasis added).

Identities are momentarily fused. His razor slips, drawing blood. Dracula's eyes 'blazed with a sort of demonic fury' and he 'made a grab at my throat' but Harker's crucifix, gift of a peasant woman, gives Dracula pause. After smashing the mirror on the pavement far below, he remarks, 'Take care how you cut yourself. It is more dangerous than you think in this country.' When Harker falters in his lawyerly duty, Dracula recalls him to it.

> I will take no refusal. When your master, employer, what you will, engaged that some one should come on his behalf, it was understood that my needs only were to be consulted. I have not stinted. Is it not so? (p 35).

'What could I do but bow acceptance?' Harker writes.

> It was Mr Hawkins's interest, not mine, and I had to think of him, not myself. The Count saw his victory in my bow, and his mastery in the trouble of my face, for he at once began to use them, but in his own smooth resistless way.

It is a tribute to Harker's training and loyalty to his firm that, despite his growing fear of Dracula, he continues to advise him, completes the real estate transaction, expedites his passage to England and attests to the confidentiality of his legal affairs. Adherence to professional duty is the solicitor's ethical salvation. It is nearly the undoing of the modern West.

Does neutral lawyering cultivate evil? A century later, the popular and even professional consensus might be 'yes'. The adversarial model championed by defence counsel in the US and Canada is an extreme variation on this paradigm, stressing the paramountcy of the lawyer's duty to the client to the exclusion of all else. 'The adversarial system emerged in England as advocates developed concrete responses to the exercise of state power'.[48] The ethos of the new advocacy is most famously located in Lord Brougham's 1820 speech in defence of Queen Caroline.[49] 'To save that client by all means and expedients, and at all hazards and costs to other persons, and, amongst them, to himself, is his first and only duty' is a central tenet of criminal defence work. The speech is quoted in the Canadian Bar Association *Code of Professional Conduct* to support the rule that '[t]he lawyers's duty is to protect the client as far as possible from being convicted.' He must 'disregard his private opinion as to credibility or merits'. This is the essence of neutral lawyering—to have no interests other than those of the client and to prefer those interests above all others. Canada abolished the death penalty in 1976 but its use in the

[48] W Wesley Pue, 'Lawyers and Political Liberalism in Eighteenth- and Nineteenth-Century England' in Terence C Halliday and Lucien Karpik (eds), *Lawyers and the Rise of Western Political Liberalism: Europe and North America in the Eighteenth to Twentieth Centuries* (Clarendon, Oxford, 1997), 271.

[49] 'An advocate, in the discharge of his duty, knows but one person in all the world, and that person is his client. To save that client by all means and expedients, and at all hazards and costs to other persons, and, amongst them, to himself, is his first and only duty; and in performing this duty he must not regard the alarm, the torments, the destruction which he may bring upon others. Separating the duty of a patriot from that of an advocate, he must go on reckless of consequences, though it be his unhappy fate to involve his country in confusion.' This speech of Lord Henry Brougham in his 1820 defence of Queen Caroline to George IV's charge of adultery was a veiled threat to reveal the King's secret marriage to a Roman Catholic, a revelation which would have deposed him and led to civil war. In deconstructing the 'institutional excuse', David Luban asks whether morally culpable conduct is excused by one's institutional role; see 'The Adversary System Excuse' in D Luban (ed), *The Good Lawyer: Lawyer's Rules and Lawyer's Ethics* (Rowman and Allenheld, Totawa, NJ, 1984). Also see Gerald J Postema, 'Moral Responsibility in Professional Ethics' (1980) 55 NYU L Rev 63, asking for a radical rethinking of the 'standard concept' of the lawyer's role as neutral and partisan. Brougham's speech continues to be inspirational to defence lawyers; see Eddie Greenspan and George Jonas, *The Case for the Defence* (Macmillan, Toronto, 1987).

[50] Austin Sarat, 'Between (the Presence of) Violence and (the Possibility of) Justice: Lawyering against Capital Punishment' in Austin Sarat and Stuart Scheingold (eds), *Cause Lawyering: Political Commitments and Professional Ethics* (Oxford University Press, Oxford, 1998) 317–346.

US intensified and, with it, the extremes of neutral lawyering in criminal cases. The Canadian defence bar may be absorbing a professional ethos developed in the shadow of lethal injection and the electric chair.[50] Under this model, even the concealing of real evidence by defence council has been defended.[51]

The adversarial model is set against an 'ethical' model which seeks to balance duty to the client and duty to the administration of justice, victims and their families and the public. Proponents of this model divide almost equally into calls for a return to a golden age of lawyering—the legal gentleman, the Christian lawyer, the Aristotelian advocate, the lawyer-statesman[52]—and to a post-1960s 'new lawyering' in which the lawyer is transformed by identifying not with, but through, the client to a just cause.[53] In some variations, lawyers are to be governed by conscience, while others call for comprehensive codes of conduct, far-reaching professional discipline and stricter governance of training and

[51] In the infamous Lake Pleasant 'bodies case,' the accused told his lawyers where he left the bodies of two girls he killed. Parents asked the lawyers for information and the lawyers denied knowledge, yet the lawyers had found and photographed the bodies. Charges of obstructing justice and disciplinary proceedings failed. The story is told by Tom Alibrandi with Frank Armani, *Privileged Information* (Dodd, Mead, New York, 1984). For a defence of the lawyers' conduct, see Monroe H Freedman, *Lawyers' Ethics in an Adversary System*, ch 1 (Bobbs-Merrill, Indianapolis, 1975). For a spirited criticism, see Alvin Esau's review of *Privileged Information* in *Headnotes and Footnotes* (The Manitoba Bar Association, Winnipeg, Manitoba, 1988). The issue arises in Paul Bernardo's lawyer's trial for obstruction of justice and disciplinary hearings: Ken Murray removed videotapes recording the sexual assault and torture of three young girls from Bernardo's house on his client's instructions, and hid them for 17 months. The lack of hard evidence against Bernardo necessitated the infamous plea bargain with his wife Karla Homolka; see McGillivray, n 44.

[52] The legal gentleman was the dominant ideal of the lawyer within the legal profession until well into the twentieth century. The 1921 Manitoba Law Society *Code of Professional Conduct* stressed gentlemanly conduct above all else. See W Wesley Pue, 'Becoming "Ethical": Lawyers' Professional Ethics in Early Twentieth-Century Canada' (1990) 20 *Manitoba Law Journal* 227.

[53] See Sarat and Scheingold, n 50. Hundreds of addresses, essays and monographs mourn the demise of the ethical tradition, reflect deep dissatisfaction with legal practice and set out models of lawyering going beyond that of client mouthpiece or neutral technician. See eg Donald E Buckingham, Jerome E Bickenbach, Richard Bronaugh, and The Hon Bertha Wilson (eds), *Legal Ethics in Canada: Theory and Practice* (Harcourt Brace, New York, 1996) and Anthony Kronman, *The Lost Lawyer: Failing Ideals of the Legal Profession* (The Belknap Press of the Harvard University Press, Cambridge MA, 1993) on the lawyer-statesman, a model which in many respects harks back to the gentleman of law. Aristotelian virtue ethics, civil rights models of identification with the client's cause, radical lawyering, religious lawyering, responsible lawyering *ad infinitum* are called for, while changes in the nature of legal practice—mega firms, extreme specialisation, billable hours as bottom line, professional conduct which meets the letter but not the spirit of professional ethics—are blamed for making lawyers unhappy with themselves as well as their public image.

professional upgrading. Running through these late twentieth-century debates is a recurrent anxiety about professional image and the dichotomy between being neutral and being ethical. A mourning for a lost craft or art, or a lost moral or civic high ground, underlies them. These anxieties and melancholies resonate with the modernism of the late nineteenth century and with lost battles in the cause of legal professionalism in that era. Harker acted in accord with the most 'up-to-date' nineteenth century ideal of lawyering, that of the trained and skilled neutral technician of law. The ethics of lawyering lie in the excellence of client service. Personal approval of the client's cause and identification with the client's person form no part of the paradigm. In solving his client's legal problems, Harker embodies the ideals of his profession and the expectations of his principal Hawkins, yet he facilitates the vampire's predation. His first problem is that the client-centred ethic of neutral lawyering does not readily permit a lawyer to refuse a client whose person or case the lawyer finds disagreeable ('I could not repress a shudder'). Severing relationships with a client requires cause and notice. As he is acting on behalf of his principal ('It was Mr Hawkins's interest, not mine'), he lacks the authority to refuse to act.[54] His second and more serious problem is that he is not a gentleman, nor is Hawkins.[55] While the circumstances of his meeting with his client are decidedly ambiguous, it may well be that a gentleman, unawed by Dracula's wealth and status, might soon spot him for a bounder and a cad and throw him out, so to speak, or die trying.[56]

Harker is an orphan raised in the service of a solicitor who stands as a father to him (he 'has grown into manhood in my service,' Hawkins writes), takes him on as partner and wills him his practice and country estate. Mina marvels on the rise in her social station, 'now, married to Jonathan, Jonathan a solicitor, a partner, rich, master of his business, Mr Hawkins dead and buried' (p 156), his funeral attended by the President of the Incorporated Law Society. Harker rejoices in his move 'to master from man'. 'Suckled and cradled an attorney', in the phrase of solicitor Sir George Stephen, Harker has risen in station, wealth and

[54] This ethic is questioned by David Luban, n 49.

[55] Being a solicitor did not preclude the possibility of gentlemanly birth. The occupational category of the modern solicitor of the nineteenth century spanned 'an enormous arena of social status, from landed gentry to lower-middle class'. Harris, n 13, 9.

[56] Had Harker been a gentleman with a gentleman's instinct and privilege, things might have turned out differently but it is difficult to know what he might have done imprisoned in a deserted castle, his mail stopped, his clothes stolen, the threat posed by Dracula not fully known. Had he dissembled his legal advice, Dracula might have caught it, given his knowledge of English law. In the ethical tradition of the common law, the true Englishman would prefer death to abetting Dracula's cannibalism, as the House of Lords ruled in the cannibal seamen case *Reg v Dudley and Stephens* (1884), 14 QBD 223, a case that Stoker would have certainly known (below).

prospects. Stephen, testifying before the 1846 Select Committee on Legal Education, agreed that his 'class' of solicitors 'consisted certainly of inferior men'[57]:

> They are young men who have probably been introduced in early days, at their early boyhood, at the age of 10 or 12 or 13, as soon as they could write, into an attorney's office, and employed as copying clerks. They pick up a great deal of practical knowledge, more especially a great deal of familiarity with the peculiar business and paper of the clients of their employer; they remain in his office for five or six years, or perhaps seven or eight years, and they become of extreme value to him; and then the attorney, with a view to retain them upon a very moderate salary, and probably with a view of ultimately making them partners, to take off the burthen of his business, will article them; and you may say with respect to a man of that sort, that he is suckled and cradled as an attorney.

If images of corrupt barristers disturbed the late Victorian psyche, counter-images of solicitors generated by intra-professional dialectics were ugly. Charles Rann Kennedy argued before the Committee on Legal Education that barristers were superior to solicitors because of their classical education and, in a later address to the Mutual Law Society, attested that:

> there has sprung up a tribe of a different character; the tribe of rascal pettifoggers; creatures that formerly crept not into the light of day, but now swarm like locusts over the country.[58]

The speech recalls Burton's 'unsensible plague' of lawyers. Brook's account of attorneys and solicitors in early modern England, *Pettyfoggers and Vipers of the Commonwealth*, documents the widening image gap between barristers and solicitors. 'Lawyer-bashing' centred from the sixteenth century onward on differences in education and social status between barristers and solicitors, with solicitors and attorneys taking the brunt.[59] The proliferation of lawsuits resulting from new courts and causes of action, and increased public access to legal redress in the preceding century, was equated with the proliferation of human misery.

[57] W Wesley Pue, 'Guild Training vs. Professional Education: The Committee on Legal Education and the Law Department of Queen's College, Birmingham in the 1850s' (1989) 33 *American Journal of Legal History* 241.

[58] Pue, 'Guild Training', n 57, 245.

[59] CW Brooks, *Pettyfoggers and Vipers of the Commonwealth: The Lower Branch of the Legal Profession in Early Modern England* (Cambridge University Press, Cambridge, 1986). 'By 1600, the enormous increase in litigation which had taken place since the 1550s began to produce concern among the observers, both inside and outside the legal profession, that there were too many lawsuits. In the space of a mere half-century, England seemed to have become an extremely litigious country' (p 75). The proliferation of courts, as well as lawsuits, meant that the same matter could be taken up through multiple courts, further complicating legal matters. Lawyers' images took a severe beating as a result; see ch 7.

Lawsuits over property challenged the divine order as reflected in rights of property foundational to English social order. In later republican discourses in the United States, lawyers and lawsuits were seen as attempts to upset the constitutional ideal of equality. 'Petty Foggers and Vipers of the Common Wealth . . . set Dissention between man and man'.[60] Calls for better governance of attorneys and solicitors centred on requiring association with an Inn of Court or Chancery but it was clear by the opening of the nineteenth century that there was no room at the Inns for the junior solicitor branch of the legal profession.

By the 1880s, Parliament had established the solicitors' profession in its modern form, with relatively uniform standards of admission, education and practice. Harker is a product of the these reforms. Even so, plague images and claims about the unfitness of solicitors persisted. In his analysis of mid-nineteenth century discourse on the legal professions and the 1846 Report of the Select Committee on the Legal Professions, W Wesley Pue shows that solicitors were perceived as lacking not professional training and competence but, rather, certain qualities associated with the aristocratic tradition.[61] Barrister privileges of class and education guaranteed gentlemanly behaviour. Liberal studies, writes the *Law Times* in 1843, 'make up the scholar and the gentleman' and the cost of establishing a barrister's practice ensures 'the necessary union of education and property.' This is a guarantee 'that a man is a gentleman'.[62] Any inadequacies in the barrister's legal education were compensated by the solicitor's expertise. The barrister could occupy a moral high ground and rely on his solicitor's donkey-work, as 'a mechanical agent for carrying out the practical process of the profession.'[63] The professional stake of keeping costs low, and barrister status correspondingly high, was accomplished by disparaging both the value of solicitors' work and their social status. W Shaen, Secretary of the Metropolitan and Provincial Law Association, notes in his 1855 circular that over 90 per cent of law is administered by solicitors and 'ours is the most valuable experience with regard to that which is included under the term "practice".' A circular put out by J. Bulmer that same year complained that barristers made up barely more than a fourth of the legal profession, yet enjoyed almost every 'office of distinction and emolument'.[64] The Education Committee

[60] Brooks, n 59, quoting the 1601 parliamentary speech of lord keeper Thomas Egerton arguing for the listing of 'the most expert and honest' attorneys and solicitors, as one of several reforms needed to prevent the 'Infinite multiplicytie of Sutes'. The need for reform of the profession was so often expressed and so little addressed with any teeth, 'the need to limit attorneys, like the suppression of ale-houses or the punishment of sturdy beggars, had become a commonplace.'

[61] Pue, 'Guild Training', n 57.

[62] Pue, 'Guild Training', n 57, 243.

[63] Pue, 'Guild Training', n 57, 255, quoting the Committee report.

[64] Pue, 'Guild Training', n 57, 246.

endorsed the opinion that solicitors 'should be so educated as to be qualified for carrying on that intercourse as gentlemen' but this could be attained only by 'educating them as gentlemen'.[65] This education, Pue suggests, lay less in the university course of studies proposed, than in exposure of solicitors through university studies to the culture of the gentleman.

The junior solicitor Jonathan Harker, educated in the law, 'full of energy and talent . . . faithful . . . discreet and silent,' is poised against the pettifogging solicitor Marquand and the corrupt and corrupting Dracula, arguably the image of old barristry and old corruption. Plague metaphors originating in the seventeenth century and focussed on the junior branch are now turned on the noble advocate. In his depiction of Harker, Stoker had a powerful image to disrupt, that of solicitors as a plague of pettifogging rascals, ungentlemanly, dishonourable and untrustworthy. Harker's professionalism in the novel is above reproach. Yet the plot points to a central problem with this image of the modern lawyer: that neutrality may facilitate predation. The solicitor's engagement with the vampire highlights the disjunction between the new professional standard and a larger morality in which ethical service is consumed in an evil cause. Harker is transformed by, and into, the vampire. His engagement with his client destabilises modernity itself.

'WHICH MERE "MODERNITY" CANNOT KILL': SOLICITOR–CLIENT TRANSFORMATIONS

> *Here I am, sitting at a little oak table where in old times possibly some fair lady sat to pen, with much thought and many blushes, her ill-spelt love-letter, and writing in my diary in shorthand all that has happened since I closed it last. It is nineteenth century up-to-date with a vengeance. And yet, unless my senses deceive me, the old centuries had, and have, powers of their own which mere 'modernity' cannot kill* (p 38).
>
> *Jonathan Harker's Diary*

Modernity in its melancholic sense of lost histories informs Harker's musings on old centuries and dead gentlewomen. Careless of the Count's warning to sleep only in his room ('I took pleasure in disobeying it', p 38), Harker wanders into a dust-shrouded sitting room and updates his shorthand diary, 'nineteenth century up-to-date with a vengeance'. The power of 'old centuries' cannot be killed by 'mere modernity.' Mimicking the habits of vampires, he chooses a bed of dust. 'I drew a great couch out of its place near the corner . . . and unthinking and uncaring for the dust,

[65] Pue, 'Guild Training', n 57, 257.

composed myself for sleep' (p 39). Three female vampires, cruel inversions of his imagined lady, appear in the moonlight with

> brilliant white teeth, that shone like pearls against the ruby of their voluptuous lips. There was something about them that made me uneasy, some longing and at the same time some deadly fear. I felt in my heart a wicked, burning desire that they would kiss me with those red lips.

His seduction is complete.

> I could feel the soft, shivering touch of the lips on the supersensitive skin of my throat, and the hard dents of two sharp teeth, just touching and pausing there. I closed my eyes in a languorous ecstasy.

Dracula bursts into the room, shouting with demonic wrath, 'This man belongs to me! . . . when I am done with him you shall kiss him at your will. Now go! go! I must awaken him, for there is work to be done' (p 41). He gives them the squirming sack he carries and Harker hears a child's cry as the *lamia* disappear with their meal.

Harker, horrified, awakens in his own room. Although 'nothing can be more dreadful than those awful women, who were—who *are*—waiting to suck my blood' (p 43), he 'must know the truth' and returns to the sitting room, now locked.[66] His transformation, presaged in his mirror, is begun while Dracula's is almost complete. Harker watches him 'crawl down the castle wall over that dreadful abyss, *face down* with his cloak spreading around him like great wings.' He asks, 'What manner of man is this, or what manner of creature is it in the semblance of man?' (p 37) but, watching the next day, sees that the 'semblance' is his own:

> I had been at the window somewhat less than half an hour, when I saw something coming out of the Count's window. I drew back and watched carefully, and saw the whole man emerge. It was a new shock to me to find that he had on the suit of clothes which I had worn whilst travelling here, and slung over his shoulder the terrible bag which I had seen the women take away. There could be no doubt as to his quest, and in my garb, too! This, then, is his new scheme of evil: that he will allow others to see me, as they think, so that he may both leave evidence that I have been seen in the towns or villages posting my own letters, and that any wickedness which he may do shall by the local people be attributed to me (p 46).

The lawyer's legal identity has been stolen and he is divested of the law.

> It makes me rage to think that this can go on, and whilst I am shut up here, a veritable prisoner, but without that protection of the law which is even a criminal's right and consolation.

[66] On Freud's account of his weird experience of wandering back to wicked women, resonating with Harker's subconscious fascination and return to the *lamia*, see Heinzelman, n 19.

The mother of the baby eaten by the *lamia* sees Harker as Dracula. 'When she saw my face at the window she threw herself forward, and shouted in a voice laden with menace:– "Monster, give me my child!" ' It gives him some relief that she is soon torn apart by wolves.

Harker follows Dracula's route down the precipitous castle wall and makes his third visit to the sitting room of the *lamia* by climbing through the window. The room is empty. He proceeds to the crypt. Here the nature of his client and the consequences of his legal services are driven home.

> There lay the Count, but looking as if his youth had been half renewed . . . on the lips were gouts of fresh blood. . . . It seemed as if the whole awful creature were simply gorged with blood; he lay like a filthy leech, exhausted with his repletion. . . . This was the being I was helping to transfer to London, where, perhaps, for centuries to come he might, amongst its teeming millions, satiate his lust for blood, and create a new and ever-widening circle of semi-demons to batten on the helpless. The very thought drove me mad (p 54).

The danger now understood, the solicitor attempts to murder his client. He seizes a shovel to smash in his head. 'The head turned, and the eyes fell full upon me, with all their blaze of basilisk horror.' The shovel twists, gashing Dracula's forehead and leaving a scar mirrored on Mina's forehead in the next turn of the transformation. Harker escapes, has a nervous breakdown and is nursed by nuns, married by Mina and returned to Exeter. Mina's friendship with Lucy, Lucy's encounters with Dracula and Harker's diary bring Mina to the centre of the vampire hunt and Dracula's seductive attentions.

Wilhelmina Murray Harker, assistant school-mistress, childhood friend and tutor to the wealthy Lucy Westenra, solicitor's wife and Dracula's bride-elect, is educated, intelligent and resourceful. She is the crux of the Harker-Dracula transformations. If modernity is the pivot of the identity exchange between Dracula and Harker, of Dracula's expropriation of Harker's legal knowledge and identity and Harker's vamping by the power of old centuries, then there is a second pivot when Mina is vamped by Dracula and, through her, identities are re-fused and restored. Ancient powers forced upon her by Dracula's baptism of blood war with her version of modernity. Jonathan can be seduced yet maintain his integrity. Mina must be raped to preserve hers. She walks a difficult line. Van Helsing enthuses, 'Ah, that wonderful Madam Mina! She has a man's brain—a brain that a man should have were he much gifted—and a woman's heart' (p 209). She is a 'pearl among women' (p 197) maintaining the balance between gender and knowledge.

Dracula is an epistolary novel and Mina edits it. She co-ordinates vital information from Harker's diary with Van Helsing's and Seward's notes, takes down meetings in shorthand, types up in manifold their journals, diaries, letters and phonograph records (Seward uses the new recording technology but must play an entire cylinder to find a bit of information) and takes a portable typewriter to Translyvania for the final stage of the vampire hunt. 'I feel so grateful to the man who invented the "Traveller's" typewriter. . . . I should have felt quite astray doing the work if I had to write with a pen' (p 307). Yet her redaction reduces the evidence of the vampire's predation to 'a mass of type-writing' (p 332), thus erasing all holographic proof of his existence. If Harker epitomises the modern solicitor, Mina is the modern solicitor's wife, one of the few openings for women at a time when women's place in the public sphere was contested even among contemporary feminists:

> I have been working very hard lately, because I want to keep up with Jonathan's studies, and I have been practising shorthand very assiduously. When we are married I shall be able to be useful to Jonathan, and if I can stenograph well enough I can take down what he wants to say in this way and write it out for him on the typewriter, at which also I am practising very hard (p 57).

But Mina is not to be cast as the New Woman of the 1890s. Of her tea with Lucy, she writes, 'I believe we should have shocked the "New Woman" with our appetites. Men are more tolerant, bless them!' (p 90).

> Some of the 'New Women' writers will some day start an idea that men and women should be allowed to see each other asleep before proposing or accepting. But I suppose the New Woman won't condescend in future to accept; she will do the proposing herself. And a nice job she will make of it, too! (p 91).

Despite her proven courage, her superb organisation of their collective knowledge and her co-ordination of the campaign against Dracula, the vampire fighters exclude her from their deliberations in an excess of chauvinism. 'It was a bitter pill for me to swallow' (p 215). This is the night that Dracula first visits her. His final visit seals their relationship.

Lucy's dreamy defloration and Jonathan's languorous dreams of *lamia* are erotic seductions. Mina's 'baptism of blood' (p 284) is something else. The scene, told from the viewpoint of the vampire fighters, contains images of virginal defloration and forced fellatio. Off on yet another unsuccessful hunt, they return to find Dracula with Mina in his grip and Harker in a trance beside her. Blood streams from her neck and her mouth is smeared with blood:

> With his left hand he held both Mrs. Harker's hands, keeping them away with her arms at full tension; his right hand gripped her by the back of the neck, forcing her face down to his bosom. Her white nightdress was smeared with blood, and a thin stream trickled down the man's bare breast which was shown by his torn-open dress. The attitude of the two had a terrible resemblance to a child forcing a kitten's nose into a saucer of milk to force it to drink (p 249).

Mist at her window, Mina writes, turned into the figure of 'a tall, thin man, all in black' with a 'red scar on his forehead where Jonathan had struck him'. After 'refreshing' himself with her blood and assuring her he is no stranger to her, he forces his blood into her mouth. He admonishes her.

> And so you, like the others, would play your brains against mine. You would help these men to hunt me and frustrate me in my designs! . . . you are to be punished for what you have done. You have aided in thwarting me; now you shall come to my call (p 255).

But he joins his cause to hers.

> And you, their best beloved one, are now to me, flesh of my flesh, blood of my blood; kin of my kin; my bountiful wine-press for a while; and shall be later on my companion and my helper. You shall be avenged in turn; for not one of them but shall minister to your needs.

This is heady stuff for a woman ejected from male council on the basis of her sex.

She rejects the offer, but the ingestion of vampire blood makes her part vampire, in telepathic contact with Dracula at sunrise and sunset. The vampire-prophylactic host wielded by Van Helsing sears her forehead 'as though it had been a piece of white-hot metal' (p 263), leaving a scar mirroring that on Dracula's forehead and exposing her as part-damned. Her teeth sharpen and her pallor deepens (p 261). Her vampiric transformation in turn makes Harker a mirror image of Dracula:

> Last night he was a frank, happy-looking man, with strong youthful face, full of energy, and with dark brown hair. To-day he is a drawn, haggard old man, whose white hair matches well with the hollow burning eyes and grief-written lines of his face. His energy is still intact; in fact he is like a living flame . . . (p 267).

Seward seeks a scientific explanation of Mina's condition:

> I suppose it is some of that horrid poison which has got into her veins beginning to work. The Count had his own purposes when he gave her what Van Helsing called 'the Vampire's baptism of blood'. Well, there may be a poison that distils itself out of good things; in an age when the existence of ptomaines is a mystery we should not wonder at anything! The same power that compels her silence may compel her speech (p 284).

Ptomaine, we now know, is the nitrogenous product of decay. It is a more accurate metaphor for the vampire's bite than Seward (or Stoker) could have known.

Mina does speak, under hypnosis administered at her suggestion by Van Helsing as she enters telepathic contact with Dracula. The vampire-fighters acknowledge their reliance on her intellect and her quasi-vampirism. Van Helsing writes,

> We want all her hope, all her courage; when most we want all her great brain which is trained like a man's brain, but is of sweet woman and have a special power which the Count gave her (p 298).

Her 'man's brain' draws on degeneration theory to predict Dracula's flight to Transylvania and interpret maps in order to trace his route home; and her 'special power' to track his coffined journey. The vampire-fighters travel to Dracula's castle in separate parties, Van Helsing with Mina. 'Unclean' if not yet Un-dead, Mina is sister to the Transylvanian *lamia,* her husband's seducers who mock her in the Transylvanian nights

> They smiled ever at poor dear Madam Mina; and as their laugh came through silence of the night, they twined their arms and pointed to her, and said in those so sweet tingling tones that Jonathan said were of the intolerable sweetness of the water-glasses: 'Come sister. Come to us. Come! Come!' (p 322).

Mina resists their pleas.

> That poor soul who has wrought all this misery is the saddest case of all. Just think what will be his joy when he too is destroyed in his worser part that his better part may have spiritual immortality. You must be pitiful to him too, though it may not hold your hand from its destruction (p 272).

Although the rapist has forgotten his victim as he dreams his way home in his coffin, she, having understood him, desires his reform. Whether it is salvation or revenge that drives the death blow, her husband Harker cuts Dracula's throat:

> [T]he red eyes glared with the horrible vindictive look which I knew too well. As I looked, the eyes saw the sinking sun, and the look of hate in them turned to triumph. But, on the instant, came the sweep and flash of Jonathan's great knife. I shrieked as I saw it shear through the throat; whilst at the same moment Mr. Morris's bowie knife plunged into the heart. It was like a miracle; but before our very eyes, and almost in the drawing of a breath, the whole body crumbled into dust and passed from our sight (p 330).

Mina with Dracula is cured. As the setting sun reveals her scarless forehead, she writes:

> I shall be glad as long as I live that even in that moment of final dissolution, there was in the face a look of peace, such as I never could have imagined might have rested there,

Mina's vamping foregrounds and suspends the problem of her identity as a woman with a man's brain. With Dracula's death, she will employ these qualities as solicitor's wife. Harker pays a high price for his neutral lawyering and Mina for her man's brain. Modernity has been admonished by the powers of old centuries. Dracula's death confirms the new order. A year later, Mina gives birth to a son named for 'all our little band of men' (p 332) but, oddly, not for her, Wilhelmina, Wilhelm or *vil-helm,* dauntless helmet, protector of men. It is Mina, not Lucy, who wived these men. She slew their dragon and bore their communal child. Although all proof of the vampire's existence is lost in her heroic mass of type-writing,

Van Helsing writes, 'We want no proofs . . . He will understand how some men so loved her, that they dare much for her sake.' Whether she would have made a wonderful solicitor would have occurred neither to her nor to Stoker. Both The Law Society and the Inns of Court excluded women until the *Sex Disqualification Act* (1919), prohibiting gender-based discrimination in the professions. The first woman solicitor in the United Kingdom was admitted in 1922.[67]

'A PECULIAR RATIONALITY': WRITING LAW INTO *DRACULA*

> *But there is one more thing worth lingering over, before we come to our list itself, and that is the sources of the information and skill of our 'legal' novelists. Where did they learn their legal lore?*
>
> *John Henry Wigmore*[68]

Bram Stoker, 38 years of age 'of Trinity College Dublin MA, the second son of the late Abraham Stoker of Rathgar, Co. Dublin, civil servant' was admitted to the Honourable Society of the Inner Temple on the 3 May 1886 and called to the Bar of England and Wales 30 April 1890. Mr IG Murray, Archivist of the Inner Temple, London, writes 18 May 1995 that the records of the Inn 'tell us nothing about his previous history or his private occupation'.[69] Mrs JE Edgell, Librarian and Keeper of the Records, Middle Temple, writes 14 June 1995,

> As a (qualified) barrister his name appeared in the 'Counsel' section of the Law Lists from 1891 until 1912, but the absence of any chamber's address from his entry each year suggests that he did not practice as a barrister in the courts (whether or not he employed his legal talents elsewhere).[70]

As Stoker managed the most successful London theatre of his day, Sir Henry Irving's Lyceum, his failure to practise is not surprising. He did not buy a pupilage, not a requirement until early in the next century, and there was no reason why he would, given his consuming career. He did use his legal talents elsewhere, advising Hallam Tennyson, son of Lord Tennyson, on the law of copyright and royalties in 1892 in the Lyceum

[67] Abel, n 47 at 79 and 172. The *Black Books* of Lincoln's Inn, entry 7 Jan 1904, records the Petition of suffragist Christabel Harriette Pankhurst 'to be admitted as a Student of this Society'. 'I am very desirous of being admitted a Member of the said Society, and I humbly pray that I may be heard by the Masters of the Bench of the said Society in my own behalf in support of my application.' The petition was refused without comment. *The Records of the Honorable Society of Lincoln's Inn: The Black Books* (The Society, Lincoln's Inn, 1968). vol V, 1854–1914, 357.

[68] Wigmore, n 2, 34.

[69] Letter to the author.

[70] Letter to the author.

production of *Becket*, Irving's last role.[71] Stoker's biographer Nigel Farson writes,

> With a stamina that seems colossal today, Bram Stoker managed the business affairs of the Lyceum, advised Irving on production, arranged the tours of America, and accompanied the actor on his journeys throughout Britain [and] *resumed* his legal studies and succeeded in passing his examinations (emphasis added).[72]

He does not say when these studies were begun, although he may have been thinking of the extra year required by Stoker to complete his terms at the Inn.

A call to the Bar in 1890 required little by way of legal studies as now understood. The Inns of Court had not offered legal education in any structured or consistent way since the mid-1600s and regularly engaged in debates about whether they should. While a university degree was encouraged, the central requirement of the call was 'keeping terms', a practice that the Inns still maintain. For a graduate of Oxford, Cambridge or Trinity College Dublin (Stoker's school), this meant dining at the Inn a certain number of times each term for 12 terms or three years, at some considerable cost. For other aspiring barristers, five years was required. The dinners served a central function in the socialisation and informal governance of its members. Students were imbued with the culture of their profession through contact with senior barristers and absorbed the legal gossip of the day with the port. Stoker's Inn, the Inner Temple, was the first to require student examinations, not, as might be expected, in law, but in history and Latin or Greek. Stoker may have sat this, given his extra year; the practice was abandoned in 1889, the year before his call. The Inns instituted a common, compulsory Bar admission examination in Roman and English law in 1872,[73] which Stoker certainly would have sat. Lectures were optional. Stoker's biographer Barbara Belford claims without more that Stoker did not attend lectures and had only to pass 'a written and oral examination'.[74] Questions and sample answers for the Bar examinations were published twice yearly. Crammers had begun to sell their services. Although it is difficult to imagine the

[71] Farson, n 5.

[72] Farson, n 5, 88.

[73] Abel, n 47, 41 *et seq.*

[74] Belford, n 20, 193. Belford gives no source for the claim that Stoker did not attend lectures. His Inn, the Inner Temple, is a brief walk from the Lyceum and Belford notes that Stoker made frequent use of its library (p 194). She cites its Archivist IG Murray on the issue of whether qualification as a barrister would excuse Stoker from jury duty, as this was Stoker's joking response to the question of why he decided to qualify as a barrister. (It does, since the 1870 *Juries Act*). Stoker's real motivation, she argues, was to raise him in Henry Irving's estimation and the esteem of his wife Florence (n 100). I suggest that this goes deeper, into something that Stoker wished to do for himself.

protean Stoker needing crammers, the pragmatics of his working life at the Lyceum might have necessitated a session or two as, by the 1880s, Bar examinations in Roman law required three months of study and English law six months to two years. Stoker's work ethic and appetite for learning suggest that he would have acquired some knowledge of law during his association with the Inner Temple. He would have imbibed with the dinners of the Inn the personalities, rivalries, debates, scandals and anxieties of the Bar, the Bench and the Inns. 'I have dined already, and I do not sup' (p 20), Dracula tells Harker, calling up images of Inn dinners (the bloodsucker dines on his 'sup' of blood).

Professional scandals and heated debates about the constitution and governance of the legal professions, proposed educational reforms and fusion of the senior and junior branches of the profession, would have been standard fare at the Inns. The 1846 Report of the Select Committee on the Legal Professions did not settle debates about fusion, Inn monopoly of central aspects of legal practice and, in particular, the right to speak in the privileged arena of the law courts, or the desirability, structure or control of legal education. The Inns consistently rejected recommendations for a central law school as an encroachment on their authority. Examinations, abandoned by the Inns a century before, were reinstituted in bare acknowledgement of the demand. *The Black Books of Lincoln's Inn* entry for 10 December 1889, the year before Stoker's call to the Bar, gives the report of its Legal Education committee.[75] The Council of Legal Education, a joint undertaking of the four Inns, paid the large sum of 1,000 guineas per year for four lectureships held by 'distinguished barristers.' They gave few lectures, attendance was dismal and there was no contact between student and lecturer outside of class hours:[76]

> It seems to us that the result of the Regulations is to deprive the Student of all motive for availing himself of the instruction which the Inns of Court undertake to provide.
>
> There are no Class Rooms. There is no Concert among the professors. The Lectures are delivered in the Dining Halls of the Inns. The Lecturer is not brought into contact with his Class. He has no means of judging of the attainments or requirements of those he addresses.
>
> There are over 2000 Students on the books of the Four Inns of Court.[77] Of these probably about half are still at the Universities, or are only eating dinners, and not studying the law. The remaining Students may be presumed to be preparing for their Call to the Bar. We believe that of these, not more than from 60 to 80 students (i.e. 6 to 8 per cent) attend any one of the several Courses of Lectures.

[75] *Black Books,* n 67, 262 *et seq*.

[76] These were 18 lectures on Roman Civil law, 12 on common law, equity and real property; 3 on public and private international law, constitutional law and legal history, and 6 on jurisprudence. *Black Books*, n 67, 262–3.

[77] The lion's share of admissions during this period went to Stoker's Inn, the Inner Temple. *Black Books*, n 67, 277.

The Committee observes that

> since the year 1873 the system of Education has been gradually undergoing alteration for the worse, until it has been brought into a condition which is deplorable, and we feel bound to add is unworthy of the Inns of Court

and concludes that 'the present system of Legal Education should be given up'.

Crammers or hired law tutors usurped the role of the Inn-appointed professors.

> The Crammer has taken the place of the Professor. Students are prepared by teachers who are not under the control of the Council of Legal Education . . . No instruction upon English Law can thus be given which is not shallow and transient.

Crammers, as the *Black Books* complain, were increasingly used by students at the Inns as well as by solicitors' clerks. Their pedagogy was informed by, and informed, classical juristic notions of 'relevance and identity',[78] taxonomy and certainty. The fact of their services to both branches would contribute to the establishment of joint university training in the next century. Yet they were disdained by the Inns. Crammers were central to the qualification of country solicitors like Harker, for whom The Incorporated Law Society (1825) provided no formal education.[79] Harker would not have attended its London lectures (which by 1846 included common law, conveyancing, equity, bankruptcy and criminal law)[80] but he would have been examined by the Society with his London counterparts.[81] The 'shallow and transient' crammer education complained of by the Inn's Legal Education committee reflects less a concern for inadequate legal education than a fear of losing control over barristers' socialisation. Barristers taught by crammers were not taught by gentlemen.

In his aptly-titled Article 'Exorcising Professional Demons',[82] Wesley Pue observes that 'any general discussion of legal education raised the twin spectres of enhanced status (and competitive power) of solicitors and even of a fused legal profession.' A contemporary argues,

[78] Sugarman in Fitzpatrick, n 18, 54.

[79] Sugarman in Fitzpatrick, n 18, 54.

[80] Pue, 'Guild Training', n 57, 251.

[81] Abel, n 47, 145. The Incorporated Law Society established a course of lectures for solicitors' clerks in 1833. Attendance was low and mandatory examinations were instituted shortly after. Few country clerks attended lectures, due in part to the travel involved. Incorporated Law Society members were primarily Londoners: in 1871, a decade or so before Harker would have begun his apprenticeship, only 10 per cent of country solicitors were members (p 242). Local law societies served major provincial cities by the latter part of the century but Harker's Exeter is not mentioned.

[82] W Wesley Pue, 'Exorcising Professional Demons: Charles Rann Kennedy and the Transition to the Modern Bar' (1987) 5 *Law and History Review* 135.

> This restless spirit of ambition on the part of solicitors will grown in proportion as they become more highly educated. . . . This is the argument against making [their] examinations too stiff. . . . Who will perform the drudgery of the law?[83]

Barrister Charles Rann Kennedy, the subject of Pue's study, was demonised partly for his commitment 'to a common, formal, vocational training for both branches of the divided legal professions', despite his stated dislike of solicitors, a vision that affronted 'the dignity of the bar'. Internecine rivalry continued throughout Stoker's day. A recurrent theme of the *Black Books* is the reassertion of restrictive rules for admitting solicitors to the Inn adding, among others, the requirement that a solicitor be out of practice for five years. The result was that a 'radical' solicitor seeking the privileged speaking- point of the courtroom would have to wait eight to ten years and more, by which time topical case-based issues would have evaporated.[84] The professional conduct of barristers was regulated by an unwritten code centred on conduct befitting a gentleman, loosely enforced by professional gossip and shaming and the occasional witch-hunt of non-conformists.[85] Solicitors were governed by the Incorporated Law Society but membership was optional. As only one in ten solicitors outside of London were members of the Society, Harker's membership is testimony to his professionalism. Although modern notions of professionalism are invoked in the depiction of his training, service ethic and membership, the Society had less control over members than Harker and Godalming thought in the burglary of Dracula's house.[86] In 1888, the Society was legislatively empowered to conduct preliminary hearings of complaints and recommend dispositions to the courts. It did not become self-regulating or universal until 1920. Even so, a complaint would have tainted Harker's reputation and shadowed his career.

Corruption may hide behind the facade of the gentleman but the Inns rarely took formal disciplinary proceedings against their member barristers. Such proceedings, as Pue shows, were less about barrister conduct than Inn politics aimed at defending turf. 'The Bar rules,' Dicey writes in 1867,

> are regulations which have a twofold aim: firstly, to promote honourable conduct; secondly, to check competition. All the rules which have the first aim may be summed up under the one law—thou shalt not hug attorneys.[87]

[83] Pue, 'Exorcising', n 82, 145.

[84] I am grateful to Wesley Pue for pointing this out.

[85] Pue, 'Lawyers and Political Liberalism', n 48.

[86] Abel, *Legal Professions*, n 47, 246–8.

[87] There is a long history to this rivalry. Inns excluded outsiders, defined by the Middle Temple in the sixteenth century as 'foraigners, discontinuers, strangers or other not of the society [and] *common attorney or sollicitor*' (emphasis added). 'It is an error

Keeping a social and professional distance between the two branches drove these politics. Disbarment proceedings against Kennedy were instituted by Stoker's Inn, the Inner Temple. Kennedy's vision of a fused legal profession, a Mutual Law Society for barristers and solicitors and university-based legal education continued to rise up from his professional grave—a shallow one, as the only result was a brief barring from his Midlands Mess. While England was up to the challenge,[88] the vision took root in the Canadian colonies[89] as it had in the United States where, as Tocqueville famously remarked, there was not a gentleman to be found. Lawyers could not be gentleman if, by revolutionary edict, there were no gentlemen.

Dracula raises the quandary of defining good lawyering and desirable clients by blood and birth. What if the gentleman is a cad?[90] Client loyalty is an ultimate professional ethic. What can the solicitor do when he discovers some hideous truth about his client? The question is even more difficult when he is acting under the instructions of another solicitor. 'It was Mr Hawkins's interest, not mine, and I had to think of him, not myself' (p 32). Harker's professionalism is challenged in Transylvania but he remains, in Stoker's vision, the model of the modern legal professional, the neutral technician of law, 'of a very faithful disposition . . . discreet and silent . . . ready to attend on you when you will [and] take your instructions in all matters.' The 'up-to-dateness' of the depiction shows a decent knowledge on Stoker's part of solicitors' work and professional ideals. The structural opposition between Harker and Dracula suggests more. It reflects the heated debates of the day within and between the two

to think that the sons of Graziers, farmers, merchants, tradesmen, and artificers can be made a gentleman by their attendance or matriculation . . . at an Inne of Court; for no man can be made a gentleman but by his father . . . because it is a matter of race, and of blood and descent', Sir George Buc explains in *The Third Universitie of England* (Society of Stationers, London, 1615). Goodrich, n 41, 87.

[88] Barristers and solicitors now graduate from an accredited university programme of legal studies, after which each branch attends a separate preparatory course, completes articles of clerkship and writes professional examinations. Would-be barristers must be admitted to an Inn and 'keep terms' (dining there, usually monthly). There is little left by way of practical distinction between the professions. Solicitors appear at virtually every level of court and may be gowned. Wigs remain a barrister privilege.

[89] Even so, enrolling as barrister or solicitor was an option in some Canadian provinces but all Canadian lawyers are now automatically enrolled as 'barrister and solicitor,' still retaining the old terminology. The image of the gentleman held its power in the drafting of early Canadian codes of professional conduct; the first of which, the Manitoba Code (1921) concludes, 'He should also bear in mind that he can only maintain the high traditions of his profession by being in fact as well as name a gentleman.' See W Wesley Pue, 'Becoming "Ethical": Lawyer's Professional Ethics in Early Twentieth Century Canada' (1991), 20 *Manitoba Law Journal* 227.

[90] 'Person of low manners; person guilty or capable of ungentlemanly conduct, blackguard. . . .' *Concise OED* (Clarendon, Oxford, 1964).

branches, over control of professional qualification and the nature of the professions.

Stoker's admiration for the junior branch is evident in his portrayal of Jonathan Harker. But why is Stoker, a newly-admitted barrister, hugging a solicitor? Stoker was born in Clontarf in 1847, third of seven children of a civil servant, and graduated from Trinity College Dublin with a BA (Hons) in science in 1870.[91] He won silver medals in history and composition and was an avid debater, amateur actor and athlete, with trophies in weights and walking marathons, the more surprising as his legs were paralysed until he was five. His prescient maiden address as president of the Philosophical Society was 'Sensationalism in Fiction and Society.' He was auditor of the Historical Society, the most prestigious student position. The Irish *Times* named him the most popular man at Trinity. On completing his BA, he took a year off to clerk in the office of the Registrar of Petty Sessions at Dublin Castle. He joined the legal department of the civil service after taking an MA in mathematics. He was promoted to Inspector of Petty Sessions, a position requiring travel throughout rural Ireland with the magistrates circuit court.[92] His task was to regularise court procedures, and to collect and codify rulings on subjects ranging from paupers to stray cattle, mutineers to dog licencing.

Making law out of lore was early a Stoker concern. His first publication was the 248-page tome *The Duties of Clerks of Petty Sessions in Ireland* (1879).[93] Petty Sessions were presided over by lay magistrates and clerked by solicitors. As inspector, Stoker would have acquired a knowledge of solicitors' law and, perhaps, an admiration and affection for the junior branch not shared by the London Inns. In Stoker's Ireland, the professions remained closer than in England. Both barristers and solicitors were examined at the King's Inns in Dublin, which may explain Stoker's slip in having Harker sit his examinations at Lincoln's Inn (p 34). There is no record of solicitors being examined at Lincoln's Inn in this period, according to its Librarian, and English solicitors had no formal connection with the London Inns since the eighteenth century.[94] The Incorporated Law Society of Ireland, estab-

[91] This seems to have been a real MA rather than a 'bought-up' one, as Belford mentions his working on a thesis. Belford, n 20, ch 2.

[92] Belford, n 20, 77; *The Dictionary of National Biography Missing Persons* (Oxford University Press, Oxford, 1993).

[93] Albert Power, Law School Principal of the Law Society of Ireland, writing to the author 5 Sept 1995, notes 'I myself have a copy of this book. It is a dull tome, replete with references to dog licences, court procedures, and sundry other matters of benefit to the Clerks of the courts. I understand that the book was a regular text for those involved in the administration of justice for quite some time. It is now a rarely found and valuable curiosity.' Stoker's association with the court 'would have been very much as a civil servant rather than a lawyer.'

[94] Guy Holborn, Librarian, Lincoln's Inn, letter to the author, 12 May 1995. Wesley Pue suggests that rooms may have been let for the purpose by private practitioners at the

lished by Charter of Queen Victoria in 1852, superceded the jurisdiction of the Honourable Society of King's Inns and governed both branches.[95]

After seeing Henry Irving perform in Dublin in 1871, Stoker volunteered as drama critic for the *Dublin Mail*. His rave review of Irving's second Dublin appearance in 1876 was rewarded by a personal meeting with the actor and a private recitation of the melodramatic poem 'The Dream of Eugene Aram'.[96] Stoker's *Personal Reminiscences of Henry Irving* (1906) records this formative event.

> That experience I shall never—can never—forget . . . such was Irving's commanding force, so great was the magnetism of his genius, so profound was the sense of his dominance that I sat spell-bound . . . he was incarnate power, incarnate passion . . . Soul had looked into soul!

Irving swooned, Stoker went into hysterics and Irving presented Stoker with a signed photograph. The scene recalls Dracula's flair for the dramatic and the hypnotic. Two years later, after 13 years in the legal department of the Northern Ireland civil service, Stoker was in London, retained by Irving as his factotum and business manager of the Lyceum, bound to the actor's service until Irving's death 27 years later.

Stoker began plot notes for *Dracula* on 8 March 1890, six weeks before his call to the Bar. '[F]or a Grub Street hack, dashing off romantic adventures with little editorial revision, the six years spent composing the novel was obsessional, not to say unusual', his biographer Barbara Belford writes. 'This novel obviously meant something more to him.' Although the identity of the vampire was uncertain (the character of Vlad Tepes would come later), Stoker's notes and an early omitted chapter clearly show that the vampire's first English contact was to be a young solicitor.[97] Stoker wrote himself into Harker, a young, provincial and idealistic self, warring with vampires. His private vampire was the domineering, dramatically protean, passionate and ungovernable Henry Irving. He was the first actor ever to be knighted, fulfilling Stoker's dream of the ennobling of the profession. He shares with Dracula a commanding force,

Inns. However, the numbers of students sitting London examinations through the 1880s ranged from 495 to 634 (Abel, n 47, Table 2.2). Alternatively, Stoker's reference may have been an artifice to upgrade Harker's status by dropping the famous name of Lincoln's Inn, or even a subtle nudge in the direction of a fused profession.

[95] Power, n 93.

[96] Hood's poem 'The Death-Bed' is quoted in *Dracula* on the occasion of Lucy's death, p 148. 'We thought her dying whilst she slept,/ And sleeping when she died.'

[97] Stoker's sources for Vlad Tepes and Transylvanian vampire lore at Whitby Library include William Wilkinson, *Account of the Principalities of Wallachia and Moldavia, Etc.* (Longmans, London, 1820), from which Stoker typed copious notes, and Mme E de Laszowska Gerard, 'Transylvanian Superstitions' July 1885 *Nineteenth Century*. Joseph S Bierman, 'The Genesis and Dating of *Dracula* from Bram Stoker's Working Notes' (1977) 24 *Notes and Queries* 39.

a magnetic genius, a spellbinding dominance, 'incarnate power, incarnate passion.' Their juniors Stoker and Harker at first intensely admire them, are seduced and consumed by their enterprises and are released only by their respective deaths. The similarity of Dracula's physiognomy (minus teeth, palms and nails) to the statue of Irving behind the London National Portrait Gallery is striking confirmation of Dracula's derivation. Stoker intended the novel to found a play starring Irving as Dracula as his tribute to the ailing actor. Irving's ill-health would be accommodated by minimal but powerful stage appearances (as in the 'sheep speech') and it would raise money for the failing Lyceum. Stoker prepared a script to protect dramatic copyright, notices were posted at the Lyceum half an hour before the reading, as required, and the part of Dracula was read by a Mr Jones. Irving's opinion was given in one word, 'Dreadful!'[98]

Wigmore's question of where a legal novelist learned his legal lore is answered. Stoker's familiarity with English law and with the ethics and internecine rivalries of its practitioners has a dual heritage. It lies first with the country solicitors of Northern Ireland he met in his civil service career, and then with the London barristers with whom he dined and dealt, whose disdain of the junior branch would have been apparent during his tenure at the Inner Temple. These rivalries inform the structural opposition of Harker and Dracula. But Stoker's legal training is also seen in his richly associative imagination, his ability to interweave suggestive yet contradictory discourses without being troubled as to fit or association (the boon and bane of *Dracula* and its critics) and his easy juxtaposition of the rational and the irrational, of modern science with old fears. 'The common law frame of mind', David Sugarman writes of Stoker's time, 'straddled a contradictory field of discourses'.[99]

> A tendency towards scientific rationality was yoked to an irrational belief in the spontaneous, piecemeal, unconscious continuity of the law. The law was a residue of immutable custom. . . . Scientific rationality was forever being mediated, refracted and sustained by an omnipresent irrationality: Therein lies the peculiar rationality of the common law mind.

In the common law mind of Bram Stoker, twice trained in law, lies the 'peculiar rationality' of *Dracula*.[100] It is Stoker who would have made a wonderful solicitor.

[98] 18 May 1897. Belford, n 20, 270.

[99] Sugarman in Fitzpatrick, n 18, 34.

[100] The novel's subversive sexuality and portrayals of femininity and masculinity, the multiple meanings of the vampire, class, alterity and the foreigner, its reflection of contemporary syphilis panics (he may have died of syphilis, as Farson claims, locomotor ataxia being a euphemism; or not, as Belford argues) and Freudian incest tabus (the band of brothers kill their father Dracula and marry their mother Mina) have been all been scrutinised. Stoker's life—his distanced marriage to the Irish beauty Florence Balcombe (courted by Oscar Wilde, drawn by Burne-Jones, escorted in Stoker's absence by libret-

tist and barrister JS Gilbert), his career at the centre of fin-de-siecle London, his alien Irishness—have been examined for their impact on the novel. It has been read from feminist, post-modernist, lesbian, gay, Victorian, filmic and lit-crit perspectives. Works not cited include Christopher Craft, ' "Kiss Me with Those Red Lips": Gender and Inversion in Bram Stoker's *Dracula*' (1984) 8 *Representations* 107; John L Flynn, *Cinematic Vampires: The Living Dead on Film and Television* (McFarland, Jefferson, N Carolina, 1992); Gail B Griffin, ' "Your Girls That You All Love Are Mine": Dracula and the Victorian Male Sexual Imagination' (1980) 5 *International Journal of Women's Studies* 454; Alan Johnson, 'Bent and Broken Necks: Signs of Design in Stoker's *Dracula*' (1887) 72 *The Victorian Newsletter* 133; Rebecca Pope, 'Writing and Biting in *Dracula*' (1990) 1 *Lit: Literary Interpretation Theory 199*; Phyllis A Roth, 'Suddenly Sexual Women in Bram Stoker's Dracula' in Margaret L Carter (ed), *Dracula: The Vampire and the Critics* (UMI Research Press, Ann Arbor, Michigan, 1988) 57–69. 27 *Literature and Psychology;* David Seed, 'The Narrative Method of Dracula' in ML Carter (ed), *ibid*, 195–206 (1985) 40 *Nineteenth-Century Fiction;* and Carol A Serf, 'Dracula: The Unseen Face in the Mirror' (1979) 9 *Journal of Narrative Technique 179*. Dracula is all things to all, protean to the last.

10

The Syndicat de la Magistrature *1968–1978: Elements in the History of French White Collar Professional Unionism*

DAVID APPLEBAUM

Contemporary French legal professions are unique. Most notably, there is a basic separation between judges (*magistrats*) and lawyers (*avocats*).[1] The contemporary division took root in the establishment of an independent and distinctively French school for judges, the *Centre National d'Etudes Judiciaires* in 1958. Thereafter a distinct and discrete subculture of legal professionals developed among French judges. The recent history of these magistrates—white-collar, public sector legal professionals—is an important chapter in the cultural history of modern French legal professions.

The dominant path to a career as a magistrate requires completion of the curriculum of the school for judges, renamed the *Ecole Nationale de la Magistrature* (*ENM*) in 1970. There are national exams for admission. One exam targets individuals who have completed undergraduate degrees and are less than 27 years old. Another is for civil servants in other legal professions, eg court clerks and bailiffs, who wish to become magistrates. The second exam is limited to those who are 40 or younger. Both groups take the same written exam. Successful candidates must pass oral examinations before a professional panel. Additionally, some civil servants, eg schoolteachers, also become full time students for careers in the judiciary. Following a public ritual and oath of office, all students are *auditeurs de justice*.

Within the *ENM*, the curriculum prepares all for careers as tenured civil and criminal court magistrates or non-tenured public prosecutors. Studies include preparation for specialisation as juvenile court judges (*juge d'enfants*), investigating judges (*juge d'instruction*) and probation

[1] For a detailed description of the two professions see Hubert Pinsseau, *L'organisation judiciare de la France*, (Paris, Documentation Française *France*) 75–114.

and parole judges (*juge de l'application des peines*). During the 1970s, the best students filled positions in Paris at the Ministry of Justice.

Increases and decreases in the professional population develop at a snails pace, circumscribed by budgetary constraints. Changes in the law and modulations in citizen use patterns of the civil and criminal courts have minimal impact on the numbers and distribution of judges and prosecutors. This makes it possible to plan for recruitment of candidates for professional schooling.

Professional education divides into two periods: *formation initial* and *formation permanente*. The first phase of education began as a three-year programme. Studies were cut back to 24 months in 1978. The program is now 28 months. The curricular sequence is stable. It begins with classroom work in Bordeaux, followed by clinical training in the field along with extra-legal internships. A Parisian study phase of one to three months ended in 1976. The capstone experience is a final stage in Bordeaux, home of the *ENM*. The curriculum prepares everyone for all careers. The shared knowledge and training frames working relationships among prosecutors and judges. At the same time, the design for learning creates a social separation between the judiciary and other legal professionals. In sum, 1958 marked a turning point in the relationships among members of the judiciary and between the judiciary and other legal professionals.

At the end of professional study, individual assessments generate class rankings that correlate with job openings and placements. Evaluation, ranking and promotion form an important and contentious part of professional life. Throughout their careers, magistrates attend compulsory post-graduate training. It is possible to change from a tenured judgeship to a non-tenured position as a prosecutor. Individuals switch specialities and move between courts in the tenured sector of the judiciary.

The history of the formation of the culture of professional judges is an important chapter in the contemporary cultural history of French legal professions. My approach to the study of this history is to focus on one key professional minority group. They were chosen because of their hyper-critical perspective on the professional sub-culture, the mentalities of magistrates and the place of law in society. They are the *syndicat de la magistrature*.

The *syndicat de la magistrature*, the first of more than four French labour unions of judges, was founded on 8 June 1968.[2] This essay

[2] Under the Fifth French Republic courts are divided into two sectors; judicial and administrative. The structures have become parallel since the creation of administrative appeals courts. All court decisions are subject to appeal to the *cour de cassation*. Jurisdictional battles between the two sections of the court system are handled by the *tribunal des conflicts*. There are common law jurisdictions that handle civil and criminal law as well as special courts. The former are staffed by professional judges. The latter

sketches the birth and growth to maturity of the union and a professional counter-culture in contemporary France. It is a story of collective challenges to the interplay between state and society and collaborative efforts to refashion judge-citizen relationships. It is a history that illuminates efforts by judges to enhance the possibility for broader changes in French society. In other words, the transformation of judicial culture and work was imagined as part of broader and deeper changes in day to day life in France.

The French magistrates' construction of their unique legal culture yielded efforts to connect the personal, the political and the professional in the exercise of judicial power. In the face of dominant forms of liberal, and Marxist (communist and socialist) legal realism, the union developed a worldview that embraced professional subjectivity, informed by post-modernism and feminism. The legal subject coupled with study of French citizen-subjects. The union project created a new empiricism, grounded in rigorous study and analysis of judges, courts and society.

Union members and leaders challenged modernist views of the rational-legal order. Their alternative professional culture differed from Old Regime and nineteenth century expressions of corporatism. At the same time, their white-collar professional unionism was influenced by a stream of criticism of modern French syndicalism, developed within the *Confederation Francaise Democratique du Travail* (the *CFDT* was a major innovative force in the worker's movements of the late 1960s). The union debated and published presentations by invited speakers such as Michel Foucault. Union militants reflected upon feminist criticisms of engendered French justice. Moreover, members questioned themselves as much as they interrogated state and public power. An important factor in the development of this critical perspective was the feminisation of the profession. Women became a majority of the membership and union leaders.

By constructing a white-collar labour union of highly educated women and men, the militants in the counterculture changed the face and altered

(*tribunaux de commerce* and *conseils de prud'hommes*) are staffed by elected judges (3,200 and 14,600 respectively). There are also assize courts that are not permanent jurisdictions but hold sessions when there are cases to be heard. Three judge panels and jurors drawn from electoral lists sit on the assize courts (paid and unpaid, professional and citizen). (See Pierre Kramer, 'L'Appareil judiciaire,' in *Après-demain 355–356: Journal mensuel de documentation politique*, Paris: Henry, 1993. This is the magazine published by the *Ligue des droits de l'homme*).

There are four levels of professional magistrates. The base and second tier of the pyramid has 70% of the membership. The first level employees work at appeals courts or in special jurisdictions and make up 25% of the group. Approximately 300 judges—5% of the professional group of 6,000 are *conseilliers* (decision makers—people who give advice), attorney-generals, general prosecutors and presidents of the courts. There has been some dissociation between grade and employment, as there has been a growing recognition of difference among and between courts at the same and different levels.

the world of French justice. Their movement emerged from a patriarchal and paternalistic professional mind-set. Satire and parody became tools for shattering a myth of separate spheres between public and private life. Under the Fifth French Republic, abstract and essentialist ideas of justice had been linked to a system of training. The dominant professional culture claimed to nurture independence and autonomy. It also fostered isolation and atomisation in a model that can be characterised as Foucauldian deindividuation. The legalism-law worldview constructed by and for mainstream French judges stressed the complex truth-seeking role of the skilled professional in applying the law. The union generated the framework for forming a dynamic collaborative consciousness, developing discussions of personal life and private experiences and concrete real life situations. The union fashioned a collective voice that reconfigured the connections between life and work.[3] Absent the dominant culture, the meaning and significance of the alternative vision of judicial theory and practice would not have developed along the lines of syndicalist professionalism. In turn, the possibility of objective truth drained away.

The union's articulation of the alternate worldview for the professional judges, courts and society connected with a transformation in the modalities of communication. There were new patterns of conversations among judges. Dialogues included spontaneous exchanges as well as planned exchanges among judges at local, regional and national union meetings. Annual national conventions and union retreats at Goutelas, near Lyon, informed joint actions with citizen groups and other sectors of the judicial administration (*Commission National de Liaison de Justice*).[4] Contacts with journalists and experiments in changing judge-journalist relationships were developed by the union sponsored *Commission Presse-Justice*. The union examined the paradoxes and dilemmas of legal limits on public professional speech. Experiments with court-based press offices modified the form and content of communications. Investigating judges challenged—in theory and practice—unequivocal rules about silence. Study of the problem judge-journalist relationships showed that the obligation of reserve (silence) could undermine the presumption of innocence, weaken the legitimacy of justice and, most importantly, endanger democratic values. Unionists held conversations with a host of political, social and cultural groups inside France, eg labour unions, immigrant groups, and civil liberties organisations. The union created regular connections to legal professionals [judges as well

[3] Membership of the union was '1,200 out of 4,000' according to the report made at the second national convention (*Justice 70:4*, 7). In the 2001 elections for professional representation, the union gained 34% of the ballots cast.

[4] The first union convention took the initiative to create this group of 18 labour and professional organisations (*Justice:70:5*, Feb 1970, 20).

as lawyers] in other European countries, eg Italy, Germany, Belgium, the Netherlands and Portugal. Union representatives monitored trials, joined in the deliberations of the Russell Tribunal on War Crimes and worked with judges in other countries in expressing outrage at the failures of the judiciary to defend democracy and civil liberties. Events in Greece, Chile, Argentina, Germany and Italy produced union statements about dictatorships and the right wing threat to freedoms. Films like '*Z*' and '*L'Homme de Kiev*' (Bernard Malamud's *The Fixer*) were recommended to members. The new lines of connection and the broader sweep of judges' interests, actions and statements modified the process and the content of professional discussions. The union energised and intensified voices of the professional counter-culture.

The union's repertoire of actions included strikes, press conferences and informational picketing where they distributed tracts about the problems and issues of French justice. At the same time, there were new dialogues between professionals and citizens (called *justiciables* [those subject to justice] in the discourse of French legalism, renamed *JUDICIABLES* [those subject to judgment] by Michel Foucault in his workshop for the union at Goutelas in 1977). These dialogues reshaped left leaning or post-structuralist critics of the court system and changed the vision of justice and the image of judges. Union members challenged myths about men in black robes and sought to reveal artificial and dangerous mysteries of legal language.

The union voice was broadcast throughout France. The *Institut National de l'Audiovisuel* in the *Bibliotheque François Mitterand* has an extensive collection documenting national conventions, press conferences, appearances on television talk shows and radio call-ins. Union archives document the strategy and tactics planned and executed to break out of the boundaries and borders of courthouses. The records preserved include external and internal criticisms of methods and goals. Magazines (*Justice*, *J'assume* and *J'essaime*) were published for audiences of professionals and interested lay persons. Books for judges and non-specialists as well as an historical collection of critical and frequently self-deprecating cartoons eg *Des juges croquent la justice*, (Maspero, 1979) brought humour and humanity to the union cause. The union voice reinvigorated the unique French version of cynical professional-political satire and the particular legacy of Honoré Daumier's critique of the mentality of men of justice in the nineteenth century.[5]

[5] By the late 1980s, Pierre Jaquin a professional journalist, trained at the *Institut National des Sciences Politique* had become the editor in chief of the union magazine, bringing exceptional and unique qualities of national political satire to the most important union publication.

The literature of the modern professional counter-culture revealed secrets in the relationships among judges and between French judges and a) elected state officials, b) political parties, c) labour groups, d) non-governmental organisations and e) the press. Mainstream publications from the conservative *Figaro* to the modernist *Le Monde,* communist *L'Humanité* and socialist *Libération* along with underground papers reported on the union, its activities and its ambitions. While isolated union members observed the ritual and requirements imposed by the obligation for professional reserve and silence, collective union voices from Troyes[6] to Lille and Paris crafted an instrument for speaking out in new ways in new settings. There were regular interchanges between Gaullist and Giscardien conservatives and liberals wielding administrative and legislative power, on the one hand, and the repoliticised, reinvigorated left-leaning professional community, on the other hand. The conversations shaped the elaboration of a sub-culture of professional and juridico-political dissent. New forms of sociability among judges were a part of the changes that were celebrated by the union.

The official union story had its formal beginnings with the foundation of the organisation in the midst of the crisis of the May–June uprisings in France, on 8 June 1968.[7] This sketch ends with the bombings of union headquarters in the fashionable sixteenth arrondissement of Paris in 1978 by right wing fanatics who opposed the unions positions on civil liberties and capital punishment.[8] The history continues to unfold in the present as founders and members of this labour union of judges continue to struggle with the day to day problems of professional culture and judicial service in the Fifth French Republic.[9]

[6] The first members of the union brought to trial for violation of rules on public pronouncements spoke out against corruption by private legal professionals (*notaires*) in the Troyes jurisdiction. The individuals were punished for their remarks and the right of judges to unionise was recognised as protected by the Constitution of the Fifth French Republic. Thereafter there were repeated efforts to either restrict or eliminate this right.

[7] In the midst of the May–June crisis, the founding moment which had taken several months of planning was almost cancelled as transport workers across France joined in the wave of strikes, preventing individuals from going to Paris to make the announcement and hold a TV press conference.

[8] After the bombing, the union headquarters moved to a manufacturing section of the city. Access to the offices is limited and mail is only received at the central post office.

[9] The most recent battles between the union and the government focused globalisation of fear and implementation of a 'zero tolerance' policy in criminal justice cases modeled upon the practices of Rudi Giuliani in New York City. Earlier battles developed over the 1993 reform of the French Constitution and the *Loi Pasqua* and legislation expanding police powers in searches for illegal immigrants, regarded by the union as being racist in nature and likely to lead to the abuse of fundamental rights (in much the same way the Vichy government handled illegal immigrants in France after 1940).

THE GOLDEN AGE OF THE SYNDICAT DE LA MAGISTRATURE 1968–1978

The second half of the twentieth century in France is haunted by memories of the German invasion of 1940 and the Vichy Regime. This is as true for French judges as for any other professional group who witnessed, participated in and struggled against the Pétainist Regime. The role of judges in carrying out state law as well as the part played by judges in restoring democracy to France posed paradoxical problems. The Fourth French Republic added to the debates about the nature of the meaning of contemporary justice and the appropriate role of professional judges in a modern democracy. The dilemmas of modern state action and the role of judges is shown most clearly in the context of the development and application of colonial programmes and policies in Indochina and Africa. French judges had to address their role in the use of torture in overseas criminal cases during Francois Mitterand's tenure as Minister of Justice in the government of Prime Minister Guy Mollet.[10] The revelations forced consideration of the danger to justice created by professional rules of silence imposed in arcane processes, obscured by secrecy.

In 1958, the founders of the Fifth French Republic demoted the 'third power' of the Fourth Republic. The judiciary in France came to be called the 'judicial authority'—linked to democratic sovereignty by selection and appointment by the President of the Republic. The founders of the Fifth French Republic abolished the office of *juges de paix* (founded in 1790), altered the *Conseil Superieur de la Magistrature*[11] and created a new system of judge education at the *Centre National d'Etudes Judiciaires*. Michel Debré looked forward to the new school for judges to mirror the role of the *Ecole National d'Administration* in the preparation of national administrators.

The transformation of the judiciary and redefinition of professional knowledge and culture built upon national entrance exams (*concours*). The examination pre-selection process and control of students' access to the judiciary, however, did not solve on-going problems of recruitment.

[10] Recent scholarship by Megan Koreman, *The Expectation of Justice: France 1944–1946* (Duke University Press, Durham, 1999) and Sylvie Thénault, *Une drôle de justice: Les magistrats dans la guerre d'Algérie* (La Découverte, Paris, 2001) combined with revelations about the career of Mitterand as well as Henry Rousso's *The Vichy Syndrome: History and Memory in France Since 1944,* translated by Arthur Goldhammer (Harvard, Cambridge, Mass, 1991) document the ambiguities in the legacy of judicial responses to fascism and neo-colonialism.

[11] Under the Fifth French Republic, the President was able to control membership of this governing body and, thereby, control the *commission d'avancement*. In 1993, Mitterand in coalition with Balladur made minor changes in the selection of members of the *Conseil superieur* which were opposed by most members of the judiciary.

Despite the changes of 1958 intended to elevate and revive the stature of judges, there were persistent low levels of recruitment and problems of morale in the profession. Moreover, the cohort of men and women who came to the *CNEJ* developed a critical perspective on the French judiciary. They formed the *Association des Auditeurs et Anciens Auditeurs de Justice*. The group held meetings and published critiques of legal learning and judicial service. These activities built up over time and the challenge to the system reached a climax just before the beginning of the May–June uprising of 1968. The connection between the revolution *manquée* of 1968 and the union is reflected in the post-June 1968 history of the union rather than in the simultaneity of the events themselves. The blueprint for change in undergraduate studies of law—in the stenciled pamphlet, *L'Université Critique—Faculté de Droit,* combined with the pre-1968 history of challenges of the creation of professional knowledge and culture at *CNEJ* (renamed the *Ecole National de la Magistrature*). These documents reveal a conjuncture between long-term dissent and short-run protest. The counterculture emerged from the double history and resulted in the most durable movement and institution born during the events of 1968. Union militants connected with the tradition of the *magistrats résistant* and the men who kept the history of opposition to judicial abuse of power under Vichy alive. They were able to embrace the theme of co-determination that was central to the student uprisings of 1968.

The process of fashioning an alternative strategy for learning and a new curriculum for judicial training came onto the national stage after publication of *La Formation du magistrat: livre blanc sur le centre national d'etudes judiciares*. The 114 page description and critique of the design for learning of the school for judges was co-authored by the *syndicat* and the Bordeaux alumni association. This booklet was followed by union publication of *La Formation du magistrat: livre blanc sur la formation permanente*, in 1973. The first white paper focused upon entry into the profession and the creation of the *mentalité* of a magistrate. The second white paper stressed nurturing a post-professional school activist role of self-constitution in the production of knowledge/power in professional life. The second volume on lifelong learning grew out of a questionnaire designed to generate discussion and debate about the form, content and control of professional life and culture.

While the *syndicat* pressed forward in its effort to transform the theory and practice of training judges, the national government took unilateral action. The claim was that a shortage of judges was the key factor in reaching the decision to change the system. Union militants argued that the hidden agenda was to destroy the school for judges. *Justice 70:4* (February 1970 p 4) announced a special union congress to deal with the crisis of *CNEJ*. The magazine restated approval for an educational reform project (p.10) which included 'authentic co-determination' (the union's version of *autogestion* [self-determination] advocated by students as well as anti-imperialists in May–June of 1968), a new collaborative pedagogy, specialised assignment of magistrates to schools for judges to train and teach others, and a change in cost accounting for educational payments (*a posteriori* to replace *a priori* calculations of student payments).

The published works on education for thc judiciary and lifelong learning dispelled the myth that professional training was limited to uniform, universal and objective applications of increasingly complex positivist civil and criminal code law. The view of judges as skilled bureaucrats who applied yet never engaged in interpretative and subjective decision-making was rejected. All decisions came to be regarded as political. Connections between the subject (the field of law) and the Subject (the person in search of justice) became central to professional self-consciousness. Evidence was presented to show that traininng for the judiciary required more than creating technicians who were automatons. Union pamphlets framed acquisition of skills in a wider context of knowledge that would enable critical understanding of subjective and interpretative components of judicial decision-making within code law processes. They refuted the sharp distinction of common law judges and 'government by judiciary' from code law judges and the continental tradition. This vision ran counter to the works of figures like Maurice Garcon and the liberal-conservatives who dominated French and Gaullist thinking about judges, courts and society. The ghost of Charles DeGaulle, mediated and channelled through the voice of Minister of Justice Alain Peyrefitte, warned of government by judiciary. They raised the spectre of corrupt and politicised judicial subjectivism as the antithesis of indivisible democratic sovereignty. At the same time the Gaullist views expressed by Peyrefitte regarded courts and judges as an appropriate tool in the elaboration of public policy, especially in the elaboration of criminal justice programmes and practices. It is significant and ironic that critics of the *syndicat's* counterculture applied their principles through practices associated with service to the courts of Vichy, in dealings with the FLN in Algeria and after 1962 in the trials of opponents of Algerian independence. Events of the past did not suggest to them that there was any fundamental flaw in the two hundred year history of republican subordination of justice and legal institutions. The *Ecole National de la Magistrature*, constructed to emulate and replicate the technocratic work of the *Ecole National d'Administration* (historically viewed as a continuation of a corollary to Vichy patterns and practices) became the source of a critical counter-culture. It's graduates challenged the claims of equity and fairness. They revealed patterns of bias and subjectivity that compromised the law and contradicted claims that professional judges only applied the law. The assault of the legal system on the disfavoured (*défavroisée*) became a core component of the critique of French justice as practised by so-called impersonal, objective, and highly proficient skilled legal professionals.

Throughout the 'golden age' of the union there was a regular chorus of governmental reform proposals and student challenges to the status quo at Bordeaux. (The *ENM* was the only one of the French 'grandes ecoles' located outside Paris—a political plum for the Gaullist Mayor of Bordeaux, Jacques Chaban Delmas.) The themes of change in education are expressed in the publications in *Justice* and the minutes of the Executive Council and the Executive Board of the Union [see archives in Paris]. For example, in 1976, *Justice 76* repeated concerns about the *ENM*. They deplored and protested the *Loi Foyer*, designed to increase lateral recruitment to the judiciary and break the monopoly of the school on the construction of judicial culture. They saw it as a plan to foster a return to the traditional power of older judges in shaping the culture of the younger recruits to the profession. The *syndicat* was particularly disturbed by proposals to switch the sequence of study. A modified return to a system of isolated apprenticeships in the field was seen as an effort to isolate, indoctrinate and weed out dissident voices. This was a case where the spatial reconfiguration and redistribution of authority would promote tighter control on new members of the profession. The union opposed training schemes that evaded supervision and control from Bordeaux. They wanted pedagogical preparation for mentors. They called for a system for monitoring of internship placements and training for mentors in order to insure that critical learning could take place. Militants questioned the authoritarian orientation towards certain functions of the *ENM* and the addition of a post-graduate probationary period. The dissidents warned that the governments plan to give decision-making power to those serving in apprenticeships would be declared unconstitutional (as it had been in 1970). Following the presentation of the union critique, the government denied that they had offered anything more than a trial balloon. The story is evidence of efforts to dismantle or transform the construction of the counter-culture in Bordeaux and restore the dispersed hegemonic power enjoyed by French judges in the pre-1958 hierarchical structures of the French judiciary. In fighting to preserve and protect *scolarité* in Bordeaux and stressing the importance of spending the last part of professional learning in the setting of a school for judges, the union was indirectly reaffirming a core factor in the development of syndicalist possibilities—the shared experience of a common professional education.[12]

[12] See *Justice 74:28* Jan 1974, 48 'La crise a L'Ecole Nationale de la Magistrature' for details of the declaration of 11 Dec 1973 by union members of the school when they voted against reducing the period of study at the school in Bordeaux, opposed

The union critique of reforms proposed by the Ministry of Justice argued that 'Piecemeal responses to problems are proof that the structures for participation are not fulfilling their function.' The dissidents argued that there was an 'over-representation of persons from the top of the judicial hierarchy and the extra-judicial hierarchy and an under-representation of students' in Bordeaux. At the same time, the dissident students who were members of the union noted that 'we did not run for positions because of the electoral system being used'.[13]

Reference to one collaborative project by graduating students gives some sense of the critical interdisciplinary nature and intellectual orientation of work that was possible in the Bordeaux programme. Thirteen members of the school joined in a final project called '*ENM/AIR*' '*Le Langage du Juge et son incidence sur les rapports entre la justice et la societe* (The Language of the Judge and its incidence in the relationships between justice and society).

> The students looked to use complex theories of linguistics and communication to uncover the influence of Jacques Derrida, Roland Barthes, JL Austen [allocutionary, illocutionary and perlocutionary acts], Pierre Bourdieu and Benvenitse on self-critical analysis among French magistrates.

Without Bordeaux and the union, it is less than likely that magistrates in training would have addressed these questions or considered the methodologies of post-structuralist analysis. Other legal cultural-anthropological perspectives on contemporary French justice emerged as an important part of union analysis and reflect on-going links to cutting-edge work in French social sciences.[14]

As members of the union trained their voices and pursued critical research, they developed the ability and capacity to speak on a wide

ending the Parisian period of study arguing that it was critical to witness and learn about the day-to-day operations of power in the Ministry in Paris and to develop a clear view of the role of judicial authority (the ministry) and its relationships with the executive and legislative branches of the government.

[13] See *Justice 74: Supplement au Numéro 31* (One of several special supplements in the sequentially numbered sequence of magazines.) 'Le Syndicat de la Magistrature et la Formation du Magistrat'—June 1974—for details on meeting held and the expulsion of students from the meeting room who continued to meet in the hallway of the school.

[14] Among the later publications by judges, Antoine Garapon's *L'ane portant les reliques* is a valuable tool in understanding the mentality of judges *and* demonstrating the influence of a critical and dissident sub-culture in the analysis of the day-to-day work and life of professional judges. Garapon's study reflects keen understanding of the works and methods of Pierre Bourdieu. His analysis is a key to the meaning of the rituals of French Civil and French Criminal court proceedings and the professional roles and relationships among tenured and non-tenured members of the judiciary as they go about work. A critical perspective on Garapon's method is offered by Katherine Fischer Taylor's *In the Theater of Criminal Justice: The Palais de Justice in Second Empire Paris* (Princeton Univesity Press, Princeton, 1993).

variety of subjects related to professional life and broader concerns of French Justice. At a meeting between René Pleven, Minister of Justice and the executive of the union, Pleven expressed his distress about the *means* used by the union to speak out about legislative proposals. He was 'especially upset about the ways in which public opinion was brought into the dynamic of the dialogue. . . .' Pleven preferred '*concertation prealable*' (discussions behind closed doors in private spaces) to statements made in a public space with invited guests from the press where perspectives and arguments could be witnessed and discussed by a still wider audience of citizens. The president of the *Union Fedéral de la Magistrature*, Ropers, [the older professional organisation] expressed similar concerns regarding the pattern of use of the syndicalist voice and recommended conversations similar to those sought by Pleven.[15] (See *Justice 71:11* February 1970 p 2–3). Despite these admonitions, the union established that it could and would speak out on proposed legislation as well as the logic and implications of specific legal decisions.[16]

Two examples of 'speaking out' by the dissident voice of the judges' counter-culture illuminate the key characteristics of counter-cultural action in the 'golden age' of the union: the first involved workplace safety and the second focused upon the right to political asylum in France.

The problem of safety in the workplace came to the fore at international meetings in Brescia, Italy in 1974 (*Justice 74:31* p 11) at a two day study session with members of Magistratura et Democratia (according to David Nelkin, a communist union of Italian judges). The report made by *syndicat* judges noted that there were 2,383 work-related deaths in France in 1971. Of these, 921 were in the construction trades. Industrial accidents were associated with 28,000,000 days of lost work calculated to cost 7.5 billion francs. A local investigation in the Lyon Court Region found that there had been 32 deaths, with 21 of the 32 among immigrants and eight of the 21 were Italian. Syndicalist judges, working 'in collaboration with work inspectors' found the need to force 'compliance with the law on the books' to stem the deaths and secure safety in the workplace. Comparisons of political pressures placed on workplace inspectors with political pressures placed on judges confirmed similar patterns of political interventions in the separated branches of the state administrations.

[15] At first, it was possible to maintain membership in the *Union Federal* and the *Syndicat de la Magistrature*. There was a break in 1974 as the older group objected to concerted action by the autonomous union in association with the two largest French labour federations, the Confederation General du Travail and the Confederation Francis Democratique du Travail.

[16] To date, the most intensive study I have completed has focused on the development of the union position on French abortion law reform in 1973 and 1974. A manuscript, *Images of Justice, Visions of Judges: The Syndicat de la Magistrature, 1968–1981* is nearing completion.

Shortly after the Brescia conference, Judge Patrice de la Charette (See 'L'affaire Chapron *Justice 75: supplement* 5 October 1975) developed a strategy to use French criminal law to highlight the problem of industrial accidents. His spontaneous individual action developed as a wider arena for judicial action. Charette's opponents, in the community of business leaders (*patronat*) and the government came to see his action as a more elaborate left-wing conspiracy with media collaborators. The action became a factor in forcing public action—on employers and on members of the public administration who were not fulfilling regulatory obligations. The 15 page stenciled special edition of the union magazine *redefined* public order and transformed the definition of public space to include the workplace. Moreover, the union was able to reconnect the traditional arena of court power to new fields of action in the techno-administrative bureaucratic state. Charette reinvigorated nineteenth century concerns about justice into a twentieth-century regulatory setting. The symbolic act of placing the head of the company in jail as part of preventive detention in order to preserve public order produced immediate attacks by the government on the dissident sub-culture. Emotions and debates following this case illustrate one more time the revelatory role of justice. The union reported, Charette's actions

> reminds us that industrial accidents have an uninterrupted flow that permanently disturb public order, threaten the security of citizens, and have been generally ignored by justice. There is one industrial accident in France every seven seconds, one death every 40 minutes and only a small number ever make it to court because of the lack of means for industrial inspections.

State and business leaders responded to Charette's action and worked to prevent his strategy from becoming part of the repertoire of tactics used by dissident judges in defence of immigrants and French workers. The magistrates' union concluded by expressing regret that others (members of the *patronat* and right wing journalists, politicians and bureaucrats) had tried to 'personalize the issue and elude their responsibility in order to receive special treatment outside the common law.'

The Chapron case and Judge Charette's creative jurisprudence illuminate the larger meanings of syndicalist connections—international and national. *Syndicat* action reinforced the left-wing view of silence and lack of imagination as tools in a conscious strategy to preserve judicial inactivity. For the left, the control of judges was a component in a right-wing conspiracy. The status quo, reinforced the powers of giant and mid-sized enterprises. Profits stabilised through control of the legal system and the judiciary. Elites drawn from big business and upper levels of administrative state profited when administrative actions stalemated judicial intervention and regulatory enforcement.

The second case that illustrates the 'golden age' also had international origins. In 1974, Mitterand organised a committee to study the problem of civil liberties and responses to terrorism in the German Federal Republic. There were regular meetings and frequent correspondence about German policies and practices. Members of the *syndicat de la magistrature* were active in the debate and discussion. Events reached a climax in 1978.

Monique Guémann, Vice-President of the union spoke out against the deportation of Klaus Croissant, a German lawyer and counsel for the Baader-Meinhoff Group. Croissant was one of several lawyers who belonged to the informal association of international leftist judges and legal professionals and represented the group. Invited to speak in France with several German colleagues, Croissant was refused permission to leave the country. He slipped into France and immediately asked for political asylum. The French Ministry of Justice moved as rapidly as possible to deny Croissant's request and ship him back to Germany. He was sent home with the explanation that he was not a person seeking political asylum because the Croissant case involved an a-political simple criminal matter.

Speaking in November of 1978, in her court in Draguignan, Monique Guémann said,

> As a Magistrate with a mission given by the constitution to guarantee liberties, it is my duty to express my concern that the defence cannot make use of the High Court of Appeals and the *Conseil d'État* regarding the immediate execution of the extradition order which appears to me to be a violation of the rights to a legal defence.

She was careful to craft the timing of her statement—before the opening of the official court session—in a space she thought was within the narrow boundaries of legality to manoeuvre.

Guémann's disciplinary hearing before the *Conseil Superieur de la Magistrature* was swift and quickly followed by disciplinary action for violation of the obligation of judicial reserve (*Justice 78 Supplément*). The union executive issued a press release saying:

> Without the liberty of the judge, what will become of the liberty of the citizen? Does Peyrefitte want to condemn judges to silence? What might magistrates do if tomorrow there were grave threats to liberties? For its part, it [executive bureau] will not renounce liberty.

Guémann's enemies regarded her speech as a violation of the requirement of judicial reserve. They reasoned that if one judge questioned the rulings of another court the system would lose legitimacy. Minister of Justice Peyrefitte initiated disciplinary charges against her which were ultimately heard by the *Conseil Superieur de la Magistrature*. She was censured, demoted and transferred to Nanterre. The message was clear.

Judges were prohibited from speaking out and questioning state decisions involving juridico-political acts of courts and legal panels that were outside their jurisdiction or competence. At the same time, the issues of technologies of power, structural divisions within the judiciary, the role of professional disciplinary bodies—theorised in debates among Dominique Charvet (a Marxist critic of Foucault and protege of Nicos Poulantzas), Michel Foucault (in his workshop excoriating dissident judges for advocating the amplification of juridical power in France—prepared for the union at Goutelas in 1977) and Michel Miaille (in his assessment of possibilities for dissident action by professional judges, published in *Justice*) became real in the Guémann case. Guémann's position fit the Charvet model and there is every indication that her speech was carefully planned to generate public debate—about the deportation of Croissant, the significance of civil liberties and the centrality of an independent judiciary as guardians of human rights.

There were marches, demonstrations and public challenges to Minister of Justice Peyrefitte after he censured Guémann. The National Union of Psychiatrists and Psychiatrists in Training called the censure of Guémann a 'grave attack on liberties' and 'an act of authoritarianism that proves once again that freedom of opinions does not belong to civil servants of the Republic' The magazine F published by Claude Servan-Schreiber referred to Guémann as a modern-day Antigone (more likely Anouilh's than Sophocles') while Odile Dhavernas, founder of a feminist group of legal professionals wrote to Guémann on behalf of the group expressing solidarity with her struggles against the oppressive, gendered French Republican establishment. (See Dossier Guémann, Archives of the Syndicat de la Magistrature).

A *Confederation Francais Democratique du Travail* group from the Haute Saône, representative of the 'second left' based in the secularised Catholic trade union movement, wrote, 'When judges refuse to serve as the eyes and fingers of the political class in power, they experience repression and undergo punishments reserved up until the recent era for union militants in private enterprise.'

Opposition to Guémann's public remarks was equally vocal and much more violent. There was an unsigned card sent to 'MG' at the Palais de Justice in Draguignan. It had a pencil drawing '*Poubelle Guémann*' (Guémann Garbage) with a line drawing supposed to be a person and labeled M. Croissant. Under the sketch, the writer said, 'VIDEZ ORDURES DANS LA POUBELLE S.V.P.' (throw refuse into the garbage please). Two bombs were placed in the offices of the syndicat de la magistrature; the first failed to detonate, and the second—made up of 12 sticks of dynamite—destroyed the lift. The terrorists note defended 'order and security,' praised the right wing bombing of the Bologna Train Station in Italy , and warned that if the judges continued to speak out or if they succeeded in putting an end to capital punishment in France, they would return and kill judges. (Envelope and handwritten note from the Archives of the union).

The decision to censure Guémann and transfer her to Nanterre was linked to yet another arena concern for dissident professional judges. Union voices challenged state structures—especially the *Conseil Superieur de la Magistrature* and its *Commission d'Avancement* (See Supplemental Issue of *Justice 76: 45*) They noted that they had received 40 per cent of the ballots but *none* of the seats because of the 'winner takes all' system of representation on the commission. They protested against the hierarchical pattern of awarding seats on the commission and called for a doubling of the representativeness of the commission. The dissident judges wanted a combination of proportional representation of organisations alongside proportional representation of a stratified profession. They claimed that their system of membership would reduce the power of the elite within the profession over those in lower level positions. They wanted a system of guarantees of fairness 'similar to other civil servants.'

At the same time, the syndicalists requested that the system of grading be reformed, with quantitative analysis restored alongside qualitative analysis, the development of individual rights to read, review, question and appeal against specific grading and professional evaluations. These steps were all designed as part of the larger critique of the interplay between hierocratic power and political interference in judicial decision-making. The reform proposals were a strategy to reduce the ability of politicians to pressure judges through manipulations of opportunities for professional promotions.

The democratic impulse in the union combined support for the division of labour with opposition to conversion of that division into the hierarchy of the pyramidical state judicial apparatus.

The proposed reforms of state structures were connected to the kind of democratic and participatory syndicalism stressed by the founders of the union. There were strict term limits on leadership positions. Emphasis was placed on local level sectional meetings. National conventions presented themes for debate and conversation. Resolutions were presented within the context of setting aside time and space for pre-convention development and small group debate and discussion. Materials were mailed in advance, opposing perspectives published and difference was stressed in order to avoid the problems of subjugated knowledges. Polls were designed as much for generating new questions and stimulating critical thinking as they were for crystallising a union position on an issue. The French obsession with numbers and divergent views was tailored to the needs of developing new ways of thinking about problems and issues.

The national government waged an active campaign against white collar judicial unionism. Individuals were prosecuted, the state opposed the right of judges to unionise, legislation was proposed to take away the right to unionise after courts made the decision that judges were covered by legislation allowing all public employees in France to form unions.

Struggles with Ministers of Justice and administrators played a constitutive role in shaping union history. Key aspects of the nature and meaning of the counter-culture was developed in the adversarial relationships between the union and the government. These conflicts expanded the range of union experiences from the inclusive, democratic and participatory model of syndicalism to the conflict model that is more usually associated with the processes of inquisitorial and accusatorial judicial discourses.

CONCLUSIONS

In 1974, Etienne Bloch, speaking about the union said

> we affirm our vocation to be on the side of the weak, in other words, the workers in relation to the employers, the tenants in relation to the landlords, the consumers in relation to the merchants. But this is not because we are obliged to render partisan justice. Our position reverses an old tendency . . . we will restore equilibrium . . . we cannot do otherwise. (*Justice 74:28* January 1974.)

Albert Petit, another union militant said,

> When a judge makes a decision he acts in the legal form imposed upon him. The law is not neutral, procedures are not neutral and means of legal action are not neutral. Our decisions are necessarily marked by political choices of the political power. . . . Like teachers, the military and bureaucrats . . . our reference point must be the values that are the common patrimony of modern democracy. The state belongs to no one, political parties are only tenants.

These views continued to shape and inform the syndicalist voice of legal professionals in 1978. In 1978, a small group in the union published two issues of a special publication called *J'assume* (this stenciled newsletter is different from *J'essaime*—to swarm/form hive and clearly is in the tradition of Zola's *J'accuse*.) The creators of *J'assume* spoke of the need of magistrates to reaffirm taking responsibility in efforts to reinvigorate debate on 'jurisprudence and speed up presentation of union news.' Themes included, 'syndicalist strategies and professional practices, the defence of liberties, prioritising professional practice.' They focused on the importance of giving union militants information so that they could use decision-making power so that ideas developed by the union would become part of 'democratic and egalitarian justice controlled by the citizen.' (*J'assume, 1*:5).

The second and final issue of *J'assume, 2*: was a retrospective self-assessment printed for the May 1978 debate at the union retreat at Goutelas. It began by describing the judges of 1968 as a group characterised by 'profound lethargy' made up of a 'sick, amorphous, debilitated body, on the path to decomposition.' The text said, ' It took one breath to reactivate it '

> The *syndicat de la magistrature* arrived with the May sun. It proceeded empirically and created a critical analysis of the functioning of justice. Each judge saw views held in silence brought into the public place. Justice was not equal for all, Justice was controlled by the power (meaning the strong executive) and was at its service. Law was not the expression of the general will but the result of the relationship between forces. Judges were not independent. The union gave lessons . . . on internal democracy, on justice, on democracy itself .

The text went on to state,

> Justice cannot exist if society itself is not just. The *syndicat de la magistrature* is not a political movement. It cannot work to change the politics of society. But it can bring its support to those, victims of social structures who struggle to establish new social relationships. (*J'assume, 2*: 9).

REFERENCES

ARCHIVAL SOURCES

Anon. Unsigned press release with one page on 'Special Jurisdictions' (addressed to Interim Minister of Justice (Jeanneney). The document has to have been written in 1969. The text condemns the preservation of special tribunals from the era of the Algerian War and the *Cour de Sureté de l'État* created by Prime Minister Pompidou. It labels them regressive and links the special court system with the lack of independence of the judiciary. The press release also contains a condemnation of the *Conseil superieur de la magistrature* adopted at the first congress of the Syndicat de la Magistrature along with a statement by one member.

Anon. Stenciled *Note complémentaire sur les modalités de l'approche généalogique* (Notes on genealogic method—(the research strategy of power/knowledge central to Foucauldian analysis—filed with papers belonging to the union in a 1977 dossier).

Charvet, Dominique (1977) ('member of the Syndicat de la Magistrature') *Foucault aux marchés du Palais*. Seven page typed memo, written in response to Foucault's presentation at Goutelas. Comité des Intellectuels pour L'Europe des Libertes (January 1978) *Manifesto*. Paris (No publisher named)

Foucault, Michel (1977) 'a propos de '*liberté, libertés*' (Typed copy with handwritten notes and changes found in envelope mailed to Monsieur Aynard, Magistrat, Tribunal d'instance de Lille, Avenue du Peuple Belge, 59 Lille. From Tribunal d'instance, Villejuif (just outside Paris). 'TOPO: Boutiques de droit—used for article on legal system' This was Foucault's response to the 1976 collaborative text that appeared under the name of Robert Badinter, introduced by François Mitterand. See Robert Badinter, *Liberté, Libertés: Comité d'étude et reflexion pour une charte des libertés* (Paris, 1976).

Groupement d'action judiciare (1977) 'Last Reminder for the June 1977 Congress,' *Justice Moderne: Tribune du Justiciable* Ecully: V Quester-Semeon.

Invitation (1 February 1977) Meeting of the Coordinating Committee Against Repression in the German Federal Republic.

Jeol, Michel, Marc Robert and Michel—Press Release from 11 June 1969 regarding the independence of the judiciary made in response to statement by Alain Poher, interim president of the Fifth French Republic. Request to *each* presidential candidate to state views on the independence of the judiciary. Follow-up correspondence with Pompidou and Mitterand in same file.

Simon, Gerald (1975) *Un syndicat dans la magistrature: Le Syndicat de la Magistrature* Dissertation Proposal in Political Science—Proposal sent to union and Jury (Vaudieaux and Baud, Courvoisier).

Syndicat de la Magistrature (1978) *Justice 78 Supplement*—Stenciled text includes synopsis of Guémann disciplinary hearing at *Conseil Superieur de la Magistrature* including pleading of Antoine Lyon-Caen (brother of Pierre), calling for a 'national day of solidarity in support of Monique Guemann.' Issue concludes with press release of 11 Feb 1978.

Syndicat de la Magistrature (1980) 'Peyrefitte contre le libertés,' *Press Release.* Rouen: Norm'Imprim.

Universite de Lille II—Faculté des sciences juridiques et politiques et Syndicat de la Magistrature (1983) *Magistrature et democratie: Présentation du colloque.* Seven pages of stenciled material prepared for the sessions. Also a red programme prepared for participants.

PUBLISHED SOURCES

Anon., (20 July 1993) 'Dépolitiser la justice,' *Le Monde.*

Badinter, Robert (1976) (ed) *Liberté, Libertés: Reflexions du comité pour une charte des libertes* (Ceres, Paris).

Bestard, Gabriel (magistrat) (1972) 'Les "Gens" de Justice,' *Les Cahiers Francais 156–157* (Documentation Francais, Paris).

Bloch, Etienne (1981) 'Faire carrière sous la Ve Republique?,' *Pouvoirs 16,* Paris.

—— (1983) 'Le Conseil superieur de la magistrature: De la Constitution du 2 Octobre 1946,' in Jean-Pierre Royer (ed), *Etre juge demain* (Presses Universitaires de Lille, Lille).

Bouchery, Rene (1993) 'Quelle independance pour les magistrats?,' *Après-demain 355–356: Journal mensuel de documentation politique* (Henry, Paris).

Bresson, Gilles and Nicole Gauthier, 'Constitution: Le Consensus Interruptus,' *Libération.*

Brunhes, Jacques, 20 July 1993. 'La Justice toujours sous tutelle,' *L'Humanité.*

Copin, Noel (20 July 1993) 'Justice: Le Pouvoir prend ses distances,' *La Croix.*

Desaubliaux, Patrice-Henri (20 July 1993) 'Constitution: Balladur s'oppose a toute autre reforme,' *Le Figaro.*

Documentation Francaise (1992) *L'Etat de Droit en France: Ombres et Lumieres* (Documentation Francaise, Paris).

Documentation Francaise (1993) *Documents d'etudes: Droit Constitutionnel et institutions politiques* (Documentation française, Paris).

D.M. (5 July 1993) 'Débat à retardement sur la bombe humaine,' *Le Parisien.*

Fears, JR (1981) 'Civil Liberties—ch 11,' *France in the Giscard Presidency* (Allen and Unwin, London).

Foucault, Michel (1980) *Power/Knowledge: Selected Interviews and Other Writings 1972–1977* (ed) Colin Gordon (Pantheon, New York).

Foucault, Michel (1987) 'Inédit: Michel Foucault a Goutelas,' *Justice 1987:115* Paris: Editions Polyglottes (Published version of printed remarks, sub-titles added by editors of the journal).

Gaboriau, Simone (1983) (President of the Syndicat) Introduction to *Etre juge demain.*, edited by Jean-Pierre Royer (Presses Universitaires de Lille, Lille).

Jaquin, Pierre (1993) 'La Mort hors-la-loi d'Eric Schmitt: Interview of Pierre Lyon-Caen by Pierre Jaquin, Editor Justice,' *Justice 93: 138* (Polyglottes, Paris).

Jeol, Michel (1978) *Changer la justice* (Jean-Claude Simoen, Paris).

Kramer, Pierre (1993) 'L'Appareil judiciaire,' in *Après-demain 355–356: Journal mensuel de documentation politique* (Henry, Paris).

Lecrubier, Daniel (1993) 'Carrière des juges et justice,' *Après-demain 355–356: Journal mensuel de documentation politique* (Henry, Paris).

Lemoine, Yves and Frédéric Nguyen (1991) *Le livre noir du syndicat de la magistrature* (Albin Michel, Paris).

Lyon-Caen, Pierre (1981), 'L'experience du Syndicat de la Magistrature: Temoignage,' *Pouvoirs 16*

Lyon-Caen, Pierre (1993) 'Le Conseil Superieur de la Magistrature,' *Après-demain 355–356: Journal mensuel de documentation politique* (Henry, Paris).

Miaille, Michel (1977) 'Goutelas: Des Pistes de Reflexion,' *Justice 77:56* (Paris).

Miller, Jonathan (1993) *The Passion of Michel Foucault* (Simon and Schuster, New York).

Mitterand, Francois (1976) 'Introductions,' *Libertés, Libertés*

Mitterand, Francois (14 June 1976) 'La Liberté,' *Le Nouvel Observateur,* Paris (30–31).

Nicod, Jean-Claude (1992) 'Allocution de Jean-Claude Nicod,' *L'Etat de droit en France: Ombres et lumieres* (Documentaiton Francaise, Paris).

Paillard, Henri (20 July 1993) 'La Constitution au pied de la lettre. . .,' *Le Figaro.*

Pinsseau, Hubert (1985) *L'organisation judiciare de la France* (Documentation Francaise, Paris).

Robert, Marc (1976) *On les appelle les juges rouges,* Paris: Tema-Editions.

Royer, Jean-Pierre (1983) *Etre juge demain* (Presses Universitaires de Lille, Lille).

Simmonot, Dominique (20 July 1993) 'Conseil de la magistrature: le texte suscite les critiques,' *Libération.*

Syndicat de la Magistrature, (1969) 'La Reforme Statuaire,' *Justice 69:2 Journal du Syndicat de la Magistrature* (Lang-Grandemanage, Paris).

Syndicat de la Magistrature (1969) *La Formation du magistrat: Livre blanc sur le Centre National d'Etudes Judiciaires.*

Syndicat de la Magistrature (1969) *La Formation du magistrat: Livre blanc sur la formation permanente.*

Syndicat de la Magistrature (1970) 'Syndicalisme, Justice et Liberté: Le juge, garant des libertés, est-il libre lui-même? *Justice 70:8 Journal du Syndicat de la Magistrature* (Lang-Grandemanage, Paris).

Syndicat de la Magistrature (1974) *Au nom du Peuple Francais* (Stock, Paris).

Syndicat de la Magistrature (1981) *Des juges croquent la justice* (Maspéro, Paris).

Syndicat de la Magistrature (1979) 'XXe Congres: Justice et Democratie,' (especially page xiii) *Justice 1979:74 Journal du Syndicat de la Magistrature* (LITO, Paris).

Syndicat de la Magistrature, (1983) 'Statut de la magistrature: Propositions pour un réforme,' *Justice 1983:94 Journal du Syndicat de la Magistrature* (Corbiere et Jugain, Paris).

Syndicat de la Magistrature (1990) 'Reforme de l'Ordonnance de 45: Un progres ver les libertes mais quelques reserves,' *Justice 90:129 Journal du Syndicat de la Magistrature* (Polyglottes, Paris).

Syndicat de la Magistrature (1992) 'Environnement: La Justice Face aux autres pouvoirs,' *Justice 92:134 Journal du Syndicat de la Magistrature* (Polyglottes, Paris) 9.

PART IV

Lawyers and Colonialism

11

Together We Fall, Divided We Stand: The Victorian Legal Profession in Crisis 1890–1940[*]

ROB McQUEEN

> *The members of the Solicitors branch of the profession are largely disunited. A leading solicitor said recently there was no profession so disintegrated. . .*
>
> *(GF Pitcher* (President of the Law Institute of Victoria) *The Lawyer and the Community, Law Institute Journal, 1/12/1933)*

INTRODUCTION

In a recent article Allen Hutchinson notes the declining homogeneity of the legal profession[1]. He suggests that a lack of homogeneity amongst members of the legal profession carries with it significant implications for simplistic notions of what might constitute 'legal ethics'. Hutchinson, however, also notes that the supposedly univocal and homogenous legal profession of the past may never have existed. There have, he observes, always been fault lines and divisions within the profession as between barristers and solicitors, as between sole practitioners and their counterparts in large city firms, as between practitioners from different ethnic and class backgrounds and so on. It is simply the case that the complexity of the divisions within the profession have apparently increased of late. It has also, in such a rapidly changing world, become more and more

* The author wishes to acknowledge the assistance provided by the staff of the State Library of Victoria and the University of Melbourne Archives in accessing relevant research materials, and the Schools of Law and Legal Studies and the Faculty of Law and Management, La Trobe University, for providing funding to undertake the research. Last, but not least, the author wishes to acknowledge the constructive comments offered by Wes Pue on an earlier draft of the paper. All errors and omissions are, of course, the sole responsibility of the author.

[1] A Hutchinson, 'Legal ethics for a fragmented society: between professional and personal', in W Pue (ed), Lawyering for a fragmented world: professionalism after God, Special Issue (1998) 5 *International Journal of the Legal Profession* 175–193.

difficult to sustain the 'myth' of a single code of ethics and ideal to which all legal practitioners subscribe.

Whilst Huthchinson's account of the present disintegration of the 'legal profession' is quite persuasive it should also be noted that this is not the first time that the legal profession has been under significant stress, both in the public eye and from within. Of course these previous crises have been different in nature from that which we are currently experiencing. Nevertheless, they were crises which were regarded with great seriousness by contemporaries, and seen to carry with them portents of the implosion of legal professionalism itself. Indeed, some of these past periods of upheaval were so traumatic that they have been, in effect, written out of the history of the profession.[2]

The periods in the 'life' of the Law Institute of Victoria which I am concerned with in this paper are those corresponding with the severe economic crisis of the 1890s, and those cognate with the Great Depression (roughly 1928–1936). The reason I have chosen these two periods is that in both, the legal profession was under significant stress. Such times of crisis are precisely the times at which the claims of 'professionalism' might be best tested, as too might the assumption of homogeneity amongst members of the profession. These are, of course, the times at which any fault lines between different factions of the legal profession might be most clearly exposed to public view.

Both periods under examination also corresponded (in Victoria) with significant changes in the formal regulatory framework of the profession itself. In the 1890s the major reform which was announced and ushered through Parliament was that of the formal fusion of the two branches of the profession. The major justifications for this reform were (i) to save clients money by allowing them to choose from a much wider pool of advocates than were available solely from the ranks of 'qualified barristers' and (ii) to make it far easier for clients to obtain representation in court in cases which were heard in remote locales where no barristers were generally available. As we will see, despite the laudable motives for amalgamation of the profession, which were formalised by changes to the Legal Profession Practice Act in 1891, and significant support from the community at large for the reform, it did not work in practice. The reasons for this failure are complex, but were largely a consequence of the resistance on the part of barristers to this 'attack' on their monopoly of advocacy in the superior courts. How they were able to achieve this victory 'against the odds' and sustain their monopoly is only properly to be

[2] For instance the early history of the legal profession in Australia, founded as it was by emancipist convicts, and the subsequent crisis which occurred when these 'practitioners' were excluded from the courts has generally been passed over by historians. It is only due to the energies of historians such as Bruce Kercher that we are again beginning to recover this 'lost' past.

understood in terms of specific aspects of the political, social and economic environment of late nineteenth century Victoria which was in many ways different from those extant in other Australian colonies in the same time period. These differences in context will be examined below.

The second period under examination in this paper, the Great Depression, was largely dominated by internal and external pressure for a scheme of fidelity insurance for solicitors. The failure of large numbers of legal practices, combined with the regular discovery of deficiencies in practitioners trust accounts led to a clamour from the public for the introduction of a scheme of fidelity insurance for solicitors and compulsory annual audits on trust accounts. Elements within the profession (and more particularly within the Council of the Law Institute) favoured the introduction of some such scheme. The reasons for this were (i) a real dismay at the low standard of ethics within the profession, combined with a determination to ensure that high professional standards were restored and (ii) a perception that if nothing was done public regard for the profession would be virtually non-existent and as a consequence of this abject failure of 'professionalism' on the part of practitioners the state would intervene to directly regulate the profession, rather than let it continue to regulate itself.

The saga of the ensuing debate as to the necessity or otherwise of fidelity insurance exposed the depth of the fault lines, both within the ranks of the legal profession itself, and as between it (in the guise of its representative body—the Law Institute of Victoria) and the wider community. The concept of a single unified profession which subscribed to high ethical ideals in its relationship with clients was simply unsustainable in the economic and social maelstrom of the Depression years.

HISTORICAL APPROACHES TO THE LEGAL PROFESSION

The predominant approach (at least until recently) to the 'history' of specific legal professions has been one which sees the 'history' of these professions as the unfolding of a series of universalistic 'professional' values over time. The maturity of the legal (and other) professions in any society is an indicia of how 'modern' and how 'civilized' that particular society was. Of course, the more sophisticated of such histories can accommodate in their explanatory framework periods in which there are eruptions of 'bad' or unethical behaviour on the part of members of the legal profession. Also, not all such histories are unaware of the important role of both the state and public opinion in shaping the 'profession'. Nevertheless it would be true to say that most historical examinations of the legal profession, at least until quite recently, considered 'professionalisation' as a predominantly linear process. Periods of crises in the legal profession in particular places and particular periods were generally accounted for in such histories as minor disturbances in the otherwise steady development of the legal profession towards a state of 'maturity'. This was usually measured against a benchmark (at least in the common law world) such as the English or the United States legal profession.

Dissatisfied with the assumptions made in such historical accounts; a group of critical scholars, often referred to as 'market control theorists', have examined the less disinterested aims of professional norms. These scholars have challenged the idea that the 'modern' form of the legal profession is the result of the unfolding of a series of 'universalistic' values. In particular, they have questioned the evolutionary assumption that the history of 'the legal profession' is characterised by the unfolding of an altruistic commitment to a set of professional values and an adherence to certain forms of ethical behaviour. These scholars also dispute the 'progressive' role performed by the imposition of 'higher' educational standards on applicants for the profession. They suggest that the imposition of such academic standards, with the consequent effect of disaccrediting non-elite law schools, excluded both the financially disadvantaged and ethnic minorities from the profession.

It is also suggested by these 'market control' theorists that the imposition of 'standards of conduct' on members of the profession has had the effect of excluding non-conformists and political radicals from the profession. By arrogating for themselves the authority to define what constituted 'misconduct' professional associations were able to exercise enormous power over who did and who did not practise law. It is also argued by these critical scholars that professional associations often used their disciplinary powers to exclude the ethnically, socially or politically 'undesirable' from the profession, rather than use them to generally raise the standards of behaviour amongst practitioners.

Additionally, it is claimed that the imposition of 'professional' standards and the establishment of self-regulatory mechanisms is simply a means by which to better assert control over the market in legal services and supply of practitioners. In addition to excluding 'undesirables' from practice the imposition of 'professional standards' ensures that paralegals and 'professionals' in associated disciplines are excluded from a wide variety of self-defined 'legal' tasks. The labelling of particular tasks as 'legal' prevents those without professional qualifications in law from performing those tasks, irrespective of their competence to do so. This narrowing of the range of individuals who can perform these 'legal' tasks, of course, has the salutary effect of lessening competition, and the unfortunate result for consumers of 'legal' services of substantially increasing the cost of having such services performed.

Richard Abel and his associates have been the main proponents of this 'market control' thesis of the history of the legal profession and its professional associations. They assert that the consumer gleans little benefit from such mechanisms, whilst the profession gains considerable influence and prestige. Abels' formulation of the 'market control' thesis clearly delineates the principal characteristics and implications of such an approach:

> [Professionalism is] a specific historical formation in which members of an occupation exercise a substantial degree of control over the market for their services, usually through an occupational association. . . .
>
> The foundation of market control is the regulation of supply . . . occupations that produce services constrain supply principally by regulating the production of producers . . . Market control is inextricably related to occupational status, not only symbolizing status but also enhancing it instrumentally, both by restricting numbers . . . and by controlling the characteristics of entrants. Professions pursue market control and status enhancement through collective action. Having erected barriers to entry, professional associations seek to protect their members from competition, both external and internal. In order to avert external surveillance they engage in self regulation.[3]

The 'market control' thesis itself has recently been subjected to criticism.[4] The loose grouping of legal scholars represented in this volume are all, in some way or other, united by an implicit or explicit unease with the 'market control' thesis as advanced by Abel and his associates. These scholars reject the meta-theoretical role assigned to a desire for market control by Abel and his associates. This loose grouping of scholars suggest that local 'cultural' factors have often played a far more significant role in the evolution of specific legal professions than the desire to control the market in legal services. A number of recent studies have indeed demonstrated the need to qualify the 'market control' thesis in specific contexts. Such studies complement, rather than completely displace, the 'market control' thesis. They suggest that market factors may indeed have been of great significance in specific legal professions during some

[3] R Abel, 'England and Wales: A Comparison of the Professional Projects of Barristers and Solicitors' in R Abel and P Lewis (eds), *Lawyers in Society: Volume One, The Common Law World* (University of California, Berkeley, 1988) 23–24.

[4] In the course of his excellent analysis of the history of legal aid in Victoria Lynch comments on the flawed assumption at the heart of the 'market control' thesis, that there is an homogeneous profession pursuing a common goal of market control:

> The notion of a professional demand creation project of the type suggested by Larson and Abel has been criticised because conspicuous, collective and intentional striving for this type of goal seems inherently implausible given that sectional groups within the profession pursue divergent interests.

(JA Lynch, *Legal Aid and the Legal Profession in Victoria 1841–1995* (Unpublished PhD thesis, Latrobe University, 1996,) 33).

periods of their history. However, what these studies also show is that at other times and in other places the desire for market control was of little importance in shaping specific legal professions.

Wes Pue's work on the development of the legal profession on the western prairies of Canada is an example of such a study.[5] In introducing this study Pue states that as the suppression of non-lawyer competitors and fee control was integral to the development of the profession on the prairies 'it would be possible to conclude . . . that "professionalism" is a sham and that professions are "essentially" about market control'.[6] He then goes on, however, to assert that any such characterisation of the process of 'professionalization' on the western prairies of Canada would be a gross misrepresentation of the real nature of developments in that context. Elsewhere, in a review of Abels' contribution to the history of the legal profession, Pue has remarked:

> Scholarship about the legal profession will have to transcend market control rather than merely renounce it. Scholars will have to direct considerably more attention than in the past to the multiple fracturings of professions from within, to the contested nature of professionalism both within and without. Visions of lawyering will need to be related much more directly than has been the norm to wider cultural understandings. Clients—who are largely ignored in most studies of professionalism—will need to be acknowledged as central. The role of lawyers outside of narrowly defined professional roles merits attention.[7]

A common assumption which is shared by 'traditional' teleological histories of the legal profession *and* those studies inspired by Abel and Lewis' work on 'market control' is that there is a high degree of homogeneity within the legal profession. In the case of 'traditional' histories it is often assumed that there is a common belief system shared by legal practitioners regarding the core attributes of professionalism. In the case of Abel and Lewis' work, and others advocating the 'market control' thesis, there is an assumption of a shared value system amongst legal practitioners as to the need to ensure that certain 'standards' be maintained in order to exclude undesirables from entry to the profession and to prevent competitors from encroaching on 'legal work'. Whilst most practitioners certainly would not articulate their shared system of values and standards as one that was designed to entrench monopoly and arrogate privileges to themselves, the assumption in Abel and Lewis' work is that there is nevertheless a consensus around a number of matters which have that effect in practice.

[5] W Pue, *Becoming Professional: Western Canadian Lawyers* (Unpublished paper presented to the ISA Working Party on the Cultural History of the Legal Profession, Aix en Provence, June 1992).

[6] *Ibid*, 4–5.

[7] W Pue, ' "Trajectories of Professionalism?": Legal Professionalism After Abel' (1991) *Manitoba Law Journal*, 417–418.

As we will observe below the high degree of homogeneity in the profession which has been assumed in previous historical analyses of the legal profession (whether 'traditional' or 'critical') is often confounded by studies of specific legal professions. Whilst in some places for short periods of time there may be a considerable degree of homogeneity in the legal profession, usually such a state of affairs does not last for long. As we will see in the following, there are, and always have been, significant fault lines between different groupings within the legal profession in the various colonies/states in Australia. The legal profession in Victoria is no exception.

THE DEVELOPMENT OF AN 'ORGANISED' LEGAL PROFESSION IN VICTORIA: THE DOMINANCE OF DEBATES REGARDING AMALGAMATION OF THE PROFESSION 1859–1917

In its early years the Law Institute of Victoria was neither representative of the profession or influential in matters pertaining to policy. In fact it was such an inconsequential body that only six members attended the Annual Meeting in 1865.[8] Most practitioners were at this time still located outside urban areas and consequently belonged to regional Law Societies, rather than to the small but growing Law Institute situated in the metropolis of Melbourne. The Institute had grown to over a hundred members by the 1890s, but nevertheless was still a small and unrepresentative body, covering less than 20 per cent of all solicitors and barely 10 per cent of solicitors in country areas. Before the 1890s it principally operated as a social club, occasionally making comments on proposed legislation and intermittently, through its complaints committee, referring cases of 'misconduct' to the Supreme Court for further action.[9]

The problems being encountered by the Law Institute in Victoria were not unique. Similar attempts to retain rural members, and thus ensure that the local association remained representative of both metropolitan and country solicitors, were being made by the NSW Law Society at the same time. The historian of the New South Wales Society has noted that even when fees were increased in the early twentieth century that 'country subscriptions were kept low to try to encourage country membership, which continued to be small'.[10]

However, despite these considerable efforts to recruit members it was still the case that, as late as 1909, membership of the Institute was still the

[8] *Centenary History of The Law Institute of Victoria 1859–1959* (Law Institute of Victoria, Melbourne, 1959), 34.

[9] *Ibid*, 35.

[10] JM Bennett, *A History of Solicitors in New South Wales* (Legal Books Limited, Sydney, 1984), 184.

exception, rather than the rule, amongst practitioners in Victoria. This was particularly the case for country solicitors. Whilst only 27.8 per cent of solicitors practising in Melbourne in 1909 were members of the Institute an even lower proportion of country solicitors bothered to join—in 1909 only 13.1 per cent of country solicitors belonged to the Institute.[11]

In addition to their difficulty in recruiting country members from the 'lower branch' of the profession the Law Institute at this stage did not represent the 'upper branch' of the profession. Even though they had a Rule, introduced in 1891, which encouraged barristers to join, the practice was for barristers to belong to the Bar Association . The representative status of the Bar Association was effectively recognised in 1903 when it was given separate representation on the newly established Council of Legal Education.[12]

Nevertheless, the relationship between the two branches of the legal profession in Victoria was a matter which was unclear for some time: there was no legislation or regulations prescribing the type of work which could be undertaken by practitioners of either branch of the profession, the only guide for most of the nineteenth century being the 'usual practice in England'.[13] Even then, this was rarely adhered to. Due to the scarcity of qualified practitioners in many locations solicitors often performed tasks traditionally associated with the 'upper branch' and barristers quite often performed tasks traditionally ascribed to their brethren in the 'lower branch'. As one historian of the legal profession in Victoria notes:

> The sole thing which seemed clear was that only a barrister could appear and conduct a case in the Supreme Court. The County Court Act of 1852 provided that a party to a case where the claim exceeded (10 might appear in person or by a solicitor or attorney or agent. Attorneys were also entitled to appear in the Court of Mines (for many years an important Court), in the Insolvency Court and all inferior Courts. In the country attorneys did a considerable part of the business of these courts . . . [on the other hand] many persons admitted as barristers found it

[11] Percentages based on membership figures cited in the President's Jubilee speech, 1909, LIV Annual Report, 1909, 4.

[12] *The Centenary History of the Law Institute of Victoria*, op cit at 35 observes:

> After the two branches of the profession were amalgamated by the Legal Profession Practice Act 1891, the Institute accepted the situation and amended the by-laws to provide for membership of any person admitted to practice as a barrister and solicitor of the Supreme Court of Victoria. A few who had previously practiced as barristers accepted the invitation and became members of the Institute, but the majority agreed amongst themselves to maintain a separate Bar which has continued de facto to the present day.

[13] A Dean, *A Multitude of Counsellors: A History of the Bar of Victoria* (FW Cheshire, Melbourne, 1968), 86.

> more profitable in the country than in Melbourne, and it seems plain enough that away from Melbourne little regard was paid to the rules of etiquette governing the respective functions of barrister and attorney. In any case such rules were not reduced to writing and were vague and uncertain.[14]

The history of the first half century of the profession in Victoria could almost be said to be dominated by the debate surrounding fusion of the two branches of the profession. Even before separation from New South Wales it was being argued by the Legislative Assembly member for the District of Port Philip (ie Victoria), Dr Brewster (a barrister himself), that there should be a fusion of the profession. He introduced a Bill into the House of Assembly to that effect in 1846.[15] Whilst the Bill was not passed into legislation it nevertheless was reflective of the thinking of 'liberals' of the time with respect to the appropriate structure of the profession in a colonial setting. At intermittent intervals over the next 25 years Bills were introduced proposing fusion of the profession, but none were enacted into legislation. Then, in 1871, the then Attorney General of Victoria called a meeting of interested parties to ascertain support for a proposal to amalgamate the profession.[16] This seemed eminently sensible, as over three quarters of the litigation in the Colony of Victoria was conducted by solicitors in courts where barristers did not have exclusive rights of appearance. All this meeting revealed, however, was the sharp divisions between practitioners on the question of fusion. At the meeting of barristers called by the Attorney-General, those who practised in the country were generally supportive of fusion—many were effectively already practising both as barrister and solicitor. A number of these country barristers operating 'fused' practices indicated that they could only make an adequate living in rural areas if they practised functions traditionally regarded as the sole preserve of the 'lower branch'. One gave evidence that in five months in the country he had earned 250 pounds whereas in the five preceding years in Melbourne, practicing solely a barrister, he had not even earned 50 pounds.[17] It was true that for most of the latter half of the nineteenth century whilst in Melbourne there was a relatively close adherence to the 'etiquette' practised in England as to the respective functions of the two branches of the profession, in country areas most practitioners, from whichever branch of the profession they

[14] *Ibid.*

[15] A Bill to Amalgamate the Professions of Barrister and Solicitor, NSW, 1846. One of the strong allies of Brewster in proposing this legislation was the young Robert Lowe who was then very active in 'liberal' political circles in New South Wales (later to be President of the Board of Trade and even later, as Viscount Sherbrooke, Chancellor of the Exchequer in the 'home' country).

[16] See the report of the meeting in *The Argus*, 21 Oct 1871.

[17] A Dean, *A Multitude of Counsellors: A History of the Bar of Victoria* (FW Cheshire, Melbourne, 1968), 88.

originally came, practised as if the profession was already amalgamated. This reality is reflected in yet another report on possible amalgamation of the profession in 1884. The Committee appointed by the Attorney-General to make this report on the possible amalgamation of the profession noted:

> As to the relations of the Bar towards solicitors in Victoria, these relations are in practice different in different parts of the Colony. In Melbourne and its suburbs the relations maintained and the professional etiquette observed are professedly and as a rule those maintained and observed in England, but in all other places in the Colony the distinctions between the two branches of the profession are virtually ignored.[18]

A new Bill was introduced into Parliament regarding amalgamation in 1884.[19] The views of a range of interested parties were sought, and these again reflected nothing but the high degree of division between practitioners (particularly the differences in attitude between rural and city practitioners) as to the desirability of fusion.[20] The 1884 Bill was the most radical and sweeping of the various attempts to effect amalgamation of the profession in the late nineteenth century. Its drafters were quite aware of the practices in other countries, in particular those in the United States, where there was an undivided profession. In the course of argument on the Bill in Parliament one Member asserted that reason would suggest that a client who engaged a solicitor to transact a case on their behalf would prefer that practitioner to carry that case to its conclusion.[21] The same Member also noted that the principal effect of the so-called rules of etiquette as to division of responsibilities between practitioners often only led to an inflation in costs to the client, something that clients, if given a choice, would not support. Australian clients were of the same democratic temper as their United States counterparts where clients objected to being 'lathered in one shop and shaved in another'.[22] This was even more so the case in circumstances where the 'two shops' were not available—a reference to the difficulty often experienced in rural areas of obtaining a barrister at all to argue ones' case before a court.

On the other side of the argument a number of members of the Bar tried to argue the case for separation on the basis of the preservation of English traditions of 'independence'. These arguments, whilst infused with a healthy dose of romanticism did not really address the real questions of cost and availability of counsel which lay at the core of many of

[18] See (July 1884) 6 *Australian Law Times Journal*, xiii.

[19] Legal Profession Practice Bill, Victoria, 1884.

[20] A Dean, *A Multitude of Counsellors: A History of the Bar of Victoria* (FW Cheshire, Melbourne, 1968) 94.

[21] *Ibid* 98.

[22] *Ibid.*

the debates surrounding amalgamation. Sir John Madden,[23] one of the then leaders of the Bar in Melbourne (and later Chief Justice, Vice Chancellor of the University of Melbourne and President of the exclusive Melbourne Club), defended separation by reference to the 'special' gentlemanly qualities of those called to the 'upper branch':[24]

> At the very outset of his career, during his education, a barrister is supposed to be trained apart from the whole community, with a view to educate feelings of independence and a knowledge of the principles upon which that independence exists. An attorney earns a livelihood as an articled clerk; he comes into contact from day to day with all classes, and a barrister is kept perfectly aloof from them in order that he may be trained to disassociate himself from the everyday life of the public, as constituting in due time, as part of the education necessary for a judge; because as I take it, that quality of independence, both in barrister and in a judge, is a matter of education . . . he must absolutely ignore all the community and know no man. That is a thing which cannot be easily be done, unless a man is trained to that particular direction, and therefore it is that a barrister from the earliest period does not see his client direct. He does not know them.[25]

As unconvincing as this rationale for separation may seem to us today there were nevertheless enough 'traditionalists' to prevent the enactment of the Amalgamation Bill in 1884. However, it was only by a slim margin that the creation of a single, undivided profession was averted. One upshot of this wide-ranging discussion of the profession in 1884 was the introduction of Victoria's first comprehensive Bar Regulations, and the establishment of a body which could argue the case for the 'upper

[23] Madden was himself subject to a scathing, if improvident, attack in the local press as to his suitability when he was appointed Chief Justice by an incumbent Supreme Court judge, and soon to be colleague. One of the most senior of the existing Justices of the Supreme Court, Justice Hartley Williams, stated in a letter to *The Argus* that he considered Madden to be simply 'an advocate' and not a 'lawyer' and that his 'skills were not those of a judge' . Justice Williams concluded this open letter to the major Melbourne daily newspaper by stating that under the leadership of 'such a person' he would do no more than his 'bare duty' and that the appointment of such 'an advocate' to such a preeminent position was 'an insult to the present occupants of the Bench'. (The letter published in *The Argus* of 8 Jan 1893 is reprinted in A Dean, A *Multitude of Counsellors*, op cit (n 20 above), at 153–154).

[24] This notion of the 'barrister as gentlemen' also characterised the profession in a number of other colonial settings. In their book, *Professional Gentlemen: The Professions in Nineteenth Century Ontario* (Ontario Historical Studies Series, Toronto, 1994), RD Gidney and WPJ Millar, note the hierarchical and class boundaries between barristers and attorneys in mid-nineteenth century Ontario. They cite an article from the *Upper Canada Law Journal* of 1855 which contrasts the gentlemanly characteristics of the 'upper branch' of the profession with the 'illiterate and unrefined' members of the body of attorneys. This article was written in the context of moves to allow attorneys to represent clients in some superior courts, a move which the author of the article saw as 'unacceptable' (at 76–77).

[25] A Dean, A *Multitude of Counsellors*, op cit. (n 20 above), 95.

branch'—the Bar Committee of Victoria.[26] One of the noteworthy aspects of the Bar Regulations of 1884 was the manner in which they hedged their bets on the question of 'fused' practice. Presumably this was an attempt not to alienate country barristers, whilst at the same time satisfying some of the demands of city barristers to establish a formal basis for professional etiquette. Regulation 10 stated:

> A barrister may, without breach of professional etiquette, see his client, advise him and earn a fee without a solicitor attorney or proctor being employed unless and until the litigation shall have actually been commenced by a writ or process issued. In no case, however, . . . is a barrister practicing in Melbourne or its suburbs to act as an attorney, by suing out process, conducting correspondence on behalf of a client, effecting the engrossment of deeds or other documents, preparing briefs, paying money into Court or by acting in any similar manner.[27]

Despite this spirit of compromise the issue of the amalgamation of the profession refused to go away. After the collapse of the Victorian economy in the early 1890s the issue again rose to prominence. In a depressed economy, in which litigation against fraudulent corporate promoters was rampant, there was a demand for cheap and ready access to legal services. Amalgamation of the legal profession promised this. Also, the Law Institute, somewhat weakened by a loss of members through financial failure, saw this as an opportunity to pick up coverage of the 'upper branch' and become the sole representative of the legal profession in Victoria. Consequently they strongly supported legislation for the amalgamation of the profession, which was introduced into Parliament in 1891.[28] This legislation repeated the terms of the 1884 Bill almost word for word. However, in the vastly different social and economic circumstances prevailing in the early 1890s the legislation this time passed both Houses of Parliament. The Legal Profession Practice Act of 1891 formally ended the separation of the two branches of the profession in Victoria.[29] However, as we shall see, subsequent events meant that the practical result of this legislation was nil. So too did the aspirations of the Law Institute of Victoria to be the sole representative of the profession in Victoria come to nix.

[26] For details on its formation see (1884) 6 *Australian Law Times Journal*, xiii.

[27] The Regulations can be found in (1884) 6 *Australian Law Times Journal*, clxxvi.

[28] However, Dean disputes this fact, and notes that in its annual report for 1891 the Council of the Institute had stated that the Institute was 'neutral' on the question of amalgamation of the profession: see A Dean, *A Multitude of Counsellors*, op cit (n 20 above) 99–101.

[29] Ss 3 and 4 were the provisions which provided for the cessation of 'separation': s 3 stated that any person heretofore admitted (in the State of Victoria) as a barrister was now also admitted as a solicitor from the date of the passing of the Act, whilst s 4 stated that any person previously admitted as a solicitor in the State of Victoria was also admitted as a barrister form the date of the passing of the Act.

Indeed the attempted fusion of the two branches of the legal profession in 1891, with the enactment in that year of the Legal Profession Practice Act, proved ultimately to be counterproductive to the development of the Institute as a professional organisation representing the legal profession in Victoria. The Institute had, as we have noted above, initially supported the 'fusion' of the profession, hoping that as a consequence of the amalgamation of the profession they would become the *sole* representative of the profession in the colony of Victoria. The Council of the Institute, in anticipation of numerous applications to join from members of the Bar, changed their Rules in 1892 due to the fact that 'the Rules heretofore only provided for the admission of Solicitors'. At the same meeting of the Council of the Institute:

> It was also thought fit to suggest . . . the desirability of increasing the number of members of Council from ten to fifteen, there being every prospect of a large influx of members during the coming year.[30]

The expected flood of applications from members of the Bar, however, never transpired. The Institute remained almost exclusively an organisation of solicitors despite the fusion of the profession. The Institute found that the existence of a *de jure* amalgamation hindered, rather than helped, their ambitions to obtain corporate status and statutory recognition for their complaints committee along the lines of the Incorporated Law Societies in England and in New South Wales.[31] Rather than becoming members of the Law Institute, practitioners at the Bar formed their own rival organisation in 1891, the Bar Association. Though this body was, in its first manifestation, short-lived, another similar body was again quickly formed. This rival organisation was granted formal recognition with the enactment of the legislation establishing the Council of Legal Education in 1903. That legislation provided for separate representation from the Law Institute of Victoria and the Committee of Counsel on the Board of the Council.[32] As Dean comments:

> The final triumph of the Bar as a separate body came in 1903 when Parliament by the Legal Profession Reciprocity Act . . . created a Council of Legal Education [which provided for three representatives to be nominated by both the Law Institute and the Bar Association (formally referred to as the Committee of Counsel)] . . . This recognition by Parliament of the separate existence as a

[30] Law Institute of Victoria, *Annual Report*, 1892, 3.

[31] Space does not permit a fuller discussion of the whole question of why the Law Institute and other similar bodies so ardently sought corporate status. 'Incorporation' must have meant something more to these bodies and their members than simply obtaining corporate status as they could have done this under the Companies Act if they were so minded. Incorporation under an Act of Parliament or Royal Charter surely must have conjured up something more like an ancient and venerable guild to these bodies rather than a modern, limited liability enterprise.

[32] *Legal Profession Reciprocity Act 1903*.

respectable body of the Bar which only twelve years before it had set out to destroy must have been a source of satisfaction to the Bar.[33]

Throughout the late nineteenth and early twentieth century barristers and their representative professional association continued to exercise their influence to prevent the Institute from obtaining statutory identity. The 'upper branch' of the profession was unlikely to accept such a development until all controversial matters pertaining to fusion were resolved to their satisfaction. The Law Institute itself recognised this impediment, lamented it, but could do very little in the short term. The Address of the President of the Institute to the Annual General Meeting in 1897 commented in this regard:

> I feel disappointed that the members of the practising Bar, as a body, still stand aloof from us, but trust in the near future advances will be made towards effecting a union which members of the Institute feel would be beneficial to both branches of the profession, and which, I am sure, could be accomplished without in any manner trenching upon any little differences of opinion which may exist in reference to the adoption by any gentleman of the whole of the principles involved in the Legal Profession Amalgamation Act. Until such a union is effected there appears little or no possibility of our obtaining an Act of Incorporation, without which the services of this Institute cannot, to my mind, be efficiently employed.[34]

The reasons for the failure of fusion in Victoria and the 'triumph' of the Bar are relatively straightforward. After the collapse of the Victorian economy in the 1890s, along with declining returns from gold mines in the Colony, there was a significant decline in the prosperity of many rural areas. Many of the rural barristers who had been strong supporters of fusion were now either forced out of business or back into the city of Melbourne. With less work to go around the 'upper branch' became more jealous of the rules of etiquette in place in England. Whilst the formal fusion of the profession had been provided for in 1892, this was possibly the worst time at which it could have occurred if it were to be a success. If the 1884 Act had not been narrowly defeated and the amalgamation legislation had been passed during the boom, the 'one shop' practice of Australian practitioners' American counterparts may have become so entrenched by the turn of the century that it would have become 'normalised'. Even such speculation must be doubtful, however, as the other significant event which occurred between 1884 and 1903 which turned the tide against the amalgamation movement within the profession was the creation of the Australian Federation. With Federation, Parliaments in all former colonies had to address the question of reciprocal recognition of

[33] A Dean, *A Multitude of Counsellors*, op cit (n 20 above), 107–108.

[34] Address to the Annual Meeting of the Law Institute of Victoria by SG Pirani, Esq., President, 26 Nov 1897.

legal practitioners. Victoria was out of step with the other States, and thus it is not surprising that it was indeed the Legal Profession Reciprocity Act 1903 which effectively brought to an end the possibility of a real fusion of the profession occurring in Victoria.

A final important factor in the failure of the Legal Profession Practice Act 1891 to lead to a truly amalgamated profession was the relatively weak political position of the Law Institute after the collapse of the Victorian economy in the 1890s. At the time of the enactment of the Legal Profession Practice Act a number of solicitors, and in particular powerful allies in the form of sympathetic company promoters, sat in the Victorian Parliament. This was no longer the case by the mid 1890s. Whilst the Bar Association of the day was quite weak organisationally compared to the Law Institute, it nevertheless held one trump card. Even after the economic collapse of the early 1890s many barristers, former barristers and aligned members of the local 'aristocracy' were still members of the Victorian Upper House of Parliament and continued to exert considerable political power. The sympathies of this powerful political bloc with respect to fusion of the profession naturally lay with the Bar. Using their political clout this group of interests sympathetic to the concerns of the Bar delayed the grant of the very thing which the Law Institute wanted most—formal recognition of the Institute by Parliament and the grant of corporate status along the lines of the English Incorporated Law Society. Whilst the Law Institute clung on to some grandiose notion of representing all practitioners in Victoria and maintaining in its Rules a provision which stated that it was the representative of both branches of the profession the Bar Association (however called at the time) would (and did) consistently oppose the granting of corporate status to the Law Institute[35]. In this opposition they knew they could rely upon their political allies in the Victorian Upper House. It was only after the Law Institute removed its Rule allowing it to represent members of the 'upper branch' of the profession in 1912 that the momentum toward incorporation gathered[36].

[35] The Law Institute acted quite provocatively in the late 1890s, electing two practising barristers as senior office bearers in 1898—Sir Samuel Leon, QC as President and O'Hara Wood, a prominent member of the Bar, as Honorary Secretary. However, the Bar Association retaliated by making it practically impossible for any 'solicitor' (who were ineligible to join the Bar Association) to practise as an advocate. A practitioner who had attempted to practise as an 'amalgam', Mr TP McInerney, stated in his evidence to the Royal Commission on Legal Reform 1897–1899 that: '. . . any member of the bar who [was not] a member of the Association was practically a pariah. The whole profession was combined against him. He could not get any legal opinion nor any legal assistance , or hold a brief from any member of the bar It is the strongest trade union that was ever formed.'

[36] Indeed, the Bar Committee and the Law Institute were at loggerheads as late as 1906 when it was proposed to appoint the then Victorian Attorney-General JM Davies, a

The leaders of the Institute had hoped that fusion of the profession would both accelerate the process of obtaining statutory recognition and augment the importance of the Institute as a professional association. The Council of the Institute had envisaged that after fusion the Law Institute would become the sole representative of the legal profession in Victoria. They were quite wrong in this prediction. Fusion, whilst a legislative reality, was never, as we have seen, a practical reality in Victoria. Former members of the Bar in Victoria continued to practise at the Bar after 'fusion', and members of the 'lower branch' of the profession continued to practise as solicitors after 'amalgamation'. Instead of accelerating the process of statutory incorporation of the Institute, as anticipated, the legislative attempt to fuse the profession in Victoria delayed the attainment of this objective at least a decade. Commenting on the deleterious effect the practical failure of fusion had caused in obtaining statutory recognition for the Institute the President, Robert Beckett, in his 1909 address to members stated:

> The incorporation of the Institute has been a matter frequently discussed . . . [it is now, however, recognised] that the amalgamation of what were formerly distinct branches of the profession and the recent constitution of the Council of Legal Education have added to the difficulties [nevertheless] it is still hoped that the incorporation will, at an early date, receive the sanction of the Legislature. The Incorporated Law Society of New South Wales and the Incorporated Law Society of England are models that, with such modifications as will fit with local conditions, we ought to be able safely to adopt.[37]

Implicit, however, in Beckett's speech is also the recognition that the Law Institute would need to take a different political tack with regard to fusion if it was to obtain its *desiderata* of corporate status. This was only achieved through a compromise with the Bar Association after two decades. Once it gave up hope of representing members of the Bar as their professional association, the Law Institute was no longer faced with the influential opposition of key members of the Bar with connections in high places to legislation granting them corporate status.[38]

'solicitor', to the Supreme Court. The Law Institute had strongly supported the appointment whilst the Bar Committee had just as vehemently opposed it. In the end the Bar Committee prevailed and Sir Leo Cussen, destined to be one of the most renowned of Victorian judges, was appointed.

[37] Law Institute of Victoria, Annual Report, 1909, Address on the Jubilee of the Profession by Robert Beckett, President, 31.

[38] The Bar was well represented in the Legislative Council, the Upper House of the Victorian Parliament, and had sufficient numbers in that House to foil any legislation incorporating the Law Institute. Gidney and Millars' wry observation that the Benchers within the Law Society of Upper Canada were not simply influential with the 'levers of power' in the mid-nineteenth century; they *were* the 'levers of power', is also to some degree true of the position of the Bar in Victoria in the late nineteenth century (see R Gidney, and W Millar, *Professional Gentlemen*, op cit, 74.

CREATING ANOTHER MONOPOLY? STATUTORY RECOGNITION AND INCORPORATION OF THE LAW INSTITUTE AND ITS EFFECTS ON THE COUNTRY LAW ASSOCIATIONS

Attaining corporate status, along the lines of the Incorporated Law Society in Great Britain, had long been a concern of the Law Institute. In the very first report of the Law Institute of Victoria in August 1859 the question of incorporating the organisation and thus placing it on a firmer footing was discussed:

> At the meeting of the Council [later this month] the question of applying for an act of Incorporation will be considered, and any remarks with which they may in the meantime be favoured will meet with due attention.[39]

The consideration of the above matter by the inaugural Council of the Law Institute was provided for in the Rules of the organisation. Those Rules recited:

> That as soon as practicable after the election of the first Council under these rules, it shall be lawful for, and the Council are hereby empowered to adopt, such proceedings as they may deem advisable for obtaining an Act of the Parliament of Victoria for incorporating the members of the Institute.[40]

The representations made by the Council of the Institute in 1859 with respect to incorporation must have fallen on deaf ears as the matter was again raised in the minutes of the Institute in 1868. The matter, however, did not come before Parliament for consideration until 1875, when a private bill was introduced into the Legislative Council by the then President of the Law Institute, the Hon RS Anderson.[41] This bill, however, was not passed, the matter of incorporation being deferred until the resolution of the other important matter concerning the profession then under Parliaments' notice—that of the possible fusion of the profession. As we have seen the saga respecting the amalgamation of the profession in Victoria dragged on for over 30 years, and was a major impediment to Parliament even considering incorporation of the Institute.

It was only during the First World War that the Law Institute began to finally make significant progress in accomplishing its objective of being granted statutory recognition. This followed the enactment of legislation in 1916 granting statutory identity to the South Australian Law Council. When the Victorian legislation was finally enacted in 1917 the Institute

[39] Annual Report of the Law Institute of Victoria, 1859.

[40] Rules of the Law Institute of Victoria, 1859.

[41] *Centenary History of The Law Institute of Victoria 1859–1959*, op cit (n 8 above), 42.

was composed exclusively of members who did not practise at the Bar (due to the Rule change respecting membership noted above).[42]

Despite the failure of the Institute to achieve its goal of being the sole representative of the legal profession in Victoria, there were nevertheless a number of significant gains made as a consequence of statutory recognition. One of the most noteworthy of these improvements in its position was the effective marginalisation of the rural Law Societies. In the past these associations had independently represented the views of country solicitors on matters which affected the profession. Now, they were effectively relegated by the Law Institute Act 1917 to a lesser role. By reason of its corporate status the Institute now constituted the only 'legitimate' voice on professional matters affecting solicitors in the State of Victoria.

The Ballarat and District Law Association, the Bendigo Law Association and the Geelong Law Association all had histories dating back as far as the Law Institute itself. Prior to the Law Institute Act of 1917 each of these associations had no formal connection with the Institute and independently lobbied on behalf of and represented the interests of those country solicitors in their geographical area of coverage. As noted earlier the Law Institute had an extremely small membership in rural areas, and thus would have seen these country associations as significant rivals, rather than as subsidiary organisations. The Law Institute Act, however, constituted a new hierarchy amongst these rival representatives of the 'lower branch' of the profession. The legislation provided that the President of each of the above country associations should be given *ex officio* membership of the Council of the Law Institute.[43] However, the only body which was granted statutory recognition was the Law Institute of Victoria.[44]

In addition to the significant enhancement to the Law Institutes' status consequent upon the above arrangement this solution also had implications with respect to the ability of the Institute to control the market in legal services for the whole of Victoria. This was not lost on those opposed to the legislation incorporating the Institute. One of the principal Parliamentary opponents of the legislation, Mr Hannah, expressed the opinion that it was extremely undesirable to concede sweeping powers to the Institute :

> There is to be vested in these gentlemen power to say who shall be admitted to the inner circle of this very powerful and very far-reaching trade union. I do not

[42] See *Centenary History of The Law Institute of Victoria 1859–1959*, and A Dean, *A Multitude of Counsellors,* op cit (n 20 above), 161.

[43] Compare with the position in Queensland where this did not occur: see H Gregory, *The Queensland Law Society Inc 1928–1988: A History* (Queensland Law Society, Brisbane, Australia, 1991) 134–152.

[44] *Centenary History of The Law Institute of Victoria 1859–1959*, op cit, Introduction by JR Burt, President, LIV, 24.

> think honourable members representing rural districts can, for a moment claim that such a provision is wise, because it has a narrowing effect . . . this Institute appears to be a junta of juntas.[45]

In addition to enhancing its control over the market in legal services in Victoria by neutralising its principal rivals, the country law associations, the Law Institute also at this time consolidated solicitors professional claims to have a monopoly on all categories of 'legal' work. In defending this 'right' the Institute resisted the claims of law clerks and conveyancers to professional recognition for the categories of work which they performed. In 1909 the then President of the Institute, Robert Beckett, noted in this respect:

> The Council has also been vigilant in guarding the entrance to the profession against those who sought to be admitted without passing the necessary examinations, or submitting to the usual service under articles. More than once conveyancers tried to establish special legislation in their favour. At another time conveyancers and notaries public secured the support of the Hon. George Higinbotham in a Bill before the House. On several occasions law clerks urged their claims to admission, and in all these cases strenuous and generally successful opposition was presented by the Council.[46]

All of these powers of admittance and exclusion conferred on the Institute, and regarded today as a 'natural' adjunct to the profession, were at the time of their adoption and/or introduction, subject to quite significant contestation. It was not considered by contemporaries that these powers were benign. Nor was it uniformly considered that the Law Institute should have an exclusive right to exercise such powers. Many bemoaned the demise of the country law associations, asserting that the interests of rural and urban practitioners were quite different and could not be represented by the same organisation. Others suggested that the 'exclusion' of law clerks and conveyancers from professional recognition was the result of self-interest on the part of the Law Institute and had little or nothing to do with the preservation of 'standards' and/or a concern with the quality of legal services provided to the public. A number of contemporaries resisted the granting of public recognition to the complaints committee of the Institute, arguing that this would be tantamount to giving the Institute a statutory right to exclude the politically radical and/or the ethnically unacceptable.[47]

[45] Victorian Parliamentary Debates (Assembly Debates), 9 Oct 1917, 2100.

[46] Law Institute of Victoria, Annual Report, 1909, Address on the Jubilee of the Profession by Robert Beckett, President, 31.

[47] In delivering his speech to Parliament on the occasion of the Law Institute being finally granted a corporate identity by Parliament in 1917 one member, Mr Hannah, expressed concern that the disciplinary powers of the Institute might be used to exclude political dissidents and other 'undesirables': '[I]f this organization (the Law Institute) is clothed with such powers, it is possible that brainy men . . . may be precluded from it

Despite considerable opposition to these developments it was the case that the Institute convinced the government of the day that these were essential reforms. Nevertheless the form and nature of contemporary opposition to these innovations should not be ignored or trivialised. Such antagonism to the profession and the Institute was never completely submerged. Subsequent to the consolidation of the position of the Institute with the enactment of the Law Institute Act 1917 it was not until the late 1920s that public disquiet with respect to the profession again emerged, with doubt being again expressed as to the ability of the Institute to properly regulate its members.

FIDELITY FUNDS FOR SOLICITORS

One of the issues which animated the various State Law Societies and Law Institutes in Australia as the Great Depression took hold was in determining how to deal with the then increasing numbers of defaulting solicitors. A spate of misappropriations of trust funds and other financial improprieties by solicitors led, in the late 1920s and early 1930s, to a campaign in most Australian States for increased public regulation over the management of trust funds by solicitors. The growing number of solicitors who had breached their obligations towards their clients by raiding their trust accounts represented a real threat to the reputation of the profession. More particularly it also constituted a real danger to the various Australian Law Societies' and Institutes' claims to legitimacy in respect to the self-regulation of the profession. The failure of the various schemes of self-regulation then in place to deal with this apparent rash of dishonest colleagues led to proposals for compulsory audits of solicitors trust accounts and for the introduction of fidelity insurance schemes. The tenor of public concern over defaults by solicitors (and support for the introduction of tighter financial controls on solicitors' trust funds combined with the introduction of a scheme of fidelity insurance) is reflected in the following comment from one of the leading Melbourne daily newspapers:

> Default is a form of delinquency which appears to increasing in frequency and audacity. Instances of solicitors misapplying or misappropriating clients' money are becoming distressingly familiar items of news in all States . . . There is no suggestion that dishonour and dishonesty are exclusive to the legal profession; every profession and occupation is at some time or other similarly disfigured. But special prominence has been conferred upon the solicitor in this matter, because within the present generation particularly, he has tended to enlarge the image of

because of their radical proclivities (Victorian Parliamentary Debates (Assembly Debates), 9 Oct 1917, 2100).

> his activities: he is primarily a solicitor, but, as a profitable side line, he has to a surprisingly wide extent assumed the role of financial adviser, investor and money lender . . . The Law Institute is the corporate custodian of the legal profession's honor in this State, and it is to warmly commended for taking steps in the right direction [ie the initial proposals to introduce tighter audit controls on solicitors and to provide for fidelity insurance] . . . In England legislation is at present being introduced to control solicitors dealing with trust funds. A measure having an identical purpose is now under consideration in the Parliament of New South Wales. There is no need to stress unduly the ugly facts which constitute the basis of the Law Institute's request that the legislation outlined should be passed.[48]

As we might note from the above newspaper report similar proposals to those being advocated by the Law Institute of Victoria in the early 1930s were being considered in England at the same time. In a recent article by Lunney the complex range of interests cohering around these proposed reforms is examined. Lunney suggests that in England, despite the threat to the Law Society's perceived capacity to self-regulate, which the then increasing numbers of defaulting solicitors represented, the members of the Incorporated Law Society were significantly divided with respect to the manner in which the Society should respond to these developments:

> London solicitors were not uniform in their views; neither were their country brethren, and any attempt to factionalise solicitors must be made carefully and with reservations. This division made it difficult for the Law Society to introduce reforms, yet it was held accountable for the failure of all solicitors to do so. The history of the Law Society, and of the wider profession, can only be told by abandoning monolithic views of the profession, for only then can the profession's response to external pressures for reform be understood. Nowhere is this better illustrated than in the history of self-regulation.[49]

Lunney's observations on the dilemma presented to the Incorporated Law Society in England by the large numbers of defalcations of solicitors at the time of the Great Depression is equally true of the situation prevailing in Victoria during the 1930s. The Law Institute of Victoria was put into the difficult position of having to react to the public disquiet over these developments and the potential they contained for bringing the profession into disrepute, whilst at the same time keeping opposing interests within the profession satisfied with their handling of the issue of fidelity insurance. This was, as we shall see, an impossible task. These difficulties were complicated in Victoria, as they were in England, by the fact that the Law Institute had also to avert the possibility of the government of the day taking a direct hand in the regulation of the profession,

[48] *The Age*, 18 Aug 1930.

[49] M Lunney, ' "And the Lord knows where they might lead"—the Law Society, the fraudulent solicitor and the Solicitors Act 1941', (1997) 4(3) *International Journal of the Legal Profession*, 235–266 at 235.

as a consequence of public concern over the inability of the Institute to properly regulate its own members.

After a series of press reports on the increasing numbers of financial defalcations by solicitors the Institute responded in 1930 by holding a special meeting of Council. There was considerable division of opinion amongst members of the profession as to how to respond to the 'problem' of financial mismanagement of trust funds which had led to a significant deterioration in the profession's standing within the community. Even though it was generally considered that greater regulation of the management of trust funds should occur, it was nevertheless the case that members of the Institute were not prepared to commit themselves to a policy on how this might be achieved.[50] When one of the members moved a motion that a solicitors indemnity fund be established by statute no seconder could be found for the motion. Further discussion of the issue of how to deal with the 'problem' of financial mismanagement was then postponed.[51]

However, even if the Institute might wish to postpone consideration of the matter the press and the public were not similarly minded. The enactment of legislation providing for compulsory indemnity insurance in New Zealand led to renewed demands for similar legislation in Victoria. The failure in New Zealand of legislation requiring annual audits of solicitors' trust accounts to stop the numbers of defaulting solicitors led directly to the institution of a system of compulsory insurance. The similarities with the situation in Victoria was commented on in a number of newspaper articles at the time:

> The provisions of the New Zealand Act requiring annual audit and certificate of the solicitor did not prove effective in preventing defalcations . . . defalcations by an average number of 1400 practicing solicitors in the Dominion during the last ten years amounted to 38,000 pounds. This, of course, was disastrous to clients, and involved the legal profession in discredit . . . [as a consequence of the failure of these provisions new provisions providing for compulsory insurance have been introduced] . . . which became law because [they] had the support as it was said of 1499 out of the 1500 solicitors in the Dominion.[52]

The press continued to popularise the issue throughout 1930, running numerous articles on defaults by legal practitioners, both in Victoria and in other States. Alarm raged amongst members of the Council of the Institute. On 1 May 1930 another special meeting of the Council of the

[50] To capture the flavour of public criticism over the indecision of the Law Institute on this matter see the newspaper reports in the *Sydney Morning Herald*, 16 Jan 1930 and *The Age*, 18 Aug 1930.

[51] *Centenary History of The Law Institute of Victoria 1859–1959*, op cit (n 8 above), 50–51.

[52] *Sydney Morning Herald*, 16 Jan 1930.

Institute discussed whether the public had lost confidence in the profession. Defenders of the *status quo* suggested that members of the Council were over-reacting and should not allow themselves to be panicked into agreeing to 'unwise' legislation. A motion was however passed to the effect that a sub-committee be charged with the task of drafting a Bill on the matter of indemnity insurance for submission to, and consideration by, the Institute.[53]

At a meeting on the 19 May 1930 the Council rescinded all the motions passed at the earlier 1 May meeting. It would appear that the rural members on the Council were instrumental in getting the earlier motions reversed. The Bendigo Law Association was implacably opposed to the introduction of any form of indemnity insurance for solicitors and lobbied its local members of Parliament on the matter throughout 1930 and 1931.[54]

Despite considerable opposition from its own rank and file and the uncertainty of a number of members of its own Council, the Law Institute of Victoria nevertheless recommended to its membership in August 1930 that legislation should be adopted which provided for the establishment of separate trust accounts by solicitors and the creation of a fidelity guarantee fund. The majority of members supported these recommendations at a meeting on 14 August 1930. A Bill was drafted and went before Parliament.[55] The press reports at the time were supportive

[53] *Centenary History of The Law Institute of Victoria 1859–1959*, op cit (n 8 above), 50–51.

[54] The *Centenary History of the Law Institute*, op cit, notes:

> . . . there was a great deal of concern on the part of members of the profession, some of them not members of the Institute, against the Bill, and also a number of country law associations, particularly the Bendigo Law Association, were bitterly opposed to it. Solicitors practising in Bendigo and Warrnambool indicated that they would attempt to obtain deferment of the Bill through their local members. (at p 51).

At least one country member of the Institute, Mr J Burt Stewart of Murchison was indefatigable in his protests to the various leading newspapers as to the unrepresentative nature of the Council of Law Institute and the unfairness of an indemnity insurance scheme in dealing with the mounting problem of defalcations by 'black sheep' within the profession:

> It is a moot question to what extent the Law Institute is representative of the legal profession in the bill now before parliament. I suggest that means be sought to test the mind of the rank and file of practitioners . . . There must be many solicitors in practice who in face of such legislation as proposed would prefer, if means allowed, to retire from practice rather than carry the odium that their integrity is doubted . . . I regret that I should draw the lance with the institute, but it is to be borne in mind that its influence behind the bill may cause the prosed legislation to be enacted without the consideration that is due to those to be affected by it. (Letter to *The Argus*, 6 Dec 1930).

[55] *The Age* of 11 Dec 1930 reported on the introduction of the Bill to Parliament:

> Protection for clients against the risk of loss through the misuse of funds entrusted to solicitors is provided in the Legal Profession Practice Bill, which was introduced into the Legislative Assembly by the Attorney General (Mr Slater) last night. *cont./*

of these initiatives and noted the need to 'do something'. They noted the ever-increasing number of delinquencies by legal practitioners and the disastrous effects of these delinquencies on clients. They also observed that these indiscretions were having a corrosive effect on the reputation of the legal profession itself.[56] However, after the Bill had reached the Third Reading stage, the Law Institute had a change of heart and agitated to have the Bill withdrawn. This reversal of the previous stance of the Institute occurred after a well-attended meeting of practitioners, not officially sanctioned by the Institute, had passed a motion criticising the Institute and urging withdrawal of the Bill. The matter again went before the Council of the Institute which, during 1932, passed a motion to the effect that Institute policy was now against the establishment of an indemnity fund. The motion went on to state that the Institute now favoured the strengthening of penal provisions for fraud to discourage practitioners from defaulting, rather than a scheme which would effectively constitute a 'tax' on honest practitioners to pay for losses brought about by the dishonesty of a small number of their colleagues.[57]

Despite their considerable unpopularity with the public and the imminence of government intervention on the matter of financial defalcations, the Institute nevertheless decided in the end to 'tough it out' on the question of compulsory insurance. The reason for this change of heart was a 'palace revolt' by its country members. Membership of those eligible members in the country climbed from less than 15 per cent to about 70 per cent in the early 1930s. This led, in turn, to the defeat or retirement (in 1932) of a number of the incumbent members of the Council of the Law Institute who supported the introduction of a scheme of fidelity insurance and/or the imposition of annual audits on solicitors' trust accounts.

One of the casualties of the above coup was Mr CH Lucas, who continued to fight a rearguard action in the letters pages of the major newspapers of the day in regard to the imposition of tighter standards on solicitors in the management of trust funds. He was an ardent advocate of the necessity of introducing a scheme of compulsory fidelity insurance along the lines of those in New Zealand and Queensland. He considered that one of the corollaries of being part of a profession was a range of

In moving the second reading of the bill Mr Slater said that if the proposals as set out in the bill had been in effect years ago it was likely there would have been sufficient money at the disposal of the Law Institute of Victoria to reimburse all those persons who had lost money at the hands of fraudulent solicitors. The Bill provided protection for the community.

[56] See, for instance, the report in *The Age*, 18 Aug 1930.

[57] A Report entitled 'Trust Funds: Another Bill Proposed' in *The Argus* of 9 Aug 1933 contains a brief history of the tortuous passage of the Bill through Parliament between 1931 and 1933 (see also below at n 53) .

obligations towards the public (ie ones clients). Amongst those obligations was the duty to ensure that members of the profession acted honestly in their dealings with their clients, and when they did not, that the culprits should be punished and affected clients be restored to their former financial position. Mr Lucas had laid out his position as early as 1929 and stuck with it throughout the ensuing years of tension within the community at large and the Law Institute itself. Commenting in 1929 on the responsibilities of the profession in respect to the clients of defaulting members Lucas stated:

> The severity of the economic depression during the last year has caused the history of such occasions to repeat itself in the increase of crime against money and other property . . . People lacking rigid principles of honesty have stolen what they could not earn. Those whose callings have been connected with the handling of money have succumbed to the same temptation, and, being prevented by the high cost of commodities from maintaining their previous degree of comfort, have embezzled . . . Unfortunately solicitors are not absent from the list . . . solicitors are alive to the serious fact that in recent times there has been a distressing increase in [defalcations of trust funds]—distressing to the professional man as well as the victim of the dishonesty. To tell the sufferer that his case is relatively a rare one would be a mockery.
>
> Restitution is his need, and if he has not in any way contributed to the wrongdoing, the writer of these lines submits to the profession that the client is entitled to restitution, and submits with equal confidence that it is possible to give it to him . . . restitution . . . is what the client requires, and statutory provisions to that end should take precedence over all preventative measures. We enjoy the unbounded confidence of our clients, and the writer submits we should show our gratitude for it by protecting them by paying a moderate annual subscription to an Indemnity Fund.[58]

By 1932 Lucas, and others like him who advocated the introduction of indemnity insurance, were in a minority within the Law Institute. For a brief, but crucial, period in the 1930s urban solicitors from larger practices lost control of the Institute. This change of leadership was behind the withdrawal of support for the legislation with regard to trust accounts and fidelity insurance. The rural members (with the support of a number of practitioners with small, family practices in the city and suburbs) were largely concerned with their own economic survival rather than broader issues of professionalism. Many country practices were small and the cost of an annual audit, plus a substantial annual payment into a fidelity insurance fund would, so it was perceived, send many of these smaller, country practices to the wall. Resentment in the country was also considerable in regard to having to pay for what they perceived to be the improvidence of their city colleagues. Most defaults were those of members of city

[58] CH Lucas, 'Solicitors Trust Funds and an Indemnity', *Law Institute Journal*, 1 Dec 1929, 228–229.

practices. It was asserted by those in the country that it was extremely unfair that they, who could least afford it, should then have to pay for the improvidence and dishonesty of their city counterparts.

The tenor of the country opposition and its effectiveness in stalling the passage of legislation regarding the institution of a scheme of compulsory insurance for solicitors in Victoria can be gauged from the following report on the (still stalled) passage of the legislation in 1933:

> In 1931 the Hogan Ministry introduced a bill to safeguard trust funds handled by solicitors, its principal object being the establishment of an indemnity fund of contributions from solicitors, which would be used to meet clients' needs. The Bill reached the Legislative Council, but there it was practically shelved. As nine out of every ten solicitors are said to oppose this method, it is understood it will not be recommended to Cabinet. Opponents of the indemnity fund contend that it would be tantamount to making honest practitioners pay for the misdeeds of the dishonest ones, without solving the primary difficulty of preventing the misuse of trust funds altogether. It has also been suggested that solicitors should be required to have their trust funds audited at intervals of six months or a year, but this method is opposed chiefly on the ground of expense, particularly to country solicitors.[59]

The Bill which was ultimately introduced into Parliament contained no provisions regarding either compulsory insurance or audit, despite the public clamour for the introduction of such measures. There was an immediate response in the letters pages of the major daily newspapers in Melbourne. Large numbers of correspondents put pen to paper to suggest that the legal profession in Victoria was a 'disgrace'. Characteristic of the letters published is one from J Elder Walker of Ringwood who expressed the view that if one listened to the members of the legal profession closely they 'couldn't help being struck by the fact that clients and their interests seem to be a secondary issue'. Mr Walker continued:

> The main issue [in the debate surrounding indemnity insurance] seems be to ensure that solicitors should not suffer any inconvenience, owing to having their accounts audited or to having a burden cast upon them having to give a bond to ensure their honesty . . . The legal profession is very jealous of its status and its monopoly in all manners which touch its honour and its pocket, and it seems strange that in this matter, which is the issue most vital to the honour of the profession, it should adopt such a helpless attitude. The general public is not greatly interested in the steps which may be taken by the legal profession to deal with members who fail to conform to the ethics of the profession. What the public wants is to be assured against loss in dealings with the legal profession, as in dealing with any other. If the profession cannot agree to be guaranteed by fidelity insurance for which each person would pay his premium according to the extent of his possible liability, there seems no alternative to forcing restitution by legislation.[60]

[59] *The Argus*, 9 Aug 1933.

[60] Letters to the Editor, *The Argus*, 12 Aug 1933.

In addition to the general public, members of a range of other professions and quasi-professions, who were themselves subject to some form of fidelity insurance, wrote to the papers expressing outrage at the special treatment being given to the legal profession. Whilst the Law Institute became more entrenched in its opposition to fidelity insurance, public opinion became more and more strident in the face of their intransigence. So too were the voices of the opposition within the Law Institute itself (such as the indefatigable Mr CH Lucas) raised more loudly with respect to the damage they perceived was being done to the integrity and public esteem of the profession. Even the professional bodies representing lawyers in other States looked askance at the policy of the Law Institute of Victoria on compulsory audits of trust accounts and fidelity insurance. At the inaugural Australian Legal Convention in 1935 many of the papers contained thinly veiled criticisms of the Law Institute of Victoria and the damage it was doing to the profession.[61]

This inscrutability on the part of the Law Institute in the face of almost daily defaults of practitioners and considerable financial losses to the public, estimated in the mid-1930s to amount to over 100,000 pounds per year, is in stark contrast to the treatment of the same issue in England. The (English) Incorporated Law Society's response to a similar dilemma was to ultimately cave into public criticism, even in the face of internal opposition to such a capitulation on the part of the members of the Associated Provincial Law Societies (a body not unlike the country law associations in Victoria). The unfolding of events in Victoria were even at odds with developments in the rest of Australia and in New Zealand.

It is hard to pinpoint exactly the reasons for the failure of fidelity insurance and audit proposals in Victoria and their success elsewhere. Perhaps the answer lies in the level of organisation of country solicitors in key rural districts in Victoria, and a certain timidity on the part of Parliament to legislate for the reforms in the face of opposition from sectors of the profession. Lunney's analysis of the relative power balances in England indicates a different mix than that prevailing in Victoria. Despite the vigorous opposition to the reforms by rural practitioners in England, through the aegis of the Associated Provincial Law Societies, these voices

[61] For instance, *The Age* of 30 Oct 1935, quite pointedly reported a speech to the Convention by Mr PT Cross, a Queensland solicitor and member of the Council of the Law Society of Queensland, on the experience in that State of an indemnity insurance scheme similar to that proposed for Victoria: 'The solicitors of Queensland, Mr. Cross said increasingly approved of what had been done, and 95% of them would not think of reverting to the old system . . . the society [had supported the scheme on the basis] that it was practising a very honourable profession, and one worthy of public trust, and that whenever a member defaulted it wished to make what redress it could. The experience of the society had been eminently satisfactory. The standing of the profession in Queensland was better than ever it had been, and commanded more respect.'

of opposition were eventually silenced by the perception that if nothing was done by the profession itself then the government would take measures to remove the privilege of self-regulation from the profession and legislate to take control of the its affairs:

> The usual effect of a rejection by the Associated Provincial Law Societies of a proposal for reform was to kill off the reform for the immediate future. On the issue of defalcations, however, pressure began to mount from outside the Incorporated Law Society for action.[62]

Lunney observes that a crucial turning point in the acceptance on the part of the profession of the inevitability of audits and fidelity insurance was the trial of a leading and apparently respectable member of the profession for fraud whilst these proposals were being considered by Parliament. This fortuitous event largely silenced opposition from provincial solicitors.

However, despite the effect such legal actions and publicity surrounding the defaults of leading and respected solicitors might have on public opinion it was by no means inevitable that such exposure of the professions 'dirty linen' would necessarily lead to support for indemnity insurance and annual audits of trust accounts. This is borne out by the fact that similar cases emerged in Victoria (and most other States in Australia) at crucial stages of the debate as to the introduction of indemnity insurance without the same result as in England. The leading daily papers in Victoria, *The Age* and *The Argus* and *The Herald*, all featured a story on a 50,000 pounds deficiency in the trust fund of a well-known and respected Sydney solicitor during August 1933.[63] Whilst this, and a number of other articles on lesser defalcations in Victoria, fuelled public dissatisfaction with the handling of the issue it did not lead to a significant change in opinion within the Law Institute. With the 'hard-liners' in control of the Institute and the perception amongst opposition forces

[62] M Lunney, ' "And the Lord knows where they might lead"—the Law Society, the fraudulent solicitor and the Solicitors Act 1941' (1997) 4(3) *International Journal of the Legal Profession*, 237.

[63] Mr Arthur Davies was the solicitor. His case was all the more dramatic for the fact that upon discovery of his defalcations Davies had committed suicide on the 18 April 1932. *The Herald* of 17 Aug 1933 reported the statements of the trustee in bankruptcy charged with dealing with the case: 'The books and general accounts of the bankrupt were in a terrible state and form them little information could be obtained . . . I came to the conclusion that Davies was a solicitor with a very large practice . . . and there was at the time of his death a large number of clients who had confidence in him.

Miss Tattersall, the bankrupts clerk, advised me that there were no books kept and the only records of transactions with trust moneys were the cheque butts . . . To imagine such a state of affairs is permissible is hardly conceivable, but I regret that the law of the land as it stands does not render it necessary that a person handling trust funds shall keep proper books.'

within the Law Institute that the majority of lawyers in the State were against the introduction of indemnity insurance, even scandals such as this were insufficient to dampen the Institute's continuing opposition to the introduction of indemnity insurance and compulsory audits.

Another factor, which may have made the trajectory of the debate on fidelity insurance and compulsory audits somewhat more laboured in Victoria than elsewhere was the growing concern on the part of the Council of the Law Institute that by supporting measures such as annual audits and indemnity insurance they might further alienate their already hostile country and suburban membership. It was noted with concern by members of the Council of the Law Institute that a number of semi-employed and unemployed practitioners were engaging in a flirtation with the organised fascist movement in Australia. Indeed as war drew closer this expression of discontent on the part of disenchanted practitioners became a matter of considerable disquiet within the Council of the Law Institute .

This disquiet may, at our considerable distance from events, seem an unlikely factor in preventing the adoption of as sensible a measure as the introduction of indemnity insurance for legal practitioners. However, at the time, it was felt by the Council of the Law Institute that further impositions on members of the legal profession would lead disenchanted members into political activism. Already quite a number of frustrated and disillusioned practitioners had joined extremist organisations, particularly Australian fascist groups, and it was felt that further administrative and financial demands on practitioners would lead ever increasing numbers of underemployed practitioners to follow in their footsteps.

The dissatisfaction of under-employed and financially straitened members of the profession was, by the late 1930s, quite significant. The professional life they had envisaged had not materialised. Instead of being financially comfortable and respected by the community in which they practised, legal practitioners with small practices were, by the middle of the 1930s, more likely to be in severe financial difficulties and sometimes also in disgrace within the communities in which they lived and practiced. The disillusionment of a number of these less successful members of the legal profession found its expression in political extremism. Some of these practitioners became advocates of fascism and joined the then fledging Australian fascist movement. This flirtation by some members of the profession with extremist movements was one of the main preoccupations of the leadership of the Law Institute during the mid- to late 1930s. Their concern was not entirely without foundation. In New South Wales over a third of the key activists in the New Guard (the proto-fascist organisation in that State, which had been modelled on Moseley's black shirts in England) were members of the legal profession.[64] The historian of the New Guard notes that 'one group strongly represented [in the membership of the New Guard] was the legal profession, the Guard being able to count among its members at least six kings counsels'.[65] Similarly, in Victoria, a large number of key members of the White Army (the Victorian equivalent to the New Guard) were members of the legal profession.

In his President's Annual Address to the Law Institute in 1935 Mr G O'Crowther voiced his concerns as to the dangerous propensities of under-employed legal practitioners:

> The existence of an underpaid, or worse still, an unemployed professional class, constitutes a definite danger to the social structure of the community. Professional associations and professional men are normally stabilising elements in a community. Their traditions and habits of thought run along the lines of peaceful evolution rather than revolution. Per contra the unemployed professional man seems, from the experience of other countries, to pass to violent extremes of doctrine and practice that threaten the stability of the State itself.[66]

This was not the first instance in which these concerns had been expressed. In 1934 an editorial in the Law Institute Journal had expressed grave concerns as to the prospects of many of those then studying law. The University of Melbourne was continuing to enrol about 350 students a year at a time when high levels of un- and under-employment already existed within the profession. As the editorial noted the profession was significantly 'overmanned', with a 'substantial proportion of the solicitors admitted during the past few years being unable to establish themselves in practice'. The editorial continued in much the same vein as the President of the Law Institute in his speech to the Institute a year later:

> . . . [I]t seems likely that there will be a serious over-supply in the profession. An unemployed intelligentsia, particularly one trained in law, has been found to be a grave mischief in other countries. Possibly a similar fear is groundless in Australia. But, however that may be, there can be little doubt that to the profession itself over-supply is likely to be a menace.[67]

Fortunately, these dire predictions proved wrong. Whilst numbers of legal practitioners did join the Australian fascist movement during the

[64] This figure has been arrived at by matching the lists of members of the New Guard command structure contained in K Amos, *The New Guard Movement 1931–1935* (Melbourne University Press, Melbourne, 1976), 116–118 against the NSW Law List for 1933.

[65] K Amos, *The New Guard Movement 1931–1935* (Melbourne University Press, Melbourne, 1976), 44–45.

[66] Presidential Address, G O'D Crowther, President of the Law Institute of Victoria, reported in the *Law Institute Journal*, Vol IX 1 Jan 1935.

[67] 'The Prospects of the Profession', in May 1934(8) *La w Institute Journal*, 71–73 at 73.

1930s their flirtation with extremist political doctrines did not ultimately threaten the State, nor prove to be enduring. However, even if the concern of the Council of the Law Institute with respect to the 'dangerousness' of un- and under-employed solicitors ultimately proved to be misplaced, for a short time in the 1930s their paranoias of a *fascisti* led by disenchanted legal practitioners seemed very real possibility to themselves and their contemporaries. The minutes of a number of the meetings of the Council of the Law Institute during the mid 1930s reflect this concern. This fear of the political volatility of their unemployed members combined with the vigorous opposition of country members of the Council to the introduction of a scheme of indemnity insurance was enough to steel the Council of the Law Institute against public criticism. They felt that by delaying the introduction of these measures until times again became more prosperous they were holding the profession together. The Council was acutely aware of the fracture lines within the profession and wished to avoid making matters worse than they already were.

Through a range of circumstances, perhaps unique to Victoria, the Law Institute of Victoria was able to delay consideration of indemnity insurance and annual audits far longer than was the case for any other equivalent professional body in Australia. It was not until 1936 that the matter again came before Parliament. The Law Institute had submitted a draft bill which had proposed that the Institute itself be responsible for the regulation of solicitors' trust accounts. Parliament had responded by enacting the Legal Profession Practice Act 1936 which required by law the keeping of separate trust accounts and gave the Attorney General, upon a complaint being made, the power to inspect and audit a solicitors' trust account. These measures proved to relatively ineffectual and led to a further attempt to legislate on the topic in 1939. In that year the Council proposed the introduction of a 'relief' fund for indemnifying clients affected by the defaulting solicitors. They proposed that the annual contributions of solicitors to the fund should vary between five and ten pounds per annum, depending upon the number of years of practice. The terms upon which the Council proposed this scheme were that membership of the Law Institute should be made compulsory. Unlike the Council of the early 1930s who were voted out of office on the basis of their support for a similar scheme, the Council in 1939 proclaimed that 'in principle it has the majority of the profession behind it in its latest move' and that Parliament should consequently legislate for such a measure. Unfortunately, due to the exigencies of war the proposed legislation was again put on hold. Thus, the question of fidelity insurance for members of the profession remained unresolved for almost a further decade.

It was only after a decade and a half of wrangling that a Solicitors Guarantee Fund was finally established in Victoria, 15 years later than was the case in New Zealand and most other States in Australia. This

Guarantee Fund was established under the terms of the Legal Profession Practice Act 1946. The legislation provided for a fidelity fund to which every practising solicitor in the State was required to subscribe. In the case of pecuniary losses resultant upon a misappropriation of trust monies the aggrieved client would be compensated from the fund if recovery was not possible against the defaulting solicitor.[68]

The Institute, despite the considerable delay in achieving its original objective of establishing a solicitors' guarantee fund, nevertheless further entrenched its position as the voice of the lower branch of the profession by having the legislature tie membership of the Institute to the issue of practising certificates. The Rules established in association with the Legal Profession Practice Act of 1946 provided for the payment of a solicitors practising fee to the Institute and stipulated that forthwith membership subscriptions should be credited in payment of the members' practising fee. The tying together of practising fees and membership of the Institute ensured that the Institute would forthwith command a much greater and more representative membership as, in practice, it meant that membership of the Institute was now virtually compulsory. Membership of the Institute immediately sky-rocketed from a mere 20 per cent[69] of practising solicitors to a more than respectable 80 per cent of all Victorian practitioners (excluding 'barristers' who separately belonged to the Bar Council).[70]

The considerable delay in introducing fidelity insurance in Victoria might be mistaken for an example of the conservatism of the Institute and its power to delay reforms. This, however, would be too simplistic an explanation. The question of the introduction of a scheme of fidelity insurance was not a matter over which the Institute had a single view. It was internally divided on the matter, with the city-based leadership of the Institute initially supporting the measure, and a loose amalgam of country law associations and urban solicitors in sole practice opposed to it. The internal friction around this issue was so great that some long standing leaders of the Institute were defeated in election for Council during the 1930s.[71] This indicates that there were considerable differ-

[68] *Centenary History of the Law Institute*, op cit (n 8 above), 51–52.

[69] What is noteworthy in this figure is that the battle around the introduction of fidelity insurance and audits had led to a haemorrhaging of city members from the Institute in the mid to late 1930s. from being a largely city-based Institute it had become an almost exclusively rural club in the late 1930s. Membership of solicitors had dropped from over 40% of those eligible to 20% in the late 1930s.

[70] These figures are based on a comparison of the 1939 and 1947 Law Lists for Victoria.

[71] *Centenary History of The Law Institute of Victoria 1859–1959*, 51. CH Lucas, a long time member of the Council of the Law Institute had retired from the Council in 1931 rather than face almost certain defeat at the hands of the members after his unequivocal support for a compulsory scheme of insurance in 1930.

ences of opinion during these years within the Institute on major matters of policy. City-based practitioners were more concerned with maintaining the reputation of the profession, whilst country solicitors and sole practitioners in the city were more concerned with keeping costs low and maintaining market control, particularly in bread and butter areas of practice.

CONCLUSIONS

In his presidential speech to the Law Institute at its 1939 Annual Meeting, Mr Frederick Gubbins speculated on the role of professional associations such as his own in the post-depression environment:

> . . . [T]he chief object of a professional body such as ours . . . is the establishment of friendly relations amongst those members of the profession who desire to uphold its dignity and reputation . . . I think the establishment of friendly understanding should be the first aim of the Law Institute; friendly understanding amongst our members and with other bodies whose opinions and friendships mean a great deal to us.

At the beginning of this speech Mr Gubbins had noted that this was the first presidential address to the Law Institute for some considerable time and then proceeded with his call for unity and friendship. He concluded by noting that in 'recent years' members of the profession had been accustomed to hearing that the profession 'was deteriorating and disunited'. He then went on to deny that this was the case and that the profession was, as ever, united by a 'strong sense of professional duty'.

The unsaid and the passing remark often reveals more than a ream of official documents. This is certainly the case with Gubbins' speech. The fact that there had not been a presidential address since 1936 was not serendipitous. It was a consequence of deep divisions within the Institute over important matters of policy. The profession had fractured into warring camps over the related issues of compulsory audits of trust accounts and the establishment of a fidelity insurance scheme. In the early 1930s country and suburban members had vigorously denounced the then leadership of the Law Institute as 'not representing' their views on these issues. For a brief period these humbler members of the profession gained control of the Institute and caused it to reverse its policy on these key issues. Arguably this reversal in policy cost the Law Institute and the profession dearly in respect to their credibility with the public. It also demonstrated in vivid relief the fact that the 'legal profession' was by no means a homogenous entity. Whilst idealised versions of the 'profession' see it as a body united by a common set of ethical and professional ideals the truth is that is characterised by a series of divisions over those very ideals.

However, despite these significant differences between sections of the profession there is nevertheless also some congealing force which seems to bind the profession together. The legal profession is, in this respect, not unlike other groupings (such as political parties) in which there is a commitment to some broad notion of what it means to belong to that particular group, but in which there is wide difference of opinion on matters of detail.

Sugarman rightly points to the error of conceiving legal (or for that manner any other form of professional practice) as monolithic. The legal profession is full of ambiguity, cohering around some issues, and fragmenting over others. Sometimes one can point to a 'single' unified profession, and in other instances one can only observe the incoherent and often conflicting views held by sectional groupings within the profession. In the course of introducing the complexity of the forces that shape the 'legal profession' Sugarman has made the following observations:

> Transcending the divisions between lawyering and business and the private and public roles of lawyers in society helps to focus attention on a related set of connections that are often neglected within the history and sociology of the profession: namely, the relationship between the ideas and culture of the profession, the work lawyers undertake, the organisation of legal practices and their economic context, how they change over time, and the larger cultural and political significance of lawyers in society . . . An examination of these issues . . . illuminates the in-built conflicts of interest and the plurality of voices, logics, 'traditions', audiences and spheres of action that are an important feature of legal work, thought, culture and authority. From this broader perspective, we can investigate the relative elasticity of the ideology of legal professionalism and the ways in which that ideology sustains apparently divergent conceptions of the profession, while asserting a common culture and history binding lawyers together as a community (my emphasis).[72]

At the outset of this account of the Law Institute of Victoria Allen Hutchinson's remarks on the 'declining homogeneity' of the legal profession in recent times were noted. At least in respect to the Law Institute of Victoria one might wish to revise such remarks. The legal profession in Victoria has always been subject to considerable division. In the 1890s the divisions were as between barristers and solicitors, and as between rural and city based members of the profession. In the Great Depression of the 1930s significant fault lines appeared as between city and country members of the profession. Whilst these divisions were repaired after the immediate crises passed, it is nevertheless the case that the level of homogeneity claimed by both 'institutional' historians of the profession and by

[72] D Sugarman, 'Blurred boundaries: the overlapping worlds of law, business and politics' in C Harrington and M Cain (eds), *Lawyers in a Postmodern World: Translation and Transgression* (Open University Press, Buckingham, 1994), 105–106 (my emphasis)

'market control' theorists never appear to have existed within the profession in Victoria. Dissent and friction between sectors of the profession have been the 'norm'. These divisions are most obvious at times of crisis such as those which existed during the financial depressions of the 1890s and 1930s, but are never far from the surface. Sometimes these divisions might produce benefits to the wider public or lead to an improvement in professional practice, and sometimes they will not. The divisions of the 1890s within the legal profession in Victoria, for instance, could not be said to have improved the position of the public *vis-à-vis* the profession. The continuing division between barristers and solicitors simply led to increased costs for clients. Nor could it be said that the public was a major beneficiary of the friction between different sectors of the profession over indemnity insurance in the 1930s. Many clients lost their life savings whilst the Law Institute and the legislature prevaricated. Even the delayed resolution of the matter in 1946 mainly benefited the Law Institute. Insurance was introduced in return for practising solicitors being forced to take out Law Institute membership—giving the Law Institute a guaranteed membership and augmenting their power base. Also, whilst clients had somewhat better protection from rogue solicitors after the legislation, this was of little comfort to those clients who had lost hundred of thousands of pounds as a consequence of dishonest lawyers absconding with their trust funds in the 1930s.

As historians of the legal profession such as David Sugarman[73] and W Wesley Pue[74] have reminded us on a number of occasions, bodies such as Law Societies (or Institutes) have had to balance a range of contradictory interests in their activities. On the one side they have to act as a form of trade union for their members, ensuring that other professions do not encroach on that of the legal profession, and that monopolies in specific areas of practice are preserved. On the other side, representative bodies of lawyers have to maintain the professional ideals and standards of the profession and ensure that members act with honesty and integrity when dealing with clients. Sometimes these two roles of the professional bodies are impossible to reconcile and the profession breaks down into contending camps. This is what happened in the 1890s and 1930s in Victoria. Some members considered the civic responsibilities and ideals of the profession as pre-eminent whilst others saw the need to keep costs low and protect their incomes as the most important goal for the Law Institute.

[73] For example, see D Sugarman, 'Bourgeois collectivism, professional power and the boundaries of the State. The private and public life of the Law Society 1825 to 1914', (1996) 3(1/2) *International Journal of the Legal Profession*, 81–134, in particular at 121.

[74] See W Pue, 'Exorcising Professional Demons: Charles Rann Kennedy and the Transition to the Modern Bar', (1987) 5 *Law and History Review* 135–187; Pue, W, 'Moral Panic at the English Bar: Paternal vs Commercial Ideologies of Legal Practice in the 1860s', *Law and Social Inquiry* (1990), 49–118.

The manner in which these irreconcilable concepts of the role of representative professional bodies is played out is always contingent on a range of factors, some within the profession itself, such as the relative balance of power as between the groups representing these contending views; and some external to the profession, such as political pressures being exerted on the profession by public opinion and government.

12

Cultural Chasm: 'Mennonite' Lawyers in Western Canada 1900–1939

HAROLD DICK

INTRODUCTION

In a real sense, there were no Mennonite lawyers in Western Canada in the first four decades of the twentieth century. To be sure, at least seven members of the legal profession in this period had been born into Mennonite homes and had grown up speaking Plattdeutsch, eating verenike, roll kuchen and zweibach and attending Mennonite churches.[1] In addition, three of these men had attended a Mennonite High School and two had married Mennonite women.[2] It is also true that all but one of these men practised law near Mennonite settlements for some period of time during their careers, using their connections with the Mennonites to build a clientele.[3] Moreover, at least two of these men used their skills

[1] These men were: Abraham Buhr (1880–1960), Henry Vogt (1886–1968), Peter J Hooge (1886–1963), John E Friesen (1895–1987), David Vogt (1900–1979), Erdman Friesen (1904–1969) and Elmer A Driedger (1914–1985). For more information concerning these men, see HJ Dick, *Lawyers of Mennonite Background in Western Canada Before the Second World War* (Winnipeg, Manitoba, Legal Research Institute of the University of Manitoba, 1993) at 97–157. Plattdeutsch is also referred to as Low German. It is a dialect adopted by the Mennonites while living along the Vistula River in Prussia (now Poland) and has not traditionally been a written language. Verenike, roll kuchen and zweibach are Mennonite dishes of German or Ukrainian origin.

[2] Abraham Buhr, Henry Vogt and David Vogt all attended the Mennonite Collegiate Institute in Gretna, Manitoba. Henry Vogt married Agenetha Buhr and David Vogt married Katherine Wiens: *Ibid.* at 97–157.

[3] Abraham Buhr practised law for many years in Winnipeg, Manitoba which contained a sizeable Mennonite population, and maintained an office in Steinbach, situated well within the East Reserve of Manitoba which had originally been set aside for Mennonite settlement. Henry Vogt practised for a time in Morden, Manitoba, near the West Reserve which had also been set aside for Mennonite settlement. Peter Hooge practised law in Rosthern, Saskatchewan for several years, near a sizeable Mennonite settlement. Both John and Erdman Friesen had their beginnings in law in Herbert, Saskatchewan, the site of a Mennonite settlement, and later moved to Swift Current, Saskatchewan, about 30 miles away. Only Elmer Driedger never practised law near any significant Mennonite settlement; after brief periods in Saskatoon and Yorkton, Saskatchewan, he moved to Ottawa: *Ibid* at 97–157.

in an extra-legal capacity to defend the interests of the Mennonite community before the government and society at large.[4]

Nevertheless, despite these connections with the Mennonite community, none of these men can be considered Mennonites by the standards of that community at that time and, almost certainly, by their own standards as well.[5] As will become clear, the cultural distinctives of Mennonites on the Canadian prairies in this era cannot be separated from their faith, their language and their agrarian lifestyle. By choosing a career which required residence in an urban environment, these seven lawyers had abandoned one key stake which held erect the 'sacred canopy' of Mennonite culture. The loss of Plattdeutsch as the language of everyday speech represented the surrender of another stake. Most importantly, however, the fact that none of these men joined or even regularly attended a Mennonite church signalled a conscious choice to reject their cultural community in favour of another.

The reality and the implications of this choice would have been readily apparent both to these seven individuals and the Mennonite community. Few of them made any significant attempts to retain ties to the Mennonite community other than by maintaining contact with relatives. Even more significantly, they did not pass on the Mennonite faith or other cultural distinctives to their children.[6] As for the Mennonites, while they

[4] Abraham Buhr was the most heavily involved in representing the interests of the Mennonite community to that of Canadian society. He helped form Mennonite Immigration Aid, an organisation dedicated to assisting Mennonites from the Soviet Union to settle in Canada. He also engaged in a series of radio broadcasts which explained Mennonite distinctives. Professionally, Buhr represented numerous Mennonites who had been drafted during World War II and wished to obtain conscientious objector status: See, for example, *R v Giesbrecht*, [1944] 1 WWR 353 (Man CA). See also *Ibid* at 110–114. Henry Vogt was also involved in defending Mennonites from the outside world; for example, in 1917 and 1920, he wrote letters to the Premier of Saskatchewan, advancing the position of the conservative Mennonites who rejected provincial curricula and the use of English in their schools: W Janzen, *Limits on Liberty: The Experience of Mennonite, Hutterite, and Doukhobor Communities in Canada* (University of Toronto Press, Toronto, 1990) 107–113.

[5] The one possible exception is Abraham Buhr, the first Mennonite who entered the legal profession. Despite marrying an Icelandic woman, living in an urban environment and failing to attend a Mennonite church, Buhr gave indications throughout his life that he continued to consider himself a Mennonite: Dick, *supra*, n 1 at 113–114.

[6] The extent to which the children of these men felt distanced from their fathers' Mennonite pasts is notable. One was unaware that her father had a Mennonite background until after his death; another, in his autobiography, referred to his father's ancestry as 'Dutch' and failed to mention the word 'Mennonite' at all. Even the children of Abraham Buhr, the man who, arguably, remained most connected to his faith and community, never considered themselves to be Mennonite despite describing their cousins (who lived in the same town) as Mennonites. Significantly, all of Buhr's sons who were able to do so entered the Canadian Armed Forces in the Second World War, a violation of a major tenet of the Mennonite faith: *Ibid* at 97–157.

may have preferred legal services provided by these lawyers over that of lawyers without a Mennonite background, they could not have helped but recognise that these men had chosen a life outside the Mennonite community. A choice had been made and a chasm leapt. From the perspective of the Mennonite community, these lawyers might be good men who spoke Plattdeutsch and understood Mennonite culture, they might be people to turn to in times of need, especially when relations with the larger world involved legal issues, but they were not Mennonites.

The fact that every one of the seven 'Mennonites' who entered the legal profession in the early decades of this century also left behind the Mennonite community may not necessarily say a great deal about either Mennonites or the legal profession in that era. One possible explanation is that the experiences of these seven individuals were coincidental. Every decision is the result of an individual's personality, experiences and circumstances; it may be that all of these men chose to practise law and, for entirely independent reasons, also decided to abandon participation in the Mennonite community. Yet coincidence appears a weak explanation for the unanimous experience of seven individuals who entered the profession over a 26 year period.[7]

Another obvious hypothesis is that the legal community demonstrated such prejudice against lawyers from immigrant communities that aspiring immigrant practitioners felt compelled to divest themselves completely of their linguistic and cultural heritage. This theory must be taken seriously; there is no doubt that prejudice toward certain ethnic groups existed in the legal profession during this period. Nevertheless, no evidence has been discovered which suggests that prejudice was directed against these men or against Icelanders who also entered the legal profession during this period. In fact, the success enjoyed by several of these Mennonite lawyers in their legal careers suggests just the opposite.[8]

A more subtle and compelling theory is that 'Mennonite' lawyers were forced to abandon full participation in the Mennonite community, not because of prejudice directed against immigrants personally, but because of a bias within the legal profession against immigrant cultures. The legal profession of Western Canada in this era was dominated by Anglo-Canadian lawyers and the belief in the superiority of British culture and tradition, as we shall see, was widespread. Certainly, the period examined here preceded by many decades an era in which multiculturalism was celebrated as a cornerstone of Canadian identity. Yet, this theory also appears inadequate. For example, it fails to account for the ability of

[7] Abraham Buhr, the first of these men to enter the legal profession, was called to the Saskatchewan Bar in 1911 while Elmer Driedger, the last, was called to the same Bar in 1937: *Ibid* at 103 and 154.

[8] Of the seven Mennonites who entered the legal profession during this period, two became judges and one a respected legal academic: *Ibid* at 97–157.

Icelandic lawyers to achieve prominence in the legal profession while not only remaining firmly within the Icelandic community but becoming leaders of it.[9]

Still, the uniform experience of 'Mennonite' lawyers in Western Canada prior to the Second World War strongly suggests that a convincing explanation must take into account the two cultures which these men had in common. In this paper, I will briefly examine these two cultures and argue that Mennonites inhabited a culture which was, in critical areas, incompatible with that of the legal profession. Moreover, while committed to starkly different visions of the future, each of these two cultures sought to occupy the same geographical territory on the Canadian prairies; conflict between them was therefore inevitable. The incompatibilities of and conflict between these cultures in the early decades of this century made it impossible to straddle the two communities. Therefore, unlike their Icelandic counterparts, the seven 'Mennonites' who wished to practise law were forced to choose between remaining within their ethnic community and entering the legal profession; they could not do both.

First, then, brief accounts of the two cultures in question.

MENNONITE CULTURE

The Mennonites of Western Canada have their roots in the Radical Reformation of the sixteenth century. Mennonites are one branch of the Anabaptist Movement, which also produced the Amish and Hutterites.[10]

[9] Two examples are sufficient to demonstrate the pattern. Walter J Lindal (1887–1976) enjoyed a successful legal practice and served as a Manitoba County Court Judge for 20 years. He was the first President of the Canada Press Club of Winnipeg and the Citizenship Council of Manitoba. He was also active in the Icelandic community, however, serving as President of the Icelandic Canadian Club of Winnipeg and the Viking Club of Manitoba. He was awarded the Coronation Medal and made a Knight of the Order of the Falcon by the Icelandic Government.

Joseph T Thorson's (1889–1978) achievements in the legal and political fields are even more spectacular. A successful lawyer, he served as Dean of the University of Manitoba School of Law, Member of Parliament, Canadian delegate to the League of Nations, Canadian Minister of National War Services during the Second World War, President of the Exchequer Court of Canada for 20 years and President of the International Congress of Jurists. Yet, although his formal positions within Icelandic circles do not match Lindal's, he took pains to retain his command of the Icelandic language and connections to the Icelandic community. He too was named to the Order of the Falcon and a Grand Cross Knight by the Icelandic government: J Collins, DT Anderson and A Esau, *Iceland Law and Lawyers in Manitoba: A Research Guide* (Legal Research Institute of the University of Manitoba, Research Report Number 5) 91–96, 156–158.

[10] The term 'Mennonite' was applied to the followers of Menno Simons, an Anabaptist leader in the Netherlands. Nevertheless, it has subsequently come to describe

Those Mennonites who eventually arrived in Western Canada can trace their history to the Netherlands of the sixteenth century.

Anabaptist theology was not a systematic affair. It placed great emphasis on ethics and very little on intellectual and academic theory.[11] This is encapsulated in a famous early Mennonite adage: 'No one can know Christ truly unless one follows him in life'.[12] For Anabaptists, true knowledge was not a result of education, logic or original thought but of obedience to God in daily life.[13] Partly as a result of this belief and partly because much of the persecution experienced by the Anabaptists was instigated by academics and the clergy of the Roman Catholic and Lutheran churches, Mennonites traditionally displayed a deep-seated suspicion of higher learning.[14]

One of the more distinctive ethical positions of the Anabaptists was the doctrine of non-resistance or non-violence. This doctrine gave rise to

other descendants of Anabaptists whose roots may be traced to Switzerland and Southern Germany. However, Hutterites and the Amish, groups which also grew out of the Anabaptist movement, are not usually identified as Mennonites.

[11] C Redekop, *Mennonite Society* (The Johns Hopkins University Press, Baltimore, 1989) at 55 states the the Anabaptist belief system should be seen: 'in the context of a continuing dialectic with the majority of Christendom on the issue of ethic or lifestyle—that is, on the concrete expression of the Christian faith.'

The controversy that ultimately caused the formation of the Anabaptist movement seemed to be basically an issue of accepting the Christian teaching at face value *and living it* . . . The conclusion that naturally emerges is that the Anabaptist-Mennonite utopian movement was much more an ethical response than a creedal one. The ideological and philosophical dynamic of the movement was a derivative one, focusing on the application of the basic Christian beliefs in personal and social life, rather than on an emphasis on abstract doctrine which was then expressed in elaborate ecclesiastical liturgy and litanies.

[12] The original phrase in German is '*Christsein heist Christum im Leben nachfolgen*' and is attributed to Hans Denk: L Driedger, *Mennonite Identity in Conflict* (The Edwin Mellen Press, Lewiston and Queenston, 1988) at 38 and CJ Dyck, *An Introduction to Mennonite History* (Herald Press, Scottdale, Pennsylvania, 1967) at 47.

[13] According to WE Keeney, *The Development of Dutch Anabaptist Thought and Practice From 1539–1564* (B de Graaf, Nieuwkoop, The Netherlands, 1968) at 192: 'The Mennonite stress upon the obedient will rather than reason as the primary means for obtaining spiritual knowledge led to and reinforced their interpretation of the Scriptures. Their approach to the Scriptures affected most directly the Mennonite position on teachers and preachers. The moral consequences of a man's life gave the evidence for judging whether he had the charismatic gift which confirmed a call to the ministry. The qualifications for office were not dependent upon education or formal training.'

[14] Melchoir Hoffman, an early Anabaptist leader, said: 'Therefore, I warn all lovers of truth that they do not give themselves over to lofty arguments which are too hard for them, but that they hold themselves to the straightforward words of God in all simplicity': Redekop, *supra*, n 11 at 107. Menno Simons echoed this view in replying to his critics: 'You say, we are inexpert, unlearned and know not the Scriptures. I reply: the Word is plain and needs no interpretation': JC Wenger (ed) *The Complete Writings of Menno Simons*, trans L Verduin (Herald Press, Scottdale, Pennsylvania, 1956) at 214.

their refusal to participate in war[15] and also contributed to their somewhat ambivalent view of the State. On the one hand, they acknowledged that the State was ordained by God to maintain order and limit evil in a sinful and fallen world and they recognised that violence was necessary to achieve that goal.[16] On the other hand, they saw the State as itself sinful and fallen.[17] This resulted in their advocacy of a radical separation of Church and State.[18] They refused to participate in the activities of the State while simultaneously demanding that the State remove itself from all issues of religion and personal ethics which they considered *ultra vires* the State's divinely-ordained jurisdiction.

The Mennonite commitment to pacifism was actually only one manifestation of a larger ethic of love for one's neighbour. This ethic was most fully manifested within the Mennonite community. Mennonites self-consciously committed themselves to the creation of a community rather than an institutional church. Made up only of those who had made a personal commitment to Christ (as evidenced by adult baptism),[19] the Mennonite congregation was to be a community which encompassed all forms of human relationship and which was characterised by 'personal intimacy, emotional depth, moral commitment, social cohesion and continuity in time'.[20]

Although early Mennonites were highly evangelistic and did not advocate a physical separation from the world,[21] the persecution inflicted upon them by the authorities in Holland reinforced a tendency toward an

[15] See, for example, Menno Simons' contention that the Bible teaches Christians not to take up the sword: *Ibid* at 423.

[16] The Dordrecht Confession, an early Anabaptist confession of faith, stated: 'God has instituted civil government for the punishment of the wicked and the protection of the pious; and also further for the purpose of governing the world . . . and to preserve its subjects in good order and good conditions': GF Hershberger, *The Way of the Cross in Human Relations* (1958) 165 in Redekop, *supra*, n 11 at 217. Menno Simons said, 'That the office of the magistrate is of God and His ordinance I freely grant . . .' *Ibid*, n 14 at 922.

[17] The Schleitheim Confession, an early Anabaptist statement of faith, describes civil authority as 'outside the perfection of Christ': JC Wenger, *Glimpses of Mennonite History and Doctrine* (Herald Press, Scottdale, Pennsylvania, 1947) at 210 as cited in Redekop, *supra*, n 11 at 127.

[18] A Friesen, *Emigration in Mennonite History with a Special Reference to the Conservative Mennonite Emigration from Canada to Mexico and South America After World War I* (MA Thesis, University of Manitoba, 1960) at 2. See also Redekop, *supra*, n 11 at 11 and W. Klaassen, *Anabaptism: Neither Catholic Nor Protestant* (Conrad Press, Waterloo, Ontario, 1981) at 46–52.

[19] The term 'Anabaptist' is derived from Latin for 'rebaptised': Dyck, *supra*, n 12 at 36.

[20] RA Nisbet, *The Sociological Tradition* (Basic Books, New York, 1966) as cited in Redekop, *supra*, n 11 at 129.

[21] CH Smith, *Smith's Story of the Mennonites* (Faith & Life Press, Newton, Kansas, 1981) at p 14 and Redekop, *supra*, n 11 at 31.

inward-looking and self-reliant community.[22] This tendency was further strengthened by their emigration from the Netherlands to Prussia (in what is now Poland) in the seventeenth century and later to southern Russia, near the Crimean peninsula. In a new place, unfamiliar with the local language, they found comfort in old traditions and language and over time began to resemble an ethnic as well as a religious group.[23] This was especially the case in Russia where State policy deliberately kept Mennonites separate from the surrounding Ukrainian and Russian population and granted them a high level of autonomy to manage their own affairs.[24]

Early Mennonites had practised a variety of trades and were largely urban dwellers.[25] However, they became increasingly rural during their sojourn in Prussia; in 1776, two-thirds of the heads of Mennonite households in West Prussia were farmers.[26] The trend toward an agricultural community was reinforced by the Mennonite migration to Russia in the late eighteenth century. In the early years of settlement, almost all Mennonites earned their livelihood from the soil and, although various crafts and trades emerged as the Mennonite colonies in Russia developed, these commercial enterprises were viewed as second-best occupational pursuits.[27] The Mennonite ideal was that of a simple farmer living in harmony with God, his community and the rhythms of nature.[28]

After 80 years in Russia, the Mennonites had developed a distinct identity. They retained the use of Plattdeutch, the German dialect they had absorbed during their years in Prussia, but spoke High German in church and on formal occasions. In addition to their unique faith, they developed a unique cuisine, a distinctive style of dress and their own

[22] F Epp, *Mennonite Peoplehood: A Plea for New Initiatives* (Conrad Press, Waterloo, Ontario, 1977) at 23 as cited in Redekop, *supra*, n 11 at 138.

[23] F Epp at 28–29 as cited in in Redekop, *supra* n 11 at 139.

[24] The Mennonite settlers were granted such significant autonomy that their secular leaders 'held all the powers and duties of authorities in the modern secular state': Redekop, *supra*, n 11 at 81. For example, they had the authority to develop and maintain roads, schools and hospitals, to regulate commerce and to deal with social deviance. This latter authority included the power to impose fines or imprisonment and, with the consent of the Russian authorities, to impose corporal punishment: J Urry, *None But Saints: The Transformation of Mennonite Life in Russia 1789–1889* (Hyperion Press, Winnipeg, Manitoba, 1989) at 72.

[25] C-P Clausen, *Anabaptism: A Social History, 1525–1618* (Cornell University Press, Ithaca, New York, 1972) as cited in Driedger, *supra*, n 12 at 17.

[26] H Penner, *Die Ost- und Westpreussischen Mennoniten in ihren Religiosen und Sozialen Leben in ihren Kulturellen und Wirdschaftlichen Leisstungen* (Mennonitischer Geschichtsverein, Weirhof, West Germany, 1978) at 414–469 as cited in Driedger, *supra*, n 12 at 19.

[27] Redekop, *supra* n 11 at 200 and J Urry, *supra*, n 24 at 144–45.

[28] R Friedman (ed and trans), 'Faith and Reason: The Principles of Mennonitism Reconsidered in a Treatise of 1833' (1948) 22 *Mennonite Quarterly Review* 75 at 91.

traditions.[29] They lived in villages, holding some land for common pasture and dividing the rest into small portions in an 'open field' pattern. They were largely self-sufficient, operating their own schools and local governments, both at the village and colony levels. They lived quite independently; to a significant extent, they were physically separated from Russians and Ukrainians and years might pass between visits from Russian government officials. The need for communication in Russian or Ukrainian was minimal.[30] In this secluded environment, Mennonites began to feel a commitment, not only to their village or even their colony but to all Mennonites in Russia. They began to refer to themselves as '*das Mennonitische Volk*'.[31]

By the mid-nineteenth century, Mennonites were also becoming increasingly wealthy, especially in comparison to neighbouring Russians and Ukrainians. Through hard work, frugality and a commitment to one another, they had succeeded beyond all expectations and had turned barren steppes into the 'breadbasket of Europe'. Their material success had been assisted by a modernisation initiative within the Mennonite community which had introduced new farming techniques, new breeds of livestock and new strains of vegetables, fruits and grains as well as contributing to the emergence of large-scale commercial farming operations.[32] Mennonites also began to industrialise, sometimes establishing large industries in towns and cities near the Mennonite colonies.[33]

Of course, modernisation benefitted some Mennonites more than others. Mennonites who had adopted progressive agricultural practices or had invested in modern industries grew extraordinarily wealthy. Some bought vast estates outside the Mennonite colonies.[34] At the same time, however, commercial farming drove numerous subsistence farmers off the land and many traditional crafts were virtually eliminated by indus-

[29] C Redekop, 'Anabaptism and the Ethnic Ghost' (1984) 58 *Mennonite Quarterly Review* 133 at 143.

[30] The Russian government deferred to the Mennonite settlers to the extent of dealing with the leaders of the community rather than with individual Mennonites and using German as the language of official correspondence: EK Francis, *In Search of Utopia: The Mennonites in Manitoba* (DW Friesen & Sons, Altona, 1955) at 21 and Urry, *supra* n 24 at 71.

[31] Urry, *supra*, n 24 at 103 and J Urry, ' "The Snares of Reason"—Changing Mennonite Attitudes to "Knowledge" in Nineteenth-Century Russia' (1983) 25 *Comparative Studies in Society and History* 306 at 320.

[32] Urry, supra, n 24 at 134–35.

[33] GK Epp, 'Urban Mennonites in Russia' in J Friesen (ed), *Mennonites in Russia: Essays in Honour of Gerhard Lohrenz* (CMBC Publications, Winnipeg, 1989) 239 at 241; J Urry, 'Mennonite Economic Development in the Russian Mirror' in J Friesen (ed), *Mennonites in Russia: Essays in Honour of Gerhard Lohrenz* (CMBC Publications, Winnipeg, 1989) 99 at 102.

[34] Urry, *supra*, n 24 at 143 notes that, by 1841, over 130,000 acres of land were owned by nine Mennonites outside the Mennonite colonies.

trially-produced goods. A landless working class, prohibited from participation in civic affairs, grew increasingly restless.[35]

Reforms also affected the Mennonite education system. Historically, elementary schooling had been required for all Mennonite children because it was thought that everyone should have the ability to read the Bible and to become proficient at basic arithmetic needed for farming. Nevertheless, teachers were not expected so much to instruct as to maintain order in the classroom while older children taught the younger.[36] Higher education had been traditionally frowned on both because it tended to disrupt to the community by giving rise to sins of pride and envy and because it created an opportunity for new and dangerous ideas to enter the community.[37] Truth, to most Mennonites, was the known rather than the knowable; it was to be maintained and lived, not discovered.

The modern approach to education flew in the face of this traditional understanding. It centralised control of schools, expanded the curriculum, introduced grades and competition to the classroom, improved school buildings and resulted in the hiring of teachers who were prepared to teach rather than merely to supervise. Secondary schools were established to train teachers, civic administrators and agricultural experts.[38]

All of these changes were resisted by conservative Mennonites who regretted the loss of the small, egalitarian village ideal. They complained of a spiritual malaise, a loss of humility and a desire for wealth, education and status within the Mennonite community.[39] One conservative Mennonite leader expressed the anxiety of many in this fashion:

> Therefore, presumptuousness comes first, then pride, ostentation and arrogance and this was already happening to us, because we already drove in large, magnificant buggies and coaches, and when we passed the native Russians, they hardly knew whether we were aristocrats or only German farmers. That is how the farmers had already changed, and this led to our downfall, for God grants grace only to the humble, but He resists the arrogant.[40]

[35] *Ibid* at 143–146.

[36] Besides its practicality, this was seen as giving children an opportunity to practise concepts of community and mutual aid: Urry, *supra*, n 31 at 313.

[37] Urry, *supra*, n 24 at 153–155 and *Ibid* at 312.

[38] Urry, *supra*, n 24 at 160–165.

[39] Urry, *supra*, n 24 at 217–218 notes: 'Although recent government reforms, especially those that affected the status of the colonists, had acted as a catalyst forcing many to reconsider their position in Russia, long-term tensions within the Mennonite communities undoubtedly contributed to their decision to emigrate . . . There were serious, long-standing doubts among many concerning the direction of Mennonite life in Russia. These doubts included not just the willingness of many to accept official policies, but also the eagerness of some to seek economic reward at the expense of their fellow brethren, as well as the enthusiasm and the desire for new kinds of knowledge and higher learning. . . .'

[40] G Wiebe, *Causes and History of the Emigration of the Mennonites From Russia to America*, trans H Janzen (Manitoba Mennonite Historical Society, Winnipeg, 1981) at 23.

The conservative Mennonites saw the majority of the Mennonite community becoming ensnared by 'reason' (*Vernunft*) rather than seeking 'understanding' (*Verstand*). 'Reason' sought higher education, more efficient civic administration, industrialisation and greater wealth; it resulted in worldly attitudes, ambition and pride. By contrast, 'understanding' permitted one to live a simple, humble and godly life in community with one's neighbours.[41] This was the goal of the conservative group.

Besides their unease with the direction of the Mennonite community, conservative Mennonites were also upset about policy changes instituted by the Russian government which was intended to integrate the Mennonite colonies more fully within the broader Russian empire. In particular, they rejected plans to require Mennonite young men to spend several years in the State forestry service (as an alternative to military service),[42] the requirement that Russian be taught in Mennonite schools and the elimination of some self-governing powers, including the power to own land collectively.[43]

Eventually, both internal and external concerns resulted in a decision by many of the conservative Mennonites to leave Russia for North America. Of the group which left Russia, however, the most conservative chose to settle in Manitoba rather than the United States. They preferred Manitoba over the better land in the American mid-west because of the better prospects for autonomy and isolation; the Canadian government had promised them an exemption from military service, block settlements exclusively reserved for Mennonites and the right to educate their children free of state interference.[44] In other words, they were not principally interested in achieving wealth or success but rather saw Canada as

[41] Friedman, *supra*, n 28 at 75. See also Urry, *supra*, n 31 and Urry, *supra*, n 24 at 123.

[42] The claim that the emigrants left because of their refusal to compromise on the issue of military service 'seems to have reached the status of myth in Mennonite circles at the time,' according to H Loewen, 'A House Divided: Russian Mennonite Non-Resistance and Emigration in the 1870s' in J Friesen (ed), *Mennonites in Russia: Essays in Honour of Gerhard Lohrenz* (CMBC Publications, Winnipeg, 1989) 127 at 127. Although Loewen contends that Mennonites had in fact long since abandoned any commitment to non-resistance as a way of life, the fact remains that, in the minds of the emigrants, this was a key reason for their departure. See, for example, K Peters, *The Bergthaler Mennonites* (trans M Loewen Reimer) (CMBC Publications, Winnipeg, 1988) at 8 who states: 'It was not hardship or persecution in the Fatherland that motivated us to cross the vast ocean to a distant land, but the fact that we were soon to lose our exemption from military service. . . .'

[43] Francis, *supra*, n 30 at 32ff and J Urry, *supra*, n 24 at 210.

[44] JH Warkentin, *The Mennonite Settlements of Southern Manitoba* (PhD Dissertation, University of Toronto, 1960) at 32; FH Epp, *Mennonites in Canada, 1786–1920: The History of a Separate People* (Macmillan, Toronto, 1974) at 195.

a potential utopia where they could return to an idyllic simple and communitarian life-style which they believed was being lost in Russia.[45]

In keeping with this vision, Mennonite settlers began by reproducing on the Canadian prairies a lifestyle identical to that of the steppes. They built homes patterned after those in Russia in small villages with the surrounding land divided into a traditional 'open 'field' arrangement. They maintained the same style of dress used in Russia, cooked many of the same dishes and spoke High German on Sundays and Plattdeutsch on weekdays.[46] They also brought with them and re-established in Western Canada many of the customs and 'legal' institutions developed in Russia.[47]

Very quickly, however, their dreams were under attack by the same forces they had faced in Europe. The prairies were virtually unsettled when the Mennonites arrived in the 1870s but in the next 50 years they experienced an explosion of growth.[48] As the Mennonite settlers became surrounded by other immigrants and as merchants began establishing towns near or within Mennonite block settlements, pressure to adopt alien ideas, practices and language increased. Natural inclinations toward individualism, modern technology and the accumulation of wealth threatened traditional Mennonite values. In addition, whether to find sufficient land, to relieve the growing pressure to assimilate or to escape the conservatism of the Mennonite community, the Mennonite settlements became extended geographically; many Mennonites seized the chance to move west, to Saskatchewan and Alberta, in order to find yet another fresh start.[49]

The Mennonite community was also threatened by more formal forces. The Canadian government had been willing to offer Mennonites a substantial level of autonomy in order to encourage settlement by a

[45] Urry, *supra*, n 24 at 217–218.

[46] Warkentin, *supra*, n 44 at viii.

[47] One such institution was the *Waisenamt* which can be described as a combination of an estates court, insurance company, social agency, trust company and bank. The administrators of the *Waisenamt* sorted out inheritances, held inheritances in trust for minors, lent money within the community, appointed guardians for orphans and removed children from abusive homes. See J Peters, *The Waisenamt: A History of Mennonite Inheritance Custom* (Mennonite Village Museum, Steinbach, Manitoba, 1985).

[48] G Friesen, *The Canadian Prairies: A History* (University of Toronto Press, Toronto, 1984) at 202 notes that, between 1870 and 1886, the population of Manitoba grew from 19,000 to 109,000. In the same period, Winnipeg grew from a population of 200 to 20,000.

[49] PD Zacharias, *Reinland: An Experience in Community* (Reinland Centennial Committee, Altona, 1976) at 197–200; Epp, *supra,* n 44 at 304, 335–336; A Sawatsky, *The Mennonites of Alberta and their Assimilation* (MA Thesis, University of Alberta, 1964) at 44.

successful group of farmers on empty land.[50] However, soon both the Canadian and provincial governments saw dangers in permitting the existence of an effectively self-governing entity within its borders. These governments were anxious to impose their own control over this territory and began to adopt policies which were designed to assimilate the newcomers. Initially passive in nature,[51] government policies became increasingly aggressive, culminating in a successful initiative to wrest control of their schools from the Mennonites. After two decades of conflict, and the imprisonment of many Mennonite parents who refused to send their children to government schools, a court challenge to the authority of the provincial government to compel Mennonite children to attend government schools was heard by the Manitoba Court of Appeal. Despite the fact that the Canadian government's promise of freedom to educate their children had been critical to the Mennonites' decision to locate in Canada, the Court held that this promise was not binding on the Province of Manitoba because the Province, rather than the Canadian government, had constitutional jurisdiction over education.[52]

This legal defeat and other external pressures prompted some of the most conservative prairie Mennonites to emigrate once more; in the 1920s, several thousand Mennonites left Western Canada to attempt to build their utopias in Mexico and Paraguay.[53] Their departure coincided with a second wave of immigration of Mennonites who arrived in Canada after fleeing the horrors of revolution and civil war in Russia.[54]

[50] A Canadian government internal communication indicated that the lands designated for the Mennonites in southern Manitoba was considered 'unfit for settlement by their being destitute of timber': PAC, Department of the Interior, File 3129(1), Telegram, Donald Codd to JS Dennis, 23 July 1875 as cited in Warkentin, *supra*, n 44 at 37.

[51] One example of a passive but effective assimilationist policy concerns the ownership of land. As noted, the traditional Mennonite approach to land ownership was for a village to own some land in common and to divide the rest into strips. The Canadian government's policy in the West was to award homestead land to individuals in quarter sections after they had lived on it and farmed it for three years. Because of their eagerness to attract the Mennonites as settlers, the government was prepared to permit several quarter sections to be farmed by several Mennonite families as a group rather than insisting that each family live on and farm a separate quarter section. This allowed Mennonites to settle in Manitoba in a traditional village style. However, Canadian law imposed no impediments which prevented an individual from leaving the village to set up a homestead on the land which was legally his. If the village happened to be located on the land of the dissenting individual, he could force the other villagers to relocate. Therefore, Canadian law was able to undermine the traditional arrangement simply by failing to support it.

[52] *R v Hildebrand*, [1919] 3 WWR 286 (Man CA). See GJ Ens, '*Die Schule Muss Sein: A History of the Mennonite Collegiate Institute 1889–1989* (Mennonite Collegiate Institute, Gretna, Manitoba, 1990) at 5–6; Francis, *supra*, n 30 at 169–186; JJ Bergen, 'The World Wars and Education Among Mennonites in Canada' (1990) 8 *Journal of Mennonite Studies* 56 at 158.

[53] Francis, *supra*, n 30 at 191.

[54] *Ibid* at 207.

These newcomers were better educated than those who left Canada, more open to new ideas and the English language and more willing to live in urban centres.[55] Nevertheless, although these 'liberal' tendencies would be influential in determining the shape of the Mennonite community in subsequent decades, for the time being, poverty and the alien nature of life in Canada drew them closely together and apart from the rest of Canadian society.[56]

Therefore, despite the existence of assimilationist pressures they had not anticipated, the Mennonites of the Canadian prairies were largely able to maintain the integrity of their vision in this era. The tightly-knit community and traditional agricultural lifestyle of the Mennonites offered comfort and security which served to negate to a significant degree the attractions offered by the non-Mennonite world. Their conservative and communitarian instincts were reinforced by elders and ministers of the Mennonite churches who defended Mennonite traditions, principally by sacralising nearly every aspect of Mennonite life and punishing departures from the norm by imposing church discipline. Depending on the church group to which they belonged, Mennonites could be excommunicated for moving from the farm to town, selling their land to non-Mennonites, allowing their children to attend public school or adopting a variety of 'worldly' practices.[57]

The result of these natural conservative inclinations and formal religious sanctions was a Mennonite community which was characterised by

> strong social coherence, intensive interaction on a face-to-face level, readiness to cooperate and offer mutual aid, and a common value system which [left] few alternatives in one's everyday conduct. . .[58]

Mennonites remained heavily rural,[59] spoke German and Plattdeutch,[60]

[55] See, for example, H Loewen, Intellectual Developments Among the Mennonites of Russia: 1880–1917' (1990) 8 *Journal of Mennonite Studies* 89 at 89; NJ Klassen, 'Mennonite Intelligentsia in Russia' (1969) *Mennonite Life* 51.

[56] Francis, *supra*, n 30 at 220–226.

[57] A Mennonite could, for example, be disciplined for owning a sleigh with bells or dressing in clothes deemed too fashionable. See E Epp-Tiessen, *Altona: The Story of a Prairie Town* (DW Friesen & Sons, Altona, Manitoba, 1982) at 64, 288; Redekop, *supra*, n 11 at 207; Epp, *supra*, n 44 at 208.

[58] Francis, *supra*, n 30 at 64.

[59] Francis, *supra*, n 30 at 243 notes that, in 1955, the Mennonites were the least urbanised group in Manitoba. Driedger, *supra*, n 12 at 84 points out that, of 20 religious groups identified in the 1981 Canadian census, Mennonites were the only group with more than half of its members living in rural areas.

[60] Francis, *supra*, n 30 at 275 surveyed 40 Mennonite students at the University of Manitoba in 1955 and found that over half spoke only German or Plattdeutsch at home. A study of Mennonites in North-Central Saskatchewan in 1972 found that 97% could speak either German or Plattdeutsch and 69% did so frequently: A Anderson,

rarely married outside the community[61] and retained the church as an important, if not the primary, focus of their identity.[62] In other words, Mennonites remained a distinct and largely separate cultural group on the Canadian prairies until the Second World War and beyond.

CULTURE OF THE LEGAL PROFESSION

This brief account of Mennonite ideology and culture provides some obvious reasons why Mennonites would not be inclined to enter the legal profession. For example, the Mennonite view that no Christian could participate in a fallen, sinful structure such as the legal system seems to preclude the idea of a Mennonite lawyer from the outset. Nevertheless, there are deeper, more profound incompatibilities between the Mennonite culture and the culture of the legal system which, although few Mennonites could have articulated them, made full and simultaneous membership in both communities impossible.

In his work on early lawyers in Manitoba (and therefore in Western Canada), Richard Willie notes the extent to which they achieved a prominent place in the developing industrial Anglo-Canadian community, primarily made up of settlers from Ontario.[63] This community was characterised by a strong commitment to the English language, a parliamentary form of government, the English common law and the British Crown.[64] However, while proud of their British heritage, immigrants from Eastern Canada were not satisfied merely to transplant in the West institutions and ideas from more settled regions.[65] Their vision for the thinly-populated vastness of the prairies was of a new civilisation where

> 'Britishness' crossed the Atlantic to be freed from the fetters of an outmoded political and class system, released from a tiny island economy to flourish in the

Assimilation in the Bloc Settlement of North-Central Saskatchewan: A Comparative Study of Identity Change Among Seven Ethno-Religious Groups in a Canadian Prairie Region (PhD Dissertation, University of Saskatchewan, 1972) as cited in Driedger, *supra*, n 12 at 81.

[61] Anderson's study of Mennonites in North-Central Saskatchewan found that 97% had married other Mennonites and more than half expressed disapproval of marriage outside their ethnic group, the highest percentage of the nine ethnic groups in the study: Anderson, *ibid* as cited in Driedger, *ibid* at 81–82.

[62] Anderson's study found that 86% of Mennonites in North-Central Saskatchewan attended church regularly: *Ibid* at 82.

[63] RA Willie, *'These Legal Gentlemen': Becoming Prominent in Manitoba, 1870–1900* (PhD Dissertation, University of Alberta, 1989) at 76.

[64] G Friesen, *The Canadian Prairies: A History* (University of Toronto Press, Toronto, 1984) at 342 describes a 'militant view of British civilization' as 'a crucial aspect of the western Canadian image.'

[65] D Laycock, *Populism and Democratic Thought in the Canadian Prairies, 1910 to 1945* (University of Toronto Press, Toronto, 1990) at 27.

> open spaces, fresh air, pure environment and fertile soils of Canada. The best traits of all the European 'races' would be mixed, talent would rise, British freedom would be perfected.[66]

This was a dream as enormous as the prairies themselves.

> The frontier in western Canada as in the United States was the land of new beginnings. Where all citizens started as social equals, merit and virtue rather than class would be rewarded. Where farms and rural life, rather than factories and cities, were the foundations of the economy, true wealth would be created. Where life was lived close to nature, individuals learned the lessons of God at first hand. Calculations of prairie greatness and imperial power inevitably ran together; the west would have a population of 100 million; it would be the breadbasket of the world; it would be the centre of gravity of all Canada; and, if it ruled Canada, and Canada led the empire (as it soon would), then, as anyone could see, the west would lead the world.[67]

Nevertheless, although the Anglo-Canadian community quickly took control of the levers of government and business,[68] its members were well aware of the possibility of failure. The raw enormity of nature, manifested in floods, drought, pestilence and bitter cold, threatened to overwhelm tiny outposts of civilisation. Foreigners, whose labour was needed to settle the vast landscape, could prove recalcitrant, clinging to ancient and misguided superstitions while refusing to acknowledge the superiority of British culture and leadership. Democracy could be perverted, suppressing real talent and leading to government by the mediocre or self-interested. British freedoms could be twisted, allowing alien ideas to flourish and producing anarchy or despotism. Newly emergent capitalism, the engine of British dominance world-wide, could be overthrown by revolutionary and socialist ideologies emerging from the sordid hovels of the industrial, Eastern European proletariat.[69]

This was the nightmare, the dream gone terribly wrong, and its implications were terrifying for the Anglo-Canadian community. If it were allowed to prevail, Canada would fail to assume its place at the head of the Empire, its mission to the world would be unrealised and the future of humanity itself would be placed in jeopardy.[70]

66 W Wesley Pue, 'Revolution by Legal Means' in *Contemporary Law 1994: Canadian Reports to the 1994 International Congress of Comparative Law, Athens, 1994* (Les Editions Yvon Blais Inc, Cowansville, Quebec, 1994) 1 at 17.

67 Friesen, *supra*, n 64 at 342.

68 H Palmer, 'Strangers and Stereotypes: The Rise of Nativism, 1880–1920' in RD Francis and H Palmer (eds), *The Prairie West: Historical Readings* (University of Alberta Press, Edmonton, 1992) 308 at 308 notes that urban areas were 'universally dominated by Anglo-Saxon Protestants.'

69 Pue, *supra*, n 66 at 17.

70 *Ibid* at 17. The dream of Western Canada as 'the city on the hill' and the fear of its failure to achieve this destiny prompted much of the activity of Christian organisations,

As the prairies became increasingly settled, some aspects of these nightmarish fears abated. Sheer numbers of settlers, assisted by modern technology, proved successful in subduing nature. The foundations of the civilisation being developed in the West were increasingly invulnerable to natural disaster. But what sort of civilisation was it? The flood of immigrants from Eastern and Southern Europe had been welcomed initially but was now viewed with increasing suspicion. Speaking a bewildering variety of languages and engaging in bizarre cultural and religious practices, these settlers demonstrated a distressing lack of appreciation of the benefits of Anglo-Canadian culture.[71] For the most part, they showed little inclination to assimilate, typically choosing to reside near others of their own ethnicity and establishing organisations designed to preserve ethnic ties. The fact that the First World War was fought against many of the nations from which these immigrants had come exacerbated concerns about the perceived failure of these newcomers to become 'Canadian'.[72]

These anxieties grew to near terror after the war, when agitation and unrest in the immigrant working class and the rise of what were understood to be dangerously anti-democratic, anti-capitalist and anti-British ideas culminated in the Winnipeg General Strike of 1919. The workers of Winnipeg, having eked out an existence in crowded, cold and unsanitary conditions for decades,[73] brought virtually the entire city to a halt. The strike was contained with the help of the Committee of 1000 ('men of substance' in the City who had organised to combat the strike) and 'specials' (who had been deputised when the regular City police force had been fired for demonstrating sympathy for the strikers) and was eventually put down when the RCMP fired into a crowd of demonstrators on Main Street, killing two and wounding dozens. Nevertheless, the General

especially Presbyterians and Methodists. For a discussion of this chapter in the history of the prairies, see DL Butcher, C MacDonald, ME McPherson, RL Smith, AM Watts (eds), *Prairie Spirit: Perspectives on the Heritage of the United Church of Canada in the West* (University of Manitoba Press, Winnipeg, 1985), especially C MacDonald, 'James Robertson and Presbyterian Church Extension in Manitoba and the North West, 1866–1902' and M Owen, ' "Keeping Canada God's Country": Presbyterian School Homes for Ruthenian Children'.

[71] Friesen, *supra*, n 64 at 352–354.

[72] Palmer, *supra*, n 68 at 322–324. One example of this rising nativism can be found in the Introduction to *Strangers Within Our Gates*, by socialist icon JS Woodsworth's book. Principal JW Sparling of Winnipeg's Wesley College wrote: 'We must see to it that the civilization and the ideals of Southeastern Europe are not transplanted to and perpetrated on our virgin soil': JS Woodsworth, *Strangers Within Our Gates* (Toronto; University of Toronto Press, Buffalo, 1909) at 4.

[73] A 1909 federal government survey in Winnipeg found 837 people living in just 41 houses—about 20 people per house. Moreover, an investigator compared the sanitary conditions in Winnipeg in the early years of the twentieth century to those of medieval European cities: Friesen, *supra*, n 64 at 287–288.

Strike made clear in stark and unambiguous terms what optimistists and 'boosters' had long overlooked—their dream of prairie settlement was not shared by all.

Although the Winnipeg General Strike represented the most serious threat to the dominance of the Anglo-Canadian culture in Western Canada, the prairies continued as a breeding ground for unrest, discontent and new ideas in subsequent decades. A multitude of movements emerged in the 1920s and 1930s, all demanding change. Numerous co operative institutions, the Non-Partisan League, communists, socialists, labour activists, agrarian reformers and xenophobes (including the Ku Klux Klan) flourished. Populist parties of great variety sprang up and some, like the United Farmers, Social Credit and the Cooperative Commonwealth Federation, were elected to form provincial governments. The dream of a shining prairie civilisation which would lead the world was fracturing into a thousand pieces.[74]

There can be no doubt that prairie lawyers identified fully with both the dreams and the concerns of the Anglo-Canadian cultural community in the years surrounding World War I. Not only were most lawyers ethnically part of this community but they considered their profession and the establishment of Canadian law to be essential to the vision of prairie greatness it espoused. As one prominent prairie lawyer put it: 'This youngest of nations, heir of all the ages, was not born for a position of insignificance but of greatness. It needs the leadership of our best jurists and lawyers'.[75]

Lawyers on the prairies knew that the success of Canadian civilisation in the West required more than formal declarations of sovereignty over the territory, the defeat by force of Métis uprisings and the arrival of the North-West Mounted Police. It was necessary to blanket the empty space with law, stitching together each settled area and bringing each segment under the comforting canopy of British justice. In a real sense, lawyers saw themselves as the frontline troops of civilisation, extending the law's coverage to the whole and eliminating anomalous pockets of aboriginal or foreign custom.[76] They knew that

> all the projects, hopes, fears and plans of financiers, captains of industry and statesmen are only so much raw material until legal machinery is devised and set up by which they may be turned to account for human uses.[77]

[74] *Ibid* at 339–417. See also Laycock, *supra*, n 65

[75] J Aikins, 'The Advancement of the Science of Jurisprudence in Canada' (1915) 51 *Can LJ* 161 at 177 in W Wesley Pue, *Common Law Legal Education in Canada's Age of Soap, Light and Water* (University of Manitoba Canadian Legal History Project Working Paper Series, Winnipeg, 1993) at 27.

[76] Pue, *supra*, n 66 at 28.

[77] IA MacKay, 'The Education of a Lawyer' (speech delivered December 1913 to the Third Annual Meeting of the Law Society of Alberta), (1940–42) *Alberta Law Quarterly* 103 at 115.

Once the 'legal machinery' had been established, the lawyer's task was to maintain and operate it for the benefit of the newly established institutions of civilisation. In this, his (invariably 'his')[78] role was no less important for, without the proper functioning of the legal system, prairie communities could never achieve the wealth or prominence for which they were destined. Ira MacKay, a Saskatchewan law professor and leader of the Western Canadian Bar, argued:

> The lawyer's office is unquestionably the most important office in the community, and that for the obvious reason that the lawyer is really the only man in the community who really makes it his business to understand the delicate and complex organization of government and law by which the community directs its activities for common ends. . . . All our institutions depend implicitly upon their solicitors to guide them . . . The state itself is an edifice constructed solely out of legal material. It is literally made of law.[79]

The institutions to which the legal profession devoted its considerable energies were intended to produce a thoroughly liberal and capitalistic West. Like others in the Anglo-Canadian community, lawyers 'simply assumed that a capitalistic labour market, private property, and individualism were part of the environment, like the plains and the river valleys'.[80] Often personally engaged in 'exploring the parameters of expectant capitalism',[81] lawyers explicitly identified their profession as essential for the success of business and the prosperity of Western Canada:

> All that commerce has of security it derives from the law. Step by step, there has been laid down for it by the great sages of the profession the stones of foundation principles that define and safeguard its rights. Upon them has been built up the great fabric of credit and mutual confidence that has brought the vast world of commerce into being.[82]

Having identified themselves as leaders of the dominant Anglo-Canadian culture, lawyers were especially susceptible to the challenge mounted

[78] The reader's indulgence is requested for the occasional use of the male singular in this article. Its use is important because, as I later argue, the image, training and work of a lawyer in this era was overwhelmingly and profoundly masculine. It is not an attempt to slight those women who overcame considerable obstacles to enter the practice of law but rather to underline the fact that within the legal profession in this era they were almost universally considered to be unfortunate exceptions to the rule of what a lawyer should be.

[79] MacKay, *supra*, n 77 at 115. For an account of McKay's role in early legal education in Saskatchewan, see Beth Bilson, ' "Prudence Rather Than Valour": Legal Education in Saskatchewan 1908–23' (1998) 61(2) *Sask LR* 341.

[80] Friesen, *supra*, n 64 at 242

[81] Willie, *supra*, n 63 at 173.

[82] WH Trueman, 'The Place of the Lawyer in the Business Life of Western Canada' (1917) 37 *Can LT* 92 at 103.

against the prevailing culture in 1919. The sobering effect of the Winnipeg General Strike on the legal profession can be clearly seen in the Presidential Address delivered by Sir James Aikins to the Canadian Bar Association (CBA) meeting in Winnipeg in the summer of 1919.

A Winnipeg lawyer, Aikins was a national figure when he addressed the legal profession in 1919. President of the Winnipeg Bar Association when it expanded to become the Manitoba Bar Association in 1911, he had later been a driving force behind the creation of the CBA and was elected its first President. Aikins had also served as a Member of Parliament and leader of the Manitoba Conservative Party. At the time of his 1919 Presidential Address, he was also serving as the Lieutenant Governor of Manitoba.[83]

Aikins' 1919 speech reveals a man whose dream for the prairie west and the future of Canada had been badly shaken. Early references to 'an intellectual, temperamental and spiritual ferment' in which there are those 'who declare the principles of Adam Smith and Mill to be quite unsound' give way to denunciations of those who advocate 'collectivism and enslavement to system', 'class control' and 'Bolshevism'.[84] Moreover, Aikins was prepared to make clear to his listeners that the revolutionary threat exhibited in Winnipeg had been directed at the legal profession; he reported that one of the strike leaders had shouted 'Damn the lawyers!' only months earlier in the very city in which they were now meeting.[85]

From the distance of eight decades, it seems obvious that the goal for Aikins and the legal profession in 1919 and thereafter was two-fold: to ensure the survival and growth of a British, liberal, capitalistic and democratic society in the West and to entrench the position of the legal profession within that society. However, most Western Canadian lawyers at the time would have been baffled by any such distinction; they believed the interests of the legal profession and those of civilised society to be identical. In their minds, the Anglo-Canadian vision of the West could not be constructed without the leadership of a powerful and successful legal profession. In instituting a programme of reform designed to regenerate the threatened legal profession, therefore, the leaders of the Bar were not prompted by mere narrow self-interest. For them, a failure to act

[83] For more information about the career of Sir James AM Aikins, see D Gibson and L Gibson, *Sir James Aikins' Seamless Web: Finding Fortune and Fame as a Lawyer in the Adolescent Canadian West* (1992) 21:2 *Man LJ* 161. See also D Gibson and L Gibson, *Substantial Justice: Law and Lawyers in Manitoba, 1670–1970* (Peguis Publishers, Winnipeg, 1972), especially at 219 ff.

[84] Sir James Aikins, 'Address of the President to the Canadian Bar Association Annual Meeting, Winnipeg' (August, 1919) (1919) 39 *Can LT* 537 at 539.

[85] *Ibid* at 544.

vigorously to strengthen the legal profession placed the dream of Western Canadian civilisation in grave jeopardy.[86]

The reform agenda which developed during and shortly after the First World War and which was evident during the 1919 CBA meetings in Winnipeg, therefore, was driven by lawyers from the prairie West who felt most acutely the need for a new professional vision.[87] Western Canadian lawyers were more aware than their eastern colleagues of the peril they faced. They also understood, especially after the events of 1919, that the West required new approaches which may not have been necessary in 'older' parts of the country. In the newly-settled prairies, it was inadequate to assume an unquestioning belief on the part of the laity in the values held by lawyers or an automatic deference to their status. The 'land of new beginnings' had developed a myth of social equality, 'a distrust of all elites and deep faith in the common sense and ethical wisdom of the common people'.[88] In the cauldron of ideas and philosophies which was the West after the First World War, acceptance of the beliefs advanced by the legal profession and lawyers' right to leadership would have to be earned by appealing to the cultural values of prairie dwellers.

In response to this challenge, prairie lawyers focused their efforts on two complementary initiatives—the adoption of 'legal science' as a way of teaching and thinking about law and the creation of a new breed of lawyers.

In their restructuring and repositioning, the leaders of the profession turned naturally for ideas to two sources—their profession's ancestral home in Great Britain and to the United States. Looking south came most naturally to Western Canadian lawyers. The legal profession in Western Canada had developed close associations with the profession in the US.[89] Moreover, in general, Western Canadian thought had been greatly influ-

[86] Aikins' vision and that of the Western Canadian Bar was that '[n]ational regeneration would be attained through regeneration of the legal profession': Pue, *supra*, n 66 at 24.

[87] *Ibid* at 20 and 24; Pue, *supra*, n 75 at 21–34; WW Pue, 'Becoming "Ethical": Lawyers' Professional Ethics in Early Twentieth Century Canada' in D Gibson and WW Pue (eds), *Glimpses of Canadian Legal History* (Legal Research Institute of the University of Manitoba, Winnipeg, 1991) 137 at 269–271.

[88] Laycock, *supra*, n 65 at 37.

[89] W Wesley Pue, *Becoming Professional: Western Canadian Lawyers* (Paper presented at the 'Law for the Beaver, Law for the Elephant' Conference, Victoria, British Columbia, 22–25 February, 1991) [unpublished] at 7. (Used with permission of the author.). See also Pue, *supra*, n 75 at 31–32 and Pue, *supra*, n 87 at 268. Sir James Aikins had developed such a close relationship with the Chicago legal profession that, during his final year as President of the Canadian Bar Association, the Chicago Bar Association honoured him with a special dinner during which Aikins was serenaded with popular songs to which his admirers had composed personalised lyrics: Gibson and Gibson, 'Sir James Aikins' Seamless Web', *supra*, n 83 at 187–188.

enced by social and political developments in the United States.[90] American thinking seemed particularly appropriate in the context of the challenge facing Western Canadian lawyers because the American Bar had faced and defeated similar challenges in the late nineteenth century.

The decades following the Civil War brought about massive changes in the United States. Industrialisation, mechanisation, massive urbanisation, political disruption and business disorganisation had created a 'distended society' and a general sense of dislocation and bewilderment.[91] The anxiety caused by these huge social forces produced responses not unlike those found in Western Canada in the early years of the twentieth century: populism, labour unrest, temperance movements and xenophobia, among others.[92] Moreover, many of these social forces had been produced by the same impulses which were characteristic of Western Canada—a yearning for wealth, status, personal achievement—and were made possible by the same rejection of class divisions, elites and permanent social divisions which characterised the Western Canadian ethos.[93] Nevertheless, while rejecting traditional structures, Americans, like their counterparts in Western Canada, exhibited a profound desire for stability, order and permanence. They longed for integrity, discipline and coherence as well as personal freedom and an outlet for their relentless ambition.[94]

The modern professional vision grew out of these contradictory desires. During the *laissez faire* Jacksonian era, entry to a professional body in the United States had been only minimally restricted; elevating an occupation to professional status was often simply a matter of making the claim.[95] In the late nineteenth century, however, this state of affairs was no longer acceptable; a means had to be found to imbue the term 'profession' with meaning.

Science provided the solution. A 'true' profession came to be identified with 'rational, expert, neutral, universal and verifiable knowledge'.[96] 'True' professions

[90] Sir James Aikins revealed the influence of American political rhetoric on his own thought in his speech to the Canadian Bar Association in 1919 when he characterised Canadian democracy as 'government by the people, of the people, for the people': Aikins, *supra*, n 84 at 539.

[91] RH Wiebe, *The Search for Order: 1899–1920* (Hill and Wang, New York, 1967) at 5–43.

[92] *Ibid* at 45–78.

[93] BJ Bledstein, *The Culture of Professionalism: The Middle Class and the Development of Higher Education in America* (WW Norton & Company, New York, 1976) at 5–7 and 30. See also Wiebe, *supra*, n 91 at 62–77.

[94] *Ibid* at 30–34.

[95] *Ibid*at 34; Wiebe, *supra*, n 91 at 13–14;

[96] W Wesley Pue, 'Trajectories of Professionalism: Legal Professionalism after Abel' (1990) *Man LJ* 384 at 416.

> attempted to define a total coherent system of necessary knowledge within a precise territory, to control the intrinsic relationships of their subject by making it a scholarly as well as an applied science, to root social existence in the inner needs and possibilities of documentable worldly processes.[97]

As scientific pursuits, professions came to be associated with higher learning; a place for a profession's programme of instruction in a university curriculum guaranteed its status while the failure of a profession to secure such a place cast serious doubts upon its claims.[98]

The notion that a profession had to be based on an area of scientific study posed difficulties for law. Although it was one of the traditional professions, the scientific claims of legal study were shaky, at best. Indeed, far from being logical and scientific in nature, the common law was described at the time as 'the empire of chaos and darkness'.[99] Undaunted, legal educators, led by Harvard's CC Langdell, carved out a place at the university by contending that:

> . . . law, considered as a science, consists of certain principles or doctrines. To have mastery of these as to be able to apply them with constant facility and certainty to the ever-tangled skein of human affairs is what constitutes a true lawyer . . . Moreover, the number of legal doctrines is much less than is commonly supposed.[100]

Similar impulses were evident in legal thinking on the other side of the Atlantic. Jurists in England argued that:

> . . . although the law may appear to be irrational, chaotic and particularistic, if one digs deep enough and knows what one is looking for, then it will soon become evident that the law is an internally coherent and unified body of rules. This coherence and unity stem from the fact that law is grounded in, and logically derived from, a handful of general principles; and that whole subject-areas such as contract and torts are distinguished by some common principles or elements which fix the boundaries of the subject. The exposition and systematization of these general principles, and techniques required to find and to apply them and the rules that they underpin, are largely what legal education and scholarship are all about.[101]

[97] Bledstein, *supra*, n 93 at 88.

[98] See. P Axelrod, *Making a Middle Class: Student Life in English Canada During the Thirties* (McGill-Queen's University Press, Montreal and Kingston, 1990) 10–11. See also Bledstein, *supra*, n 93 at 121–126.

[99] J Austen, *Lectures in Jurisprudence* 5th edn (1885) in D Sugarman, 'Legal Theory, the Common Law Mind and the Making of the Textbook Tradition' in W Twining (ed) *Legal Theory and Common Law* (Basil Blackwell, Oxford, 1986) at 29.

[100] CC Langdell, *A Selection of Cases on the Law of Contracts* at vii in R Stevens, *Law School: Legal Education in America from the 1850s to the 1980s* (University of North Carolina Press, Chapel Hill, 1983) at 52.

[101] Sugarman, *supra*, n 99 at 26.

By demonstrating that 'the grubby, disorderly world of the court room and the law office could, in fact be regarded as "science in action" '[102] these legal educators staked law's claim to professional status in a contest where science was increasingly the sole yardstick.

Western Canadian lawyers were quick to echo the claims of their colleagues in England and the United States. Sir James Aikins endorsed the view that 'the number of legal principles [is] few' and could be taught in a systematic manner.[103] While conceding that some problematic legal judgments might be 'binding and awkward for the time being', another Winnipeg lawyer argued that these were, in reality, 'wholly of no account' because 'what is not founded on reason has and can have no place in English law'.[104] Law schools, established in all three prairie provinces during this era, reflected this view by rejecting a practical and technical legal education in favour of Harvard's 'scientific' model.[105]

There is little doubt that the claims to a scientific basis for the study and practice of law would have impressed many Western Canadians. The inter-war years in Canada were 'an era in which faith in science and expertise had reached unprecedented if not mystical proportions'.[106] Western Canadian populists, in particular, 'were attracted by the apparently scientific, conflict resolving and abundance-producing elements of technocratic thought'.[107] Reform movements of many stripes were thoroughly enthralled by the prospects of the scientific administration of society.[108] The 'science of law' would have appealed mightily to this large and growing stream of prairie culture.

In order to justify their claim to be teaching law as a science, legal scholars in both the United States and England embarked on an ambitious project to identify the principles at the core of each area of law and the many corollaries and sub-rules flowing from them. Of course, the 'discovery' of the relatively few legal principles on which the whole of the

[102] *Ibid* at 29–30.

[103] Sir James Aikins, 'Formal Opening of the Manitoba Law School, Inaugural Address to the Students by Sir James Aikins, KC, MP' (1914) 34 *Canadian Law Times*, 1183 at 1189.

[104] Trueman, *supra*, n 82 at 92–93.

[105] Pue, *supra*, n 75 at 10, 11 and 19–20. See also WW Pue, 'British Masculinities, Canadian Lawyers: Canadian Legal Education, 1900–1930; in Robert McQueen and W Wesley Pue (guest eds), Misplaced Traditions: The Legal Profession and the British Empire, Symposium Issue (1999) 16(1) *Law in Context* 80–122. WW Pue, ' "The disquisitions of learned Judges": Making Manitoba Lawyers, 1885–1931' in J Phillips and GB Baker (eds), *Essays in the History of Canadian Law: In Honour of RCB Risk* (Toronto, Osgoode Society, 1981–1990) (Used with permission of the author).

[106] Axelrod, *supra*, n 98 at 66.

[107] Laycock, *supra*, n 65 at 10.

[108] *Ibid* at 52–54. See also M Valverde, *The Age of Light, Soap and Water: Moral Reform in English Canada, 1885–1925* (McClelland & Stewart, Toronto, 1991).

common law was based involved a strong evaluative element.[109] Inevitably, those who analysed, organised and provided definitive statements of the law in order to teach it 'scientifically', found within its immutable principles support for their own views.[110]

One of the core propositions 'discovered' within the ostensible chaos of the common law by legal scholars was a highly individualistic liberalism. According to this view, the common law had always demonstrated a 'firm grasp of the rights of the individual citizen' who was dealt with as 'a centre of force, an active atom, whirling about among other atoms, a person in whom there inheres certain powers and capacities, which he is entitled to assert and make effective, not only against other citizens, but against all other citizens taken together; that is, against the state itself. . .'[111] The legal principles reflecting this philosophy were meant to carve out for each individual a zone of activity within which the individual could act with complete freedom.

Closely identified with the rise of modern capitalism, this form of liberalism was fundamentally optimistic. In the same way as the 'invisible hand' of the market would ensure that self-interested economic decisions would benefit all, liberals believed that freeing individuals to act in their own best interests would eliminate domination, oppression and conflict.[112] Science and technology would be allowed to flourish, progress would be accelerated and society would become wealthier, fairer and more free.

Legal science's defence of economic liberalism and modern capitalism would have been most helpful in justifying the aggressive capitalism of the Western Canadian business elite, the 'boosters' who thought progress could go on forever.[113] A weapon which could demolish the objections of

[109] 'The task of systemization . . . both simplifies and idealizes. The complexities of actual statements are replaced by generalizations. These, at best, represent but dominant patterns discernable amid the various pronouncements. More often, they are but the writer's views as to what the law ought to be, expressed in language which speaks of principles of what the law is. . .' Montrose, 'Return to Austin's College' (1960) *Current Legal Problems* 9 in Sugarman, *supra*, n 99 at 27.

[110] See *ibid* at 27.

[111] J Bryce, The Influence of the National Character and Historical Environment on the Development of the Common Law (Address delivered to the American Bar Association at its Annual Meeting, Portland, Maine, August, 1907) in J Bryce, *University and Historical Addresses Delivered During a Residence in the United States as Ambassador of Great Britain* (The Macmillan Company, New York, 1913) at 45–46.

[112] RW Gordon, 'Legal Thought and Legal Practice in the Age of American Enterprise: 1870–1920' in G Geison (ed) *Professions and Professional Ideologies in America* (University of North Carolina Press, Chapel Hill, 1983) 70 at 93.

[113] 'Boosterism', prevalent in the early years of prairie settlement and present throughout the era was the conviction that, by pulling together, communities could harness progress and achieve unlimited prosperity and success. 'Boosters' optimistically sought to encourage almost unrestricted development and ignored the huge social and

socialists and communitarian Aboriginal and immigrant communities was eagerly grasped by the ideological defenders of that corner of the 'vast world of commerce' established on the prairies. In his 1919 address, for example, Sir James Aikins noted that '[t]he essential unit of democracy is the individual' and asserted that

> the strong bent of the profession has been to uphold and develop the law of personal liberty, freedom to contract, and the right to hold property, checked only by the reciprocal liberty and rights of others.[114]

Despite the freedom it proclaimed, liberalism was not anarchy. The atomised individual of classic liberal imagery did not only act autonomously. The individual sphere of freedom was bounded by others' autonomous zones as well as by contractual and other obligations to them. Moreover, the State retained legitimate authority in liberal theory to ensure 'peace, order and good government' which, in this era, included the power to enact and enforce aggressive social and moral regulation aimed at prostitution, alcohol consumption, illegitimacy, obscenity, divorce and other social evils.[115]

Nevertheless, the focus of liberalism in this era was the individual's freedom to act within a zone of complete autonomy. To maintain this freedom, the law was seen as essential. Indeed, only within the context of the 'rule of law' in which the rights of each individual were scrupulously observed could freedom flourish. The task of the law was not only to protect individual rights against incursions by the State, but also to referee conflicts between individuals' spheres of freedom, ensuring by the impartial application of objective rules that everyone would enjoy the benefits of freedom. The message of liberalism, therefore, was that:

> . . . law (primarily through case law) and the legal profession (centrally, the judiciary) play a major role in protecting individual freedom; and that the rules of contract, torts and constitutional law, for example, confer the maximum freedom on individuals to act as they wish without interference from other individuals or

economic inequities which were evident to the 'knockers'. See AFJ Artibise, 'Boosterism and the Development of Prairie Cities, 1871–1913' in RD Francis and H Palmer (eds), *The Prairie West: Historical Readings* (The University of Alberta Press, Edmonton, 1992) 515 at 517–522. See also Friesen, *supra*, n 64 at 283–284.

114 Aikins, *supra*, n 84 at 539.

115 For example, after advancing the image of 'the individual citizen' as 'an active atom, whirling about among other atoms', Bryce hastened to characterise the State as 'entitled to require and compel the obedience of the individual wherever and whenever it does not trespass on the rights which are legally secured to him.' Moreover, outside the protected sphere of rights, it was the individual's duty, not only to obey but to cooperate with the State in imposing its will: Bryce, *supra*, n 111 at 46. For an excellent discussion of social and moral reform and regulation in Canada in this era, see Valverde, *supra*, n 108.

> the state. Policing the boundaries within, and between, legal subject areas constitutes a major foundation of the rule of law.[116]

In this way,

> the form as well as the content of the law [became] synonymous with [the] very definitions of individual freedom and liberty, and thereby acquire[d] an additional patina of reverence and universality.[117]

Veneration for the common law to the point where it could be fairly described as a 'civil religion'[118] led naturally to an association of the Anglo-Saxon race (of which the common law was a reflection) with a unique respect for the rule of law and a love of personal liberty. Authorities claimed to be able to trace 'an unbroken genetic preference for freedom and individual rights, from the Teutonic forests via the village communities of Anglo-Saxon England to America.'[119] At the same time, Anglo-Saxons were described as possessing an unequalled commitment to law and order. An Ambassador of Great Britain to the United States asserted in a 1907 speech:

> Our forefathers were fierce and passionate, like other half-civilized peoples, but they had this power [of self-control] and they restrained themselves from overriding the process of law and letting passion work injustice many a time when men of other races, Greeks, or Slavs, or Celts, would have yielded to their impulses.[120]

This reverence for the common law was also common among prairie lawyers. One prominent Winnipeg lawyer waxed poetic in his description of the law of partnership 'worked out by the master minds of the English Bench':

> To consider that piece of workmanship and to perceive its grasp of sound and balanced principles and to realize the far-reaching provision it makes for well-nigh every conceivable case is to comprehend the claim that the Common Law is the highest product of human wisdom.[121]

[116] E Mensch, 'The History of Mainstream Legal Thought' in D Kairys (ed) *The Politics of Law: A Progressive Critique* (Pantheon Books, New York, 1982) at 23–24.

[117] D Sugarman, '"A Hatred of Disorder": Legal Science, Liberalism and Imperialism' in P Fitzpatrick (ed) *Dangerous Supplements: Resistance and Renewal in Jurisprudence* (Pluto Press, London, 1991) at 35. The irony of the law being trumpeted as the guarantee of individual liberty while simultaneously being wielded to impose on often recalcitrant individuals moral reforms ranging from prohibitory offensives against prostitution and alcohol to legislation which forcibly subjected the mentally challenged and mentally ill to the most 'modern' and 'beneficial' treatment is considerable.

[118] Sugarman, *supra*, n 99 at 40.

[119] Sugarman, *supra*, n 117 at 57.

[120] Bryce, *supra*, n 111 at 53. Bryce fails to provide any evidence to support this astounding statement.

[121] Trueman, *supra*, n 82 at 92–93.

A view of the common law as 'the perfection of reason'[122] could only have reinforced the belief, widely held by the Anglo-Canadian cultural group on the prairies that 'the Anglo-Saxon peoples and British principles of government were the apex of both biological evolution and human achievement. . .'[123]

The Anglo-Canadian conviction that the English common law was 'the highest product of human wisdom' and therefore superior to all other legal systems permitted the belief that its application must be universally beneficial. If the common law was the 'perfection of reason', the guarantor of personal freedom and human flourishing, then imposing it on other people, far from being oppressive, must necessarily be liberating.[124] Indeed, the Anglo-Canadian imperial project could be pursued with missionary zeal as a means of freeing pre-modern peoples from the chains of irrational and superstitious beliefs. If the bearers and implementers of this gospel of liberalism and the rule of (the common) law were Anglo-Saxons, uniquely qualified by reason of their ancestry to lead a multi-ethnic society, so much the better.

'Legal science', as developed in England and the US therefore supplied the leaders of the Western Canadian Bar with a powerful bulwark against the forces of disintegration and destruction. Faced with 'scientific socialism', the profession could counter with 'legal science' which demonstrated the superiority of liberalism and capitalism. The genius of the evolutionary common law was put forward as superior to revolution; the belief that those who were of British stock were more fit to steer the ship of state and guide the community provided an antidote to the alien notions of immigrants from Eastern and Southern Europe. Moreover, legal science provided an offensive weapon; it granted the legal profession the legitimacy to proceed with the implementation of modernity and progress despite the objections of the working classes, communitarian immigrant groups and other naysayers. Finally, and best of all, legal science allowed lawyers to act within a cloak of disinterested neutrality. Their authority, like that of other professionals, 'transcended the favoritism of politics, the corruption of personality, and the exclusiveness of partisanship'.[125]

While powerful, however, 'legal science', was recognised by the leaders of the prairie Bar as insufficient in itself to accomplish the task of creating in Western Canada a civilisation which would surpass that of the Old World. Prairie lawyers were practical men; they knew that law could not

[122] *Ibid* at 92.

[123] Palmer, *supra*, n 68 at 311.

[124] P Fitzpatrick, 'Imperialism and Law in the Experience of the Enlightenment' in A Carty (ed) *Post-Modern Law: Enlightenment, Revolution and the Death of Man* (Edinburgh University Press, Edinburgh, 1990) 90 at 90–106.

[125] Bledstein, *supra*, n 93 at 90.

exist as an abstraction, in the form of statutes or judicial pronouncements on paper alone. Law had to be transformed into reality in the cities, towns, villages and farmsteads of the west. Even more importantly, it had to conquer the 'psychic space' of the prairies—the minds and hearts of those living there. Ever realistic, Ira MacKay pointed out:

> The law is what the consensus of legal opinion in the community believes it to be, first the judges, next the lawyers, and finally the mass of intelligent laymen who direct the organized activities of the state.[126]

No less down-to-earth, Sir James Aikins acknowledged: 'That what gives sanctity to law in a democratic country is not the passing of it by a legislature but the fact that it represents the calm judgment of right-minded citizens'.[127]

If their dreams for the West were to become reality, the leaders of the Bar recognised that it would be necessary to develop a 'consensus of legal opinion' on the prairies, not only among lawyers but also among the laity; it was necessary to create sufficient numbers of 'right-minded citizens'. This would not be easy. As the events of 1919 had demonstrated, the verities of the Anglo-Canadian community would not necessarily be accepted as self-evident. For hard-bitten prairie-dwellers, a point of view was only as credible as the person who advanced it. Therefore, if the Canadian West was to be won, its residents would have to be convinced of these truths by credible and respected advocates. In 'the land of new beginnings', where citizens believed that virtue and merit would be rewarded, the necessary credibility would have to be earned through unimpeachable integrity, strength of will, hard work and intelligence. In other words, the success of the legal profession, of the common law and, indeed, of Anglo-Canadian civilisation on the prairies, depended on the creation of lawyers of competence, virtue and character.

The legal profession in the West turned to two mechanisms in order to create these lawyers. The first was the Code of Legal Ethics, adopted by the Canadian Bar Association in 1920. A formal ethical code was not endorsed by all leaders of the Bar; a minority, led by Ontario Supreme Court Justice Riddell, mounted several arguments against the introduction of a written code of conduct. One of these was that, fundamentally, ethics could not be codified; a man was either a gentleman or he wasn't. Riddell asserted:

> . . . there is and can be nothing in the practice of law inconsistent with the highest type of scholar, gentleman and Christian. With that as text, all else follows—the lawyer, a gentleman, will act as such, he will treat all, whether professional

[126] MacKay, *supra*, n 77 at 108.
[127] Aikins, *supra*, n 84 at 540.

> brethren or laymen, as he would be treated in like case—that, it seems to me, is the whole of the law and the prophets. . .[128]

As Pue notes, the difference of opinion within the CBA about a code of conduct was based on geography. The CBA was dominated by prairie lawyers and they carried the day on this issue over the objections of the minority, primarily from Eastern Canada.[129]

In contrast to their eastern colleagues, Western Canadian lawyers would have had several reasons to support a written code. Despite a recent and massive influx of immigrants, Western Canada was still sparsely settled in comparison to the East. Opportunity for easy contact with fellow practitioners was limited in many cases. Creating a consensus of opinion among these far-flung practitioners was therefore a difficult task, made more difficult by the diversity of backgrounds represented by prairie lawyers.[130] A code of ethics was undoubtedly therefore, at least in part, an attempt to develop a consensus on ethics or, if that proved impossible, to inform practitioners of what their leaders had determined that consensus to be.

It is also clear that prairie lawyers, especially after 1919, were acutely aware of the scepticism and occasional hostility with which they were viewed by the lay public. In the raw and turbulent West, unlike the East, it was not possible to rely on a traditional deference to an ancient profession in order to achieve credibility; it was necessary to demonstrate the ethical commitment and public spirit of prairie lawyers in an explicit and unequivocal manner.[131]

Despite the value of the Code of Legal Ethics to the Western Canadian profession, however, it suffered from the same deficiency as statutes and judicial decisions—it was only an abstraction until put into practice. The legal profession in Western Canada knew that it could not rely on practising lawyers to consistently consult and comply with a code of ethics nor on law societies to detect and punish all violations of the Code. A 'by the book' approach to legal practice provided, at best, a tool by which the worst offenders could be removed from the profession and those committed to ethical practice guided. A far better solution would be to ensure

[128] Justice WR Riddell, 'A Code of Legal Ethics' (1919) 39 *Can LT* 620 at 623.

[129] Pue, *supra*, n 87 at 269.

[130] Pue argues, perhaps cynically but plausibly, that the imposition of a code was considered especially critical on the prairies because, to a greater extent than in the east, the Western Canadian Bar was in danger of being infiltrated by immigrants whose moral qualities were considered to be dubious by Anglo-Canadians. Pue, *supra*, n 87 at 258, 271; Pue, *supra*, n 66 at 24. I am only prepared to go so far as to suggest that the arrival in the legal profession of individuals from non-British communities made the task of creating and disseminating a consensus on ethical matter both more urgent and more difficult.

[131] Pue, *supra*, n 87 at 269–270.

that those admitted to practice would have, not only the requisite knowledge, but the commitment and dedication required to practice competently and ethically. Western Canadian lawyers were prepared to disagree with their Eastern colleagues about the need for a code of ethics but they were in complete agreement over the need for the law to be administered by 'the highest type of scholar, gentleman and Christian.'

In order to produce lawyers with 'the qualifications of mind and character'[132] fit to serve as ambassadors of the law on the prairies, the leaders of the Bar put their faith in the instrument which had served the US profession well—the university law school. Moreover, to ensure the best possible results, law schools in all three prairie provinces adopted the most modern pedagogical techniques—the study of cases and the Socratic method of instruction.[133] Manitoba's Law School, in particular, was considered on the cutting edge of Canadian legal education. The first law school in Canada to embrace the case method, it was also the first to adopt the CBA's model curriculum in 1921 and in 1926 and 1927 it was recognised by the Carnegie Foundation's 'Annual Review of Legal Education' as the best law school in Canada.[134] Saskatchewan's law school featured one of the foremost early practitioners of the Socratic method, Thaddeaus Hebert, and Alberta introduced a 'full-time, three year programme, entrance standards set at two years of college work, stiff examinations, and instruction by means of "large, well organized casebooks containing leading English and American decisions" '.[135]

There is little doubt that the decision to associate law schools with universities in all three provinces was heavily influenced by the American experience. American professions had discovered that the association of professional training with universities was important, not only because it certified the scientific credentials of the profession, but because it guaranteed that scientific methods would be employed in the selection and training of students. In this way, it ensured that only the most meritorious would be permitted to enter and graduate from professional programmes.[136] A professional university education was a test of mental

[132] In his 1919 speech, Aikins argues in favour of limiting entry to the legal profession to those 'who possess the qualifications of mind and character' necessary for this task: Aikins, *supra*, n 84 at 546.

[133] Pue, *supra*, n 75 at 10, 11 and 18. See also Pue, 'Colonizing Canadian Space', *supra*, n 105. For a sense of the faith invested in these schools by leaders of the Bar, see Aikins, *supra*, n 103 at 1189 and MacKay, *supra*, n 77 at 112–113.

[134] Pue, *supra*, n 75 at 20. See also Pue, 'The disquisitions of learned Judges', *supra*, n 105 at 14–25.

[135] Pue, *supra*, n 75 at 11. See also Pue, 'The disquisitions of learned Judges', *supra*, n 105.

[136] According to Bledstein, *supra*, n 93 at 127, 'By invoking the highest ideals—talent, merit, achievement—the educational system sanctioned the privileges, indeed, the

acuity and physical endurance. Graduation certified that one was among the brightest and the best, an important source of credibility in the merit-driven cultures of the United States and Western Canada.

Similarly, the adoption in all three prairie law schools of the study of case law and the Socratic method of instruction, pioneered at Harvard, was driven by some of the same impulses as had been in play in the United States. One of these was an attraction to the rigour of this system. Students were expected to study legal cases on their own and be prepared to respond correctly to queries about these cases tossed at them like hand grenades by professors. Students who were unprepared faced humiliation before their classmates. The Harvard system no doubt encouraged study and honed students' ability to think on their feet, but it also provided a very public means of separating the weak scholars from the strong:

> The case method fulfilled the latest requirements in modern education: it was 'scientific', practical and somewhat Darwinian. It was based on the assumption of a unitary, principled system of objective doctrines that seemed or were made to provide consistent responses. In theory, the case method was to produce mechanistic answers to legal questions; yet it managed to create an aura of the survival of the fittest.[137]

Pue argues, convincingly, that other factors also contributed to the enthusiasm for the case method expressed by the leaders of the Western Canadian legal profession. He suggests that the case method grew out of a belief that sufficient and direct exposure to the actual words of judges who were both learned in the law and distinguished gentlemen would result in some of these qualities rubbing off.

> [T]he logic of the case method was an 'irrational' logic founded on mystical notions that exposure to 'great' literature *in their original* would make not just better scholars (or lawyers) but also better people, better gentlemen, better 'souls'.[138]

Related to this belief was the view that requiring students to engage in a process of self-discovery of the text would ensure that the lessons learned would be fully internalised. By refusing to explain the text and, in fact, challenging students' insights into the text with rapid-fire and difficult questions, the Socratic method was intended to force students to wrestle with the case law, resulting eventually in a more profound understanding of it. However, the ultimate goal of the Socratic method was not simply to ensure that the legal principles set out in each case was firmly

affluence, of an accredited individual in American society. Theoretically, neither birth nor prejudice nor favoritism restricted those privileges.'

[137] R Stevens, *Law School: Legal Education in America from the 1850s to the 1980s* (University of North Carolina Press, Chapel Hill, 1983) at 55.

[138] Pue, 'Colonizing Canadian Space', *supra*, n 105 at 37.

imbedded in the student's mind. Rather, the purpose of this enforced struggle was

> inner transformation, understandings of self so intimately bound with doctrinal truth . . . that the transformation would endure for a lifetime, withstand all temptation, be immune from challenge from those who understand not.[139]

The frustration and struggle forced upon students by the Harvard model was itself seen as valuable because it was thought to build a student's character. 'Character' was highly important on both sides of the border and of the Atlantic in this era. For Americans,

> [t]he person with an ideal character was distinctive, intellectually and emotional confident. He paced life properly, heard the true rhythm of the universe; and chose the real over the illusory, the natural over the artificial. He demonstrated such judiciousness, discretion, equanimity, and balance that right and wrong became clear to him, duty defined and worldly matters set straight, perhaps for a lifetime. . . Beyond confusion the person of character discovered meaning, beyond chaos he perceived a rational order, beyond doubt he settled upon hard facts, beyond youthful experimentation he pursued a career that suited his nature. The person of character never wandered aimlessly in a bleak and dessicated world.[140]

The importance of character was equally obvious to leading Canadians. Indeed, the development of character among the Canadian elite was considered critical if the nation was to acheive its destiny.

> An individual without character . . . was a miniature mob: disorganized, immoral, and unhealthy as well as an inefficient member of the collectivity. . . character-building was an inner, subjective task. It involved learning to lead a morally and physically pure life, not only for the sake of the individual health and salvation but for the sake of the nation.[141]

In the United States, a professional university faculty was considered the best place to build one's character. Unlike the carefree time of drinking, gambling, sexual excapades and campus hijinks associated with an undergraduate degree, a professional education was a serious undertaking, designed to develop the character of the young men enrolled in it.

> The earnest young man regenerated himself during his college years; he purified his character and reformed his intelligence in order to fight the battle of an American life on the terms of his own permanent choosing.[142]

Leaders of the Western Canadian Bar took a similar view of the purpose of law schools. In his address at the formal opening of the Manitoba

[139] Pue, 'Colonizing Canadian Space', *supra*, n 105 at 42.
[140] Bledstein, *supra*, n 93 at 147.
[141] Valverde, *supra,* n 108 at 27.
[142] Bledstein, *supra*, n 93 at 250.

Law School in 1914, for example, Aikins exhorted law students to exert control over themselves and to avoid excesses, especially alcohol. He stressed the importance of integrity, moral fibre, honour and character.[143] Ira MacKay scorned what he described as the 'dilletantism and intellectual play' of arts programmes. 'But', he said, 'a law course is a serious matter. An arts course is intended for boys, a law course for men'.[144]

It was, of course, the creation of 'men' which was a basic function of law schools as far as leaders of the Bar were concerned. When they thought of the ideal ambassadors and administrators of the law, these men pictured men. The law schools they created reflected the masculinity of the ideal student. Complete with '[c]lassroom battles of wits and aggressive contests for "true" understandings' of case law, '[e]verything about the Socratic engagement was "masculine" '.[145] At the same time, however, shared hardships of law school also created a sense of camaraderie akin to that of a fraternity.[146] Whether intended or not, the law school experience created bonds between students which often lasted for life.

The masculine ideal which the law schools were designed to produce was grounded in a vision of the British gentleman. 'He' was, of course, a scholar and a Christian but was also convinced to his bones of 'the intrinsic superiority of British ways, the virtues associated with British law'[147] and the absolute necessity that both flourish on the prairies. Accordingly, prairie law schools were charged to 'teach law in a big way' in order to create lawyers who would be 'leaders in thought, promoters of the intellectual and moral development of our young nation, so that it may become a strong and forceful leader in the Empire.'[148]

For those who saw a strong legal profession as a critical component in the struggle for civilisation on the prairies, the creation of a new sort of lawyer through study at a law school provided hope. They believed that law schools would transform individuals who in turn might transform Canada, the Empire, the world.[149] Despite the challenge to the dream of a shining prairie civilisation posed by recalcitrant Aboriginal and immigrant groups, labour unrest and radical political thought, the creation in law schools of disciplined, rational, scientific, educated, authoritative

[143] Aikins, *supra*, n 103 at 1183–1187. RW Lee, Dean of McGill's Law School also expressed the need to 'instill into the student a sense of professional honour and civic duty', to create a man who was learned, reflective, ethical and public-spirited: RW Lee, 'Legal Education: A Symposium' (1919) 39 *Can LT* 138 at 141 in Pue, *supra*, n 75 at 31.

[144] MacKay, *supra*, n 77 at 108

[145] Pue, 'Colonizing Canadian Space', *supra*, n 105 at 44.

[146] *Ibid* at 43.

[147] *Ibid* at 9.

[148] Aikins, *supra*, n 103 at 1190.

[149] Pue, *supra*, n 75 at 30.

men, full of character and devoted to patriotic ends, held out a promise that Western Canada could be led to its rightful destiny after all.

CONCLUSION

Both Mennonites and lawyers of the prairie West in the early decades of the twentieth century inhabited cultures which controlled their perceptions, guided their thoughts and motivated their actions. These cultures were, however, profoundly incompatible and, because they each sought to occupy the same geographical space at the same time, were destined to come into conflict.

Lawyers were, and understood themselves to be, part of a larger Anglo-Canadian cultural community. Primarily of British stock, lawyers were proud of their heritage and of their place within an Empire which spanned the globe. Like the rest of the Anglo-Canadian community on the prairies, they were animated by the dream of constructing a prairie civilisation which would not only incorporate Western Canada fully within Canada and the British Empire, but would result in the prairies achieving national and even imperial prominence.

This was a modern project conceived by an optimistic and forward-looking culture. Anglo-Canadians believed that modern technology, education and science could overcome social ills, including alcoholism, promiscuity and poverty, and could produce superior people—healthier, more intelligent and more virtuous. They were convinced that knowledge could be used to create a better society on the prairies—wealthier, fairer and more free—than existed anywhere else. The solution to virtually any problem could be found by right-thinking people applying the appropriate scientific and techological solutions.

Lawyers on the prairies during the first decades of the twentieth century fully embraced this modern vision. Although the common law was itself vulnerable to the accusation that it was an irrational vestige of an ancient past which ought to be abandoned in favour of a more modern and rational legal system, the legal community was able successfully to contend that the apparently disordered common law was in fact, upon close and scientific examination, 'the perfection of reason', the culmination of centuries of evolution and ideally suited to the modern age. To certify this claim, the legal profession moved to establish law as an appropriate subject of academic inquiry by creating law schools at Western Canadian universities. Taught in a university law school, law could lay claim to the authority of a neutral and objective science which, like other sciences, was essential for progress and prosperity. The placement of law in a university setting alongside medicine, engineering and other professional faculties whose scientific credentials were unassailable not only lent weight to the depiction of law as a science but also helped to secure the position of law as a profession, worthy of the same respect as professions whose achievements were more self-evidently valuable.

In contrast to the modern values and vision embraced by lawyers and the Anglo-Canadian community, the Mennonites of the Canadian prairies were a pre-modern people. Despite having travelled from Russia to reach the prairies, Mennonites lived in a much smaller world than Anglo-Canadians; their vision was deliberately and resolutely bounded by the Mennonite community. Mennonite culture looked more to the past than to the future, stressed tradition rather than progress, and valued a simple agrarian lifestyle more than prosperity. Emphasising practice over thought, right-living over education, and established truths over new ideas, Mennonites instinctively rejected education, rationality and science as incapable of sustaining moral values. They were deeply suspicious of higher education and sought nothing more than the opportunity to live out known religious truths in daily life.

It was taken for granted by the Anglo-Canadian community that the civilisation under construction in the West would be one in which individuals would be freed from the bonds of class, ethnicity and ancient traditions to flourish on the strength of their own abilities and hard work. By releasing the full potential in each individual, progress and prosperity were assured. Though attacked by socialists and resisted by the communitarian cultures of the First Nations and many of the immigrant communities in the West, this liberal philosophy was endorsed by 'legal science'. The common law, 'scientifically' understood, was portrayed by legal scholars and the legal profession as vindicating a view of the individual as an entity with personal prerogatives free of society's control. It was the function of the law to protect the autonomy of each individual from improper interference by the State and other individuals. The law was therefore essential liberty and human flourishing.

This commitment to individual freedom was alien to prairie Mennonites. Mennonites viewed society, not as a collection of autonomous individuals, but as a collectivity. Individuals were defined, not by a sphere of autonomy, but by their place within their immediate family, their larger circle of relatives, their village, church and, ultimately, *das Mennonitische Volk*. An individual could be understood only within the complex web of relationships which defined his or her life. These relationships were held together by shared values and behavioural norms which left little room for independent thought or action. Mennonites were trained from childhood to subordinate their personal desires to the interests of the group. In return, they received a level of security and support which was rare in a more individualistic society.

In economics, the liberalism of the Anglo-Canadian elite supported a *laissez faire* approach to business and commerce, a result enthusiastically embraced by prairie lawyers. If allowed to flourish, they believed, capitalism would create on the prairies the prosperity and greatness for which they believed the region was destined. They were convinced that only unfettered trade, industry and business could develop the West's economic potential. Themselves often privately involved in business ventures, lawyers saw their primary task as creating a legal environment which would provide the stability and freedom needed by business. They vigorously resisted challenges to the aggressive and free-wheeling business practices of the day.

The Mennonites of the Canadian prairies had had experience with the emergence of modern capitalism in the Mennonite colonies in Russia and had emphatically rejected it. In fact, they had abandoned Russia in large part because of the social strife, economic dislocation and loss of simple community associated with these economic changes. They were, consequently, suspicious of the raw, energetic capitalism of Western Canada. For the most part, Mennonites viewed the offer of material prosperity held out by modern capitalism as dangerous, threatening their faith, their traditional way of life and their closely-knit communities.

To secure their position within Western Canadian society, lawyers could not afford to rely exclusively on the status of law as a science and their association with other, more clearly 'scientific' professions. They sought to create an elite corps of legal professionals whose personal qualities would be so worthy of admiration and respect that the position of the legal profession would be unquestioned. The adoption of a formal and written code of ethical conduct assisted in this project but a law school education played a more critical role. The study of case law and the Socratic method of instruction were only partially intended to ensure that students mastered the relevant subject matter. Their more important function was both to instil and to demonstrate in law school graduates the full spectrum of gentlemanly attributes: perseverance, virtue, force of will, intelligence, self-discipline and character. These, as much or more than claims to unique skills and knowledge, were meant to justify the influence, prestige and wealth afforded lawyers in prairie society.

Like other prairie dwellers, Mennonites respected self-discipline, hard work, honesty, and character. However, the undisguised goal of the legal profession—to achieve prestige, wealth and power—was antithetical to Mennonite values. The Mennonite commitment to community was such that actions which could give rise to pride on the part of the individual and envy on the part of others were discouraged or even prohibited. Competition, school grades, public performances and conspicuous wealth were all seen as dangerous because they threatened to result in envy and conflict, disrupting the cohesiveness of the community. Those who stood out from the group were generally viewed with suspicion. Humility was seen as a key attribute for leadership; indeed, a desire for prominence was likely to scuttle the leadership ambitions of anyone who displayed it.

Of course, the desire of lawyers for respect, influence and leadership in Western Canada was not solely or even principally due to self-interest. Most genuinely considered the success of their profession to be crucial to the achievement of the Anglo-Canadian dream for the West. Lawyers saw themselves as the bearers of the common law, its front-line troops, its missionaries, its planters and gardeners. It was up to them to replace the superstitious, irrational and alien traditions of Aboriginals and ethnic immigrants with a system of justice which was 'the highest product of human wisdom.' It was their task to blanket the West with the common law, eliminating anomalies until it could be presented as a single, uniform whole.

The Mennonites were one of the ethnic immigrant groups whose very existence as a distinct cultural entity stood in the way of the Anglo-Canadian dream. Their traditional, semi-formal legal system offered an unacceptable alternative to the common law. Unsurprisingly, they were targeted by the legal system and the legal profession; both passive and aggressive methods were used to force Mennonites into the patterns of the Canadian legal system. The hegemonic impulses inherent in Anglo-Canadian culture, and especially within that of the legal profession, and the tenacity with which Mennonites defended their traditional way of life, inevitably resulted in conflict. On questions of land ownership, education and numerous other issues, tensions and clashes between Mennonites and the Canadian legal system were the norm.

The Mennonite dream was to re-create the early years of their settlement in Russia. Plenty of good land for every man to live as a simple farmer, closely-knit villages in autonomous block settlements with Mennonite control over schools and local government, freedom to practise their faith and to maintain their own culture—this was the vision which had led them to abandon prosperity in Russia and to choose the Canadian prairies over better land in the American mid-west. The Mennonite utopia held no place for non-Mennonites or the society outside the Mennonites' cultural and geographical frontier. Indeed, all Mennonites asked of Canadian governments and Canadian society was to be left alone.

Such a vision was unacceptable to Anglo-Canadian society and the lawyers who were its central and leading figures. Itself threatened by the fractured and chaotic enormity of the prairies, this cultural group was driven by a vision of coherence and uniformity. It set itself the task of civilising the West, bringing it firmly within Anglo-Canadian (and British imperial) control and encouraging those progressive and modern institutions which would allow it to attain its destiny. It was the specific task of the legal profession to fill up the terrifying space of the prairies with law, binding it together and eliminating unseemly anomalies. From this perspective, the pockets of traditional Mennonite culture were intolerable flaws in the tapestry of Canadian culture which had to be eliminated if the dream of the West was to be realised.

These were the two cultures in which the seven 'Mennonite' lawyers of this era lived their lives. Born and raised in a traditional, tightly-knit and besieged community, each one at some point turned his back on this world and embraced the modern, individualistic and ambitious culture of the dominant Anglo-Canadian community and the legal profession. As each did so, however, he must have been profoundly aware that the vast differences between these cultures meant that it would not be possible to hold membership in both simultaneously. The chasm between these cultures could not be straddled; it could only be leapt.

13

Cultural Projects and Structural Transformation in the Canadian Legal Profession[1]

W WESLEY PUE

> The problem of state power . . . is a problem of how to distill a 'single will—or rather, the constitution of a unitary, singular body animated by the spirit of sovereignty—from the particular wills of a multiplicity of individuals'.
>
> . . .
>
> The ultimate end of **government** is not the achievement of a coexistence of autonomous sovereignties, but the production of a happy, healthy, virile and integrated social body.
>
> Anne Barron, 1990[2]

A group of lawyers met in a small, dusty railway town in cattle-country east of the Rocky Mountains in the spring of 1899. Their meeting established the *Calgary Bar Association*, reflecting their consensus

> that the Bar of Calgary were sufficiently numerous to form an association for the purpose of cultivating a feeling of professional brotherhood, discussing various matters affecting the interests of the profession and taking united action thereon. . . .[3]

[1] This paper draws on research supported by the Social Sciences and Humanities Research Council of Canada, the Legal Research Institute, University of Manitoba, and the University of British Columbia. I am grateful for the advice, encouragement and assistance of colleagues at the University of Manitoba (Professors Anderson, Esau, Gibson, Harvey, McGillivray in particular) and elsewhere (L Gibson, A Diduck, T Halliday, L Karpik, L Spelman, D Sugarman and R McQueen), and to excellent research assistants (B Williams, J Bermel, M McVicar, and J Bliss). Thanks are due also, to archivists and officials who facilitated access to significant records at the Law Societies of Manitoba, Alberta, British Columbia and Ontario, the Alberta Legal Heritage Society, and the Glenbow Institite. The University of Adelaide provided an outstanding environment for research and writing during my term as Distinguished Visiting Professor in History, Law and British Studies from May to September, 1999.

[2] Anne Barron, 'Legal Discourse and the Colonisation of the Self in the Modern State' in Anthony Carty (ed), *Post-Modern Law: Enlightenment, Revolution and the Death of Man* (Edinburgh University Press, Edinburgh, 1990), 107–125, at 108 and 117.

[3] Minute Book of the *Calgary Bar Association*, dated 12 May 1899 (Glenbow Institute).

The matters most urgently in need of collective action, they thought, were the development of a conveyancing tariff, agreement on uniform office hours, and confronting the problem of 'unlicenced conveyancers'. I wish to demonstrate that such objectives were integrally related to the project of government sketched out by Anne Barron in the introductory quotation.The Calgary Bar Association, in common with the Canadian Bar Association and similar bodies, participated in professional projects oriented toward creating the preconditions for effective state governance in a land which was, in principle, ungovernable.

From some viewpoints the lawyers' projects discussed in this essay seem to provide inauspicious origins for organised professionalism, even in the cowboy capital of British Empire. Whereas professional rhetoric makes much of public service—sometimes elevating professional self-governance to the status of an entrenched constitutional 'right'[4]— the nitty-gritty of professional organisation *seems* to have been self-interest. Their specific objectives were classic trades-union stuff: money, work-week and monopoly. From one viewpoint this hints of professional conspiracy against clients, community and state.

Alluring though it may be, such interpretations dreadfully caricature processes of professionalisation. I wish to interrogate the history of the 'professionalisation' of Canadian lawyers in order to develop broader understandings of professionalism and lawyers alike. There is more here than meets the eye.

THE NOVELTY OF LAWYERS' PROFESSIONALISM

Lawyers west of Ontario spearheaded the movement which created modern professional forms in Canada. Although historical antecedents of some sort exist for every 'innovation', this is almost entirely a twentieth Century story. The forms and cultures of the professionalism we experience did not exist anywhere before the twentieth Century.[5] The high water mark of European Imperialism, the spatial extension of both the USA and the Canadian Dominion, and the creation of modern professional structures occured simultaneously. Each process affected the others.

In it's paradigmatic expression professionalism incorporates demanding admission standards, mandatory and extended formal education,

[4] I have reviewed such arguments in 'In Pursuit of Better Myth: Lawyers' Histories and Histories of Lawyers', (1995) 33(4) *Alberta Law Review*, 730–767.

[5] I do not wish to be taken as making the nonsense argument that 'professionalism' or 'professions' did not exist in earlier times, only that twentieth century Canadian professionalism is distinctive in its forms, manifestations and cultures. Earlier forms of professionalism are also to be treated seriously in their own right: see Wilfrid Prest (ed), *The Professions in Early Modern England* (Croom Helm, London, 1987).

examinations, admissions screening, state licencing, prohibitions on 'unauthorised' practice, self-regulation, written 'codes' of conduct and technocratic or meritocratic culture. In its peculiar combinations and in its relationship to a culture which was being consumed by 'galloping hegemony of instrumental reason', all this is very much part of larger twentieth century phenomenon.[6] The whole, distinctly greater than the sum of its parts, combined in our grandparents' and great-grandparents' generations to form the core 'structures' or forms of contemporary professionalism.[7] North American professionalism was a new social technology for new times.

Noting this suggests the importance of several oft-overlooked themes. Most obviously, the *novelty* of contemporary professional form deserves greater emphasis than it is generally accorded. This is particularly so in the case of the legal profession. Because 'law' is obviously an 'ancient' profession the suggestion that some essence of the existing profession might be of recent origin strikes many as very nearly heretical. Understandings of lawyers' professionalism in Canada and in other 'British Diaspora' lands (including the United States) characteristically assume that, although much changes in professional *culture*, the essential forms or structures have a timeless quality about them. The distilled 'essence' of professionalism—corporate structures, codes of ethics, effective 'self-regulation', rigorous training programmes and admissions standards—are often assumed to have existed since time immemorial, only relatively inconsequential matters of 'detail' changing over the generations. Not infrequently, key features are traced back through presumed

[6] Charles Taylor, *The Malaise of Modernity* (House of Anansi, Concord, Ontario, 1991) 112 (and on the nature of instrumental reason see 5–6).

Cf the tracings-out of professionalism provided by Harold Perkin, *The Rise of Professional Society: England since 1880* (Routledge, London, 1989), James C Foster, *The Ideology of Apolitical Politics: Elite Lawyers' Response to the Legitimation Crisis of American Capitalism, 1870–1920*, (Garland Publishing, NY, 'Distinguished Studies in American Constitutional and Legal History,' second series, 1990), Jerold S Auerbach, *Unequal Justice: Lawyers and Social Change in Modern America* (Oxford University Press, NY, 1976), Andrew Abbott, *The System of Professions: An Essay on the Division of Expert Labor* (University of Chicago Press, Chicago, 1988). cf Dorothy Ross, *The Origins of American Social Science* (Cambridge University Press, Cambridge, New York, 1990); John McLaren and Hamar Foster 'Hard Choices and Sharp Edges: the Legal History of British Columbia and the Yukon' in Foster and McLaren (eds), *Essays in the History of Canadian Law, Vol. VI: British Columbia and the Yukon*, ch 1, 3–27 at 18–19.

[7] I invoke this convenient and commonsensical understanding of professional 'structures' in order to avoid the necessity of taking on the full-blown debate as to what, precisely, constitutes 'structure' in social analysis. My work-a-day approach to professional structures in the twentieth century seems to fit Sewell's definition that 'Sets of schemas and resources may properly be said to constitute structures only when they mutually imply and sustain each other over time': William Sewell, 'A Theory of Structure: Duality, Agency, and Transformation' (1992) *American Journal of Sociology* 98, 1–29, at 13.

genealogies to mysterious origins at the English Inns of Court in a time before recorded professional history. A heavy overlay of myth needs to be peeled back if the cultural origin of professionalism in our age is to be understood.[8]

STRUCTURES AND CULTURES OF LEGAL PROFESSIONALISM

The second theme is more complex. Broadly, it is that professional forms themselves need to be understood as cultural artifacts, that 'culture' and 'structure' are properly understood as mutually constitutive, not as distinct forces. There is no 'base', no bedrock professional core which is unmoved by the currents of time. Equally, there is no superstructure, no 'determination', no 'overdetermination'. The case study of Canadian legal professionalism adds support to the 'general theoretical argument that conceptual distinctions between structure and culture have lost force and utility in providing compelling theoretical maps, accounts, and images of the social world'.[9] Amongst many possible ways of understanding the relationships between culture and form, I wish to canvass four, for convenience labelled 'structural determinism', 'disengagement', 'metasomatism' and 'cultural efficacy'.

Structural determinist understandings treat structures as timeless (or, in a more modest version, as immutable over the longue durée) *and* assume that structures *determine* the essential features of professional culture. Conversely, approaches based on some notion of *disengagement* between the two spheres perceive professional culture as dynamic and important whereas professional form is thought of as static, unchanging—and hence rather uninteresting. Structural determinism sees professional culture as mere epiphenomena, barely noteworthy. On the other hand, research premised on the assumption of disengagement commits an opposite error, tending to focus exclusively on the most visible forms of cultural change—such as the poetry, plays, books, classroom dynamics, politics, sporting activities or the homosociability of gentlemen lawyers—without taking structure seriously into account.

Founded on opposite errors, neither approach is satisfactory. Form is *neither* everything *nor* nothing. Structures and cultures influence each

[8] See Pue, 'Better Myth', (n 4 above); Sewell, (n 7 above), addresses the ways in which actors often falsely invoke history in order to effect transformation. See also Eric Hobshawm and Terence Ranger (eds), *The Invention of Tradition* (Cambridge University Press, Cambridge, 1983).

[9] Lyn Spillman, 'How are structures meaningful? Cultural Sociology and theories of social structure', (1996) 22(2) *Humboldt J of Social Relations*, 31–45 at 41; See also P Bourdieu, *Outline of a Theory of Practice*, translated by R Nice (Cambridge University Press, Cambridge, 1977).

other through innumerable feed-back mechanisms: 'Structures shape people's practices, but it is also people's practices that constitute (and reproduce) structures. . . . human agency and structure, far from being *opposed*, in fact *presuppose* each other'.[10] Certainly, structures frequently demonstrate an impressive durability by contrast with the ephemeral, seemingly fleeting, realm of 'culture'. This indeed is precisely why revolutionaries or legislators labour mightily to demolish, transform or create structures: they hope to give permanence to their visions.

Structural transformation unaccompanied by cultural revolution is, however, doomed to failure. Noting the complexity of all this, we should seek to transcend habits of thought and speech which treat structure and culture as distinct spheres, preferring instead to recognise that such language crudely parses a hugely complex web. Our limited descriptive vocabularies should not be permitted to legislate our perceptions: structures are, as Giddens reminds us, 'both the medium and the outcome of the practices which constitute social systems'.[11] The language seems inescapable and, *modestly* understood, the fictions of structure and culture provide convenient entry into a rather complexly integrated whole. Bearing all this in mind, two further models of the relationship are helpful in approaching the history of legal professions.

Models which foreground *cultural efficacy*, emphasise that structures themselves are cultural artifacts. Whether deliberately created in fulfillment of a self-conscious plan or emerging from ad hoc or contingent processes, professional forms are human creations, constructs made and remade from generation to generation. In many circumstances a time 'lag' between cultural change and the transformation of structures can be expected, but the relationship is always mutually constitutive, the forces never unidirectional. On occasion, structural projects can take concrete form with dramatic speed. The argument for cultural efficacy is especially strong in understanding the history of legal professionalism in newly colonised places or in the wake of revolution.[12] Just as rock forms

[10] Sewell, n 7 above, at 4.

[11] Anthony Giddens, *A Contemporary Critique of Historical Materialism, Vol. 1: Power, Property and the State* (Macmillan, London, 1981), 27 as quoted in Sewell, *ibid.*

[12] In studies of the history of the legal profession, scholars who emphasise the economic monopoly of professions tend to appreciate that many professional structures are of relatively recent vintage or, alternatively, that inherited structures have been transformed to new use during the nineteenth or early twentieth century. Surprisingly, however, most such studies fail to recognise the 'cultural' rather than merely 'economic' significance of such transformations. The same, to lesser degree, might be said of even the 'power' theorists of professionalism. See, for example, Richard L Abel, 'The Rise of Professionalism' (1979) 6 *British Journal of Law and Society* 82; Richard L Abel, *The Legal Profession in England and Wales* (BH Blackwell, Oxford, 1988); Richard L Abel, *American Lawyers* (Oxford University Press, New York, 1989) (monopoly theory); Terence J Johnson, *Professions and Power* (The Macmillan Press Ltd, London, 1972)

can be made, transformed and shaped either slowly and subtly (over 'geological time') or rapidly by catastrophic event, so too social transformations take place on many different time-scales. Discontinuities are possible.

The second social process is less catastrophic. In human affairs 'social institutions may change their substance, though not necessarily their form, in unplanned response to events', producing a metasomatism of sorts.[13] Incremental change 'at the level of culture' can transform or even reverse the meanings, functions and effects of enduring structures. Such change occurred in England's legal profession during the course of the eighteenth and nineteenth centuries, when a series of molecular-level transformations turned the English Inns of Court from loosely structured gentlemen's guilds into modern, efficient (more or less), 'professional' regulatory bodies. The transformation was real and substantial even though surface forms proved remarkably resilient. The Bar remained organised around four separate 'Inns of Court' in London and circuit 'Messes' outside of the capital. Customs of dining and debate persisted, boundary lines between solicitors and barristers remained important, and governance continued to be the prerogative of unelected 'benchers'. All this survived a period of massive political, economic and social dislocation relatively unscathed. Despite apparent stasis in structure both meaning and effect were culturally and dynamically constructed.[14]

In the twentieth century history of Canadian legal professions both processes have been at play. A cultural revolution of sorts transformed the

('power' theory), W Pue, 'Trajectories of Professionalism: Legal Professionalism after Abel' in Alvin Esau (ed), *Manitoba Law Annual*, 1989–1990 (Legal Research Institute, Winnipeg, 1991), 57–92 [reprinted from (1990) 19 *Manitoba Law Journal*, 384–418).

13 James Willard Hurst, *The Growth of American Law: The Law Makers* (Little Brown & Co, Boston, 1950) at 273. The geomorphological process of metasomatism is one in which essential transformation is achieved by the migration of elements in and out of an apparently unchanging structure. Though Hurst does not use the term the analogy is apt.

14 These transformations are sketched in W Pue, 'Moral Panic at the English Bar: Paternal vs. Commercial Ideologies of Legal Practice in the 1860s' (1990) 15 *Law and Social Inquiry*, 49–118; 'Rebels at the Bar: English Barristers and the County Courts in the 1850s' (1987) 16 *Anglo-American Law Review*, 303–352; 'Exorcising Professional Demons: Charles Rann Kennedy and the Transition to the Modern Bar' (Spring, 1987) 5 *Law and History Review*, 135–174; 'Lawyers & Political Liberalism in 18th & 19th Century England', in Lucien Karpik and Terrence Halliday (eds), *Lawyers and the Rise of Western Political Liberalism: Legal Professions and the Constitution of Modern Politics* (Clarendon Press, Oxford; Oxford University Press, New York, 1997), 239–302; 'Trajectories of Professionalism', n 12 above.

The contemporaneous transformation of the Paris Ordre des Avocats from association into 'corps' is analagous: David A Bell, *Lawyers and Citizens: The Making of a Political Elite in Old Regime France* (Oxford University Press, NY, 1994), 52. Cf Lucien Karpik, *French Lawyers: A Study in Collective Action, 1274–1994* (Oxford University Press, Oxford, 1999).

structures of legal professionalism between 1867 and the Second World War. The lawyers who led these efforts imagined that, by getting the structures of legal professionalism 'just right', they would transform the country as a whole. Once their goals of structural transformation were attained, however, the larger cultural project fell into disfavour. Less perceptible, lacking dramatic moment, subsequent changes were real nonetheless.

This paper identifies changes in the first third of the twentieth century, illustrating how professional forms emerged from the cultural predispositions of reforming lawyers. Though subsequent metasomic processes cannot be explored here, they need to be noted so as to avoid leaving a misleading impression of the *effects* of the transformations described in this essay. Often operating in directions *opposite* to those intended by the cultural revolutionaries of the earlier decades, a narrow and constrained technocratic pragmatism supplanted the essentially moral vision of modern professionalism's founding fathers.

DOMINION AND EMPIRE

Before considering professional transformations in detail it is useful to pause briefly to consider the social contexts from which they emerged. The bursts of Canadian professional reform between 1910 and 1939 occurred in the best of times, the worst of times.

For a brief period Canadians fantasised that the world was theirs to lead and believed in turn that Canada's future lay in the west:

> Calculations of prairie greatness and celebrations of imperial power inevitably ran together; the west would have a population of 100 million; it would be the bread-basket of the world; it would become the centre of gravity for all Canada; and, if it ruled Canada, and Canada led the empire (as it soon would), then, as anyone could see, the west would lead the world.[15]

Not surprisingly, many reform initiatives originated in the Canadian west and especially in the prairie provinces (Manitoba, Saskatchewan and Alberta). This now forgotten periphery was once an important place, simultaneously the object and the soul of Canadian imperialism. Conditions were ripe for social experimentation.

Numerically small and finding themselves in a 'new' land, prairie legal professions lacked the inherited social capital enjoyed by lawyers in Ontario and the east. They faced special difficulties in attempting either to assert cultural leadership or to establish its condition precedent, a secure market niche. The political communities of the prairies were

[15] Gerald Friesen, The Canadian prairies: a history (University of Toronto Press, Toronto, 1984) 342–43.

hostile to privilege, infused with an egalitarian and reform ethos. Even the structures of Government itself could not be taken for granted. The mood was riotously democratic, consistent both in its rejection of hierarchy, and in its questioning of the authoritative voice. At the same time, extraordinarily rapid social change was under way. Outside forces perpetually destabilised the region economically, socially and politically. The effects of a newly industrialising continent's 'distended society'[16] were powerfully felt. Successive waves of populist politics threatened status, wealth, privilege, hierarchy, order.

The region participated in a reforming culture shared with other parts of Anglo-Canada,[17] but it was less inhibited by the constraint of convention or the gravitational pull of congealed hierarchies. In Canada's 'new' lands relatively greater emphasis was placed on freedom and its prerequisite, the governance of the good and the deserving (rather than to mere submission to hierarchy). Amongst the Anglo-elite, frontier egalitarianism combined creatively with pride in 'Britishness', and a belief in pioneer virtue. They held out the hope that this new land 'could recreate the individual just as it improved upon the social order'.[18] A 'militant view of British civilization' emerged and 'the goal of prairie social leaders—a Protestant, law-respecting, English-speaking community in which democracy and social equality were fundamental assumptions—seemed within reach'.[19] Proud of their Britishness, western leaders were nonetheless 'not complacent about British social achievements' and they insisted on their 'freedom to improve upon the parent culture'.[20]

Yet, the first three decades of the twentieth century brought unusual challenges. The newness and social fluidity which promised so much also appeared in threatening guise. The Dominion seemed to totter on a knife-edge between heaven on earth and a hell of human making. Massive urbanisation, industrialisation, recession, war and growing xenophobia all took their toll. Economic dislocations corroded confidence in the future of governance. Class, ethnic, and rural-urban divisions were accentuated, culminating in a post-War burst of radicalism more pervasive than any other in North America. Winnipeg's crippling

[16] Robert H Wiebe, *The Search for Order, 1877–1920* (Hill and Wang, New York, 1967), 39.

[17] Marianna Valverde, *The Age of Light, Soap, and Water: Moral Reform in English Canada, 1885–1925* (McClelland & Stewart, Toronto, 1991); Carl Berger, *The Sense of Power: Studies in the Ideas of Canadian Imperialism, 1867–1914* (University of Toronto Press, 1970); Ramsay Cook, *The Regenerators: Social Criticism in Late Victorian English Canada* (University of Toronto Press, 1985).

[18] Gerald Friesen, *The Canadian Prairies: A History*, n 15 above, 303–304, discussing the novels of Ralph Connor.

[19] *Ibid*, 343.

[20] *Ibid*, 343.

General Strike of 1919 was stunningly effective.[21] Anglo-élites experienced a rapid, discomforting, erosion of confidence in their ability to assimilate newly 'dangerous' others into proper British ways. Buffeted by temperance, women's suffrage, social gospel, labour radicalism, progressivism, the farmer's and co-operative movements, socialism and maternal feminism, regional consciousness threatened to disintegrate under the pull of centrifugal forces.

Knowing that lasting social peace could not grow from the barrel of a gun, élites faced the conundrum of how best to contain radical urges in a society where deeply-held commitment to an open, democratic, egalitarian social order co-existed with quite contrary cultural currents and with immense class and ethnic inequities. Lawyers kept all options under review as they contemplated their professional and civic futures. A degree of professional cohesion was attained through multiple professional and social connections, including those formed through the work of the Canadian Bar Association. Regional, Dominion-wide and international webs of professional interconnection provided ideas, promoted consensus, and provided legitimation for novel professional projects.

Looking southward they discovered a social vision which held forth the promise of founding a better world on terrain mid-way between the Bolshevik abyss and a sort of *ancien régime* repression. The middle ground was professionalism.

REMAKING CANADIAN LEGAL PROFESSIONALISM

During the first half of the twentieth century Canada was divided into nine provinces (Newfoundland not yet having joined the Dominion) and

[21] Frieson, *ibid*, 355–64. The strike, which seemed to substitute government by 'strike committee' for the ordinary organs of municipal government from 15 May to 21 June 1919, registered powerfully on elite consciousness. The establishment of a 'proletarian dictatorship' was explicitly threatened.

For a useful review of existing historiography and of previously unexplored archival records relating to the Winnipeg General Strike see: Ken Kehler and Alvin Esau, *Famous Manitoba Trials: The Winnipeg General Strike Trials—Research Resource* (University of Manitoba, Legal Research Institute, 1990); Craig Heron (ed), *The Workers' Revolt in Canada, 1917–1925* (University of Toronto Press, Toronto 1998); Tom Mitchell, 'To Reach the Leadership of This Revolutionary Movment': AJ Andrews, the Canadian State and the Suppression of the Winnipeg General Strike' (Fall 1993) 18(2) *Prairie Forum*, 239–255; Tom Mitchell, 'Repressive Measures': AJ Andrews, the Committee of 1000 and the Campaign Against Revolution After the Winnipeg General Strike' Fall 1995–Spring 1996, *left history* 3.2 & 4.1, 132–167.

The USA experienced similar concerns which also motivated its 'Bar Association Movement'. See: James C Foster, *The Ideology of Apolitical Politics: Elite Lawyers' Response to the Legitimation Crisis of American Capitalism, 1870–1920* (Garland, NY, 1990), 97 ff.

extensive, sparsely populated, northern territories which were administered as colonies of the Dominion government. Quebec was—and remains—distinct from all the others, a civil law jurisdiction living in complex relationships to common law Canada. Its legal professions, cultures and history are distinctive. Respecting that difference I make no attempt to fold Quebec into the larger Canadian whole. This essay focuses on legal professions in the 'rest of Canada'.

Each of the eight common law provinces had its own structures of professional regulation, typically featuring a provincial 'law society' or equivalent body established under provincial legislation.[22] All solicitors *and* barristers were required to be members of the law society of their province. Although Canadian federalism precludes any possibility of a pan-provincial regulatory body, reform-minded lawyers of the early twentieth century developed a national voluntary association through which to promote their professional visions. The 'Canadian Bar Association' (CBA), which emerged as an important force in 1914, was the creature of lawyers who had become frustrated in varying degree by the inaction of provincial law societies (the formal regulatory bodies). Formed quite deliberately within the realm of culture, part of its purpose was to spur those bodies into action. It was backed up or egged on by an array of local 'bar associations', law student organisations, and similar voluntary bodies, organised with varying degrees of formality, ambition, and effectiveness.[23] Although Canada was a self-governing colony or 'British Dominion', it did not follow the English model of a 'divided profession'. In each of the common law provinces barristers and solicitors, though *formally* distinct, were members of a single professional body. Most lawyers were both 'barrister and solicitor' (a usage which continues

[22] A consequence of the division of powers under the Canadian constitution.

[23] The Vancouver Law Students Association was a particularly important locus of professionalising activity. It and the Vancouver Bar Association played key roles in the development of British Columbia legal education. See Pue, *Law School: the Story of Legal Education in British Columbia* (Faculty of Law, University of British Columbia, Vancouver, 1995). For writings on other similar bodies see: William CV Johnson (ed), *The First Century: Essays on the History of the County of Carleton Law Association by Various Hands on the Occasion of the Association's Centenary, 1888–1988* (Bonanza Press, Ottawa, Ontario, 1988); Robert Crawford, 'The New Westminster Bar Association, 1894–1994' (1994) *The Advocate* 221–226. The story of the Calgary Bar Association is to be found in its own minutes, housed with the Glenbow Archive in Calgary and in 23 Volumes of transcripts of oral history inverviews pertaining to the legal history of southern Alberta ca. 1900–1982. Professionalsing movements in Manitoba, Ontario, and British Columbia are discussed respectively in D Gibson and L Gibson, *Substantial Justice: Law and Lawyers in Manitoba, 1670–1970* (Peguis, Winnipeg, 1972), Christopher Moore, *The Law Society of Upper Canada and Ontario's Lawyers, 1797–1997* (University of Toronto Press, Toronto, 1997), and Alfred Watts, *History of the Legal Profession in British Columbia, 1869–1984* (Law Society of British Columbia, Vancouver, 1984)

to the present) and, although some élite lawyers earnestly wished to create a distinctive and élite barristers' profession,[24] this never came about.

The Canadian Bar Association (confusingly, never restricted to barristers) provided a focal point for new initiatives. Its influence was felt across Canada and the patterns of professionalism which emerged were strongly shaped by it. Canadian professional reformers spearheaded a fundamental re-shaping of their common law structures of legal professionalism. Significant reforms were implemented with regard to qualification, education and admission, professional ethics, the regulatory powers of professional organisations and the assertion of a lawyers' monopoly over 'legal' services.

Taken together they radically reworked existing structures of professionalism to the point where something new and distinctive had emerged.

QUALIFICATION, EDUCATION AND ADMISSION

The training, education and socialisation of aspiring lawyers was central to the reform agenda. During the early twentieth century Canadian lawyers moved decisively away from their English inheritance. In the place of almost exclusive reliance upon apprenticeship they created ambitious blueprints for a new sort of legal education. The new model was explicitly cultural in content, university focussed, rigorous and taught in novel ways. New law schools emerged in Winnipeg, Regina, Saskatoon, Calgary, Edmonton, Victoria and Vancouver (later consolidated in Winnipeg, Saskatoon, Edmonton and Vancouver). Most were affiliated with the Provincial university. Moreover, there were significant developments in curriculum, staffing and programme delivery at the older law schools in Fredericton, Halifax, Montreal (where McGill uncomfortably straddled the common law and civil law worlds) and Toronto. Early twentieth century reformers sought to raise the pre-law educational requirements so that only University graduates would be admitted to legal education (a goal attained only in late century).

The founders of twentieth century Canadian legal education sought nothing less than to impose a uniform 'cultural curriculum'. Their objective involved more than merely producing better legal technicians. By restricting entry to the right persons and subjecting them to the right sort of legal education, they sought to achieve an enduring transformation of the law students' inner essence. They expected a new class of graduate

[24] This was, for example, briefly considered within the Law Society of Manitoba during the 1920's. A short period of formal division was ended in Ontario in 1854: Christopher Moore, 'Law Society of Upper Canada', n 23 above, 109.

lawyer to emerge: lawyers who were technically competent but also *better people*, permanently converted to a deep inner understanding of the virtues of British law. Inculcating the wisdom, judgement and the ethics of gentlemen was the central goal. It was hoped that an army of gentlemen lawyers would emerge, to be dispersed over Canada's enormous and varied territory, carrying the life-blood of British civilisation within them. Lawyers were to become missionaries in service of a secularised triune: law, Britishness, civilisation.[25]

LAW SOCIETIES

Reformers also sought to mutate existing provincial law societies into active agents of a new professionalism. They wished to do so in part to achieve *particular* instrumental goals. Symbolism was equally important, however. Law societies which played an active role in the project of professionalism would enjoy enhanced prestige *and* enlarge the dignity of the profession as a whole. Lying below the field of vision of most late twentieth century observers, such symbolic objectives were viewed as considerable and distinct 'goods' in and of themselves. The dignity of the profession and the prestige of its collective leadership were no small matters in an era when notions of honour, dignity and gentlemanliness still carried considerable social freight.

In this respect the reform of law societies was nestled within a larger vision of social ordering. Reformers wished to implant in Canadian soil forms of social governance which were neither narrowly economic nor exclusively 'political'. Law societies, like Bar Associations, gentlemen's clubs and volunteer associations of all sorts were thought to occupy an important space in civil society. They were to secure their niche in a realm which was neither fully 'public' nor fully 'private', acting for the good of public and state alike—but distinctly *not* as 'State' agents. A particular understanding of constitutional governance informed professional reform.[26]

This repositioning was most apparent with regard to revamped law society roles respecting ethics policing, admissions and qualification, discipline and monopoly protection.

[25] See: W Pue, 'British Masculinities, Canadian Lawyers: Canadian legal education, 1900–1930', in *Misplaced Traditions: The Legal Profession and the British Empire*, Symposium Issue, (1999) 16(1) *Law in Context*, guest edited by Robert McQueen and W Wesley Pue, 80–122, and sources cited therein.

[26] The connections between professional organisation and constitutional structures of governance in society at large are sketched out in Lucien Karpik and Terence Halliday, 'Politics Matter' in Halliday and Karpik (eds), *Lawyers and the Rise of Western Political Liberalism*, n 14 above, 15–64.

Law Society Roles I: Ethics Policing

A radical re-making of approaches to policing the 'ethics' of practicing lawyers took place, the most tangible marker being the development of an ethics code. Undertaken at the initiative of the Canadian Bar Association this appears in retrospect to have been a logical, perhaps a necessary, development of modest proportions. In fact however the move was highly controversial at the time. It marked a striking deviation from British models of lawyers' professionalism.[27]

The Canadian Bar Association's cultural authority was powerfully felt and most provincial law societies soon embraced the notion that a formal promulgation of professional ethical standards was desirable. They in their turn sought changes in their statutory powers so as to expand their disciplinary reach into new territory. The *content* of Canada's first code of lawyerly ethics has provoked insightful scholarly commentary focussed on its coverage, gaps and omissions[28] but for present purposes it is the novelty of this form of 'ethical' regulation rather than its particulars which most bears noting.

Law Society Roles II: Admission & Education

In and of themselves, the development of more formalised legal education for *some* aspiring lawyers (mandatory formal education for *all* aspiring lawyers came much later) and the promulgation of hortatory ethical codes operate 'only' in the realm of culture. The matter was not left there however. Further innovations gave force to the cultural aspirations of élite lawyers.

One area related to the 'gatekeeping' function of law societies. Issues surrounding the eligibility of women for admission to the legal professions of Canada came to a head in some jurisdictions. There were also statutory changes relating to the enrollment of 'foreign', aboriginal, or foreign qualified lawyers. Both types of initiative clearly involved responses to centrally important questions regarding just what sort of person from what sort of background could properly embody law in a

[27] An earlier attempt to create a code had been turned back in Ontario and the CBA initiative was strongly resisted by prominent Ontario judge William Renwick Riddell on a number of grounds involving professional tradition and principle. See Pue, 'Becoming 'Ethical': Lawyers' Professional Ethics in Early Twentieth Century Canada' (1991) 20 *Manitoba Law Journal*, 227–261 [also published in Dale Gibson & W Wesley Pue (eds), *Glimpses of Canadian Legal History* (Legal Research Institute, University of Manitoba, Fall 1991), 237–277.]

[28] JW Hamilton, 'Metaphors of Lawyers' Professionalism' (1995), 33 *Alta L Rev* 833–58.

new British Dominion, a question not yet adequately explored in Canadian historical writing.[29]

Other changes expanded the ambit of discretion exercisable by the governing boards of law societies ('Benchers') in making decisions about admissions and qualifications. In some cases statutory redefinitions of law society powers were passed (sometimes retroactively) in order to facilitate the creation of full-time professional law faculties.[30]

[29] See however Mary Kinnear, *In Subordination: Professional Women, 1870–1970* (McGill-Queen's UP, Montreal, 1995); Joan Brockman, ' "Not By Favour But By Right": The History of Women and Visible Minorities in the Legal Profession of British Columbia', in John McLaren and Hamar Foster (eds), *Essays in the History of Canadian Law, Volume 6: The Legal History of British Columbia and the Yukon* (University of Toronto Press and The Osgoode Society, Toronto, 1995), 508–561; Carol A Aylward, *Canadian Critical Race Theory: Racism and the Law* (Fernwood Publishing, Halifax, 1999), 44–45; Lois K Yorke, 'Mabel Penery French (1881–1955): A Life Re-Created' (1993) 42 *University of New Brunswick Law Journal* 3; Constance Backhouse, *Petticoats & Prejudice: Women and Law in Nineteenth Century Canada* (Women's Press, Toronto, 1991); Constance Backhouse, 'To Open the Way for Others of My Sex: Clara Brett Martin's Career as Canada's First Woman Lawyer', (1985) 1 *Canadian Journal of Women and the Law*, 1–41; Pue, *Law School*, n 23 above; Peter M Sibenik, 'Doorkeepers: Legal Education in the Territories and Alberta, 1885–1928' (1990) *Dal LJ*, 419–464; Alfred Watts, *History of the Legal Profession in British Columbia*, n 23 above; Dawna Tong 'A History of Exclusion: The Treatment of Racial and Ethnic Minorities by the Law Society of British Columbia in Admissions to the Legal Profession' *The Advocate* (March 1998) 56(2), 197–208; Pue, 'British Masculinities', n 25 above, Margaret Thornton's, *Dissonance and Distrust: Women in the Legal Profession* (Oxford University Press, Melbourne, 1996) is, in part, an outstanding study of the embodiment of law in lawyers. The book is discussed by Ramshaw and Pue in 'Feminism Unqualified: (review essay) (1997) 15:1 *Law in Context*, 166–178.

Statutory changes included: Sask 1912–13 (Amendment to s 37 by adding new section 37a, allowing benchers in their discretion to make rules providing for the admission of women to practise as barristers and solicitors); Man 1912, An Act to amend 'The Law Society Act' (interpretation section, s 2 amended adding that 'persons' includes females within the Act); eg, 1907 The Legal Profession Act; Alta. 1911–12, c4, s 29(2) (modest changes to provisions for enrolment of British, colonial or foreign legal practitioners; s 29(3) (change to the oath sworn and provisions for custody of roll of society); The Legal Profession Act; Alta. 1911–12, c4, 29(2) (change in provisions for enrolment of British, colonial or foreign legal practitioners); s 29(3) (change to the oath sworn and provisions for custody of roll of society).

[30] Eg, Man 1909 An Act to amend 'The Law Society Act', s 54(d) (the admittance of attorneys not practicing in the province rendered subject to rules framed by the Benchers); Man 1911, An Act to amend 'The Law Society Act' (increasing discretion of Benchers regarding the admission of members and students-at-law in special cases); Man 1915, An Act to amend 'The Law Society Act', s 40 (powers of Benchers to make rules for improvement of legal education amended by specifically including the establishment and maintenance of a Law School, permitting regulations respecting attendance at classes or instructions at law, and so on); Alta 1921, An Act to amend the Legal Profession Act, (new provision—s 32 in 1922 amendments—35 providing for the admission of university of Alberta Graduates having completed degree in law and served articles); Alta 1947, An Act to Amend the Legal Profession Act, (adding s 62a permitting Benchers to make

Such changes were important both in themselves and for their symbolic impact. The honour of the legal profession and hence its cultural authority was thought to be much bound up with its discretionary authority: the wider the discretion, the greater the honour and, hence, the greater the cultural capital of the profession. A high point in this movement (in one way of seeing things) was the judgment of Hunter CJ in *Re Hagel* holding that there 'is no right of admission' to the Law Society. Mr Justice Hunter explained that:

> the discretion to call or to admit ought to be left exclusively to the Benchers . . . it would not be in the public interest to permit any right of review. It must be evident that a judge is not in as good a position to pass on a matter of this kind as the Benchers. . . . There is a latitude and discretion in such a matter inherent in such a tribunal as the Benchers which is not available to a Court.

The *ratio decidendi* (reasons for decision) of the Hagel case could have been narrowly expressed as limited to circumstances in which a fully qualified lawyer who just happens to be a convicted bank robber seeks admission to the legal profession in another province after his release from prison. Chief Justice Hunter however sought to establish the broadest possible scope of cultural authority for the benchers. In so doing he imagined himself to be according the colonial law society a gentlemanly *status* and a role equivalent to that of England's ancient Inns of Court.[31] Similar cultural presuppositions also underlay the British Columbia courts' decisions in the late 1940s upholding the Law Society's rejection of a communist who, political conviction apart, was fully qualified. The patterns of decision-making in *Martin v Law Society of B.C.* have conventionally been understood as manifesting a sort of hysteria-driven conspiracy of the legal élite. That interpretive frame, rendered plausible by the subsequent McCarthyite purges in the USA and by the fact that the judges undoubtably shared the Benchers' opinion that communism was a 'pernicious creed', obscures other aspects of the case. The Benchers' genuine commitment to an ideal of lawyering as a gentlemanly service and to visions of professional governance which were thought to advance this were shared with the judiciary. The assertion that 'it is not for the Court to substitute its view for that of the Benchers' (expressed by Coady J at the Supreme Court of British Columbia, and endorsed by the Court of Appeal) simultaneously reflects a constitutional commitment of sorts

provision for enrolment of students from other universities than the University of Alberta under certain conditions).

Some related developments are discussed in works such as Peter M Sibenik, 'Doorkeepers', n 29 above; Dale Gibson, and Lee Gibson, 'Substantial Justice', n 23 above, Alfred Watts, 'Legal Profession in British Columbia', n 23 above; Christopher Moore, 'Law Society of Upper Canada', n 23 above.

[31] *Re Hagel*, per Hunter CJ, 31 BCR, 75–77, at 77.

within 'administrative law' *and* an understanding of the roles of Canadian legal professions which would have been unintelligible before the reforms spearheaded by the early Canadian Bar Association.[32]

Law Society Roles III: Discipline

The historical antecedents of the contemporary legal professions' disciplinary powers over its members is easily misunderstood. Most post-World War II observers tend to *assume* that such powers are somehow inherent in the idea of legal professionalism (they are not). Hence it is commonly assumed that such bodies have always (or practically always) had full, unfettered, discretion to discipline lawyers by means of censure, suspension or expulsion. It also seems logical, from our vantage point, to assume that the power to expel a member necessarily has the consequence that that person is thereafter prohibited from earning a living from the practice of law. We take for granted the effective policing of a monopoly on legal services.[33] Such assumptions, each of them false, are frequently reflected in hurriedly-produced professional apologetics but also underlie some of the more reflective writing on professional history.[34]

At least three further factors contribute to confusion. First, the waters are muddied by a rather unreflective North American elision of the histories of the barristers' and solicitors' professions.[35] Secondly, confusion arises when the historic roles of courts and of lawyers' organisations are misunderstood. The inherent right of superior courts to limit *who* can appear before them and *how* those people (whether solicitors/attorneys or advocates) may conduct themselves has long been recognised. It should never be mistaken for the exercise of disciplinary powers by an

[32] *Re Legal Professions Act, Re Martin, Reasons of the Benchers for the Refusal of the Application*, 30 October, 1948 [1949] 1 DLR 105–114; *Re Legal Professions Act, Re Martin*, [1949] 2 DLR, 559–567 (BCSC, Coady J); *Martin v Law Society of British Columbia* [1950] 3 DLR 173–199.

[33] Note however the recent case of Maurice Sychuk, disbarred by the Law Society of Alberta for murdering his wife, and denied reinstatement at the conclusion of his sentence. (The Law Society of Alberta, 'Reasons for the Benchers' decision re. Maurice Sychuk's Application for Reinstatement as a member of the Law Society of Alberta' October 1999). The press reported that Mr Sychuk nonetheless earned a living from working in Calgary in the field of 'oil and gas', an area within his established legal expertise. cf F Edge, *The Iron Rose—The Extraordinary Life of Charlotte Ross, MD* (University of Manitoba Press, Winnipeg, 1992), providing an account of a woman physician who was able to practise medicine despite being refused recognition by formal regulatory bodies.

[34] One among many misperceptions of the histories of legal professions found in professional apologetics. See Pue, 'Better Myth', op. cit. n 4 above.

[35] See Pue, 'Better Myth', n 4 above.

organised professional body. These are quite distinct matters.[36] Finally, and most confusingly, the organised legal professions' long-standing exercise of power to expel convicted criminals is all too easily mistaken for a plenary disciplinary power. Though the former is of relatively ancient vintage within the Anglo-Canadian tradition, the latter has only been asserted in relatively recent times.[37]

Curiously, the writings of Mr Justice William Renwick Riddell have added to the confusion. A prominent figure in the early twentieth century legal profession, Riddell was both a Canadian legal historian and a student of legal professionalism.[38] His conclusion that Ontario's Law Society (the 'Law Society of Upper Canada') had enjoyed full disciplinary powers over members of the Bar, attorneys, solicitors and articled clerks since 1876 (or 1881)[39] is easily misconstrued as having a more expansive meaning than intended. It stands in apparent self-contradiction to his forceful argument against the adoption of codes of professional 'ethics' by Canadian law societies. On *that* matter he argued vigorously that

> [i]f it were proposed to make the Code a Penal Code violation of which would render the offender liable to disbarment, legislation would be necessary, and

[36] This aspect, which raises a question of professional discipline in the context of a constitutional separation-of-powers is ably dealt with in James Willard Hurst, *The Growth of American Law: The Law Makers* (Little Brown & Co, Boston, 1950) at 278–79. The relationship between courts and professional bodies in the USA is complex and leads to some confusion between these quite different exercises of power. These matters are ably dealt with in William H Hurlburt, *The Self-Regulation of the Legal Profession in Canada and in England and Wales* (Law Society of Alberta and Alberta Law Reform Institute, Calgary and Edmonton, 2000).

[37] Robert Baldwin's fascinating report on the Law Society of Upper Canada's disciplinary powers, prepared in relation to the case of James Doyle, who had been removed from the Court of King's Bench list of attorneys for misconduct, merits further scrutiny. See Christopher Moore, n 23 above, 70. Note however that in this case the primacy of the courts as the locus of discipline is taken entirely for granted.

[38] See Law Society of Upper Canada Archives, *The Riddell Collection in the Great Library at Osgoode Hall*, Text from an Exhibition prepared by the Law Society of Upper Canada with financial support from the Law Foundation of Ontario (LSUC, 1992)

[39] William Renwick Riddell, *The Bar and Courts of the Province of Upper Canada or Ontario* (MacMillan, Toronto, 1928), 111–112. The legislative changes which Riddell addresses are ably explained in Curtis Cole, *'A Learned and Honorable Body': The Professionalization of the Ontario Bar, 1867–1929* (Faculty of Graduate Studies, University of Western Ontario, London, Ontario, 1987), ch 5, ' "To Purge the profession of those who bring disgrace upon their Brethern": The Bar's Assumption of Autonomous Professional Self-Discipline.'

See also Christopher Moore, 'Law Society of Upper Canada', n 23 above, 149: 'Discipline in the legal profession was also transformed. Though barristers had been disbarred for ungentlemanly behaviour as early as 1820, only in 1876 had the society's disciplinary power been made explicit in the Law Society Act, and judges had continued to assert a right to discipline the solicitors enrolled by their courts.'

> many considerations would arise . . . which to my mind would be fatal to the proposition.[40]

The apparently glaring inconsistency is easily resolved when it is recalled that when one wrote *in 1926* of a law society having 'full disciplinary powers', this in no way implied a plenary and exclusive jurisdiction over lawyers' conduct of the sort we now take for granted. Though the *idea* that law societies should be entirely sufficient *and* efficient in the control of their members' conduct was 'in the air' in the early twentieth century, no such plans had yet come to fruition. Existing powers were constrained by quasi-constitutional understandings regarding the autonomy of individual lawyers, by the jealousy of the courts in preserving *their* traditional authority over the legal profession and by the terms of legislation in various provinces.

The idea that the organised legal professions should be the sole locus of disciplinary power over lawyers was in fact boldly innovative. So too the related notion that powers of discipline and punishment should be enforced in a field as nebulous as professional 'ethics'.[41] The hidden hand of the Canadian Bar Association was felt as a series of statutory changes which transformed Canadian legal professions. The direction of movement was from rather loose gentlemanly guilds into something closer to the modern disciplinary apparatus we now take for granted. These changes gave clearer definition to Law Society powers over discipline, regularised or streamlined procedures, increased the ambit of that authority, and—over time—moved the supervisory jurisdiction of the courts further and further into the background. But none of this was part of any ancient English heritage. It was only in the first half of the century that law societies were actively transformed into organisations with public regulatory roles which far surpassed those of earlier guild structures.[42]

[40] William Renwick Riddell, 'A Code of Legal Ethics,' (1919) 4 *Reports of the Can Bar Assn*, 136–149, at 139.

[41] Riddell's objections were cogent. See Pue, 'Becoming "Ethical" ', n 27 above, Peter M Sibenik's research has traced out developments in relation to professional discipline in Alberta. See Sibenik, ' "The Black Sheep": The Disciplining of Territorial and Alberta Lawyers, 1885–1928' (1988) 3 *Canadian Journal of Law & Society/ Revue Canadienne Droit et Société*, 109–139.

[42] This shift was reflected in a series of legislative changes to the framework of regulation by law societies including: Man 1915, An Act to amend 'The Law Society Act'; Sask 1919–1920, An Act to Amend the Legal Profession Act; Alta 1921, An Act to amend the Legal Profession Act; Sask 1923, An Act to Amend the Legal Profession Act; Alta 1924, An Act to amend the Legal Profession Act; Alta 1925, An Act to amend the Legal Profession Act; Alta 1926, An Act to amend the Legal Profession Act; Man 1926 An Act to amend 'The Law Society Act'; Alta 1928, An Act to amend the Legal Profession Act; Sask 1933, An Act to amend The Legal Profession Act; Sask 1936, An Act to Amend the Legal Profession Act; Man 1943, An Act to amend The Law Society Act. Generally these

Importantly, as their powers increased, so too did their 'dignity'. This mattered immensely to a generation less obsessed than our own with the efficacy of power and less exclusively focussed on narrowly, pragmatically conceived instrumentalism.

Law Society Roles IV: Asserting Monopoly

The final element of early twentieth century transformations in Canadian legal professions was the extension of a lawyers' monopoly beyond its traditional domain (rights of audience or agency before superior courts) and increased protection within the widening 'competition-free' zone. The protected zone expanded consistently during the second and third decade of the twentieth century. Saskatchewan, for example, made it unlawful to act under false pretenses by holding oneself 'out to be a barrister and solicitor' whether or not the individual did so in appearing before the Court of Kings' Bench (1923). Manitoba extended lawyers' monopoly, first prohibiting unqualified individuals from threatening legal procedures or using documents simulating court forms (1932) and then protecting lawyers' monopolies over conveyancing (1933). Similar provisions were enacted in Alberta in 1936. In neighbouring Saskatchewan non-lawyers were prohibited from threatening legal proceedings on behalf of a creditor (1933). In that province the policing of monopoly by means of annual certification was strengthened in 1936. Manitoba again reinforced its unauthorised practice prohibitions in 1943.[43]

provisions extended the powers of the benchers to regulate the conduct of lawyers, limiting the authority of the courts in these matters.

For accounts of law society disciplinary powers see Alfred Watts, n 23 above, ch 10, 'Discipline', 117–132; Lee Gibson, 'A Brief History of the Law Society of Manitoba', in Cameron Harvey (ed), *The Law Society of Manitoba, 1877–1977* (Peguis Publishers Limited, Winnipeg, 1977), 28–51, at 50; Dale Gibson and Lee Gibson, *Substantial Justice: Law and Lawyers in Manitoba 1670–1970* (Peguis Publishers, Winnipeg, 1972), 128, 171–2, 240, 252, 257, 267, 305; Christopher Moore, *The Law Society of Upper Canada and Ontario's Lawyers, 1797–1997* (University of Toronto Press, Toronto, 1997), 61, 70, 125–6, 149–51, 300–2, 323–4, 326–9; Peter Sibenik, ' "The Black Sheep": The Disciplining of Territorial and Alberta Lawyers, 1885–1928', (1988) 3 *Canadian Journal of Law and Society/Revue Canadienne de droit et société*, 109–139, especially, 'The Locus of Disciplinary Power', 113–120; Curtis Cole, *'A Learned and Honorable Body': The Professionalization of the Ontario Bar, 1867–1929* (Unpublished PhD thesis, University of Western Ontario, 1987), ch 5, ' "To Purge the profession of those who bring disgrace upon their Brethern": The Bar's Assumption of Autonomous Professional Self-Discipline' (pointing out that the courts' exercise of disciplinary jurisdiction concurrent with that of the Law Society in Ontario continued well into the twentieth century).

[43] Sask 1923, An Act to Amend the Legal Profession Act, s 37 (1); 1932 An Act to amend The Law Society Act, s 53; Man 1933 An Act to amend The Law Society Act, s 53 (The Manitoba Act to amend The Law Society Act, 1937, added s 53A, specified that the prohibition extended to corporations as well as to natural persons. Fines were imposed

Beneath the surface of legislative change, law societies invested considerable effort in *enforcing* prohibitions on 'unauthorized practice'.[44] Future research will, in all likelihood, reveal that this hidden terrain was where 'the action' was.

RE-MAKING THE LEGAL PROFESSION: SUMMARY

All told then, the contours of professionalism shifted significantly, even if we restrict our gaze to the most formal level. Less visible transformations were advanced by means of the delegated rule-making authority and less formal policies of law societies and, in part, through the creative interaction of all aspects of lawyering with wider social, cultural and intellectual contexts.[45]

The more important questions, perhaps, are *why* these changes? *Why* in this place? *Why* at this time? We are taken part way to an answer by

on unauthorised individuals preparing instruments for conveyancing of real and personal property); Alta 1936, An Act to Amend the Legal Profession Act, s 59 amended by adding 59a, imposing penalties for preparation of instruments (for reward) in relation to any real or personal estate or incorporation of joint stock proceedings; Sask 1933, An Act to amend The Legal Profession Act. (amending s 64 of the Legal Profession Act. Sask 1936, An Act to Amend the Legal Profession Act, enacting 'No person except those enrolled as barristers and solicitors of Saskatchewan and holding subsisting annual certificates issued to them pursuant to the rules and bylaws of the society shall practise at the bar of any court of civil or criminal jurisdiction in Saskatchewan. . .' and making it an offence for anyone without a subsisting annual certificate to willfully pretend to be qualified to act as a barrister or solicitor; Man 1943, An Act to amend The Law Society Act, ss 53 and 54 repealed and replaced by a new, wider, s 53, expressly including the drawing of wills within the lawyers' monopoly, prohibiting simulating court procedures, prohibiting employment of disbarred persons. The new legislation allowed for injunctions to be obtained against unauthorised persons. Statutory exceptions to the ambit of unauthorised practice prohibitions protected public officers, notaries and persons acting for themselves.

On similar developments in British Columbia during this time period see Alfred Watts, *History of the Legal Profession in British Columbia, 1869–1984* (Law Society of British Columbia, Vancouver, 1984), 119–120.

[44] This is revealed in the records of the Manitoba Law Society. See also Watts, n 23 above, 120; Peter Sibenik, *The Doorkeepers: The Governance of Territorial and Alberta Lawyers, 1885–1928* (MA Thesis, U of Calgary, 1984), 'The Protective Impulse', 170–180.

[45] The full cultural import of legal education, for example, cannot be discerned from statutory histories alone but needs to be understood in relation to universities, curriculum and wider cultural contexts. See Pue, 'British masculinities', n 25 above, and sources cited therein.

Further evidence of the sorts of changes which might be involved at this 'hidden' level are documented in PJ Giffen, (1961) 'Social control and professional self-government: a study of the legal profession in Canada,' in SD Clark, *Urbanism and the Changing Canadian Society* (University of Toronto Press, Toronto) 117–134.

noting that this professional renewal was carefully planned in advance. Structural innovation, even in relatively narrow fields takes time, labour, energy. These are not tasks to be under-taken lightly, even where strong leaders find developed blue-prints of change readily available for appropriation. Nor is it 'rational' for individuals to undertake such projects—at least if rational behaviour is understood in terms of narrow self-interest. The time and energy demands are far in excess of any conceivable benefit individuals might derive from successful completion of such tasks. If we are to appreciate *why* leading lawyers invested so heavily in reforming their profession it is necessary to look outward to their beliefs and to their larger social contexts. The founders of Canada's modern legal professions did not undertake these tasks for personal profit nor in order to advance guild interest as an end in itself. They believed that developing a certain kind of lawyers' hegemony was essential to the preservation of constitutional monarchy, liberal governance and Britishness. It is their deep and public-spirited commitment to these ideals which explains their actions. Professionalisation was part of larger projects aimed at securing a safe future for all they held dear. Their parochial work in transforming their own profession was part of their contributions to a much larger cultural revolution.

The context from which these changes emerged is well behind us, the culture of moral reform which spawned them invites ridicule. Nonetheless, their professional structures endure. This is so even though subsequent social changes have very nearly *inverted* the cultural ethos which originally gave them meaning. Subsequent processes have indeed transformed professionalism but have done so within inherited frames which sit oddly out of time at the turn of a new century.

CANADA, AN 'AMERICAN' NATION

Canada is an 'American' nation[46] and despite the then widespread affection for the British Empire it is arguable that the dominant cultural influence on Canadian lawyers in this period came from the United States of America. By the early twentieth century a ready-made template of professionalisation had been developed there, drawing upon conceptions of social ordering which resonated with contemporary concerns. North American social thought conceived of professionalism as the only acceptable bulwark capable of protecting ordered society from descent into 'lawlessness and anarchy'.[47] Never fully implemented in the United

[46] Allan Smith, *Canada—An American Nation? Essays on Continentalism, Identity, and the Canadian Frame of Mind* (McGill-Queen's UP, Montreal, 1994)

[47] Julius Henry Cohen, *The Law:—Business or Profession?*, ch VII 'The American Lawyer (Continued)' (Banks Law Publishing Co, New York, 1916) 109.

States, a neatly packaged ideology of legal professionalism was available there. It came in a form which simultaneously advanced the cause of professional reform and deflected criticism, hostility, and 'anti-lawyer sentiment.'

On both sides of the border an intensely *moral* professionalism developed, designed to advance the rule of the 'righteous' and the rule of law rather than the government of either the masses or of those who were merely knowledgeable. Lawyers commonly thought of their profession in such terms. British Columbia's Justice O'Halloran, for example, gave voice to such a view:

> Moreover, the law student's training is not manual training, but is training of the mind, not only in law, but if he wishes to be something more than a mere legal mechanic, he must study logic, history, in particular constitutional history, political science and economics, a certain amount of philosophy and acquire a reasonable familiarity with English literature, and know something at least of the literature of other countries. The job of a lawyer is basically to advise people upon all manner of things arising out of the complexities of life and the frailties of human nature. As such he cannot fail in time to acquire an influence upon others, impossible to reduce to purely material terms. It is not too much to say that the training and experience a lawyer undergoes fits him for leadership to a greater or less degree. Obviously such men should not be partial to political philosophies and movements that conflict with the interests of their own country.
>
> By reason of these things, all countries throughout the ages have given the lawyer a correspondingly high place in society—particularly so in the case of the lawyer who pleads in the higher Courts. The object of law training is to attract young men of high character, and to train them in a manner that they will be trustworthy, honourable and competent in the performance of their legal duties, and will use such influence as they have to maintain and improve but not destroy our Canadian constitutional democracy. They are to be the defenders and not the destroyers of liberty. They are expected to be sufficiently well-informed and experienced to distinguish between liberty and licence.[48]

It mattered deeply in other words that lawyers be gentlemen, right-thinking, and politically safe. Such understandings provided a pervasive common language which gave direction to developing legal professionalism *and* rendered the projects of professional elites palatable—even attractive—to a wider public.

In developing a 'moral' vision of professionalism Canadians looked south for inspiration rather than 'home' to Britain. They did so for several reasons. Proximity as well as ease and density of social contact account for much. So too does social fit. The United States, like Canada, had suffered the disruptions associated with immigration, internal colonisation, and the industrialisation of an immense federation. It also

[48] *Martin v Law Society of British Columbia* [1950] 3 DLR 173–199, at 189, per O'Halloran, JA.

was avowedly democratic, heterogeneous in ethnicity, language, and religion, regionally diverse, and heavily marked by a migrating frontier of European settlement. The USA experienced continuous change and was racked with uncertainty, at times overwhelmed by the sense of 'the irrationality of life'.[49] By the turn of the century it had become a 'distended' society marked by business and political disorganisation, a widening 'cultural gap between city and countryside', '[i]rresponsibility' and 'ethical evasions.' 'Respectable' citizens feared that 'the true and simple America [was] in jeopardy from foes of extraordinary, raw strength—huge, devouring monopolies, swarms of sexually potent immigrants, and the like'.[50]

Seeking ordered freedom, 'science' stepped in to fill the governmental void left by the overthrow of traditional sources of authority.[51] A novel political and cultural project emerged, a 'culture of professionalism' in which lay persons were required to trust the integrity and omnicompetence of an emergent educated class: 'Science as a source for professional authority transcended the favoritism of politics, the corruption of personality, and the exclusiveness of partisanship'.[52]

The political corollary of all this was the rise of progressivism in its various mutations, the development of the bureaucratic state, 'reform', an abandonment of party loyalties, and a search for mechanisms whereby authority in discrete areas of social life might be entrusted to 'experts' for the good of all.[53] Reformers of many stripes looked forward hopefully to a world made better by rational planning, education, proper procedures, regularity, and the creation of means by which to infuse '*ethics*' into the interstices of everyday life.[54] Religion transmuted into 'social gospel' and the notion that ethical life could be segmented was eroded. Regulation seemed desirable to generations who perceived change as fundamental, inevitable and rapid but who had not yet forgotten the moral claims of a 'public sphere'.[55]

[49] Burton Bledstein, *Culture of Professionalism: the middle class and the development of higher education in America*, 322 (discussing the 1860s and 1870s).

[50] Robert H Wiebe, *The Search for Order, 1877–1920* (Hill and Wang, New York, 1967) 19, 28, 14, 39, 52.

[51] Bledstein, n 49 above, 326.

[52] Bledstein, n 49 above, 90. Cf Robert Wiebe, n 50 above, 161. 'Science' did not necessarily stand in opposition to religion in this period. For many God, science and cultural tradition for a time lived in mutually constitutive relations. See, for example, Ramsay Cook, 'Regenerators,' n 7 above.

[53] The development of standardised testing was part of this process. A splendid account is found in Nicholas Lemann, *The Big Test: The Secret History of the American Meritocracy* (Straus & Giroux, LLC, Farrar, 1999).

[54] Robert Wiebe, n 49 above, 153–157, 164–169, 222.

[55] Julius Cohen, n 47 above, ch VII 'The American Lawyer (Continued)' p 107: 'Within two decades we have been whisked about and hurdled over Interstate Commerce Commissions, Public Service Commissions, Minimum Wage Laws, Industrial Boards,

In this era lawyers presented themselves as specialists in law but also as guardians of cultural knowledges, in effect, 'universal experts'.[56] 'Professional' principles held forth the promise of containing social discontent and maintaining order.[57] One formulation had it that

> if the down-pull of government by plebiscite is to be arrested, if the vortex movement of democracy is to be counter-balanced, it will be accomplished mainly by the grace of the professional spirit.[58]

Curious admixtures of conservatism, reverence for property, social elitism, community spiritedness, *laissez-faire*, 'service' and 'duty' resulted.

OBVIOUS UNSUITABILITY OF OTHER MODELS

Whatever the emotional tugs on colonial heartstrings, it was clear to all that English models of legal professionalism could not practicably be sustained in North America.

The 'fit' was difficult enough in Ontario and Atlantic Canada, impossible in Quebec and the west. Key elements of English legal professionalism could not be transplanted. A strong egalitarian ethos combined with the small numbers of lawyers in the west to make a rigid demarcation of solicitors from barristers impracticable—in sharp contradistinction to the experience of some other British 'Dominions' and colonies.[59] The legal professions in the western provinces were of recent origin, created by statute, and far removed in origin, structure and governance from the English Inns of Court. Features central to the English barristers' profession were palpably absurd in the newest part of the New World at the dawn of 'Canada's Century'. Governance by a self perpetuating oligarchy, qualification on the basis of meals eaten, expected (but largely *unenforced*) conformity to imprecise principles of 'etiquette' and regula-

Workmen's Compensation Acts, Income Taxes, Inheritance Taxes. . . . Truth is, the conservatives have turned progressives, the progressives have turned socialists, and the socialists are looking about for new wearing apparel.'

[56] For development of this notion see Peter L Berger and Thomas Luckmann, *The Social Construction of Reality* (Doubleday, Garden City, NY, 1967), 117. Berger & Luckmann's insight is deployed to good effect in relation to the USA legal profession in James C. Foster, n 21 above, at 12.

[57] For example, 'Ontario Bar Association. Address of Mr Henry R Rathbone, of Chicago, Delivered at the Last Annual Meeting', 55 *Can LJ*, 1919, 168–175.

[58] Robert N Wilkin, *The Spirit of the Legal Profession* (Oxford University Press, Yale University Press, 1938), 160.

[59] Contrast, for example, the state of Victoria in Australia: Rob McQueen, 'Together We Fall, Divided We Stand: the Victorian Legal Profession in Crisis 1890–1940', in this volume; JRS Forbes, *The Divided Legal Profession in Australia: History, Rationalisation and Rationale* (The Law Book Co, Sydney, 1979)

tion by itinerant dining clubs, to pick only the most obvious examples, could not be transplanted into a new place.

Ontario's Law Society or its' younger cousin, the Law Society of England and Wales, provided models more suited to transplantation. USA models proved more compelling however. A significant trans-boundary intercourse took place amongst professional leaders.[60]

The evolving culture wove six strands of a new professionalism together. Not surprisingly, these bear striking resemblance to innovations actually implemented in common law Canada during the early twentieth century. The new model was founded on a confidence in professional meritocracy which in turn was to be constructed from stringent admission standards, formal education, examined expertise *and* practical experience. It relied on an ongoing cleansing of the bar by means of the enforcement of ethical standards by professional governing bodies operating independently of state control. Minimum fee schedules and the creation of a secure monopoly over the right to provide legal services were seen as providing a necessary quid pro quo for such constraints on ordinary market principles and, of course, the suppression of all and any 'unlicensed competitors' was necessary if the new structures were to be effective.

First taking shape as a coherent, deliberate and workable 'project' in the early twentieth century USA, this web of professionalism had come to constitute a professional 'common sense' by the time the Canadian Bar Association began to assert itself.[61] The individual components, moreover, were understood as constituting a unitary structure, a 'whole cloth' of inseparable strands. A compelling logic bound the whole together. It was thought, for example, that individuals would not be willing to pursue an extensive professional education unless certain privileges (eg the dignity attached to self governance) and financial benefits (mandatory fee schedules and protected monopoly) could be guaranteed. This in turn required statutory prohibition on unlicensed practice and the enforcement of codes of 'ethics'. Otherwise, the privileges could not be justified, the benefits could not flow.[62] Because only practising lawyers

[60] Reports of proceedings for both the 'American Bar Association' and the 'Canadian Bar Association' during the early decades of the Century reveal patterns of elite interaction which have yet to be properly assessed. For one example see Sir James Aikins, 'Inaugural Address of the President. Sir James Aikins, KC, Knt, Lieutenant-Governor of Manitoba', 54 *Can LJ*, 1918, 344–357, 348 (discussing the immense US influence on Canada). Cf ' "Our Arctic Brethren: Canadian Law and Lawyers as Portrayed in American Legal Periodicals, 1829–1911' in Jim Phillips and G Blaine Baker (eds), *Essays in Canadian Law, Vol. VIII: In Honour of Richard Risk* (Osgoode Society, Toronto, 1999) 241–280.

[61] This is broadly the agenda set forth by Julius Henry Cohen, n 47 above.

[62] See, for example, Julius Henry Cohen, n 47 above, ch XIV, ' "It Pays to Advertise." Does It?' 173–200.

could appreciate both the constitutional principles on which legality was based and the concrete problems which arose in day to day legal work, their own professional bodies, independent of state and lay interference alike, needed to be given charge of ethical and professional matters.[63]

Idealised 'traditions' of the professional guild (emphasising service orientation and anti-commercialism) were melded with the new ideology of regulation, bureaucratic regularity, 'scientific' credentialling, and ethical policing to produce a distinctly twentieth century, *uniquely North American*, version of professionalism.[64] Julius Cohen's remarkable book, *The Law:—Business or Profession?*, for example, is replete with self-conscious references to the ways in which a new 'evolution of a new public opinion',[65] a 'new philosophy which is to be American democracy's great gift to the world',[66] mandated professional reforms. It called for nothing less than an entire new formulation of professionalism, emphasising 'duty', 'service rather than profit,' rigorous educational standards, professional conscience, and enforcement of ethical codes so as to 'purge' the dishonourable from the profession.[67] Of necessity, 'unauthorized practice' would have to be prohibited and effectively punished.[68]

Canada's reform-minded lawyers too articulated a vision of professionalism as an immutable whole. This involved careful attention to defining the limits of acceptable society with an almost obsessive cultural emphasis on structured knowledge, rational education and the virtues of

[63] According to Julius Henry Cohen, n 47 above, xvi, Dr Felix Adler in 1908 'presented to the public his conviction that the further solution of problems of ethics, in industry, in business, and in the professions, must come from the definite assistance of men who live with these problems; that it is not enough for our day and generation to have a general philosophy of ethics, but that there must be daily application of the philosopy to the fact, and that this can be best done by the experts in the line.'

[64] An English version of 'professional society' arose at a similar time period. See: Harold Perkin, *The Rise of Professional Society: England since 1880* (Routledge, London, 1989). In its English manifestation however 'professionalism' never attained the fully 'modern' character of its North American mutation. See, for example, Richard Abel, *The Legal Profession in England and Wales*, n 12 above.

[65] Julius Henry Cohen, n 47 above, 144. Cohen observes that 'Unless we grasp the meaning of these changes in American thought, we shall pass by an understanding of the momentous changes taking place in the practice of the law.' (143)

[66] Julius Henry Cohen, n 47 above, 146.

[67] Cohen, op cit, 158, 159, 127, 143–144, 155, 151.

[68] See Cohen, ch XIV, ' "It Pays to Advertise." Does It?', 173–200; Chapter XX, 'The Missouri Idea of Suppressing the Unlawful Practice of Law' (277–285). Ideas of this sort were commonplace.

See also 'Unauthorised Practice of Law' 55 *Can LJ*, 1919, 375–376, reproducing an article from Law Notes (Northfield, USA). The article establishes linkages between questions relating to lawyers qualifications, ethical regulation, competition, bar organisation, and the need to suppress competitors. Typical of the period, it amounts to a complete project of professionalisation similar to that advanced in Cohen's work and implemented in Canada through the influence of the Canadian Bar Association.

science.[69] Finally, they shared the widespread notion that professionalism provided a magic key capable of maintaining authority in a society rent by centrifugal forces.

The most articulate advocate of American-style professionalism in the period was the intensely proud British Canadian Lawyer, Sir James Aikins. Variously a leading lawyer, Royal Commissioner, Manitoba Governor-General, and founding President of the Canadian Bar Association, Aikins worked hard in the cause of professional reform. His address on the topic of 'The Legal Profession in Relation to Ethics, Education and Emolument,' delivered at the Canadian Bar Association meeting in Winnipeg in August 1919 makes clear the extent to which reforms of legal professionalism were implemented as part of an integrated plan. Like Cohen, his remarks point to the absolute imbrication of the political, economic, cultural and 'professional' spheres.[70]

Asserting that the lawyer's first duty is to the State, Aikins developed arguments against open admissions and in favour of both more rigorous educational requirements and more active 'moral' policing:

> It is a false notion of democracy that the right to practice law should be free for all, that anyone can practice it, and without serious loss to the public, operate or help to operate the expensive and intricate machinery of justice which the State creates for its safety and well-being. The administration of justice has always touched the nadir of its decline when the profession has been lowest in morals and least educated. In such times there is seen a tendency on the part of practitioners to regard the work of the Bar as a trade and not a profession, a thing to be bartered and not a national service to be sought after; then also is found the pettifogger, the ambulance chaser, the fabricator of evidence and the trickster, and the man who is alien to the professional spirit and its traditions, destitute of *gentlemanly* instincts, *disrespectful* to his seniors, and a *slanderer* of Judges.[71]

In tone and in content this echoes contemporary professional apologetics in the United States of America.[72] The Queen's Representative was remarkably 'American' in his professionalising role.

[69] See David Laycock, *Populism and Democratic Thought in The Canadian Prairies, 1910 to 1945* (University of Toronto Press, Toronto, 1990). On Canadian legal education see: Pue, 'British Masculinities', n 25 above; ' "The disquisitions of learned Judges": Making Manitoba Lawyers, 1885–1931', in Jim Phillips and G Blaine Baker (eds), Essays in the History of Canadian Law: In Honour of RCB Risk (Osgoode Society, Toronto, 1999), 825–914; 'Common Law Legal Education in Canada's Age of Light, Soap and Water' in *Canada's Legal Inheritances*, Symposium Issue, edited by W Wesley Pue and D Guth, (1995) 23 *Manitoba Law Journal*, 654–688.

[70] Sir James Aikins, 'The Legal Profession in Relation to Ethics, Education and Emolument' 55 *Can LJ*, 1919, 335–338.

[71] Sir James Aikins, 'The Legal Profession in Relation to Ethics, Education and Emolument' 55 *Can LJ*, 1919, 335–338, at 335, emphasis added.

[72] Cf, for example, Julius Henry Cohen's extended comparative 'history' of professional admission standards and the cause of 'justice' in Cohen, op. cit.

One central feature of this new vision was the articulation of a code of professional conduct coupled with a new determination on the part of professional governing bodies to actively seek out and expunge 'undesirable' practitioners. This was thought necessary for professional cohesion, utility and security. As Aikins said on another occasion,

> [i]f the legal profession refuses to ruthlessly *rid itself of its barnacles and fungus*, how can the public be expected to extend to the profession, as a profession, the high honor, the dignity and revenue which that profession rightly deserves.[73]

This project of defining the good practitioner turned toward explicit class bias or nativism and wartime prohibitions on the admission of members of non-charter ethnic groups reflected a deep-seated fear of 'foreigners'.[74]

Proceeding to develop the case in favour of a more thorough education of aspiring lawyers, Aikins acknowledged that this would require 'adequate rewards for meritorious services' and, hence, 'Standard Solicitor's Tariffs'.[75] Even this was presented as being for the benefit of society in that it would 'create a higher type of barrister and advocate, well skilled in the law, gentlemanly in conduct, kindly disposed to his fellow practitioners and of a public spirit'.[76] This was to be reinforced by 'the frequent meetings of the members of each of the Provincial Bars.' These, 'official law and Bar societies' were, he said, invaluable 'bulwarks protecting the people against incompetent and unscrupulous men posing as lawyers, and thus guarding the honour of the profession'.[77]

Similarly, and for much the same reasons, it was necessary to clearly demarcate lawyers from 'unauthorised practitioners.' These latter would not have the same education as lawyers, would not be subject to the same ethical codes, and therefore could not be trusted to provide competent service to their clientele. Aikins warned that those 'without suitable qualifications would batter on a too credulous and unsuspecting public,' and called upon the Benchers of the various law societies to adopt 'the best methods and best ways possible' to 'fulfil the statutory and traditional

[73] 13 December 1927, *Vancouver Sun*, 'Vancouver Benchers,' (reporting on Sir JAM Aikins' view of the general reputation of the legal profession.)

[74] See, for example, 'Inaugural Address of the President. Sir James Aikins, KC, Knt, Lieutenant-Governor of Manitoba', 54 *Can LJ*, 1918, 344–357, arguing that the experience of 1914–1918 demonstrated the desirability of careful immigration controls—'Even before the war that error was made manifest in industrial dissensions, in the ignorant, too often corrupt, use of the franchise and failure to understand the privileges and responsibilities of our free institutions . . . Detached by distance from their own people they generally are all for self and none for the adopted nation' (354–5). Aikins indicates however that US, UK, French immigrants are not the subject of concern.

[75] *Ibid*, 336.

[76] *Ibid*, 338.

[77] *Ibid*, 338.

obligations cast upon them and protect the profession from encroachment upon its sphere'.[78]

There was a symmetry and mesh of components here, a vision of professionalism cut of whole cloth.

KEYSTONE OF SOCIAL COHESION

The rhetoric of service infused professional discourse during and after the Great War.[79] Lawyers were said to be qualified by training, experience and commitment to service, as '*natural leaders of the people* in public affairs'.[80] As such they could provide an anti-dote to various undesirable ideologies which were then in circulation:

> A special duty rests upon our profession both on the Bench and at the Bar, for we are the agents and ministers of the law. . . . Through a general neglect of that service in our country of popular suffrage our people are in *imminent danger of the despotism not so much of individuals as of classes,* organized on the principle of every one for himself. . . .[81]

The whole package of legal professionalism was conceived as a bulwark against social unrest, despotism and class warfare.[82] It was hoped that

> *greater unity of the profession would lead to the much needed and greater unity in the thought and action among the peoples of Canada and to like mindedness and singleness of heart and soul in the interest of our country.*[83]

Thus, it was cultural revolution first and foremost that Canadian lawyers sought. The goal was to avert political disaster. More than anything else, the craving for national integration on such terms spurred lawyers toward modern 'professionalisation'. Seeking to avert radical social change, they discovered their profession.

[78] 28 August 1928, 'Aikins is Again Head of Governing Body,' Western Canadian Legal History Archives (University of Manitoba), Clipping File 1928–1933, 2, (Summary 2nd Annual conference on Benchers). In the result, a Committee on Encroachments recommended investigating the areas in which the public should look to lawyers for service. 'Archive of Manitoba Legal-Judicial History' within the Provincial Archives of Manitoba.

[79] Eg 'Inaugural Address of the President. Sir James Aikins, KC, Knt, Lieutenant-Governor of Manitoba', 54 *Can LJ*, 1918, 344–357.

[80] 'Canadian Bar Association. Proceedings at Fifth Annual Meeting, The President's Address' 56 *Can LJ*, 1920, 308–325, at 308.

[81] 'Canadian Bar Association. Proceedings at Fifth Annual Meeting, The President's Address' 56 *Can LJ*, 1920, 308–325, 309.

[82] A somewhat similar point is made with reference to USA developments by James C Foster, who argues that the 'bar association' movement was a deliberately 'ideological' response to the crises of USA capitalism. See: Foster, n 6 above.

[83] 'Canadian Bar Association. Proceedings at Fifth Annual Meeting, The President's Address' 56 *Can LJ*, 1920, 308–325, 308–309.

CONCLUSIONS

This vision of professionalism resonated at many levels with popular conceptions of appropriate social organisation. Ironically, it was imbricated with the very modernity which, in other manifestations, its proponents resisted. This period, this time and the peculiar circumstances relating to the opening of Canada's western empire provided the habitat from which emerged the form of professionalism which Canadian lawyers now take for granted. The vision of social life which it incorporates however has little currency in our time or among contemporary lawyers.

The conclusions to be drawn from this can be traced along two axes. The first is in relation to theories of professionalism, the second in relation to wider issues in cultural history.

i) Theories of professionalisation

The theories of professionalisation which have enjoyed currency during the past 50 years have fallen into functionalist or 'rational choice' camps (the latter manifesting itself in both 'market control' and 'work jurisdictions' variants). Two of the pre-eminent theorists of legal professionalism, Terence Halliday and Lucien Karpik, have described these approaches as focussing on (i) the achievement of 'a service relationship', (ii) 'the monopolistic strategy of extracting market rent and thus social privilege', and 'the deployment of knowledge for the creation and defence of work jurisdictions as a way to define boundaries between work domains'. Each approach is inadequate, they assert, on account of what each of them overlooks: 'politics'.[84]

Certainly, the history of lawyers' professionalisation in Canada provides strong support for the critique of *both* functionalist approaches premised on 'client-service' *and* narrowly economic interpretations of professionalism.[85] The 'market control paradigm' and its cousins, even when qualified and re-worked to the highest level of sophistication, cannot adequately account for the very obvious non-market motivations of legal professionals who struggled to create their profession.[86] Nor can it

[84] Halliday and Karpik, n 14 above,15.

[85] Cf Stuart A Scheingold, 'Taking Weber Seriously: Lawyers, Politics, and the Liberal State' (1999) 24(4) *Law and Social Inquiry*, 1061–81; Michael Burrage, 'Escaping the Dead Hand of Rational Choice: Karpik's Historical Sociology of French Advocates' (1999) 24(4) *Law and Social Inquiry*, 1083–124.

[86] Hurlburt, n 36 above, lends some support to what he calls the 'honour' model of legal professionalism as developed by Michael Burrage, 'From a gentleman's to a public profession: status and politics in the history of English solicitors' (1996) 3 *International Journal of the Legal Profession*, 45.

account for the very important non-market effects of legal professionalism. Much more is at stake than who gets what portion of the economic pie. To the extent that Canada's legal professionals re-created their profession in an attempt to stave off political and social change, to warp discourses of politics and civic life by confining them in 'acceptable' channels, their project can seem to carry an almost conspiratorial and anti-democratic import of far greater significance than 'market control' ordinarily implies.[87]

Canadian lawyers clearly had *political objectives* of sorts in mind as they went about the work outlined above. Because of this their story might be taken as buttressing an emerging interpretive frame which postulates a necessary and causal relationship between lawyering and the rise of western political liberalism.[88] There can be little doubt that 'the politics of lawyers directly engage one of the great ideological and institutional movements of the past several centuries—the construction of political liberalism'.[89] Equally, there can be little doubt that the lawyers who created the twentieth century Canadian common law legal professions were 'liberals' in the broad sense. They were committed to private property (within limits), individual freedom (within limits), *laissez-faire* (within limits), a moderate state, civil society and a rights-based form of citizenship which encompassed both British constitutionalism and the rule of law. By the same token however these lawyers do not appear in *quite* so heroic and unambiguous a guise as those who struggled to create political liberalism in more authoritarian places.[90] Their story points to an unseemly under-side to liberalism which is not always immediately apparent. Not all lawyers have played key roles in the overthrow or containment of absolutist regimes and it is dangerous to build theory on a few well documented case studies which may turn out to be abberational. Political theorists have properly emphasised that the success of liberal governance rests on the preadaptation of subjects to self-governance. It is

[87] Cf James C Foster, n 21 above, 47: 'But the political importance of lawyers' trade association involves considerably more than restricting competition. . . . The American bar's prerogatives are not simply occupational. . . . By insisting we see through all that lawyers professed, to the 'proprietary' motives behind their words, Auerbach directs our attention away from the very real imperative that both conservative and progressive lawyers perceived to shore up the hegemony of the liberal-capitalist steering principles underlying their power. What elite lawyers said is as significant as what they did.'

[88] Lucien Karpik and Terence Halliday, 'Politics Matter: a Comparative Theory of Lawyer in the Making of Political Liberalism' in Halliday and Karpik (eds) n 14 above. Stuart A Scheingold, 'Taking Weber Seriously', n 85 above.

[89] Terence C Halliday, 'The Politics of Lawyers: An Emerging Agenda' (1999) 24:4 *Law and Social Inquiry*, 1007–1011, at 1010.

[90] See various of the contributions to Lucien Karpik and Terence Halliday (eds), 'Lawyers and the Rise of Western Political Liberalism', n 14 above.

dependent, at least in the context of large 'nation states', on mechanisms of social control which contain difference, Barron's point in the quotation which heads this essay.[91] Where long-standing tradition or custom does not 'naturally' contain difference substitutes must be found. Cultural projects operating through temperance societies, welfare, state, education, policing and professions are the result. Legal professionalism, like moral regulation movements, can be a manifestation of 'an anxiety of freedom that haunts modern liberal forms of rule' where there 'is no 'natural' system of order'.[92] It is important that the developing literatures on lawyers and liberalism take into account this seemingly anti-democratic zone of professional activity, as well as the more obviously 'liberal' contributions of individual lawyers and (less often) organised legal professions alike.

ii) Lawyers' histories and cultural history

The second general conclusion that might be suggested by the example of legal professionalism in twentieth century Canada is with regard to the relationships between professional forms and cultures. In this zone of liberal lawyers' 'illiberal' activity it is cultural projects which come to the fore. They do so only in part to advance a political vision as such. We do well in this area to heed Alan Hunt's caution against taking conceptual categories too seriously:

> We conventionally make distinctions, such as those between social, economic and moral realms; such categories are useful, even necessary, so long as we do not fall into the trap of imagining that these terms create real separations as if there is some field, realm or space that is exclusively social, moral or economic. . . . Our conceptual distinctions are elaborated for analytical purposes only; in the real world they are always found in complex connection with other elements.[93]

The founding fathers of modern legal professionalism in Canada knew full well that their profession, their personal ethics, religion, economic beliefs, and political convictions were bound together in some fashion. It was not an absolutist binding together however. For some purposes Baptists or Jews or Catholics could be tolerated just as in politics disagreements between Liberals and Conservatives were both legitimate and genuine. Nonetheless, a cultural web held the whole together and most leading lawyers would have understood the urges which led Michel

[91] Cf Alan Hunt, *Governing Morals: A Social History of Moral Regulation* (Cambridge University Press, Cambridge, 1999) at 25 on the relationship between moral politics, 'nationalism, population and sexuality'. See also Richard V Ericson and Nico Stehr (eds), *Governing Modern Societies* (University of Toronto Press, Toronto, 2000).

[92] Alan Hunt, n 91 above, 215.

[93] Alan Hunt, n 91 above, at 7–8.

Foucault to describe one project of western states as being to 'constitute the populace as a moral subject'.[94] This was no idle philosophy in their time and their place. In common cause with other prominent Canadians acting in many realms, it was very much *what Canadian lawyers were on about*.

What is interesting in the work of the legal professions is the extent to which lawyers combined agendas which were explicitly moral and reforming with a profound restructuring of their profession. Their efforts to reform the curriculum of formal legal education, for example, is not altogether dissimilar from near contemporaneous efforts to introduce public schooling, to reform private boys schools, to educate imperial civil servants or to fashion universities anew so as to meet the needs of a changing world.[95] Though it is less immediately obvious perhaps with respect to their desire to attain self-regulation, monopoly, professional independence and plenary disciplinary powers, these too were directed to 'cultural' ends. They built structures on cultural foundations, drawn to blue-prints of moral origin.

This, of course, is a limited conclusion. To assert that Canadian legal professionalism originated in cultural projects in the early twentieth century is not to assert that *all* legal professions, *everywhere*, *always* have originated in these ways (only imperial centres and obviously important places—such as London, New York, Los Angeles or Paris—can plausibly hope to turn *their* parochialisms into social theory).

Moreover the argument that structures emerge from deliberate, self-conscious agency cannot be made at all places and all times. Some professional structures may indeed have important origins which are lost in the mists of time and others may accrete slowly in *ad hoc* response to periodic crises (the English Bar comes to mind in both categories). It is also undoubtably the case that much cultural, economic and political change takes place *within* frameworks provided by more or less durable structures. The late twentieth century legal profession, for example, leaves little room for the rhetoric of moral reform. No contemporary lawyer can adopt the role of a 'high priest' of law, just as no university law teacher could now seriously adopt as his or her mission the inculcation of the virtues of British gentlemanliness.

Even modestly understood, however, the findings reported here are not *de minimis*. They direct our attention to questions of cultural agency and structural revolution that are too easily overlooked. They suggest connections between market control, political lawyering, culture, liberalism and professionalism that have yet to be adequately explored.

[94] Michel Foucault, 'Prison Talk' in Colin Gordon (ed), *Power/Knowledge: Selected Interview and Other Writings, 1972–1977* (Harverster Press, Brighton, 1980), 37–54 at 41.

[95] See Pue, 'British Masculinities', n 25 above.